DATE DUE

	PRINTED IN U.S.A.

INTRODUCTION TO
CRIMINOLOGY

INTRODUCTION TO CRIMINOLOGY

Order and Disorder

CLEMENS BARTOLLAS
University of Northern Iowa

SIMON DINITZ
The Ohio State University

HARPER & ROW, PUBLISHERS, New York
Cambridge, Philadelphia, San Francisco, London,
Mexico City, São Paulo, Singapore, Sydney

1817

Editor in Chief: Judith Rothman
Sponsoring Editor: Alan McClare
Project Editor: Eric Newman
Text Design Adaptation: Barbara Bert/North 7 Atelier Ltd.
Cover Design: Joan Greenfield
Cover Illustration: Untitled 1959–60; Helen Frankenthaler; oil on canvas mtd. on
  masonite; 16⅝″ × 13⅝″; courtesy of Vanderwoude Tananbaum Gallery, New
  York, New York
Photo Research: John Schultz, PAR/NYC
Production Manager: Jeanie Berke
Production Assistant: Paula Roppolo
Composition and Text Art: ComCom Division of Haddon Craftsmen, Inc.
Printer and Binder: R. R. Donnelley & Sons Company
Cover Printer: Lehigh Press

INTRODUCTION TO CRIMINOLOGY: ORDER AND DISORDER

Library of Congress Cataloging-in-Publication Data

Bartollas, Clemens.
    Introduction to criminology : order and disorder / Clemens
  Bartollas, Simon Dinitz.
      p.   cm.
  Includes bibliographies and index.
  ISBN 0–06–040518–X
  1. Crime and criminals.   I. Dinitz, Simon.   II. Title.
HV6025.B35 1989
364—dc19   88-14891 CIP

88   89   90   91   9   8   7   6   5   4   3   2   1

To a balance between individual
freedom and collective well-being

Brief Table of Contents

Detailed Table of Contents   ix
Preface   xix

1   The Ordered Society   1

2   Law and Society   29

3   Crime as Disorder   57

4   Free Will and Crime   93

5   Biological and Psychological Explanations of Crime   125

6   Sociological Positivism: Structural Causes   159

7   Social Process Theory   193

8   Conflict Theory and Crime   223

9   Crimes of Violence   253

10   Property Crimes   283

11   Crimes Against the Public Order   317

12   The Criminal Justice System   349

13   The Police   379

14   The Courts   411

15   The Prison   447

16   Probation, Parole, and Community-Based Corrections   479

17   Coping with Criminal Behavior Through Technology   515

Glossary   547
Name Index   559
Subject Index   566

Detailed Table of Contents

Preface   xix

1   **THE ORDERED SOCIETY   1**

    Order and Disorder   2
    Disruptive Effects of Crime   5
    Roots of Social Disruption   6
        Human Nature   6
        Industrial Society and the Impact of Social Change   11
    Modern Nations with Little Crime   18
        Japan   19
        Switzerland: Cities with Little Crime   21
    Criminology: The Scientific Study of Crime   23
    Summary   24
    References   25
    Notes   25

2   **LAW AND SOCIETY   29**

    Constitutional Order   31
        Respect for the Law   33
        Disobedience of the Law   35
    Purpose of the Law   37
    Nature and Function of Criminal Law   38
        Substantive Criminal Law   38
        Procedural Criminal Law   40
    Social Context of the Law   44

Perspectives on the Law 46
   Consensus Perspective 46
   Pluralist Perspective 47
   Conflict Perspective 48
Analysis 49
   Law: The First Condition of an Ordered Society 50
   Due Process Ideal and Bureaucratic Reality 51
   The Rule of Law 52
Summary 52
References 53
Notes 54

3   CRIME AS DISORDER 57

Enduring Aspects of Crime in America 58
   Enforcement of Public Morals 59
   Poverty and Dangerousness 59
   Violence as an Accompaniment to Crime 61
   Intractable Nature of Crime 64
   Vigilante Justice 65
Extent of Crime 66
   Measurement of Official Crime 66
   Unofficial Measurement of Crime 76
The Costs of Crime 81
   The Fear of Crime 82
   Criminal Victimization 83
   The Economic Cost of Crime 84
   Disruption to Community 84
Analysis 85
   Social Disorder and Its Relationship to Crime 85
   Crime and the Frustrations of Public Policy 86
Summary 88
References 88
Notes 89

4   FREE WILL AND CRIME 93

Classical School of Criminology 95
   Right to Punishment 95
   Utility of Punishment 95
   Effectiveness of Punishment 96
   Degree of Punishment 96
   Administration of Punishment 98
   Contribution of Jeremy Bentham 98
   Revolutionary Criminology of the Eighteenth Century 99
   Summary 100

Utilitarian Punishment Philosophy   101
Assumptions About Social Order   101
Components of the Utilitarian Punishment Philosophy   106
Summary   108

Retribution or "Just Deserts" Philosophy   109
Assumptions of the Justice Model   110
Components of the Justice Model   111
Summary   111

Analysis   112
Can the State Be Trusted?   112
Is Criminal Behavior Rational?   113
Does Punishment Deter?   116

Policy Implications   118
Danger of Repression   118

Summary   119
References   120
Notes   120

5   BIOLOGICAL AND PSYCHOLOGICAL EXPLANATIONS OF CRIME   125

Development of Positivism in Criminology   127
Biological Positivism   127
Early Theories of Biological Positivism   128
Sociobiology or Contemporary Biological Positivism   131

Psychological Positivism   138
Psychological Abnormality and Crime   138

Punishment and Personal Responsibility   146

Analysis   148
Badness to Sickness   148
Sickness to Dangerousness   149
Sickness to Responsibility   150

Policy Implications   151
Summary   151
References   152
Notes   153

6   SOCIOLOGICAL POSITIVISM: STRUCTURAL CAUSES   159

Cultural Deviance Theories   160
Clifford R. Shaw and Henry D. McKay   160
Lower-Class Culture and Delinquent Values   166
Violence and Lower-Class Culture   168

Strain Theory   170

Robert K. Merton and the Theory of Anomie   170
Albert K. Cohen and the Theory of Delinquent Subculture   173
Richard A. Cloward and Lloyd E. Ohlin and Opportunity Theory   176

Theories of Upper-World Crime and Delinquency   179

Subculture Theories   179
Socialization Theories   179
Strain Theories   180

Analysis   180

Disorder of Economic Inequality   181
Disorder of the Breakdown of Social Rules   185
Disorder of Hard-Core Lower-Class "Losers"   186

Policy Implications   187

Summary   188

References   189

Notes   189

7   SOCIAL PROCESS THEORY   193

Differential Association Theory   195

Propositions of Differential Association Theory   196
Evaluation of Differential Association Theory   197

Delinquency and Drift   200

Evaluation of Drift Theory   201

Control Theory   202

Containment Theory   202
Social Control Theory   204

Labeling Theory   208

Frank Tannenbaum: The Dramatization of Evil   208
Edwin M. Lemert: Primary and Secondary Deviation   208
Howard Becker and the Outsider   209
Evaluation of the Labeling Perspective   210

Analysis   211

Transmission of Individual Patterns   211
Development of Deviant Identity and Career   214
Escape from a Deviant Label   216

Policy Implications   217

Summary   218

References   219

Notes   219

8   CONFLICT THEORY AND CRIME   223

Nature of Conflict Theory   225

Dimensions of Conflict Theory   226

Socioeconomic Class and Marxist Criminology   226

Power and Authority Relationships   227
Group and Cultural Conflict   229

Marxist Criminology and Explanations of Criminal Behavior   230
Oppressiveness of the Law   231
Alienation and Powerlessness in the Lower Class   233
Economic Exploitation of the Lower Class   234
Social Injustice   238

Evaluation of Conflict Theory   239

Analysis   242
Equality and Liberty   242
Social Cost of Upper-World Crime   242
Legitimacy of the State   245

Policy Implications   246
Summary   247
References   248
Notes   248

9   CRIMES OF VIOLENCE   253

Adult Street Crime   254
Murder and Nonnegligent Manslaughter   255
Forcible Rape   259
Robbery   261
Aggravated Assault   264

Domestic Violence   264
Child Abuse and Neglect   265
Spouse Abuse   267
Abuse of the Elderly   268

Juvenile Violence   270
Delinquent Career   270
Violent Juvenile Gangs   271

Terrorism   272
Trends Regarding Terrorism in the 1980s   273

Analysis   275
Violence and the Social Order   275
Violence and Global Disorder   276

Policy Implications   277
Summary   277
References   278
Notes   278

10   PROPERTY CRIMES   283

Traditional Property Crimes   285
Burglary   286

Larceny-Theft   288
Motor Vehicle Theft   291
Fraud   292
Arson   293

White-Collar Crime   293
Occupational White-Collar Crime   294
Corporate Crime   299

Organized Crime   304
Structural Versus Process Views of Organized Crime   305
The Mafia   307
Services   308

Analysis   309
Property Offenders Differentiated   309
Social Disorder of Property Crimes   311

Policy Implications   311
Summary   312
References   312
Notes   313

11   CRIMES AGAINST THE PUBLIC ORDER   317

Substance Abuse   319
Alcohol   320
Marijuana   321
Cocaine   321
The Opiates   322
Enforcement and Drugs   323

Prostitution   325
Varieties of Prostitutes   328
Legality and Prostitution   329

Homosexuality   331
Gambling   333
Illegal Markets   334
Legality and Gambling   335

Vagrancy   336
Analysis   340
Disorder of Choosing Safety over Freedom   340
Disorder of Becoming a Victim   341
Disorder of Enforcing Public Order Laws   342

Policy Implications   343
Summary   344
References   345
Notes   345

12 THE CRIMINAL JUSTICE SYSTEM 349

Development of Social Control in American Society 351
Early American Practices 351
Social Control in the Nineteenth Century 352
The Twentieth Century: A Time of Change 357

Criminal Justice: A Search for Order 361
Structure of the Criminal Justice System 361
Functions of the Criminal Justice System 365

Criminal Justice: A System in Chaos 370
Fragmentation 371
Overload 372
Limited Capacity 372

Policy Implications 373
Summary 374
References 375
Notes 375

13 THE POLICE 379

Guardians of the Social Order 381
Divergent Cultures Within the Police 382
Professionalism: The Bureaucratization of Policing 382
The Police Culture 385

Crime Reduction 387
Community-Oriented Policing 389
Policing Repeat Offenders 389
Arresting Spousal Assaulters 389

Police Discretion 391
Constitutional Protections and the Police 392
Police Corruption 397
Police Brutality 398

Integration of Women and Minority Groups into Policing 400
Women as Police Officers 400
Minority Police Officers 401

Analysis 402
Freedom and Order 402
Order and the Police 403

Policy Implications 403
Community-Oriented Policing 404
Resolution of Conflict Between Management and Police Cultures 404
Reduction of Stress 405

Summary   405
References   406
Notes   406

14   THE COURTS   411

Structure of the Criminal Courts   413
The State Court System   416
The Federal Court System   420

Pretrial Processes   424
The Charging Decision   424
Pretrial Release   424
Pretrial Diversion   428
Plea Bargaining   429

Criminal Trial   431
Steps in the Criminal Trial Process   431

Sentencing   434
Indeterminate or Determinate Sentencing   434
Sentencing Hearing   436

Analysis   437
Order and Disorder   437
Structured Order Within the Courthouse   440

Policy Implications   441
Plea Bargaining Reform   441
Sentencing Reform   441

Summary   442
References   443
Notes   443

15   THE PRISON   447

A Sociological Analysis of the Prison   449
The Changing Administration of the Prison   449
Services and Programs   452
The Inmate World   454
Problems of American Prisons   458
The Invasion of the Courts   462

Analysis of the Prison   466
Perseverance of the Prison   466
Microcosm of the Larger Society   467
Freedom Versus Order   468

Policy Implications   468
Reduction of Overcrowded Prisons   469
Humane Prisons   470

Summary 473
References 473
Notes 474

16   PROBATION, PAROLE, AND COMMUNITY-BASED CORRECTIONS   479

Overview of Community-Based Corrections   **481**
    Social Context of the 1960s and Early 1970s   481
    Philosophical Underpinnings   482
    Administrative Strategies   483
    ''Get-Tough'' Policies   484
    Trends in the Late 1980s   485
Probation   **485**
    Changing Goals of Probation Services   488
    Risk Assessment   490
    The Probation Officer   492
Parole   **495**
    Parole Under Attack   495
    Parole Guidelines   498
    Supervision of Ex-offenders   499
Evaluation of Probation and Parole   **501**
Residential Programs   **502**
Analysis   **505**
    The Quest for Order   505
    Disorder in Community-Based Programs   506
Policy Implications   **507**
    Reconstruction of Urban Communities   507
    Coordinated Administration of Community-Based Programs   508
Summary   **508**
References   **509**
Notes   **509**

17   COPING WITH CRIMINAL BEHAVIOR THROUGH TECHNOLOGY   515

The American Contribution   **519**
Target Hardening   **524**
Biomedical Intervention   **526**
    Critical Organ Surgery   527
    Drug Treatment   531
Ethical Problems   **536**
    Intrusion   537

Irreversibility   537
Involuntary Administration   537
Overcontrol   538
Summary   538
Notes   539

Glossary   547
Name Index   559
Subject Index   566

Preface

The theme of this text is the relationship between order and disorder and its application to the study of criminology. The fascinating relationship between order and disorder can be seen on three levels: the social order of the larger society, the institutions of public order, and those individuals who, by violating the rules of society, come to the attention of the institutions of public order. A major advantage of this approach is that it uses an analytical and integrative method to examine the study of crime.

The ordered society has long been the quest of humankind. Such a society is characterized by such factors as individuals' accepting their roles, complying with society's values and norms, and obeying the rules. The achievement of an ordered society depends upon the socialization skills of the family and schools, upon the cohesiveness of societal norms and values, and upon a stable economic life and structure of government. However, contemporary Western societies resemble the disordered society far more than the ordered one.

Industrialized and urbanized modern societies constantly face new and persistent forms of social disorder. Criminal behavior and civil disobedience have dramatically increased in most Western societies since the 1950s. A major problem in any attempt to restore public order is that most Western societies prefer tolerant, humanitarian policies in dealing with violators of the law. A principled conviction, under attack at the present time, is that a substantial level of disorder is more tolerable than the annihilation of civil liberties in the service of revolution or reaction. But neither the liberal policies of humanitarian approaches nor the authoritarian solution of brutalizing punishments is currently working well in reducing crime.

In our world, order and disorder blend together. Too much order and a society becomes stifling; too little order, and a society can unravel and disintegrate. Many Americans today feel that the disorder of crime poses a real threat to the quality of life. But the American system is one that allows the rights, or freedoms, of the individual to be protected from abuse by the state. The balance between the rights of the individual and the security of society continues to pose problems in maintaining public order.

Our development of the "order and disorder" theme springs from the writings of other criminologists. Some criminologists view crime as an indicator of a disorganized society; others claim that tolerable amounts of deviant and criminal behavior may even strengthen the social order. Still others have studied crime as a means of understanding the assumptions about order held by members of that society, assumptions upon which these individuals base decisions that contribute to everyday order and disorder. Finally, order is regarded by some criminologists as emerging from competition and conflict among various interest groups, and the disorder of crime is seen as endangering the interests of some groups while promoting those of others.

The organization of this text is unique. Chapter 1 begins with an examination of crime in contemporary urbanized and industrialized society. As a necessary starting point in this investigation of order and disorder, we give special emphasis to the effects of modernization on crime. The second chapter examines the means by which the law orders society. The criminal law depends on the position that humans have free will and, therefore, are responsible for their behavior. As citizens of the state, individuals become involved in a social contract that gives the state the right to punish those who violate the law. However, the decline of respect for and obedience of the law is resulting in higher rates of crime in the United States. The third chapter examines the enduring aspects, the extent, and the costs of crime in the United States.

Chapters 4 through 8 examine why criminals violate the law. Chapter 4 suggests that criminal behavior is purposeful activity resulting from rational decisions in which pros and cons are weighed, and the acts that promise the greatest potential gains are performed. This emphasis on free will and responsibility is quite different from that of the next four chapters, which argue that the disorder of crime results because individuals are impelled by psychological or biological deficiencies or by sociological factors.

The types of criminal behavior, or public disorder, are discussed in Chapters 9 through 11. Violent, property, and victimless crimes are the general categories of public disorder examined. The disorder that these crimes bring to the social order is emphasized, and the world views and techniques of those involved in these crimes are also investigated. The ever-changing nature of disorder and order is dramatically illustrated by examining the micro-perspective of those who refuse to comply with the rules of society.

The social control of crime receives attention in the final six chapters of this text. The structure of the criminal justice process, the police, the courts, community-based corrections, prisons, and social control methods of the future are the subjects of these chapters. The main emphasis is on how institutions of public order handle the disorder of crime. However, as microcosms of the larger society, political, cultural, and economic forces shape the policies of these social control institutions.

The format of each chapter is another unique feature of this text. The social context of crime, the philosophical ideas underpinning crime, and the theory of law all receive special emphasis in this text. An analysis section in each chapter examines the major issues related to order and disorder on the societal, institutional, and individual levels and also considers the cultural, political, and economic forces in defining and handling public disorder. Moreover, policy recommendations throughout this text suggest more fruitful directions for the social control of crime.

We believe that this emphasis on order and disorder will be helpful in understanding crime in American society. We hope that students will find this a refreshing and stimulating text. We have been fascinated by our study of order and disorder in American society, and we trust that our enthusiasm will be shared by our readers.

ACKNOWLEDGMENTS

We would first like to express our gratitude to those pioneers in criminology, teachers, and colleagues who have influenced our thinking and writing. Edwin H. Sutherland, Walter C. Reckless, Thorsten Sellin, Marshall B. Clinard, Jerome Hall, George Vold, Edward Segarin, and John Conrad are names that quickly come to mind. We also want to thank our students for their helpful comments and reactions to our major theme, order and disorder.

We want to express our appreciation to our editor, Alan McClare, who was patient with us to the end. We are very grateful to Judith Sutton and Linda Dippold Bartollas, who edited the manuscript; Linda also prepared the index. Dean Wright and David Shichor are two reviewers whose comments and suggestions were particularly helpful. The following academic reviewers also provided many helpful comments: John A. Conley, The University of Wisconsin–Milwaukee; John E. Holman, North Texas State University; and Calvin J. Swank, Youngstown State University. Colleagues who made various contributions to the development of this project are B. Keith Crew, Kurt Mielke, Loras A. Jaeger, and Bill Kinney. Rosemarie Skaine assisted in many ways. Kristin Bartollas spent much time incorporating revisions and doing library research. Finally, we are grateful to those inmates and offenders who helped shape our perspective and understanding of crime in America. We especially acknowledge the help of Walter Sheets.

Clemens Bartollas
Simon Dinitz

CHAPTER 1

The Ordered Society

ORDER AND DISORDER

DISRUPTIVE EFFECTS OF CRIME

ROOTS OF SOCIAL DISRUPTION

Human Nature

    Humans Are Wicked

    Humans Are Pleasure Seekers

    Human Behavior Is Determined

Industrial Society and the Impact of Social Change

    Effects of Modernization

MODERN NATIONS WITH LITTLE CRIME

Japan

Switzerland: Cities with Little Crime

CRIMINOLOGY: THE SCIENTIFIC STUDY OF CRIME

SUMMARY

REFERENCES

NOTES

KEY TERMS

born criminal   humanization   rehabilitative ideal
criminology   industrial society   social contract
demodernization   modernization   social disruption
disorder   nationalization   third industrial revolution
feudalism   order   traditional society
"get-tough" approach

> . . . *Order and disorder are created by humans to serve their needs and ambitions. Order serves one group and disorder another. As peace does not equal progress for everyone, some employ disorder to advance. Order can encroach on liberty, so it is resisted. People also use order or disorder, or both, to protect their interests. Some who induce disorder may eventually join the order they sought to disrupt, which is where they wanted to be all along. Others, such as successful revolutionaries, may establish a new system of their own, but it [any social system] will always have its challengers. In this persistently unsettled environment, individuals can shift from compliance to dissent and return to order with unsuspected ease. Why they do it, and when, is linked to the galaxy of individual motivations and historical circumstances that make generalizations elusive, if not useless.*
>
> —Paul J. Vanderwood[1]

We are about to embark on an exciting intellectual journey into the field of criminology, a journey that we hope will lead us to an understanding of crime. **Criminology,*** most commonly defined as the scientific study of crime, deals with street crime, including murder, rape, armed robbery, and auto theft; public order crime; organized crime; white-collar and corporate crime; and political terrorism. Some forms of crime, such as prostitution, are old, others, such as computer crime, are new. The study of criminology examines why crime takes place; the extent of crime; and the impact of the wider society, the immediate neighborhood, and the family on crime. It also discusses the measures and programs needed to prevent and control criminal behavior.

ORDER AND DISORDER

The excitement of our particular journey is coupled with the fact that we will use the relationship of **order** and **disorder** to be the unifying theme of this text. Indeed, the study of criminology, or criminal behavior, is part of a basic quest—that of understanding the relationship between order and disorder. The criminologist is concerned with the collective aspects of human life, as well as with understanding

---

*Key terms are highlighted by boldface type on first significant use throughout this text. For ease of reference, key terms are listed at the beginning of each chapter.

how societal conditions influence individuals to engage in behaviors that are socially approved or disapproved. These concerns translate into the following questions of order and disorder:

- What is social order?
- How is it created?
- How is it maintained?
- What explains social disruption?
- What spells the difference between orderly change and collapse into disorder?[2]

An examination of order is relevant because humankind has always sought the ordered society. Prehistoric humans desired order because they feared the catastrophes of nature and the disruption of their already fragmented communal existences. To humans throughout history, the ordered society has meant structured and stable communal lives. In the ordered society, people feel safe; traditional values are preserved; human behavior is predictable; and those who play by the rules are honored as valued members of the community.

Order can be defined as "a condition in which every part or unit is in its right place or in a normal or efficient state" and as "the condition brought about by good and firm government and obedience to the laws."[3] The definition of order, however, varies from society to society, and, therefore, no one absolute definition of order can stand over time or among cultures. For example, order in feudal society is quite different from order in industrial society, and order in a Marxist society is quite different from order in a capitalist society. Thus, what is order in one society may be seen as something that causes stress or is defined as deviance or crime in another.

But in the midst of order, there is always disorder. Disorder, according to Ted Robert Gurr, can be defined as "a threatening lack of predictability in the behavior of others."[4] In communal societies, disorder is viewed as "chaotic, uncoordinated, and allowing accidental conflict, waste, or needless destruction."[5] In industrial societies, disorder is defined as disorganization, cultural conflict, normlessness or anomie, norm erosion, disconsensus, and entropy. *Webster's Dictionary* adds the following definitions: "a lack of order, confusion; neglect or disregard of system; breach of public peace, a riot; and irregularity, disarrangement, tumult, bustle, disturbance."[6]

An examination of Western society during the nineteenth and twentieth centuries shows that the balance between order and disorder is precarious and temporary, and that the balance can be altered by conditions that cannot always be contained. The competition between the two states is relentless. Too much order triggers disorder, and there is order even in disorder, such as a natural disaster.

Every society has had to control socially disruptive behavior, and, therefore, all societies require some means of effective social control.[7] The primary means of social control has come from religious beliefs, an autocratic ruler, a benevolent landlord, a social contract, or the rule of law. As contemporary society has

---

BOX 1.1   **FINDING ORDER IN DISORDER**

James Gleick's *Chaos: Making a New Science* is an exciting book, and it is particularly relevant to this examination of order and disorder. He states:

> Everything tends toward disorder. Any process that converts energy from one form to another must lose some as heat. Perfect efficiency is impossible. The universe is a one-way street. *Entropy must always increase in the universe and in any hypothetical system within it.* However expressed, the Second Law [of thermodynamics] is a rule from which there seems no appeal. In thermodynamics that is true. But the Second Law has had a life of its own in intellectual circles far removed from science, taking the blame for disintegration of societies, economic decay, the breakdown of manners, and many other variations on the decadent theme. These secondary, metaphorical incarnations of the Second Law now seem especially misguided. In our world, complexity flourishes, and those looking to science for a general understanding of nature's habits will be better served by the laws of chaos.

According to Gleick, the premise of chaos theory is that beneath disorder lurks order. Although it may never be possible to predict precisely the weather or the stock market or even the path of a roulette ball, a number of scientists in a wide range of fields have discovered that one can foresee patterns of behavior. Significantly, these patterns are the order within the chaos.

Chaos, says Gleick, is offering scientists their best chance to learn the secrets of nature. But the emergence of chaos was a "story not only of new theories and new discoveries, but also of the belated understanding of old ideas. Many pieces of the puzzle had been seen long before—by Poincaré, by Maxwell, even by Einstein—and then forgotten."

As part of a long history, social scientists today are also turning to disorder to explain the social world. The authors of this text contend that the best way to understand criminology is through an examination of disorder and its underlying order. We describe how crime is disorder and how the effects of crime are creating chaos for American society. We have found it far easier to portray fruitless efforts to remove the disorder of crime than to explain the patterns of order within the disorder of crime or the patterns of order within society itself. In the final pages of this book, we conclude that the order within the disorder of the social world represents the ultimate hope of humankind.

Source: James Gleick, *Chaos: Making a New Science* (New York: Viking, 1987), pp. 181, 308.

become more complex, with the result that humans deal with each other more impersonally and formally than in the past, the law has been more widely used to establish social control.[8]

An examination of order and disorder is particularly relevant today, for in the late 1960s and early 1970s, social disorder on nearly every front made the public wonder whether American society was losing its steering mechanism. Events ranging from the takeover at Attica to the killings at Kent State, from urban riots to student protests, from the rise of the women's liberation movement to the emergence of humanistic secularism, and from failure in Vietnam to corruption in the Oval Office all combined to rob citizens of their confidence in the prevailing order.[9] The public became convinced that an intolerable point had been reached: the rules were no longer clear, the legal constraints were no longer effective, and the moral consensus was no longer present.

In this context, rising crime rates became a source of special concern and fear because they signified, in Richard Quinney's words, "the ultimate crack in the armor of the existing order."[10] Crime became the symbol of the breakdown of the status quo. The public, whose perceptions had been influenced by the media as well as by real increases in the crime rates, began to advocate a "get-tough" strategy for dealing with crime. The media, in alerting the public to the chilling realities of crime, played a significant role in making crime-control strategies more attractive to the American public.

Our study of crime in American society begins with a discussion of the disruptive effects of crime, the roots of social disruption, and the relationship between modernization and crime.

DISRUPTIVE EFFECTS OF CRIME

Emile Durkheim, a French sociologist of the late nineteenth and early twentieth centuries, stated that crime is functional for a society, because it helps unite citizens against lawbreakers. He contended that people react to crime by increasing their social contacts and pulling together, thereby enhancing the solidarity of the community. "Crime is, then, necessary; it is bound up with the fundamental conditions of all social life," he asserted, "and by that very fact is useful, because those conditions of which it is a part are themselves indispensable to the normal evolution of morality and law."[11] He further explained:

> Crime brings together upright consciences and concentrates them. We have only to notice what happens, particularly in a small town, when some moral scandal has just been committed. [People] stop each other on the street, they visit each other, they seek to come together to talk of the event and to wax indignant in common.
>
> [If the offended sentiment] is strong, if the offense is serious, the whole group attacked masses itself in the face of the danger and unites, so to speak, in itself. As soon as the news of a crime gets abroad, the people unite, and although the punishment may not be predetermined, the reaction is unified.[12]

Kai T. Erikson, in his study of the Puritan society of New England, found that crime fused individuals into a stronger entity by focusing group feelings and drawing attention to the values of the collective conscience, thus defining and maintaining boundaries of acceptable, or normative, social behavior. Erikson noted: "Deviant forms of behavior, by marking the outer edges of group life, give the inner structure its special character and thus supply the framework within which the people of the group develop an orderly sense of their own cultural identity."[13]

However, the concept that the disorder of crime and social deviance is necessary for progress or is functional for society has little support today. Since the mid–1960s, public opinion polls show, crime has been regarded by the American public as one of the top three social problems.[14] In the 1970s, such catch phrases as "the crime problem," "law and order," and "crime in the streets" came to symbolize the public's fear of the disorder of crime.

James Q. Wilson, a proponent of a **"get-tough" approach** to crime, tells what the fear of crime can do to a community: "Predatory crime, in particular crime committed by strangers on innocent victims, causes the kind of fear that drives people apart from one another and thus impedes or even prevents the formation of meaningful human communities."[15] In Columbus, Ohio, a son and a daughter of the mayor and governor, respectively, were assaulted within a month in separate incidents in different parts of the city. Elliott Currie concludes that the United States is wracked by criminal violence:

> To live in the urban United States in the 1980s is to feel that the elementary bonds of society are badly frayed. The sense of social disintegration is so pervasive that it is easy to forget that things are not the same elsewhere. Violence on the American level comes to seem like a fact of life, an inevitable feature of modern society. It is not. Most of us are aware that we are worse off, in this respect, than other advanced industrial countries. How much worse, however, is truly startling.[16]

ROOTS OF SOCIAL DISRUPTION

Social disruption can be blamed either on human nature or on society itself. These theoretical ideas form the background for our beliefs about the causes of crime.

Human Nature

There are three basic philosophies in which human nature is held accountable for **social disruption**: that humans are sinners and wicked by nature; that humans are pleasure seekers and abuse the rights of others; and that humans are driven into antisocial behavior.

Humans Are Wicked   Ever since Biblical times, Christians and Jews have believed that humans have sinned and fallen short of the glory of God. John Calvin,

Violence on the streets: disorder in American cities. (*Source:* Michele Dogre/Sygma.)

one of the fathers of the Protestant Reformation, was particularly mindful of the sinfulness and limitations of humans, whose "insolence and wickedness" is so great that they "can scarcely be restrained by extremely severe laws."[17] Calvin had little hope that malefactors or criminals could be rehabilitated, and he believed that public order depended on restraining such individuals by the infliction of severe penalties.[18]

The seventeenth-century philosopher Thomas Hobbes argued that the defective or wicked nature of human beings requires repressive social controls by the state to avoid widespread social disruption. He stated that one of the basic questions of social order is: How can humans, naturally endowed with an infinity of desires, an unbounded passion for getting what they want and an "equality of hope" in their ability to get what they want by using force or fraud, live with one another without the ever-present fear of a violent death? Hobbes's answer was that a strong and repressive government is the only effective cure for disorder.[19]

Hobbes believed that without the lawlike restraints of the sovereign state, social life would collapse into an ongoing war between individuals with conflicting self-interests. The naturalness of this sovereign state was dictated by the inability of humans to live together without force and law. Hobbes's renowned treatise *Leviathan* spells out the essential principles of this sovereign state: monopoly of force by the state, the naturalness of centralized sovereignty, the supremacy of national values, and the atomlike character of the individual citizen.[20] Hobbes's support of the all-powerful state was based in part on the belief that almost any other approach would fail and that humankind without strict controls would end up destroying itself.

The notion that wicked people create social disruption continues to be accepted today. As James Q. Wilson put it in *Thinking About Crime,* a "sober" or "unflattering view of man" tells us that "wicked people exist" and that "nothing avails but to set them apart from innocent people."[21] President Ronald Reagan told a convention of police chiefs that "some men are prone to evil, and society has a right to be protected from them."[22] Edward C. Banfield, a Harvard political scientist, quotes Henry George, the American economist, to show the chaos that will erupt if strong forces of social control are not used on wicked people:

> Let the policeman's club be thrown down or wrested from him, and the foundations of the great deep are opened, and quicker than ever before chaos comes again. Strong as it may seem, our civilization is evolving destructive forces. Not desert and forest, but city slums and country roadsides are nursing the barbarians who may be to the new what Hun and Vandal were to the old.[23]

Feudalism, the economic system that developed in Europe during the ninth century and endured until the fourteenth century, is one of the best examples of a society created to control the wickedness of human nature. During the feudal age, almost all the rural land was divided into large estates, owned by absentee lords or nobles, managed by landlords, and farmed by peasants. The owners of the large estates would entrust parcels of land, or fiefdoms, to persons of noble background. The obligation of the landlord was to protect the peasants, their families, and their possessions. The land in each fief was generally divided into two parts. The landlord kept the smaller parcel of land—ordinarily the land nearest the landlord's house (sometimes called the manor)—to manage for his own profit. The remainder of the land was distributed among many peasant families, who usually lived in cottages grouped around the manor.[24]

Each peasant family, from generation to generation, cultivated the same allotment of land, which typically was made up of several small parcels scattered over the fief. The peasants kept the products of the land, but in exchange they owed dues and services to the fiefholder. These dues and services varied in accordance with the agreements made at the outset of the fiefholder-peasant relationship or with the custom of the surrounding area.[25]

The ability to repress dissent among the peasants, who were clearly the "inferior" and "wicked" class, was one of the chief reasons why the feudal society survived so long. The isolated and self-sufficient society of the fief prevented peasants from being "corrupted" by processes of social change or by revolutionary ideas. Religious beliefs and pressures helped the peasants to accept the misery of their lives, but the peasants also knew that if they broke the rules (and the rules were very clear), they would be severely punished. Dissent among the peasants also was discouraged by a castelike consciousness that made everyone aware of his or her status and by cultural and economic conditions that encouraged an acceptance of one's role in the feudal society. Finally, the interdependence of the lord, the fiefholder, and the peasant made it difficult for peasants to alter long-standing economic and social arrangements.

Humans Are Pleasure Seekers Jean-Jacques Rousseau, the French social-contract theorist of the eighteenth century, planted the seeds for social change and the development of a new order as he challenged the prevailing intellectual thought of his day. Rousseau contended that each individual possesses an irrational and unceasing drive for more of everything and anything, a drive that will generate massive social conflict unless it is checked. Thus, according to his view, social disruption arises because human nature is hedonistic, or pleasure seeking; that is, the more one has, the more one wants.[26] In this regard, Rousseau asked: "If, in order to fall heir to the property of a rich mandarin living at the farthest confines of China, whom one had never seen or heard spoken of, it were enough to push a button to make him die, which of us would not push that button?"[27]

To avoid the war of all against all, Rousseau stated, "the rich man, who was the most severely affected because he had the most to lose, . . . proposed to his fellows that they institute rules of peace and justice to which everyone would have to conform, that all individual forces be united into one supreme power which would protect and defend all the members of the association."[28] He argued that it is through this social contract that humans are willing to permit restraints on their behavior and to restore order to society. According to Rousseau, the purpose of civil government is to establish this social contract between citizens and their social order.

Cesare Beccaria and Jeremy Bentham, founders of what is known as the classical school of criminology, applied the notion of social contract to the study of crime. They contended that humans are aware that without law and constraints on their behavior, they would live in a barren and primitive state. Beccaria and Bentham viewed humans as rational creatures who are willing to surrender enough liberty to the state so that society can establish rules and sanctions for the preservation of the social order.[29] Thus, the government under law is the means by which contemporary nations can avoid social disruption.

Beccaria and Bentham, in an effort to reform the punitive and unfair court procedures used during the eighteenth century, added three more ingredients to the concept of the **social contract**. First, they stated that human beings are rational creatures who, being free to choose their actions, can be held responsible for their behaviors. This concept of free will holds that human behavior is purposeful; therefore, individuals choose those actions that will give pleasure and avoid those that will bring pain. Second, they added that a system of rational punishment is necessary to remind individuals of their common interest in preserving the social order. Punishment "should be public, immediate, and necessary; the least possible in the case given; proportioned to the crime; and determined by the laws."[30] Finally, these classical reformers concluded that the purpose—and consequence—of punishment is to deter humans from criminal behavior.

Human Behavior Is Determined   Social disruption has also been explained by the belief that human behavior is constitutionally, psychologically, and/or enviromentally determined. A critical assumption of this viewpoint is the existence of scientific determinism. Crime, like any other phenomenon, is seen as determined by prior causes; it does not just happen. The deterministic approach rejects the position that the individual exercises freedom, possesses reason, and is capable of choice.[31]

Lombroso, an Italian criminologist of the late nineteenth century, argued that some humans are biologically impaired. Lombroso coined the term **born criminals** for these individuals; he believed that such individuals represent an earlier stage of evolutionary development and are more likely to become involved in crime.[32] Sigmund Freud argued that some individuals are psychologically impaired. According to Freud and his many successors, individuals who have suffered severe emotional damage may manifest effects of this damage in the form of criminal behavior in the present or future.[33] Others have claimed that individuals who have grown up impoverished, who have lived in disorganized communities, or who have been environmentally deprived have not been socially processed to live by "the rules." Such individuals, according to this sociological explanation, simply have not been socialized to live in a society without robbing and hurting others.

The means of social order proposed by scientific determinism is the rehabilitative ideal. The goal of rehabilitation is to change an offender's character, attitudes, or behavior patterns so as to diminish his or her criminal propensities.[34] The criminal is sick, according to the medical model of rehabilitative philosophy, and needs to be cured of his or her criminality. Donal E. J. MacNamara, in his noteworthy essay on the medical model, provides a definition of that model:

> In its simplest (perhaps oversimplified) terms, the medical model as applied to corrections assumed the offender to be "sick" (physically, mentally, and/or socially); his offense to be a manifestation or symptom of his illness, a cry for help. . . . Basic to the medical model, although rather surprisingly denied by many of its proponents, is that the criminogenic factors are indigenous to the individual offender and that it is by doing "something" for, to, or with him that rehabilitation can be effected.[35]

Francis Allen, in an essay that has become a classic on the **rehabilitative ideal**, clarifies the basic assumptions of the medical model: (1) that "human behavior is a product of antecedent causes"; (2) that it is the obligation of the scientist to discover these causes; (3) that knowledge of these antecedent causes makes it possible to control human behavior; and (4) that measures employed to treat the offender "should be designed to effect changes in the behavior of the convicted person in the interest of his or her own happiness, health, and satisfaction."[36]

In sum, there are three general philosophies in which human nature has been blamed for social disruption, and each philosophy offers a prescribed means of social control. First, humans are viewed as being sinners or wicked, and, therefore, what is needed to restore order is firm social controls. Second, humans are viewed as pleasure seekers, but as individuals who have the good sense to join together in a social contract, or civil government, to restrain disruptive behavior. Third, human behavior is defined as determined by prior causes. Rehabilitation therefore is needed for those who are constitutionally, psychologically, or sociologically flawed; cured of their criminality, these rehabilitated individuals can become responsible, law-abiding citizens.

Industrial Society and the Impact of Social Change

Society also has been blamed for socially disruptive behavior. The basic assumption here is that industrialized and urbanized society has been unable to assimilate the broad processes of social change, and widespread disruptive behavior has resulted. An examination of **traditional society** and **industrial society** is helpful in assessing the impact of social change and its consequences in terms of disruptive behavior.

The traditional society is so small and limited that all its members know each other well and most remain in close contact all their lives. Few individuals stray beyond the geographical limits of their own society, so they seldom realize that those in other societies have different norms. The primary unit of social organization is the kin group, which is the center of all activity within the society, makes all decisions, and preserves and transmits all norms. Thus, the traditional society is composed of economically self-sufficient groups that face life's problems in conventional ways with traditional and automatic behavior that is expected and is seldom questioned or criticized.[37] The members of a folk society, with their continuous interaction, are all very much alike, both genetically and socially. Norms are clear and consistent and deviation is minimal. The society as a whole is characterized by a strong sense of identification and togetherness.[38]

The industrial society, as exemplified by the nations of Western society, is in direct contrast to the traditional society. The kin group is largely replaced by other distinct and specialized economic, political, religious, and educational organizations. The industrial society is a large society, characterized by social role differentiation and specialization, with the result that many new institutional areas are created that have no precedent in the past and thus require new norms. The society is so complex that, within the institutions themselves, subgroups evolve and use social, economic, or political pressure to maintain or extend their own norms.

An industrial society depends upon a large working force. In the United States, this need has been in large part satisfied by immigration. Of course, apart from the members of Indian tribes, all Americans are either immigrants or the descendants of immigrants. At the time of the Revolutionary War, there were only four million people here to begin this nation, but during the next hundred years, over thirty-five million people left Europe and came to the United States because of the political and economic unrest and displacement caused by industrialization. They came by the millions, found jobs, and stayed. Although this mass movement from Europe was interrupted by World War I and virtually halted by restrictive legislation in 1921 and 1924, the United States retained a heritage of eight million people from Central Europe, six million from Eastern Europe, five million from Italy, four million from Ireland, four million from England, three million from the Balkan countries, and two million from Scandinavia.[39]

The need for labor throughout the United States resulted in a high rate of internal migration. People took literally Horace Greeley's advice to "go West," where land could be acquired cheaply and developed, at first for agriculture and later for industry. Industry's needs caused another geographical shift, from rural to urban areas. But geographical mobility has greater overall significance than these patterns of westward and rural migration. From 1950 to 1960, for example, over 30 million people moved each year; and, though two-thirds of this movement was local, from block to block or across town, five million people went to a new county and another five million moved to different states.

Mobility, then, is one cause of confusion and conflict among the members of an industrial society, but work also can create dissension and disorder. The term *mass production* evokes an image of a long conveyor belt attended by lines of people, each putting a slightly different part into something that will eventually emerge as a finished product. But the factory assembly line of mass production is only one aspect of bureaucratization, an industrial society's system for organizing all levels of social life. Before industrialization, individuals performed their work largely at home, set their own pace, and started and stopped whenever they wished, within the limits of necessity. But when the worker moved to factory or office, he or she became one part of a larger economic organization, and his or her task merely one part of a broad operation requiring the combined efforts of other parts.[40]

This new work world became more and more specialized, partly because individuals are different, and their individual strengths must be cultivated and utilized so that they can function with maximum efficiency as working parts within massive economic organizations. The work world also began to center around a regular routine. It has been suggested that the clock, not the steam engine, is the machine that made industrialization possible. Moreover, the work world is impersonal and contractual. The intense interest in time results from the regularity and precise coordination expected at all levels of life. Individual workers' relationships with fellow workers and superiors reinforce this impersonality. In traditional society, individuals could share the risks involved in earning a living with their kin group or with the whole community, but workers in industrial society are valued chiefly for their labor. Another aspect of impersonality in industry is represented by the contract, an implicit or written agreement between workers and their company that limits each individual to those formal responsibilities and activities that constitute a specific job.

An industrial society also is characterized by a heterogeneous population, as a result of the different levels of experience necessary in a complex division of labor. To fulfill the specialized tasks a division of labor requires, individuals often must move from place to place, leaving behind those with whom they have shared common experiences. The mobile heterogeneous population of an industrial society is often confronted with new norms that arise from unique experiences, or different norms that conflict with traditional patterns, as the presence of new norms compels a reevaluation of older ones.

The industrial society, then, is far more complex than the traditional society because of shifts in population, an extensive division of labor, economic interdependence with other societies having other norms, and technological changes that create innovations in experience and behavior for which traditional norms are inadequate. The social control of the kin group is replaced by complex sets of institutional norms that often conflict, so that dissension and deviation are plentiful and social problems arise.

Some theorists have suggested that the growth of totalitarian governments in the twentieth century can be interpreted as an attempt to "solve" the disorder of modern society. Modernization has created the demand for a new kind of existence, where isolation and anxiety would be minimized and maximum consensus could exist. Authoritarian governments offer individuals a sense of security and order. They have arisen not only in situations where a small group of leaders seized power by force; many Germans and Italians relinquished their freedom willingly. The Nazis and Fascists offered a "folk society" with which the individual could identify, and that gave him or her direction and consistency.

Effects of Modernization   An important subject in the unfolding essay on order and disorder is how the effects of **modernization**, or Westernization, have shaped the ways in which crime is defined and dealt with in Western societies. Ted Robert Gurr suggests that crime in the Western world has been shaped by four aspects of modernization: (1) industrialization; (2) the growth of cities; (3) the expansion of the state's powers and resources; and (4) the humanization of interpersonal relations.[41]

Industrialization   Industrialization, according to Gurr, has had three basic socioeconomic consequences for Western societies, beginning in the late eighteenth and early nineteenth centuries. First, this process pulled a mass of rural workers together into cities. Second, the specialization and diversification of economic activity and the emergence of distinctive groups led to the rapid increase of social heterogeneity. Third, industrialization brought about an unprecedented increase in material wealth; this growth was accompanied at first by increased economic inequality, but was then followed in some industrialized societies by a lessening of inequality.[42]

The incidence of crime, not surprisingly, is affected by industrialization. First, people are more likely to steal when they are abruptly and unexpectedly afflicted by economic distress. The early stages of industrialization changed the focus and extent of economic hardship, and, as there were fewer opportunities for

Effects of the industrial society. (*Source:* John Benton-Harris/Archive Pictures, Inc.)

those skilled only in the traditional occupations, increased property crimes resulted. Second, advanced industrialization was accompanied by changes in the character of property crime. Once industrialized societies pass the threshold at which most individuals' material needs are satisfied, property crime becomes a function of increased opportunity. From this threshold onward, theft increases with the growth of material prosperity. For example, before the Great Depression of the 1930s, economic slumps tended to be accompanied by increased property crime. But since then, especially since about 1950, rising prosperity has meant rising property crime in nearly every Western society.[43]

The politics of public order have been affected by the impact of industrialization on crime. A major consequence of the early stages of industrialization was a rising demand for the protection of private property. The upper middle classes, who benefited substantially from the wealth generated by early capitalism, were typically the strongest advocates of a "get-tough" policy toward property offenses. But as industrial societies matured and moved into the stage of mass consumption, the earlier demands for protection of private property shifted to an increased concern about "victimless" and nuisance activities. Thus, in time, the force of the law was brought to bear on the problems of alcoholism, gambling, prostitution, drug use, loitering, vagrancy, and juvenile delinquency.[44]

Urbanization Urban growth, which has gone hand in hand with industrialization, has had a number of distinctive effects on the problems and politics of public order, independently of industrialization:

1. It has involved selective migration to the cities, especially by young people with few ties and fewer resources—a group that in all places is especially susceptible to crime.

2. Migration from culturally diverse regions, and from other countries, has brought about increased interaction among heterogeneous people. As a consequence, the traditional, and mainly informal, social controls that operated in rural communities lost much of their force.
3. New mechanisms of social integration have developed to replace traditional ones, including occupational associations, new religious creeds and organizations and, in some settings, the re-creation of community at the neighborhood level—the so-called "urban villages." Some of these new communities have developed deviant, and occasionally predatory, subcultures that pose a threat and challenge to public order as conceived by dominant social groups.[45]

Although the effects of urbanization on crime tend to vary across time and among societies, large cities consistently have higher crime rates than towns or rural areas.[46] The higher rates of crime attributed to cities can be questioned, because crime generally has been better recorded and more carefully policed in cities than in rural areas. But crime is certainly more visible in cities, as more people are likely to know about any given offense. The fear of crime is also more concentrated in cities and is more threatening to the social order.[47]

The concentrated fear of crime among the upper and middle classes in growing cities increased the demands for more effective criminal justice policies. This urban bourgeoisie began to favor rationally articulated legal codes, professional policing systems, efficient courts, and a penal system that applied punishment in proportion to the seriousness of the social harm.[48]

Nationalization   Gurr defines **nationalization** as "the growth of the power and resources of the state."[49] He defines four dimensions of nationalization that have affected the politics of public order and the character of the criminal justice system. First, political authority has become centralized at the national level. Second, the state has increased its command of resources to a level higher than in the past. For example, democratic governments have dramatically increased their absolute and proportional share of national products over the last two centuries, especially since the early decades of the twentieth century. The development of mechanisms of group participation and representation in government is a third important dimension of nationalization. These mechanisms refer not only to electoral systems but also to the multitudes of channels by which class, corporate, and associational groups exert influence on local and national politicians. Finally, governments have vastly expanded their scope of action as they have assumed responsibility for a host of general and specialized social and economic functions.[50]

This expansion of the state has been accompanied by a steady increase in political expectations and demands on governments for public order. The scope or range of order for which the state is expected to assume responsibility includes the politics of public order. The earlier emphasis on the protection of person and property shifted in the late nineteenth and early twentieth centuries to a concern with the criminalization and control of victimless crimes and nuisance behavior.

More recently, in Western societies, the decriminalization of what was criminal a century ago has occurred. The contention that the state has the right to punish behavior that outrages the sensibilities of any significant interest group has become a fixed feature of Western political and social thought.[51]

Crisis in confidence is a term currently used in describing present attitudes toward political and legal institutions of American society. Confidence in the criminal justice system appears to be at an all-time low.[52] The loss of confidence in the political institutions did not start with the Watergate affair, but it was certainly highlighted by it. Watergate and the related scandals (Agnew, Vesco, and ITT) involved government officials of the highest rank who were committing such criminal acts as burglary, "bugging," extortion, fraud, bribery, tax evasion, misuse of funds, obstruction of justice, and destruction of criminal evidence.[53]

Jody Powell, former press secretary to President Jimmy Carter, commented on the situation:

> If people keep getting told that their leadership is poor, or ineffective, and that they don't have any real choices, you'll see a fairly steady erosion in the legitimacy of government. That's going to have a real impact on anybody's ability to govern—Reagan's or ours.[54]

Humanization   Gurr also contends that the processes of economic modernization have been accompanied by a shift in prevailing values that he calls **humanization**. The problems and policies of public order have been particularly affected by three of these value changes. First, there are now much stronger internal and external controls on interpersonal aggression than was once the case. Second, a change in the value and respect accorded individuals, regardless of their status, has resulted in a long-term decline in interpersonal violence. Third, a gradual change has taken place with respect to the once-unchallenged assumption that criminals and deviants were morally flawed. In the twentieth century, positivist criminologists first shifted the blame of criminal behavior to physiological and psychological factors and, more recently, to environmental and biomedical causes.[55]

The effects of humanization on the policies of public order have been widespread. These effects can be seen in the steady decline in reliance on capital punishment during the nineteenth century; since the early part of the twentieth century, only South Africa, China, some Middle Eastern countries, and the United States have used the death penalty. A reevaluation of the validity of corporal punishment of prisoners and the criminalization of the physical abuse of children and spouses have been other effects of Gurr's "humanization." The emphasis on rehabilitative practices has had an even far greater impact on the practices of criminal justice. Such rehabilitative policies—now challenged by the "just deserts" and other philosophies—are the products of the principle that criminals, like others, deserve humane treatment and can be led, rather than coerced, away from criminal activities.[56]

Another political manifestation of humanitarian trends involves the increased concern for protecting individuals from lesser forms of interpersonal violence. Aggressive acts formerly viewed as acceptable, or at least looked upon as private matters outside of the state's competence, have now been brought within the purview of the state. These trends involve such diverse matters as petty assault and disorderly conduct, more sensitivity to victims of sexual assault, and, as noted, the criminalization of wife beating and child abuse. Reformers also have urged the decriminalization of "moral offenses" (homosexual acts, drunkenness, prostitution) on grounds that they represent the individual's right to engage in unconventional acts provided that others are not injured by them.[57]

Variations in the effects of modernization   The ways that policies of public order in Western societies have been affected by modernization have varied. Some Western societies are more prosperous, urbanized, and centrally controlled than others, and these factors have shaped distinctive patterns of institutional development. Wars and revolutions have sharp short-term impacts on the incidence of crime, and economic depression, inflation, unemployment, and shortages all cause short-term variations in the problems and policies of public order.[58]

There is some evidence that the United States is beginning to experience a **third industrial revolution,** one built around brain power rather than tools and hard labor. The assembly line is being replaced by robots, but a new assembly line of paper is emerging. Achievement is the basic work ethic of this new industrial revolution, and new ecological patterns are developing as cities are emptying out. The rise of computer fraud is one of the ways the third industrial revolution is affecting crime in America. The reduced need for unskilled workers for laboring jobs is likely to increase street crime, and the emptying of the cities will probably result in higher rates of suburban crime.

Furthermore, there is some evidence that **demodernization,** or a gradual erosion of humanitarian values, is taking place in Western societies. Serious crimes against the person have risen sharply in most Western societies during the last twenty years, a trend that may reflect an increased tolerance of and willingness to do violence to one another. This increase in violence has also been attributed to the explosion in the size of the youth population in the 1960s, the public legitimization of violence under the guise of entertainment and politics, and the development of a hedonistic set of values among many young people.[59]

The rise of violent crimes has reduced the support for humane policies of criminal justice, as evidenced in the United States by a return to the death penalty and by more frequent and severe sentencing of offenders. In the mid–1970s, the politics of law and order began to dominate our crime control policies. Conservative policymakers, beginning with presidential candidate Barry Goldwater in 1964, assured the public that a "get-tough" approach was needed to restore order.

In sum, the definitions of crime and the ways in which crime has been handled in Western societies have been greatly influenced by the processes of industrialization, urbanization, nationalism, and humanization. The rise of industrialization and urbanization has contributed to a number of social problems in urban areas, such as unemployment, poverty, lack of housing, and disorganized communities; these problems, in turn, have led to higher rates of serious crimes

Youth engaging in violent crime. (*Source:* Mark Ellen Mark/Archive Pictures, Inc.)

among the poor. Industrialization has also influenced the rise of white-collar and corporate crime in Western societies. The state has assumed a greater role in public order policies, but a crisis in confidence in some nations is making it difficult at present to fulfill this role. A gradual erosion of humanitarian values in relation to punishing criminals also appears to be taking place. The United States is especially visible in supporting the belief that a "get-tough" approach is needed to restore order, but other Western countries have also embraced this posture.

MODERN NATIONS WITH LITTLE CRIME

With a few notable exceptions, such as Japan, Switzerland, the Low Countries, and Scandinavia, the crime and delinquency rate is increasing at an unprecedented pace throughout the world. The rise is particularly steep in the most highly developed countries, such as the United States, Canada, and England, and in the rapidly developing countries of the Third World. This should come as no great surprise since development has always seemed to impose some uninviting payments for a healthier, longer, and more affluent lifestyle.

Japan

It is a widely accepted fact that Japan, an island nation of enormous density (with a population approximately half that of the United States), has achieved modernization without the social disorganization and other undesirable consequences associated with urban, industrial, secular societies.[60]

Table 1.1 shows that while the Japanese population of legally responsible adults grew from 53 to 88 million in the years 1948 through 1977, conventional offenses known to the police and local authorities *fell* from 2995 to 1437 per 100,000 adults. The number of suspects per 100,000 *fell* from 1003 to 409, the number of persons prosecuted from 444 to 161, and the number of persons convicted from 427 to 118. Detailed inspection of Table 1.1 also shows that most of this decline occurred prior to 1970. Since then, the rates of offenses known, and of offenders handled in the system, have declined less sharply. Still, this general decline occurred precisely during the time when other developed countries were experiencing great increases in nearly every category of crime, especially in the safety offenses.[61]

The decrease in the rate of crime in Japan is not an artificial drop caused by changes in the Japanese penal code, of reporting and recording procedures, or of alterations in the processing of complaints. Insofar as any criminal justice data, from any country, can be used with confidence, these Japanese figures are undoubtedly more reliable than crime trend data from elsewhere. Few can dis-

Table 1.1 NON-TRAFFIC PENAL CODE OFFENDERS—SUSPECTED, PROSECUTED, AND CONVICTED: SELECTED YEARS (COMPUTED PER 100,000 CRIMINALLY RESPONSIBLE POPULATION)

Year	Criminally Responsible Population Unit: 1,000	Rate Computed per 100,000 of the Criminally Responsible Population			
		Offenses Known	Suspects	Persons Prosecuted	Persons Convicted in the First Court of First Instance
1948	53,413	2,995	1,003	444	427
1955	61,443	2,337	799	297	254
1966	76,459	1,690	564	245	206
1969	79,740	1,570	470	204	167
1970	80,500	1,587	470	198	159
1971	81,364	1,526	442	182	148
1972	82,947	1,473	417	185	151
1973	83,885	1,416	423	166	137
1974	84,792	1,425	425	153	126
1975	86,323	1,428	419	170	118
1976	87,195	1,429	409	169	118
1977	88,145	1,437	409	161	—

Source: White Paper on Crime, Government of Japan, 1977.

agree with the assertion that it is usually in the interest of every criminal justice system to increase the magnitude of the problem it confronts, if only for budgetary and personnel reasons, to say nothing of political pressures and motives. Given this bias towards the exaggeration of the crime problem, the Japanese trend line is even more impressive.

The overall Japanese crime rate was separated into the major components of property, violent, heinous, sex, negligence, and miscellaneous offenses. It is noteworthy that only the property crime category showed a substantial increase from 1973 through 1977; the rate in all other categories fell dramatically. Most of the yearly increases in property crimes were caused by the greater numbers of theft (larceny) offenses reported and by a very substantial rise in the rate of reported embezzlements. In contrast, the number of violent offenses investigated by the police declined systematically and substantially. Comparing 1973 and 1977, the rate of reported violent crimes decreased no less than 21 percent. The sharpest decline of all, however, was in the sex offense rate. All of these data, by specific category, are presented in Table 1.2.

In comparison to the United States, for example, Japan has about 22.5 percent of the murder rate, 20 percent of the rape rate, and 0.95 percent of the robbery rate. Reversed, this means that the United States has 4.5 times as many murders per 100,000 persons, 5.0 times the rapes, and 105 times the robberies. It should also be noted that substance abuse is no real problem in Japan, but the high suicide rates are a genuine concern.

Despite the intrusion of Western ways, there is little alienation in Japan's homogenous population, fewer structural and ascriptive barriers to achievement, and great social cohesion. The Japanese family, still extended, remains strong. Its strength is reinforced by other socializing agencies such as the school and neighborhood groups and by a profound respect for governmental agencies and the police. Enforcement is significantly easier because the population is cooperative.

Some examples should suffice: the "cleared by arrest" rate (a measure of police efficiency) in the United States is about 22 percent. That is, the police arrest

Table 1.2   RATES OF MAJOR CRIMES KNOWN TO THE POLICE PER 100,000 POPULATION IN DEVELOPED AND DEVELOPING COUNTRIES AND IN JAPAN, 1970–1975

Crime	Developing Countries Group	Developed Countries Group	Japan
Homicide	5.1	2.7	2.1
Assault	253.1	115.3	49.9
Sex Offense	24.3	24.0	5.8
Kidnapping	1.2	0.2	0.2
Robbery	58.8	33.3	2.1
Theft	354.3	1,370.5	927.3
Fraud	30.1	136.4	45.7

Source: Figures are based on *UN Report on Crime Prevention and Control,* 1977.

someone or solve the crime in about 22 percent of the cases reported to them. The Japanese police "cleared" 77 percent of the reported robberies, 83 percent of the rapes, 96 percent of the murders, and 86 percent of the arson cases. The Japanese are also relentless in their pursuit of a case through the criminal justice process to conviction. Once the latter is accomplished, however, the punishment is quite light by U.S. standards, for both juveniles and adults. Finally, the Japanese police and social control apparatus is aided greatly by crime prevention associations of local citizens in each district. These associations are especially valuable in the juvenile area. A wayward juvenile is soon made to feel the shame of his or her deviant behavior. Family, police, school, and neighborhood "good citizens" combine to keep such youths in place.

The social cost of this network of control agents, some will argue, is to produce maximum conformity to existing standards—but, in so doing, it restricts innovative and rebellious behaviors that are socially desirable. The right to be different, to be left alone, falls victim to the number one priority: the need to be part of the cohesive whole. This need is seen as a functional necessity in a land of great tradition, holy rituals, and limited natural resources. Suicide is a likely option for those who fail to become part of the cohesive whole. This social cohesion also protects, or insulates, the overseas Japanese from deviant conduct— even into the second and third generation. The delinquency rates of overseas Japanese are characteristically the lowest of any group except the Chinese.

Switzerland: Cities with Little Crime

Marshall B. Clinard contends that Switzerland represents an exception to the high crime rates of other industrialized and urbanized Western societies. He found that even in the largest Swiss cities crime is not a major problem.[62] In analyzing the reduced rates of crime in Switzerland, Clinard says:

> The incidence of criminal homicide and robbery is low, despite the fact that firearms are readily available in most households, owing to the nature of the country's military system. The low incidence of crime in Switzerland is even more intriguing in view of the fact that the criminal justice system is neither harsh nor repressive. In German-speaking Switzerland, constituting nearly three-fourths of the country, persons are generally not arrested and booked for a crime but are given a citation; if they are prosecuted there is no plea bargaining. Sentences are generally short, even for serious crimes, with the exception of murder. They rarely exceed a year, and most convicted offenders sentenced to prison are given suspended sentences. For the most part, those who do go to prison receive short sentences, and a large proportion of them are released prior to the expiration of the sentence.[63]

Clinard asserts, with ample empirical data to back him up, that "one of the major explanations of Switzerland's lower crime rate is that it has a consistently lower percentage of offenders among its youth."[64] He then suggests several explanations for the reduced youth crime rates in Switzerland. First, the Swiss family retains tighter control over its members than do families in other Western countries. For example, home discipline is more rigid; children (up to age 20) have less flexibility in their lives than their peers elsewhere. Fewer mothers work; the family remains intact to a remarkable extent. Second, the school buttresses this disciplined life. Permissiveness is at a minimum, and achievement is expected. The schoolmaster is respected, and an assault on him or her would be beyond comprehension. Third, surveys of the attitudes of youth indicate little intergenerational conflict. Fourth, there are no slums in Switzerland, as defined by any national norms. There is no culture of poverty, no disorganized communities, no delinquent gangs, and no drug subculture. In all of Switzerland, the police counted about a dozen youth gangs, but none were committed to delinquent and criminal acts as a way of life.

Fifth, Switzerland has no underclass in the American or British sense. There are no black ghettos, as in the United States; nor Indian, Pakistani, or West Indian enclaves as in London and Midland English cities. The Swiss, like the West Germans and the Benelux countries, have been importing "guest workers," legal aliens on fixed terms, to do the menial and "dirty" work which needs to be done. These migrants are the underclass and, in their segregated areas, are to Swiss society what illegal, undocumented Mexicans are to California. With the guest workers from Greece, Turkey, Italy, Spain, and Yugoslavia doing the lowly jobs, Swiss youth necessarily are pushed up to a higher social status. The Swiss, in other words, produce no "losers." Unemployment, poverty, and the slums are for others; the bottom is reserved for the foreigners. The system probably largely accounts for the lack of alienation of Swiss youth.

Finally, Swiss society, like Japanese society, is homogenous, and this facilitates consensus on values, lifestyle, and social structure. About 65 percent of the Swiss are German speaking, less than 50 percent speak Romansh, and the rest are more or less evenly divided between the French and Italian speakers. Each language group is more than merely a community of speakers. It is an autonomous community—homogeneous by area, by endogamy, and by custom. The Swiss federal system has allowed for these divisions by making the canton (the local community) the governing authority in all but national matters. So, the controls from the family, school, and political areas are harmonious and integrative. In this context, traditional values can be taught and absorbed, intergenerational conflict reduced, and alienation minimized. The segregation is voluntary; ethnicity is the common denominator.

In summary, Japan has high suicide rates and Switzerland has had several recent urban riots connected with squatters, but these nations have distinguished themselves as low crime societies. The homogeneity of these societies produces a very low level of cultural conflict and enables these societies to maintain a high level of integration and cohesiveness. This homogeneity is maintained either through the division of a complex and heterogeneous society into homogeneous particles—like the cantons in Switzerland—or through ethnic segregation, as in the case of Japan. The canton system in Switzerland creates a lateral identification and participation; in Japan the same effect is achieved through a strong ascriptive system in which belonging to the family, the class, and the nation is the dominant pivot for citizen identification. This structure facilitates strong and efficient informal controls that keep people in line. Thus, these societies produce only low levels of alienation, and they strengthen the bonding of the individual to his or her immediate social surroundings.

CRIMINOLOGY: THE SCIENTIFIC STUDY OF CRIME

Edwin Sutherland's definition of criminology is one of the most widely accepted:

> Criminology is the body of knowledge regarding crime as a social phenomenon. It includes within its scope the process of making law, of breaking laws, and of reacting toward the breaking of law. The objective of criminology is the development of a body of general and verified principles and of other types of knowledge regarding this process of law, crime, and treatment.[65]

A relatively young field, criminology dates back roughly a hundred years. Most criminologists today received their academic training in the social sciences, frequently taking their degrees in sociology, but the pioneers in the field were trained in other disciplines. Cesare Lombroso (1835–1909), who is known as the father of criminology, was a physician and surgeon. Raffaele Garofalo (1852–1934) was a professor of law and a magistrate, and Enrico Ferri (1856–1929) was a criminal lawyer and member of the Italian parliament.[66] These three are known collectively as the Italian School of Criminology.

Criminology gained wide acceptance in American universities during the early decades of the twentieth century. Although the early criminology textbooks were written primarily by sociologists, other criminologists received their primary training in such fields as psychiatry, public administration, criminal law, anthropology, and political science. One positive aspect of the interdisciplinary nature of criminology is that the input of individuals with these varied types of training has expanded the understanding of the criminalization process. For example, understanding the criminalization process requires the study of criminal law, an insight into psychiatry, a grasp of public administration and political science, and a knowledge of the components of the criminal justice system.[67]

However, criminology has been widely attacked in the United States and elsewhere in recent years. Some scholars have even questioned the capacity of criminology to deliver its promises of a scientific understanding of crime.[68] The most frequent criticisms of criminology include charges of being tied too closely to the state and thereby failing to document adequately the futility of the state's crime control policies; of focusing too much on the individual offender and ignoring the larger issues related to crime; of lacking an integrative and analytical approach; and of neglecting the importance of social policy.[69]

The order and disorder approach of this text will be helpful in avoiding these deficits attributed to criminology. First, viewing the study of crime through the perspective of order and disorder neither accepts the crime control policies of the state—as is done by traditional approaches to criminology—nor rejects the "evilness of the state"—as radical criminologists have done. Second, one of the fascinating aspects of the order and disorder approach is that it includes an analysis of crime on the societal, institutional, and individual levels, thereby encompassing both the macro and micro issues related to crime. Third, the order and disorder approach provides a needed integrative and analytical approach to understanding crime. Although the quantification of crime has made rapid gains in the past two decades, few integrative or theoretical advances have taken place in criminology during this same period. Finally, the attention given to social disorder leads to an emphasis on policy analysis. Criminologists too frequently regard policy analysis as polemical or ideological, because they limit their role to using value-free and scientific means to study and understand crime. But we question whether criminology, or any other academic field, can or should be value-free. Individuals bring background assumptions, or beliefs, to any study of crime, and these background assumptions shape what is studied, how the data are interpreted, and what conclusions are drawn from the data. Jon Snodgrass expressed this point very well:

> Criminology was not . . . the value-free, objective, and scientific postulations that creators professed it to be. The personal outlook on the nature of American society had deep and lasting ramifications for the discipline; it permeated the intellectual production; it shaped the structure of the theories, oriented the empirical research and the data (facts) selected as evidence, determined the subjects of theory and research, restricted the breadth of variables open to investigation and causal attention, molded the concepts, colored interpretations and conclusions, and provided the American criminological tradition with a rather homogeneous and pervasive ideological quality.[70]

SUMMARY

Humans have always quested for the ordered society. Surveys show that social disruption, especially the disruption of crime, is currently perceived as one of the most disturbing social problems facing American society. The historical and social background contained in this chapter will later become critical in our attempt to explain crime and provide the United States with a response to the social reality of crime.

In the ordered societies of the past, such as that under feudalism, the social classes understood their place and how they were supposed to act. The social strata, especially those who were exploited, accepted their roles and felt powerless to alter their stations in life. The consensus of values clearly provided cement for these societies. But the social stability of the feudal society and the more recent folk community made it much easier to establish and maintain an ordered society than in the ever-changing contemporary social situation. The modernized and industrial societies of the present typically have high rates of social disorder, including high rates of violent and property crimes. Major exceptions are Japan and Switzerland, both of which are characterized by a homogenous population, supportive community, strong family unity, and stable social structure.

While few dispute the fact that crime is a serious social problem today, the question of what to do about crime causes wide disagreement in all Western societies. We do know that the study of crime can tell us much about the society in which we live. We know that crime is affected by changes in societal understanding and values, as well as by the political and economic climate of society. Although this text focuses on crime in America, many of the insights it presents about the disruption of crime could be applied to other Western societies.

REFERENCES

Bernard, Thomas J. *The Consensus–Conflict Debate: Form and Content in Social Theories.* New York: Columbia University Press, 1983.

Course, Keith, et al. "The False Promises of Criminology and the Promise of Justice." Paper presented at the American Society of Criminology Annual Meeting, Toronto, Canada, 4–6 November 1982.

Currie, Elliot. *Confronting Crime.* New York: Pantheon, 1985.

Davis, William Stearns. *Life on a Mediaeval Barony: A Picture of a Typical Feudal Community in the Thirteenth Century.* New York: Harper & Row, 1923.

Durkheim, Emile. *The Rules of Sociological Method.* Translated by Sarah A. Solovay and John H. Mueller. Edited by George E. G. Catlin. New York: Free Press, 1938.

Friedrichs, David O. "An Age of Violence and Disillusionment: Two Viewpoints on the 'Legitimacy Crisis.' " *Justice Reporter* I (Spring 1981), pp. 2–8.

Gleick, James. *Chaos: Making a New Science.* New York: Viking, 1987.

Gurr, Ted Robert. "Development and Decay: Their Impact on Public Order in Western History." In *History and Crime: Implications for Criminal Justice Policy,* edited by James A. Inciardi and Charles E. Faupel. Beverly Hills, Calif.: Sage, 1980, pp. 31–52.

Hobbes, Thomas. *Leviathan.* New York: Macmillan, 1947.

Vanderwood, Paul J. *Disorder and Progress: Bandits, Police, and Mexican Development.* Lincoln, Neb.: University of Nebraska Press, 1981.

Wilson, James Q. *Thinking About Crime.* revised ed. New York: Basic Books, 1983.

NOTES

1. Paul J. Vanderwood, *Disorder and Progress: Bandits, Police, and Mexican Development* (Lincoln, Neb.: University of Nebraska Press, 1981), p. xi.

2. Joseph F. Sheley, *America's "Crime Problem": An Introduction to Criminology* (Belmont, Calif.: Wadsworth, 1985), p. 2.

3. *Oxford Paperback Dictionary* (New York: Oxford University Press, 1979), p. 445.

4. Ted Robert Gurr, *Rogues, Rebels, and Reformers: A Political History of Urban Crime and Conflict* (Beverly Hills, Calif.: Sage, 1976), p. 9.
5. Rosabeth Moss Kanter, *Commitment and Community: Communes and Utopias in Sociological Perspective* (Cambridge: Harvard University Press, 1972), p. 39.
6. *Webster's New Twentieth Century Dictionary of the English Language Unabridged,* 2d ed. (New York: Simon and Schuster, 1968), p. 527.
7. David J. Rothman, *The Discovery of the Asylum: Social Order and Disorder in the New Republic* (Boston: Little, Brown, 1971).
8. Donald Black, *The Behavior of Law* (New York: Academic Press, 1976.
9. Francis T. Cullen et al., "Explaining the Get Tough Movement: Can the Public Be Blamed?" (Paper presented at the Annual Meeting of the American Society of Criminology, November 1984), p. 10.
10. Richard Quinney, *The Problem of Crime: A Critical Introduction to Criminology,* 2d ed. (New York: Harper & Row, 1977), p. 13.
11. Emile Durkheim, *The Rules of Sociological Method,* trans. Sarah A. Solovay and John H. Mueller, ed. George E. G. Catlin (New York: Free Press, 1938), pp. 67–69.
12. Ibid., pp. 102–104.
13. Kai T. Erickson, *Wayward Puritans: A Study in the Sociology of Deviance,* 2d. ed. (New York: Wiley, 1983), p. 5.
14. Thomas E. Cronin et al., *U.S. v. Crime in the Streets* (Bloomington, Ind.: Indiana University Press, 1981), p. 60.
15. James Q. Wilson, *Thinking About Crime,* revised ed. (New York: Basic Books, 1983), p. 5.
16. Elliot Currie, *Confronting Crime,* (New York: Pantheon, 1985), p. 5.
17. See Book IV, Chapter 25, in John Calvin, *Institutes of the Christian Religion,* trans. John McNeil (Philadelphia: Westminster Press, 1958).
18. Ibid.
19. Thomas Hobbes, *Leviathan* (New York: Macmillan, 1947).
20. Ibid.
21. Wilson, *Thinking About Crime,* p. 260.
22. Quoted in Currie, *Confronting Crime,* p. 23.
23. Edward C. Banfield, *The Unheavenly City: The Nature and Future of Our Urban Crisis* (Boston: Little, Brown, 1968), p. 158.
24. Charles Seingnobos, *The Feudal Regime* (New York: Holt, 1908), pp. 3–4.
25. Ibid.
26. Thomas J. Bernard, *The Consensus–Conflict Debate: Form and Content in Social Theories* (New York: Columbia University Press, 1983), p. 81.
27. Quoted in William Bonger, *Criminality and Economic Conditions* (Bloomington, Ind.: University of Indiana Press, 1969), pp. 126–127.
28. Bernard, *Consensus-Conflict Debate,* p. 81.
29. Cesare Beccaria, *Of Crimes and Punishment,* trans. Fr. Kenelm Foster and Jane Grigson (New York: Oxford University Press, 1964).
30. Ibid.
31. Donald C. Gibbons, "Differential Treatment of Delinquents and Interpersonal Maturity Level: A Critique," *Social Service Review* 44 (1970), p. 68.
32. Cesare Lombroso, introduction to Fina Lombroso Ferrero, *Criminal Man According to the Classification of Cesare Lombroso* (New York: Putnam, 1911).
33. Sigmund Freud, *An Outline of Psychoanalysis* (reprint ed., New York: Norton, 1963).
34. Andrew von Hirsch, *Doing Justice: The Choice of Punishments* (New York: Hill and Wang, 1976), p. 12.

35. Donal E. J. MacNamara, "The Medical Model in Corrections: Requiescat in Pace," *Criminology* 14 (February 1977), pp. 439–440.

36. Francis A. Allen, *The Borderland of Criminal Justice* (Chicago: University of Chicago Press, 1964), p. 26.

37. The following discussion is adapted from Russell R. Dynes, Alfred C. Clarke, Simon Dinitz, and Iwao Ishino, *Social Problems: Dissensus and Deviation in an Industrial Society* (New York: Oxford University Press, 1964), pp. 12–34.

38. Robert Redfield, "The Folk Society," *American Journal of Sociology* (January 1947), pp. 293–308.

39. Oscar Handlin, *The Uprooted: The Epic Story of the Great Migrations That Made the American People* (Boston: Little, Brown, 1951), p. 3.

40. Lewis Mumford, *Technics and Civilization* (New York: Harcourt, Brace, 1934), p. 14.

41. Ted Robert Gurr, "Development and Decay: Their Impact on Public Order in Western History," in *History and Crime: Implications for Criminal Justice Policy,* ed. James A. Inciardi and Charles E. Faupel (Beverly Hills, Calif.: Sage, 1980), pp. 31–52.

42. Ibid., p. 33.

43. Ibid., pp. 33–34.

44. Ibid., pp. 34–35.

45. Ibid., pp. 36–37.

46. For other explanations of why crime is higher in urban areas, see Ferdinand Tonnies, *Community and Society,* trans. Charles P. Loomis (New York: Harper & Row, 1957), and Emile Durkheim, *The Division of Labor in Society* (New York: Free Press, 1964).

47. Gurr, "Development and Decay," pp. 37–38.

48. Ibid., p. 39.

49. Ibid., pp. 40.

50. Ibid.

51. Ibid., p. 41.

52. Ibid., pp. 41–42.

53. David O. Friedrichs, "Part I: The Crisis of Confidence and Criminal Justice," *Justice Reporter* 1 (Spring 1981), p. 3.

54. Quoted in *Time,* 17 November 1980.

55. Gurr, "Development and Decay," p. 44.

56. Ibid., p. 45.

57. Ibid.

58. Ibid., p. 47.

59. Ibid., p. 48.

60. Discussion adapted from Gideon Fishman and Simon Dinitz, "A Country with Safe Streets" (Unpublished paper, n.d.).

61. White Paper on Crime, Government of Japan, 1977.

62. Marshall B. Clinard, *Cities with Little Crime: The Case of Switzerland* (Cambridge: Cambridge University Press, 1978), p. 1.

63. Ibid.

64. Ibid, p. 122.

65. Edwin H. Sutherland and Donald R. Cressey, *Criminology,* 10th ed. (Philadelphia: Lippincott, 1978), p. 3.

66. Hugh D. Barlow, *Introduction to Criminology,* 2d ed. (Boston: Little, Brown, 1981), p. 21.

67. Harry E. Allen, Paul C. Friday, Julian B. Roebuck, and Edward Sagarin, *Crime and Punishment: An Introduction to Criminology* (New York: Free Press, 1981), p. 23.

68. Keith Course et al., "The False Promises of Criminology and the Promise of Justice" (Paper presented at the American Society of Criminology Annual Meeting, Toronto, Canada, 4–6 November 1982), p. 11.
69. Ibid.
70. Jon Snodgrass, "The American Criminological Portraits of the Men and Ideology in a Discipline" (Ph.D. dissertation, University of Pennsylvania, 1972), p. 25.

CHAPTER 2

Law and Society

CONSTITUTIONAL ORDER
Respect for the Law
Disobedience of the Law
PURPOSE OF THE LAW
NATURE AND FUNCTION OF CRIMINAL LAW
Substantive Criminal Law
Procedural Criminal Law
    Sources of Procedural Criminal Law
    Due Process Model Versus Crime Control
        Model
SOCIAL CONTEXT OF THE LAW
PERSPECTIVES ON THE LAW

Consensus Perspective
Pluralist Perspective
Conflict Perspective
ANALYSIS
Law: The First Condition of an Ordered
    Society
Due Process Ideal and Bureaucratic Reality
The Rule of Law
SUMMARY
REFERENCES
NOTES

KEY TERMS

actus reus
Bill of Rights
bureaucratic justice
civil law
common law
conflict model
consensus model
constitutional model
courtroom team
crime
crime control model
criminal law

due process model
justice model
mens rea
pluralist model
procedural criminal law
retribution
rule of law
substantive criminal law
utilitarian
utilitarian punishment philosophy
vagrancy

> *Criminology, however scientific, can never divorce itself from the mythos that underlies it. If we see* homo delinquent *as the protagonist of his own story, then justice has one kind of meaning; if we see him as victim, it has another. Ever since the rise of biological determinism in the late nineteenth century, law and criminology have diverged because their assumptions are different. Where the law posits free will, criminology, both biogenic and sociogenic, posits determinism. Where the law sees a criminal who acts rationally, criminology sees someone who does not—who is, in fact, driven by forces beyond his control or understanding. It is not that the law is less "scientific" than the biological and the behavioral sciences, rather that it operates in the classic Christian tradition, under different assumptions about human nature. The law appeals to precedent and common sense, criminology to its data; but at bottom, the real, if unrecognized, difference between them is philosophical. The reason we argue fruitlessly over what should be done about criminals is that we cannot agree on who-and-what is man.*
>
> —Ysabel Rennie[1]

Ysabel Rennie correctly surmises that the law is based upon the view of rational citizens who acknowledge their responsibility as members of a society and who want a society ordered by legal rules. The type of ordered society that existed under feudalism in Europe disappeared with the demise of that economic and social system. But another type of ordered society appeared in the eighteenth century with the rise of philosophical rationalism, and it is described in the writings of the classical school of criminology. Cesare Beccaria and Jeremy Bentham, previously mentioned as founders of the classical school, proposed that human beings are rational persons who, being free to choose their actions, can be held responsible for their behavior.[2]

Beccaria based the legitimacy of sanctions against criminals on the social contract. This concept, the major tenet of the Enlightenment thinkers of the eighteenth century, holds that an individual is bound to society only by his or her consent and that both society and the individual have responsibilities to each other. Beccaria believed that each individual surrenders only enough liberty to the state so that society can establish rules and sanctions for the preservation of the social order.[3] He explained individual choice in this way:

> Laws are the conditions of that fellowship which unites men, hitherto independent and separate, once they have tired of living in a perpetual state of war and of enjoying a liberty rendered useless by the uncertainty of its preservation. They will sacrifice a portion of this liberty so that they may enjoy the rest of it in security and peace.[4]

In sum, the founders of the classical school contended that the social contract between citizens and the state enables the law to establish a set of rules, or sanctions, to bring order to a disordered society.

Law is only one means of social control, but over the broad span of history, the use of law has broadened. The rates of legislation, litigation, and adjudication have increased because of the reduced control that cultural groups, religious beliefs, and social institutions have over people's lives. Further, as American society has become more industrialized and urbanized, with the result that humans deal with one another more impersonally and formally than in the past, the law has been more widely used to establish social control.[5]

Criminal law and **civil law** are the two basic types of law. Criminal law deals with public peace and safety. The idea behind criminal law is that a criminal violation against any member of a society represents a criminal violation against the entire society. When such a violation takes place, society has not only the right but also the obligation to take corrective and retaliatory action. The person injured by a criminal act is entitled to have the entire society represent him or her. Thus, the law frees the injured party from having to risk further injury in the act of seeking revenge.[6]

Civil law, on the other hand, is essentially private law governing the relationships among persons or groups. In civil law, the role of the state is to be a neutral umpire among disputants. Civil suits are listed with the name of the person or party bringing suit first *(Jones* v. *Smith)*. Civil law encompasses a wide range of rights and duties; courts enforce the civil law by making the wrongdoer, or transgressor, pay the injured party for losses. Civil cases have two kinds of outcomes: monetary compensation, or damages, for injuries sustained; and court orders, called *injunctions,* obligating the person or government in the wrong to terminate the misconduct.[7]

CONSTITUTIONAL ORDER

Throughout history, various ideas, thoughts, justifications, and rationalizations have produced theses explaining the origins of law, defining whose order the law is serving, and interpreting how law is to be judged. For example, Plato believed that the law was to serve the philosopher kings at the expense of the masses;

Socrates held that the law, or justice, was designed for the individual at the expense of the group; and Aristotle felt that the law was created for the benefit and concern of the group at the expense of the individual. These same philosophies concerning the origins of law, the control over law, and the interpretation of law have endured to the present, for the questions about the law that troubled past societies are the same questions that trouble contemporary societies.

The origins of American criminal law can be traced to the Code of Hammurabi (1750 B.C.), to the Draconian Code in Greece (800 B.C.), and to the Law of the Twelve Tables in Rome (450 B.C.). But in actuality most of America's legal concepts are derived from English common law and Blackstone's *Commentaries*.

As the term itself suggests, the basis of **common law** was custom and tradition. Criminals were tried by juries in England to establish guilt, but the law was applied and interpreted by judges. Thus, common law was judge-made law, in that the laws were molded, refined, examined, and changed as each decision was made. Judges were supposed to draw their decisions from existing precedents or principles of law, but these principles actually reflected the evolving values, attitudes, and ethical ideas of the English people. Judges relied on their own past actions and continued to modify their actions under the pressure of changing times and changing patterns of litigation.[8]

The English common law was imported to the colonies, and its precedents and procedures were maintained until the American Revolution. At that time, a written constitution was ratified, and state legislatures and Congress gained the power to pass criminal laws, as long as they did not conflict with the Constitution and its Bill of Rights.

Two decades before the American Revolution, Blackstone's *Commentaries*, with their exposition of the rights of Englishmen, set forth ideas about the rights and freedom of the individual that the colonists later used in the political controversies that led to the Declaration of Independence. Blackstone's *Commentaries* also influenced the criminal procedures that were later adopted in the American colonies. The rules regarding arrest and the system of bail were the same, as were the systems of arraignment, trial procedures, appellate review, reprieve, and pardon.[9]

The American revolutionaries were deeply impressed with the dangerous potential of criminal prosecution as an instrument of political and religious repression and, therefore, they made important changes in the system of criminal justice through constitutional provisions. The value of legality, the cornerstone of this constitutional system, is summed up by the Bill of Rights: No person shall be deprived of life, liberty or property without due process of law. The intent of the Bill of Rights was to protect the individual against coercive government action, except for that exercised in conformity with a previously stated legal grant of power.

Any government official has the power to kill, confine, or seize the property of those who offend him or her only when it is granted by the law. The writers of the Constitution wanted to assure that the process of being governed by law would be monitored by independent, law-trained judges, who would review the legality of the exercise of coercive power and monitor it. Thus, the executive cannot carry out punishment until an independent court has issued a formal judgment.[10]

The **constitutional model** of the criminal justice system process is based on a radical view of the personality of the accused and a much altered position of the individual whom the state seeks to punish. Although the accused has occupied a subordinate and passive place throughout much of the history of the law, underlying the American system is the concept that the accused is an equal contestant. The accused is to be given competent counsel and the opportunity to challenge the legal basis for any action proposed against him or her. The accused is even permitted the right to stand silent without his or her action being interpreted as proof of guilt.[11] In Box 2.1 Stuart A. Scheingold aptly describes how the Constitution was seen as the means by which order would be brought to the emerging American society.

According to Scheingold, three key ideas undergird the theory of government under law. First, the U.S. Constitution lays the foundation for a just political order. Second, legal reasoning as employed by judges provides a subtle tool for updating constitutional principles. Third, American politics are responsive to constitutional principles; that is, when judges talk, politicians listen. Taken together, these ideas ground "faith in the political efficacy and ethical sufficiency of law as a principle of government."[12]

Scheingold argues that the influence of legal symbols is indirect but powerful in American life, because they "condition perceptions, establish role expectations, provide standards of legitimacy, and account for the institutional patterns of American politics."[13] He adds that the reason legal values have such a grip on the American people is that these values take root early; indeed, research has indicated that even young children seem to associate successful social ordering with rules.[14]

Respect for the Law

The law provides the framework for an ordered society because of the respect it is given by the public. This respect for the law is a traditional norm in American society, even though an individual may disagree with the law and seek to change it. Thus, the law is important not only because it authorizes distribution of particular values, but also because it has symbolic effect. Once enacted, laws tend to command respect even from those who oppose them.

This respect for the law has at least two consequences for the judicial process. First, it imbues court proceedings with a dignity and a ritualism that is unmatched in other branches of American government. Courtrooms are often built to resemble temples; that is, they tend to be dimly lit and richly paneled and to have high ceilings. More importantly, the law provides rules for society, and members of society have felt enough respect for the law that they usually have been inclined to obey these rules.[15]

Jonathan D. Casper, who interviewed criminals convicted of violating the criminal law, found that (with the exception of some convicted narcotics viola-

BOX 2.1

THE CONSTITUTION

The law writers trace the justness of our constitutional document to the very careful balances it strikes between stability and change and between freedom and social responsibility. Any constitution is supposed to have a stabilizing effect on the policy, because it specifies in advance the rights and obligations of citizens and of authorities as well. Our Constitution is additionally defended on more substantive grounds. The particular mix of rights and obligations is said to promote a decent relationship between the people and their government—one anchored firmly in mutual respect and responsibility; one in which the citizen has a stake in the system and is, in turn, respected by its officials.

The case for constitutionalism rests on the alternative it offers to force and violence as a means of resolving conflict within the polity. The claim of constitutionalists is that in bringing the protean world of politics under the influence of legal norms, a constitution lends a welcome measure of stability to the political order. . . . So long as the rules of the game are enforced in a systematic and even-handed fashion—so long as the authorities take the rights seriously—all those with a stake in the existing system will have good reason not to take the law into their own hands. Forbearance and restraint are, in other words, the price of a secure social setting. . . .

The theory of constitutional government also implies a legal approach to political change. If the Constitution does actually express our most fundamental political ideas, it becomes a timeless document. Properly interpreted by the judiciary, constitutional standards encourage us to constantly reexamine and upgrade the ethical tone of our society. As such, they enable us to adjust peacefully to changing conditions, but in a manner consistent with values we have agreed to live by as a people. Rather than tieing us irrevocably to the past, constitutional standards are presented as indispensable guides to the future.

Source: This material appears in Stuart A. Scheingold, *The Politics of Rights: Lawyers, Public Policy, and Political Change* (New Haven: Yale University Press, 1974), pp. 16, 24–26.

tors) these individuals believed the law they violated was in fact a valid one. When asked what would happen if the law against their crime did not exist, almost all of the interviewees indicated that repeal of the law would result in a crime epidemic. They viewed a society without law as one in which everyone would steal from others or engage in assaults upon those whom they disliked. These criminals tended to perceive the purpose of the law as constraining such behavior by setting up mechanisms to protect persons and their property against unscrupulous individuals.[16] In short, the interviewees who had been unwilling to follow the law in their own lives still argued that the rules of society were necessary because individuals need controls placed upon their behaviors.

Disobedience of the Law

Over the past several decades, however, respect for the law has increasingly been replaced by disobedience and defiance. This attitude of disobedience toward the law first became obvious to American society during Prohibition, with the widespread disregard of the liquor laws, but disobedience turned to defiance in the 1960s, with riots in more than 200 cities, on college campuses, and in prisons across the nation. Refusal to register for the draft, as well as the widespread use of illegal drugs among the youth, were further testimonies that respect for the law had broken down. Watergate and the increase of street crime in the 1970s were further evidence of the decline of respect for the law.

Then, in the 1980s, as illustrated by Box 2.2, the widespread disregard of the law among well-known business and government figures was brought to the public's attention. More than one hundred members of the Reagan administration had ethical or legal charges leveled against them. Improper activities, according to a *Time* editorial, are "more general, more pervasive, and somehow more

Draft dodgers fight the law. (*Source:* Michael D. Sullivan/Texa-Stock.)

BOX 2.2   **HYPOCRISY, BETRAYAL, AND GREED
            UNSETTLE THE NATION'S SOUL**

Just about every place you look, things are looking up. Life is better—America's back—and people have a sense of pride they never thought they'd feel again.

—*Voice-over from 1984 Ronald Reagan TV commercial*

Once again it is morning in America. But this morning Wall Street financiers are nervously scanning the papers to see if their names have been linked to the insider-trading scandals. Presidential candidates are peeking through drawn curtains to make sure that reporters are not staking out their private lives. A congressional witness, deeply involved in the Reagan administration's secret foreign policy, is huddling with his lawyers before facing inquisitors. A Washington lobbyist who once breakfasted regularly in the White House mess is brooding over his investigation by an independent counsel. In Quantico, Va., the Marines are preparing to court-martial one of their own. In Palm Springs, Calif., a husband-and-wife televangelist team, once the adored cynosures of 500,000 faithful, are beginning another day of seclusion.

Such are the scenes of morning in the scandal-scarred spring of 1987. Lamentation is in the air, and clay feet litter the ground. A relentless procession of forlorn faces assaults the nation's moral equanimity, characters linked in the public mind not by any connection between their diverse dubious deeds but by the fact that each in his or her own way has somehow seemed to betray the public trust: Oliver North, Robert McFarlane, Michael Deaver, Ivan Boesky, Gary Hart, Clayton Lonetree, Jim and Tammy Bakker, maybe Edwin Meese, perhaps even the President. Their transgressions—some grievous and some petty—run the gamut of human failings, from weakness of will to moral laxity to hypocrisy to uncontrolled avarice. But taken collectively, the heedless lack of restraint in their behavior reveals something disturbing about the national character. America, which took such back-thumping pride in its spiritual renewal, finds itself wallowing in a moral morass. Ethics, often dismissed as a prissy Sunday School word, is now at the center of a new national debate. Put bluntly, has the mindless materialism of the '80s left in its wake a values vacuum?

Source: This material appears in "What's Wrong: What Ever Happened to Ethics?" *Time*, 25 May 1987, p. 14. Copyright 1987 Time Inc. All rights reserved. Reprinted by permission from *Time*.

ingrained than those of any previous administration."[17] In addition, not since the reckless 1920s, adds another *Time* editorial, "has the business world seen such searing scandals. White-collar scams abound: insider trading, money laundering, greenmail. Result: What began as the decade of the entrepreneur is becoming the age of the pinstriped outlaw."[18]

The decline in respect for and obedience to the law in American society appears to be related to a number of factors. First, the social and economic structure has failed to meet the needs and aspirations of many citizens. Second, an increased acceptance of deviant norms and values has led to the breakdown of the law. Third, the "overreach" of the law into moral areas has contributed to disobedience of the law. Finally, reduced respect for other means of social control, including the family, school, community networks, religion, and the criminal justice system, has contributed to disobedience of the law. Judge Lois G. Forer, in documenting the decline of these social institutions, states:

> The only identifiable power remaining in the community with authority to compel obedience to a code or standard is the law. Law alone is insufficient to replace all of the other institutions and shared beliefs upon which society has relied for stability.[19]

PURPOSE OF THE LAW

One of the oldest questions concerning criminal law is whether its purpose is retributive or utilitarian.[20] For thousands of years punishment has been retributive and backward looking. The believer in **retribution** wants to punish an individual for what he or she has done in the past. If the question "Why was J. put in jail?" is asked, the retributive answer is, "Because he or she robbed a bank, was tried, and was convicted." Sir James Fitzjames Stephens suggested that "the criminal law stands to the passion of revenge in much the same relation as marriage to the sexual appetite."[21] Retribution holds that the person being punished meant to do harm and is blameworthy. Retribution also attempts to administer a "just" amount of pain to "pay back" wrongdoing.

The **utilitarian**, however, looks to the future rather than to the past. He or she is concerned with accomplishing some socially desirable future outcome from criminal sanctions, such as protection of society or criminal rehabilitation. The utilitarian asks the question "Why do people put other people in jail" and answers, "To protect good people from bad people."[22] Bentham and Beccaria added that the law should place no more restrictions on individual freedom than are needed to promote the welfare of society, "the greatest happiness of the greatest number."[23]

In the 1970s the debate on this issue broke out again. But the opponents this time were the proponents of the **justice model** and those of **utilitarian punishment philosophy** (see Chapter 4). "Just deserts" was acknowledged as one of the key concepts undergirding the justice model, while the protection of society and the deterrence of crime were regarded as the basic goals of the utilitarian punishment philosophy.

NATURE AND FUNCTION OF CRIMINAL LAW

The word *crime* is derived from the Latin *crimen,* meaning judgment, accusation, and offense. Its roots, therefore, are clearly legalistic.[24] Hence, it is not surprising that the disorder of crime is typically defined as a violation of criminal law. Paul W. Tappan's definition of crime has been widely used: "Crime is an intentional act of omission [of right behavior] in violation of criminal law [statutory and case law], committed without defense or justification, and sanctioned by the state as a felony or misdemeanor."[25]

After a person commits illegal acts and is arrested, he or she is tried by law. The means by which the criminal receives punishment is divided into substantive and procedural law. Substantive law is based on statutes passed by state legislatures and Congress, interpreted by judges, and applied by juries. Substantive law is primarily concerned with the question: What is illegal? Procedural law sets forth the rules governing how violators of the law should be handled.

Substantive Criminal Law

The basic concept of **substantive criminal law** is that one cannot be punished for an offense unless that offense is prohibited by the law. Jerome Hall's formulation of the main principles of law is helpful in understanding what constitutes a crime. According to Hall, seven interlocking principles must be present to constitute a crime: (1) legality, (2) *actus reus,* (3) *mens rea,* (4) harm, (5) concurrence, (6) causation, and (7) punishment.[26]

The doctrine of *actus reus* means that thoughts do not constitute a crime. Although one can fantasize a violent crime, such as rape or murder, no crime has been committed as long as the thoughts do not result in action *(actus reus).* But, interestingly enough, speech must be separated from thoughts, because when two or more persons agree to commit a crime, a criminal conspiracy is said to have taken place.

Mens rea requires that a guilty mind be present. That is, a person has not committed a crime unless he or she has this state of mind. To show *mens rea,* it must be proven that an individual intentionally and purposefully, knowingly, or negligently behaved in a certain manner or caused a given result. Persons who are insane when they commit a crime are not considered to have *mens rea* and, therefore, are not legally responsible for committing a crime.

Social harm also must be provable against persons, property, or reputation in order for a crime to have taken place. Harm to public safety is now increasingly being defined as a crime. Motorcyclists in some states are required to wear helmets because their injury or death may have harmful effects on others, such as their dependents. The use of seat belts in automobiles is also becoming mandatory in most states for the same reason.

Causation relates to the causal link between the act and the harm. That is, an individual's conduct must have produced the harm. For example, A shoots B and, believing B is dead, leaves his body on the Interstate. B then is killed when C—who does not see B lying on the road—runs over him. Subject A can be convicted of B's murder only if it can be demonstrated that A's conduct was a substantial factor in bringing about B's death or that what happened to B was a foreseeable consequence of A's behavior.[27]

Finally, punishments that are to be applied to the crime must be stipulated by the criminal law. This means that citizens cannot be convicted of a crime unless the criminal law clearly defines that behavior as unlawful.

In summary, the elements of a crime are defined as the act *(actus reus),* the attendant circumstances, and the state of mind *(mens rea)* of the accused. However, a number of defenses against the responsibility for a crime exists: (1) self-defense, (2) necessity, (3) duress, (4) immaturity, (5) mistake of fact, (6) intoxication, and (7) insanity.

Self-defense has to do with the legal right to ward off an attack from another if a person thinks that he or she is in immediate danger of being harmed. Necessity may be claimed as a defense when the accused was faced with a choice of evils. For example, a driver who races through traffic lights to get an injured person

A woman displays the gun and guard dog she uses to protect her pharmacy. She has been robbed repeatedly. (*Source:* Michael O'Brien/Archive Pictures, Inc.)

to the hospital is exonerated by the law. Duress is involved when the accused was forced or coerced by another into doing the illegal act; the courts have upheld this defense when it is shown that the defendant could not have done otherwise without the fear of receiving bodily harm or death.

Immaturity (the infancy defense) can be used as a defense for children under the age of seven on the grounds that children under this age are immature and are not responsible for their actions. In addition, children who are seven to fourteen have limited responsibility for their behavior because of their immaturity.

A person can occasionally use mistake of fact as a defense if he or she accepts the law but believes it does not apply in the context of a given situation. For example, a person could use this defense if she took property believing it was her own. Intoxication can be used as a defense only when a person has been tricked into consuming a substance that he or she did not know would result in intoxication.

Finally, insanity, a defense that has provoked considerable controversy, can be used when a defendant fails the test of sanity for a particular jurisdiction. To plead successfully the defense of insanity, the defendant must establish that he or she was insane at the time the criminal act was committed.

Procedural Criminal Law

Procedural criminal law is intended to ensure that accused persons are given certain rights and that they are tried according to legally established procedures. The sources of procedural law and the conflict between the due process and crime control models are important in understanding procedural criminal law.

Sources of Procedural Criminal Law   The sources of procedural criminal law are set down in such official documents as the U.S. Constitution and its Bill of Rights, statutory law, court decisions or case law, and administrative regulations.

In June 1789, James Madison proposed 12 constitutional amendments, and Congress approved 10 of them in September 1791. These ten amendments have become known as the **Bill of Rights** (see Box 2.3).

The Fourth, Fifth, Sixth, and Eighth Amendments are particularly important in understanding the constitutional rights of those citizens who break the law. The Fourth Amendment prohibits "unreasonable" searches, not all searches. The changing rules handed down by the U.S. Supreme Court concerning search and seizure have made the Fourth Amendment one of the most controversial amendments. The Fifth Amendment provides two important rights—protection against self-incrimination and against double jeopardy. Protection against self-incrimination gives an individual the right not to answer questions that may tend to incriminate him or her. Double jeopardy protects an individual charged with a criminal act from being subjected to more than one prosecution or punishment for that offense. The Sixth Amendment provides the right to counsel, to a speedy and public trial, and to an impartial jury. Finally, the Eighth Amendment prohibits excessive bail and fines and the infliction of cruel and unusual punishment.

The substantive and procedural rules for criminal law of most states are found in their statutes. Each state has a penal code that defines the acts constituting criminal behavior. Congress has also passed statutes pertaining to federal criminal law. In addition to those dealing with the more commonly known federal crimes such as counterfeiting, robbing a bank, and transporting kidnapped victims across state lines, there are federal statutory laws concerning draft evasion, subversive activity, organized crime, and political terrorism.

Local ordinances provide a body of statutory law. Although local ordinances vary from one jurisdiction to another, they cover such matters as traffic regulations, health regulations, and liquor controls. For example, in the early 1980s, Morton Grove, Illinois, made the ownership of a handgun illegal in that town.

Sources of procedural law also are found in court decisions, or case law, and in administrative regulations. Although most of common law has been replaced by statutes, judges and lawyers, especially those in appellate courts, continue to use precedents to interpret the cases before them. Administrative regulations refer to the laws and rulings made by federal, state, and local agencies to deal with such contemporary problems as wage and hour disputes, pollution, automobile traffic, industrial safety, and the purity of food and drugs.

Due Process Model Versus Crime Control Model   The due process model—described by Herbert Packer as "an obstacle course"—is the theoretical basis upon which procedural law of the criminal justice system operates.[28]

The due process model starts with the assumption that the transition from probable (factual) guilt to established (legal) guilt must be made difficult, for only if this process is slow, cumbersome, and individualized will it be certain or almost certain that crime suspects whose cases eventually end in conviction and penal sanction are truly deserving of their fate. Whatever else the criminal justice system may succeed or fail to do, it is argued that it must not convict innocent defendants.[29]

Hence, the due process model demands the strictest adherence to constitutional requirements and prohibitions that have been implicit or explicit in Supreme Court rulings over the years. In the due process model, there can never be too many legal impediments to overweigh or even balance the might of the state. Although the protection of society is a primary goal, the ultimate and absolute goal must be the protection of the individual rights of crime suspects, of those convicted, and even of those being punished.

The **due process model** requires the following constitutional safeguards:

1. The presumption of innocence until the accused is proved guilty beyond a reasonable doubt.
2. The privilege against self-incrimination.
3. Prohibition against unreasonable search and seizures.
4. The right to the assistance of counsel.
5. Arraignment with all possible speed.

BOX 2.3   **THE BILL OF RIGHTS**

I. Congress shall make no law respecting an establishment of religion, or prohibiting the free exercise thereof; or abridging the freedom of speech or of the press; or the right of the people peaceably to assemble, and to petition the government for a redress of grievance.

II. A well-regulated militia being necessary to the security of a free state, the right of the people to keep and bear arms shall not be infringed.

III. No soldier shall, in time of peace, be quartered in any house without the consent of the owner, nor in time of war, but in a manner to be prescribed by law.

IV. The right of the people to be secure in their persons, houses, papers, and effects, against unreasonable searches and seizures, shall not be violated, and no warrants shall be issued but upon probable cause, supported by oath of affirmation, and particularly describing the place to be searched, and the persons or things to be seized.

V. No person shall be held to answer for a capital or otherwise infamous crime, unless on a presentment or indictment of a grand jury, except in cases arising in the land or naval forces or in the militia when in actual service in time of war or public danger; nor shall any person be subject for the same offense to be twice put in jeopardy of life or limb; nor shall be compelled in any criminal case to be a witness against himself; nor be deprived of life, liberty, or property, without due process of law; nor shall private property be taken for public use without just compensation.

VI. In all criminal prosecutions the accused shall enjoy the right to a speedy and public trial, by an impartial jury of the State and district wherein the crime shall have been committed, which district shall have been previously ascertained by law, and to be informed of the nature and cause of the accusation; to be confronted with the witnesses against him; to have compulsory process for obtaining witnesses in his favor.

VII. In suits at common law, where the value in controversy shall exceed twenty dollars, the right of trial by jury shall be preserved, and no fact tried by a jury shall be otherwise reexamined in any court of the United States, than according to the rules of the common law.

VIII. Excessive bail shall not be required, nor excessive fines imposed, nor cruel and unusual punishments inflicted.

> **IX.** The enumeration in the Constitution of certain rights, shall not be construed to deny or disparage others retained by the people.
>
> **X.** The powers not delegated to the United States by the Constitution, nor prohibited by it to the States, are reserved to the States respectively, or to the people.

6. The right to know the precise nature of the charge being made so that the accused may prepare a defense.
7. The right to reasonable bail.
8. Trial by jury.
9. The right to call witnesses and confront adverse witnesses through cross-examination.
10. The right to an impartial judge.
11. The right to an impartial prosecutor.
12. Prohibition against cruel and unusual punishment.
13. Through writ of habeas corpus, the opportunity for those imprisoned to have the legality of their detention reviewed by the courts.[30]

However, Packer has also suggested that the **crime control model** rivals the due process model. Packer compares the crime control model to a well-regulated, functioning assembly line, noting that law enforcement is the key element in this model. The police apprehend factually guilty or probably guilty suspects, and the other actors in the system—prosecutors, defense attorneys, judges—play their specialized roles in converting factual or probable guilt into legal guilt with the rules and constraints of the adversarial format.[31]

Packer describes this assembly line in these words:

The image that comes to mind is an assembly line which moves an endless stream of cases, never stopping, carrying them to workers who stand at fixed stations and who perform on each case as it comes by the same small but essential operation that brings it one step closer to being a finished product, or, to exchange the metaphor for the reality, a closed file.

The criminal process is seen as a screening process in which each successive stage—pre-arrest, investigation, arrest, post-arrest, investigation, preparation for trial, trial or entry of plea, conviction, disposition—involves a series of routinized operations whose success is gauged primarily by their tendency to pass the case along to a successive conclusion.[32]

Abraham Blumberg, one of the most persistent critics of the criminal courts, charges that the law in action is much closer to the crime control than the due process model. Blumberg, along with others, suggests that innocent people may not come to think of themselves as factually guilty, but they come to the conclusion that it is fruitless to resist the label of guilty.[33] Blumberg adds that the practice of criminal law too often becomes a "confidence game," in which the defense counsel is a "double agent," whose loyalty is with the criminal court rather than the defense of the client.[34]

Arthur Rosett and Donald Cressey argue that the defense counsel is part of **bureaucratic justice** and, therefore, the counsel's organizational role frequently requires him or her to place pressure on a defendant to negotiate a plea.[35] Jonathan Casper, in an interview with a criminal defendant, describes the coercion that is frequently found in this negotiated plea:

> CASPER: Did you eventually plead guilty?
> DEFENDANT: Yes, he told me, "With your record and stuff, you better plead guilty."
> CASPER: Who told you that?
> DEFENDANT: The lawyer. . . . He told me I would probably get a year; that's why I pleaded guilty.
> CASPER: Did he first ask you what you wanted to plead?
> DEFENDANT: Yes, I said, "I want to plead not guilty; I'm not guilty of it." And then—see, I'd been in prison before; so he says, "Well, you take this to a jury trial, you might get you a year." So I said OK, and then I got up there, and I got five years.[36]

In sum, the crime control model, or the law in action, presumes defendants to be guilty rather than innocent. Defendants may have to pay a high price to assert their rights in the justice system, for court officials generally can outwait defendants. Jails are particularly well suited to the purpose of wearing down defendants.[37] Moreover, defendants frequently are told that if they go to trial, they are likely to receive much longer sentences than the negotiated pleas they are being offered.[38]

SOCIAL CONTEXT OF THE LAW

The social context of the law is reflected in the law's focus on preventing the predatory behavior of the poor while largely excusing the crimes of the rich.[39] Indeed, the means by which the rich, or upper classes, have exempted themselves from punishment fill a fascinating chapter in legal history. In England during the early Middle Ages, the "benefits of clergy" was a plea often utilized by the rich to escape severe punishment. This provision was designed to permit a cleric accused of a crime to be tried in an ecclesiastical court, but the privilege was soon extended to anyone who could read or write. Under the "benefits of clergy," the accused was allowed to swear an oath of innocence, after which 12 character witnesses would swear they believed him; then defense witnesses only were examined. The accused was generally acquitted in this system.[40]

The duality that existed in English law between property crime and violent crimes also favored upper-class criminals. Up until the late seventeenth century, the most violent crimes against the person were treated as misdemeanors, punishable generally by fines. Rennie reasons that it is possible such leniency existed because the upper classes often became involved in crimes of violence. Property crimes, on the other hand, were punished severely, frequently by death, because the rich feared theft and robbery by the lower classes. The most minor theft could result in the state's administering its most severe punishment, that of taking the life of the perpetrator of the crime.[41]

William J. Chambliss has argued persuasively that **vagrancy** became a crime only when the criminalization of such behavior suited the needs of the English industrial system.[42] In analyzing the vagrancy statutes that were passed in England in the fourteenth century, Chambliss concludes that these statutes were designed for the expressed purpose of forcing "laborers (whether personally free or unfree) to accept employment at a low wage in order to insure the landowner an adequate supply of labor at a price he could afford to pay."[43] These laws were a legislative innovation, adds Chambliss, designed to provide an abundance of cheap labor to landowners "during a period when serfdom was breaking down and when the pool of available labor was depleted."[44] Punishment for the crime of vagrancy became increasingly severe, until the punishment of death was applied early in the sixteenth century.[45]

Jerome Hall, in examining the growth of modern theft laws, traced the growth of property and theft statutes to the Carrier's Case of 1473.[46] In that case, a defendant was charged with a felony because he failed to carry out properly an assignment from a merchant. This carrier had been hired to carry certain bales to Southampton, England, but he broke them open and appropriated the contents. In the ensuing deliberations, sharp debate took place among the judges. Some judges argued that no felony had been committed because the carrier could not steal what he had already had in his possession. This line of argument supported previous decisions that the taking of property meant, literally, the physical removal of it. But the defendant was ultimately found guilty on the grounds that he had broken open and taken for himself the contents of the bales. Although he had possession of the bales, it was ruled that he did not have possession of their contents. Hall concluded that the judiciary revised existing rules because the emergence of commerce and industrialization in the Western world required that merchants receive greater protection against theft.[47]

A more recent example of the social construction of the law is found in Edwin H. Sutherland's work concerning sexual psychopath laws.[48] First passed in Illinois in 1938, sexual psychopath laws, which provide for the detention and treatment of certain types of sexual offenders in a state hospital, have been created in response to public outcries for action after a series of sex offenses. Sutherland has commented on such situations:

> The hysteria produced by child murders is due in part to the fact that the ordinary citizen cannot understand a sex attack on a child. The ordinary citizen can understand fornication or even forcible rape of a woman, but he concludes that the sexual attack on an infant or a girl of six years must be the act of a fiend or maniac. Fear is the greater because the behavior is so incomprehensible.[49]

Another example of the social construction of law is found in Joseph Gusfield's inquiry into the social background of the Volstead Act.[50] Passed in 1919, that legislation was designed to enforce the Eighteenth Amendment of the Constitution, which banned the sale of beverages containing more than one-half of 1 percent alcohol. Gusfield concluded that this law reaffirmed the basic interests of native, white, rural, Protestant Americans, who perceived their values as under attack by foreign-born groups within the population. By getting their statute adopted, this Protestant group hoped to assert the dominance of their values over "alien" ones.[51]

In sum, crime is ultimately defined in terms of the range of behavior of young people and adults socially accepted in a given community at a given time. That is, each community decides which crimes are to be enforced at any given time. Accordingly, city officials may direct police administrators to ignore certain behaviors and to arrest individuals involved in other behaviors. But a community tends to change its laws and enforcement from one generation to the next, so that the seriousness of particular behaviors and sometimes even the definitions of criminal behavior may change.

PERSPECTIVES ON THE LAW

Raymond J. Michalowski, identifying the major perspectives that have been used to explain the relationship between law and society, calls them the *consensus, pluralist*, and *conflict* **models** of social organization.[52] Each of these perspectives is based on somewhat different organizing principles and different values concerning the nature of humanity and society, and each suggests different directions for the study of crime. The three perspectives can be viewed along a continuum moving from right to left, from conservative to radical:

Consensus	Pluralist	Conflict
(Conservative)	(Liberal)	(Radical)

Consensus Perspective

The consensus model of law and social organization is derived from the more general consensus model of society. The organizing principles or assumptions of this model are that: (1) society is a relatively persistent and stable structure, (2) society is well integrated, and (3) a functioning social structure is based on agreed-upon values.[53] When applied to questions of law and social organization, the consensus perspective has several organizing principles:

1. *There are core values,* universally held, which are the touchstone of universal law. The acts which violate these values are criminal by everyone's definition, e.g., murder, treason, incest, kidnapping, theft, and vandalism.

2. *Law reflects the collective will of the people.* All members of a society agree upon the basic definitions of right and wrong, and the law is merely the written statement of this collective agreement.
3. *The law serves all people equally.* Because it reflects the collective will of all the people, the law neither serves nor represses the interests of any particular group of individuals.
4. *Those who violate the law represent a unique subgroup.* Because the majority agree upon the definitions of right and wrong, the small group who violates the law must share some common element, which distinguishes them from the law-abiding majority.[54]

The respected American legal scholar Roscoe Pound supported this understanding of the law, arguing that the law is a social product that reflects the conscience of society. He interpreted the law as a necessary means of social control to constrain individuals, to deter them from "conduct at variance with the postulates of social order, and to uphold civilized society." Thus, Pound saw the function of the law as an integrative mechanism to resolve conflicting interests and maintain order in society:

> Looking at [it] functionally, the law is an attempt to satisfy, to reconcile, to harmonize, to adjust these overlapping and often conflicting claims and demands, either through securing them directly and immediately, or through securing certain individual interests, so as to give effect to the greatest total of interests or to the interests that weigh most in our civilization, with the least sacrifice of the scheme of interests as a whole.[55]

In sum, a consensus perspective assumes that the law reflects general agreement concerning the basic values of social life. This perspective has had a major impact on the development of the positivist philosophy, which guided the development of criminology from the late nineteenth century until the late 1960s. The consensus perspective is most commonly applied as a justification for laws and the enforcement of these laws. Indeed, the legal system of our democratic society, as well as our means of social control, is based on the assumption that laws and their enforcement represent what the public wants. Or, to express this another way, the laws and their enforcement reflect the collective will of the people.

Pluralist Perspective

The pluralist perspective reflects a somewhat more complicated view of society. Although the consensus perspective assumes general agreement upon basic values and interests, the pluralist model recognizes the existence of a multiplicity of social groups having different and competing interests and values. Law is necessary, then, precisely because people disagree rather than agree upon a definition of right and wrong. Because individuals recognize the need for some mechanism for conflict resolution, they agree upon a legal structure within which conflicts can be resolved without placing the overall welfare of society in jeopardy. Chambliss and Seidman made this observation:

It is a popular viewpoint of present-day political theory in the United States, that while society is no doubt made up of interest groups with divergent goals and values, it is in everybody's interest to maintain a political framework which permits these conflicts to be resolved through peaceful bargaining, always reserving the right of the minority group to object through peaceful persuasion and dissent.[56]

Accordingly, in the pluralist perspective, general consensus about the nature and operation of law and justice permits conflict to be resolved through peaceful means. The basic organizing principles of this perspective are:

1. *Society is composed of diverse social groups.* This diversity results from the presence of regional, economic, religious, sex, age, race and ethnic variations in the population.
2. *There exists among these groups differing, and sometimes conflicting, definitions of right and wrong.* The various groups have different values, goals, and interests, and at times these may come into conflict with one another.
3. *There is collective agreement on the mechanisms for dispute settlement.* All groups agree upon the establishment of a legal system within which these conflicts can be peacefully settled.
4. *The legal system is value-neutral.* The legal mechanisms for dispute settlement are above the dispute themselves. The legal system exists simply as a value-free framework or arena in which the disputes can be fairly and peacefully settled.
5. *The legal system is concerned with the best interests of the society.* While it stands above the specific value-laden disputes between individual social groups, the system's overriding concern is with the general well-being of the society as a whole.[57]

This perspective has had a major impact on the development of American political thought in the twentieth century, and it is the primary basis for much of the concern for individual rights in the administration of justice. It also has been influential in the development of the labeling approach in the study of crime.

Conflict Perspective

The conflict model of law and justice, like the consensus perspective, is derived from a more general perspective on the nature of society itself. The organizing principles of this perspective are that: (1) at every point society is subject to change, (2) society displays at every point dissension and conflict, (3) every element contributes to change, and (4) society is based on the coercion of some of its members by others.[58]

As a model for the study of law and society, the conflict perspective emphasizes the coercive and repressive nature of the legal system. The legal system, rather than being viewed as an impartial tool for dispute settlement, is seen as a mechanism by which those with the greatest amount of political power can advance their own interests. According to this perspective, law reflects neither a general consensus about values nor a mutually agreed-upon mechanism for the settlement of disputes. Instead, law represents the interests of those with the power to make and enforce the law, without particular regard for the interests of those without such power. This perspective assumes that one of the major interests of those with the power to make and enforce the law is the maintenance of that power. The law, then, serves not only to advance the specific interests of those in power but also to advance their interest in retaining power. The means by which the interests of those with this power are advanced is the definition as criminal of those behaviors that conflict with these interests. The governing principles of this perspective are:

1. *Society is composed of diverse social groups.*
2. *There exist differing definitions of right and wrong.* Social groups have diverse values, goals, and interests, and at times these conflict with one another.
3. *The conflict between social groups is one of political power.* At all times there is an imbalance of political power, with those who have it struggling to maintain it, and those who do not have it struggling to obtain it.
4. *Law is designed to advance the interests of those with the power to make it.* The law is not a value-neutral forum for dispute settlement. It is a mechanism for those with the power to make the law advance their own interests, without particular concern for the overall good of the society.
5. *A key interest of those with the power to make and enforce the law, is maintaining their power.* Much of law is concerned with keeping those with interests different from those in power from gaining political power.[59]

William Chambliss states, "What makes the behavior of some criminal is the coercive power of the state to enforce the will of the ruling class."[60] Richard Quinney argues that "unlike the pluralistic conception of politics, law does not represent a compromise of the diverse interests in society but supports some interests at the expense of others," and "whenever a law is created or interpreted, the values of others are either ignored or negated.[61]

The conflict perspective and the pluralistic perspective concur on the fact that society is composed of groups with differing interests that lead to conflict among social groups. But these two perspectives disagree over how such conflicts should be resolved. The pluralistic perspective proposes that the conflicts be solved by the development of a mutually agreed-upon, value-neutral legal system. According to the conflict perspective, however, the only way conflicts can be resolved is for one group to acquire sufficient power to force its will upon others.

ANALYSIS

The purpose of law is to establish order in society. An examination of the means by which law establishes order requires that its purpose and role in the American criminal justice system be examined.

Law: The First Condition of an Ordered Society

In the United States, law is the means to order our free and democratic society. The constitutional order established early in the history of this nation is based upon several key principles. First, constitutional order is shaped by the classical definitions of humankind, which presume that citizens are rational beings who prefer pleasure over pain and who are willing to accept the responsibility of sacrificing a portion of their freedom so that the larger society may enjoy security and peace. Second, this classical understanding of law presumes that humans are willing to play by the rules, and, therefore, it presents a reform-oriented approach to criminal sanctions. Third, the Constitution and its Bill of Rights were designed to protect the individual against coercive government action. The writers of the Constitution attempted to strike a balance between freedom of the individual and the security of the state. This protection of the rights of the individual placed a heavy burden on the state to prove the guilt of suspects of criminal behavior.

However, this constitutional order was established at a time when society was simpler and the family, religion, and community had much more influence than they have today. Not too surprisingly, with a changing social context, the law began to lose respect among the American people. Disobedience, and even defiance, of the law became more widespread. Indeed, as recent investigations have indicated, crime has become a normative behavior of both the upper and lower classes.

Riding the subway: taking your life in your hands. (*Source:* Bruce Davidson/Magnum Photos, Inc.)

Due Process Ideal and Bureaucratic Reality

The manifest purpose of the criminal law is to set standards of expected behavior or to establish rules of conduct for society, but the purpose of the criminal courts is to identify and sanction the law's failures. Dealing with the failures is the way the law ensures that order is maintained in society. In the Anglo-American legal tradition, the institutional means for accomplishing this goal is adjudication, which represents a special and highly developed form of problem solving. Adjudication is rooted firmly in a belief in the value of the rule of law, a belief that places a premium on due process.[62]

The goal of due process has attained a new importance in the criminal law, and concern for justice is inextricably linked to the notion of due process. However, as previously discussed, the organizational demands of dealing with overcrowded court dockets have resulted in new rules designed to process cases more efficiently through the courts.

The **courtroom team**—consisting of the prosecutor, the defense attorney, and the judge—has developed a legal culture, or a set of informal rules, to guide decision-making in plea bargaining or negotiating pleas.[63] Plea bargaining presumes the assumption of guilt, rather than the innocence mandated by the Constitution and its Bill of Rights. The courthouse team insists that the negotiated plea process is needed to maintain an orderly system; in fact, these officials commonly believe that without plea bargaining, total chaos (absolute disorder) would erupt in the court system.

Legal actors claim that the systematic needs of bureaucratic justice are balanced by fairness in the way defendants are actually treated. A prosecutor in New Jersey, for example, asserts that this presumption of guilt does not negate the due process principles of fairness and justice: "In other words, we're not interested in just convicting people; we're interested that they be convicted fairly."[64] That prosecutor, along with most officials in the court system, is aware that the presumption of guilt serves the bureaucratic imperative of efficient dispositions, but, at the same time, these officials claim that the aims of law are still served by the just and fair way defendants are handled.[65]

Court officials contend that, at present, freedom and order are brought into balance through the court process. They argue that the liberty of individuals is not sacrificed by these informal ways of processing cases, as defendants benefit by pleading guilty to their crimes. The end result of reduced charges, they claim, is less severe sanctions than defendants would receive if they insisted on a criminal trial.

Although this assertion may be generally true, its flaws become apparent when individual cases are examined. Some innocent defendants plead guilty because they are afraid of the severity of the criminal law if they insist upon a jury trial. Illegal arrest procedures that would result in the dismissal of the case if it came to trial are concealed by the use of plea bargaining. Moreover, plea bargaining enables prosecutors to attain convictions in weak cases that would likely be lost if they went to trial. Finally, some defendants, assured of receiving a specific sentence for a guilty plea, find upon pleading guilty that they are sentenced to a harsher-than-expected punishment. Obviously, in these examples, order has resulted not in equitable disposition but in injustice and unfairness.

The Rule of Law

Americans have a commonsense inclination to invoke written or unwritten rules in most ongoing social relationships. The appeal of the law in American society consists of three essential advantages claimed for legal ordering:

1. The legal approach is realistic. It is based on a willingness to accept things as they are rather than as one might ideally wish them to be.
2. The legal approach is neither complicated nor demanding. The principles to guide action are easily understood; their implementation may be confidently left to professionals.
3. The legal approach rests firmly on an ethical base. Typical American values like personal responsibility and equality of opportunity are inherent in the legal frame of reference.[66]

The American public is assured that judges and lawyers, trained in the legal paradigm, are able to determine just what kinds of behaviors are consistent with existing rights and obligations. Trained in the language, as well as the rationale, of the law, these legal actors—or so it is believed—are able to step back from the relevant rule to some higher law or even to principles inherent in that higher law.[67] Theoretically, the process of becoming a lawyer is one in which rules rather than people become the focus and govern one's way of thinking. The lawyer, then, does not have to be concerned with the outcomes or the people involved as long as the rules of the legal game are followed.[68]

However, as countless examples throughout legal history reveal, the **rule of law** does not treat all individuals alike. Donald Black, as well as many others, contends that "whatever the crime, wealth is an advantage for the offender"; he adds that "at every stage of the legal process, a marginal person is more vulnerable to law," and "when anything goes wrong, those who are more marginal to social life are more likely to be blamed."[69] In short, Black is making the point that the law in action has always been and is likely to remain inequitable.

SUMMARY

The rule of law in the United States is guided by the ideal of the rationality of human beings, who possess free will and can be held accountable for their behavior. The law further presumes that individuals are committed to the social contract because they acknowledge the legitimacy of criminal sanctions when they violate the law. Both of these assumptions are required for law to order social relations in society. On the one hand, our society could not in good conscience punish individuals for uncontrollable illegal behavior. On the other, it is only because the vast majority of citizens choose to obey the law and to refrain from taking collective actions against the government that law is able to order social relations.

Law is needed to maintain order in this or any society. A government under law promises a stable political order and a reliable structure of authority. The doctrine of constitutional rights is rooted in a vision of a society dedicated to maximizing individual freedoms. The Bill of Rights, in this regard, serves as a protective shield against unwarranted governmental intrusion.[70]

The symbolic role of the law in defining the rules of human behavior continues to be held in high esteem by the American public. Respect for the law is a necessary barrier against anarchy and in fact is a chief reason why there have been so few attempts in the history of this nation to overthrow the government. Respect for the law encourages citizens to obey legal rules. Furthermore, respect for the law imbues court proceedings with a dignity and a ritualism unmatched in other branches of American government.

However, declining respect for and obedience to the law is creating a moral crisis in America. Such violations of the law as cheating on income tax forms, speeding on the highways, stealing from motel rooms, committing petty theft on the job, and violating drug laws are becoming common and acceptable behavior for American citizens. In addition to the emerging acceptability of criminogenic norms, there is the fact that the law in action is often quite different from the law on the books. For example, although constitutional law promises due process and an adversarial system, the law in action tends to be preoccupied with justifying the legal guilt of defendants. This presumption of guilt, as expressed in plea bargaining, often benefits both the courtroom team and defendants. But this unfair exchange breaks down when defendants plead guilty only because they are afraid of the severe sanctions they will receive if convicted in a jury trial.

It has been said that much can be learned about a society by entering its prisons: it is even more true that the quality of life in a society can be determined by reading its lawbooks and by observing the law in action. Balance is always needed between the freedom of the individual and the security of a society. Today, the emphasis is tilting toward reducing the liberty of the individual because of the concern with the disorder of crime. Justice is clearly the proper end of a society under law. The wisest use of law in American society is to be guided by the following questions: Is it fair? Is it decent? Is it worthy of civilized society?

REFERENCES

Beccaria, Cesare. *Of Crimes and Punishment.* Translated by Fr. Kenelm Foster and Jane Grigson. New York: Oxford University Press, 1964.

Bentham, Jeremy. *An Introduction to the Principles of Morals and Legislation.* 1823; reprint ed., New York: Hafner, 1948.

Black, Donald. *The Behavior of Law.* New York: Academic Press, 1976.

Blumberg, Abraham S. *Criminal Justice: Issues and Ironies.* 2d ed. New York: New Viewpoints, 1979.

Casper, Jonathan D. *American Criminal Justice: The Defendant's Perspective.* Englewood Cliffs, N.J.: Prentice-Hall, 1972.

Clark, Malcolm. *The Enterprise of Law.* St. Paul, Minn.: West, 1987.

Hall, Jerome. *General Principles of Criminal Law.* 2d ed. Indianapolis: Bobbs-Merrill, 1947.

————. *Theft, Law and Society.* 2d ed. Indianapolis: Bobbs-Merrill, 1952.

Michalowski, Raymond J. "Perspectives and Paradigm: Structuring Criminological Thought." In *Theory in Criminology,* edited by Robert F. Meier. Beverly Hills, Calif.: Sage, 1977, pp. 17–39.

Nardulli, Peter. *The Courtroom Elite: An Organizational Perspective on Criminal Justice.* Cambridge, Mass.: Ballinger, 1978.

Packer, Herbert L. *The Limits of Criminal Sanction.* Stanford, Calif.: Stanford University Press, 1968.

Rennie, Ysabel. *The Search for Criminal Man: A Conceptual History of the Dangerous Offender.* Lexington, Mass.: D.C. Heath, 1978.

Rosett, Arthur, and Cressey, Donald R. *Justice by Consent: Plea Bargains in the American Courthouse.* Philadelphia: Lippincott, 1976.

NOTES

1. Ysabel Rennie, *The Search for Criminal Man: A Conceptual History of the Dangerous Offender* (Lexington, Mass.: D.C. Heath, 1978), pp. 149–150.
2. Cesare Beccaria, *Of Crimes and Punishment,* trans. Fr. Kenelm Foster and Jane Grigson (New York: Oxford University Press, 1964); Jeremy Bentham, *An Introduction to the Principles of Morals and Legislation* (1823; reprint ed., New York: Hafner, 1948).
3. Beccaria, *Of Crimes and Punishment,* p. 14.
4. Ibid.
5. Donald Black, *The Behavior of Law* (New York: Academic Press, 1976), pp. 3, 131.
6. Bruce Jackson, *Law and Disorder: Criminal Justice in America* (Urbana and Chicago: University of Illinois Press, 1984), pp. 4–5.
7. James P. Levine, Michael C. Musheno, and Dennis J. Palumbo, *Criminal Justice in America: Law in Action* (New York: Wiley, 1986), p. 37.
8. Lawrence M. Friedman, *A History of American Law* (New York: Simon and Schuster, 1973), p. 17.
9. Roscoe Pound, *Criminal Justice in America* (New York: Holt, 1930), pp. 3–4.
10. Arthur Rosett and Donald R. Cressey, *Justice by Consent: Plea Bargains in the American Courthouse* (Philadelphia: Lippincott, 1976), p. 50.
11. Ibid., p. 51.
12. Stuart A. Scheingold, *The Politics of Rights: Lawyers, Public Policy, and Political Change* (New Haven: Yale University Press, 1974), pp. 17, 23.
13. Ibid., p. xi.
14. Ibid., p. 23.
15. Herbert Jacob, *Justice in America: Courts, Lawyers, and the Judicial Process,* 3d ed. (Boston: Little, Brown, 1978), p. 9.
16. Jonathan D. Casper, *American Criminal Justice: The Defendant's Perspective* (Englewood Cliffs, N.J.: Prentice-Hall, 1972), p. 48.
17. "Morality Among the Supply-Siders," *Time,* 25 May 1987, p. 18.

18. "Having It All, Then Throwing It All Away," *Time,* 25 May 1987, p. 22.

19. Lois Forer, *The Death of the Law* (New York: McKay, 1975), p. 335.

20. Rennie, *Search for Criminal Man,* p. 20.

21. Sir James Fitzjames Stephen, *A History of the Criminal Law in England,* vol. 2 (London: Macmillan, 1983), p. 80.

22. Rennie, *Search for Criminal Man,* pp. 24–25.

23. Beccaria, *Of Crimes and Punishment,* and Bentham, *Principles of Morals and Legislation.*

24. *Webster's New Twentieth Century Dictionary of the English Language Unabridged,* 2d ed. (New York: Simon and Schuster, 1983), p. 527.

25. Paul W. Tappan, *Crime, Justice, and Corrections* (New York: McGraw-Hill, 1960), p. 10.

26. Jerome Hall, *General Principles of Criminal Law,* 2d ed. (Indianapolis: Bobbs-Merrill, 1947), p. 18.

27. Harold J. Vetter and Leonard Territo, *Crime and Justice in America: A Human Perspective* (St. Paul, Minn.: West, 1984), p. 55.

28. Herbert L. Packer, *The Limits of Criminal Sanction* (Stanford, Calif.: Stanford University Press, 1968).

29. Ibid.

30. Abraham S. Blumberg, *Criminal Justice: Issues and Ironies,* 2d ed. (New York: New Viewpoints, 1979), pp. 162–167.

31. Packer, *Limits of Criminal Sanction,* pp. 176–178.

32. Ibid, p. 21.

33. Blumberg, *Criminal Justice,* pp. 159–161.

34. Ibid., pp. 242–246.

35. Rosett and Cressey, *Justice by Consent,* pp. 22–24.

36. Casper, *American Criminal Justice,* pp. 56–57.

37. W. Boyd Littrell, *Bureaucratic Justice: Police, Prosecutors, and Plea Bargaining* (Beverly Hills, Calif.: Sage, 1979), pp. 191–192.

38. See Conrad G. Brunk, "The Problem of Voluntariness and Coercion in the Negotiated Plea," *Law and Society Review* 13 (Winter 1979), pp. 527–553.

39. For a masterful review of the history of English and American law, see Raymond J. Michalowski, *Order, Law, and Crime: An Introduction to Criminology* (New York: Random House, 1985), pp. 69–133.

40. Rennie, *Search for Criminal Man,* p. 32.

41. Ibid., p. 5.

42. William J. Chambliss, "A Sociological Analysis of the Law of Vagrancy," *Social Problems* 12 (1964), pp. 67–77.

43. William J. Chambliss, "The Law of Vagrancy," in *Crime and the Legal Order,* ed. by William J. Chambliss (New York: McGraw-Hill, Inc., 1969), p. 54.

44. Ibid., p. 61.

45. Ibid., p. 57.

46. Jerome Hall, *Theft, Law and Society,* 2d ed. (Indianapolis: Bobbs-Merrill, 1952).

47. Don C. Gibbons, *Society, Crime, and Criminal Behavior,* 4th ed. (Englewood Cliffs, N.J.: Prentice-Hall, 1982), pp. 65–66.

48. Edwin H. Sutherland, "The Diffusion of Sexual Psychopath Laws," *American Journal of Sociology* 56 (September 1950), pp. 142–148.

49. Sutherland, "The Diffusion of Sexual Psychopath Laws," in *Crime and the Legal Process,* p. 75.

50. Joseph R. Gusfield, *Symbolic Crusade* (Urbana, Ill.: University of Illinois Press, 1963).

51. Gibbons, *Society, Crime, and Criminal Behavior,* p. 69.
52. The following discussion on the three perspectives is drawn largely from Raymond J. Michalowski, "Perspectives and Paradigm: Structuring Criminological Thought," in *Theory in Criminology,* ed. Robert F. Meier (Beverly Hills, Calif.: Sage, 1977), pp. 17–39.
53. Ralf Dahrendorf, "Toward a Theory of Social Conflict," *Journal of Conflict Resolution* 2 (1958), p. 174.
54. Michalowski, "Perspectives and Paradigm," p. 23.
55. R. Pound, "A Survey of Interests," *Harvard Law Review* 57 (October 1943), p. 39.
56. W. J. Chambliss and R. Seidman, *Law, Order and Power* (Reading, Mass.: Addison-Wesley, 1971), p. 51.
57. Michalowski, "Perspectives and Paradigm," pp. 24–25.
58. Dahrendorf, "Theory of Social Conflict," p. 174.
59. Michalowski, "Perspectives and Paradigm," pp. 26–27.
60. William J. Chambliss, "Toward a Political Economy of Crime," in *The Sociology of Law,* ed. C. Reasons and R. Rich (Toronto: Butterworth, 1978), p. 193.
61. Richard Quinney, *The Problem of Crime* (New York: Dodd, Mead, 1970), pp. 35, 37.
62. Malcolm M. Feeley, *The Process Is the Punishment: Handling Cases in a Lower Criminal Court* (New York: Russell Sage, 1979), p. 22.
63. See David W. Neubauer, *Criminal Justice in Middle America* (Morristown, N.J.: General Learning Press, 1974); Littrell, *Bureaucratic Justice;* and Peter Nardulli, *The Courtroom Elite: An Organizational Perspective on Criminal Justice* (Cambridge, Mass.: Ballinger, 1978).
64. Littrell, *Bureaucratic Justice,* p. 153.
65. Ibid.
66. Scheingold, *Politics of Rights,* pp. 40–41.
67. Ibid., p. 50.
68. Malcolm Clark, *The Enterprise of Law* (St. Paul, Minn.: West, 1987).
69. Black, *Behavior of Law,* pp. 25, 50, 55.
70. Scheingold, *Politics of Rights,* pp. 59–60.

Crime as Disorder

ENDURING ASPECTS OF CRIME IN AMERICA
Enforcement of Public Morals
Poverty and Dangerousness
Violence as an Accompaniment to Crime
Intractable Nature of Crime
Vigilante Justice
EXTENT OF CRIME
Measurement of Official Crime
  Uniform Crime Reports
  Trends in Crime
Unofficial Measurement of Crime
  Victimization Surveys
  Self-Report Studies

THE COSTS OF CRIME
The Fear of Crime
Criminal Victimization
The Economic Cost of Crime
Disruption to Community
ANALYSIS
Social Disorder and Its Relationship to Crime
Crime and the Frustrations of Public Policy
SUMMARY
REFERENCES
NOTES

KEY TERMS

corporate violence

criminal victimization

dangerous class

economic costs of crime

enforcement of public morals

reliability

self-report studies

Uniform Crime Reports

validity

victimization surveys

vigilante

war on crime

Don't get the idea that I'm one of those . . . radicals. My rackets are run on strictly American lines, and they're going to stay that way. . . . The American system of ours, call it Americanism, call it Capitalism, call it what you like, gives each and every one of us a great opportunity if we only seize it with both hands and make the most of it.

—Al Capone[1]

Be not afraid of any man,
  No matter what his size;
When danger threatens, call on me
  And I will equalize.

—Inscription on the nineteenth-century
Winchester rifle

Crime and violence have been recurrent themes throughout American history. Indeed, as Al Capone suggested, twentieth-century free enterprise values provide a great opportunity for both rule-keepers and rule-breakers. The emphasis placed on winning and on success encourages Americans to violate rules that "get in the way" and to feel justified in doing so. The individualistic spirit of this society, with its distrust of authority, also leads to the admiration of someone who pulls off a "big job" and is able to get away with it, especially if "the government" seems to come out in last place.[2] Not surprisingly, within this social context, such well-known criminals as Jesse James, Billy the Kid, John Dillinger, Bonnie and Clyde, and Frank Costello have been romanticized as folk heroes.

In examining crime in America, this chapter focuses on several questions: What are the durable aspects of crime? How big is the crime problem? How much does it cost? Who pays? What is the relationship between crime and the social order?

ENDURING ASPECTS OF CRIME IN AMERICA

The disorder of crime has been a regular part of the American experience since the settlement of the colonies. The most enduring aspects of crime in this nation are related to: the enforcement of public morals, the definition of the poor as "the

dangerous class," violence as an accompaniment to crime, the intractable nature
of crime, and the public's dissatisfaction with the institutional control of crime.

Enforcement of Public Morals

Colonial Americans believed that their social order had divine approval; indeed,
the early settlers were convinced that they had been commissioned to establish
the Kingdom of God on earth. Belief in the divine approval of their society caused
these seventeenth- and eighteenth-century Americans to develop attitudes and
practices toward the poor, the insane, the orphan, the criminal, and the delinquent that were to be far different from those of subsequent generations.[3]

Poverty and crime, two critical sources of social disorder in nineteenth- and
twentieth-century America, were not defined as disruptive to colonial society. The
colonists did not interpret the presence of the poor as symptomatic of basic flaws
in their social order or as an indicator of personal or communal failing. Instead,
they strongly believed that the presence of the poor offered a God-given opportunity to do good.[4]

The leaders of colonial society adopted elaborate precautions and procedures to control deviancy because they were far more apprehensive about the
deviant than they were about the poor, but they did not regard the crime problem
as symptomatic of a basic flaw in community structure, nor did they expect to
eliminate it. They viewed crime as an inevitable part of the social order, because
humans were born to corruption. To combat the evilness of crime, they warned,
chastised, corrected, banished, flogged, and/or executed offenders.[5]

When faced with the inherent sinfulness of humans that led to wrongful
behavior, the colonists looked with confidence to the family, the church, and the
network of community relations as important weapons to battle sin and crime.
They believed that these social control mechanisms would provide stability and
order. But when these means proved ineffective, brutal punishments frequently
were used.[6]

The **enforcement of public morals** continues to guide the defining and
handling of crime in America. Acts that offend public morality, such as drunkenness, prostitution, and disorderly conduct, are disturbing to "respectable" people
and, therefore, are not allowable in society. Norval Morris and Gordon Hawkins
charge that too much of the criminal law expresses the moralistic concerns of
particular groups that are offended by the behavior of others. They recommend
removing a broad range of crimes from the statutes, especially those that are
concerned with the "overreach," or moralistic expressions, of the criminal law.[7]

Poverty and Dangerousness

Early in the twentieth century, the poor began to be regarded as "the **dangerous
class.**" Between 1790 and 1820, as 5000 immigrants a year streamed into the
nation, the population greatly increased and so did the number and density of
cities. The fact that these newcomers to America came largely from different
cultural, ethnic, and religious backgrounds raised the fear that they would

BOX 3.1   **DEVIANCY IN COLONIAL AMERICA**

The colonists judged a wide range of behavior to be deviant, finding the gravest implications in even minor offenses. Their extended definition was primarily religious in origin, equating sin with crime. The criminal codes punished religious offenses, such as idolatry, blasphemy, and witchcraft, and clergymen declared infractions against persons or property to be offenses against God. Freely mixing the two categories, the colonists prohibited an incredibly long list of activities. The identification of disorder with sin made it difficult for legislators and ministers to distinguish carefully between major and minor infractions. Both were testimony to the natural depravity of man and the power of the devil—sure signs that the offender was destined to be a public menace and a damned sinner. This attitude underlies the heavy-handedness of eighteenth-century codes, which set capital punishments for crimes as different as murder and arson, horse-stealing, and children's disrespect for parents. . . . By linking murder with sin and sin with every transgression against man and God, clergymen taught the colonists to find terrifying significance in even casual offenses.

Source: This material appears in David J. Rothman, *The Discovery of the Asylum: Social Order and Disorder in the New Republic* (Boston: Little, Brown, 1971), pp. 15–16.

threaten the order of the new republic. Democratic, economic, and intellectual developments of the period also raised the question of whether or not the traditional mechanisms of social control were becoming obsolete.[8] David J. Rothman describes the impact of these social changes:

> Americans in the Jacksonian period could not believe that geographic and social mobility would promote or allow order and stability. Despite their marked impatience and dissatisfaction with colonial procedures, they had no ready vision of how to order society. They were still trapped in many ways in the rigidities of eighteenth-century social thinking. They knew well that the old system was passing, but not what ought to replace it. What in their day was to prevent society from bursting apart? From where would the elements of cohesion come? More specifically, would the poor now corrupt the society? Would criminals roam out of control? Would chaos be so acute as to drive Americans mad?[9]

The changing economic conditions soon made the poor the scapegoats of the emerging society. The depressions of 1807, 1819, and 1837 forced many of the unskilled immigrants, such as the displaced Irish farmers, out of work; this mass of poor, unskilled, and unemployed immigrants came to be seen as the source of an expanding pool of criminality. It was widely perceived that the poor could no longer be assimilated into the social order and, therefore, that institutions were needed to protect society against the dangerous poor.[10]

The association of poverty with dangerousness has continued to the present. For example, throughout the nineteenth century, each succeeding wave of immigration, with the poverty each new group lived in at first, was perceived as threatening a new crime wave. More recently, a "get-tough" approach has been directed against street criminals, most of whom are from the poorer classes, because they have been defined as most dangerous to the public order. Thus, throughout this nation's history, the need has been to protect the existing social order, as defined by political and economic elites, against the dangerous poor.[11]

In contrast, the crimes of the rich have been largely ignored. As Ysabel Rennie has observed, "In modern times as in ancient, the poor and dangerous are seen as dangerous, while the rich and dangerous are simply rich."[12] Jeffrey Reiman makes this same point:

> I have tried to argue . . . that this is not a simple process of selecting the dangerous and the criminal from among the peace-loving and the law-abiding. It is also a process of weeding out the wealthy at every stage, so that the final picture . . . is not a true reflection of the real dangers in our society but a distorted image. . . . My point is that people who are equally or more dangerous, equally or more criminal, are not there [in prison]; that the criminal justice system works systematically, not to punish and confine the dangerous and the criminal, but to punish and confine the poor who are dangerous and criminal.[13]

Violence as an Accompaniment to Crime

Each generation of Americans has felt itself threatened by rising violent crime. In 1767, Benjamin Franklin, in his capacity as agent for Pennsylvania, petitioned the British Parliament to stop shipping convicted felons to the American colonies. He complained that transported felons were terrorizing the rest of the population with burglaries, robberies, and murders. Decades later, in one of his first speeches, Abraham Lincoln argued that internal violence was America's major domestic problem and decried "the increasing disregard for law that pervades the country."[14]

By the middle of the nineteenth century, the increasing violence in the cities was well documented. On December 2, 1839, Phillip Hone, a former mayor of New York, wrote in his diary, "One of the evidences of the degeneracy of our morals and of the inefficiency of our people is to be seen in the frequent instances of murder by stabbing." In 1844 (more than one hundred years before the Goetz subway case), a Philadelphian noted that citizens were arming themselves because they did not expect adequate protection from the law. And just prior to the Civil War, a U.S. Senate committee investigating crime in Washington, D.C., concluded that "riot and bloodshed are of daily occurrence, innocent and unoffending persons are shot, stabbed, and otherwise shamefully maltreated, and not infrequently the offender is not even arrested."[15]

In the undeveloped West, bandits and settlers engaged in continued violence after the Civil War. American folklore, as well as television and motion pictures, tells of the violent adventures of Jesse James and Cole Younger, Butch Cassidy

Severity of punishment in pre–Civil War America. (*Source:* Library of Congress [LC-USZ62-5365].)

and the Sundance Kid, and other lesser-known outlaws. But what is not commonly known is that as much of this violence of the West was committed by lawmen as by desperadoes. Indeed, many of the "lawmen" were desperadoes; these gunslingers were sometimes marshals, sometimes outlaws, and sometimes both.[16]

In the 1920s and early 1930s, the prohibition of liquor sales in the United States brought the violent gangster to the attention of the public. As captured in folklore, Eliot Ness and his "Untouchables" fired machine guns through the open windows of a 1925 Packard to combat such underworld figures as Al Capone, George "Baby Face" Nelson, and Charles "Pretty Boy" Floyd. But far more lethal for the gangsters of this era was the full-fledged guerrilla warfare that broke out among rival groups. Between September 1923 and October 1926 alone, some 215 Chicago gangsters died as they battled for control of the beer business.[17]

In the early 1970s, the media began to target the violence of street crime, reporting vicious murders, pistol whippings and robberies, rapes, child molestations, and assaults on the elderly. In the early 1980s, several disturbing and different expressions of violent crime came to the attention of the American

---

BOX 3.2   **THE MEXICAN RURALES, DOUBLE AGENTS
OF ORDER AND DISORDER**

The thin line between order and disorder characteristic of the lawmen of the West also applied to the Mexican police, the famed Rurales. Porfirio Diaz, who became the president of Mexico in the mid–nineteenth century, carefully crafted the reputation of the Rurales, or rural police corps. People constantly read and talked about the thousands of elite Rurales on duty for the nation. The Rurales were hailed as national heroes; indeed, to criticize the Rurales was to attack the president, even Mexico itself.

Bandits were heavily recruited to become Rurales and, thus, the lawless became the law-enforcers. But when the bandits became Rurales, many remained bandits as well. Endless stories were circulated about how they continued to operate on both sides of the law. In one incident, six bandit–police officers got drunk, robbed several stagecoaches assigned to their protection, and then headed for the mountains as out-and-out bandits. In another, a detachment of Rurales arrived in the company of bandits at a town they were assigned to patrol, and together they raided the village. In effect, these bandit–police officers became double agents of order and disorder.

Source: Paul J. Vanderwood, *Disorder and Progress: Bandits, Police, and Mexican Development* (Lincoln: University of Nebraska Press, 1981).

---

public—the kidnapping of children; "copycat" crimes committed by a number of individuals who placed cyanide poisoning in Tylenol capsules, harmful substances in baby food and Girl Scout cookies, or razor blades in Halloween candy; and serial murders by vicious criminals who sexually molested their victims and then tortured and mutilated them.

However, what has been ignored until recently is the means by which state and private violence have contributed to the long history of violence in American society. Examples include the use of the militia to clear off the Indian nation; the use of the militia or National Guard by private corporations to suppress coal miners', railroad employees', and steel-mill workers' strikes; the use of public police by private companies in various cities to break strikes; and the use of public police to protect the social order against civil rights workers, Vietnam protesters, and political discontents.

Corporations are currently under attack for the way they contribute to this legacy of violence. **Corporate violence** can be defined as "behavior producing an unreasonable risk of physical harm to consumers, employees, or other persons as a result of deliberate decision-making by corporate executives or culpable negligence on their part."[18] Clinard and Yeager suggest that "far more persons are killed through corporate criminal activities than by individual criminal homicides; even if death is an indirect result, the person has died."[19]

Corporate violence includes losses due to sickness and even death resulting from air and water pollution and the sale of unsafe foods and drugs, toys, tires, autos, appliances, and clothing. It also includes the disabilities resulting from injuries to plant workers, including those caused by contamination by chemicals and other hazardous substances.[20]

Intractable Nature of Crime

The United States has a history of seeking cure-alls to solve the crime problem, but there are no simple solutions to this age-old problem. The search for a panacea for crime began in the early nineteenth century, or Jacksonian period, when the young American nation was thought to have an unlimited capacity to solve its social problems.[21] The institutions that emerged to create better environments for deviants represented an attempt to promote the stability of society at a time when traditional ideas and practices seemed to be outmoded, constricted, and ineffective.

Legislators, philanthropists, and local officials all were convinced that the nation faced both unprecedented dangers and unprecedented opportunities. It was hoped that the penitentiary for adults and the house of refuge for juveniles, as well as the almshouse for the poor, the orphan asylum, and the insane asylum, would restore a necessary balance to the new republic, and, at the same time, eliminate longstanding problems. The fact that these institutions eventually came to be viewed as failures did not prevent another generation of reformers from seeking new ways to cure the crime problem.[22] Ysabel Rennie aptly summarizes this history of seeking a cure-all for crime:

> . . . There is nothing more disconcerting than the realization that what is being proposed now for the better management of crime and criminals—to get tough, to increase sentences and make them mandatory, and to kill more killers—has been tried over and over again and abandoned as unworkable. It is sad but true that the reformation of criminals through education, psychology, and prayer has not worked either. As for that great rallying-cry of the positivists, the individualization of punishment, its chief, if not its only, effect has been an unconscionable disparity in judicial sentences. Thus we are left to contemplate the evidence that we have for centuries been going in circles.[23]

One of the most vexing characteristics of crime is its apparent ability to survive all the policy assaults against it. Street crime, which is the principal concern of public order institutions and which affects one in four households every year, represents a crude and reprehensible activity that is conducted by individuals who are largely without any sort of talent or training. Arrayed against these social outcasts is an impressive army of trained professionals backed by committed political leaders and an aroused public. Common sense tells the American people it should be no contest, and so when crime continues to flourish the public becomes frustrated and angry.[24]

Vigilante Justice

Americans will take justice in their own hands when their dissatisfaction with the institutions of public order reaches a certain level. In the mid-eighteenth century, the first **vigilante** movement took place in South Carolina, when a group of about a thousand citizens developed an organization called the Regulators, with the expressed purpose of restoring order to communities in the hinterlands. Frontier vigilante groups developed elsewhere as well; new communities typically lacked the resources to hire police officers and judges, and vigilante movements arose in response to the absence of formal means of social control.[25]

The wealthy and the politically powerful have usually taken the lead in vigilante movements. As such movements have proceeded to impose their own notions of what constitutes the good community, "popular justice" has been directed against such "undesirables" as criminals; political opponents; racial, ethnic, and religious minorities; and the poor.[26] Richard Maxwell Brown, a widely respected authority on the subject, sees vigilantism as a violent and ugly scar on the history of criminal justice in America.[27]

The Ku Klux Klan has been one of the most notorious vigilante groups. In the last sixteen years of the nineteenth century, a total of 2500 recorded lynchings took place in the United States, the majority of them attributed to the Klan. In 1900 alone more than 100 blacks were lynched; the victims were primar-

Bernhard Goetz, the "subway vigilante." (*Source:* Allen Tannenbaum/Sygma.)

ily southern blacks. Not surprisingly, lynch-mob participants did not need to fear prosecution with the machinery of justice firmly in white hands.[28]

In our era, dissatisfaction with the justice system has become so intense that increased numbers of citizens are turning to various expressions of vigilantism. For example, Bernhard Goetz, a 37-year-old electronics engineer since dubbed the "subway vigilante," gained nationwide recognition in the December 1984 shootings of four youths on a New York City subway train after one or more of the group asked him for money. The debate on crime and self-protection prompted by the Goetz case led President Reagan to say in January 1985, "In general, I think we all can understand the frustration of people who are constantly threatened by crime and feel that law and order is not particularly protecting them."[29] Goetz was acquitted of all but one charge, unlawful possession of a weapon, in May 1987. Polls showed great support for the verdict, but many criminologists were mortified by the verdicts on the many charges. In October 1987, at Goetz's sentencing hearing for his conviction on the illegal gun possession charge, he was sentenced to six months in jail and ordered to undergo psychiatric treatment.

EXTENT OF CRIME

In the following section, we will detail the extent of "official" and "unofficial" crime in American society.

Measurement of Official Crime

The *Uniform Crime Reports* (UCR) and cohort studies are the chief sources of official crime data in the United States. The *Uniform Crime Reports'* findings are discussed here, while those of the cohort studies are analyzed in Chapter 9.

Uniform Crime Reports The *Uniform Crime Reports* are part of a process that began in 1870, when Congress created the U.S. Department of Justice and authorized federal record keeping. Greater support for the task of record keeping by state and local police departments was provided when the International Association of Chiefs of Police created a committee on Uniform Crime Reports. In 1930, the U.S. Attorney General authorized the Federal Bureau of Investigation to serve as the national clearinghouse for data collected by the UCR program.

In 1931, Thorsten Sellin stated that "the value of a crime for index purposes decreases as the distance from the crime itself in terms of procedure increases."[30] This opinion was widely shared and led to an emphasis on gathering statistics on actual crimes reported to and recorded by the police, rather than data on arrested suspects, defendants in courts, or prisoners in jails and prisons. The *Uniform Crime Reports* were issued monthly at first, then quarterly until 1941, semiannually through 1957, and annually to the present. The FBI gathers data from over 15,000 law enforcement agencies throughout the nation, covering about 98 percent of the population.

The FBI divides the crimes for which it collects information into Part I and Part II offenses. Part I offenses, also known as Index crimes, are subdivided further into crimes against the person, such as murder, rape, robbery, and aggravated assault, and crimes against property, such as burglary, larceny, auto theft, and arson. Part II offenses are such property offenses as simple assault, forgery and counterfeiting, fraud, embezzlement, and vandalism.

The police report monthly the number of Part I offenses that are "cleared." Offenses are cleared either by the arrest of a suspect who is turned over to the justice system for prosecution or by circumstances beyond the control of the police. The "clearance rate" represents the number of crimes solved expressed as a percentage of the total number of crimes reported to the police (see Figure 3.1 for the Part I crimes cleared by arrest in 1986). This rate is important, because the higher the number of crimes solved by arrest, the more effective deterrence this nation will have over crime.

Trends in Crime The level of crime in the United States has always been high, but there have been upward and downward trends. The trend was clearly upward from the turn of the twentieth century until the early 1930s. For example, the

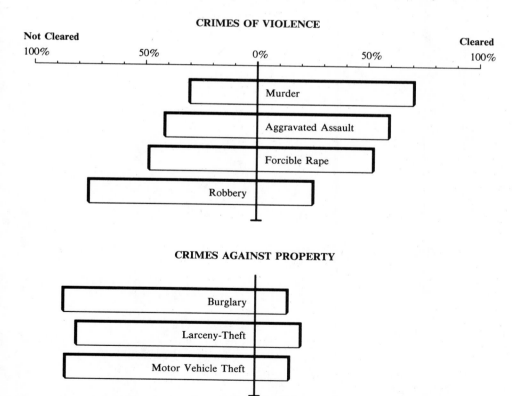

Figure 3.1 Crimes Cleared by Arrest, 1986 (*Source:* Federal Bureau of Investigation, *Uniform Crime Reports 1986* (Washington, D.C.: U.S. Department of Justice, 1987), p. 155.)

Table 3.1 TOTAL ARREST TRENDS, 1977–1986

Offense Charged	Number of Persons Arrested								
	Total All Ages			Under 18 Years of Age			18 Years of Age and Over		
	1977	1986	Percent Change	1977	1986	Percent Change	1977	1986	Percent Change
Total	7,524,937	9,526,389	+26.6	1,824,712	1,603,497	−12.1	5,700,225	7,922,892	+39.0
Murder and nonnegligent manslaughter	13,668	14,833	+8.5	1,301	1,297	−.3	12,367	13,536	+9.5
Forcible rape	21,232	28,471	+34.1	3,527	4,316	+22.4	17,705	24,155	+36.4
Robbery	99,267	116,636	+17.5	31,661	26,380	−16.7	67,606	90,256	+33.5
Aggravated assault	186,506	267,817	+43.6	30,887	34,141	+10.5	155,619	233,676	+50.2
Burglary	383,306	342,672	−10.6	198,132	123,037	−37.9	185,174	219,635	+18.6
Larceny-theft	851,980	1,089,672	+27.9	369,801	347,046	−6.2	482,179	742,626	+54.0
Motor vehicle theft	112,612	117,190	+4.1	60,514	45,907	−24.1	52,098	71,283	+36.8
Arson	13,787	13,949	+1.2	7,137	5,619	−21.3	6,650	8,330	+25.3
Violent crime[a]	320,673	427,757	+33.4	67,376	66,134	−1.8	253,297	361,623	+42.8
Property crime[b]	1,361,685	1,563,483	+14.8	635,584	521,609	−17.9	726,101	1,041,874	+43.5
Crime Index total[c]	1,682,358	1,991,240	+18.4	702,960	587,743	−16.4	979,398	1,403,497	+43.3
Other assaults	328,237	547,846	+66.9	61,726	79,391	+28.6	266,511	468,455	+75.8
Forgery and counterfeiting	54,840	70,884	+29.3	7,510	6,587	−12.3	47,330	64,297	+35.8
Fraud	183,816	268,047	+45.8	21,362	17,360	−18.7	162,454	250,687	+54.3
Embezzlement	5,701	9,678	+69.8	682	657	−3.7	5,019	9,021	+79.7
Stolen property; buying, receiving, possessing	87,716	105,049	+19.8	29,076	26,651	−8.3	58,640	78,398	+33.7

Offense							
Vandalism	164,327	202,729	+23.4	99,842	86,674	−13.2	116,055	+80.0
Weapons; carrying, possessing, etc.	107,696	144,996	+34.6	17,642	23,092	+30.9	121,904	+35.4
Prostitution and commercialized vice	60,514	92,555	+52.9	2,572	2,106	−18.1	90,449	+56.1
Sex offenses (except forcible rape and prostitution)	52,017	76,543	+47.1	9,435	12,512	+32.6	64,031	+50.4
Drug abuse violations	477,387	632,225	+32.4	111,945	62,399	−44.3	569,826	+55.9
Gambling	39,448	24,524	−37.8	1,425	559	−60.8	23,965	−37.0
Offenses against family and children	42,261	43,514	+3.0	2,525	2,416	−4.3	41,098	+3.4
Driving under the influence	944,344	1,313,421	+39.1	20,699	20,147	−2.7	1,293,274	+40.0
Liquor laws	270,566	433,837	+60.3	101,355	117,748	+16.2	316,089	+86.8
Drunkenness	1,047,121	731,771	−30.1	42,439	24,348	−42.6	707,423	−29.6
Disorderly conduct	436,970	519,560	+18.9	90,621	77,446	−14.5	442,114	+27.6
Vagrancy	41,570	26,581	−36.1	5,028	2,313	−54.0	24,268	−33.6
All other offenses (except traffic)	1,265,600	2,097,060	+65.7	263,420	259,019	−1.7	1,838,041	+83.4
Suspicion (not included in totals)	19,582	7,006	−64.2	5,305	2,519	−52.5	4,487	−68.6
Curfew and loitering law violations	75,672	66,757	−11.8	75,672	66,757	−11.8	—	—
Runaways	156,776	127,572	−18.6	156,776	127,572	−18.6	—	—

[a] Violent crimes are offenses of murder, forcible rape, robbery, and aggravated assault.

[b] Property crimes are offenses of burglary, larceny-theft, motor vehicle theft, and arson.

[c] Includes arson.

Source: Federal Bureau of Investigation, Uniform Crime Reports 1986 (Washington, D.C.: U.S. Government Printing Office, 1987), p. 168. Data reported by 8494 agencies; 1986 estimated population was 180,790,000.

homicide rate, which is the only crime for which reasonably accurate long-term statistics are available, virtually exploded during the first three decades of this century. Then, for about twenty-five years after the end of Prohibition, the United States enjoyed a period in which crime rates were either stable or declining; the fear of crime during this period was also relatively low. The crime rate remained well below the levels of the 1920s and early 1930s until the current crime wave began to hit the nation in the early 1960s.[31]

The *Uniform Crime Reports* documented a sharp increase in crime during the 1960s and 1970s. However, according to the *UCR,* the crime rate began to level off in the final years of the 1970s. In 1980, the crime rate increased again, with record levels of murder, robbery, and burglary reported in New York, Los Angeles, Miami, and Dallas. But between 1981 and 1984, the crime rate declined sharply, with overall drops of 7 percent in 1983 and 7 percent in 1984; then the rate began to climb again in 1985 and 1986.[32] For the arrest trends between 1977 and 1986, see Table 3.1 (pages 68–69).

Demographic variations in crime   There are three demographic variables that are often considered in the study of the distribution of crime: sex, age, and race.

1. Sex Distribution of Arrests.   Arrest rates in the United States reveal that males are far more frequently involved in violational behavior than are females. In Table 3.2, the sex ratios by offense category are reported. In 1986, four of every five arrestees throughout the nation were males. Males accounted for 79 percent of arrests for Index crimes, 89 percent of those for violent crimes and 76 percent of those for property crimes. Males were most often arrested for driving under the influence (15 percent of all male arrests). Females were most often arrested for larceny-theft, which accounted for 81 percent of the arrests for Index crimes and 20 percent of all female arrests. Male arrests increased 6 percent from 1985 to 1986, while females were up 5 percent.[33]

2. Age Distribution of Arrests.   Conventional crime in the United States, as well as in other Western countries, since World War II appears to be committed primarily by relatively young persons. The FBI reported that of the 10,392,177 crimes in which individuals were arrested in 1986, juveniles under 18 were arrested for 1,747,675. Juveniles between the ages of 10 and 17 constituted about 15 percent of the general population, but youths in this age group were arrested for 15.4 percent of the violent crimes and 33.5 percent of the property crimes.[34] Juveniles were arrested most frequently for curfew, loitering, and runaways.

Adults over the age of 18 were arrested for 8,644,502 crimes in 1986, 84.6 percent of all violent crimes and 66.5 percent of all property crimes. Violent crime is usually committed by older offenders, with 25 to 29 being peak years.[35] The rates of crime greatly drop in the late 30s and continue to decrease thereafter. For a crime by age breakdown of all arrestees, see Table 3.3 (page 75).

3. Racial Distribution of Arrests.   Whites are arrested nearly three times more than blacks; 71.3 percent of all arrestees in 1986 were white, compared with 27.0 percent for blacks. But the percentages were much closer in the specific category of serious crimes. For violent crimes, 52.3 percent of all arrestees were

Table 3.2 SEX RATIOS BY OFFENSE CATEGORY, 1986

Offense Charged	Total	1986 % of Males	Ratio Male to Female
Total	10,392,177	82.6%	4.7 to 1
Murder and nonnegligent manslaughter	16,066	87.7%	7.1 to 1
Forcible rape	31,128	98.9%	89.9 to 1
Robbery	124,245	92.2%	11.8 to 1
Aggravated assault	293,952	86.8%	6.6 to 1
Burglary	375,544	92.1%	11.7 to 1
Larceny-Theft	1,182,099	69.3%	2.3 to 1
Motor vehicle theft	128,514	90.5%	9.5 to 1
Arson	15,523	86.3%	6.3 to 1
All other assaults	593,902	84.8%	5.6 to 1
Forgery and counterfeiting	76,546	66.1%	1.9 to 1
Fraud	284,790	56.7%	1.3 to 1
Embezzlement	10,500	63.6%	1.7 to 1
Stolen property; receiving, possessing, etc.	114,105	88.6%	7.8 to 1
Vandalism	223,231	89.5%	8.5 to 1
Weapons; carrying, possessing, etc.	160,204	92.6%	12.5 to 1
Prostitution	96,882	34.6%	.52 to 1
Sex offenses (except forcible rape and prostitution)	83,934	92.1%	11.7 to 1
Drug abuse violations	691,882	85.5%	5.9 to 1
Gambling	25,839	82.8%	4.8 to 1
Offenses against family and children	47,327	85.0%	5.7 to 1
Driving under the influence	1,458,531	88.5%	7.7 to 1
Liquor laws	490,436	83.2%	5.0 to 1
Drunkenness	777,866	91.1%	7.7 to 1
Disorderly conduct	564,882	81.8%	4.5 to 1
Vagrancy	32,992	88.1%	7.4 to 1
All other offenses (except traffic)	2,272,589	84.6%	5.5 to 1
Suspicion (not included in totals)	7,455	83.4%	5.0 to 1
Curfew and loitering law violations	72,627	74.5%	2.9 to 1
Runaways	138,586	42.3%	.73 to 1

Source: Federal Bureau of Investigation, *Uniform Crime Reports 1986* (Washington, D.C.: U.S. Government Printing Office, 1987), p. 181. Data reported by 10,743 agencies; 1986 estimated population was 198,488,000.

white, compared with 46.5 percent black.[36] In this regard, blacks, who constitute only between 12 and 13 percent of the U.S. population, committed more robberies than whites and nearly as many murders and rapes as whites, but whites committed such crimes as drunkenness and driving under the influence far more frequently than blacks. For the percentage of arrests of blacks for Part I and Part II offenses, see Table 3.4 (page 76).

Ecological variations in crime Arrests are unevenly distributed not only by population characteristics but by geographic variables as well. With several exceptions, urban arrest rates exceeded rural arrest rates in all Part I and Part II offense categories in 1986. For all offenses, urban rates were more than twice as high as rural rates. The degree of disparity varied with the offense, but the greatest differentials occurred for such offenses as prostitution and vice, drunken-

| *BOX 3.3* | **THE NEW WOMAN CRIMINAL** |

Today's debate on the subject of crime committed by women focuses on three questions: Are women committing more crimes now than in the past? Are they committing more violent and aggressive crimes? Has the increased criminality of women been influenced by the women's rights movement?

The public's contention that women are committing more crimes appears to be confirmed by the *Uniform Crime Reports* and several studies on women and crimes. Official statistics of the *Uniform Crime Reports* document a dramatic increase in crime committed by women over the past several decades. In 1953, about one in every 12 persons arrested was a woman, but by 1974, this figure had increased to one in every five persons. In 1986, this figure remained one in every five persons. The change is in arrests for larceny or theft: The rate for women committing this offense has increased three to four times as much as the rate for men. Rita J. Simon explains that the reason why female crime rates have been increasing in larceny/theft is that more women are in the labor force, and, therefore, they have greater opportunities to commit these property offenses.

In the mid–1970s, Freda Adler's *Sisters in Crime* appeared, seemingly in answer to the public's bewilderment over what to make of the new woman criminal. In her book, Adler offered one answer: The violent, aggressive woman criminal was now committing crimes which in the past were committed only by men. Women, she contended, were becoming murderers, muggers, and bank robbers and were even penetrating organized crime. Adler's appearance on a number of television programs gave her views nationwide publicity.

However, Rita J. Simon, Laura Crites, and Darrell J. Steffensmeier have challenged this concept of the violent, aggressive woman criminal. Using the *Uniform Crime Reports,* they found that arrests of women for crimes of violence demonstrated no clear upward or downward trend from the mid–1950s to the mid–1980s. According to the *Uniform Crime Reports,* female arrests constitute but 11 percent of the arrests for violent crimes in 1986, compared with 13 percent in 1956. Steffensmeier adds that "women may be a little more active in the kinds of crime they have always committed," but they are "still typically nonviolent, petty property offenders." These researchers contend, in effect, that women may be hungrier, greedier, or unhappier, but, as a group, they do not appear to be any more violent than they were in the past.

Freda Adler also endorses the viewpoint that the women's liberation movement has resulted in increased criminality among women:

All that is changing. Women are no longer behaving like subhuman primates with only one option. Medical, educational, economic, political, and technological advances have freed women from unwanted pregnancies, provided them with male occupational skills, and equalized their strength with weapons. Is it any wonder that, once women were armed with male opportunities, they should strive for status, criminal as well as civil, through established male hierarchical channels?

Laura Crites challenges the assumption that the increase in arrests of women is directly related to the women's liberation movement. Her statistical analysis shows that women offenders most often are from minority groups. Frequently unemployed and seeking work, they are generally responsible for their own support and often for that of their children. Furthermore, their employment potential is limited in that more than half have not graduated from high school and their work experience has usually been in low-wage, low-status occupations. Crites concluded that the psychological independence and expanded economic opportunities of the women's rights movement are almost meaningless for this group, since the typical female offender is caught up in an all-consuming struggle for economic, emotional, and even physical survival.

Steffensmeier, in examining female delinquency, concludes that female delinquents continue to reflect traditional female sex roles and that the women's liberation movement has had little effect on them. Joseph W. Weiss's examination of self-reports of middle-class delinquency also led him to conclude that the alleged relationship between women's liberation and the emergence of a new type of female delinquent is a social invention, not reality.

Source: Freda Adler, *Sisters in Crime* (New York: McGraw-Hill, 1975), pp. 10–11; Laura Crites, "Women Offenders: Myth vs. Reality," in *The Female Offender,* edited by Crites (Lexington, Mass.: D.C. Heath, 1976), pp. 33–41; Rita James Simon, *Women and Crime* (Lexington, Mass.: D.C. Heath, 1975), pp. 36–42; Darrell J. Steffensmeier, "Organizational Properties and Sex-Segregation in the Underworld: Building a Sociological Theory of Sex Differences in Crime," *Social Forces* 61 (June 1983), pp. 1010–1032; and Joseph G. Weiss, "Liberation and Crime: The Invention of the Female Criminal," *Crime and Social Justice* 6 (Fall–Winter 1976), p. 24.

ness, vagrancy, and gambling—all of which are more typically urban violations.[37] Significantly, John M. Stahura and C. Ronald Huff's recent work indicates that increasing amounts of crime are found in suburbia, or "the white belt."[38]

Evaluation of Uniform Crime Reports   The chief findings of the *Uniform Crime Reports* are as follows:

1. There is widespread crime in American society, but crime appears to be leveling off.
2. Males commit more offenses than females, with the differences larger in serious offenses than in minor ones.
3. Lower-class individuals are involved in more frequent and more serious offenses than middle-class individuals; indeed, serious crime is primarily focused among lower-class individuals.

4. Blacks proportionately commit more frequent and more serious offenses than whites.
5. Urban individuals commit more frequent and more serious offenses than suburban or rural individuals.

However, experts challenge the validity of the UCR statistics for several reasons. The police can make arrests only when crimes come to their attention; because most crimes are hidden or not reported to the police, the UCR greatly underestimate the actual amount of crime in this nation. The offenses that are most likely to go unreported are white-collar crimes, thefts that go undiscovered until inventory time, prostitution, narcotics sales, and illegal gambling.

The reports also vary in accuracy and completeness, partly because not all police departments submit reports. Then, it is the individual patrol officer who both decides if a report is to be filed and makes the decision on what goes into the report, and officers vary in terms of how they interpret and handle the incidents that come to their attention. Furthermore, political reasons may cause a police department to underreport or overreport certain crimes. For example, city administrators and chiefs of police may have a vested interest in keeping the violent crime rates down. If the rate for rape is rising and the citizenry is becoming concerned, something is indeed done about the rate of rape—increasing numbers of rapes are tabulated as aggravated assaults.

Moreover, federal crimes are not reported, and, in cases of multiple crimes, usually only the most serious crime is reported. In addition, increases in rates of

Symbionese Liberation Army in bank robbery. (*Source:* ISP.)

Table 3.3 TOTAL ARRESTS, DISTRIBUTION BY AGE, 1986

Offense charged	Total All Ages	Ages Under 15	Ages Under 18
Total	10,392,177	536,609	1,747,675
Percent distribution	100.0	5.2	16.8
Murder and nonnegligent manslaughter	16,066	156	1,396
Forcible rape	31,128	1,514	4,798
Robbery	124,245	6,615	27,987
Aggravated assault	293,952	10,816	37,528
Burglary	375,544	47,080	134,823
Larceny-theft	1,182,099	156,033	378,283
Motor vehicle theft	128,514	11,961	50,319
Arson	15,523	3,837	6,271
Violent crime	465,391	19,101	71,709
Percent distribution	100.0	4.1	15.4
Property crime	1,701,680	218,911	569,696
Percent distribution	100.0	12.9	33.5
Crime Index total	2,167,071	238,012	641,405
Percent distribution	100.0	11.0	29.6
Other assaults	593,902	30,411	85,905
Forgery and counterfeiting	76,546	1,101	7,234
Fraud	284,790	6,722	17,727
Embezzlement	10,500	52	696
Stolen property; buying, receiving, possessing	114,105	7,613	28,739
Vandalism	223,231	45,247	95,479
Weapons; carrying, possessing, etc.	160,204	6,394	25,170
Prostitution and commercialized vice	96,882	247	2,192
Sex offenses (except forcible rape and prostitution)	83,934	6,110	13,753
Drug abuse violations	691,882	9,374	68,351
Gambling	25,839	105	610
Offenses against family and children	47,327	1,255	2,521
Driving under the influence	1,458,531	456	22,749
Liquor laws	490,436	10,163	132,335
Drunkenness	777,866	3,283	26,589
Disorderly conduct	564,882	22,517	82,986
Vagrancy	32,992	539	2,550
All other offenses (except traffic)	2,272,589	70,918	276,876
Suspicion	7,455	846	2,595
Curfew and loitering law violations	72,627	19,260	72,627
Runaways	138,586	55,984	138,586

Source: Federal Bureau of Investigation, *Uniform Crime Reports 1986* (Washington, D.C.: U.S. Government Printing Office, 1987), p. 174.

Data reported by 10,743 agencies; 1986 estimated population was 198,488,000.

crime may be partially related to new reporting procedures and computerization that make the reporting and recording of offenses easier than ever before. Finally, developments in medical science have caused changes in crime statistics. For example, improved emergency room practices have reduced the number of homi-

Table 3.4 CRIME BY RACIAL BREAKDOWNS

Offense	Total Arrests	% Black
Total	10,335,942	27
Murder and nonnegligent manslaughter	15,953	48
Forcible rape	30,777	46.6
Robbery	123,649	62
Aggravated assault	293,121	39.8
Burglary	374,081	29.5
Larceny-theft	1,179,482	30.1
Motor vehicle theft	127,749	34.7
Arson	15,440	23.6
All other assaults	591,372	32.7
Forgery and counterfeiting	76,442	32.6
Fraud	284,903	33.0
Embezzlement	10,495	28.8
Stolen property; receiving, possessing, etc.	113,430	37.4
Vandalism	222,615	19.9
Weapons; carrying, possessing, etc.	159,391	34.4
Prostitution	96,564	38.8
Sex offenses (except forcible rape and prostitution)	83,736	20.4
Drug abuse violations	688,815	31.8
Gambling	25,385	46.1
Offenses against family and children	46,071	32.3
Driving under the influence	1,440,862	9.7
Liquor laws	487,930	9.8
Drunkenness	772,861	17.7
Disorderly conduct	560,888	30.7
Vagrancy	32,974	29.4
All other offenses (except traffic)	2,262,963	33.6
Suspicion (not included in totals)	7,444	22.9
Curfew and loitering law violations	72,088	21.9
Runaways	138,461	13.4

Source: Federal Bureau of Investigation, *Uniform Crime Reports 1986* (Washington, D.C.: U.S. Government Printing Office, 1987), p. 182. Data reported by 10,699 agencies; 1986 estimated population was 197,663,000.

cides. In the 1930s, the mortality rate from a gunshot wound in the abdomen was about 50 percent; by the 1970s/1980s, it had dropped to about 12 percent.[39]

Unofficial Measurement of Crime

Victimization surveys and self-report studies are the main sources of unofficial accounts of criminal behavior. Victimization surveys ask people to tell about the crimes committed against them, while self-report studies ask people to tell about the crimes they have committed.

Victimization Surveys   In 1972, the Census Bureau began victimization studies to determine the extent of crime in the United States. Three different procedures were involved in these surveys. The largest component of the program is the

National Crime Panel, which oversees the interviewing of a national sample of approximately 125,000 people in 60,000 households every six months, for up to three and one-half years. Since 1973, the Bureau of Justice Statistics and its predecessors have published an annual national report called *Criminal Victimization in the United States*. **Victimization surveys** revealed that nearly 35,000,000 Americans were victims of crime in 1985, a figure nearly four times that reported by the *Uniform Crime Reports* (see Table 3.5).[40]

The National Crime Survey has also revealed that blacks are far more likely to be victims than whites. The rates of victimization are higher among the unemployed and the poor than among the employed. Furthermore, males are much more likely than females to be victims of violent crimes, with the rates for robbery and assault twice as high for men as for women. The elderly, somewhat surprisingly, given their fear of crime, are the least frequent victims, and those persons 12 to 24 years of age are most frequently victims. Males are more likely than females to be attacked by strangers, and whites are more likely than blacks to be attacked by strangers.[41]

One-fourth of the households in the United States were touched by a crime of violence or theft in 1986, the same proportion as in 1985 and well below the one-third of all households touched by crime in 1975 (the first year for which this measure is available). Five percent of the households in America had a member who was the victim of a violent crime in 1986; five percent of all households were also burglarized at least once during the year.[42]

The Bureau of Justice Statistics, in analyzing the 1974–1985 National Crime Survey, estimates that at current homicide rates, 1 of every 133 Americans will become a murder victim; for black males the proportion is estimated to be 1 of every 30. It is estimated that 5 out of 6 people will be victims of violent crimes (rape, robbery, and assault), either completed or attempted, at least once during their lives. Moreover, it is estimated that more than 2 in 5 black males will be victimized by a violent crime three or more times; this projection is almost double the likelihood for black females and more than triple the likelihood for white females.[43]

Evaluation of victimization surveys Some of the principal findings of the victimization surveys are as follows:

1. Far more crime is committed than is recorded, but the discrepancy between the number of people who say they have been victimized and the number of crimes known to the police varies with the type of offense.
2. The likelihood of being victimized varies with where one lives; the centers of large cities are the most probable sites of violent crimes.
3. The crimes that affect the most victims are thefts of property worth less than $50 and malicious mischief.
4. Men are about twice as likely as women to be victims of robbery and assault. Blacks experience violent crimes at a much higher rate than whites, and members of the lowest income groups are by far the most likely victims of violent crime.

Table 3.5   NUMBER AND PERCENT DISTRIBUTION OF VICTIMIZATIONS, BY SECTOR AND TYPE OF CRIME

Sector and Type of Crime	Number	Percent of Crimes Within Sector	Percent of All Crimes
All crimes	34,863,960	—	100.0
Personal sector	19,296,460	100.0	55.3
Crimes of violence	5,822,650	30.2	16.7
Completed	2,060,300	10.7	5.9
Attempted	3,762,350	19.5	10.8
Rape	138,490	0.7	0.4
Completed	70,700	0.4	0.2
Attempted	67,790	0.4	0.2
Robbery	984,810	5.1	2.8
Completed	651,750	3.4	1.9
With injury	211,320	1.1	0.6
From serious assault	119,780	0.6	0.3
From minor assault	91,540	0.5	0.3
Without injury	440,430	2.3	1.3
Attempted	333,060	1.7	1.0
With injury	82,810	0.4	0.2
From serious assault	41,490	0.2	0.1
From minor assault	41,320	0.2	0.1
Without injury	250,250	1.3	0.7
Assault	4,699,340	24.4	13.5
Aggravated	1,605,170	8.3	4.6
Completed with injury	507,730	2.6	1.5
Attempted with weapon	1,097,440	5.7	3.1
Simple	3,094,170	16.0	8.9
Completed with injury	830,110	4.3	2.4
Attempted without weapon	2,264,060	11.7	6.5
Crimes of theft	13,473,810	69.8	38.6
Completed	12,764,480	66.1	36.6
Attempted	709,330	3.7	2.0
Personal larceny with contact	522,740	2.7	1.5
Purse snatching	106,260	0.6	0.3
Completed	82,670	0.4	0.2
Attempted	23,590	0.1	0.1
Pocket picking	416,480	2.2	1.2
Personal larceny without contact	12,951,070	67.1	37.1
Completed	12,265,330	63.6	35.2
Less than $50	5,918,190	30.7	17.0
$50 or more	5,778,480	29.9	16.6
Amount not available	568,660	2.9	1.6
Attempted	685,740	3.6	2.0
Total population age 12 and over	194,096,690	—	—

Table 3.5 (*Continued*)

Sector and Type of Crime	Number	Percent of Crimes Within Sector	Percent of All Crimes
Household sector	15,567,500	100.0	44.7
Completed	13,243,990	85.1	38.0
Attempted	2,323,510	14.9	6.7
Burglary	5,594,420	35.9	16.0
Completed	4,353,970	28.0	12.5
Forcible entry	1,827,060	11.7	5.2
Unlawful entry without force	2,526,910	16.2	7.2
Attempted forcible entry	1,240,450	8.0	3.6
Household larceny	8,702,910	55.9	25.0
Completed	8,067,300	51.8	23.1
Less than $50	3,886,200	25.0	11.1
$50 or more	3,757,570	24.1	10.8
Amount not available	423,530	2.7	1.2
Attempted	635,610	4.1	1.8
Motor vehicle theft	1,270,170	8.2	3.6
Completed	822,720	5.3	2.4
Attempted	447,450	2.9	1.3
Total number of households	89,262,830	—	—

NOTE: Detail may not add to total shown because of rounding. Percent distribution based on unrounded figures.

—Not applicable.

Source: Bureau of Justice Statistics, *Criminal Victimization in the United States* (Washington, D.C.: U.S. Government Printing Office, 1987), p. 12.

5. Juveniles are more likely to commit crimes, particularly property offenses, than those in any other age groups, and they are more likely to be victims than members of any other age group.
6. Injury is more likely to occur when the offender is known to the victim than when the offender is a stranger.
7. The elderly have substantially lower victimization rates than do younger people in nearly every category. The exception is purse snatching and pickpocketing, for which the rates for the elderly are about the same as for the rest of the population.[44]

Victimization surveys have several limitations. These surveys cover only a small portion of the behaviors covered by either criminal justice statistics or self-report studies. They do not include information on victimless crimes, such as drug abuse, prostitution, and drunkenness, and information on white-collar crimes is difficult to gain from victim surveys. Moreover, victims may forget the victimizations they have experienced, may deliberately exaggerate or fail to admit victimization, or may state that a specific crime took place within the research year when it actually occurred before or after the relevant period.

Self-Report Studies   Another indication of the extent of crime is the data from self-report studies, in which criminologists ask people with and without arrest records to reveal any crimes they have committed. The self-report method has been widely used for two reasons: (1) self-report studies enable researchers to examine the nature and extent of hidden crime or delinquency; and (2) self-report studies are thought to eliminate the lower-class bias of official studies produced by law enforcement data.

Self-report studies, which first became widely used in the 1960s, commonly agree that practically every youth commits some form of delinquency. These studies specifically suggest that adolescents should not be divided into "offenders" and "nonoffenders," as the majority commit at least minor offenses and the youth who never violates the law is a rarity.[44] Those offenders who commit violent or predatory crimes are, not surprisingly, more likely than minor offenders to be arrested and referred to the juvenile court.[46]

J. S. Wallerstein and C. J. Wyle studied the self-reported crimes of adults in New York City. They asked more than sixteen hundred people whether they had violated any of forty-nine laws during their adult life. Of the people asked, 99 percent admitted having committed one or more of the named offenses. Men admitted to an average of eighteen crimes; women admitted to an average of eleven crimes. As with most self-report studies, the number of people admitting the commission of any particular offense varied inversely with the seriousness of the offense. Of the men, 89 percent admitted some form of petty larceny; 85 percent, disorderly conduct; and 77 percent, acts of indecency; but only 17 percent admitted to burglary; only 13 percent, grand larceny; and only 11 percent, the commission of a robbery.[47]

The Rand Corporation conducted self-report surveys of prisoners in California, Michigan, and Texas. Of those inmates convicted of either robbery or burglary, high offense rates were related to the following seven factors: (1) prior conviction for the same offense; (2) incarceration for more than 50 percent of the two-year period preceding the current arrest; (3) an adjudication, or finding, of delinquency before age 16; (4) time served in a state juvenile facility; (5) drug use in the two years preceding the current arrest; (6) drug use as a juvenile; and (7) employment for less than 50 percent of the two-year period preceding the current arrest.[48]

Further examination of this recidivist population revealed that offending rates appear to be remarkably skewed even among those who commit offenses serious enough and frequent enough to put them in prison. This study also revealed how active high-rate offenders appear to be: individuals serving time in California admitted to committing on the average 53 robberies per year when free; "working" burglars in California reported committing 90 burglaries per year.[49]

Evaluation of self-report studies   The principal findings of self-report studies include the following:

1. Most citizens break the law in minor ways.
2. A smaller percentage, sometimes called repeated offenders, recidivists, or chronic offenders, break the law over and over.
3. Females commit more criminal and delinquent acts than official statistics indicate, but males still appear to commit more criminal and delinquent acts and to commit more serious crimes than females do.
4. Most criminal and delinquent behavior is group-related, but some kinds of criminal and delinquent acts are less likely to be performed by groups than others.
5. Drug and alcohol abuse is one of the most important predictors of delinquent and criminal behavior.
6. Although most self-report studies have shown no relationship between social class and self-confessed criminality, several recent studies marked by greater sophistication and sensitivity in data collection analysis have shown that lower-class individuals appear to commit more frequent and serious criminal and delinquent acts.[50]

Self-report studies have been criticized for three reasons. First, their research designs have often been deficient, resulting in the failure to include those who commit more serious forms of criminal and delinquent behavior.[51] Second, the varied nature of social settings in which the studies have been conducted makes it difficult to test hypotheses, or theoretical notions. Third, these studies often have questionable reliability and validity.[52]

The most serious questions concerning self-report studies rest with their **reliability** and **validity**. Validity is concerned with the question: how can researchers be certain that respondents are telling the truth when they fill out questionnaires? Also, individuals may not remember their offenses—and may therefore underreport crime—or they may remember offenses that occurred before the period in question—and thus may overreport crimes. Furthermore, respondents may conceal their activities or exaggerate them, depending on the image they want to project to the researcher.[53]

Reliability is related to the consistency found in answers given on a questionnaire or in an interview. The crucial issue of reliability is whether repeated administration of a questionnaire will elicit the same answers from the same individuals when they are questioned two or more times. The late Michael Hindelang, in examining the reliability of self-report studies, concluded that "reliability measures are impressive, and the majority of studies produce validity coefficients in the moderate to strong range."[54]

THE COSTS OF CRIME

The costs of crime to American society are enormous. Among these costs are pervasive fear, emotional and physical trauma, direct and indirect economic costs, and social disruption.

BOX 3.4   **TYLENOL SCARE AND COPYCAT KILLERS**

The 1982 Tylenol scare shows how the fear of violent crime can grip an entire nation. The first victim of the Tylenol scare was 12-year-old Marty Kellerman of Elk Grove Village, Illinois, whose parents had given her an Extra-Strength Tylenol capsule to relieve a runny nose and sore throat. The next victim was 27-year-old Adam Janus, who collapsed upon taking a Tylenol capsule in his Arlington Heights, Illinois, home. Hours later, Adam's grief-stricken brother and sister-in-law were admitted to the hospital after taking the Extra-Strength Tylenol they had found in his house. By the weekend, they were counted among the seven Chicago-area residents who lost their lives after taking the Tylenol capsules.

The extensive media coverage of the Tylenol tragedy soon spread the fear of Tylenol capsules far beyond Illinois. Copycat killers turned up elsewhere, following nationwide television and newspaper coverage. Indeed, a hundred copycat poisonings occurred in the next weeks alone. In more than a dozen states across the nation, poison was discovered in pies, candy, mixed nuts, eyedrops, mouthwash, and a variety of over-the-counter drugs. By October 31, 1982, parents in communities across the nation were panic-stricken with the fear that their children might be victimized by a Tylenol-type Halloween trick. Dozens of communities banned trick-or-treating or restricted it to the daylight hours.

Source: Jack Levin and James Alan Fox, *Mass Murder: America's Growing Menace* (New York: Plenum Press, 1985), p. 24.

The Fear of Crime

According to a mid–1980s NBC survey, almost half of all Americans believed that they were in greater danger from serious crime than they were three years earlier. The level of fear is greatest in the major cities, but 46 percent of the people living in the suburbs said they also felt more fearful than they had three years earlier.[55]

The fear of crime varies from one group to another, but the variations are usually related in fact to a group's vulnerability to crime. The fear of crime tends to be higher among blacks than whites.[56] Women fear crime more than men, and the elderly fear crime more than younger people.[57] Those with lower family income and education levels tend to fear crime more than individuals with higher family income and education levels.[58] Individuals who live in neighborhoods with high rates of crime are more fearful than those from more placid communities. People who are socially isolated are more fearful, as are those with fewer resources for coping with the consequences of crime. Recent victims are also more worried, more concerned with the amount of crime around them, and more likely to take actions to protect themselves and their families.[59] Some evidence exists to

The fear of crime: extending to the drugstore.
(*Source:* Steve Leonard/Sygma.)

show that the more serious the previous injury from crime, the greater the consequent fear.[60]

Criminal Victimization

Criminal victimization is the most obvious cost of the disorder of crime. Robberies, assaults, and burglaries leave victims in their wake. Victims are often in pain and frightened. While many of their losses are concentrated in the moments, days, and weeks immediately following an attack, some consequences linger. Physical injuries suffered in a criminal attack may become permanent disabilities.[61] Psychological problems arise when victims draw negative conclusions about themselves based on their failure to cope.[62] Indeed, Gerald Caplan claims that being a crime victim can be as psychologically upsetting as suffering through a disaster or a war.[63] Criminal victimization disputes the idea that the world is a just and fair place and destroys trust in the safety of home or community, as well as the capacity to trust others.

Victims' families and friends also experience losses, through empathy and economic interdependence. Other individuals in the community, hearing of the victimization, may not experience the same emotional or financial losses, but they may take time-consuming and expensive actions to protect themselves.[64] In fact, if many people are afflicted with fear and if the material and emotional consequences of fear are large enough, criminal victimization may be the smaller part of the overall problem.[65]

The Economic Cost of Crime

The **economic costs of crime** in American society are added to the social costs of the suffering of victims, the anguish of friends and relatives, and the widespread fear. If an uninsured victim sustains financial loss from stolen property, medical payments, and continuing disability, long-lasting financial hardship may result. If the attack was particularly traumatic, involving injury or sexual attack at home, the victim may invest time and money in elaborate precautions that, in the end, fail to restore the sense of security enjoyed before the attack.

The economic costs can be divided into direct and indirect costs, but because a great deal of crime is hidden, it is impossible to calculate accurately the real cost. The direct costs are basically the out-of-pocket expenses of victims and witnesses, the loss of money or property and consequent inability to buy goods and services, and the cost of having to appear at court hearings. The costs of personal injury, as well as mental problems that may result from being a victim of or a witness to a violent crime, also are important.[66]

Indirect costs are those that affect the community generally. For example, families often must pay more for goods and services because a victimized business is forced to raise prices to cover its losses. Indirect losses also result when businesses must increase their insurance coverage against losses and must pay for better security systems. Other indirect costs include increased taxes to pay for public and private victim compensation programs, unemployment compensation, welfare, and the processing of offenders through the criminal justice system.[67]

Disruption to Community

In the late 1960s and early 1970s, the increased awareness of the declining quality of urban life became another disturbing indicator of the costs of crime. Residents of urban communities became so fearful of violent street crime that they modified their behavior accordingly. They used the streets less often and, when on the streets, stayed away from others, moving with averted eyes and hurried steps.[68] The brutal slaying of Kitty Genovese in the mid–1960s shocked the nation because 37 witnesses had heard her cries for help and watched her being stabbed, but the first call to the police did not come until several minutes after her death. A "don't get involved" attitude increasingly became the credo of urban dwellers in the 1970s.

In the late 1980s, it has become even clearer that we are becoming a nation of strangers. As a daily reality, Samuel Walker suggests, crime "afflicts us like a plague, casting a pall over every part of our lives. It affects how we think, how we act, and how we behave toward one another. The fear of crime," he concludes, "exerts a corrosive effect on interpersonal relations cautioning us against small acts of friendliness toward strangers."[69]

It is particularly disturbing that the elderly must live like prisoners in the decaying sections of some cities. *Time* correspondents, in surveying the plight of the elderly in three cities, noted:

When they go out—if they go out—they listen anxiously for the sound of foot-steps hurrying near, and they eye every approaching stranger with suspicion. As they walk, some may clutch a police whistle in their hands. More often, especially after the sun sets, they stay at home, their world reduced to the confines of apartments that they turn into fortresses with locks and bars on every window and door. . . . [T]hey share a common fear—that they will be attacked, tortured, or murdered by the teenage hoodlums who have coolly singled out old people as the easiest marks in town.[70]

ANALYSIS

Disorder and its relationship to crime and the frustrations of public policy to eliminate crime are two critical themes relating to crime as disorder in American society.

Social Disorder and Its Relationship to Crime

American society was founded on the concept of the ordered society. The colonists, many of whom were seeking relief from religious persecution, sought to establish the perfect Kingdom of God on earth. In this homogeneous society, religious law was the guiding force to preserve the social order. As with many ordered societies throughout history, those who did not play by the established rules faced either banishment or brutal corporal punishments.

Then, at the end of the eighteenth century, ideas of liberty and equality gripped the colonists and spurred revolution. The successes or failures of war often dramatically change the course of a nation's history, and a successful revolution against Mother England made the colonial leaders heroes rather than traitors. The freedom of the individual became the cornerstone of the new society, and the organizing concept of the newly ratified Constitution was that of a decent and humane society. Thus, the order of the new republic was based on the rights of the individual over the security and domination of the state.

But the new nation had to face a variety of social disorders throughout the nineteenth century. Large-scale immigration, especially in the first and last decades of the century, brought to America many who were different in terms of cultural values and religious preferences. Furthermore, several waves of economic depressions early in the century for the first time made poverty a problem that communities could not handle. The rise of the industrial state and the urbanized society gave birth to more expressions of social disorder. The economics and morality of slavery became a dividing issue between the North and the South and led to a bloody and costly war whose effects lasted long beyond Lee's surrender in a small courthouse in central Virginia. Finally, the conflict between owners of industry and workers generated social disorder in the final decades of the nineteenth century.

Crime became a major expression of social disorder in the new republic. The impoverished were regarded as the dangerous class, and citizens became fearful, especially in the rapidly growing cities of the Northeast. When the formal means of social control did not appear adequate to preserve the existing social order, citizens often took justice into their own hands.

The United States has had to face more extensive social disorder in the twentieth century than at any previous time in the history of this nation. First, a world war was fought and won. The era of prohibition showed the tendency of Americans to disobey the law if it did not agree with what they wanted. A depression settled in that continued to plague the country until the outbreak of the Second World War. Then, the United States became involved in two wars in Korea and Vietnam that it did not win. In the 1960s, the order of the American society seemed to be in grave jeopardy. The civil rights movement; urban, college, and prison riots; the expressions of antiwar sentiments by American youth in reaction to the Vietnam War; and the rise of a drug-using counterculture among young people were sobering reminders to political leaders and their constituents that unrest had gone far enough. Conservatives, who promised the return of order, were elected to all levels of government.

In the 1960s and early 1970s, mirroring the social disorder of the larger society, the rates of crime seemed to rise dramatically. The actual increases in crime, as well as the sometimes exaggerated coverage by the media, brought fear to urban dwellers. Politicians found that the public responded strongly to "get-tough" crime proposals. Law and order became the theme of the political right, but even the mainstream found that they could not stray far from this theme. Crime became symbolic of all that was wrong in American life, and the public was promised that proper doses of punishment would reaffirm communal values and restore the ordered society of the past.

In the 1980s, crime continues to be acknowledged, both in public opinion polls and in many other indicators, as a major impediment to achieving an ordered society. Current political sentiment, in fact, focuses on crime more than on the decay of the cities, the breakup of the family, the decline of mainstream religious influence, the growing economic needs of the underclass, the failure of the schools, or the plight of the farmers.

Crime and the Frustrations of Public Policy

In 1964, during his unsuccessful bid for the presidency, Barry Goldwater announced that it was time to declare **"war on crime"**:

> Tonight there is violence in our streets, corruption in our highest offices, aimlessness among our youth, anxiety among our elderly. . . . The growing menace in our country tonight, to personal safety, to life, to limb and to property, in homes, in churches, in the playgrounds and places of business, particularly, in our great cities, is the mounting concern of every thoughtful citizen in the United States.[71]

Most of the presidential elections since that of 1964 have made crime a major political issue. Presidents Nixon, Ford, and Reagan have taken particularly strong stances against the disorder of crime. The public order figures and institu-

| *BOX 3.5* | **RESULTS OF THE WAR ON CRIME** |

- Recent U.S. Supreme Court decisions have reduced procedural restraints, while police personnel, training, and technology have increased dramatically. But no evidence exists that these changes have led to more arrests or to reduced levels of crime.
- The population of state and federal institutions skyrocketed from 169,000 in the early 1970s to over 500,000 by 1986. But no evidence exists that the policy of increased incapacitation has contributed to greater community safety or protection.
- Mandatory (fixed-term) sentencing acts were passed in state after state across the nation, and 13 states also adopted determinate sentencing acts in the late 1970s and early 1980s. But no evidence exists that mandatory and determinate sentences have reduced recidivism.
- In 1977, Gary Gilmore became the first criminal to be executed in nearly a decade in the United States. At the end of 1986, nearly 1800 persons were under a sentence of death. By 1987, some 68 persons had been executed since the U.S. Supreme Court affirmed the death penalty in 1976. Texas and Florida have contributed nearly half the executions in this period. Yet the rates of violent crimes have continued to rise.
- The courts have continued to use plea bargaining to dispose of 90 percent of their cases. In addition, in spite of the hard-line mood of society, the use of probation has increased by 57.5 percent since 1979.
- No evidence exists that the law-and-order approach has had any effects on the amounts of drugs available or the use of drugs in this nation.
- There is little evidence that serious juvenile criminals are being treated differently from the way they were in the past. For example, the population of training schools continues to remain stable in the 1980s, with marked decreases over the levels of the 1960s.

Source: Bureau of Justice Statistics, *Capital Punishment, 1986* (Washington, D.C.: U.S. Government Printing Office, 1987), and Bureau of Justice Statistics, *Probation and Parole 1984* (Washington, D.C.: U.S. Department of Justice, 1986).

tions, especially permissive judges, have frequently been attacked for their contribution to this out-of-control problem. Ronald Reagan fought the war on crime with great diligence. His emphasis during his first term in office was on violent street crime; during his second term, he focused on violent crime, drug trafficking, and organized crime.[72]

The war on crime has not been restricted to the White House. In state legislatures, as well as governors' offices, politicians have passed tougher laws— including the institution of the death penalty—aimed at the hardened criminal.

The public's greater intolerance toward street crime, along with an intensive campaign by the media, convinced policymakers that it was time to enforce more aspects of the hard line model in the policies and practices of the criminal justice system.

However, from every vantage point, the war on crime has been a dismal failure. Hard-liners have promised the public that crime will be reduced by arresting more offenders, by targeting career criminals for special attention, by reducing the use of plea bargaining, by granting probation only for minor offenses, by sentencing more defendants to imprisonment for longer terms, by declaring a war on drugs, and by developing a "get-tough" policy toward serious juvenile criminals. Meanwhile, legislatures have come under pressure to pass into legislation a wider use of determinate and mandatory sentencing acts and death penalty statutes.

In sum, the institutions of public order are receiving a clear mandate today to "get tough" on criminals. But the reality is that the daily workings of criminal justice are not really affected by the law and order approach.[73] Nor is there any convincing evidence that hard-line measures are reducing recidivism.

SUMMARY

Crime and violence have always been recurrent themes of American life. The individualism of our society tends to give respect to those who will not bow to the whims, or obey the rules, of Big Government. But, as the fear of crime increased in recent decades, the tendency to romanticize the criminal has diminished. In the 1960s, social unrest on every front made the public question whether or not the institutions of American society were able to perform as advertised in a fair, just, and efficient way and to enforce the prevailing values. The decline of all social institutions, including the family, the school, and the church, made the citizenry more conscious of disorder than ever before.

In the turmoil, crime became the symbol of all our problems, and the public—whose perceptions had been influenced by the media as well as by real changes in the crime rates—began to advocate a "get-tough" strategy for dealing with crime. Politicians then promised the public that proper doses of punishment would reaffirm communal values and restore the ordered society of the past. Although the politicalization of crime has promised more than the war on crime could deliver, this still does not deny the social and economic costs of public disorder in American society. Disorder connotes a threatening lack of predictability in the behavior of others in one's social environment, and crime is seen by many citizens as the final blow to the quality of life.

REFERENCES

Brown, Frank, and Gerassi, John. *The American Way of Crime.* New York: Putnam, 1980.
Currie, Elliott. *Confronting Crime.* New York: Pantheon Books, 1985.

Moore, Mark H., et al. *Dangerous Offenders: The Elusive Target of Justice.* Cambridge, Mass.: Harvard University Press, 1984.

Rennie, Ysabel. *The Search for Criminal Man: A Conceptual History of the Dangerous Offender.* Lexington, Mass.: Lexington Books; Heath, 1978.

Rothman, David J. *The Discovery of the Asylum: Social Order and Disorder in the New Republic.* Boston: Little, Brown, 1971.

Rubin, Lillian B. *Quiet Rage: Bernie Goetz in a Time of Madness.* New York: Farrar, Straus & Giroux, 1986.

Scheingold, Stuart A. *The Politics of Law and Order: Street Crime and Public Policy.* New York: Longman, 1984.

Silberman, Charles E. *Criminal Violence, Criminal Justice.* New York: Random House, 1978.

Skogan, Wesley G. "The Impact of Victimization on Fear." *Crime and Delinquency* 33 (January 1987), pp. 135–154.

Walker, Samuel. *Sense and Nonsense About Crime: A Policy Guide.* Monterey, Calif.: Brooks/Cole Publishing Company, 1985.

Wilson, James Q. *Thinking About Crime.* Revised ed. New York: Basic Books, 1983.

NOTES

1. Ysabel Rennie, *The Search for Criminal Man* (Lexington, Mass.: Lexington Books, 1978), p. xiii.
2. Charles E. Silberman, *Criminal Violence, Criminal Justice* (New York: Random House, 1978), p. 21.
3. David J. Rothman, *The Discovery of the Asylum: Social Order and Disorder in the New Republic* (Boston: Little, Brown, 1971), p. 3.
4. Ibid., pp. 3, 7.
5. Ibid., p. 15.
6. Ibid., p. 16.
7. Norval Morris and Gordon Hawkins, *The Honest Politician's Guide to Crime Control* (Chicago: University of Chicago Press, 1970), chap. 1.
8. Rothman, *Discovery of the Asylum,* pp. 57–58.
9. Ibid., p. 58.
10. Frank Browning and John Gerassi, *The American Way of Crime* (New York: Putnam, 1980), pp. 127–128.
11. See Stephen J. Pfohl, "The 'Discovery' of Child Abuse," *Social Problems* 24 (1977), pp. 310–323.
12. Rennie, *The Search for Criminal Man*, p. 273.
13. Jeffrey Reiman, *The Rich Get Richer and the Poor Get Poorer: Ideology, Class and Criminal Justice* (New York: Wiley, 1979), p. 97.
14. Silberman, *Criminal Violence, Criminal Justice,* pp. 21–22.
15. Browning and Gerassi, *American Way of Crime,* p. 241.
16. Ibid.
17. Ibid., pp. 328–329.
18. John Monahan, Raymond W. Novaco, and Gilbert Geis, "Corporate Violence: Research Strategies for Community Psychology," in *Challenges for the Criminal Justice System,* ed. Daniel Adelson and Theodore Sarbin (New York: Human Sciences Press, 1979), p. 118.

19. Marshall B. Clinard and Peter C. Yeager, *Corporate Crime* (New York: Free Press, 1980), p. 9.
20. Ibid.
21. Rothman, *Discovery of the Asylum,* p. 78.
22. Ibid.
23. Rennie, *Search for Criminal Man,* p. 273.
24. Stuart A. Scheingold, *The Politics of Law and Order: Street Crime and Public Policy* (New York: Longman, 1984), p. 3.
25. Samuel Walker, *Popular Justice: A History of American Criminal Justice* (New York: Oxford University Press, 1980), pp. 32–33.
26. Ibid.
27. Richard Maxwell Brown, *The Strain of Violence: Historical Studies of American Violence and Vigilantism* (New York: Oxford University Press, 1975), pp. 95–133.
28. Walker, *Popular Justice,* p. 119.
29. Lillian B. Rubin, *Quiet Rage: Bernie Goetz in a Time of Madness* (New York: Farrar, Straus, & Giroux, 1986.
30. Thorsten Sellin, "The Basis of a Crime Index," *Journal of Criminal Law and Criminology* 22 (September 1931), p. 346.
31. Silberman, *Criminal Violence, Criminal Justice,* p. 28.
32. Federal Bureau of Investigation, *Crime in the United States: 1986* (Washington, D.C.: U.S. Government Printing Office, 1987), p. 43.
33. Ibid., p. 181.
34. Ibid., p. 174.
35. Ibid.
36. Ibid., p. 181.
37. Ibid., p. 182.
38. See John H. Stahura and C. Ronald Huff, "Crime in Suburbia, 1960–1980," in *Metropolitan Crime Patterns,* ed. Robert Figlio, Simon Hakeim, and George F. Rengert (Monsey, N.Y.: Criminal Justice Press, 1986), pp. 55–71.
39. For criticisms of the *Uniform Crime Reports,* see Franklin E. Zimring, "The Serious Juvenile Offender: Notes on an Unknown Quantity," in *The Serious Juvenile Offender: Proceedings of a National Symposium* (Washington, D.C.: U.S. Government Printing Office, 1978), pp. 22–23.
40. Bureau of Justice Statistics, *Criminal Victimization in the United States, 1985* (Washington, D.C.: U.S. Government Printing Office, 1986), p. 1.
41. Ibid.
42. Bureau of Justice Statistics, *Households Touched by Crime, 1986* (Washington, D.C.: U.S. Department of Justice, 1987), p. 1.
43. Bureau of Justice Statistics, *Likelihood of Victimization* (Washington, D.C.: U.S. Department of Justice, 1987), pp. 1–3.
44. Most of these findings are from Gwynn Nettler, *Explaining Crime* (New York: McGraw-Hill, 1974), pp. 68–70.
45. Silberman, *Criminal Violence, Criminal Justice,* p. 41.
46. William T. Pink and Mervin F. White, "Delinquency Prevention: The State of the Art," in *The Juvenile Justice System,* ed. Malcolm W. Klein (Beverly Hills, Calif.: Sage, 1976), p. 9.
47. J. S. Wallerstein and C. J. Wyle, "Our Law Abiding Law Breakers," *Probation* 25 (1947), pp. 107–112.
48. Peter W. Greenwood, *Selective Incapacitation* (Santa Monica, Calif.: Rand, 1982).
49. Ibid.

50. See Delbert S. Elliott and Suzanne S. Ageton, "Reconciling Race and Class Differences in Self-Reported and Official Estimates of Delinquency," *American Sociological Review* 45 (February 1980), pp. 95–110.

51. Paul Brantingham and Patricia Brantingham, *Patterns in Crime* (New York: Macmillan, 1984), p. 60. See also Elliott and Ageton, "Reconciling Race and Class Differences," pp. 95–110.

52. Nettler, *Explaining Crime,* p. 86.

53. Gary F. Jensen and Dean G. Rojek, *Delinquency: A Sociological View* (Lexington, Mass.: Heath, 1980), p. 94.

54. Michael Hindelang et al., *Measuring Delinquency* (Beverly Hills, Calif.: Sage, 1981), p. 126.

55. Public Agency Foundation, *Crime: What We Fear, What Can Be Done* (Dayton, Ohio: Domestic Policy Association, 1986), p. 5.

56. A. D. Biderman, L. A. Johnson, J. McIntyre, and A. W. Weir, *Report on Victimization and Attitudes Toward Law Enforcement.* (Washington, D.C.: U.S. Government Printing Office, 1967); F. J. Fowler, Jr., and T. W. Mangione, *The Nature of Fear* (Boston: Survey Research Program, University of Massachusetts, 1974); W. G. Skogan, "Crime in Contemporary America," in *Violence in America,* ed. H. Graham and T. R. Gurr, 2d ed. (Beverly Hills, Calif.: Sage, 1979), chap. 14; W. G. Skogan and M. G. Maxwell, *Coping with Crime: Victimization, Fear, and Reactions to Crime* (Beverly Hills, Calif.: Sage, 1981).

57. Skogan and Maxwell, *Coping with Crime,* p. 46.

58. James Garofalo, *Public Opinion About Crime: The Attitudes of Victims and Nonvictims in Selected Cities* (Washington, D.C.: U.S. Government Printing Office, 1977), p. 20.

59. Wesley G. Skogan, "The Impact of Victimization on Fear," *Crime and Delinquency* 53 (January 1987), p. 151.

60. Skogan and Maxwell, *Coping with Crime.*

61. Mark H. Moore et al., *Dangerous Offenders: The Elusive Target of Justice* (Cambridge, Mass.: Harvard University Press, 1984), p. 10.

62. Steve Berglas, "Why Did This Happen to Me?" *Psychology Today* (1985), p. 44.

63. Ibid.

64. Moore et al., *Dangerous Offenders,* p. 10.

65. Ibid.

66. H. Reynolds, *Cops and Dollars: The Economics of Criminal Law and Justice* (Springfield, Ill.: Thomas, 1981), p. 139.

67. Ibid.

68. James Q. Wilson, *Thinking About Crime,* Revised ed. (New York: Basic Books, 1983), p. 5.

69. Samuel Walker, *Sense and Nonsense About Crime: A Policy Guide* (Monterey, Calif.: Brooks/Cole, 1985), p. 3.

70. *Time,* 29 November 1976, p. 21.

71. "Goldwater's Acceptance Speech to GOP Convention," *New York Times,* 17 July 1964.

72. Scheingold, *Politics of Law and Order,* pp. 59–60.

73. *Ibid.*

CHAPTER **4**

Free Will
and Crime

CLASSICAL SCHOOL OF CRIMINOLOGY

Right to Punishment

Utility of Punishment

Effectiveness of Punishment

Degree of Punishment

Administration of Punishment

Contribution of Jeremy Bentham

Revolutionary Criminology of the Eighteenth Century

Summary

UTILITARIAN PUNISHMENT PHILOSOPHY

Assumptions About Social Order

Humans Require Strong Social Controls
Declining Quality of Life Today
Low Cost of Crime Today
Punishment and the Criminal
Incentives and Disincentives to Crime
Lower-Class Status and the Crime Problem

Components of the Utilitarian Punishment Philosophy

Increased Use of Incapacitation
Greater Use of Determinate and Mandatory Sentences
Development of a More Effective Court System

Hard-Line Policy Toward Serious Juvenile Offenders
Get-Tough Policy with Drug Offenders
Greater Use of the Death Penalty

Summary

RETRIBUTION OR "JUST DESERTS" PHILOSOPHY

Assumptions of the Justice Model

"Just Deserts"
Distrust of the State
The Criminal Justice System Needs Reform

Components of the Justice Model

Summary

ANALYSIS

Can the State Be Trusted?

Is Criminal Behavior Rational?

Does Punishment Deter?

POLICY IMPLICATIONS

Danger of Repression

SUMMARY

REFERENCES

NOTES

KEY TERMS

classical school of criminology

determinate sentencing

deterrence

Enlightenment

felicific calculus

free will

indeterminate sentencing

just deserts

mandatory sentencing

parens patriae philosophy

selective incapacitation

> *The problem of social order is fundamental: How can mankind live together in reasonable order? Every society has, by definition, solved that problem to some degree, but not all have done so with equal success or without paying a high cost in other things—such as liberty—that we also value. If we believe that man is naturally good, we will expect that the problem of order can be rather easily managed; if we believe him to be naturally wicked, we will expect that provision of order to require extraordinary measure; if we believe his nature to be infinitely plastic, we will think the problem of order can be solved entirely by plan and that we may pick and choose freely among all possible plans. Since every known society has experienced crime, no society has ever solved that problem of order. The fact that crime is universal may suggest that man's nature is not infinitely malleable, though some people never cease searching for an anvil and hammer sufficient to bend it to their will.*
> —James Q. Wilson and Richard J. Herrnstein[1]

The problem of how humankind can live together in an ordered society, as Wilson and Herrnstein surmise, is a key issue facing every nation. The answer given is ultimately related to both assumptions about the basic nature of humanity and the reasons for criminal behavior. This chapter, the first of five on explanations of criminal behavior, offers a definition of such behavior as purposeful activity resulting from rational decisions in which the pros and cons are weighed and the acts that promise the greatest potential gains are performed.[2] Therefore, because criminals have **free will** and know what they are doing, a position that goes back to the eighteenth-century **classical school of criminology**—they deserve to be punished.

This emphasis on free will and responsibility, also the basic philosophical premise of criminal law, is quite different from the premises of the next four chapters, which assume that criminals cannot help committing their socially undesirable behavior. The disorder of crime, according to the positive school of criminology, results because individuals are controlled by internal factors (psychological or biological deficiencies) or external factors (environment, poverty, criminogenic peers, or societal labeling). The final chapter of this unit presents the viewpoint that lower-class individuals cannot help committing conventional criminal acts because of economic exploitations by the economic and political elites.

CLASSICAL SCHOOL OF CRIMINOLOGY

Cesare Boneseana, Marchese of Beccaria, was born to noble parents in 1738. His early education took place at the Jesuit College of Parma, and he studied law at Pavia in Italy. As part of a group of Milanese youth whose members were disenchanted with the archaic organization of European society, Beccaria was highly influenced by two brothers, Pietro and Alessandro Verri. Alessandro, a prison official in Milan, exposed Beccaria to the existing practices and practitioners in criminal justice, including capricious judges, excessive discretionary justice, politically motivated magistrates, and brutal methods of punishment.[3] In 1764, encouraged by the group and incensed by the corruption and brutality of the existing system, Beccaria published a slim volume called *On Crimes and Punishment*.[4]

This essay was published anonymously because Beccaria feared reprisals if his authorship was known. But such caution proved to be unnecessary, for the book was avidly read and translated into nearly all the languages of Europe. Beccaria gained a reputation from this book that has endured for more than two centuries. The eminent mathematician D'Alembert rightly predicted that "this book is sufficient to assure the author of an immortal name," adding, "What philosophy, what trust, what logic, what precision, and at the same time what emotions and what humanity."[5]

Beccaria's *On Crimes and Punishment* examines five concerns about punishment: right to punishment, utility of punishment, effectiveness of punishment, degree of punishment, and administration of punishment.

Right to Punishment

Beccaria believed that human beings are rational creatures who, being free to choose their actions, can be held responsible for their behavior. The concept of free will, according to Beccaria, is that behavior is purposive and that it is based on hedonism; that is, individuals choose those actions that will give pleasure and avoid those that will bring pain. Beccaria based the legitimacy of criminal sanctions on the social contract. He believed that the individual surrenders only enough liberty to the state so that the society can establish rules and sanctions for the preservation of the social order.[6]

Utility of Punishment

The authority of making laws rested with the legislator, who had only one aim in sight, "the greatest happiness for the greatest number."[7] To achieve this happiness, Beccaria argued, the purpose of punishment is to deter persons from the commission of crime, *not to provide social revenge*. Thus, punishment was justified because of its practical usefulness as a deterrent. It was valuable in protecting society and in deterring individuals from crime.[8]

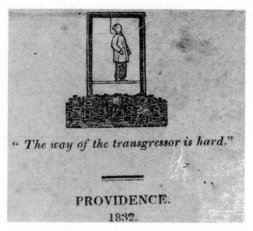

" *The way of the transgressor is hard.*"

PROVIDENCE.
1832.

Punishment and the criminal offender. (*Source:* Warshaw Collection/Archive Center, Smithsonian Institution.)

Effectiveness of Punishment

Beccaria maintained that the punishment must be sure and swift and penalties determined strictly in accordance with the social damage created by the crime.[9] "For a punishment to attain its end," he wrote, "the evil which it inflicts has only to exceed the advantage derivable from the crime."[10]

Beccaria argued that "the more prompt the punishment and the sooner it follows the crime, the more just it will be and the more effective."[11] He contended that the promptness of punishment is necessary "because the shorter the time between punishment and misdeed, the stronger and more durable in human spirit is the association of these two ideas of *crime* and *punishment.*"[12] But the certainty of punishment, according to Beccaria, is a greater check upon crime than the severity of punishment. This certainty, or inevitability, or punishment, reasoned Beccaria, "always makes a stronger impression than the fear of another worse punishment . . ."[13]

Beccaria was aware that ultimately the effectiveness of punishment depended upon the willingness of citizens to obey the law, and he believed that citizens would be more willing to obey just rather than unreasonable and unjust statutes. However, Beccaria admitted that regardless of the efficiency of punishment, it is impossible to prevent all or even most crimes that arise in the universal conflict of human passion. He went on to argue that the disorder of crime rises with the growth of population, with the expansion of private interests, and with the development of empires.[14]

Degree of Punishment

Beccaria believed that the degree of punishment should be proportionate to the amount of evil caused by the social harm against society. The degree of punish-

Cesare Beccaria: a reformer. (*Source:* Picture Collection, New York Public Library.)

ment should also be the least necessary to protect society and to deter criminal behavior. He is acknowledged as a reformer because he opposed the brutal means that traditionally were used to punish crimes. Beccaria advocated that:

- Secret accusations and torture in criminal procedures should be abolished.
- There should be speedy trials.
- The accused should be treated humanely before trial and must have every right and facility to bring forward evidence in his or her behalf.
- Crimes against property should be punished solely by fines, or by imprisonment when the person is unable to pay the fine.
- Banishment is an excellent punishment for crimes against the state.
- There should be no capital punishment. Life imprisonment is a better deterrent. Capital punishment is irreparable and hence makes no provision for possible mistakes and desirability of later rectification.
- Imprisonment should be more widely employed, but its mode of application should be greatly improved through providing better physical quarters and by separating and classifying the prisoners into age, sex, and degree of criminality. [15]

Elio Monachesis wrote in 1955 that "it is not an exaggeration to regard Beccaria's work as being of primary importance in paving the way for penal reform for approximately the last two centuries." [16] Beccaria largely inspired the transition from reliance on capital and corporal punishment to dependence on incarceration. He further emphasized the necessity to control discretion in order to defend individual rights, and he argued that fixed and predictable sentences represented the best way to ensure the certainty needed for promoting deterrence.[17]

Administration of Punishment

Beccaria believed that criminal law should have those qualities that would make it easy to administer. It should be "clear and simple," should have the support of society, should favor individuals more than classes, and should be both respected and feared by mankind.[18] Beccaria claimed that uncertainty in law is likely to generate disorder in a society:

> If climate makes a nation indolent, uncertainty in its laws will maintain and aggravate that indolence and that stupor. If a nation likes its pleasures but is lively, uncertainty in its laws will dissipate that liveliness in numberless little cabals and intrigues, which sow distrust in every heart and establish treachery and dissimulation as the foundation of prudence. If a nation is courageous and strong, all uncertainty in its laws will in the end disappear, but only after much wavering between freedom and slavery, slavery and freedom.[19]

Beccaria had far more confidence in the ability of legislatures than in that of judges to administer the law. He felt that judicial discretion, as well as other arbitrary means in dealing with the disorder of crime, had to be minimized. The sole business of the judge, according to Beccaria, was to discover whether an individual had broken the law. If he or she had, then the judge should pronounce sentence from a rational scale of punishments developed by the legislature.[20]

Contribution of Jeremy Bentham

Jeremy Bentham, a contemporary of Beccaria and a British philosopher, was the other leading proponent of the classical school. Bentham's most famous concept was the *felicific calculus*, which assumed that people are rational creatures who will choose pleasure and avoid pain.[21] He believed that a rational person will do what is necessary to achieve the most pleasure and the least pain, and, therefore, he contended that punishment would deter criminal behavior providing "the value of the punishment must not be less in any case than what is sufficient to outweigh the profit of the offense."[22] Thus, if a thief gained X units of pleasure from a crime, it would be up to the court to assign, for example, X + 10 units of pain to deter criminal behavior.[23]

Bentham added that punishment has four objectives: (1) if possible, to prevent all offenses; (2) if an individual does decide to commit an offense, to persuade him or her to commit a less serious rather than a more serious one; (3) if an individual has resolved upon a particular offense, "to dispose him to do not more mischief than necessary to his purpose," and (4) to prevent the crime at as cheap a cost to society as possible.[24]

Jeremy Bentham's writings led to reforms in British criminal law. John Howard, sheriff of Bedfordshire, England, was stimulated by Bentham's ideas to recommend more humane conditions in jails and hulks (ships used to imprison felons). Sir Samuel Romilly, Sir James MacKintosh, and Sir Thomas Burton all urged the reform of the English criminal code. William Penn, the Quaker leader who prescribed imprisonment as a means to correct the behavior of criminals, brought the concept of more humanitarian treatment of offenders to the colonies.

In summary, the basic theoretical constructs of the classical school of criminology were developed from the writings of Beccaria and Bentham and their contemporaries. Human beings were looked upon as rational creatures who are free to choose their actions and, therefore, can be held responsible for their behavior. Classical thinkers contributed the concept of utility in the punishment of criminal behavior. Punishment was justified because of its practical usefulness, for the aim of punishment was the protection of society, and its dominant theme was deterrence. Furthermore, the human being was seen as a creature governed by a *felicific calculus,* which presumed that people will choose pleasure rather than pain. It was necessary for sanctions to be proportionate to the offense and to outweigh the rewards of crime. Beccaria and Bentham put order where there had been the untidiness of arbitrary discretion. They tried to make sentences more uniform and less severe. A rational scale of punishment was designed to deter criminals from further offenses and to prevent others from following their example.[25]

Revolutionary Criminology of the Eighteenth Century

In the eighteenth century, William Godwin and the Marquis de Sade proposed an alternative criminological paradigm, a perspective that had much in common with the views of radical criminologists of the twentieth century. In 1790, Godwin wrote that it was the inequality of the existing property system that caused crime. He rejected all claims that could be made in favor of the state, because he charged that the laws inevitably favored the rich, a fact that was obvious from the tendency of laws not to punish the socially harmful acts of the rich. He saw no justification for punishment, because he reasoned that science had already shown free will to be mythical. Godwin believed that crime arose from factors within society and could only be removed by changing that society. Finally, he rejected reformation and rehabilitation as appropriate ideas for a system of reform; coercion would only alienate the mind of the prisoner, regardless of the good intentions of the interventionist.[26]

The criminology of the Marquis de Sade in the late eighteenth century was viewed as even more revolutionary. He imagined a primitive age when the world was divided between the weak and the strong. The strong had seized a certain amount of material goods by theft and violence. Society then was created to draw a line against further thefts and violence, so that anyone who attempted to do what the strong had already done was defined as a criminal. The weak, according to de Sade, agreed to the social contract only to safeguard the little they had left. De Sade reasoned that punishing theft meant punishing the weak for attempting to reclaim what had once belonged to them. He summed up his viewpoint by saying that laws were a worse form of oppression than anarchy and that property was in itself a fundamental crime against society.[27]

Summary

The rapid acceptance of the principles of the classical school, rather than those of the revolutionary criminology of Godwin and de Sade, is explained by the intellectual, political, sociocultural, and economic factors present during the late eighteenth century in Europe. The intellectual climate was especially receptive to the philosophies of the classical school. This era, the **Enlightenment,** was one in which the explanations of crime based on sin and demons were being replaced by those espousing individual responsibility and free choice. Philosophers were advocating the primacy of the rights of the individual over those of the state. Enlightenment thinkers were particularly indignant at the injustice of the criminal law in its widespread use of torture, corporal punishment, and the death penalty. They blamed these brutal measures on the authorities' lack of regard for human life.[28]

Beccaria and Bentham's themes also were widely accepted because they offered an increasingly educated society a rational and enlightened view of human behavior without resorting to the radical materialism of Godwin and de Sade. Furthermore, the public responded to the fact that the classical criminologists defined the disorder of crime in terms of acts that were typical behaviors only of the lower classes. Moreover, Beccaria and Bentham's desire to make punishment more humane suited the moral sensibility of middle-class interest groups.[29]

Beccaria and Bentham's ideas were well received in the political arena because they provided propaganda for the intelligentsia and the bourgeoisie to use in attacking the aristocracy and the Church. Absolutist rulers realized that by supporting the principles of the classical school of criminology, they were able to prove that their power did not rest solely on tradition and heredity. Furthermore, because classical criminology did not require any major structural changes in society or in traditional institutions, its views were much preferred to the revolutionary criminology of Godwin and de Sade.[30]

Finally, middle-class interest groups responded favorably to the economic implications of classical criminology, especially the protection of private property. Beccaria and Bentham did not question the social and economic inequality at the time, but instead created a legal system that would punish those who interfered with the ownership and the distribution of property. Thus, in a period that was undergoing incredibly rapid social change—from the transformation of the feudal economy into early forms of capitalism to the emergence of the modern nation-state—classical criminology promised an ordered society that would preserve the existing economic and social system and would promote criminal justice reforms.[31]

Utilitarianism became the dominant theoretical idea guiding the development of criminal justice in both the United States and Europe over the next century. Criminal deterrence, social reform, and prisoner rehabilitation were justified because of their presumed social advantages. Eventually, the utilitarian punishment philosophy came under attack on two fronts; it was threatened first by the rise of positivism, or the treatment model, and then by the development of "just deserts," a retributive punishment philosophy. Significantly, however, a neoclassical, utilitarian punishment philosophy became the dominant model guiding criminal justice during the 1970s and the 1980s.

UTILITARIAN PUNISHMENT PHILOSOPHY

In the late 1960s, political scientists and economists began to apply the theory of rational choice to explain criminal behavior just as that theory had been used to explain the actions of voters, consumers, and investors.[32] James Q. Wilson and Ernest van den Haag, spokespersons for this position in the 1970s, were particularly critical of those who suggested that "crime could be curtailed by reducing poverty, increasing educational attainments, eliminating dilapidated housing, encouraging community organization, and providing troubled or delinquent youth with counseling services."[33]

Utilitarian punishment philosophy, like the classical school of criminology, is grounded on the belief that punishment is necessary to deter criminals and to protect society from crime. Punishment, then, is justified because of its presumed social utility. Those who favor this utility of punishment argument suggest that because we are unable to reform offenders through rehabilitative programs, we should at least assure ourselves that they are punished and that potential criminals are deterred by the consequences paid by those who break the law.[34]

The utilitarian punishment philosophy is sometimes referred to as "neoclassical," because this hard-line approach updates the eighteenth-century classical school. Yet, while the concept of utility may tie this movement of the 1970s and 1980s to the classical school, *utilitarian punishment philosophy* appears to be a better title because it lacks the social and legal reform emphasis of the classical model.

Assumptions about Social Order

Proponents of utilitarian punishment philosophy display considerable diversity in terms of backgrounds and beliefs, but they are generally united in supporting six assumptions about social order: (1) humans require strong external social controls to preserve the social order; (2) the breakdown in order today reflects grave losses in the quality of life; (3) crime has too little cost today; (4) the disorder of crime is caused by individuals rather than by social conditions; (5) punishment is effective in maintaining public order; and (6) the conventional crime problem is mostly a lower-class male phenomenon.

Humans Require Strong Social Controls   The viewpoint that humans require social controls has a long history. Ernest van den Haag and Edward C. Banfield, the hard-liners of present-day utilitarian punishment philosophy, blame crime on the lack of individual moral responsibility. They tend to dwell on the more lurid and reprehensible crimes, and they argue that criminals who choose to prey on others show clearly they are wicked or defective human beings.[35] They add that the wicked nature of humans mandates that force, or the big stick, is the only appropriate response to criminality; that is, it is only through "get tough" measures that order will be restored to American society.[36] To paraphrase James Q. Wilson, evil men exist and nothing avails but for society to separate them from the rest of us.[37]

Declining Quality of Life Today   Current proponents of the utilitarian punishment position are also unified in their resentment at what they see as the declining quality of life caused by the problem of criminality. Supporters of this approach are fond of expressing nostalgia for an earlier period of American society, in which, they claim, the values were clear, the moral consensus was overwhelming, and the future was predictable and inviting.[38]

James Q. Wilson, who is somewhat more moderate in his views than van den Haag and Banfield, expresses grave concern about the losses in the quality of American life caused by the threat of violent, or predatory, crime. He argues that because of the disruptive social consequences of street crime, urban dwellers have only two choices: either they can curtail their activities so as to reduce the hazards of urban life, or they can try to lead relatively normal lives while risking injury and property loss. Either way, they are forced to live with a fear that drains pleasure from their lives and plants seeds of distrust of those around them.[39] Once again, the Goetz case speaks to this fear and panic.

Wilson also sees crime as symptomatic of a general breakdown of society, signified by a rising school dropout rate, widespread drug abuse, the declining structural unity of the family, and too much reliance on welfare. He adds that "the social bonds—the ties of family, of neighborhood, of mutual forbearance and civility—seem to have come asunder.[40] In the excerpt in Box 4.1, Wilson analyzes how social disorder at the community level leads to higher rates of crimes.

Low Cost of Crime Today   Advocates of the utilitarian punishment philosophy argue that in the current climate crime does pay, and, therefore, they generally are critical of society for being too easy on crime. They feel that most of the people who commit crime have very little to lose and a lot to gain. These individuals know that the chances of being punished are very small; for them, crime is a perfectly rational choice.[41]

Most proponents of this "raising the ante" philosophy also claim that the criminal justice system has contributed to the low cost of criminal behavior. They decry the establishment of legal and constitutional rights that "protect" predatory criminals from prosecution and punishment. The due process reforms of the U.S. Supreme Court under Chief Justice Earl Warren are prime targets of advocates of this position, who believe that these reforms made it more difficult to apprehend and convict criminals.[42] They are particularly bitter about the "exclusionary rule"; some even resent the presumption of the innocence of arrested defendants.

Advocates of utilitarian punishment philosophy also charge that making

BOX 4.1

CRIME AND THE BREAKDOWN OF COMMUNITY CONTROLS

Philip Zimbardo, a Stanford psychologist, reported in 1969 on some experiments testing the broken-window theory.[43] He arranged to have an automobile without license plates parked with its hood up on a street in the Bronx and a comparable automobile on a street in Palo Alto, California. The car in the Bronx was attacked by "vandals" within ten minutes of its "abandonment." The first to arrive were a family (father, mother, and young son) who removed the radiator and battery. Within twenty-four hours, virtually everything of value had been removed. Then random destruction began—windows were smashed, parts torn off, upholstery ripped. Children began to use the car as a playground. Most of the adult "vandals" were well-dressed, apparently respectable whites. The car in Palo Alto sat untouched for more than a week. Then Zimbardo smashed part of it with a sledgehammer. Soon, passersby were joining in. Within a few hours, the car had been turned upside down and utterly destroyed. Again, the "vandals" appeared to be primarily respectable whites.

Untended property becomes fair game for people out for fun or plunder, and even for people who ordinarily would not dream of doing such things and who probably consider themselves law-abiding. Because of the nature of community life in the Bronx—its anonymity, the frequency with which cars are abandoned and things are stolen or broken, the past experience of "no one caring"—vandalism begins much more quickly than it does in staid Palo Alto, where people have come to believe that private possessions are cared for, and that mischievous behavior is costly. But vandalism can occur anywhere once communal barriers—the sense of mutual regard and the obligations of civility—are lowered by actions that seem to signal that "no one cares."

Source: This material appears in James Q. Wilson, *Thinking About Crime,* revised ed. (New York: Basic Books, 1983), pp. 78–79.

rehabilitation the purpose of sentencing has resulted in a permissive justice system. They feel that rehabilitation does not work, for there is insufficient evidence that rehabilitation reduces recidivism. In addition, they question whether undergoing rehabilitation is a sufficient penalty for the social harm offenders have done. Proponents are further indignant about the injustice of indeterminate sentencing, because of the fact that offenders who have committed the same crimes under the same circumstances often receive very different sentences. Finally, they question the ability of a parole board to know when a person has been rehabilitated.[44]

Punishment and the Criminal   Proponents of utilitarian punishment philosophy assume that punishment is deserved and that it will work. Punishment is de-

The broken-window theory in action. (*Source:* Charles Harbutt/Archive Pictures, Inc.)

served, they assert, because offenders can reason and have freely chosen to violate the law.[45] Wilson, in the revised edition of *Thinking About Crime,* defends the position that punishment will work by saying:

> [Public] consensus had much in common with what the first edition of this book said and what the revised edition repeats: rehabilitation has not yet been shown to be a promising method for dealing with serious offenders, broad-gauge investments in social progress have little near-term effect on crime rates, punishment is not an unworthy objective for the criminal justice system of free and liberal society to pursue, the evidence supports (though cannot conclusively prove) the view that deterrence and incapacitation work, and new crime-control techniques ought to be tried in a frankly experimental manner with a heavy emphasis on objective evaluation.[46]

Wilson, however, does not support harsh sanctions. He points out that making sanctions more harsh does not increase the likelihood of catching more criminals. He also notes that indiscriminate increases in criminal penalties are likely to be self-defeating, because "the more severe the penalty, the more unlikely that it will be imposed."[47]

Incentives and Disincentives to Crime   Proponents of the utilitarian punishment philosophy presume that individuals respond rationally to incentives. Banfield notes, "The present scheme implies that when probable costs exceed probable benefits, an individual will not commit the crime. Indeed, he will not commit it even when probable benefits exceed probable costs if another noncriminal action promises to be *more* profitable."[48] But, "The assumption that individuals tend to respond rationally to incentives and disincentives does not imply that all individuals respond to the *same* incentives or that they respond to *particular* incentives with equal sensitivity."[49]

Van den Haag also comments on this key assumption of utilitarian punishment philosophy:

> However, if a given offender's offenses are rational in the situation in which he lives—if what he can gain exceeds the likely cost to him by more than the gain from legitimate activities does—there is little that can be "corrected" in the offender. Reform will fail. It often fails for this reason. What has to be changed is not the personality of the offender, but the cost-benefit ratio which makes his offense rational. That ratio can be changed by improving and multiplying his opportunities for legitimate activity and the benefits they yield, or by decreasing his opportunity for illegitimate activities, or by increasing their cost to him, including punishment.[50]

Lower-Class Status and the Crime Problem   Advocates of the utilitarian punishment model argue that it is the lower-class male who is the major player in the crime drama. Wilson, for example, states that white-collar crime may be expensive to the social order, but it is street crime that strikes fear in the hearts of citizens, causes injuries, and disrupts community life.[51]

Banfield, in one of the most derogatory discussions of the lower class in contemporary literature, blames its habits, living conditions, and alienation from society as leading to its high rates of crime. He says, "This political danger in the presence of great concentrations of people who feel little attachment to the society has long been regarded by some as *the* serious problem of the cities—the one problem that might conceivably produce a disaster that would destroy the quality of the society."[52] He then elaborates upon his perceptions of the inferior nature of the lower class:

> So long as the city contains a sizable lower-class, nothing basic can be done about its most serious problems. Good jobs may be offered to all, but some will remain chronically unemployed. Slums may be demolished, but if the housing that replaces them is occupied by the lower-class it will shortly be turned into new slums. Welfare payments may be doubled or tripled and a negative income tax instituted, but some persons will continue to live in squalor and misery. New schools may be built, new curricula devised, and the teacher-pupil ratio cut in half, but if the children who attend these schools come from lower-class homes, they will be turned into blackboard jungles, and those who graduate or drop out from them will, in most cases, be functionally illiterate. The streets may be filled with armies of policemen, but violent crime and civil disorder will decrease very little. If, however, the lower-class were to disappear—if, say, its members were overnight to acquire the attitudes, motivations, and habits of the working

class—the most serious and intractable problems of the city would all disappear with it.[53]

Components of the Utilitarian Punishment Philosophy

An increased use of incapacitation, a greater use of determinate and mandatory sentences, more effective court systems, a hard-line policy toward serious juvenile offenders, a get-tough policy with drug offenders, and an increased use of the death penalty are the bases of the utilitarian punishment model.

Increased Use of Incapacitation   Proponents hold that depriving a criminal of liberty reduces the number of those free to violate the law, and, therefore, they recommend that most offenders be imprisoned and that they be held for longer periods of time. These advocates strongly emphasize the importance of incarcerating repeat offenders, who, they claim, now "suffer little or no loss of freedom."[54] In addition, they add, it is advantageous to incarcerate serious offenders because they are prevented, during the period of confinement, from committing additional crimes.[55] Not surprisingly, they have been strong supporters of the policy of **selective incapacitation** (see Box 4.2).

Greater Use of Determinate and Mandatory Sentences   Supporters of the punishment model advocate a wider use of fixed, **determinate**, and **mandatory sentences**. Because they have little confidence in the **indeterminate sentence** and in the parole board, they argue that sentences fixed by the legislature will deal with the crime problem better than those that depend on the decisions of judges and parole boards.

Development of a More Effective Court System   Proponents of this punishment model recommend that the court system be provided with increased financial and staff resources so criminals will receive sufficient punishment. As Wilson states the position:

> Anyone familiar with the police station, jails, and courts of some of our larger cities is keenly aware that accused persons caught up in the system are exposed to very little that involves either judgement or solemnity. They are instead processed through a bureaucratic maze in which a bargain is offered and a haggle ensues at every turn—over amounts of bail, degree of the charged offense, and the nature of the plea. Much of what observers find objectionable about this process could be alleviated by devoting many more resources to it, so that an ample supply of prosecutors, defense attorneys, and judges were available.[56]

Hard-Line Policy Toward Serious Juvenile Offenders   The proponents of the utilitarian punishment model are opposed to what they term the present "permissiveness" of the juvenile system, as expressed in the *parens patriae* **philosophy** of the juvenile court. They recommend instead that violent juvenile offenders should

BOX 4.2   **SELECTIVE INCAPACITATION**

Incapacitation emerged as a major objective of sentencing during the 1970s. The logic of incapacitation was that an offender who is locked up cannot commit crimes in the community. Researchers had discovered that a small number of offenders are responsible for a large portion of crimes or arrests, and, therefore, it was argued that with such a distribution, the potential exists to achieve improved crime-reduction benefits from incarceration of these high-rate offenders.

Research at the Rand Corporation, especially by Peter Greenwood and Jan Chaiken and Marcia Chaiken, sparked interest in policies of selective incapacitation. Using data on convicted robbers and burglars from the Rand survey of prison and jail inmates in three states, a seven-point scale was developed to predict the self-reported, high-crime-rate offenders in the inmate samples. This prediction instrument then was used to explore the impact of alternative sentencing policies on crime reduction and prison population. It was predicted that imposing long prison terms on high-rate robbers and sending all other incarcerated robbers to jail for one year was estimated to result in a 15 percent reduction in armed robberies by adults in California and a 5 percent reduction in the prison population for robbery.

There is no question that targeting crime-control strategies at "career offenders," "habitual offenders," or "high-rate offenders" offers far more hope in reducing the rate of criminal behavior in American society than other crime-control tactics. As studies have found, these offenders are involved in a high percentage of such crimes as robbery, assaults, and drug dealings in urban areas. But policymakers need to be cautious about embarking on a policy of selective incapacitation until a much more reliable predictive instrument can be empirically tested on non-institutional populations. The present status of predictive instruments, such as the one developed by the Rand researchers, provides much too high a proportion of "false positives," or individuals who are predicted to commit crime but do not.

Source: Jacqueline Cohen, "Selective Incapacitation: An Assessment," *University of Illinois Law Review*, Number 2 (1984), pp. 253–290; Alfred Blumstein, "Selective Incapacitation as a Means of Crime Control," *American Behavioral Scientist* 27 (September/October 1983), pp. 87–108; and Peter W. Greenwood, *Selective Incapacitation* (Santa Monica, Calif.: Rand, 1982).

be shifted from the jurisdiction of the juvenile court to that of the adult court. They also argue that the commitment of more juveniles to training schools would act as an effective deterrent to youth crime. Currently, supporters of this position are urging that the death penalty be used with older juveniles who commit vicious murders. In fact, the entire juvenile court and juvenile corrections systems are under pressure to become more like the adult system and to hand out more and harsher penalties.

Get-Tough Policy with Drug Offenders   Both Wilson and van den Haag are aware that drug addiction causes considerable criminal activity, especially in urban areas. But they refuse to regard addiction as a disease and to excuse the crimes that individuals addicted to drugs commit. Van den Haag holds that if "we punish becoming addicted, fewer persons do become addicted."[57] Wilson also agrees that drug addicts, like other offenders, are deterred when a get-tough policy is enforced. He found that when the cost [of addiction] declined sharply in 1961–1970, the number of addicts in Boston increased about tenfold; "the larger increases in the number of addicts tended to follow years in which the certainty and severity of law enforcement were the lowest."[58]

Greater Use of the Death Penalty   Proponents of the utilitarian punishment model have been the most vocal supporters of increased use of the death penalty. They argue that the death penalty should be more widely used because it is a proper and fitting punishment. Wilson is less convinced than van den Haag that the death penalty is a deterrent to crime, but he states that "the main issue remains that of justice—the point is not whether capital punishment prevents future crimes, but whether it is a proper and fitting penalty for crimes that have occurred."[59]

Summary

The late 1960s and early 1970s were years of alarming disorder in American life. Riots on college campuses in more than 200 U.S. cities and in prison settings gave notice that public order was in jeopardy. Some of the traditional values of American society (e.g., those concerning sexual mores and family attitudes) were also changing, another sign of the challenge to order. In addition, crime, both personal and property, was rising, and a "get-tough" response was hailed as an effective way to make the streets safe.

The utilitarian punishment philosophy was at first embraced enthusiastically because the public and its policymakers felt that this approach provided a rational response to crime in American society. The approach was popular because it promised a legal order that would enable citizens to be secure in their lives, their liberties, and their pursuit of happiness. Moreover, this crime control model assured the public that punishment would work. Criminals, who have free will, would be taught not to commit further crimes (through specific deterrence), and noncriminals would see what happens to those who break the law (the concept of general deterrence).

Today, the major criticism of utilitarian punishment philosophy is that a repressive public response to crime does not work as advertised. Critics define this control model as repressive because there is almost no limit to the severity of punishment prescribed, up to the death penalty. As long as proponents of this model can argue that whatever is being done is effective, it is possible to justify increasing the dosage of punishment. Critics charge that a brutal response to crime has not worked in the past—citing, for example, the period when over 200 offenses were punishable by death—and is no more likely to work in the present or future.

However, utilitarian punishment philosophy continues to have many supporters as it guides control strategies of American society. Proponents contend that their hard-line approach should be tried because rehabilitation and a permissive criminal justice system have not worked. They promise that when the cost of crime goes up, crime will be controlled and the streets again will be safe—and the quality of life in this nation will return to what they claim it was in the past.

RETRIBUTION OR "JUST DESERTS" PHILOSOPHY

The quest for order can be vividly retold in an examination of retribution throughout history. Graeme Newman found that ancient people, faced with unnerving disorders of a harsh environment and the burden of natural disasters, struck out vengefully against wrongdoers.[60] Throughout history, tribal codes and other religious laws also encouraged this reaction. Retributive philosophy basically adheres to the assumption that a wrongful act must be "repaid" in a manner that is proportionate to the wrongfulness of the act.

Stanley Grupp summarizes retributive justice in three propositions: First, an orderly, collective expression of society's natural feeling of revulsion toward and disapproval of criminal acts is desirable. Second, the criminal deserves the pain of the punitive reaction. Third, this punitive reaction vindicates the criminal law and thereby serves to unify society against crime and criminals.[61]

F. H. Bradley wrote that the purpose of retribution is the negation of wrong:

> . . . the destruction of guilt, whatever be the consequences, and even if there be no consequences at all, is still a good in itself; and this, not because a mere recognition is a good, but because the denial of wrong is the assertion of right . . . and the assertion of right is an end in itself.[62]

Thus, punishment becomes the means of negating wrong. Whatever form it takes, the assessment of punitive measures always entails the pronouncement of guilt upon the defendant. The punishment, then, becomes a remedy by which the pronouncement of guilt can be removed. Immanuel Kant thought that punishment must be delivered by the state if sanctions are to remain credible. In short, the state owes it to the offender and to itself to deliver on its promises. But once a sentence has been carried out, the wrong has been negated, and the state can lay no further claim upon the offender for his or her crime.

J. D. Mabbott's widely received 1930s essay, "Punishment," represented the first step in the contemporary application of retributive philosophy. Mabbott argued that it is unfair to deprive a person of liberty as a consequence of that person committing a criminal act for any reason other than the act "deserves" to be punished and that the person committed the act.[63]

Retribution, or the more commonly used term "just deserts," has become the basis of the justice model. In the early 1970s, David Fogel used the presumption that an offender deserves to be punished simply because of what he or she has done rather than for any social reasons to develop the justice model.

Assumptions of the Justice Model

The justice model is based upon three main assumptions: offenders deserve to be punished proportionate to the social harm they have done; the state cannot be trusted; and the criminal justice system needs reform.

"Just Deserts"   Fogel contends that offenders are volitional and responsible human beings and, therefore, deserve to be punished if they violate the law. This punishment shows offenders that they are responsible for their behavior. Decisions concerning offenders, then, should be based not on their needs, but upon the penalties they deserve for their acts. This nonutilitarian position is not intended to achieve social benefits or advantages, such as deterrence or rehabilitation, but instead is designed to punish offenders because they deserve it; it is their **"just deserts"** for the social harm they have inflicted upon society.

The punishment given offenders must be proportionate to the social harm they have done. Fogel believes that the "just deserts" approach offers a more rational ground for the construction of correctional policies and offers a "set of principles for the rehabilitation of the system itself":[64]

> The retributive position, in contrast (to rehabilitation), is essentially nonutilitarian, holding that punitive sanctions should be imposed on the offender simply for the sake of justice. Punishment is deserved; the form and severity of the punishment must, however, be proportionate to the criminal act. The right of the state to impose treatment of one sort or another on the offender holds no place in this approach.[65]

Distrust of the State   Fogel's justice model is based upon a firm distrust of the state. He feels that the unbridled discretion built into the criminal justice system is one means by which the state misuses its power over citizens and that it represents a central problem to be dealt with by justice-as-fairness.[66] He is bothered by judicial discretion that results in offenders' serving various lengths of sentences for the same offense. Fogel adds that the misuse of discretion by the parole board forces prisoners into trying to "con" the parole board into an early release. Finally, he charges that correctional administrators frequently abuse the authority given to them by denying the due process rights of inmates. Fogel believes that "one of the most fruitful ways the prison can teach the non-law-abiders to be law-abiding is to teach them in a law-abiding manner."[67]

The Criminal Justice System Needs Reform   The justice-as-fairness perspective, which is what Fogel calls his model, is extremely critical of current criminal justice practices. This perspective charges that the due process rights of offenders are violated by the justice system, that the rights of victims are ignored, and that the rights of those who work with offenders are denied. Fogel summarizes the basic approach of the justice model: "If we cannot treat with reliability, we can at least be fair, reasonable, humane, and constitutional in practice."[68]

Components of the Justice Model

To attain the desired reforms of the justice model, Fogel recommends the following practices:

- *Sentencing:* (1) The indeterminate sentence and the parole board should be replaced by a determinate sentencing structure; (2) probation, it should be remembered, is a criminal sentence and does not represent an absence of punishment.
- *Victims:* Officials of the criminal justice system are to have as much concern for the victim of crime as they have for offenders.
- *Corrections:* (1) Inmate self-government and an adequate grievance process must be fully implemented in prisons; (2) administrators of correctional institutions can no longer keep the law out of prison, nor can they treat prisoners in capricious and arbitrary ways; (3) appointment of an ombudsman is an effective means to ensure fairness in prison; (4) programs in the prison should be totally voluntary and should have nothing to do with the length of the confinement; (5) participatory management techniques will be helpful in bringing correctional staff into the decision-making process; (6) prison guards need better training, a safe environment, upgraded job classification, and a better salary to match their difficult jobs; and (7) the fortress-like prison is to be dismantled.[69]

Another expression of the "just deserts" philosophy is found in Andrew von Hirsch's *Doing Justice: The Choice of Punishments.* He recommends that "just deserts" be used as the guiding principle of the correctional process. Criminals are to be subjected to punishment because they deserve it, and they deserve it because they have engaged in illegal conduct. But the severity of punishment should be commensurate with the seriousness of the wrong. In addition, the report recommends determinate sentencing, limited use of confinement, dismantling of rehabilitative procedures, and reduced length of sentences.[70]

Summary

Throughout history, retribution has been one of the most widely used means of dealing with criminal behavior. However, it had lost favor in America until the 1970s, when critics became aware of the disorder and near bankruptcy of the criminal justice system. Prisons were exploding in riots, enforced rehabilitation was neither humane nor successful in reducing recidivism, and the misuse of discretion was in violation of offenders' rights. David Fogel concluded that this state of affairs proved the state could not be trusted and that justice-as-fairness must become the primary focus of the justice system.

In the 1970s and 1980s, the justice model provided an alternative correctional model for those criminologists who could accept neither the rehabilitation nor the utilitarian social control models. Many criminologists had become disillusioned with rehabilitative philosophy, questioning both the theoretical assumptions upon which it was based and its inadequacy in practice and implementation. Nor could these criminologists accept the repressive notions of the utilitarian punishment model.

Policymakers in some states widely supported the justice model because it emphasizes both punishment and reform. That is, it urges the punishment of criminals in a humane way and it recommends the adoption of determinate sentencing, a measure that coincided with the "get-tough-with-criminals" mood of society. These policymakers were also attracted to the victim restitution emphasis of the justice model.

In the 1980s, the justice model continues to have its supporters and its critics. The critics charge that the concept of "just deserts" or "just punishment" is a fatal weakness, because making retribution as the ultimate aim of the correctional process breeds a policy of despair rather than one of hope.[71] In this regard, it is argued that while the idea of "just deserts" has been around for centuries, it has never totally dominated the penal policy of any advanced society.[72] Critics also state that while the justice model may have broad support in theory, there is little evidence that it is producing a more humane system. They point out that determinate sentencing has even been used by state legislatures to create more punitive and prolonged sentences.[73] Furthermore, the criticism is made that prisons are worse today than in 1975, when Fogel began to gain the ear of politicians and correctional administrators. Fogel agrees that the justice model has fallen short of its intended objectives: "I am encouraged by the rhetoric of the nationwide acceptance of the justice model, but there are precious few places that have accepted it as a mission."[74]

However, supporters of this model continue to maintain that justice-as-fairness is the most humane way of dealing with offenders. Whatever else is done during the correctional process, they add, due process and fair play must be primary concerns. Proponents also contend that the systemwide reforms of the justice model provide the most viable means of humanizing the justice process.

ANALYSIS

Three basic questions about order are raised in this chapter: Can the state be trusted? Is criminal behavior rational? Does punishment deter?

Can the State Be Trusted?

The current popularity of the "get-tough-with-crime" approach raises anew the question of order in a free and democratic society. Thomas Hobbes proposed that a Leviathan, or state, with absolute power is needed to institute and maintain order. This strong state could provide the external social control that humans need, especially those who refuse to comply with society's laws and norms.[75]

However, a reluctance to grant the state too much power has always been a characteristic of American society. The basic order of this nation, as discussed in Chapter 2, is a constitutional order, one that attempts to strike a careful balance between stability and change and between freedom and social responsibility.[76] This constitutional order is careful to place controls on government, as it balances the power of the executive, legislative, and executive branches of the federal government. Thus, the national heritage of our society is based on the belief that freedom of the individual can be achieved and maintained without sacrificing the security of the state.

None of the individuals cited in this chapter is suggesting that a totalitarian government is needed to establish order in American society. But proponents of the utilitarian punishment philosophy come dangerously close to suggesting a double standard—one for law-abiding citizens and one for criminals. Good citizens, this position seems to imply, deserve every protection of a free and democratic society. But criminals, whose basic nature is wicked or antisocial, must have strong social controls, because they arouse fear, injure the innocent, and disrupt community life.

The suggestion that the power of an absolute state is needed for those who threaten the social order poses danger to a free and democratic society. "Power tends to corrupt," the English historian Lord Acton has noted, "and absolute power tends to corrupt absolutely." As other societies have discovered, a police state can inflict terrible violations upon individual liberties. A court system aligned too closely to the state also can destroy any notion of individual rights. The return to the "good old days" of corrections means treating prisoners as slaves of the state, administering corporal punishment for minor violations, and isolating troublesome prisoners for months or even years. Thus, if there are no checks and balances in how power is to be administered, the state and the justice system are likely to abuse this power.

Is Criminal Behavior Rational?

The individualistic approaches of the utilitarian punishment and justice models presume that "would-be offenders are reasonably rational and respond to their perceptions of the costs and benefits attached to alternative courses of action."[77] The rational person is expected to calculate the costs of any external and internal sanction that might be imposed as a consequence of his or her behavior, prior to choosing a course of action. Potential sanctions are then weighed against possible benefits. James Q. Wilson argues that individuals pay attention to costs even when engaging in the most emotional behaviors:

> As my colleague Richard Herrnstein likes to point out, when husbands and wives start throwing dishes at each other, they are more likely to throw the everyday crockery rather than the fine china. I can imagine getting drunk enough or mad enough to challenge somebody in a bar to a fight. I cannot imagine getting drunk or mad enough to challenge that somebody if his name happens to be Sugar Ray Leonard or Mean Joe Greene.[78]

Richard Nixon announces that he is resigning the presidency. (*Source:* AP–Wide World Photos.)

Philip J. Cook contends that it is not necessary for would-be offenders to be totally rational or fully informed in order for the criminal justice system to have an effect on them.[79] They simply need to place some value on the consequences of their actions. These would-be offenders, of course, do not want to be caught and, therefore, they operate on the basis of a crude rule of thumb about how great or small these risks are.[80]

Needless to say, some individuals do engage in unlawful behavior according to the cost of that behavior. Sally Engle Merry, in a study of young criminals in an urban neighborhood, found that they distinguished carefully between more and less affluent targets, between persons and activities more and less likely to lead to arrest and prosecution.[81]

A much stronger argument can be made that white-collar, corporate, political, and organized crimes are more likely to take place only after the perpetrators had calculated the benefits and dangers of their criminal involvements. For example, corruption in government, crimes committed by Wall Street firms, and violations of antitrust laws by corporations appear to be forms of illegal behavior that are typically based on rational decision-making. The Watergate-related crimes, designed to win the reelection of President Richard Nixon (see Box 4.3), were committed by officials of the government and represented acts of secrecy and deception. Francis T. Cullen et al. add that corporate managers are prime examples of those who become involved in illegal activities after calculating the costs and benefits of criminal behaviors:

> Their [corporate managers'] illegalities are seldom acts of passion or situational opportunism—as many street crimes are—but flow instead from calculated risks taken by rational actors. As such, they are more amenable to control by policies based on the utilitarian assumptions of the deterrence doctrine.[82]

BOX 4.3   **WATERGATE**

- Burglars, financed by funds from the Committee to Reelect the President, broke into and bugged the headquarters of the Democratic party in the Watergate apartment complex.
- These burglars were paid hush money and promised executive clemency to protect the president and his advisors.
- President Nixon's personal attorney solicited money for an illegally formed campaign committee and offered an ambassadorship in return for a campaign contribution.
- Money gathered from contributions, some illegally, was systematically "laundered" (to conceal the donors). Much of this money was kept in cash so that when payoffs were made, the money could not be traced.
- President Nixon ordered secret wiretapping of his own aides, several journalists, and even his brother. Additionally, he had secret microphones planted in his offices to record every conversation.
- The director of the FBI destroyed vital legal evidence at the suggestion of the president's aides.
- The attorney general of the United States, John Mitchell, participated in the preliminary discussions about bugging the Democratic headquarters. He even suggested that one means of gaining information about the Democrats was to establish a floating bordello at the Democrats' Miami convention.
- The White House used the CIA in an effort to halt the FBI investigation of Watergate.
- President Nixon offered aides H. R. Haldeman and John Ehrlichman as much as $300,000 from a secret "slush fund" for their legal fees after they were forced to resign.
- The president and his advisors, using the cloak of "national security," strongly resisted attempts by the special prosecutor, the courts, and Congress to obtain the facts in the case.
- Various administration officials were found guilty of perjury and withholding information.
- When the president, under duress, did provide transcripts of the tapes or other materials, they were edited.

Source: D. Stanley Eitzen and Doug A. Timmer, *Criminology* (New York: John Wiley and Sons, 1985), pp. 344–345.

However, to conclude that all criminal activity is the result of a rational process, in which individuals calculate the benefits and dangers of criminal involvement, appears to ascribe too much rationality to the criminal mind. Elliott Currie has aptly expressed this position:

. . . The idea that criminals (or anyone else) could be understood as simply atomized, rational calculators of costs and benefits, carefully weighing the gains of crime against the risks of punishment, seemed grossly inadequate. It might fit some criminals, under certain conditions; but as a model of criminal behavior in general, it strained the imagination. Criminologists were well aware that many crimes took place in the heat of passion (including many homicides and assaults between family members) or under the influence of alcohol or drugs. Others, like much young-gang violence, reflected a quest for "manhood," status, or street level "glory"—which, given the values prevalent on the street, might even be enhanced by a stint behind bars. These points remain valid. We don't have much research on what goes on in the minds of criminals before they commit crimes, but what we do have suggests that rational planning is the exception rather than the rule, even for crimes involving material gain. The enormous role of drugs and alcohol in serious crimes has likewise been reaffirmed in recent Department of Justice findings.[83]

In sum, although some offenders' involvement in crime may be related to cost-benefit decisions and to a rational thinking process, this progression does not offer a satisfactory explanation of why others become involved in criminal activities. With some, compulsive behavior, the influence of alcohol or drugs, or an intense emotional reaction to a situation appears to lead them to bypass any rational process. With others, criminal behavior arises without much forethought as they interact with the components of their environment.

Does Punishment Deter?

Deterrence, as first formulated by the classical school of criminology, is generally categorized as general and special deterrence. General deterrence refers to the threat and the use of punishment in order to prevent illegal behavior on the part of the population in general. Special deterrence has to do with the threat and use of punishment in order to prevent illegal behavior by persons who have already broken the law.[84]

For punishment to deter, according to the classical school of criminology, it must have *celerity, certainty,* and some measure of *severity.* Bentham, for example, suggested that a punishment that follows closely after the offense will result in greater pain to the offender and thus offer deterrence.[85] Several recent theorists have concurred that swifter punishment offers a greater deterrent effect than punishment that is delayed, but they question whether, in practical terms, it is possible to achieve celeritious punishment.[86] Joan E. Jacoby contends that while celerity is desirable for prosecutors, it is rarely achieved because there are many reasons for delay that are beyond the control of prosecutors.[87] Robert E. Meier also argues that the police are handicapped in the pursuit of celeritious justice by the manner in which they detect and apprehend offenders and that courts are hindered by delays in the court process, by the safeguarding of defendants' rights, and by excessive caseloads. Only the last obstacle, Meier adds, is "even potentially correctable."[88]

Another limitation of deterrence is the fact that the criminal justice system has a limited ability to identify, apprehend, and punish criminals with certainty. Theodore Chiricos and Gordon Waldo, using the *Uniform Crime Reports* and national prisoner statistics to analyze deterrent effects, found an inconsistent relationship between certainty and severity of punishment and crime rates. Even with homicide, Chiricos and Waldo found little relationship between the certainty and severity of punishment and the crime rate.[89]

To be an effective deterrent, a perceived certainty factor must attain a specific level. Charles Tittle and Alan Rowe found that level to be approximately 30 percent, but William Bailey places this figure closer to 50 percent.[90] Thus, these researchers contend that unless the certainty of identification, apprehension, and punishment is regarded by the lawbreaker to be in the 30 to 50 percent range, general deterrence policy has little value.

Nevertheless, a number of studies have supported deterrence. Alfred Blumstein and Daniel Nagin studied the relationship between draft evasion and the penalties imposed for evading the draft. After controlling for socioeconomic characteristics, they found that the higher the probability of conviction for draft evasion, the lower the evasion rates.[91] Kenneth I. Wolpin, who analyzed changes in crime rates and the chances of being arrested, convicted, and punished in England for the period 1894 to 1967, concluded that crime rates went down with the greater probability of being punished.[92] H. L. Ross examined crosscultural trends in traffic fatalities and injuries before and after the enactment of stricter drunk driving legislation and concluded that increasing the certainty of legal punishment serves as a short-term deterrent to the drinking driver.[93]

Ann Witte followed the activities of 641 men released from prison in North Carolina and concluded that the higher the probability of being punished in the past, the lower the number of arrests in the future.[94] Jan Chaiken and Marcia Chaiken, after interviewing over two thousand inmates of jails and prisons in California, Michigan, and Texas, concluded that the rate at which Texas inmates committed robberies was significantly lower and the chances of going to prison for a crime in Texas was significantly higher than in either California or Michigan. The Texas inmates committed the fewest serious crimes, the Chaikens contended, because they were least likely to believe they could get away with it.[95] Finally, researchers in Minneapolis found that spouse assaulters who were arrested were less likely to be reported to the police for a subsequent assault than were those who were counseled—and much less likely than those who were merely sent out of the house. Arrests appeared to have a deterrent effect even though the arrested persons generally spent no more than a night or two in jail.[96]

In summary, the evidence concerning the effects of sanctions on crime rates is mixed, but the majority of studies show some relationship between reduced crime rates and deterrent factors such as arrest and probability of sanction.[97] On the business of certainty, celerity, and severity, a general conclusion can be drawn: the greater the certainty and the celerity, the less the severity need be.

Policymakers need to understand how the deterrent effects of punishment actually operate for different types of people and for various types of crimes. The correct "formula" for using the threat of punishment is especially important for dealing with those individuals who are relatively resistant to societal rules.[98] A more highly developed theory of deterrence also requires more specific information about the motivation of criminals. The most difficult types of offenders to deter are career criminals, who regard crime as a way of life, and those whose crimes result from expressive, or emotional, needs.[99]

POLICY IMPLICATIONS

In the 1970s, punishment returned as the primary means to restore order in a society. The public's demand for greater punishment was felt keenly by nearly every elected official with any authority over the criminal justice system. Repression rather than benevolence became the official state crime policy. But while the public persisted in demanding more severe punishments of convicted offenders, it expressed an equally strong reluctance to provide additional resources to implement this "get-tough" policy. In the 1980s, a problem of some magnitude for policymakers is that the increased public pressure for punishment comes at a time when there is little ability within the criminal justice system to respond to such demand.[100] For example, the basic step necessary to declare war on crime is to place more offenders in prison, but the capacity of correctional institutions is already severely overcrowded—so much that overcrowded conditions have resulted in court intervention in at least 36 states.[101]

Danger of Repression

Hard-liners today are informing policymakers that a panacea is available: that is, that the simple solution to the crime problem is to increase the cost, especially for street offenders. Wilson and van den Haag, chief high priests of this "get-tough" approach, promise that such a strategy will protect the community and deter would-be offenders.[102]

The basic problem with implementing a crime control policy based on the principles of utilitarian punishment philosophy is that the celerity and certainty of punishment cannot at present be attained by the criminal justice system. No one involved seems to know how the time lag between the commission of the crime and the punishment for the crime can be made significantly shorter. Nor does anyone appear to know how the certainty of arrest and conviction can be raised to an acceptable level. But because the celerity and the certainty of punishment cannot be attained, policymakers are being urged by some to become more severe in punishing criminals.

Critics also claim that a crime-control policy based on utilitarian punishment philosophy focuses almost entirely on street crime and is blind to the more serious violations of trust inherent in economic or white-collar crime. Furthermore, advocates of this crime control model are accused of neglecting the social and structural conditions, such as poverty, unemployment, and social injustice, that may lead to crime. Radical criminologists add that this crime control position solidifies the power of the middle class, thereby preventing the structural transformation of an exploitative economic system.

The consequences of a repressive response to crime are grim indeed. First, a repressive approach drains the humaneness from the justice process. Second, blaming the crime problem on lower-class street offenders prevents society from dealing more adequately with white-collar, corporate, and organized criminals. Third, repression brings only more repression; as many inmates are fond of saying, "What goes around comes around." A repressive society brings upon itself the anger and frustration of those whom it represses. Finally, a repressive response ignores the social and structural conditions in society that lead to crime.

SUMMARY

This chapter, the first of five on causation, explains criminal behavior as purposeful activity resulting from rational decisions in which the pros and cons are weighed and the acts that promise greatest potential gains are performed. Utilitarian punishment philosophy is grounded on the assumption that punishment is necessary to deter potential criminals and to protect society from crime. Those who favor the social utility of punishment make the argument: If we are unable to improve criminals through rehabilitative programs, we can at least ensure that society is protected and that potential criminals are deterred by the consequences incurred by lawbreakers. The justice model is based on retribution or the more commonly used term "just deserts." Thus, an offender should be punished for the harm done rather than for reasons of deterrence or prevention.

The utilitarian punishment model focuses on societal disorder. The writings of James Q. Wilson, Ernest van den Haag, Edward Banfield, and others are filled with warnings about the dangers of lower-class males who prey upon innocent victims. Crime, for advocates of this punishment model, becomes synonymous with the disorder of social breakdown. The social problems of the larger society are minimized, as the criminal behavior of this largely impoverished class becomes the central and nearly exclusive focus. A central theme in the writings of those espousing the punishment model is the contention that society will be all right, that the "good old days" will return, and that America will be great again when the behavior of this criminal class can be sufficiently repressed. Critics contend that such an approach will lead to an inhumane and unfair justice system, because, short of the death penalty, punishment can always be escalated. History suggests that a punishment strategy alone is no more likely to work now or in the future than it did in other periods of social and technological upheaval.

In contrast, the justice model attempts to reform the chaotic procedures of the juvenile and adult justice systems. David Fogel suggests such reforms as abolishing the parole board and indeterminate sentencing, providing more due process rights for offenders, giving more consideration to the rights of victims in the justice process, upgrading the jobs and working environments of corrections staff, and replacing the fortress-like prison. Although policymakers have largely ignored other reforms of the justice model, legislatures in a number of states have adopted determinate sentencing laws. Critics argue that "get-tough-with-criminals" politicians have used determinate sentencing to escalate penal sanctions. In fact, in most states adopting determinate sentencing acts, mandatory minimum sentences for some crimes have doubled the time to be served.

REFERENCES

Beccaria, Ceasare. *Of Crimes and Punishment.* Translated by Fr. Kenelm Foster and Jane Grigson. New York: Oxford University Press, 1964.

Blumstein, Alfred; Cohen, Jacqueline; and Nagin, Daniel. *Deterrence and Incapacitation: Estimating the Effects of Criminal Sanctions on Crime Rates.* Washington, D.C.: National Academy of Sciences, 1978.

Bentham, Jeremy. *An Introduction to the Principles of Morals Legislation.* 1823. Reprint. New York: Hafner, 1984.

Chiricos, Theodore, and Waldo, Gordon. "Punishment and Crime: An Examination of Some Empirical Evidence." *Social Problems* 18 (1970), pp. 200–217.

Fogel, David. ". . . *We Are the Living Proof": The Justice Model for Corrections.* Cincinnati: Anderson, 1975.

Jenkins, Philip. "Varieties of Enlightenment Philosophy." *British Journal of Criminology* 24 (1984), pp. 112–130.

Miller, J. L., and Anderson, Andy B. "Updating the Deterrence Doctrine." *Journal of Criminal Law and Criminology* 77 (1986), pp. 418–438.

Sherman L. W. and Berk, R.A. "The Specific Deterrent Effects of Arrest for Domestic Assault." *American Sociological Review* 49 (1984), pp. 261–272.

Tittle, Charles, and Rowe, Alan. "Moral Appeal, Sanction Threat, and Deviance: An Experimental Test." *Social Problems* 20 (1973), pp. 490–495.

Van den Haag, Ernest. *Punishing Criminals: Concerning a Very Old and Painful Question.* New York: Basic Books, 1975.

von Hirsch, Andrew. *Doing Justice: The Choice of Punishments.* New York: Hill and Wang, 1976.

Wilson, James Q. *Thinking About Crime.* Revised ed. New York: Basic Books, 1983.

Zimring, Franklin, and Hawkins, Gordon. *Deterrence: The Legal Threat to Crime Control.* Chicago: University of Chicago Press, 1973.

NOTES

1. James Q. Wilson and J. Herrnstein, *Crime and Human Nature* (New York: Simon and Schuster, 1985), p. 20.
2. Edward Cimler and Lee Roy Bearch, "Factors Involved in Juvenile Decisions About Crime," *Criminal Justice and Behavior* 8 (September 1981), pp. 275–286.
3. Coleman Phillipson, *Three Criminal Law Reformers: Beccaria, Bentham, Romilly* (Montclair, N.J.: Patterson Smith, 1970), p. 7.
4. Ceasare Beccaria, *Of Crimes and Punishment,* 1964, trans. Fr. Kenelm Foster and Jane Grigson (New York: Oxford University Press, 1964), p. 13.
5. Ibid., p. 11.
6. Ibid., p. 14.
7. Ibid., p. 11.
8. Ibid., p. 42.
9. Ibid., pp. 42, 96.

10. Ibid., p. 43.

11. Ibid., p. 55.

12. Ibid.

13. Ibid., p. 57.

14. Ibid., p. 62.

15. Harry Elmer Barnes and Negley K. Teeters, *New Horizons in Criminology* (Englewood Cliffs, N.J.: Prentice-Hall, 1959), p. 322.

16. E. Monachesi, "Cesare Beccaria," in *Pioneers in Criminology,* ed. Herman Mannheim (Montclair, N.J.: Patterson Smith, 1972), p. 49.

17. Philip Jenkins, "Varieties of Enlightenment Criminology," *British Journal of Criminology* 24 (April 1984), p. 112.

18. Beccaria, *Of Crimes and Punishment,* p. 92.

19. Ibid.

20. Ibid., pp. 16–17.

21. Jeremy Bentham, *An Introduction to the Principles of Morals and Legislation* (1823; reprint ed., New York: Hafner, 1948).

22. Ibid., pp. 178–182.

23. Philip Jenkins, *Crime and Justice: Issues and Ideas* (Monterey, Calif.: Brooks-Cole, 1984), p. 128.

24. Ysabel Rennie, *The Search for Criminal Man: A Conceptual History of the Dangerous Offender.* (Lexington, Mass.: Lexington Books, 1978), p. 15.

25. Richard A. Ball, "Restricted Reprobation and the Reparation of Social Reality: A Theory of Punishment" (Paper presented at the Annual Meeting of the American Society of Criminology, Dallas, 1978), p. 6.

26. Jenkins, "Varieties of Enlightenment Criminology," pp. 122–125.

27. Ibid., p. 127.

28. Ibid., p. 113.

29. Ibid.

30. Ibid.

31. Ibid., p. 116.

32. Wilson and Herrnstein, *Crime and Human Nature,* p. 14.

33. James Q. Wilson, *Thinking About Crime,* Revised ed. (New York: Basic Books, 1983), p. 13.

34. John P. Conrad, *Justice and Consequences* (Lexington, Mass.: Heath, 1981), p. 157.

35. Edward C. Banfield, *The Unheavenly City: The Nature and Future of Our Urban Crisis* (Boston: Little, Brown, 1968), p. 158.

36. Stuart A. Scheingold, *The Politics of Law and Order: Street Crime and Public Policy* (New York: Longman, 1984), p. 9.

37. Wilson, *Thinking About Crime,* p. 260.

38. Francis A. Allen, *The Decline of the Rehabilitative Ideal* (New Haven: Yale University Press, 1981), p. 62.

39. Wilson, *Thinking About Crime,* p. 26.

40. Quoted in Wilson, *Thinking About Crime*, p. 13.

41. Quoted in Clemens Bartollas, *Juvenile Delinquency* (New York: Wiley, 1985), p. 113.

42. Scheingold, *Politics of Law and Order,* p. 9.

43. Philip G. Zimbardo, "The Human Choice: Individualism, Reason, and Order Versus Deindividuation, Impulse, and Chaos," in *Nebraska Symposium on Motivation,* ed. W. J. Arnold and J. P. Levine (Lincoln, Neb.: University of Nebraska Press, 1969), pp. 237–307.

44. Wilson, *Thinking About Crime,* pp. 171–172.

45. Ernest van den Haag, *Punishing Criminals: Concerning a Very Old and Painful Question* (New York: Basic Books, 1975), p. 23.

46. Wilson, *Thinking About Crime,* p. 5.

47. Wilson, *Thinking About Crime,* 1st ed., p. 201.

48. Banfield, *Unheavenly City,* p. 160.

49. Ibid., p. 221.

50. Van den Haag, *Punishing Criminals,* p. 59.

51. Wilson, *Thinking About Crime,* revised edition, p. 5.

52. Banfield, *Unheavenly City,* p. 13.

53. Ibid., pp. 210–211.

54. Wilson, *Thinking About Crime,* 1st ed., p. 224.

55. Ibid.

56. Ibid., pp. 230–231.

57. Van den Haag, *Punishing Criminals,* 1st ed., p. 127.

58. Wilson, *Thinking About Crime,* 1st ed., p. 163.

59. Ibid., p. 221.

60. Graeme Newman, *The Punishment Response* (Philadelphia: Lippincott, 1978).

61. Stanley Grupp, *Theories of Punishment* (Bloomington, Ind.: Indiana University Press, 1971).

62. F. H. Bradley, *Ethics* (Oxford, England: Clarendon Press, 1927), p. 109.

63. J. D. Mabbott, "Punishment" (1930), reprinted in Frederick A. Olafson, *Justice and Social Policy* (Englewood Cliffs, N.J.: Prentice-Hall, 1961), p. 39.

64. David Fogel and Joe Hudson, eds., *Justice as Fairness: Perspectives on the Justice Model,* (Cincinnati: Anderson, 1981), p. 1.

65. Ibid.

66. David Fogel, ". . . *We Are the Living Proof": The Justice Model for Corrections,* 2d. ed. (Cincinnati: Anderson, 1979), p. 227.

67. Ibid., p. 204.

68. Fogel and Hudson, *Justice as Fairness,* p. viii.

69. See Fogel, ". . . *We Are the Living Proof,*" for an expanded discussion of these components.

70. Andrew von Hirsch, *Doing Justice: The Choice of Punishments* (New York: Hill and Wang, 1976).

71. Willard Gaylin and David J. Rothman, "Introduction," in von Hirsch, ed., *Doing Justice.*

72. Allen, *Decline of the Rehabilitation Ideal,* p. 69.

73. See Chapter 14 for an examination of the consequences of the determinate sentencing acts across the nation.

74. Quoted in Clemens Bartollas, *Correctional Treatment: Theory and Practice* (Englewood Cliffs, N.J.: Prentice-Hall, 1985), p. 44.

75. Hobbes, *Leviathan* (New York: Macmillan, 1947).

76. Stuart A. Scheingold, *The Politics of Rights: Lawyers, Public Policy, and Political Change* (New Haven: Yale University Press, 1974), p. 24.

77. Wilson, *Thinking About Crime,* Revised ed., p. 118.

78. Ibid., pp. 127–128.

79. Phillip J. Cook, "Research in Criminal Deterrence: Laying the Groundwork for the Second Decade," *Crime and Justice* 2, ed. Norval Morris and Michael Tonry (Chicago: University of Chicago Press, 1980), p. 219.

80. Wilson, *Thinking About Crime,* 1st ed., p. 128.

81. S. E. Merry, *Urban Danger: Life in a Neighborhood of Strangers* (Philadelphia: Temple University Press, 1981).

82. Francis T. Cullen, William J. Maakestad, and Gary Cavender, *Corporate Crime Under Attack* (Cincinnati: Anderson, 1987), p. 344.

83. Elliott Currie, *Confronting Crime: An American Challenge* (New York: Pantheon Books, 1985), pp. 55–56.

84. Chris W. Eskridge, "Flaws in the Theory and Practice of General Deterrence" (Paper presented at the Annual Meeting of the Academy of Criminal Justice Sciences, San Antonio, Texas, March 1983), p. 1.

85. Bentham, *Introduction to the Principles of Morals and Legislation*.

86. Van den Haag, "The Criminal Law as a Threat System," *Journal of Criminal Law and Criminology* 73 (1982), pp. 769–785; David Lester, "Modern Psychological Theories of Punishment and Their Implications for Penology and Corrections," *Corrective and Social Psychiatry and Journal of Behavior Technology, Methods, and Therapy* 25 (1979), pp. 81–85; Michael R. Geerken and Walter R. Gove, "Deterrence: Some Theoretical Considerations," *Law and Society Review* 9 (1975), pp. 197–513.

87. Joan E. Jacoby, "The Deterrent Power of Prosecution," in *Preventing Crime,* ed. James A. Cramer (Beverly Hills, Calif.: Sage, 1978), pp. 137–161.

88. Robert F. Meier, "The Deterrence Doctrine and Public Policy: A Response to Utilitarians," in von Hirsch, ed., *Preventing Crime,* pp. 233–247.

89. Theodore Chiricos and Gordon Waldo, "Punishment and Crime: An Examination of Some Empirical Evidence," *Social Problems* 18 (1970), pp. 200–217.

90. Charles Tittle and Allan Rowe, "Moral Appeal, Sanction Threat, and Deviance: An Experimental Test," *Social Problems* (1973), pp. 490–495; and William Bailey, "Certainty of Arrest and Crime Rates for Major Felonies: A Research Note," *Journal of Research in Crime and Delinquency* (July 1976), pp. 145–154.

91. Alfred Blumstein and Daniel Nagin, "The Deterrent Effect of Legal Sanctions on Draft Evasion," *Stanford Law Review* 28 (1977), pp. 241–275.

92. Kenneth I. Wolpin, "An Economic Analysis of Crime and Punishment in England and Wales, 1894–1967," *Journal of Political Economy* 86 (1978), pp. 815–840.

93. H. L. Ross, *Deterrence of the Drinking Driver: An International Survey* (Washington, D.C.: U.S. Department of Transportation; National Highway Traffic Safety Administration, 1981); Ross, *Deterring the Drinking Driver: Legal Policy and Social Control* (Lexington, Mass.: Lexington Books, 1982).

94. Ann Dryden Witte, "Estimating the Economic Model of Crime with Individual Data," *Quarterly Journal of Economics* 94 (1980), pp. 57–84.

95. J. M. Chaiken and M. R. Chaiken, *Varieties of Criminal Behavior* (Santa Monica, Calif.: Rand, 1982), pp. 172–173.

96. L. W. Sherman and R. A. Berk, "The Specific Deterrent Effects of Arrest for Domestic Assault," *American Sociological Review* 49 (1984), pp. 261–272.

97. Franklin Zimring and Gordon Hawkins, *Deterrence: The Legal Threat to Crime Control* (Chicago: University of Chicago Press, 1973).

98. J. L. Miller and Andy B. Anderson, "Updating the Deterrence Doctrine," *Journal of Criminal Law and Criminology* 77 (1986), p. 418.

99. John E. Conklin, *Criminology* (New York: Macmillan, 1981), p. 392.

100. Alfred Blumstein, "Selective Incapacitation as a Means of Crime Control," *American Behavioral Scientist* 27 (September/October 1983), pp. 87–88.

101. *Criminal Justice Newsletter* 13 (15 March 1982), pp. 2–5.

102. Wilson, *Thinking About Crime;* van den Haag, *Punishing Criminals.*

CHAPTER **5**

Biological and Psychological Explanations of Crime

DEVELOPMENT OF POSITIVISM IN CRIMINOLOGY

BIOLOGICAL POSITIVISM

Early Theories of Biological Positivism

Lombroso and the Atavistic Criminal
Criticism and Support of Physical Anomalies
Body Types, or Somatotyping
Evaluation of Early Biological Positivism

Sociobiology or Contemporary Biological Positivism

Twins and Adoptions
Cytogenetic Studies (XYY Chromosome)
Intelligence
Physique or Constitutional Factors
Evaluation of Sociobiology

PSYCHOLOGICAL POSITIVISM

Psychological Abnormality and Crime

Psychological Characteristics of Offenders
Psychopathy
Cognitive Theories
Evaluation of Psychological Positivism

PUNISHMENT AND PERSONAL RESPONSIBILITY

ANALYSIS

Badness to Sickness

Sickness to Dangerousness

Sickness to Responsibility

POLICY IMPLICATIONS

SUMMARY

REFERENCES

NOTES

KEY TERMS

autonomous nervous system and
   delinquent behavior
ectomorphic body type
endomorphic body type
fraternal twins (dizygotic)
identical twins (monozygotic)
intelligence and crime
medicalization of deviance
mesomorphic body type
Minnesota Multiphasic Personality
   Inventory (MMPI)

moral development theory
physiognomy
positivism
psychoanalysis
psychopathy
reinforcement theory
sociobiology
XYY chromosome

He was a real fruitcake. We never knew what he would do next. He used to walk the big yard all day, talking 90 miles a minute about the case he lost. He would stick pins and stuff in his arms. He would drink stuff, stuff that would kill the rest of us. He had a real thing for shoes, always wanting to shine our shoes. I think he got off on shoes. I thought he would take the dive [kill himself], but one day a new dude happened to bump into him in the yard. Later that same day, right in front of the guards and gun tower, he jumped the new dude and stabbed him seven times. Man, we left him alone after that.

—Former San Quentin inmate[1]

Some individuals' behavior is unpredictable. As long as their behavior is not dangerous or harmful to the social order, they are generally tolerated by those who know them. Families, for example, sometimes can manage to accept quite eccentric behavior from family members, saying, in effect, "that's just the way he or she is." But when individuals' behavior becomes too dangerous or troublesome, then it is necessary to deal with these persons. Inmates of adult prisons, as the opening quotation to this chapter indicates, have real problems in dealing with unpredictable behavior in others.

What makes some offenders' behavior unpredictable, according to the theories discussed in this chapter, is that these individuals are controlled by biological or psychological factors that cause them to become involved in criminal behavior. In presuming that criminality is caused by some factor within the individual or present in the environment, this deterministic position changes the focus from the harmful act to the actor. Proponents of this viewpoint agree that criminal behavior brings disorder to society, but they argue that it is a disorder that the individual cannot help or control.

DEVELOPMENT OF POSITIVISM IN CRIMINOLOGY

Positivism is a philosophical stance that uses empirical data and the inductive method and that relies on objective evidence and on experimental approaches (when possible).[2] It focuses on the *why* of the behavior, rather than the act itself, and asserts that scientific research is needed to discover why a person commits a specific behavior. It rejects the logic of the law, especially the assumptions of free will and the rational or prudent "man." Or, to take this position to its logical conclusion, it denies the relevance of the legal and punishment process.[3] Historically, law and criminology have diverged, precisely because the two fields address different questions and use different approaches in the study of crime.[4]

Positivism makes three basic assumptions about criminal behavior.[5] First, the criminal is seen as fundamentally different from the noncriminal. The task for the researcher then is to identify the factors that have made the criminal a different kind of person. Positivism asserts that this difference is explained "by something in his physical makeup, by aberrant psychological impulses, or by the meanness of his social environment."[6] Second, the unique background of each individual explains criminal behavior. Thus, positivism, relegating the law and its administration to a secondary role, looks for the cause of deviancy in the actor. The third critical assumption of positivism is the existence of scientific determinism. That is, crime, like any other phenomenon, is seen as determined by prior causes; it does not just happen. This deterministic viewpoint rejects the position that the individual exercises free will, possesses reason, and is capable of choice.[7]

BIOLOGICAL POSITIVISM

The belief in a biological explanation for criminality has a long history. **Physiognomy**, which suggests that one's physical appearance betrays a predisposition toward brutality or crime, goes back to the ancient Greeks. Indeed, Socrates was charged by a physiognomist as having a face that reflected a brutal nature.[8] A later medieval law directed that "if two persons fell under suspicion of crime the uglier or more deformed was to be regarded as more probably guilty."[9] Shakespeare has Caesar say:

> Let me have men about me that are fat;
> Sleek-headed men, and such as sleep o' nights.
> Yond Cassius has a lean and hungry look;
> He thinks too much: such men are dangerous.

> —*Julius Caesar*, Act I, Scene II

The attention given in the United States to biological positivism can be divided into two periods. The first period was characterized by the nature-nurture debate during the latter part of the nineteenth century and the early twentieth

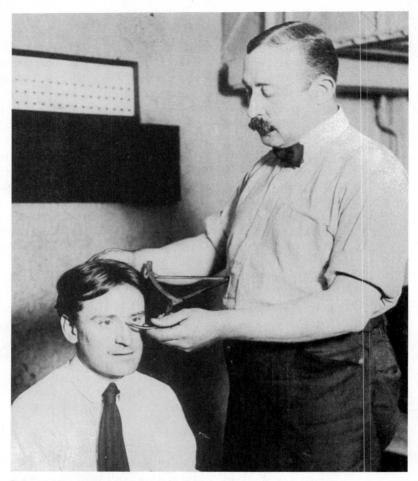

Police taking measurements at New York headquarters for identifying prisoners. (*Source:* Library of Congress [LC-USZ62-50068].)

century. Sociobiology, the focus of concern during the second and more recent period, stresses the interaction between the biological factors within an individual and the influence of the environment.

Early Theories of Biological Positivism

Lombroso's theory of physical anomalies, Goring's criticism and Hooton's support, and the various theories of human somatotyping, or body type, were the results of some of the earliest examinations of the relationship between crime and biological factors.

Lombroso and the Atavistic Criminal   Cesare Lombroso, a nineteenth-century Italian forensic psychiatrist, is known as the father of modern positivist criminology. In the process of examining many prisoners both before and after their deaths, he became convinced that there was a "criminal man" physically distinct from other human beings. According to Lombroso, the criminal was a moral imbecile who was a reversion to an earlier evolutionary form or level; that is, the characteristics of primitive men periodically reappeared in certain individuals.[10] Lombroso thought that he had discovered the secret of criminal behavior when he examined the skull of the notorious criminal Vihella:

> This was not merely an idea, but a flash of inspiration. At the sight of that skull I seemed to see all of a sudden, lighted up as a vast plain under a flaming sky, the problem of the nature of the criminal—an atavistic being who produces in his person the ferocious instincts of primitive humanity and the inferior animals. Thus were explained anatomically the enormous jaws, high cheek bones, prominent superciliary arches, solitary lines in the palms, extreme size of the orbits, handle-shaped sensile ears found in criminals, savages, and apes, insensibility to pain, extremely acute sight, tattooing, excessive idleness, love of orgies, and the irresistible craving for evil for its own sake, the desire not only to extinguish life in the victim, but to mutilate the corpse, tear its flesh, and drink its blood.[11]

Lombroso initially insisted that all criminals were born criminals, or atavistic, but study of several thousand criminals led him to modify his theory. By 1887, when the fifth edition of his book *L'Uomo Delinquente* appeared, he had reduced his estimate of the percentage of born criminals to 40 percent. He eventually concluded that environment was more responsible for crime than atavism. He also identified a continuum of "criminaloids"—individuals who fell between atavistic and other criminals.[12] Lombroso's work was so flawed that it soon met considerable criticism, primarily for the following reasons:

1. His measurement of physical characteristics was often causal, imprecise, and incompletely described. . . .
2. Criminals were compared to noncriminals without taking account of other differences between them, such as age, socioeconomic standing, and ethnic background. . . .
3. His statistical methods were rudimentary.
4. Lombrosian psychology was as weak as Lombrosian biology. Corresponding to the physical atavism, there was supposed to be moral atavism as well.[13]

Criticism and Support of Physical Anomalies   The research of Charles Goring, an English prison physician, posed the most serious challenge to Lombroso's work. Using the techniques of physical anthropology and a more sophisticated means of statistical analysis, Goring examined over three thousand male prisoners and various comparison groups of nonprisoners. In *The English Convict: A Statistical Analysis* (1913), he concluded that Lombroso's atavistic born criminal "has no existence in fact since the physical and mental constitution of both criminal and law-abiding persons, of the same age, stature, class, and intelligence, are identical."[14] Denying that there is any such thing as an anthropological criminal type, Goring did go on to say:

But, despite this negation, and upon the evidence of our statistics, it appears to be an equally indisputable fact that there is a physical, mental, and moral type of normal person who tends to be convicted of crime; that is to say, our evidence conclusively shows that, on the average, the criminal of English prisons is markedly differentiated by defective physique—as measured by stature and body weight; by defective mental capacity—as measured by general intelligence; and by an increased possession of willful antisocial proclivities—as measured, apart from intelligence, by length of sentence to imprisonment.[15]

E. A. Hooton, a physical anthropologist at Harvard University, continued the debate by conducting a large-scale study of the characteristics of criminals in ten states. He compared ten thousand convicted male criminals with about four thousand noncriminals on several dozen physical traits, along with several sociological variables such as marital status, education, and occupation. He found criminals to be generally smaller than noncriminals and noted that the larger the criminal, the more serious his crimes were likely to be.[16] Hooton interpreted his data in this way:

. . . My present hypothesis is that physical inferiority is of principally hereditary origin; that these hereditary inferiors naturally gravitate into unfavorable environmental conditions; and that the worse or weakest of them yield to social stresses which force them into criminal behavior.[17]

But Hooton found an inferiority in criminals that was not suggested in the data. A likely explanation for Hooton's lapse into a Lombrosian circularity is that he had no real alternative, as psychology had not yet developed to the point where it could trace the steps leading from static anatomical traits to dynamic events.[18] Hooton anticipated the reactions of his critics in the opening sentence of *Crime and the Man:* "The anthropologist who obtrudes himself into a study of crime is an obvious ugly duckling and is likely to be greeted by the lords of the criminological dung-hill with cries of 'Quack! quack! quack!' "[19]

Body Types, or Somatotyping   Ernst Kretscher, a German, first developed the theory that there are two body types, the cyclothyme and the schizothyme. Schizothymes, strong and muscular, are more likely to be criminal or delinquent than are cyclothymes, who are soft-skinned and lack muscle tone.[20]

William H. Sheldon was the first American researcher to examine the relationship between body type and delinquent behavior. Sheldon described three body types: **endomorphic** (soft, round, and fat); **mesomorphic** (bony, muscular, and athletic); and **ectomorphic** (tall, thin, and fragile). He developed a system for classifying or somatotyping human physique which suggested that body build correlates with behavioral tendencies, susceptibility to disease, and life expectancy. He also postulated that these somatotypes had temperamental correlates. For example, the temperamental correlations with mesomorphy pertained to such characteristics as social assertiveness, lack of submission to authority, and less inhibited motor responses.[21]

Sheldon somatotyped two hundred institutionalized youths who had been admitted to Hayden Goodwill Inn over a period of several years for antisocial or maladaptive behaviors. He found that the most striking features of this population were that they were predominantly mesomorphs deficient in ectomorphy and that their physiques included a configuration called andromorphy (broad chest flaring toward the shoulders, long arms, large bones and joints, and fat distributed throughout the body).[22]

P. Epps and R. W. Parnell compared the physiques of 177 female delinquents to those of 123 Oxford undergraduates and found the delinquents to be shorter and heavier in build, more muscular, and fatter; that is, more mesomorphic and endomorphic.[23] Sheldon and Eleanor Glueck, in comparing 500 delinquents with 500 nondelinquents matched for age, IQ, ethnic background, and socioeconomic status, found that delinquents were significantly more mesomorphic and less ectomorphic than nondelinquents. They concluded: "Among the delinquents, mesomorphy is far and away the most dominant component, with ectomorphic, endomorphic, and balanced types about equally represented but in relatively minor strength."[24]

In summary, according to body-type theories, delinquents on the average differ in physique from the population at large. They tend to be more mesomorphic and less ectomorphic. The mesomorphic physique is associated with expressive, extroverted, domineering temperaments, given to high levels of activity. Sheldon referred to the resulting temperament as "Dionysian"—the spirit of unrestrained, impulsive self-gratification.[25] Some sociologists and other experts contend that endomorphic mesomorphs are overly represented in institutional populations because the criminal justice system tends to associate the body type with dangerousness and to impose more severe sanctions. Neither the puny ectomorph nor the rotund endomorph inspires the same sort of fear as the tattooed, heavily muscled mesomorph.

Evaluation of Early Biological Positivism   The primitiveness of the research techniques of the early biological positivists won them few supporters. Lombroso's theory that the criminal had distinctive physical features was quickly dismissed. The theory that criminal genes are inherited was also discredited by most biologists and social scientists. Finally, so were the body type theories, because they ignored the importance of environment in the development of the body structure of adolescents.

Sociobiology or Contemporary Biological Positivism

Sociobiology differs from other theories of biological determinism because it links genetic and environmental factors. That is, sociobiology claims that criminal behavior, like other behaviors, has both biological and social correlates. Recent advances in experimental behavior genetics, human population genetics, the biochemistry of the nervous system, experimental and clinical endocrinology and neurophysiology, and many related areas have led to more sophisticated knowledge of the ways the environment affects the growth, development, and functioning of the human organism.[26]

This recent explosion of knowledge concerning the variety of factors influencing human behavior has caused a number of criminologists to endorse enthusiastically biosocial theories. Indeed, C. R. Jeffrey, a criminologist and one of the proponents of sociobiology, goes so far as to propose that the biosocial interdisciplinary model should become the major theoretical framework for dealing with the prevention of crime and delinquency.[27]

Sociobiologists have investigated the relationship between antisocial behavior and biological factors and environment through studies of twins and adoptions, chromosomal abnormalities, electrodermal activity and psychopathy, minimal brain functioning, intelligence, physique, and orthomolecular imbalances. The research involving twins and adoptions, chromosomal abnormalities, intelligence, and physique will be examined in this section, while the research on electrodermal activity and psychopathy will be investigated in the next section.

Twins and Adoptions   Modern quantitative genetics deals with patterns of correlations among blood relatives and among people who share common environments even though they may not be blood relatives. The comparison of **identical (MZ, for monozygotic)** and same-sex **fraternal twins (DZ, for dizygotic)** provides the most comprehensive data for exploring genetic influences on human variation. Identical twins develop from a single fertilized egg that divides into two embryos; hence, they share all their genes. Fraternal twins develop from two separate eggs that were both fertilized during the act of conception; hence, they share about half their genes.

All twins share a prenatal environment and most a common family environment, and they have either all or only about half of their genes in common. If their pre- and postnatal environments were identical, then greater similarity between MZ twins than between DZ twins would be convincing evidence for a genetic factor.[28]

In the 1920s, Johannes Lange, a German physician, did the first systematic twin study. He located thirty pairs of same-sex twins of which at least one was a known criminal. He concluded, using the limited techniques of the time, that thirteen of the pairs were identical and seventeen fraternal, but, interestingly, in ten of the thirteen pairs of MZ twins, both were criminal, while in only two of the seventeen pairs of DZ twins were both criminal. Such a large difference in "concordance" (i.e., both twins showing the same trait) between MZ and DZ twins was held by Lange as evidence for a genetic contribution to criminality.[29]

Karl Christiansen and S.A. Mednick reported on a sample of 3586 twin pairs from the Danish Twin Register, a complete listing of twins born in Denmark between 1870 and 1920. The subset used by these researchers included almost all the twins born between 1881 and 1910 in a certain region of Denmark. Criminal justice statistics turned up 926 offenses for the 7172 twins, coming from 799 twin pairs. The probability of finding a criminal twin when the other twin was a criminal was .50 for MZ twins and .21 for same-sex DZ twins. Although the concordances in this study were lower than in the earlier surveys, they were still significant and indicated a genetic contribution to criminal behavior.[30]

The largest systematic adoption study of criminality is one based on all nonfamilial adoptions in Denmark from 1924 to 1947. This sample included 14,427 male and female adoptees and their biological and adoptive parents. After exclusions—because criminal records or other kinds of demographic information were missing—the analysis involved no fewer than ten thousand parents in the four parental categories (i.e., biological/adoptive, mother/father) and over thirteen thousand adoptees. The parents were counted as criminal if either the mother or father had a criminal conviction. Of those boys who had neither adoptive nor biological criminal parents, 13.5 percent had at least one conviction. The percentage rose slightly to 14.7, if adoptive (but not biological) parents were criminal; if biological (but not adoptive) parents were criminal, 20 percent of the boys had at least one conviction. Boys with both adoptive and biological criminal parents had the highest proportion, 24.5 percent. Mednick concluded that criminality of the biological parents is more important than that of the adoptive parents, a finding that suggests genetic transmission of some factor or factors associated with crime.[31]

A large Swedish study, consisting of 862 adopted males and 913 adopted females, confirmed and expanded upon many of the Danish findings. Adopted children again were found to follow their biological parents' tendency toward crime to a greater extent than any criminal tendency identified in the adoptive family setting. The same genetic pattern was found for both sexes. For women, however, the genetic predisposition was even stronger than for men.[32]

David C. Rowe, in a recent American study, distributed questionnaires to all the twins in the eighth to twelfth grades in almost all the school districts of Ohio. Completed questionnaires were received from 168 MZ and 97 same-sex DZ twin pairs, with more females than males responding. Rowe found that self-reported delinquent behavior was greater for MZ than DZ twins for both males and females, further evidence of some genetic involvement.[33]

An American study of the adopted children of a group of convicted mothers in Iowa supported the Danish and Swedish findings regarding the importance of genetic factors in crime. The 41 mothers, who primarily had been convicted of felonies, put their children up for adoption in early infancy. The sample of their children was compared with a control group of 52 adoptees matched for age, sex, race (all were white), age of separation from mother (about 3.9 months), and socioeconomic and marital status of adopting families. The two groups clearly differed in criminal histories. Three of the sample, but none of the controls, had records of felonies; deviant behavior, other than criminal, was also more common among the sample than the controls and was of a more serious type.[34]

In sum, the evidence of these studies of twins and adoptions is impressive. The twin method does have the weakness that the differences in MZ and DZ twin similarity tell us about genetic involvement only to the extent that the MZ-DZ difference is not related to environmental differences. But if the environment makes MZ twins more alike or DZ twins more different than they would otherwise be, the environmental influence overestimates the genetic contribution.

Cytogenetic Studies (XYY Chromosome)   In 1965, P.A. Jacobs and her associates found a disproportionately high frequency of men with an extra Y chromosome among the inmates of a maximum-security state hospital in Scotland.[35] Their report raised the possibility of the **XYY chromosome** as a genetic correlate of criminality. In human beings, gender is determined by one of the 23 pairs of inherited chromosomes. A female receives an X chromosome from each parent; a male receives an X from his mother and a Y from his father. But defects in the production of egg or sperm result in certain genetic anomalities, of which one type is the XYY male, who receives two Y chromosomes from his father. Any resulting abnormalities may be postulated as caused by the extra Y chromosome.

Jacobs and her colleagues' studies, as well as population surveys in places other than Scotland, found that the frequency of XYY males in the general population is about one per one thousand. But in correctional institutions, the frequency of XYY is about ten to twenty times larger, found in from 1 to 2 percent of the institutionalized male population.[36]

Another study conducted in Denmark was the most revealing study of the XYY population. From the total Danish population of men born between 1944 and 1947, the study selected the tallest 15 percent. Sex-chromosome determinations on over 90 percent of the tall men involved 4139 cases, of which 12 were found to be XYY. Five of the XYYs had criminal records of one or more offenses, a prevalence rate of over 40 percent. The prevalence rate among XY men was only 9.3 percent, which is significantly lower. Most of the 149 recorded offenses committed by the 5 XYY criminals were minor property offenses; although they were more often criminal, XYY men did not appear to be more violent or aggressive than the XY men with criminal records. The Danish study also found that, on the average, XYY men had lower tested intelligence and educational achievements.[37]

Still, the XYY sex chromosome theory is actually a very crude postulation that does not indicate the mechanisms whereby genetic differences are translated into behavioral differences. The theory is also very restrictive because it applies only to a tiny proportion of all offenders. Offenders under six feet in height are generally excluded from consideration because of the low incidence of XYY males of short and medium height. Furthermore, there are four types of XYY males, and the most common class of XYY males by far is an anomaly even among the XYY populations studied. Were it not for Richard Speck—the multiple murderer of nurses in Chicago, who was erroneously, as it later turned out, diagnosed as an XYY—few people would have heard of this anomaly and even fewer would have linked it to predatory behavior.

Intelligence   Various studies have examined the link between criminality and low intelligence. In 1914, H. H. Goddard concluded from the available data that "25 percent to 50 percent of the people in our prisons are mentally defective and incapable of managing their affairs with ordinary prudence."[38]

It took only a decade for Goddard's conclusion about the relationship between **intellegence and crime** to be challenged. In 1926, Carl Murchison presented evidence that the scores earned by samples of enlisted men during World War I were lower than those earned by prisoners in the federal penitentiary at Fort Leavenworth. This sample, along with other comparisons around the coun-

Richard Speck: convicted murderer denied parole.
(*Source:* AP–Wide World Photos.)

try, convinced Murchison that criminals are no less intelligent than the population at large.[39]

Edwin H. Sutherland, one of the leading criminologists of his generation, concurred with Murchison. He concluded that the deficiencies were not in the criminals but in the studies purporting to find them, as demonstrated by their inadequate sampling procedures and the questionable standardization and validation of intelligence tests.[40]

With the increased popularity of sociobiology in the 1960s and 1970s, intelligence was again examined as a factor in delinquent and criminal behavior. D. J. West and D. P. Farrington conducted a longitudinal study of 411 English boys and found that those who later became criminals were characterized by lower IQs than were those who did not. The authors thus concluded that intelligence is a meaningful predictive factor of future delinquency.[41] Lis Kirkegaard-Sorensen and Sarnoff A. Mednick also conducted a longitudinal study on the value of adolescent intelligence test scores for the prediction of later criminality. They too found that adolescents who committed criminal acts later had a lower tested intelligence score than their more law-abiding peers.[42]

Robert Gordon, in comparing delinquency prevalence and incidence rates, concluded that nonwhite juvenile males had higher arrest rates and court appearance rates than white males or females, regardless of any specific geographical location, rural or urban. He proposed that differences in IQ may provide the greatest explanation of these persistent differences in unlawful behavior.[43] In another paper, Gordon stated that "IQ was always more successful in accounting for the black–white differences [in crime] than income, education, or occupational status."[44]

BOX 5.1   **INTELLIGENCE AND CRIME**

It makes intuitive sense that more intelligent criminals would be more guided by the risk of arrest and prosecution and so, as compared to less intelligent criminals, would be drawn disproportionately to crimes with lower clearance rates. The contribution of intelligence to this particular fact would be explained simply by the supposition that people with higher scores are generally more attuned to the actual contingencies and risks of various sorts of offending.

But that is at best only a partial reason for the relationship. The typical crimes of less intelligent offenders are often crimes with an immediate payoff—crimes of violence in which the reward is the damage inflicted on one's antagonist of the moment, or sexual crimes that yield immediate gratification, or minor property crimes occasioned by a target of opportunity, such as a nighttime encounter with a solitary stranger on a quiet city street. In contrast, the characteristic crimes of more intelligent offenders involve preparation, planning, occasionally even negotiation with confederates, and a payoff that may be long deferred. In short, insofar as the rate of time discounting is itself a correlate of intelligence, low intelligence will favor impulsive crimes with immediate rewards, and high intelligence, the inverse. Perhaps not coincidentally, clearance rates are lower for crimes that take longer to plan, to carry out, and to deliver the goods. What evidence there is suggests that low test scores are in fact associated with impulsive crimes.

Source: This material appears in James Q. Wilson and Richard J. Herrnstein, *Crime and Human Nature* (New York: Simon and Schuster, 1985), pp. 166–167.

Travis Hirschi and Michael Hindelang reexamined a number of research studies—Hirschi's 1969 data from California, Wolfgang and associates' Philadelphia data, and Weiss's data from the state of Washington—and found that "the weight of evidence is that IQ is more important than race and social class" for predicting delinquency. These two researchers also rejected the contention that IQ tests are race- and class-biased in that they favor middle-class whites and are therefore invalid means of comparing lower- and middle-class youths. Hirschi and Hindelang concluded that low IQ affects school performance, resulting in an increased likelihood of delinquent behavior.[45]

The excerpt in Box 5.1 is James Q. Wilson and Richard J. Herrnstein's explanation of why they believe there is an inverse relationship between intelligence and certain types of adult criminality.

In sum, sociologists thought that the IQ issue was dead in the mid–1930s, when the research consistently challenged the relationship between IQ and delinquency, but recent studies have resurrected the issue. Unquestionably, whatever the correlation between IQ and delinquency may be, the association is strengthened by other environmental factors, such as performance in school.

Physique or Constitutional Factors Some constitutional factors are more directly related to delinquent and criminal behavior than others. For example, studies of structural disorders of the limbic system demonstrate that focal brain disease can alter the propensities of the human organism.[46] Hormones, especially those related to sexual reproduction, have been cited as affecting the propensity of delinquent behavior in an individual.[47] Hans Eysenck's theory on the relationship between the **autonomous nervous system and delinquent behavior** has received wide attention.

Eysenck's theory has its origins in the earlier attempts to understand the relationship between constitutional factors and delinquency. Eysenck contends that some children are more difficult to condition than others because of the inherited sensitivity of their autonomous nervous system. Yet the conditioning of the child also depends on the quality of the conditioning the child receives within the family. Eysenck argues that types of individuals range from those in whom it is easy to excite conditioned reflexes and whose reflexes are difficult to inhibit, to those whose reflexes are difficult to condition and easy to extinguish.[48]

Eysenck adds that individuals whose consciences or autonomic nervous systems are more difficult to condition tend to be extroverts rather than introverts, and extroverts are much more likely to become involved in delinquent behavior. He sees the extrovert as a person who craves excitement, takes chances, acts on the spur of the moment, and frequently is impulsive. Eysenck also believes that the extrovert tends to be aggressive and to lose his or her temper easily, is unable to keep his or her feelings under tight control, and is not always reliable.[49]

However, the research methods used to prove Eysenck's theory have come under sharp criticism. Another major criticism of his theory is related to the basic concept of the autonomic nervous system. The fact that autonomic nervous systems differ does not mean that the differences can be directly related to delinquent or criminal behavior later in life.

Evaluation of Sociobiology Sociobiological theory is based upon several assumptions. First, sociobiologists reject the belief that all human beings are born with equal potential to learn and achieve, and they accept and recognize biological differences. Second, sociobiologists place a strong emphasis on learning, but caution that the physical and social environments interact either to limit or to enhance a person's capacity for learning. Third, sociobiologists emphasize the importance of the biological environment as a means of preventing crime and delinquency.[50]

There has been an evolution in sociobiology from single-factor biological theses to complicated biosocial ideas. The complexity of explanations has also increased, and each cycle brings more sophistication. The greater sophistication of sociobiology, based on recent scientific findings, has brought its theories increased support from criminologists.

However, for several reasons, the majority of criminologists remain reluctant to accept sociobiological theories. First, the physical processes through which behavior can be inherited have not been defined, and current explanations remain only speculative. Second, most criminologists are fearful that the moral and legal concepts of responsibility will be eroded further if the idea of determinism by heredity forces is accepted. Third, the transformation of crime into a medical problem appears to represent a return to the much-maligned medical or rehabilitation model, and criminologists are concerned about the new possibilities for abuse under the guise of treatment.[51]

PSYCHOLOGICAL POSITIVISM

Although biological factors have been given little credibility as a cause of crime until recently, psychological factors have long been an important part of the study of crime and delinquency. Psychological abnormality and crime, personality characteristics of offenders, psychopathy, and cognitive theories are examined in this section.

Psychological Abnormality and Crime

Sigmund Freud, the founder of **psychoanalysis**, devoted little attention to crime and delinquency, but his followers have identified four ways in which emotional problems suffered in childhood might lead to delinquent and criminal behavior. First, they say, criminal behavior is related to neurotic development in the personality. Freud established a relationship between desire and behavior; that is, everything is integrated in the subconscious, and external behavior is only an expression of the subconscious drives of the organism. An individual may feel guilty over a socially unacceptable desire, such as an incestuous craving for sex with a parent, or over an act he or she committed in the past. Thus, according to Freudian theory, he or she will seek punishment to expiate the feelings of guilt.[52]

Second, criminal behavior is attributed to a defective superego. The inability to develop a normally functioning superego can result in the inability to feel guilt, to learn from experience, or to feel affection toward others.[53] Those individuals with defective superegos, who are sometimes called sociopathic or psychopathic, may constantly express aggressive and antisocial behavior toward others.

Third, violent delinquent or criminal behavior is sometimes related to the tendency of children with overly developed superegos to repress all negative emotional feelings throughout childhood, with the result that their repressed feelings explode in a violent act at a later point in life. For example, "model" adolescents occasionally become involved in violent crimes toward parents and neighbors, sometimes horribly mutilating their victims.

Fourth, criminal involvements can be related to a search for compensatory gratification. According to Freud, individuals who were deprived at an early stage of development will later seek the gratification which they missed. Thus, an individual may become an alcoholic to satisfy an oral craving or may become sadistic because of poor toilet training received during the anal period.

William Healy, a psychiatrist who practiced during the early decades of the twentieth century, used the constructs of psychoanalytic theory to focus upon mental conflicts that originated in unsatisfactory family relationships.[54] August Aichhorn, another proponent of psychoanalytic theory, believed that delinquents had considerable hatred toward their parents because of the conflictual nature of the family relationship and that they transferred this hatred to other authority figures.[55] Kate Friedlander used another psychoanalytic approach in treating delinquents. She focused upon the development of antisocial characteristics, such as selfishness, impulsiveness, and irresponsibility, which she defined as the results of disturbed ego development in early childhood.[56]

Proponents of psychological positivism today contend that some criminal behavior is caused by the fact that the individuals involved have little or no control over their thoughts, feelings, or actions. They are mentally ill or suffer from a mental disease. There is no question that John Hinckley, Jr., shot President Reagan and several companions outside the Washington Hilton Hotel in 1981; this fact was never disputed by Hinckley's defense attorneys. Instead, they argued that he was the helpless victim of an insane and frustrated obsession to win the love of the actress Jodie Foster and, therefore, was driven to the crime by a pathological condition over which he had no control. The jury was convinced by this argument and voted "not guilty by reason of insanity." Hinckley was hospitalized for treatment, rather than sent to prison for punishment. Box 5.2 summarizes the various tests of insanity.

Psychological Characteristics of Offenders Proponents of psychological positivism argue that populations of offenders differ statistically in a number of ways from populations of nonoffenders.

S. Glueck and E. T. Glueck, in comparing five hundred delinquents and nondelinquents, found that there were marked personality differences between the two groups. The delinquents were assertive, unafraid, aggressive, unconventional, extroverted, and poorly socialized. In contrast, the nondelinquents were self-controlled, concerned about their relationships with others, willing to be guided by social standards, and full of such internal feelings as insecurity, helplessness, neediness, and anxiety.[57]

J. J. Conger and W. C. Miller, in a longitudinal study of male delinquents using all the boys entering the tenth grade in Denver, Colorado, public schools in 1956, found that by the age of 15, delinquents could be differentiated from nondelinquents either by the standard personality tests or by teacher evaluations. Delinquents, on the average, were characterized as emotionally unstable, impulsive, suspicious, hostile, given to petty expressions of irritations, egocentric, and typically more unhappy, worried, and dissatisfied than their nondelinquent matches.[58]

The continuity between childhood symptoms of emotional problems and adult behavior also emerged in L. N. Robins's 30-year follow-up of 526 white childhood patients in a St. Louis, Missouri, guidance clinic in the 1920s. Robins

BOX 5.2   ## THE TESTS OF INSANITY

The M'Naughten Rule: In 1843, Daniel M'Naughten was acquitted of killing Edward Drummond, whom he thought to be Sir Robert Peel, the prime minister of England. M'Naughten claimed that he was suffering from delusions, and he was acquitted. Public uproar at his acquittal caused the House of Lords to ask the court to define the law concerning mental delusions. The judges responded by saying that the finding of guilt cannot be given if, "at the time of the committing of the act, the party accused was laboring under such a defect of reason, from disease of the mind, as not to know the nature and quality of the act he was doing, or if he did know it that he did not know he was doing what was wrong."

This test, which is often called the "right-from-wrong test," is currently accepted by most states. The M'Naughten Rule has been heavily criticized through the years, both because individuals may be insane but still able to distinguish right from wrong, and because the term "disease of the mind" has not been adequately defined.

The Irresistible Impulse Rule: This modification of the M'Naughten Rule, which is used in 15 states, allows defendants to plead that although they knew what they were doing, they were unable to control the irresistible impulse to commit the crime. Thus, the Irresistible Impulse Rule excuses the defendant from responsibility when a mental disease controls his behavior.

Durham Rule: A few states and the District of Columbia use the Durham Rule. This rule, which was developed in New Hampshire in 1871, was adopted by the Circuit Court of Appeals for the District of Columbia in the 1954 case *Durham* v. *United States*. Monte Durham had a long history of both criminal activity and mental illness. On appeal of Durham's conviction for burglary, Judge David Bazelon rejected the M'Naughten Rule, but he ruled that an accused is not criminally responsible "if an unlawful act is the product of mental disease or mental defect." The Durham Rule is based on the supposition that insanity is a product of many personality factors.

Model Penal Code's Substantial Capacity Test: This rule, which is essentially a broadening of the M'Naughten and Irresistible Impulse rules, emphasizes that the test for insanity does not require that a defendant be totally unable to distinguish right from wrong. The Substantial Capacity Test is more aligned with present-day psychological concepts, and it supplies what standards are lacking in the Durham Rule.

Source: *M'Naughten*, 10 C. & F. 200, 8 Eng. Rep. 718 (1843); *Durham* v. *United States,* 94 U.S. App. D.C. 228, 214 F. 2d 862 (1954).

"I got a hunch he'll plead insanity."

Drawing by RJD; © *1937 The New Yorker Magazine, Inc.*

was looking for clues of the adult "antisocial personality," or "sociopathy."[59] Excluding cases involving organic brain damage, schizophrenia, mental retardation, or symptoms appearing only after heavy drug or alcohol use, she found that the adult sociopath is almost invariably an antisocial child grown up. In fact, she found no case of adult sociopathy without antisocial behavior prior to the age of 18. Over 50 percent of the sociopathic males showed an onset of symptoms prior to the age of 8.[60]

Starke Hathaway and Elio Monachesis examined the ability of the **Minnesota Multiphasic Personality Inventory (MMPI)** to detect criminal tendencies in advance of encounters with the law. They administered the MMPI to most of the children entering ninth grade in the Minneapolis public schools in 1947, a sample of almost four thousand boys and girls. Delinquents predominated among the boys whose highest scores had been on scales 4, 8, and 9—the psychopathic deviate, schizophrenia, and hypomania scales.[61]

Prisoners with the most deviant profiles had the highest probability of reincarceration after release and the greatest amount of trouble during imprisonment. Hathaway and Monachesis also found that prisoners deviated from the population at large in terms of those traits associated with high values on the psychopathy, schizophrenia, and hypomania scales of the MMPI—namely, deficient attachments to others and to social norms, bizarre thinking and alienation, and unproductive hyperactivity.[62]

Personality assessment has uncovered a type of violent criminal who tends to have more, rather than fewer, internalized prohibitions than those engaging in moderate or nonviolent crimes.[63] Megargee and his associates have derived a new MMPI scale, the O–H scale, to identify "Over-controlled Hostility." The high O–H offender is an individual whose hostile impulses have been held at bay by unusually strong internal controls. According to this theory, when this controlled hostility does occasionally burst forth, it is uncommonly violent. An example would be the quiet, peaceful neighbor who suddenly kills his family.[64]

Psychopathy   Few psychiatric accounts of **psychopathy** are more vivid than that provided by Hervey Cleckley, whose book *The Mask of Sanity* communicated that psychopathy is a serious illness, despite its "mask of sanity." Cleckley suggested that the essence of the disease is an inner emptiness: "We are dealing here not with a complete man at all but with something that suggests a subtly constructed reflex machine."[65] He listed 16 identifying characteristics he had noted in his practice:

1. The psychopath is charming and of good intelligence.
2. He is not delusional or irrational.
3. There is an absence of nervousness or psychoneurotic manifestations.
4. The psychopath is unreliable.
5. He is insecure, and he is a liar who can be trusted no more in his accounts of the past than in his promises of the future.
6. He is lacking in either shame or remorse.
7. His antisocial behavior is inadequately motivated. He will commit all kinds of misdeeds for astonishingly small stakes, and sometimes for no reason at all.
8. His judgment is poor, and he never learns from experience. He will repeat over and over again patterns of self-defeating behavior.
9. He is pathologically egocentric, and has no real capacity for love, although he often simulates affection or parental devotion.
10. His emotions are shallow.
11. The psychopath lacks insight to a degree usually found only in the most serious mental disorders.
12. He does not respond to consideration, kindness, or trust.
13. Drunk or sober, but especially when drunk, he is guilty of fantastic and uninviting behavior.
14. Psychopaths often threaten suicide but almost never carry it out.

15. The psychopath's sex life is impersonal, trivial, and poorly integrated.
16. The psychopath shows a consistent inability to make or follow any sort of life plan.[66]

Available clinical evidence indicates that psychopaths of both sexes may constitute from 1 to 3 percent of the adult population. According to prison classification data, at least 20 percent of the adult correctional population in the United States has antisocial personalities.[67] Whatever the figure, the antisocial personality is an economically and socially expensive mental disorder. Psychopathy has been found to be associated with a shortened life span and an unstable family life; it is a burden of conduct that, when not criminal, is often predatory or destructive.[68] Chronically antisocial persons tend to resist efforts at resocialization; in correctional institutions they are often disruptive to the point of negating any such efforts for the remaining 80 percent of the prisoners.

Four characteristics of the psychopath have been associated with increased rates of criminal behavior: lower arousal level, less susceptibility to learning and conditioning, greater impulsiveness, and lower anxiety.

There is some evidence that the psychopath is engaged in a reckless search for external stimulation to compensate for the lack of internal stimulation.[69] Such findings strengthen the idea that in an ordinary environment, psychopaths suffer from stimulation hunger, perhaps because their nervous systems provide too little internal stimulation. This diminished autonomic functioning may be what enables psychopaths to lie successfully on lie-detection tests and get away with it. These findings also largely support the fact that psychopaths have diminished resting levels of skin conductance, or diminished reactivity to stimuli.[70]

Deficiency in the ability to learn is a common characteristic of psychopathy. Cleckley's list of 16 traits includes "poor judgment and failure to learn by experience."[71] Wilson and Herrnstein, in analyzing the experiments on the conditionability of psychopaths, conclude that it is not impossible to condition psychopaths, but that the autonomic nervous system that mediates their emotional responses is insensitive. For example, the psychopath may know that punishment is coming and some of his or her responses may be conditioned normally, but the skin conductance response is typically dormant until the punishment actually arrives (and even then the response is often restricted).[72]

Psychopathy also usually is characterized by impulsiveness, a trait that makes it difficult for the psychopath to defer his or her desires to the future. Wilson and Herrnstein conclude that "to the extent that success at completing lawful pursuits depends on an ability to work for deferred benefits, so much the worse for those who discount time quickly, such as psychopaths."[73]

The early evidence suggested that the extreme psychopath is relatively free from anxiety. Fleeting resentments, irritations, and urges were usually found to take the place of the more lasting worries or goals of the nonpsychopath. Yet subsequent research has indicated that some psychopaths are at least as anxious—if not more so—as normal controls.

Benjamin Karpman has distinguished between these two types of psychopath, the "idiopathic" and the "symptomatic," or, simply, the "primary" and the "secondary." In Karpman's view, primary (or idiopathic) psychopaths behave antisocially because they are more or less untouched by fear, anxiety, and guilt. But secondary (symptomatic) psychopaths behave antisocially because they are experiencing some other emotional disturbance. In addition to being symptomatically psychopathic, they also experience intense conflict, fear, and anxiety.[74]

Whatever the etiology of psychopathy, it seems probable that the disruption of the modern family, the increased geographic mobility, the "eclipse" of a sense of community, the emergence of the single-parent household, and the social disorganization brought about by urbanization and industrialization have surely exacerbated the problem. The chronically antisocial offender creates problems for the community; the city brings out the worst in the psychopath. The spiral effect is evidenced by "children who hate,"[75] the "core" members of gangs,[76] and the changing composition of the prison population. Experienced correctional counselors are disturbed by the increasing numbers of antisocial personalities in prison and confess that they are unable to deal constructively with these highly disruptive inmates; at best, they can only contain them.

Cognitive Theories   Cognitive psychologists examine individuals' mental processes—the way they perceive and mentally represent the world in which they live. Wilhelm Wundt, Edward Titchener, and William James were the leading developers of this school. Several subcategories comprise the cognitive perspective. Gestalt psychology focuses upon whole units rather than individual parts. Humanistic psychology stresses self-awareness and "getting in touch with feelings." Moral development theory is concerned with how individuals morally perceive and deal with the world.[77]

Moral development theory has been used more to understand criminal behavior than the other cognitive theories. It is postulated that ideas about morality and justice develop in regular, predictable stages as a person passes through the various developmental stages of childhood. The idea is that interaction with others, combined with a "readiness to learn" (determined by maturation and by having achieved previous levels of development), produces a sequence of beliefs or attitudes about (1) what happens if a rule is obeyed or disobeyed and (2) what kind of distribution of scarce resources would be fair.[78]

The Swiss psychologist Jean Piaget pioneered this approach with his studies of the development of moral judgment among children. He suggests that individuals' moral reasoning develops in an orderly fashion, beginning at birth and continuing until they are at least 12 years old. According to his observations, younger children gave answers that Piaget classified as showing *heteronomous morality,* while older children displayed *autonomous morality.* Heteronomous morality is a set of beliefs that leads a person to strict obedience based on the fear of punishment. In contrast, autonomous morality is one under which children obey rules because they recognize that the rules best serve the interests of all those involved. Piaget adds that between the extremes of heteronomous and autonomous morality are several transitional stages that involve modifications of the extreme forms.[79]

Lawrence Kohlberg, in applying the concept of moral development to criminal behavior, states that individuals travel through stages of moral development, during which they make decisions on issues of right and wrong.[80] His stages of moral development are:

- *Stage 1:* Right is obedience to power and avoidance of punishment.
- *Stage 2:* Right is taking responsibility for oneself and focusing primarily on meeting one's own needs.
- *Stage 3:* Right consists of having good motives and being able to put oneself in another's shoes.
- *Stage 4:* Right is involved in maintaining the rules of society and being concerned about the welfare of a group or society.
- *Stage 5:* Right is based on recognizing individual rules within a society and complying with agreed-upon social rules.
- *Stage 6:* Right is assuming obligation to principles applied to all humankind, such as justice, equality, and freedom.[81]

L. Kohlberg and colleagues classified people according to the stage on the continuum at which their moral development ceased to grow, and they discovered that the majority of criminals could be classified in stages one and two. The majority of noncriminals, in turn, could be classified in stages three and four.[82] Kohlberg then postulated that criminal behavior is associated with the focus of one's life; the more that one is focused on satisfying one's basic needs, the more likely it is that one will commit criminal behavior. Conversely, the more that one sees one's place in a larger perspective and agrees to comply with the rules of others, the less likely it is that one will commit criminal behavior.[83] (See Table 5.1 for summaries of the biological, sociobiological, and psychological theories.)

Evaluation of Psychological Positivism Two questions must be answered to evaluate accurately the effect of psychological positivism. First, do personality differences between criminals and noncriminals actually exist? Second, do psychological problems cause criminal behavior?

K. F. Schessler and D. F. Cressey, in a 1950 survey of the empirical literature, found it "impossible to conclude from these data that criminality and personality elements are associated."[84] They reviewed more than 110 studies and found that only about 40 percent reported personality differences between criminals and noncriminals. G. P. Waldo and S. Dinitz, examining 94 additional studies, reported that in 81 percent of the studies, a statistical difference was found to exist between a criminal group and noncriminal group, but they contended that the methodological weaknesses of the studies made any reliable conclusions difficult.[85] D. J. Tennenbaum also reviewed personality studies conducted from 1966 to 1975 and presented results similar to those of Waldo and Dinitz. He found that "personality tests, per se, are no better predictors of criminal personalities now than those of ten years ago."[86]

Concerning the second question, there is no doubt that a great deal of crime is committed by individuals who appear as normal psychologically as noncriminals.[87] But psychological positivism, according to supporters, can help explain

Table 5.1   SUMMARY OF BIOLOGICAL, SOCIOBIOLOGICAL, AND PSYCHOLOGICAL THEORIES OF CRIME

Theory	Cause of Crime Identified	Supporting Research
Lombroso and the born criminal	The atavistic criminal is a reversion to an earlier evolutionary form	Weak
Body type	Mesomorphic body type	Weak
Twins and adoptions	Positive correlations between identical and fraternal twins and criminality shows the genetic influence	Moderately strong
XYY	Additional Y chromosome	Weak
Intelligence	IQ is a meaningful predictive factor in criminal behavior when combined with environmental factors	Moderately strong
Eysenck and the autonomic nervous system	Insensitivity of the autonomic nervous system, as well as faulty conditioning by parents	Weak
Psychoanalytic theory (Freud)	Unconscious motivations resulting from early childhood experiences	Weak
Psychopathic personality	Inner emptiness as well as biological limitations	Moderately strong
Moral development	Inability to recognize rights of others	Weak
Wilson and Herrnstein	Several key constitutional and psychological factors	Weak

the behavior of deeply disturbed offenders, compulsive-obsessive antisocial behavior, and the repeated failures of some offenders. The problem is that the popularity of psychological positivism has resulted in the forced administration of treatment to all offenders. Some offenders need treatment, are receptive to it, and do profit from it. But few positive results occur with countless others who neither want nor need intervention. Indeed, sometimes treatment does more damage than good.

PUNISHMENT AND PERSONAL RESPONSIBILITY

Wilson and Herrnstein's *Crime and Human Nature* contains a model of how the complex interaction of constitutional and psychological factors leads to criminal behavior. In brief, they consider potential causes of crime and of noncrime within the context of **reinforcement theory**; that is, the theory that behavior is governed by its consequent rewards and punishments, as reflected in the history of the individual. The authors are quick to dismiss evidence that is inconsistent with

---

BOX 5.3   **WILSON AND HERRNSTEIN'S THEORY**

At any given moment, a person can choose between committing a crime and not committing it (all these alternatives to crime we lump together as "noncrime"). The consequences of committing the crime consist of rewards (what psychologists call "reinforcers") and punishments; the consequences of not committing the crime (i.e., engaging in noncrime) also entail gains and losses. The greater the ratio of the net rewards of crime to the net rewards of noncrime, the greater the tendency to commit the crime. The net rewards of crime include, obviously, the likely material gains from the crime, but they also include intangible benefits, such as obtaining emotional or sexual gratification, receiving the approval of peers, satisfying an old score against an enemy, or enhancing one's sense of justice. One must deduct from these rewards of crime any losses that occur immediately—that are, so to speak, contemporaneous with the crime. They include the pangs of conscience, the disapproval of onlookers, and the retaliation of the victim.

The value of noncrime lies all in the future. It includes the benefits to the individual of avoiding the risk of being caught and punished and, in addition, the benefits of avoiding penalties not controlled by the criminal justice system, such as the loss of reputation or the sense of shame afflicting a person later discovered to have broken the law and the possibility that, being known as a criminal, one cannot get or keep a job.

Source: This material appears in James Q. Wilson and Richard J. Herrnstein, *Crime and Human Nature* (New York: Simon and Schuster, 1985), pp. 44–45.

---

their theoretical framework, but, as few have done in the field of criminology, they are able to show how the topics of gender, age, intelligence, families, schools, communities, labor markets, mass media, drugs, and variations across time, culture, and race influence the propensity to commit criminal behavior, especially violent offenses.[88] Box 5.3 expands on the basic assumptions of their theory.

Persons deficient in conscience, according to Wilson and Herrnstein, do not internalize society's rules.[89] Crimes with a higher certainty of success will be valued more by such individuals than those with less certainty, and seemingly certain punishments will be feared more than those that appear less certain. Therefore, they must be sure that "the net value of noncrime will equal the value of avoiding any legal penalties (fines or imprisonment) and social costs (family disgrace, lost social esteem, or inability to hold or get a job)."[90]

Furthermore, individuals also take into account not only what they stand to gain but what others stand to gain from what is perceived as comparable effort. Most individuals have some notion of what they are entitled to, and this notion is affected by what they see other people getting. Wilson and Herrnstein define the relationship between what one thinks he or she deserves and what he or she sees other people getting as an "equity equation."[91] They add that "the effect of a reward or punishment is inversely proportional to the strength of all the reinforcements acting on a person at a given time."[92]

Wilson and Herrnstein then raise a critical question: "What is the purpose of punishing an offender for crimes that he was doomed to commit?"[93] Their answer, consistent with Wilson's viewpoint as expressed in the previous chapter, is that progress made toward explaining criminality does not reduce the need for punishment because a biological explanation "only enables us to think more clearly about how punishment might work on people who commit, or might commit, crimes."[94]

However, Wilson and Herrnstein's theory, as set forth in *Crime and Human Nature,* does have serious flaws. Most importantly, their text consistently shows a disdain for the social context in which crime occurs. What Wilson and Herrnstein do, in effect, is to factor society out of their considerations of crime. Instead of examining criminal behavior as part of complex social mechanisms and attempting to understand the connection, they typically conclude that no conclusion is possible from the available data and that, therefore, no programs for reducing criminality among groups perceived as major sources of crime are worth their costs.[95]

ANALYSIS

The transitions from "badness" to "sickness," from "sickness" to "dangerousness," and from "sickness" to "responsibility" must be examined in order to understand the impact of biological and psychological positivism.

Badness to Sickness

One of the most interesting subjects in criminology is the gradual transformation of deviance designations in American society from "badness" to "sickness." The role of the medical profession in creating deviance designations cannot be ignored in the **medicalization of deviance**.[96]

The medicalization of deviance refers to how certain categories of deviant or criminal behavior came to be defined as medical rather than moral problems and how medicine, rather than the family, church, or state, has become the primary agent of social control for those exhibiting such behaviors. The significance of the medicalization of deviance is that the social responses to crime and to illness are different. Criminals are punished because their disruptive behavior is seen as willful; sick people are treated because their behavior is seen as out of their control.

Peter Conrad and Joseph W. Schneider's *Deviance and Medicalization: From Badness to Sickness* adds that the sick role has four components—two exemptions from normal responsibility and two added obligations:

First, the sick person is exempted from normal responsibilities, at least to the extent necessary to "get well." Second, the individual is not held responsible for his or her condition and cannot be expected to recover by an act of will. Third, the person must recognize that being ill is an inherently undesirable state and must want to recover. Fourth, the sick person is obligated to seek and cooperate with a competent treatment agent (usually a physician). For sickness, then, medicine is the "appropriate" institution of social control. Both as legitimizer of the sick role and as the expert who strives to return the sick to conventional social roles, the physician functions as a social control agent.[97]

Historically, the definitions of deviance have changed from religious to state-legal to medical-scientific interpretations. Nicholas Kittrie views these changes as the divestment of the criminal justice system and the coming of the therapeutic state.[98] Philip Rieff's sociological study of the impact of Freudian thought calls it "the triumph of the therapeutic."[99]

Conrad and Schneider provide the following examples of the medicalization of deviance:

- A woman claiming to be Lady Godiva rides a horse naked through the streets of Denver; after being apprehended by the police, she is taken to a psychiatric hospital and declared to be suffering from a mental illness.
- A prominent surgeon in a Southwestern city performs a psychosurgical operation on a young man who is prone to violent behavior.
- An Atlanta attorney who goes on drinking sprees is treated in a hospital clinic for his disease, alcoholism.
- A child in California brought to a pediatric clinic because of disruptive behavior is labeled hyperactive and is prescribed methylphenidate (Ritalin) for his disorder.[100]

The probability of medicalization increases as a particular kind of deviance becomes a middle-class rather than solely a lower-class problem. That is, there is a tendency to define deviance that is thought endemic to lower-class life as badness, but when it becomes apparent that it is also a middle-class phenomenon, it is likely to be defined as sickness. For example, when chronic drunkenness was thought common only to the lower-class alcoholic, designations of badness prevailed. But when problem drinkers were increasingly found in middle-class homes, the notion that alcoholism was a disease became more widely accepted. Another example is that lower-class schoolchildren are expected to be overactive, restless, and distracted, but when middle-class and suburban children behave that way, they are diagnosed as hyperactive and sick.[101]

Sickness to Dangerousness

The belief that permitted scientists to view criminal and dangerous behavior as evidence of a disease has been largely abandoned. Yet the search for biological explanations of violence continues. As each concept is found wanting, it is replaced by a new, but not necessarily more useful, theory. For example, the discovery of electrical activity in the brain and the identification of certain electrical patterns with convulsive disorders inspired interest in the electroencephalographic profiles of seriously antisocial individuals.[102]

Dangerous behavior often seems to provoke clinicians into the application of excessive remedies. The castration of sex offenders became a treatment of choice in some circles, with little consideration of the possible effectiveness of less radical treatments. The tragic consequences of the irresponsible legitimization of prefrontal lobotomies still haunt forensic medicine. It would seem that scientists, of all people, should know better than to expect a simple means of transforming a person prone to violence into a reliably peaceful citizen.[103]

The discouraging experiences of the past require us to be cautious in assessing the claims of the present generation of sociobiologists. It is no doubt true that some violence originates in twisted physiology, and cautious medical experimentation may play an indispensable role in treating the nervous systems of certain individuals. But the power to make peaceful citizens out of bestial thugs, if it ever becomes available, should also generate fear.[104] As Harold Goldman has commented, "What can be done to the thug for good reasons can also be done to ordinary citizens for bad reasons. The twentieth century has seen hideous abuses of power, so it is natural to be apprehensive about the creation of new means to increase it."[105]

Sickness to Responsibility

The focus today is on societal rather than individual problems because it is believed that the magnitude of the disorders of the larger society requires that they be given precedence over individual disorders. Wilson and Herrnstein take seriously the constitutional and psychological origins of criminal behavior, but they still maintain that individual pathology does not eliminate the need for punishment.[106] The work of the psychiatrist Dr. William Gaylin also reflects the current emphasis on public safety. In his account of the brutal murder of Bonnie Garland, Dr. Gaylin recognized the power of psychic determinism: "Psychiatrically speaking, nothing is wrong—only sick. If an act is not a choice but merely the inevitable product of a series of past experiences, a man can be no more guilty of a crime than he is guilty of an abscess."[107] Yet Gaylin challenges the attempts to spare Garland's killer, Richard Herrin, the legal consequences of his act. For Gaylin, the law should exact retribution even for an act that appears to be the inevitable expression of psychopathology:

> . . . A just society traditionally does some disservice to its individual members. The common good demands sacrifice of the individual. That is the lesson in the most moral of doctrines. The community under Jehovah is a community of law and justice, and yet the prophets may demand the ultimate sacrifices, even unto death, for the preservation of the law and the people of the law.[108]

The increased public disapproval of the insanity defense is a further indicator that collective disorder has become of greater concern than individual disorder. Even before John Hinckley's shooting of President Reagan, public opinion polls revealed that for some time the American people had viewed the insanity plea as a loophole that allows too many guilty people to go free.[109] The "guilty but mentally ill" legislation passed in many legislatures across the nation also reflects the reduced tolerance for individual disorders.

POLICY IMPLICATIONS

Positivist approaches to criminality have been widely criticized in recent years. The rehabilitative ideal, the basic means to put into practice the theories of positivism, has been denounced as being in conflict with basic human values. The positivist approach regards humans as disordered, and it is true that it has sometimes justified bizarre treatment to cure these disordered individuals. Rehabilitative philosophy is also criticized on the grounds that it does not work; the various studies indicate little evidence of the effectiveness of correctional treatment. Thus, the ideals of the "therapeutic state," especially when it comes to the treatment of criminals, are currently under sharp attack.

Today, the cutting issue involves what to do about the dangerous offender who appears to be emotionally disturbed as well. The solution advocated by those on the right is to use the public health model of quarantine; that is, to remove the germ by isolating germ carriers from the body politic, placing them in increasing numbers in isolated prisons. Some neuroscientists have recommended such bizarre means as psychosurgery to correct the behavior of hard-core offenders, although this solution has lost much of its earlier support. Neither medical experimentation nor incapacitation appears to be the answer to the problem of dangerous and disturbed offenders. (See Box 5.4 for a list of the issues that policymakers must resolve in order to deal with the problem of dangerousness.)

SUMMARY

Biological and psychological positivism offer individualistic explanations of crime. Criminal behavior, like other behaviors, is seen as having an organic or psychological basis. The individual criminal thus is controlled by specific organic or psychological factors. Sometimes the factors are more elusive—such as an autonomic nervous system that is difficult to condition or an inadequately developed superego—but other factors are more easily discerned—such as violence experienced in the family.

The early versions of both biological and psychological positivism have developed into more complex explanations of criminal behavior. Early biological positivism has been replaced by sociobiology, and psychoanalysis has been replaced by models less intrapsychic and more oriented to the interaction between the individual and the environment. In addition to being more interdisciplinary, research on the biological and psychological contributions to crime is more sophisticated than in the past.

BOX 5.4   **QUESTIONS ABOUT DANGEROUSNESS**

1. Is there a taxonomy of dangerousness that will enable us to differentiate decision making about violent offenders more accurately and equitably? Obviously, there is a profound and crucial difference between the offender whose violence is subcultural in origin and another whose central nervous system is so impaired as to render him prone to violent acts in provocative contexts. . . .

2. Can an offender's potential dangerousness be discriminated? Should psychologists continue to seek tests that can make such determinations? If there can never be a better predictor of the future than the offender's past record, what ethical principles should be invoked to justify social control of persons whose past behavior inspires apprehensions for the future?

3. If society must define some offenders as dangerous by a criterion of law and practice, if not by scientifically established principles, what shall be done with them? How long shall they be detained, and what principles should govern the duration of their detention? What kinds of treatment shall the prison authorities offer them and why? . . .

4. Are there any biomedical or psychological interventions that can be accepted as compatible with the values of a free and moral society? . . .

5. What kinds of intervention are appropriate for the dangerous juvenile offender? . . .

6. What actions can a community take to reduce the level of violence? What do the facts about violent behavior and its causes—as far as they can be known—indicate for relief from the fears that pervade American cities? . . .

Source: This material appears in John P. Conrad and Simon Dinitz, "What Happened to Stephen Nash? The Important Questions About Dangerousness," in *In Fear of Each Other,* ed. P. Conrad and Simon Dinitz (Lexington, Mass.: Lexington Books, 1977), pp. 7–9.

The disorder of American society has influenced the trend toward the medicalization of deviance or crime. Yet the recent concern with reestablishing public safety and security has resulted in more emphasis on the order of the larger society than on the disorder of particular criminals. The emerging feeling is that criminals, whether they are sane or insane, disturbed or nondisturbed, normal or abnormal, will be held accountable for their behavior.

REFERENCES

Aichhorn, August. *Delinquency and Child Guidance.* New York: International University Press, 1964.

Conrad, Peter, and Schneider, Joseph W. *Deviance and Medicalization: From Badness to Sickness.* St. Louis, Miss.: Mosby, 1980.

Cortes, Juan B., with Gatti, Florence M. *Delinquency and Crime: A Biopsychosocial Approach: Empirical, Theoretical, and Practical Aspects of Criminal Behavior.* New York: Seminar Press, 1972.

Erickson, Erik. *Identity, Youth, and Crisis.* New York: Norton, 1966.

Eysenck, H. J. *Crime and Personality.* 2d ed. London: Routledge & Kegan Paul, 1977.

Freud, Sigmund. *A General Introduction to Psycho-Analysis.* Translated by Joan Riviere. New York: Liveright, 1935.

Glueck, S., and Glueck, E. *Unraveling Juvenile Delinquency.* Cambridge: Harvard University Press, 1950.

Hippchen, Leonard, ed. *Ecologic-Biochemical Approaches to Treatment of Delinquents and Criminals.* New York: Van Nostrand Reinhold, 1978.

Hirschi, Travis, and Hindelang, Michael J. "Intelligence and Delinquency: A Revisionist Review." *American Sociological Review* 42 (1977), pp. 571–587.

Jeffrey, C. R., ed. *Biology and Crime.* Beverly Hills, Calif.: Sage, 1979.

Jenkins, Richard L., and Boyer, Andrew. "Type of Delinquent Behavior and Background Factors," *International Journal of Social Psychiatry* 14 (1967), pp. 66–76.

Mednick, Sarnoff A., and Christiansen, Karl O., eds. *Biosocial Bases of Criminal Behavior.* New York: Gardner Press, 1977.

Piaget, Jean. *The Moral Judgement of the Child.* London: Kegan Paul, 1932.

Schauss, Alexander. *Diet, Crime and Delinquency.* rev. ed. Berkeley, Calif.: Parker House, 1981.

Schussler, Karl, and Cressey, Donald. "Personality Characteristics of Criminals." *American Journal of Sociology* 17 (1952), pp. 704–729.

Shah, Saleem A., and Roth, Loren H. "Biological and Psychophysiological Factors in Criminality." In *Handbook of Criminology,* edited by Daniel Glaser. Chicago: Rand Mcnally, 1974. Pp. 101–173.

Wilson, James O., and Herrnstein, Richard J. *Crime and Human Nature.* New York: Simon and Schuster, 1985.

NOTES

1. Interviewed in March 1987.
2. For an expanded definition of positivism, see Piers Beirne, "Between God and Statistics: Adolphe Quetelet and the Development of Positivist Criminology" (Paper presented at the American Society of Criminology Annual Meeting, San Diego, California, November 1985), p. 4.
3. Michael Phillipson, *Understanding Crime and Delinquency* (Chicago: Aldine, 1974), p. 18.
4. For a discussion of the development of positivist criminology in early nineteenth century France, see Phillipson, *Understanding Crime and Delinquency.* For a discussion of the influence of positivism on late nineteenth-century America, see David J. Rothman, *Conscience and Convenience: The Asylum and Its Alternative in Progressive America* (Boston: Little, Brown, 1980).
5. David Matza, *Delinquency and Drift* (New York: Wiley, 1964), p. 5.
6. Donald C. Gibbons, "Differential Treatment of Delinquents and Interpersonal Maturity Level: A Critique," *Social Services Review* 44 (1970), p. 68.

7. Matza, *Delinquency and Drift,* p. 5.

8. James Q. Wilson and Richard J. Herrnstein, *Crime and Human Nature* (New York: Simon and Schuster, 1985), p. 71.

9. Ibid.

10. Ian Taylor, Paul Walton, and Jock Young, *The New Criminology: For a Social Theory of Deviance* (New York: Harper & Row, 1973), pp. 41–42.

11. Cesare Lombroso, introduction to Fina Lombroso-Ferrero, *Criminal Man According to the Classification of Cesare Lombrosco* (New York: Putnam, 1911), p. xiv.

12. F. Lombroso-Ferrero, *Criminal Man* (Montclair, N.J.: Patterson Smith, 1972).

13. Wilson and Herrnstein, *Crime and Human Nature,* pp. 74–75.

14. C. Goring, *The English Convict: A Statistical Study* (London: Darling, 1913).

15. Ibid., p. 370.

16. E. A. Hooton, *Crime and the Man* (Cambridge, Mass.: Harvard University Press, 1939).

17. E. A. Hooton, *The American Criminal: An Anthropological Study* (Cambridge, Mass.: Harvard University Press, 1939).

18. Wilson and Herrnstein, *Crime and Human Nature,* pp. 78–79.

19. Hooton, *Crime and the Man.*

20. William H. Sheldon, with the collaboration of E. M. Hartl and E. McDemott, *Varieties of Delinquent Youth* (New York: Harper, 1949).

21. W. H. Sheldon, with the collaboration of S. S. Stevens and W. B. Tucker, *The Varieties of Human Physique* (New York: Harper, 1940); Sheldon, with the collaboration of Stevens, *The Varieties of Temperament* (New York: Harper, 1942); Sheldon, *Varieties of Delinquent Youth.*

22. Sheldon, *Varieties of Delinquent Youth.*

23. P. Epps and R. W. Parnell, "Physique and Temperament of Women Delinquents Compared with Women Undergraduates," *British Journal of Medical Psychology* 25 (1952), pp. 249–255.

24. S. Glueck and E. T. Glueck, *Five Hundred Criminal Careers* (New York: Knopf, 1930).

25. Wilson and Herrnstein, *Crime and Human Nature,* p. 89.

26. Saleem A. Shah, Sarnoff A. Mednick, and C. R. Jeffery are some of the main proponents of sociobiology.

27. C. R. Jeffery, *Biology and Crime* (Beverly Hills, Calif.: Sage, 1970), pp. 16–17.

28. Wilson and Herrnstein, *Crime and Human Nature,* p. 91.

29. J. Lange, *Verbrechen als Schicksal [Crime as Destiny]* (Leipzig: Thieme, 1929 [London: Unwin, 1931]).

30. K. O. Christiansen, "A Preliminary Study of Criminality Among Twins," in *Biological Bases of Criminal Behavior,* ed. S. A. Mednick and K. O. Christiansen (New York: Wiley, 1977).

31. Ibid.

32. M. Bohman, C. R. Cloninger, S. Sigvardsson, and A.-L. von Knorring, "Predisposition to Petty Criminality in Swedish Adoptees: Genetic and Environmental Heterogeneity," *Archives of General Psychiatry* 39 (1982), pp. 1233–1241.

33. D. C. Rowe, "Biometrical Genetic Models of Self-Reported Delinquent Behavior: A Twin Study," *Behavior Genetics* 13 (1983), pp. 473–489. See also D. C. Rowe and D. W. Osgood, "Heredity and Sociological Theories of Delinquency: A Reconsideration," *American Sociological Review* 49 (1984), pp. 526–540.

34. R. J. Cadoret, C. A. Cain, and R. R. Crowe, "Evidence for Gene-Environment

Interaction in the Development of Adolescent Antisocial Behavior," *Behavior Genetics* 13 (1983), pp. 301–310.

35. P. A. Jacobs et al., "Aggressive Behaviour, Mental Subnormality, and the XYY Male," *Nature* 208 (1965), pp. 1351–1352; Jacobs et al., "Chromosome Surveys in Penal Institutions and Approved Schools," *Journal of Medical Genetics* 8 (1971), pp. 49–58.

36. Ibid.

37. H. A. Witkin et al., "XYY and XXY Men: Criminality and Aggression," *Science* 193 (1976), pp. 547–555.

38. H. H. Goddard, *Feeble-Mindedness, Its Causes and Consequences* (New York: Macmillan, 1914), pp. 6–10.

39. C. Murchison, *Criminal Intelligence* (Worcester, Mass.: Clark University, 1926).

40. E. H. Sutherland, "Mental Defiency and Crime," in *Social Attitudes,* ed. K. Young (New York: Holt, 1931).

41. D. J. West and D. P. Farrington, *Who Becomes Delinquent?* (London: Heinemann, 1973).

42. Lis Kirkegaard-Sorensen and Sarnoff A. Mednick, "A Prospective Study of Predictors of Criminality: Intelligence," in *Bisocial Basis of Criminal Behavior,* ed. Sarnoff A. Mednick and Karl O. Christiansen (New York: Gardner Press, 1977).

43. Robert A. Gordon, "Prevalence: The Rare Datum in Delinquency Measurement and Its Implications for the Theory of Delinquency," in *The Juvenile Justice System,* ed. Malcolm Klein (Beverly Hills, Calif.: Sage, 1976), pp. 201–284.

44. Robert A. Gordon, "IQ–Commensurability of Black–White Differences in Crime and Delinquency." Paper presented at the Annual Meeting of the American Psychological Association, Washington, D.C. (August 1986), p. 1.

45. Travis Hirschi and Michael Hindelang, "Intelligence and Delinquency: A Revisionist Review," *American Sociological Review* 42 (1977), pp. 471–486.

46. For a discussion of the limbic system and violence, see Harold Goldman, "The Limits of Clockwork: The Neurobiology of Violent Behavior," in *In Fear of Each Other,* ed. John P. Conrad and Simon Dinitz (Lexington Books: Heath, 1977), pp. 46–51.

47. Saleem A. Shah and Loren H. Roth, "Biological and Psychophysiological Factors in Criminality," in *Handbook of Criminology,* ed. Daniel Glaser (Chicago: Rand McNally, 1974), pp. 115–126.

48. Hans Eysenck, "The Technology of Consent," *New Scientist* 26 (June 1969), p. 689.

49. Hans Eysenck, *Fact and Fiction in Psychology* (Harmondsworth, England: Penguin, 1965), pp. 260–261.

50. Larry J. Siegel and Joseph J. Senna, *Juvenile Delinquency: Theory, Practice, and Law* (St. Paul, Minn.; West, 1981), p. 77.

51. William E. Thornton, Jr., Jennifer James, and William G. Doerner, *Delinquency and Justice* (Glenview, Ill.: Scott, Foresman, 1982), p. 83.

52. Sigmund Freud, *An Outline of Psychoanalysis* (reprint ed., New York: Norton, 1963).

53. Ibid.

54. William Healy, *Twenty-Five Years of Child Guidance, Studies from the Institute for Juvenile Research,* Series C, no. 256 (Illinois Department of Public Welfare, 1934), pp. 14–15.

55. August Aichhorn, *Wayward Youth* (New York: Viking Press, 1963).

56. Kate Friedlander, *The Psychoanalytic Approach to Juvenile Delinquency* (London: Routledge & Kegan Paul, 1947).

57. S. Glueck and E. T. Glueck, *Unraveling Juvenile Delinquency* (Cambridge, Mass.:

Harvard University Press, 1950); Glueck and Glueck, *Delinquents and Nondelinquents in Perspective* (Cambridge, Mass.: Harvard University Press, 1968).

58. J. J. Conger and W. C. Miller, *Personality, Social Class, and Delinquency* (New York: Wiley, 1966).

59. L. N. Robins, *Deviant Children Grown Up: A Sociological and Psychiatric Study of Sociopathic Personality* (Baltimore: Williams & Wilkins, 1966), p. 256.

60. L. N. Robins, G. Murphy, R. A. Woodruff, Jr., and L. J. King, "The Adult Psychiatric Status of Black Schoolboys," *Archives of General Psychiatry* 24 (1971), pp. 338–345.

61. S. R. Hathaway and J. C. McKinley, *Minnesota Multiphasic Personality Inventory* (Minneapolis: University of Minnesota Press, 1942); Hathaway and McKinley, *Minnesota Multiphasic Personality Inventory,* rev. ed. (New York: Psychological Corporation, 1951).

62. Ibid.

63. E. I. Megargee, "Estimation of CPI Scores from MMPI Protocols," *Journal of Clinical Psychology* 22 (1966), pp. 456–458.

64. E. I Megargee, P. R. Cook, and G. A. Mendelsohn, "Development and Validation of an MMPI Scale of Assaultiveness in Overcontrolled Individuals," *Journal of Abnormal Psychology* 16 (1967), pp. 22–27.

65. H. Cleckley, *The Mask of Sanity,* 4th ed. (St. Louis: Mosby, 1964), p. 406.

66. Ibid., p. 426.

67. Ibid.

68. Robins, *Deviant Children Grown Up.*

69. H. C. Quay and W. A. Hunt, "Psychopathy, Neuroticism, and Verbal Conditioning: A Replication and Extension," *Journal of Consulting Psychology* 29 (1965); and R. D. Hare, "Psychopathy, Autonomic Functioning, and the Orienting Response," *Journal of Abnormal Psychology* 73, suppl. (1968), pp. 1–24.

70. W. M. Waid, M. T. Orne, and S. K. Wilson, "Socialization, Awareness, and Electrodermal Response to Deception and Self-Disclosure," *Journal of Abnormal Psychology* 88 (1979), pp. 663–666.

71. Cleckley, *Mask of Sanity,* p. 363.

72. Wilson and Herrnstein, *Crime and Human Nature,* 203.

73. Ibid., p. 204.

74. B. Karpman, "On the Need for Separating Psychopathy into Two Distinct Types: The Symptomatic and the Idiopathic," *Journal of Criminal Psychopathology* 3 (1941), pp. 112–137.

75. Fritz Redl and David Wineman, *Children Who Hate* (Glencoe, Ill.: Free Press, 1951).

76. Lewis Yablonsky, *The Violent Gang* (New York: Macmillan, 1962).

77. Larry J. Siegel, *Criminology,* 2d ed. (St. Paul, Minn.: West, 1986), p. 165.

78. Robert L. Kidder, *Connecting Law and Society: An Introduction to Research and Theory* (Englewood Cliffs, N.J.: Prentice-Hall, 1983), pp. 247–248.

79. Jean Piaget, *The Moral Judgement of the Child* (London: Kegan Paul, 1932).

80. Lawrence Kohlberg, *Stages in the Development of Moral Thought and Action* (New York: Holt, Rinehart & Winston, 1969).

81. Ibid.

82. L. Kohlberg, K. Kauffman, Peter Scharf, and J. Hickley, *The Just Community Approach to Corrections: A Manual* (Niantic, Conn.: Connecticut Department of Corrections, 1973).

83. Ibid.

84. K. F. Schuessler and D. F. Cressey, "Personality Characteristics of Criminals," *American Journal of Sociology* 55 (1950), pp. 476–484.

85. G. P. Waldo and S. Dinitz, "Personality Attributes of the Criminal: An Analysis of Research Studies, 1950–1965," *Journal of Research in Crime and Delinquency* 4 (1967), pp. 185–202.

86. D. J. Tennenbaum, "Personality and Criminality: A Summary and Implications of the Literature," *Journal of Criminal Justice* 5 (1977), pp. 225–235.

87. Richard L. Jenkins, "Delinquency and a Treatment Philosophy," in *Crime, Law and Corrections,* ed. Ralph Slovenko (Springfield, Ill.: Thomas, 1966), pp. 135–136.

88. Wilson and Herrnstein, *Crime and Human Nature.*

89. Ibid., p. 49.

90. Ibid., p. 52.

91. Ibid., p. 56.

92. Ibid., p. 59.

93. Ibid., p. 490.

94. Ibid., pp. 490–491.

95. Edgar Z. Friedenberg, "Solving Crime," *Readings: A Journal of Reviews* (March 1986), p. 21.

96. This discussion on the medicalization of deviance and crime is adapted from Peter Conrad and Joseph W. Schneider, *Deviance and Medicalization: From Badness to Sickness* (St. Louis: Mosby, 1980), pp. 25–29.

97. Ibid., p. 32.

98. N. Kittrie, *The Right to be Different: Deviance and Enforced Therapy* (Baltimore: Johns Hopkins University Press, 1971).

99. Philip Rieff, *Triumph of the Therapeutic* (New York: Harper & Row, 1966).

100. Conrad and Schneider, *Deviance and Medicalization*, p. 28.

101. Ibid., p. 275.

102. Goldman, "The Limits of Clockwork," p. 44.

103. Ibid.

104. Ibid., p. 43.

105. Ibid.

106. Wilson and Herrnstein, *Crime and Human Nature.*

107. William Gaylin, *The Killing of Bonnie Garland: A Question of Justice* (New York: Simon and Schuster, 1982), p. 253.

108. Ibid., p. 341.

109. See Valerie P. Hans, "An Analysis of Public Attitudes Towards the Insanity Defense," *Criminology* 24 (1986), pp. 393–411.

CHAPTER 6

Sociological Positivism: Structural Causes

CULTURAL DEVIANCE THEORIES

Clifford R. Shaw and Henry D. McKay

Social Disorganization and Crime and Delinquency

Opportunity Structure and Delinquency

Evaluation of Shaw and McKay's Cultural Deviance Theory

Lower-Class Culture and Delinquent Values

Focal Concerns of Lower-Class Culture

Membership in One-Sex Peer Groups

Evaluation of Miller's Thesis of Lower-Class Culture

Violence and Lower-Class Culture

Evaluation of the Violent Subculture Thesis

STRAIN THEORY

Robert K. Merton and the Theory of Anomie

Conformity

Innovation

Ritualism

Retreatism

Rebellion

Evaluation of Merton's Theory of Anomie

Albert K. Cohen and the Theory of Delinquent Subculture

The Delinquent Subculture

Evaluation of Cohen's Theory of the Delinquent Subculture

Richard A. Cloward and Lloyd E. Ohlin and Opportunity Theory

The Criminal Subculture

The Conflict Subculture

The Retreatist Subculture

Evaluation of Cloward and Ohlin's Opportunity Theory

THEORIES OF UPPER-WORLD CRIME AND DELINQUENCY

Subculture Theories

Socialization Theories

Strain Theories

ANALYSIS

Disorder of Economic Inequality

Disorder of the Breakdown of Social Rules

Disorder of Hard-Core Lower-Class "Losers"

POLICY IMPLICATIONS

SUMMARY

REFERENCES

NOTES

KEY TERMS

Chicago Area Projects

cultural deviance theories

economic inequality

focal concerns of lower-class culture

lower-class "losers"

modes of adaptation

opportunity theory

social disorganization

social structure theories

status frustration

strain theory

subculture of violence

In the neighborhood I lived in, we didn't have what other kids had in neighborhoods a mile or so away. We used to intermingle at a playground. The other kids would have bicycles, ballbats, balls, and gloves, and we didn't have any of that. We wanted the same things they had. And so we started stealing. Progressively, we got involved in bigger and bigger things. Before I knew it, I had the cops looking for me for burglary, armed robbery, boosting drugs, and "hanging paper" [writing bad checks]. It was not long before I hit the "Pen."

—Former San Quentin inmate[1]

Sociological explanations for criminal behavior are examined in this chapter and the following one. **Social structure theories**, which are evaluated in this chapter, are based on the assumption that the basic flaw of explanations related to the individual is that such interpretations fail to come to grips with the underlying social and cultural conditions giving rise to delinquent and criminal behavior. Social structure theorists contend that there are several sources of social disorder in American society that predispose individuals to become involved in lives of crime. These sources include the antisocial cultural groups that are composed of alienated lower-class individuals, the social disorganization of communities that arises from urban decay, the impoverished conditions and continuous struggles for survival that face lower-class persons, and the status frustration that springs from the inability to attain middle-class goals.

CULTURAL DEVIANCE THEORIES

Cultural deviance theories view criminal and delinquent behavior as conformity to cultural values and norms that are in opposition to those of the larger American society. The cultural deviance theories of Clifford R. Shaw and Henry D. McKay, Walter B. Miller, and Marvin Wolfgang and Franco Ferracuti are examined in this section.

Clifford R. Shaw and Henry D. McKay

In a writing career that spanned more than three decades, Clifford R. Shaw and Henry D. McKay began with an examination of the relationship between social

BOX 6.1   **THE BACKGROUNDS OF SHAW AND McKAY**

Clifford R. Shaw and Henry D. McKay were two farm boys who came to Chicago in the 1920s to undertake graduate work in sociology at the University of Chicago. Both were born and brought up in rural areas of the Midwest. Shaw was from an Indiana crossroads that barely constituted a town, while McKay was from the prairie regions of South Dakota. Following graduate school, Shaw and McKay worked together for 30 years as a research team at the Institute for Juvenile Research, near the Chicago Loop.

The social origins of the two men were quite similar, but their personalities were strikingly different. McKay was the quiet statistician who plotted the maps, calculated the rates, ran the correlations, and described the findings that located the distribution of crime and delinquency in Chicago. Shaw was an activist who interviewed delinquents and got their life stories; he was also an organizer who created a community reform movement. McKay was a scholar, an academic who was out to prove his position with empirical evidence. Shaw was the practitioner—a professional administrator and an organizer—who was out to make his case through action and participation.

Shaw tells how the ordered community from which he came influenced his involvement in the Chicago Area Projects, which he and McKay founded in 1932:

Many of my ideas about delinquency seem to spring from the situation in which I found myself as I grew up. I grew up in the county in what was, in the real sense of the word, a community. In this situation, people were brought together by certain ties of long acquaintance and friendship, by certain common beliefs and interests. There was something under the surface which made it possible for them to rise to meet a crisis or disaster when the occasion arose. If there was an illness or death or someone's home burned, there was a reaction among all the people of the community.

Source: Jon Snodgrass, "Clifford R. Shaw and Henry D. McKay: Chicago Criminologists," *British Journal of Criminology* 16 (January 1976), pp. 1–19. The quote of Shaw was taken from "From the Inside Out: Self-Help in Social Welfare," General Session, Illinois Federation of Community Committees, *Twentieth Annual Conference on Youth and Community Service* (State of Illinois, Dept. of Public Welfare, 1951), pp. 69–70.

disorganization and delinquency and then investigated the relationships between opportunity structure and delinquency and between cultural transmission theory and delinquency. The research of Shaw and McKay contains the seeds of nearly all of the major schools of sociological criminology and delinquency.[2]

Social Disorganization and Crime and Delinquency   Shaw and McKay were exposed to the **social disorganization** approach while they were students at the

Migration to the city: social disorganization in action. (*Source:* Library of Congress [LC-USF33-2927-M2].)

University of Chicago. This approach, which dominated sociological explanations of crime from the 1920s through the 1940s, emphasized the importance of social rules in maintaining social organization. When such means of social change as immigration, rural-urban migration, and high mobility accompanied the development of an urbanized and industrialized society, social conditions began to be characterized by anonymity, impersonality, and new laws and traditions. People no longer behaved in traditionally expected ways, and the rules of society could no longer maintain the smooth functioning and interrelationships of social institutions. In such a context, crime and other forms of deviance became alternative methods of adjusting to the environment.[3]

Shaw and McKay found that adult criminality and juvenile delinquency resulted from the breakdown of social controls among traditional primary groups, such as the family and the neighborhood. Their studies, which supported the social disorganization approach, revealed that high delinquency areas were disorganized communities characterized by physically deteriorated and condemned buildings, economic dependence, population mobility, heterogeneous populations, and high rates of school truancy, infant mortality, and tuberculosis.

Shaw and McKay turned to ecology to explain the relationship between social disorganization and delinquency. Robert Park and Ernest Burgess had earlier used the concept of ecology in explaining the growth of cities. Burgess, for example, suggested that cities do not merely grow at their edges, but rather have a tendency to expand radially from their centers in patterns of concentric circles,

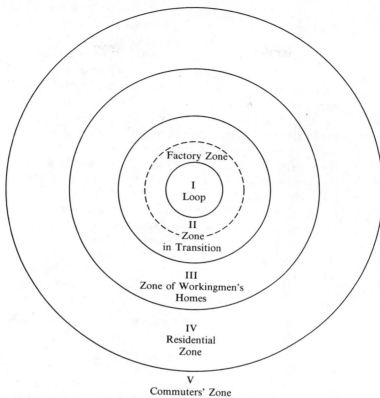

Figure 6.1 The Growth of the City. *Source:* Ernest W. Burgess, "The Growth of the City," in *The City,* ed. Robert E. Park, Ernest W. Burgess, and Roderick D. McKenzie (Chicago: University of Chicago Press, 1928), p. 51.

each moving gradually outward.[4] Figure 6.1 is a diagram of the growth zones as Burgess envisioned them.

In 1929, Shaw reported that there were variations in rates of school truancy, juvenile delinquency, and adult criminality in the different areas in Chicago. The high delinquency areas tended to have the correlates of disorganized communities. These rates varied inversely with the distance from the center of the city; that is, the closer a given locality was to the center of the city, the higher its rates of delinquency and crime. Shaw also reported that areas of concentrated crime maintained their high rates for long periods, even when the composition, or ethnic background, of the population changed markedly.[5]

In 1942, Shaw and McKay published their classic work *Juvenile Delinquency in Urban Areas,* in which they further developed these ecological insights. In studying males brought into the Cook County Juvenile Court on delinquency charges in the periods from 1900 to 1906, 1917 to 1923, and 1927 to 1933, they discovered that the vast majority of delinquent boys came from either an area adjacent to the central business and industrial areas or a community along two forks of the Chicago River.[6]

Then, applying Burgess's concentric zone hypothesis of urban growth, Shaw and McKay also constructed a series of concentric circles, like those on a target, with the bull's-eye in the central city.[7] Measuring delinquency rates by zone and by smaller areas within the zones, they found that in all three time periods studied the highest rates of delinquency were in Zone I (the central city), the next highest in Zone II (next to the central city), and so forth, in progressive steps outward to the lowest rate in Zone V.[8]

Significantly, Shaw and McKay found that although the delinquency rates changed from one time period to the next, the relationship among the different zones remained constant, although the ethnic compositions of some neighborhoods experienced a marked change. For example, during the first decade of the century, the largest portion of the population was German or Irish; 30 years later, it was Polish and Italian. Shaw and McKay concluded that delinquent behavior had become an alternative mode of socialization through which youths were attracted to deviant lifestyles. Delinquent values and traditions, which had replaced traditional ones, were passed on from one generation to the next. Thus, cultural transmission theory, as Shaw and McKay proposed, states that bad environments and the cultural values and groups resulting from these environments will cause individuals to pursue delinquent and criminal behavior.[9]

Opportunity Structure and Delinquency   Shaw and McKay eventually moved their focus of analysis of deliquency rates from the influence of social disorganization in the community to the importance of economics. They contended that the economic and occupational structure of the larger society was actually more influential in the rise of delinquent behavior than was the social life of the local community. They also argued that the reason that members of lower-class groups remained in the inner-city community was less a reflection of their recent arrival and their lack of acculturation than it was a function of their class position in American society.[10]

The existence of a differential opportunity structure, according to Shaw and McKay, led to a conflict of values in local communities, as some residents embraced illegitimate values while others maintained allegiance to conventional ones. Delinquent groups were characterized by their own distinctive standards, and Shaw and McKay became increasingly involved in examining the process through which delinquents came to learn and to pass on these standards.[11]

Shaw and McKay summarized the relationship between ecology, social disorganization, opportunity structure, and cultural transmission theories thusly:

1. Delinquency rates vary widely throughout the city. The probability of adolescents becoming delinquent and getting arrested and later incarcerated depends on their living in one of these high-rate areas.
2. Delinquency is a product of the socialization mechanisms existing within a neighborhood. Unstable neighborhoods have the greatest chance of producing delinquents.
3. High delinquency rates indicate the breakdown of social institutions and of the ability of society to care for and control its citizens.

4. Delinquency is not the property of any one ethnic or racial group. Members of any racial or ethnic group wil be delinquent if they live in the high-rate areas. Their crime rate will be reduced once they leave these areas.
5. Delinquency rates correlate highly with economic and social conditions such as poverty, poor health, and deteriorated housing.
6. Areas disrupted and in transition are the most likely to produce delinquency. After the transtion has ended, a drop in the delinquency rate occurs.
7. Since the community is the major source of delinquency, it is evident that control of delinquency should be commmunity-based.[12]

Evaluation of Shaw and McKay's Cultural Deviance Theory Shaw and McKay's studies have been so influential in the development of criminological theory because their work addressed the problem of crime in terms of multiple levels of analysis. They shifted attention away from individual characteristics of delinquents and nondelinquents to group traditions in delinquency and to the influence of the larger community. Thus, Shaw and McKay's analysis provides a theoretical framework bridging sociological and social psychological explanations.[13]

The fact that Shaw and McKay's model incorporated specific images of the delinquent in each stage of development permitted such bridging. They viewed delinquents as disaffiliated in the social disorganization stage, for delinquents were part of disorganized communities and, as such, were alienated from the values and norms of the larger society. In the functionalist stage, delinquents were viewed as "frustrated social climbers," primarily because they were poor and longed for the cultural goals that could be achieved only through illegitimate means. The third, or interactionist, stage viewed delinquents as "aggrieved citizens." Delinquents were faced with cultural groups in their own communities that provided social acceptance but also involved them in socially unacceptable behavior. Thus, to gain acceptance among peers meant rejection by the larger society and punishment from its social control agencies.[14]

A second reason for their enduring influence is that Shaw and McKay founded the **Chicago Area Projects**, one of the most significant attempts to develop community organization within local communities. Shaw, especially, was concerned with enabling lower-class youngsters to learn to deal with their own problems and to do a better job of running their own lives. He was able to persuade former delinquents and troublemakers to become involved as leaders of neighborhood groups, at first throughout Chicago and eventually throughout the state of Illinois.[15]

Third, Shaw and McKay contributed important insights on the formation of youth gangs. They regarded the delinquent gang as an expected outgrowth of the slum conditions and the social deprivations of the local environments. As part of the Chicago tradition, Shaw and McKay contributed to the development of research on gang structure, leadership, and cohesiveness. In the 1950s and 1960s, important studies that built on Shaw and McKay's insights were carried out in such urban areas as Boston, Chicago, Los Angeles, and New York.

Finally, Shaw collected hundreds of autobiographical statements from delinquents throughout his career. These statements, many of which were published, revealed the delinquents' world view and the struggles they experienced as they dealt with the deprivations of poverty and disorganized communities.

However, critics have criticized Shaw and McKay's contention that youngsters growing up in slum neighborhoods are bound to become delinquents. First, they charge that even in the neighborhoods with the highest rates of delinquency, a large percentage of young people do not turn to delinquent careers. Second, although Shaw and McKay's studies suggest that higher economic class protects adolescents from delinquency, critics point out that recent self-report studies have clearly shown that delinquent behavior is spread throughout the social classes. Critics also observe that Shaw and McKay's analysis of delinquent behavior was based upon official statistics, which distort the picture of delinquent behavior. Third, if social disorganization always leads to some degree of personal disorganization, how could such personally disorganized individuals be capable of forming gangs with a high degree of organization?[16]

Fourth, the Chicago Area Projects has been criticized because it fails to attack the political and economic sources of power. Saul Alinsky, a street worker for the Area Projects, broke with the organization because he felt that confrontational tactics were the only viable means of effecting change in disorganized communities.[17] Jon Snodgrass challenged the effectiveness of the Area Projects because it neglected the realities of Chicago politics and economics; that is, he felt that it was essentially a conservative response to the radical changes needed in disorganized communities.[18]

Yet even critics are forced to concede that Shaw and McKay have had an enduring impact on the study of crime and delinquency in the United States.

Lower-Class Culture and Delinquent Values

Walter B. Miller, in his variation of cultural deviance theory, contends that the lower class has its own cultural history and that the motivation to become involved in criminal activities is intrinsic to lower-class culture. That is,

> . . . the cultural system which exerts the most direct influence on [delinquent] behavior is that of the lower-class community itself—a long-established, distinctively patterned tradition with an integrity of its own—rather than a so-called "delinquent subculture" which has arisen through conflict with middle-class culture and is oriented to the deliberate violation of middle-class norms.[19]

Focal Concerns of Lower-Class Culture   Miller argues that the lower-class culture is characterized by a set of **focal concerns**, or values, that command widespread attention and a high degree of emotional involvement. The focal concerns are trouble, toughness, smartness, excitement, fate, and autonomy.[20]

Getting into and out of trouble, according to Miller, represents a major preoccupation of lower-class youth. The personal status of lower-class delinquent youth, including membership in adolescent gangs, is often determined by how much trouble they make. Physical prowess is also valued in lower-class culture. The tough guy who is hard, fearless, undemonstrative, and a good fighter is the ideal of many lower-class males. The value of smartness translates into the ability to outsmart, outfox, con, dupe, and "take" others. Smartness is also seen as necessary to achieve material goods and personal status without physical effort.

Miller sees these three qualities as combined in the search for excitement or "a thrill." He contends that this search has its origins in the extreme fluctuations that accompany the lower-class work cycle, with periods of exhausting and repetitive work interspersed with wild weekends "out on the town." The quest for excitement leads to the widespread use of alcohol by both sexes and to gambling of all kinds. It can also lead to the use of a deadly "Saturday Night Special" to resolve a dispute.

Lower-class individuals, according to Miller, feel that their lives are subject to a set of forces over which they have little control. They tend to believe that fate controls them and that there is little they can do to change it. This belief in fate, or the "big score," encourages the lower-class person to gamble—and to become involved in crime. Finally, the desire for autonomy, or personal independence, is an important concern in lower-class culture, primarily because the lower-class individual feels controlled so much of the time. The lack of control characteristic of lower-class life leads to a desire for freedom from external constraint and authority. But Miller also suggests that such assertions as "No one's gonna push me around" may sometimes represent a call for restraint, for being controlled also may be interpreted as "being cared for." Table 6.1 provides a comparison of the alternatives represented by these focal concerns.

Membership in One-Sex Peer Groups Miller claims that the one-sex peer group is a significant structural form in the lower-class community. The males-only

Table 6.1 FOCAL CONCERNS OF LOWER-CLASS CULTURE

Area	Perceived Alternatives (state, quality, condition)	
1. Trouble	law-abiding behavior	law-violating behavior
2. Toughness	physical prowess, skill; "masculinity"; fearlessness, bravery, daring	weakness, ineptitude; effeminacy; timidity, cowardice, caution
3. Smartness	ability to outsmart, dupe, "con," gain money by one's "wits"; shrewdness, adroitness of repartee	gullibility, "con-ability"; slowness, dull-wittedness; gaining money only by hard work; verbal maladroitness
4. Excitement	thrill; risk, danger, change, activity	boredom; "deadness," safeness; sameness, passivity
5. Fate	favored by fortune	being ill-omened, being "unlucky"
6. Autonomy	freedom from external constraint; freedom from superordinate authority; independence	presence of external constraint; presence of strong authority; dependency, being "cared for"

Source: Walter B. Miller, "Lower-Class Culture as a Generating Milieu of Gang Delinquency," *Journal of Social Issues* 14 (1958), p. 12.

group is a reaction to female-dominated homes, where the male parent is absent from the household, present only occasionally, or only minimally involved in the support and rearing of children. The male-oriented peer group represents the first real opportunity for lower-class boys to learn the essential aspects of the male role, in the company of others facing the same problems of sex-role identification. Delinquent behavior is seen as the lower-class boy's attempt to prove that he is grown up and no longer tied to his mother's apron strings.[21]

In sum, Miller argues that the lower class has a distinctive culture and set of values. On the one hand, law-abiding behavior is valued, but, on the other hand, most of the focal concerns are likely to lead lower-class youth to delinquent behavior. Lower-class individuals want to demonstrate that they are tough and able to outwit the cops. Yet the lower class is protected by the fatalistic belief that if one is going to get caught, nothing can be done about it. Crime also allows the lower-class individual to show personal independence from the controls placed upon him or her.

Evaluation of Miller's Thesis of Lower-Class Culture   Miller's theory of lower-class values appears to be most plausible when applied to the behavior of lower-class delinquent gangs, especially those of the 1950s and the 1980s. However, Miller's contention that the lower class has distinctive values has come under wide criticism. Some critics argue that the lower class holds to the same values as the larger culture. For example, Albert K. Cohen and Richard A. Cloward and Lloyd E. Ohlin, discussed later in this chapter, claim that lower-class youths have internalized middle-class values and that their delinquent acts are actually a consequence of their desire to achieve middle-class goals.[22]

Violence and Lower-Class Culture

Marvin Wolfgang and Franco Ferracuti's *The Subculture of Violence* argues that there is a **subculture of violence** among young males in the lower classes that legitimizes the use of violence in various social situations.[23] The origins of their theory date from Wolfgang's early research on homicide and the differences in the rate of homicide found among ethnic groups in Philadelphia. Wolfgang found that nonwhite males who were 20 to 24 years of age had a rate of 54.6 homicides per 100,000 population, compared to only 3.8 for white males of the same ages.[24]

This subculture's norms, according to Wolfgang and Ferracuti, are separated from the larger societal value system. An ever-present theme of violence influences life styles, the socialization process, and interpersonal relationships. It is expected that violence will be used to solve social conflicts and dilemmas. Indeed, those who do not turn to violence, especially when they are threatened or insulted, will encounter rejection by the peer group.

The subculture of violence thrives where life is worth little and where violence is a common response to life's problems and frustrations. Wolfgang and Ferracuti compare the subcultural norms of violence to those that exist throughout a culture during periods of war.[25] They state that "Homicide . . . is often a situation not unlike that of confrontations in wartime combat, in which two individuals committed to the value of violence come together, and in which chance, prowess, or possession of a particular weapon dictates the identity of the slayer and the slain."[26]

Evaluation of the Violent Subculture Thesis Wolfgang and Ferracuti's subculture of violence thesis has two major sources of support. First, both official and unofficial statistics show that violence appears to be concentrated among young males between the ages of 15 and 30 who live in urban areas. Wolfgang and associates' two cohort studies found that violent crime was concentrated primarily among 6 or 7 percent of the young males in Philadelphia.[27] In this age range, death by violent means is a leading cause of death. The high rate of violence in urban areas is one of the reasons why the Centers for Disease Control now defines violence in a health context.

Second, the constantly erupting violence of prison settings can be explained by the fact that most inmates are lower-class males who carry with them subcultural values and attitudes that make violence an acceptable behavior. Inmates typically regard superior strength as a criterion of maleness, and their machismo orientation makes them retaliate quickly against any possible attack on their manhood. Those who fail to resort to physical combat are contemptible in their eyes. Most inmates prefer privately administered justice, taking punishment into their own hands. The survival lessons they have learned on the streets dictate that

Riot-torn Watts bears scars of violence. (*Source:* AP–Wide World Photos.)

they intimidate others, exploit the weak, and protect themselves. An inmate at San Quentin put it this way:

> Hey man, when anyone gets into your face, you'd better take care of business. You can't let nothing go by. I learned my lesson when I was in the Youth Authority, and by the time I got to prison, I knew I couldn't let nobody mess with me. If you do, they'll never let you alone, and you'll end up giving up your ass.[28]

However, the subculture of violence thesis has been criticized as a circular argument. Wolfgang and Ferracuti seem to be explaining violent behavior by pointing out the prevalence of this behavior. John Hagan notes that it is not that these statements are incorrect; rather, it is that they describe what is already known.[29] Gwynn Nettler further explains: "It is as though one were to say that 'People are murderous because they live violently,' or 'People like to fight because they are hostile.' "[30] The question has also been raised of whether this violence is indeed uniquely focused among lower-class males. Howard Erlanger's analysis of data collected for the President's Commission on the Causes and Prevention of Violence found an absence of major differences by race or class in approval of interpersonal violence.[31]

In sum, Wolfgang and Ferracuti are unquestionably correct in stating that violence is overrepresented among lower-class males, but violence has always been a characteristic of American society, extending far beyond lower-class culture.

STRAIN THEORY

Strain theorists regard crime/delinquency as a consequence of the frustration individuals feel when they are unable to achieve the goals they desire. Robert K. Merton, in a revision of Emile Durkheim's theory of anomie, first explained the relationship between **strain theory** and crime; Albert K. Cohen and Richard A. Cloward and Lloyd E. Ohlin later related strain theory to urban gang delinquency.

Robert K. Merton and the Theory of Anomie

Durkheim, in an analysis of suicide, concluded that anomie (normlessness) results from the inability of society to regulate the natural appetites of individuals.[32] Merton's reformulation of Durkheim's theory of anomie points out that many of the appetites of individuals are "culturally induced." He also argues that the social structure can limit the ability of certain groups to satisfy these appetites.[33] Merton states: "Socially deviant behavior is just as much a product of social structure as conformist behavior. . . . Our primary aim is to discover how social structure exerts a definite pressure upon certain persons in the society to engage in nonconforming rather than conforming behavior."[34]

Merton considers two elements of the social and cultural systems. The first is the set of "culturally defined goals, purposes, and interests held out as legitimate objectives for all or for diversely located members of the society." These cultural goals are those that people feel are worth striving for. Cultural goals vary from society to society, but Merton claims that the acquisition of wealth is the most prominent cultural goal in American society. Wealth is generally equated with personal value and worth and it confers a high degree of prestige and social status.[35]

A second important element is the set of norms that "defines, regulates, and controls the acceptable means of reaching out for these goals."[36] Society, according to Merton, specifies the approved norms, or institutionalized means, that individuals are expected to use in pursuing cultural goals. Thus, Merton suggests, a cultural goal may be attained by a variety of means, not all of which are sanctioned by the culture.[37] Merton contends that the two elements—cultural goals and institutionalized means—must be reasonably well integrated if a culture is to be stable and smooth running. When such integration is lacking, a state of normlessness, or anomie, exists. Merton adds that contemporary American culture seems to "approximate the polar type in which great emphasis upon certain success-goals occurs without equivalent emphasis upon institutional means."[38] Lower-class persons, according to Merton, are asked to orient their behavior toward the prospect of accumulating wealth, but, at the same time, are in large part denied the means of doing so legitimately. The conflict between the cultural emphasis and the social structure creates intense pressure for deviation.

The application of Merton's theory to the study of criminal behavior suggests that the drive to commit crime lies in culture rather than in human nature. Merton argues that the forces in American society driving individuals toward crime are stronger than those in other cultures because of the emphasis on accumulating wealth in our society. The forces restraining individuals from committing crimes are also cultural, he asserts, and these forces are related to the socially accepted institutionalized norms. Merton argues that the high level of crime in American society is a result of a cultural imbalance that arises when the cultural values driving the individual toward criminal behavior are stronger than the cultural forces restraining the individual from such behavior.[39]

Merton developed a typology of **modes of adaptation** to explain how deviant behavior is produced by the social structure. In Table 6.2, five types of individual

Table 6.2 **MERTON'S THEORY OF ANOMIE**

Modes of Adaptation	Cultural Goal	Institutional Means
1. Conformity	+	+
2. Innovation	+	−
3. Ritualism	−	+
4. Retreatism	−	−
5. Rebellion	±	±

Source: Reprinted with permission of The Free Press, a division of Macmillian, Inc., from *Social Theory and Social Structure* by Robert K. Merton. Copyright © 1949, 1957 by The Free Press, renewed 1977, 1985 by Robert K. Merton.

adaptation are listed: a plus (+) signifies acceptance, a minus (−) signifies rejection, and a plus-and-minus (±) signifies a rejection of the prevailing values and a substitution of new ones.

Conformity   The conforming individual accepts the cultural goals of society as well as the institutional means of attaining them; he or she works hard in legitimate ways to become a success. Merton states that conformity to the cultural goal of society, as well as to the institutional means of attaining it, is the most common adaptation in his means-ends analysis.

Innovation   This mode of adaptation is adopted by those individuals who accept the cultural goal but reject the institutional means of attaining it. Merton contends that innovation resulting in deviant behavior is especially likely to occur in a society that proposes success as a goal for all, but simultaneously withholds from a segment of the population the opportunity of attaining success.[40]

Ritualism   Some individuals have given up on attaining cultural goals, but they continue to abide by the acceptable means for attaining them. As Merton put it, ritualism is evidenced by those who are "seeking a private escape from the dangers and frustrations . . . inherent in the competition for major cultural goals by abandoning these goals and clinging all the more closely to the safe routines and institutional norms."[41] Law-abiding bureaucrats who have given up on being promoted and are putting in their time until retirement are prime examples of ritualists.

Retreatism   Some individuals reject both the cultural goals and the institutionalized means of attaining them. They, in effect, have retreated from society. The heroin addict exemplifies this mode of adaptation, for this individual is divorced from the cultural goal of society and breaks the law to obtain and use drugs.

Rebellion   This final mode of adaptation consists of rejecting one's culture and institutions and substituting a new set of values and institutions. The terrorist, for example, may become committed to establishing a new social order that has a "closer correspondence between merit, effort, and reward."[42]

Merton contends his theory of anomie "is designed to account for some, not all, forms of deviant behavior customarily described as criminal or delinquent."[43] Thus, rather than attempting to explain all the behaviors prohibited by criminal law, Merton focuses attention on the acute pressure (strain) resulting from the discrepancy between culturally induced goals and the opportunities inherent in the social structure.

Evaluation of Merton's Theory of Anomie   Merton's revision of anomie theory has been called "the most influential single formulation in the sociology of deviance in the last 25 years and . . . possibly the most frequently quoted single paper in modern sociology."[44] The importance of this theory is also seen in its influence on later theoretical contributions of Cohen and Cloward and Ohlin.

However, like all others, Merton's theory has been subjected to wide criticism. It is argued that his theory is not logically adequate because steps are missing in his typology. In retreatism, Merton rejects both cultural goals and institutional means, and in rebellion, he establishes new goals and new means; logical development, critics note, would suggest intervening steps between retreatism and rebellion. In one step, a new set of cultural goals would be established and the institutional means rejected; in another, the cultural goals would be rejected and a new set of institutional means substituted.

This classification scheme also falls short in pragmatic adequacy, a criterion that relates to the ability of a theory to offer a solution for the particular problems that initiated the research inquiry. Merton's theory, according to critics, merely describes the effect of anomie on a success-oriented culture, without explaining why and how such behavior occurs. Accordingly, Merton does not provide solutions to the problem of deviant behavior; nor does his typology contain suggestions for controlling deviant behavior.

Moreover, this theory lacks operational adequacy; i.e., the capability of being tested. Merton's typology describes behaviors typical of those found in society, but it has not been developed to the level of working hypotheses that can be tested. His theory is also faulted because it fails to explain why some of those who have achieved success do become involved in crime. Nor does it discuss the importance of interaction with peers, a crucial variable in both juvenile and adult crime. Nor do the psychological characteristics of offenders receive adequate consideration.

But Merton appears to be on solid ground in terms of empirical adequacy; i.e., the degree of agreement between theoretical claims and empirical evidence. The types of adaptations proposed in the typology are exemplified by the lives of individuals who walk the streets of every city in the United States. Conformists, innovators, and retreatists may be more plentiful, but rebels and ritualists are also easily found.

Albert K. Cohen and the Theory of Delinquent Subculture

Albert K. Cohen's thesis in *Delinquent Boys: The Culture of the Gang* is that lower-class youths seek the goals of middle-class society, but they experience **status frustration**, or strain, because they are unable to attain these goals. This strain results in their membership in delinquent gangs and their nonutilitarian, malicious, and negativistic behavior.[45]

The Delinquent Subculture The social structure of American society, according to Cohen, has an immense hold on citizens; even very young children know about the class system.[46] The class system defines the middle-class values and norms that children are expected to aspire to and to achieve:

> These norms are, in effect, a tempered version of the Protestant ethic which has played such an important part in the shaping of American character and American society. In brief summary, this middle-class ethic prescribes an obli-

gation to strive, by dint of rational, ascetic, self-disciplined, and independent activity, to achieve in worldly affairs. A not irrebuttable but common corollary is the presumption that "success" is itself a sign of the exercise of these moral qualities.[47]

Cohen sees American society as dominated by such middle-class values as ambition, individual responsibility, the cultivation and possession of skills, an ability to postpone gratification, rationality, personableness, control of physical aggression, and respect for property. But the working class, according to Cohen, is characterized by such attributes as a dependence on primary groups, spontaneity, emotional irrepressibility, a freer use of aggression, and the disvaluing of the appearance and personality attributes necessary to make it in middle-class society.[48]

The problem, Cohen says, arises for the working-class youth when he or she enters the public school, for status at school is measured by middle-class standards. First, the teacher is expected to foster the development of middle-class personalities. Second, the teacher is likely to be a middle-class person, who values ambition and achievement and quickly recognizes and rewards these virtues in others. Third, the educational system itself favors "quiet, cooperative, 'well-behaved' pupils" who make the teacher's job easier. The school greets with disapproval "lusty, irrepressible, boisterous youngsters who are destructive of order, routine, and predictability in the classroom."[49] The working-class youth is now assessed against a "middle-class measuring rod." Cohen observes:

> To win the favor of the people in charge he must change his habits, his values, his ambitions, his speech, and his associates. Even were these things possible, the game might not be worth the candle. So, having sampled what they have to offer, he returns to the street or to his "clubhouse" in a cellar where "facilities" are meager but human relations more satisfying.[50]

Cohen suggests that working-class youngsters are attracted to delinquent subcultures because they offer alternative criteria for status. The delinquent subculture thus performs its role by redefining the criteria of status so that disvalued attributes become instead status-conferring ones. Significantly, this redefinition is done with a vengeance.[51] Underclass values and norms are reshaped into "an explicit and wholesale repudiation of middle-class standards."[52] Thus, the delinquent subculture absorbs the norms of the larger society but turns them upside down. The delinquent's conduct is right by the standards of the subculture precisely because it is wrong by the norms of the larger culture.[53]

Cohen contends that the delinquent subculture is nonutilitarian because delinquents commit crimes "for the hell of it," without intending to gain or profit from their crimes. For example, a delinquent in a subculture may steal items that are often discarded, destroyed, or casually given away.[54] The delinquent subculture is also characterized by "short-run hedonism." It has little interest in planning activities, setting long-term goals, budgeting time, or gaining knowledge or skills that require practice, deliberation, and study.[55]

Another characteristic of the delinquent subculture is that it demonstrates versatility in its delinquent acts. That is, delinquents do not specialize in their offenses as do many adult criminal gangs and "solitary" delinquents.[56] Group autonomy is a further characteristic of the subculture. Members are resistant to attempts (other than the informal pressures of the gang itself) to regulate their behavior at home, at school, or in community activities.[57]

A pivotal assumption of Cohen's theory is that lower-class boys internalize middle-class norms and values and then are unable to attain middle-class goals. Status frustration occurs, and the mechanism of reaction-formation is used to handle it. This mechanism is expressed by the delinquent who claims that the middle-class standards do not matter, but directs irrational, malicious, unaccountable hostility toward the norms of respectable middle-class society.[58] The delinquent subculture offers the lower-class boy the status he does not receive from the larger culture; yet, the status offered by the subculture is status only in the eyes of fellow delinquents. In short, according to Cohen, the same middle-class value system in the United States is instrumental in generating both respectability and delinquency.[59]

Evaluation of Cohen's Theory of the Delinquent Subculture   Cohen's theory has played an important role in the development of delinquent theory. James F. Short, Jr., and Fred L. Strodtbeck used it to design their study of youth gangs.[60] Cloward and Ohlin's subcultural theory of delinquent boys also profited from Cohen's work.[61]

In addition, Cohen's theory is important because it views deviance as a process of interaction between the delinquent youth and others, rather than the abrupt and sudden product of strain or anomie, as proposed by Merton's theory. Cohen contends that delinquency arises during a continuous interaction process whereby changes in the self result from the activities of others.[62]

However, a number of criticisms have been leveled at Cohen's theory. Travis Hirschi questions the validity of using status frustration as the motivational energy to account for delinquency, because most delinquent boys eventually become law-abiding, even though their lower-class status does not change. That is, since the delinquent's position in the economic structure is relatively fixed, his eventual reform cannot be attributed to any changes in the conditions that originally drove him into delinquency.[63]

David Matza challenges Cohen's sharp distinction between the delinquent and the nondelinquent.[64] David Greenberg argues that rather than engaging only in nonutilitarian, malicious, and negativistic behaviors, many delinquents are rational and commit crime for profit or gain.[65] Cohen's theory also ignores those individuals who commit delinquent acts alone. Finally, Cohen does not offer any empirical evidence to support his theory, and the vagueness of such concepts as reaction formation and lower-class internalization of middle-class values makes it difficult to test his theory.

Yet Cohen's *Delinquent Boys* did make a seminal contribution to the delinquency literature, and much of the delinquency research since the publication of his book has built on its findings.

Richard A. Cloward and Lloyd E. Ohlin and Opportunity Theory

Richard A. Cloward and Lloyd E. Ohlin sought to integrate the theoretical contributions of Merton and Cohen with the ideas of Edwin H. Sutherland. Although Merton argues that lower-class youths strive for monetary success and Cohen contends that they strive for status, Cloward and Ohlin conceptualize success and status as separate strivings that can operate independently of each other.[66] Cloward and Ohlin portray delinquent youngsters who seek an increase in status as striving for membership in the middle class, while other delinquent youths try to improve their economic position without changing their class position.[67]

Cloward and Ohlin propose four basic categories of delinquent youths (see Table 6.3). Disagreeing with Cohen's argument, they claim that boys of Type I and Type II, who are striving to increase their status and whose values are consistent with those of the middle-class, do not constitute the major group of delinquents. They also contend that Type IV youths, who may incur criticism from middle-class authorities for their "lack of ambition," usually avoid trouble with the law because they tend to avoid middle-class institutions and people as much as possible.[68]

Cloward and Ohlin argue that the most serious delinquents are of Type III, who are oriented toward conspicuous consumption. Type III youths experience the greatest conflict of the four groups with middle-class values, since they "are looked down upon both for what they do not want (i.e., the middle-class style of life) and for what they do want (i.e., 'crass materialism')."[69] Cloward and Ohlin refer to Merton's theory to explain the particular form of delinquency which Type III youths will commit. They assume that there are no legitimate opportunities available for these youths to improve their economic position and, therefore, they will become involved in one of three specialized gang subcultures: "criminal," "conflict," and "retreatist."[70]

The Criminal Subculture   The criminal subculture is primarily based upon criminal values. Such illegal acts as extortion, fraud, and theft are accepted as a means of achieving economic success. The criminal subculture provides the socialization by which new members learn to admire and respect older criminals and to adopt

Table 6.3   CLOWARD AND OHLIN'S CLASSIFICATION OF LOWER-CLASS YOUTH

Categories of Lower-Class Youth	Orientation of Lower-Class Youth	
	Toward Membership in Middle Class	Toward Improvement in Economic Position
Type I	+	+
Type II	+	−
Type III	−	+
Type IV	−	−

Source: Richard A. Cloward and Lloyd E. Ohlin, *Delinquency and Opportunity: A Theory of Delinquent Gangs* (New York: Free Press, 1960). Reprinted with permission of The Free Press, a division of Macmillan, Inc. Copyright © 1960 by The Free Press.

their life styles and behaviors. They master the techniques and orientations of the criminal world through criminal episodes. They become hostile and distrust representatives of the larger society, who are regarded as "suckers" and to be exploited whenever possible.[71]

The Conflict Subculture   Violence is the key ingredient in the conflict subculture, whose members pursue status, or "rep" through force or threats of force. The warrior youth gangs exemplify this subculture. The "bopper," the basic role model, fights with weapons to win respect from other gangs and to demand deference from the adult world. The role expectation of the bopper is to show great courage in the face of personal danger and always to defend his personal integrity and the honor of the gang.[72]

A reputation for toughness is the primary goal of fighting gangs. Such a "rep" ensures respect from peers and fear from adults, and it provides a means of gaining access to the scarce resources for pleasure and opportunity in underprivileged areas. Relationships with the adult world are weak because gang members are unable to find appropriate adult role models who offer a structure of opportunity leading to adult success.[73]

The Retreatist Subculture   The consumption of drugs is the basic activity of the retreatist subculture. Shut out from conventional roles in the family or occupational world, members of this subculture have withdrawn into an arena where the ultimate goal is the "kick." The "kick" may mean alcohol, marijuana, hard drugs, unusual sexual experiences, hot music, or any combination of these, but whatever

The youth gang: violence among lower-class youth. (*Source:* Tom Kelly.)

is chosen, the retreatist is seeking an intense awareness of living and a sense of pleasure that is "out of this world, man."[74]

The retreatist subculture generates a new order of goals and criteria of achievement. Instead of attempting to impose this system of values on the world of the "straights," however, the retreatist is content merely to strive for status and deference within his own subculture.[75]

Cloward and Ohlin note that while these subcultures exhibit essentially different orientations, the lines between them may become blurred. A subculture primarily involved with conflict may on occasion become involved in systematic theft; members of a criminal subculture may sometimes become involved in conflict with a rival gang.[76]

Evaluation of Cloward and Ohlin's Opportunity Theory   Cloward and Ohlin's **opportunity theory** is important because of the impact it has had on the development of public policy and criminological theory. Delbert S. Elliot and Harwin L. Voss, for example, used variables drawn from Cloward and Ohlin's study to design their influential study of school dropouts.[77] The establishment of such delinquency prevention programs as Mobilization for Youth in New York City was based on the premise that youths who do not have legitimate avenues to success will pursue illegitimate ones. The development of the 1960s War on Poverty welfare programs likewise was influenced by Cloward and Ohlin's thesis that lower-class individuals will pursue illegitimate opportunities if they are not provided legitimate ones.

However, the findings of several studies are in sharp disagreement with the assumptions of Cloward and Ohlin's opportunity theory. Gwynn Nettler has charged that the two key concepts in the theory are aspiration and opportunity and that neither term is defined very clearly.[78] A number of authors have failed to find evidence in gang delinquents of the particular kind of thought processes suggested by Cloward and Ohlin.[79] Ruth Kornhauser, in reviewing the empirical research on aspirations and expectations of delinquents, claims that it shows that delinquency is consistently associated with both low expectations and low aspirations; she suggests that delinquents may not expect to get much but they do not want much either. Thus, Kornhauser is challenging the strain aspect of opportunity theory.[80]

Cloward and Ohlin's theory has also been criticized because it portrays gang delinquents as talented youth who have a sense of injustice about the lack of legitimate opportunities available to them, a perspective in startling contrast to those studies that indicate that gang delinquents have limited social abilities.[81] Cloward and Ohlin's concept of the three types of gangs—criminal, conflict, and retreatist—is further challenged because of a lack of empirical adequacy. Studies simply have not found the existence of these three lower-class types of male gangs.[82]

On balance, however, Cloward and Ohlin's theory was designed to explain the behavior of seriously delinquent urban male gang members, and studies that focus on these youths have produced strong support of opportunity theory.[83]

THEORIES OF UPPER-WORLD CRIME AND DELINQUENCY

Theories of middle-class delinquency are usually an extension of the perspectives developed to explain lower-class delinquency. Subculture, strain, and socialization theories all have been modified to deal with the question of why middle-class youths commit crime.[84] Socialization and strain theories also can be used to explain upper-world criminality.

Subculture Theories

Subcultural theories of middle-class delinquency stress the importance of peer groups in the development of alternative values. In contrast to lower-class delinquent subcultures, which are presumed to have an inversion of middle-class morality, middle-class youth cultures are seen as determined by boredom rather than rage. Adolescents turn to peers in order to relieve restlessness and anxiety. The pursuit of pleasure is their basic concern, and clothing, cars, and precocious sexuality are used to give meaning to an otherwise empty existence. Delinquency provides a kick that is missing from the easy consumerism of daily life. The more that middle-class youth adopt these hedonistic values, the more they resemble lower-class youngsters and the more they increase their chances of engaging in delinquent behavior.[85]

Socialization Theories

Middle-class delinquency is sometimes seen as the product of lower-class youth who have only recently entered the middle class. Such youngsters were socialized in lower-class attitudes and values, and even when the families moved up to middle-class status, the children retained the values and outlook of the lower class.[86] Another popular socialization theory is that the changes in middle-class socialization patterns in the years following World War II have resulted in increased permissiveness. Parents no longer instill in their children such traditional middle-class values as self-control and deferred gratification, which can serve as barriers to delinquent behavior. Instead, an emphasis on individual development and indulgence has produced a generation that lives for the here and now and that demands immediate gratification of its needs. These new values are likened to those of the lower class and, therefore, are thought to lead to delinquency for many of the same reasons.[87]

Clinard and Yeager provide a fascinating discussion of how socialization processes contribute to the making of a corporate criminal. The socialization into corporate deviance begins with the company's recruiting of certain types of people who are willing to be team players. New employees are informed that the organization demands total allegiance and that they must pursue relentlessly the means of achieving profit and productivity.[88]

The ethic demanded in the corporate world, according to Clinard and Yeager, is the "ethic of the good soldier; take the order, do the job." As employees discover deviations from standard operating procedures and practices, they become aware that questioning these deviations may hinder their professional advancement. The outcomes desired at the higher levels require that employees question neither the ends nor the most efficient or quickest means of achieving them. Corporate executives, as well as lower-level employees, are socialized by the structure and nature of work and the status system to accept deviance as a necessary byproduct of organizational commitment. This socialization process leads to corporate deviance and, in large part, ensures that organizational deviance will escape detection.[89] Thus, the individual learns that crime is required as a natural byproduct of organizations' pursuit of profits and that the organization creates expectations of performance that may be met only by law violators.[90]

Strain Theories

Strain theories of middle-class delinquency focus on the similarities between middle-class and lower-class youths in dealing with the anxieties and frustrations of growing up in contemporary society. Many middle-class boys, like lower-class ones, grow up in female-dominated homes, and, therefore, they experience the need to prove their "manliness," which may lead them to engage in socially unacceptable behavior.[91] Another theory is that middle-class youngsters experience strain because of the difficulty of achieving meaningful increases in status over that of their parents. This status anxiety generates feelings of injustice that, in turn, can lead either to passive acquiescence or to angry retaliation in the form of delinquency.[92] Furthermore, middle-class youths further experience strain in dealing with the transition from childhood to adolescence. During this period, they are largely excluded from the labor market, yet the peer group culture places pressure on them to engage in a hedonistic social life. This pressure may lead to theft and burglary as a means of financing their pursuits of pleasure.

Strain theory can also be applied to corporate and white-collar criminals. The strain felt by corporate employees to attain organizational productivity and profits can influence them to pursue illegitimate means to attain their objectives, such as antitrust violations. In many companies, middle-level executives, especially, are constantly under stress to meet tough earnings targets. Says John Fleming, a professor at the University of Southern California Graduate School of Business Administration: "For middle managers, there is so much pressure to get a certain degree of performance that they sometimes feel they almost have to do something illegal to meet the goals set by upper management."[93]

In sum, theories about middle-class crime and delinquency commonly view middle-class individuals as caught in an affluent but largely meaningless lifestyle. The social forces operating upon them can also influence them to become involved in illegal behavior.

ANALYSIS

Cultural deviance and strain theories suggest that three disorders are directly related to crime—namely, the disorder of economic inequality, the disorder of the

"Oh, Harry! And all this time you said you had a job with ALCOA."
Drawing by Leonard Dove. © *1956 The New Yorker Magazine, Inc.*

breakdown of social rules, and the disorder of hard-core lower-class "losers." (See Table 6.4 for a summary of social structure theories.)

Disorder of Economic Inequality

Social structural explanations of crime ultimately rest on the importance of class as a significant variable. These theories suggest that an individual is more likely to become a criminal or delinquent because of **economic inequality**. Unquestionably, lower-class individuals do experience significantly greater disorder than do middle- and upper-class persons. This disorder is evident in their economic struggles for survival; in the fact that their children spend more time on the streets because of the squalor that sometimes exists at home; in their higher rates of neglect and physical abuse; in their higher rates of infant mortality, disease, and emotional illness; in their higher rates of spouse abuse; and in the deprived quality of the disorganized communities in which the poor live.

The logic of the social structural approach is very appealing. This approach takes an optimistic view of human nature. Criminals are driven to crime because

Table 6.4 SUMMARY OF SOCIAL STRUCTURE THEORIES OF CRIME

Theory	Cause of Crime Identified in the Theory	Supporting Research
Cultural Deviance Theories		
Shaw and McKay	Delinquent behavior becomes an alternative mode of socialization through which youths who are part of disorganized communities are attracted to delinquent values and traditions	Moderate
Miller	Lower-class culture has a distinctive culture of its own, and its focal concerns, or values, make lower-class boys more likely to become involved in delinquent behavior	Weak
Wolfgang and Ferracuti	Subculture of violence exists among lower-class males that legitimizes the use of violence	Moderate
Strain Theories		
Merton	Social structure exerts pressure upon those individuals who cannot attain the cultural goal of success to engage in nonconforming behavior	Weak
Cohen	Lower-class boys are unable to attain the goals of middle-class culture and, therefore, they become involved in nonutilitarian, malicious, and negativistic behavior	Weak
Opportunity Theory		
Cloward and Ohlin	Lower-class boys seek out illegitimate means to attain middle-class success goals if they are unable to attain them through legitimate means, usually through one of three specialized gang contexts	Moderate
Middle-class Theories		
Subculture	Adolescents become involved in a youth culture, and delinquency provides a kick that is missing from the easy consumerism of daily life	Moderate
Socialization	Lower-class youths move up to the middle class while retaining the values and behavior of the lower class	Weak
Strain	Middle-class juveniles, like lower-class ones, become involved in delinquent behavior because of the anxieties and frustrations of growing up	Weak

The disorder of economic inequality. (*Source:* Stephen Shames/Visions.)

they are poor; they would be law-abiding if only given a chance. The drive to commit crime is caused by the structure of American society and can not be blamed on the condition of human nature. Thus, crime is concentrated in the lower classes because of economic inequality and the other debilitating conditions that accompany economic inequality.

Two basic criticisms have been raised concerning this direct association between crime and economic inequality. First, this conclusion is challenged by the findings of various self-report studies that show that crime is distributed throughout the social strata. The recently reported findings on white-collar crime serve as a reminder of the fact that crime is found throughout the social classes. Charles Tittle and his associates, after examination of the relationship between crime and class, flatly declare that criminologists should abandon once and for all "the myth of social class and criminality," a myth these researchers attribute to "the tendency of sociologists, criminologists, and laymen to begin with the preconceived notion—the prejudice—that lower-class people are characterized by pejorative traits such as immorality, inferiority, and criminality."[94] Travis Hirschi and his colleagues announced in 1982 "the class issue is a diversion the field [of criminology] can no longer afford."[95]

In contrast, Delbert S. Elliott and David Huizinga's national sample found that class differences among males are evident in the prevalence and incidence of all serious offenses and in the incidence of nonserious and total offenses.[96] Robert Sampson and Thomas Castellano, using victim surveys, found that offense rates for both juveniles and adults were twice as high in low-income as in high-income neighborhoods.[97] John Braithwaite also found that research tends to support the existence of higher offense rates among lower-class juveniles. He concludes:

> The sociological study of crime does not need to "shift away from class-biased theories" as Tittle et al. [advocate]. What we require are class-based theories which explain why certain types of crime are perpetuated disproportionately by the powerless, while other forms of crime are exclusively the prerogative of the powerful.[98]

Robert Gillespie's survey of 57 studies shows considerable support for the existence of a relationship between unemployment and property crime.[99] Finally, Donald Clelland and Timothy Carter contend that arguments and research disputing the relationship between class and delinquency are neither theoretically nor methodologically sophisticated and that methodologically sophisticated studies would tend to find a relationship between social class and delinquency.[100] Thus, most recent evidence is supportive of a relationship between economic inequality and crime.

Second, the association between crime and economic inequality is attacked on the basis of the argument that economic prosperity causes crime. That is, crime tends to go down during a depression and to rise during the "good times." For example, declining rates of crime accompanied the Great Depression of the 1930s, and crime rates skyrocketed during the "good times" of the 1960s and the 1970s.

The evidence suggests that affluent times may have different effects on property and violent crimes. Studies generally support the finding that property crimes increase with affluence. Thus, when there is more to steal, more will be stolen or, other things being equal, increased opportunity will outstrip the declining need for theft. But the evidence strongly supports the conclusion that violent crime ordinarily goes down as societies become more prosperous.[101] Elliott Currie explains this relationship between economic inequality and criminal violence:

> . . . the fact that economic inequality and criminal violence are closely and predictably linked raises a far deeper and, I think, perhaps more compelling point than the courts and the police may treat poor people differently from others. It reminds us that harsh inequality is not only morally unjust but also enormously destructive of human personality and social order. Brutal conditions breed brutal despair. To believe otherwise requires us to argue that the experience of being confined to the mean and precarious depths of the American economy has *no* serious consequences for personal character or social behavior. But this not only misreads the evidence; it also trivializes the genuine social disaster wrought by the extremes of economic inequality we have tolerated in the United States.[102]

In sum, it may be that it is the poorest of the poor who are influenced by the variable of class, or economic inequality, to engage in criminal behavior. This population, as an abundance of research has documented, has become more involved in violent crime and is more likely to commit serious property crimes.

Indeed, within this underclass of the underclass, a small percentage tends to commit a large proportion of the violent and serious property crimes of most communities. The disorder of these individuals' lives is greater than the disorder of the working poor above them; they may feel that crime is the only viable option they have.

Disorder of the Breakdown of Social Rules

The social disorganization perspective focuses on the problems faced by groups, small geographic areas, and even whole societies when the rules guiding social behavior break down or are disturbed. Social organization demands the smooth functioning and interrelationships of social institutions, and social disorganization occurs when social rules can no longer maintain these conditions. Social relations are disrupted when societal conditions change and people no longer behave in traditionally expected ways.[103]

The social disorganization perspective presumes that at some point in the past, society was fairly stable as people accepted the rules and played their roles in an expected manner. Social institutions, such as the family and the schools, were able to satisfy both individual needs and societal requirements. Social disorganization theorists use examples of simple, rural, agrarian folk societies in Quebec, in Mexico, and in the Ozarks in the United States as models of social organization. These simple and smoothly functioning societies were characterized by well-regulated patterns of life, few ambiguities, and few opportunities for personal choice. The homogeneous populations of such communities were also guided by traditions and folk knowledge, strong kinship relations, and teamwork and high morale, with little emphasis on formal institutions and government.[104]

The social disorganization perspective thus was basically motivated by the need to answer the question of how a decent world could be created. It contends that the acceptance of social rules and smoothly functioning social institutions are key components in a stable society. But industrialized and urbanized modern societies have almost completely opposite characteristics from those identified with folk societies. The disruptive social changes in contemporary societies, especially in urban areas, have resulted in the "right" conditions for social organization to break down.

Social disorganization takes place when individuals with a way of life appropriate to a provincial social setting move to the cities. They experience intense disruption in their transition from a rural, stable, homogeneous folk society to an urban society characterized by anonymity, impersonality, and different laws and traditions. As the old rules no longer seem to apply and as these individuals have not yet internalized the new rules, crime and other forms of deviance become alternative methods of adjusting to the new environment.

In sum, the disorganized societies of urban areas appear to be breeding grounds for crime and other forms of deviance. The rules concerning family life are different. The support of extended family or kinship relations has largely dissipated. The schools, for other than the few who are both motivated and able to achieve, tend to be alienating experiences. The community, rather than being a positive force of social control, provides alluring opportunities for crime and deviant behavior.

Disorder of Hard-Core Lower-Class "Losers"

Most industrial societies, including the United States, produce a sizable group of **lower-class "losers."** These individuals have inadequate coping skills and live on the margins of society. They do not have the wherewithal to pull their own weight and are the perennial misfits of society. Indeed, these frustrated individuals have few resources. They typically are illiterate and have poor employment histories and chronic illnesses. Moreover, they are likely to be addicted to drugs and/or alcohol. The opportunity structure is not available to them because they simply are not competitive. Thus, they have no real stake in the system.

Society's response is to shunt such individuals aside, to give up on these troublesome "losers." Institutionalization, including prison, holds no terror for these individuals. They are unreceptive to traditional means of resocialization or rehabilitation. Sometimes they are merely a menace to the social order; homeless and detached, they are found on the streets of most urban areas. They also are disproportionately represented among mental patients. But at other times, they pose a real danger to society. As juveniles, these hard-core losers commit a large proportion of the serious violent and property offenses of urban areas. As adults,

The lower-class "loser." (*Source:* Michael O'Brien/Archive Pictures, Inc.)

they tend to pursue crime until they die at an early age or "burn out" after many years in prison.

These hard-core criminals have been called unsocialized delinquents, psychopaths, sociopaths, habitual criminals, repeat criminals, professional criminals, or violent, recidivist, career offenders. Researchers at the Rand Corporation; Alfred Blumstein and Judith Cohen; and others have documented their extensive criminal activities.[105] The media constantly inform the public of the vile, vicious, and violent acts they commit.

There is no doubt that hard-core criminals are destroying the quality of life and are disrupting urban communities. The most widely accepted criminal justice solution today is to remove such people from society. In many jurisdictions, prosecutors have special programs to handle the hard-core offenders. Across the nation, preventive detention laws are being passed to keep such criminals in jail during the pretrial stage. Mandatory and determinate sentencing acts are designed to keep them in prisons for prolonged periods. More recently, selective incapacitation has been proposed as a means of preventing these individuals from remaining on the streets for long periods of time.

POLICY IMPLICATIONS

Social structural theorists inform policymakers that the quality of American life—and the crime rate—will not improve until structural changes are made in the wider society. Elliott Currie contends that the "ideal" model of a violent society resembles some of the developing countries of the Third World—Brazil, the Philippines, parts of Mexico—and it also looks uncomfortably like the United States.[106]

Structural changes are needed in two basic areas to alter the course the United States is presently taking. First, greatly expanded public and private support are needed for the following measures:

- Intensive job training, perhaps modeled along the lines of supported work, designed to prepare the young and the displaced for stable careers.
- Strong support for equity in pay and conditions, aimed at upgrading the quality of low-paying jobs.
- Substantial, *permanent* public or public-private job creation in local communities, at wages sufficient to support a family breadwinner, especially in areas of clear and pressing social need like public safety, rehabilitation, child care, and family support.
- Universal—and generous—income support for families headed by individuals outside the paid labor force.[107]

Inherent in these recommendations is a strong belief in the viewpoint that every individual must be guaranteed an adequate standard of living. If American society is serious about the goal of crime reduction, then such generous and humane supports as unemployment insurance and income-maintenance benefits must be more widely used to guard against the criminogenic effects of joblessness.

Second, the social structural analysis in this chapter suggests that the answer does not rest with eliminating the group of hard-core losers or keeping them in prison, because the unhealthy conditions of lower-class life will continually replenish the supply of hard-core criminals. Instead, the solution lies in the removal of the conditions that give rise to such unsocialized individuals: The disorganized urban communities, the lack of opportunities for legitimate life styles, the criminogenic and violent values and norms of disorganized communities, the breakdown of the family support systems, the failure of education to reach hard-core losers, and the scarcity of viable options other than crime. Another strategy needed to bring these lower-class losers back into the system is to find them a place in society. This goal is likely to involve providing them with sheltered housing arrangements, sheltered workshops for employment, treatment programs for their drug and alcohol problems, and self-help programs as the need arises.

SUMMARY

This chapter proposes that social conditions relating to the cultural groups and structural conditions of a society are more important in predisposing persons to crime than are individual or biological characteristics. Cultural theorists are more concerned with the values and attitudes of individuals and the motivations they produce. Structural theorists place more emphasis on the ways in which societies are organized to satisfy or fail to satisfy human needs and wants and on the group-linked advantages or disadvantages that result. But cultural and structural theories have much in common. All essentially agree that basic conflicts in the society are part of the motivation or pressures that push some people to challenge the laws of the society in which they live. These theories suggest that this push comes in various ways.[108]

- Cultural deviance theorists state that disorganized communities provide persistent and pervasive values that are an inevitable source of crime and delinquency.
- Status frustration theorists claim that the frustrations resulting from the reality that lower-class individuals are unable to attain the middle-class standard of life, or success, are an inevitable source of crime and delinquency.
- Illegitimate opportunity theorists contend that lower-class individuals become involved in illegitimate pursuits because they are unable to attain desired middle-class goals in legitimate ways.

All of these theories see crime and delinquency as a response to inequalities. They vary in the mechanisms they describe as mediating the impact of inequalities, but their focus is still to identify a channel through which the pressure toward crime and delinquency flows. Social structure theories provide one important part of the equation of crime and delinquent behavior—as they rightly propose, disorder on all fronts results in high rates of crime, unsafe and disruptive living conditions, and the breeding grounds for a subculture of unsocialized individuals who strike out at their society. Yet this structural equation requires another element; namely, the social process involved in an individual's becoming a criminal or delinquent. The next chapter will discuss the process of becoming a criminal or delinquent.

REFERENCES

Braithwaite, John. "The Myth of Social Class and Criminality Reconsidered." *American Sociological Review* 46 (February 1981), pp. 36–57.

Cloward, Richard A., and Ohlin, Lloyd E. *Delinquency and Opportunity: A Theory of Delinquent Gangs.* New York: Free Press, 1960.

Cohen, Albert K. *Delinquent Boys: The Culture of the Gang.* New York: Free Press, 1955.

Currie, Elliott. *Confronting Crime: An American Challenge.* New York: Pantheon Books, 1985.

Kornhauser, Ruth Rosner. *Social Sources of Delinquency.* Chicago: University of Chicago Press, 1978.

Laub, John H. *Criminology in the Making: An Oral History.* Boston: Northeastern University Press, 1983.

Merton, Robert K. *Social Theory and Social Structure.* 2d ed. New York: Free Press, 1957.

Miller, Walter B. "Lower-Class Culture as a Generating Milieu of Gang Delinquency." *Journal of Social Issues* 14 (Summer 1958), pp. 5–19.

Shaw, Clifford R., and McKay, Henry D. *Social Factors in Juvenile Delinquency: Report on the Causes of Crime, Vol. II.* Washington, D.C.: National Commission on Law Observance and Enforcement; U.S. Government Printing Office, 1931.

Wolfgang, Marvin E., and Ferracuti, Franco. *The Subculture of Violence.* London: Tavistock, 1957.

NOTES

1. Interviewed in December 1985.
2. John H. Laub, *Criminology in the Making: An Oral History* (Boston: Northeastern University Press, 1983), p. 13.
3. Harold J. Vetter and Ira J. Silverman, *Criminology and Crime: An Introduction* (New York: Harper & Row, 1986), p. 297.
4. George B. Vold and Thomas J. Bernard, *Theoretical Criminology,* 3d ed. (New York: Oxford University Press, 1986), p. 163.
5. Clifford R. Shaw, *Delinquency Areas* (Chicago: University of Chicago Press, 1929), pp. 198–203.
6. Clifford R. Shaw and Henry D. McKay, *Juvenile Delinquency and Urban Areas* (Chicago: University of Chicago Press, 1942).
7. Ernest W. Burgess, "The Growth of the City," in *The City,* ed. Robert E. Park,

Ernest W. Burgess, and Roderick D. McKenzie (Chicago: University of Chicago Press, 1928), p. 62.

8. Shaw and McKay, *Juvenile Delinquency.*

9. Harold Finestone, *Victims of Change: Juvenile Delinquents in American Society* (Westport, Conn.: Greenwood Press, 1976), p. 90.

10. Ibid., pp. 83–84.

11. Ibid., p. 92.

12. Shaw and McKay, *Juvenile Delinquency,* pp. 38–39.

13. Laub, *Criminology in the Making,* p. 10.

14. James F. Short, Jr., "Introduction," in *Delinquency, Crime and Society,* ed. Short (Chicago: University of Chicago Press, 1976), p. 3.

15. For an evaluation of the Area Projects, see Soloman Kobrin, "The Chicago Area Project—A 25-Year Assessment," *Annals of the American Academy of Political and Social Science* 322 (March 1959), p. 20–29.

16. Finestone, *Victims of Change,* p. 112.

17. See Saul Alinsky, *Reveille for Radicals* (New York: Vintage Books, 1969).

18. Jon Snodgrass, "Clifford Shaw and Henry D. McKay," in *Delinquency, Crime and Society,* p. 16.

19. Walter B. Miller, "Lower-Class Culture as a Generating Milieu of Gang Delinquency, *Journal of Social Issues* 14 (1958), pp. 9–10.

20. Ibid., pp. 11–14.

21. Ibid., pp. 14–16.

22. Richard A. Cloward and Lloyd E. Ohlin, *Delinquency and Opportunity: A Theory of Delinquent Gangs* (New York: Free Press, 1960); Albert K. Cohen, *Delinquent Boys: The Culture of the Gang* (New York: Free Press, 1960).

23. Marvin E. Wolfgang and Franco Ferracuti, *The Subculture of Violence* (London: Tavistock, 1957).

24. Ibid.

25. Ibid.

26. Ibid., p. 156.

27. See Marvin E. Wolfgang et al., *Delinquency in a Birth Cohort* (Chicago: University of Chicago Press, 1972).

28. Interviewed in July 1986.

29. John Hagan, *Modern Criminology: Crime, Criminal Behavior, and Its Control* (New York: McGraw-Hill, 1985), p. 182.

30. Gwynn Nettler, *Explaining Crime* (New York: McGraw-Hill, 1974), p. 152.

31. Howard Erlander, "The Empirical Status of the Subculture of Violence Thesis," *Social Problems* 22 (1974), pp. 235–248.

32. Emile Durkheim, *Suicide,* trans. John A. Spaulding and George Simpson (Glencoe, Ill.: Free Press, 1987).

33. George B. Vold and Thomas J. Bernard, *Theoretical Criminology,* 3d ed. (New York: Oxford University Press, 1986), p. 185.

34. The following analysis of social structure and anomie is adapted from Robert K. Merton, *Social Theory and Social Structure,* 2d ed. (New York: Free Press, 1957).

35. Ibid.

36. Ibid.

37. Ibid.

38. Morton Deutsch and Robert K. Merton, *Theories in Social Psychology* (New York: Basic Books, 1965), p. 198.

39. Vold and Bernard, *Theoretical Criminology,* p. 29.

40. Merton, *Social Theory and Social Structure.*
41. Ibid., p. 151.
42. Ibid., p. 155.
43. Ibid., p. 155.
44. Marshall B. Clinard, "The Theoretical Implications of Anomie and Deviant Behavior," in *Anomie and Deviant Behavior,* ed. Clinard (New York: Free Press, 1964), p. 10.
45. Cohen, *Delinquent Boys,* p. 25.
46. Ibid., p. 82.
47. Ibid., p. 87.
48. Ibid., p. 88–91, 97.
49. Ibid., p. 113–114.
50. Ibid., p. 117.
51. Hagan, *Modern Criminology,* p. 189.
52. Cohen, *Delinquent Boys,* p. 117.
53. Ibid., p. 28.
54. Ibid., pp. 26.
55. Ibid., p. 30.
56. Ibid., p. 29.
57. Ibid., p. 30.
58. Ibid., p. 133.
59. Ibid., p. 315.
60. James F. Short, Jr., and Fred L. Strodtbeck, *Group Process and Gang Delinquency* (Chicago: University of Chicago Press, 1965).
61. Cloward and Ohlin, *Delinquency and Opportunity.*
62. Albert K. Cohen, "The Sociology of the Deviant Act: Anomie Theory and Beyond," *American Sociological Review* 30 (1945), p. 9.
63. Travis Hirschi, *Causes of Delinquency* (Berkeley, Calif.: University of California Press, 1969).
64. David Matza, *Delinquency and Drift* (New York: Wiley, 1964).
65. David F. Greenberg, "Delinquency and the Age Structure of Society," *Contemporary Crisis* 1 (1977), p. 199.
66. Vold and Barnard, *Theoretical Criminology,* p. 196.
67. Cloward and Ohlin, *Delinquency and Opportunity.*
68. Vold and Barnard, *Theoretical Criminology,* p. 197.
69. Cloward and Ohlin, *Delinquency and Opportunity,* p. 97.
70. Ibid., p. 20.
71. Ibid., p. 23.
72. Ibid., p. 24.
73. Ibid., p. 25.
74. Ibid., pp. 25–26.
75. Ibid., p. 27.
76. Ibid., p. 21.
77. James F. Short, Jr., Ramon Rivera, and Ray Tennyson, "Perceived Opportunities, Gang Membership and Delinquency," *American Sociological Review* 30 (1965), pp. 56–57.
78. Nettler, *Explaining Crime,* pp. 228–230.
79. Hagan, *Modern Criminology,* p. 196.
80. Ruth Rosner Kornhauser, *Social Sources of Delinquency* (Chicago: University of Chicago Press, 1978), pp. 139–180.

81. Gwynn Nettler, *Explaining Crime,* 3d ed. (New York: McGraw-Hill, 1984), pp. 212–218.

82. Vold, *Theoretical Criminology,* p. 200.

83. Thomas J. Bernard, "Control Criticisms of Strain Theories: An Assessment of Theoretical and Empirical Adequacy," *Journal of Research in Crime and Delinquency* 21 (November 1984), pp. 353–372.

84. Pamela Richards, Richard A. Berk, and Brenda Forster, *Crime as Play: Delinquency in a Middle-Class Suburb* (Cambridge, Mass.: Ballinger Publishing Company, 1979), pp. 10–15.

85. Ibid., p. 11.

86. Ibid., p. 13.

87. Ibid.

88. Marshall B. Clinard and Peter C. Yeager, *Corporate Crime* (New York: Free Press, 1980), p. 64.

89. Ibid, pp. 65–66.

90. Travis Hirschi and Michael Gottfredson, "Causes of White-Collar Crime," *Criminology* 25 (November 1987), p. 969.

91. Cohen, *Delinquent Boys,* p. 164.

92. Richards et al., *Crime as Play,* p. 14.

93. Quoted in "Crime in the Suites," *Time,* 10 June 1985, p. 57.

94. Charles R. Tittle, Wayne J. Villemez, and Douglas A. Smith, "The Myth of Social Class and Criminality: An Empirical Assessment of the Empirical Evidence," *American Sociological Review* 43 (October 1978), pp. 643–656.

95. Travis Hirschi, Michael Hindelang, and Joseph Weis, "Reply," *American Sociological Review* 47 (June 1982), p. 435.

96. Delbert S. Elliot and David Huizinga, "Social Class and Delinquent Behavior in a National Youth Panel," *Criminology* 21 (May 1983), p. 169.

97. Robert J. Sampson and Thomas C. Castellano, "Economic Inequality and Personal Victimization," *British Journal of Criminology* 22 (October 1982).

98. John Braithwaite, "The Myth of Social Class and Criminality Reconsidered," *American Sociological Review* 46 (February 1981), p. 49.

99. Robert Gillespie, "Economic Factors in Crime and Delinquency: A Critical Review of the Empirical Evidence," *Hearings, Subcommittee on Crime of the Committee of the Judiciary House of Representatives 95th Congress,* serial 47 (Washington, D.C.: U.S. Government Printing Office, 1978), pp. 601–625.

100. Donald Clelland and Timothy Carter, "The New Myth of Class and Crime," *Criminology* 18 (1980), pp. 319–336.

101. Elliott Currie, *Confronting Crime: An American Challenge* (New York: Pantheon Books, 1985), p. 172.

102. Ibid., pp. 159–160.

103. Vetter and Silverman, *Criminology and Crime,* pp. 297–298.

104. Ibid., p. 298.

105. Alfred Blumstein, David P. Farrington, and Soumyo Moitra, "Delinquency Careers: Innocents, Amateurs, and Persisters" (unpublished paper, n.d.).

106. Currie, *Confronting Crime,* p. 278.

107. Ibid.

108. Hagan, *Modern Criminology,* p. 199.

CHAPTER 7

Social Process Theory

DIFFERENTIAL ASSOCIATION THEORY
Propositions of Differential Association
  Theory
Evaluation of Differential Association Theory
DELINQUENCY AND DRIFT
Evaluation of Drift Theory
CONTROL THEORY
Containment Theory
  The Self-Concept as an Insulation Against
  Delinquency
Social Control Theory
  Elements of the Bond
  Evaluation of Social Control Theory
LABELING THEORY

Frank Tannenbaum: The Dramatization of Evil
Edwin M. Lemert: Primary and Secondary
  Deviation
Howard Becker and the Outsider
Evaluation of the Labeling Perspective
ANALYSIS
Transmission of Individual Patterns
Development of Deviant Identity and Career
Escape from a Deviant Label
POLICY IMPLICATIONS
SUMMARY
REFERENCES
NOTES

KEY TERMS

containment theory

control theories

deviant career

deviant identity

differential association theory

drift theory

labeling theory

neutralization theory

primary and secondary deviation

self-concept and delinquency behavior

social bond

social control theory

social process theories

symbolic interactionism

I ran wild as a kid. My parents didn't have any controls over me. I did what I wanted, came and went as I wanted. Everyone thought I was a loser; I thought I was a loser myself.

—Director of court services[1]

I wish I knew why I retired. I really wish, because these guys come in all the time that I know and they're out here enjoying themselves, they got a pocket full of money; and, believe me, there's nothing in the world harder to understand than square-john people. I understand my people—they're a bunch of bums. I know it and they know it, but I don't understand square-johns.

—Former safecracker[2]

Social process theories, the focus of this chapter, examine the environmental forces that influence individuals to become involved in criminal or delinquent behavior. These sociopsychological theories gained popularity in the 1960s because they provided a theoretical mechanism for understanding how environment influences individual decision making.

The relationship between rules and criminal behavior, a consistent theme of this text, is highlighted by social process theories. Individuals pursue criminal behavior, according to social process theorists, because they have learned antisocial rules or norms from others, because the group has given them permission to disobey the rules of society, because they have not internalized social rules that will keep them out of trouble, and because the larger society has defined them as unable to comply with the rules.

Part of the popularity of social process theories is that they provide a more dynamic analysis of criminal behavior than individual and structural explanations do. They examine how the individual is influenced by the group; why the individual moves in and out of criminal behavior; how such factors as self-concept, identity, career, and commitment push one toward or away from criminal behavior; and how the relationship between social and individual variables affect whether or not one becomes involved in criminal pursuits.

DIFFERENTIAL ASSOCIATION THEORY

Edwin H. Sutherland, in formulating the **theory of differential association**, proposed that individuals learn crime from others. His basic premise was that crime, like any other form of behavior, is a product of social interaction. In developing his theory, Sutherland was influenced by the French social theorist Gabriel Tarde (1843–1904) and by the writings on symbolic interactionism.

Tarde was concerned with the social processes whereby forms of behavior and ways of thinking and feeling are passed on from person to person and from group to group. His theory was one of "imitation and suggestion," for he defined the origins of crime as similar to the origins of fads and fashions. Crime is a socially learned acquisition, he asserted, governed by the "three laws of imitation"; namely, the law of close contact, the law of imitation of superiors to inferiors, and the law of insertion. Tarde's law of first contact is that people have a tendency to imitate the fashions and customs of those with whom they have the most contact. His second law suggests that superiors, or persons of higher social status, are more frequently imitated than those of lower social status. The law of insertion, according to Tarde, refers to the power that is inherent in newness or novelty. Tarde believed that the newer way of doing things would ordinarily win out when two approaches came into conflict.[3] The importance that Tarde placed on associative imitation is evident in the following:

Edwin H. Sutherland. (*Source:* From *The Sutherland Papers* by Albert Cohen, et al. © 1956, Indiana University Press and the University of Chicago.)

The majority of murderers and notorious thieves began as children who have been abandoned, and the true seminary of crime must be sought for upon each public square and/or each crossroad of our towns, whether they be small or large, in those flocks of pillaging street urchins, who like bands of sparrows, associate together, at first for marauding, and then for theft, because of a lack of education and food in their homes.[4]

Symbolic interactionism holds that individuals are constantly being changed as they take on the expectations and points of view of the people with whom they interact in intense small groups.[5] It is assumed that the concept of self is developed in a process that is largely characterized by the development of symbols and their interpersonal exchange. Thus, this process teaches each person to take the role of another person, to imagine one's "self" in the other person's situation. Symbolic interactionist theorists look for the explanations of social behavior in learned dispositions identified through their expression in symbolic language. These dispositions are called "attitudes," "beliefs," "meanings," "perceptions," "expectations," "values," and "definitions of the situation."[6]

Sutherland began with the notion that criminal behavior is to be expected of those who have internalized a preponderance of definitions favorable to law violations.[7] He first set forth the theory of differential association in his 1939 text *Principles of Criminology,* and he continued to revise this classic text until its final form appeared in 1947.[8]

Propositions of Differential Association Theory

Sutherland's theory of differential association is outlined in nine propositions:

1. **Criminal Behavior Is Learned.** Criminal behavior, like other behaviors, is learned from others. That is, criminal behavior is not an inherited trait, but an acquired one.
2. **Criminal Behavior Is Learned in Interaction with Other Persons in a Process of Communication.** Criminal behavior is learned through an individual's active involvement with others in a process of communication, both verbal and nonverbal.
3. **The Principal Part of the Learning of Criminal Behavior Occurs within Intimate Personal Groups.** Individuals learn criminal behavior from their most intimate social groups. The definitions derived from these intimate relationships are far more influential for individuals than any other form of communication, such as movies and newspapers.
4. **When Criminal Behavior Is Learned, the Learning Includes: Techniques of Committing the Crime, Which Are Sometimes Very Simple; the Specific Direction of Motives, Drives, Rationalizations, and Attitudes.** Individuals learn the techniques of committing crime from others. (For example, a youth may learn from a delinquent companion how to "hot wire" a car.)

5. **The Specific Direction of Motives and Drives Is Learned from Definitions of Legal Codes as Favorable and Unfavorable.** Individuals come into contact both with persons who define the legal codes as rules to be observed and with those whose definitions of reality favor the violation of the legal codes. This situation creates culture conflict; the next proposition explains how this conflict is resolved.

6. **A Person Becomes Criminal Because of an Excess of Definitions Favorable to Violation of Law over Definitions Unfavorable to Violation of Law.** This proposition expresses the basic principle of differential association. According to Sutherland, a person becomes criminal because he or she has more involvement with criminal or delinquent peers, groups, or events than with noncriminal or nondelinquent peers, groups, or events. Both an excess of contacts with criminal definitions and isolation from anticriminal patterns are important.

7. **Differential Associations May Vary in Frequency, Duration, Priority, and Intensity.** The impact that criminal peers or groups have upon individuals depends upon the frequency of the social contacts, the length of the period of time over which the contacts take place, the age at which a person experiences these contacts, and the intensity of these social interactions.

8. **The Process of Learning Criminal Behavior by Associations with Criminal and Anticriminal Patterns Involves All of the Mechanisms That Are Involved in Any Other Learning.** The learning of criminal behavior is like any other learning experience; it is not restricted to mere imitation of others' behavior.

9. **Though Criminal Behavior Is an Expression of General Needs and Values, It Is Not Explained by Those General Needs and Values Since Noncriminal Behavior Is an Expression of the Same Needs and Values.** Sutherland concludes by stating that the motives for criminal behavior are different from those for conventional behavior. What differentiates criminal from noncriminal behavior is that it is based on an excess of criminal definitions learned from others.[9]

Sutherland presumes that crime must be taught. Those who do not become involved in crime, then, have been taught other values. Sutherland develops a quantitative metaphor, in which conventional and criminal value systems are compared to elementary units called "definitions." Each unit can be weighted by the modalities of frequency, priority, duration, and intensity of contact. Thus, criminality or delinquency is determined by the algebraic sum of these weighted units.[10]

Evaluation of Differential Association Theory

Differential association theory still retains an important place in the study of criminal behavior because it is difficult to refute the argument that individuals learn crime from others. Individuals, of course, are taught their basic values, norms, skills, and perception of self from others, and, therefore, it seems irrefutable that they also learn crime from "significant others."

In this context, Jack Henry Abbott, who had spent most of his life in confinement, wrote a book about his life in prison called *In the Belly of the Beast.* [11] The convincing narration and penetrating insights into the brutality of prison life gained Abbott a reputation as a skilled author—and as a rehabilitated inmate. He was praised by New York's literary elite and was granted an early parole by state officials.

Shortly after his release, Abbott engaged in a dispute with a waiter in a New York City restaurant. Abbott wanted to use the restaurant's restroom, but the waiter informed him there was none. Accounts differ about what happened next. Some witnesses say that the waiter was escorting Abbott outside so that he could urinate in the alley; Abbott claims that the waiter was going to attack him. He reacted as if he were in prison; he had a knife and he used it. When he was apprehended and charged with the murder, Abbott claimed that he acted as he did because he had learned to act that way. Most of Abbott's life had been spent in juvenile and adult institutions, and, therefore, he contended that the state of New York, rather than he, should be held responsible for his act of violence. Thus, Abbott argued that the process of social learning, a process over which he had little personal control, was the real perpetrator of his violent act. [12]

Some support for differential association theory is found in the literature. James S. Short, Jr., tested an institutional sample of 126 boys and 50 girls in an attempt to gain information on the frequency, duration, priority, and intensity of their pre-delinquent associations. He found a moderately strong relationship,

Jack Henry Abbott. (*Source:* Nick Passemore/ Sygma.)

significant for both boys and girls, between exposure to delinquents and delinquent behavior.[13] Albert J. Reiss, Jr., and A. Lewis Rhodes obtained measures of the delinquent behavior of 299 boys and each boy's two best friends. They discovered that close friendships were "closely correlated with delinquency," but they concluded that these correlations "were well below what one expected from the learning hypothesis in differential association theory." Thus, this study provided only qualified support for differential association theory.[14] Brenda S. Griffin and Charles T. Griffin, testing differential association theory in two studies of drug use among adolescents, concluded that the findings generally supported differential association theory.[15]

The enduring impact of differential association theory is apparent in the attempts to revise this theory. Melvin DeFleur and Richard Quinney, in reformulating the nine propositions of Sutherland's differential association theory, argue that the theory could be formally tightened if it were based on the concepts of symbolic interaction and attitude formation.[16] Daniel Glaser's modification of differential association theory is called differential identification. The theory of differential identification is as follows: "A person pursues criminal behavior to the extent that he identifies himself with real or imaginary persons from whose perspective his criminal behavior seems acceptable."[17] Glaser's revision allows for human choice and stresses the importance of role models existing in the wider culture, independent of direct intimate association. Robert Burgess and Ronald Akers's differential reinforcement theory proposes a step-by-step restatement of differential association in terms of such ideas as reinforcement and punishment. They argue that criminal behavior is primarily learned "in those groups which comprise the individual's major source of reinforcements."[18]

The criticisms of differential association theory can be grouped into three areas. First, critics point out that differential association theory has no room for human purpose and meaning, because it reduces the individual to an object that merely reacts to the bombardment of external forces and can not reject the material being presented.[19] The criminal, then, is viewed as a passive recipient into which various definitions are poured, and the resultant mixture is something over which he or she has no control.[20]

Second, it is charged that differential association theory does not deal with several critical questions relating to the process of learning crime from others. Why does one individual succumb to criminal definitions while another does not? Why do individuals who are exposed to criminal definitions still conform most of the time? How did the first "teacher" learn criminal behavior and definitions to pass on? What is the effect of punishment on criminals and delinquents?

Third, the terms of differential association theory are so vague that it is nearly impossible to test the theory empirically. For example, how can "excess of definitions toward criminality" be measured? How can "frequency, duration, priority, and intensity" be studied? What defines an intimate personal group? What exact techniques, motives, and rationalizations are learned from others?

Yet, in spite of these and other criticisms, differential association theory remains one of the best known and most enduring theories of criminal behavior.

DELINQUENCY AND DRIFT

The process of becoming a delinquent, as explained by David Matza in *Delinquency and Drift,* begins when a juvenile neutralizes himself or herself against the moral bounds of the law and drifts into delinquency. Drift means that "the delinquent transiently exists in limbo between convention and crime, responding in turn to the demands of each, flirting now with one, now the other, but postponing commitment, evading decision. Thus, he drifts between criminal and conventional action."[21]

Matza's concept of drift and the theory of differential association have many assumptions in common, but Matza places far more importance than differential association theorists on the exercise of juveniles' choices and on the sense of injustice that juveniles feel about the discriminatory treatment they have received. Matza's **drift theory** also differs from differential association because he contends that their violation of legal norms does not mean that delinquents are surrendering their integration to the wider society or their allegiance to legal norms.[22]

> There are millions of occasions during which delinquency may be committed. Except for occasions covered by surveillance, virtually every moment experienced offers an opportunity for offense. Yet delinquency fails to occur during all but a tiny proportion of these moments. During most of the subcultural delinquent's life he is distracted and restrained by convention from the commission of offenses. Episodically, he is released from the moral bind of conventional order. This temporary though recurrent release from the bind of convention has been taken for compulsion or commitment. It is, instead, almost the opposite. During release the delinquent is not constrained to commit offense; rather, he is free to drift into delinquency. Under the condition of widely available extenuating circumstances, the subcultural delinquent may choose to commit delinquencies.[23]

Delinquency, states Matza, becomes permissible when the individual's sense of responsibility is neutralized. The neutralization of a sense of responsibility is the immediate condition of drift, but other conditions include the presence of a sense of injustice, the primacy of custom, and the assertion of tort. The delinquent is part of a subculture that is filled with a sense of injustice; this subculture depends on a memory file that collects examples of inconsistency and unfairness on the part of actors in the justice system.[24]

The primacy of custom refers to the delinquent's observation of the virtues of his subculture; the virtues stress the "traditional precepts of manliness, celebrating as they do the heroic themes of honor, valor, and loyalty."[25] In the group setting, the delinquent must demonstrate valor and loyalty when faced with dare, challenge, and insult.[26]

The assertion of tort occurs when the subcultural delinquent regards a harmful wrong as a tort instead of a crime. The tort is viewed as a private interaction between the accused and the victim, and subcultural delinquents frequently believe that the justice process can not be invoked unless the victim is willing to make a complaint or to press charges.[27]

Matza contends that "the breaking of the moral bind to law arising from neutralization and resulting in drift does not assure the commission of a delinquent act."[28] The missing element that provides "the thrust of impetus by which the delinquent act is realized is *will*."[29] Success in crime in the past and a sense of desperation can activate the will to commit delinquent acts. Matza explains that the delinquent is not likely to have the will to repeat an old offense if he or she has failed in the past: "Few persons—clowns and fools are among them—like to engage in activities they do badly."[30] Desperation arises when the delinquent feels pushed around and sees himself or herself as cause rather than as effect.[31]

Evaluation of Drift Theory

Matza's theory has received some empirical support. Richard Ball, in examining a delinquent population at the Fairfield School for Boys in Lancaster, Ohio, and an inner-city sample of high school boys, found that delinquents tend to give more excuses for various offenses than do nondelinquents.[32] Robert Regoli and Eric Poole concluded that delinquents may well drift in and out of delinquent behavior and that the attitudes of delinquents and nondelinquents are very similar.[33]

A major strength of drift theory is that it builds on the assumption that delinquent or criminal behavior is a learning process that takes place during interactions with others. Drift theory examines the influence of the group in encouraging youths or adults to release themselves from the moral binds of the law. Drift theory also can be used to explain the fact that the majority of adolescents commit occasional delinquent acts but then go on to become law-abiding adults.

Drift theory is also helpful in understanding the situational aspects of delinquent behavior. Matza views the delinquent as one who is pressured by a specific situational context and the norms of that context to engage in delinquent behavior. Thus, Matza analyzes the group processes that encourage adolescents to take a moral vacation from the law.

Finally, **neutralization theory**, according to Gresham Sykes and Matza, provides a means of understanding how the delinquent or the criminal insulates himself or herself from responsibility for wrongdoing. The process involves the denial of responsibility, the denial of injury to the victim, the condemnation of the condemners, and the appeal to higher loyalties.[34] Studies of juvenile and adult offenders reveal the constant use of the device of neutralizing oneself from blame for wrongdoing.

However, several criticisms have been made of drift theory. Hirschi accuses drift theory of a logical deficiency, in that "the strain that prompts the effort at neutralization" can not also be "the motive force that results in the subsequent deviant act."[35] He also accuses Matza of overstating the conformity of delinquent youth: "Many persons do not have an attitude of respect toward the rules of society; many persons feel no moral obligation to conform regardless of personal advantage."[36] Furthermore, Taylor et al. claim that Matza underestimates the resourcefulness of lower-class delinquents, whom he views as caught between a despairing and a less despairing handling of their situation.[37]

Nevertheless, Matza has provided one of the most useful expressions of how the group influences the lower-class juvenile to become involved in delinquent behavior.

CONTROL THEORY

The core ideas of control theory, which can be traced back to the early nineteenth century, contend that human beings must be held in check, or somehow controlled, if innate criminal tendencies are to be repressed. **Control theories** also explain crime as the result of a deficiency in individuals whereby they lack a controlling force. Walter C. Reckless's containment theory and Travis Hirschi's social control theory are the two best known control theories.

Containment Theory

Walter C. Reckless, another founder of American criminology, developed **containment theory** in the 1950s in order to explain crime and delinquency. He argues that individuals are affected by a variety of forces driving them toward, and a variety of other forces restraining them from, crime and delinquency. Reckless calls the driving forces *social pressures* that bear down on individuals, such as conditions associated with poverty or deprivation, conflict and discord, external restraint, minority group status, and limited access to success in an opportunity structure. *Social pulls*—including bad companions, delinquent or criminal subculture, patterns of deviancy, and criminogenic advertising and propaganda—draw the individual away from acceptable norms of living. In addition, there are inner biological or psychological *pushes* that drive each individual away from or toward crime and delinquency. These pushes include drives, motives, restlessness, disappointments, inner tensions, frustrations, hostility, aggressiveness, need for immediate gratification, rebellion against authority, and feelings of inferiority.[38]

Containment theory has two reinforcing elements: an outer control system and an inner control system. External containment represents the structural buffers in the person's immediate social world or environment that are able to hold him or her within bounds. External controls or regulators consist of such factors as the presentation of a consistent moral front; institutional reinforcement of the individual's norms, goals, and expectations; effective supervision and discipline; provision for a reasonable scope of activity, including limits and responsibilities; and opportunity for acceptance, identity, and belongingness.

Internal containment is derived from self-control, positive self-concept, ego strength, well-developed superego, high frustration tolerance, high resistance to diversions, high sense of responsibility, ability to find substitute satisfactions, goal orientations, and tension-reducing rationalizations. The inner control resulting from moral training produces five indicators of its presence: (1) a healthy self-concept, (1) goal-directedness, (3) a realistic level of aspiration, (4) the ability to tolerate frustration, and (5) an identification with lawful norms.[39]

Reckless claims that strong inner containment and reinforcing external containment provide insulation against criminal behavior. But he does note that containment theory does not explain certain categories of criminal behavior; namely, those crimes that emerge from strong inner pushes, such as compulsions, anxieties, and personality disorders, or from organic impairments, such as brain damage.[40]

Reckless reasoned that if an individual has a weak outer containment system, the external pressures and pulls must be handled by the inner control system. If an individual's outer buffer is relatively strong and effective, his or her inner defense does not have to play such a critical role. Similarly, if an individual's inner controls are not equal to the ordinary pushes, an effective outer defense may help hold him or her within socially acceptable behavior. But if the inner defenses are in good working order, the outer structure does not have to come to the rescue. Thus, individuals who have both a strong external and a strong internal containment system are much less likely to commit criminal activity than those who have only a strong external or a strong internal containment system. Individuals who have both weak external and weak internal controls are the most prone to criminal or delinquent behavior.

The Self-Concept as an Insulation Against Delinquency   Walter C. Reckless, Simon Dinitz, and their students spent over a decade investigating the effects of self-concept on delinquent behavior. The subjects of their study were sixth-grade boys living in the area of Columbus, Ohio, that had the highest white delinquency rate. Teachers first were asked to nominate those boys who, in their point of view, were insulated against delinquency; in the second phase of the study, teachers in the same schools were asked to nominate those sixth-grade boys who appeared to be heading toward delinquency. Both the "good boy" group and the "bad boy" group were administered the same battery of tests; the mothers of both groups also were interviewed.[41]

Reckless and Dinitz concluded from these studies that one of the preconditions of avoiding delinquent behavior is a good self-concept. This "insulation" against delinquency may be viewed as the result of an ongoing process reflecting an internalization of nondelinquent values and conformity to the expectations of significant others—parents, teachers, and peers. Thus, a good self-concept, the product of favorable socialization, steers youths away from delinquency by acting as an inner buffer or "containment" against delinquency.

In the 1960s, Reckless and Dinitz undertook a four-year intervention project involving all of the Columbus core city junior high schools; the project was designed to improve the self-concepts of seventh-grade boys who were seen as potentially delinquent. But the follow-up evaluation of this study indicated that the special classes had no appreciable impact.[42]

A number of other studies have examined the relationship between **self-concept and delinquent behavior**. In Hawaii, Gary F. Jensen examined specific variables of self-concept and their relationship to "inner containment." He found that the greater the self-esteem, the less likely the youth is to become involved in delinquent behavior.[43] E. D. Lively and colleagues, who investigated self-concept in teenage children in various ethnic groups in Akron, Ohio, found that self-concept appears to improve as one moves away from the inner city.[44] H. B. Kaplan and A. D. Pokorny, investigating the relationship between a broken home and self-derogation (negative self-concept), found that a broken home in itself does not lead to a poor self-concept. Such factors as race, sex, and socioeconomic class, along with instability within the home, join together to create a negative self-concept.[45] A study conducted by Franco Ferracuti and Simon Dinitz in San Juan, Puerto Rico, also supports the relationship of poor self-concept and delinquent behavior.[46] Finally, H. B. Kaplan's recent study examined delinquent behavior as a coping strategy to defend against negative self-evaluation. He found that if some students had negative experiences with nondeviant groups, they would turn to delinquent-oriented groups to achieve a positive experience.[47]

However, the major flaw of inner containment, or self-concept, theory, is the difficulty of defining self-concept in such a way that researchers can be certain they are accurately measuring the key variables involved. Dinitz and Bettye A. Pfau-Vicent, in updating the self-concept studies, summarized why measurement of the self-concept is difficult:

> In short, we do not know what the crucial variables are in defining self-concept, nor how to use what we do know to adequately predict and control delinquent behavior. What is needed now is careful and thorough research aimed at accurate operationalization of self-concept. Only when we have identified these crucial variables will improved prevention efforts find fallow ground in which to take root in our efforts to enhance a young person's self-concept in the service of the prevention and control of serious juvenile delinquency.[48]

M. Schwartz and S. S. Tangri expressed a number of criticisms of the self-concept studies. They disputed the adequacy of Reckless and Dinitz's measure of self-concept, saw the definitions of terms as confusing, questioned the effects of labeling on the subsequent behavior of both the "good" and "bad" boys, and suggested that poor self-concept might have other outcomes besides vulnerability to delinquency.[49]

In sum, Reckless's containment theory has lost popularity in recent years; indeed, even in the latest edition of Reckless's text it does not receive special prominence.[50] Furthermore, the relationship between self-concept and delinquent behavior has been basically ignored in recent criminological research.

Social Control Theory

Travis Hirschi is the theorist most closely identified with **social control theory**. In *Causes of Delinquency,* Hirschi links delinquent behavior to the quality of the bond an individual maintains with society, stating that "delinquent acts result when an individual's bond to society is weak or broken."[51] Hirschi is indebted to Emile Durkheim for recognition of the importance of the social bond to society.

He accepts the view of Thomas Hobbes, Puritan theologians, and Sigmund Freud that humans are basically antisocial and sinful. In Hirschi's words, "We are all animals and thus all naturally capable of committing criminal acts."[52] Thus, he is arguing that their basic impulses motivate humans to become involved in crime and delinquency unless there is reason for them to refrain from delinquent or criminal behavior. Instead of the standard question, "Why do they do it?" the most important question becomes, "Why don't they do it?"[53]

Elements of the Bond   Hirschi theorizes that individuals who are most tightly *bonded* to social groups such as the family, the school, and peers are less likely to commit delinquent acts.[54] The **social bond**, according to Hirschi, is made up of four main elements: attachment, commitment, involvement, and belief.

Attachment relates to the ties of affection and respect an individual has to parents, teachers, and friends. The attachment to others also relates to the ability to internalize norms and to develop a conscience. The stronger the attachment to others, the more likely it is that an individual will take this attachment and respect into consideration when he or she is tempted to commit a delinquent act.[55] The attachment to parents is the most important factor insulating a child against delinquent behavior. Hirschi asserts, "If the child is alienated from the parent, he will not develop an adequate conscience or superego."[56]

Commitment to conventional activities and values is the second element of the social bond. An individual is committed to the degree that he or she is willing to invest time, energy, and self in conventional activities, such as educational goals. Hirschi contends that if juveniles are committed to conventional values and activities, they develop a stake in conformity and will refrain from delinquent behavior.[57]

Involvement also protects a juvenile from delinquent behavior. One's time and energy, of course, are limited, and, therefore, involvement in conventional activities leaves less time for delinquent behavior. "The person involved in conventional activities is tied to appointments, deadlines, working hours, plans, and the like," Hirschi states, "so the opportunity to commit deviant acts rarely arises. To the extent that he is engrossed in conventional activities, he can not even think about deviant acts, let alone act out his inclinations."[58]

Belief is the final element in the social bond. Hirschi contends that delinquency results from the absence of effective beliefs forbidding socially unacceptable behavior. *Belief* is Hirschi's term for the acceptance of the "moral validity" of conventional rules. Respect for the law and respect for the social norms of society are two important components of belief. Hirschi develops a causal chain, "from attachment to parents, through concern for the approval of persons in positions of authority, to belief that the rules of society are binding on one's conduct."[59]

Hirschi tested the presence of these four elements in a self-report survey administered to 4077 junior high and high school students in Contra Costa County, California. He also used school records and police records in analyzing the data he received on the questionnaires.

He found that the greater the attachment to parents, the less likely the child is to become involved in delinquent behavior. The quality or the intimacy of the communication between child and parents appears to be the critical factor: the more love and respect found in the relationship with parents, the more likely it is that the child will recall the parents when and if a situation of potential delinquency arises.[60] Nor can the attachment to the school be ignored in understanding delinquent behavior. Students with little academic competence and those who perform poorly are more likely to become involved in delinquent behavior. Significantly, Hirschi found that students with weak affectional ties to parents typically have little concern for the opinions of teachers and dislike school.[61]

In terms of commitment, Hirschi found that the more committed a boy is to academic achievement, the less likely he is to become involved in delinquent acts. Also, the higher the occupational expectations of boys, the less likely it is that they will become involved in delinquent behavior. If a boy claims he has the *right* to smoke, drink, date, and drive a car, he is more likely to become involved in delinquency. The automobile, like the cigarette and bottle of beer, indicates that the youth has put away childish things.[62]

Hirschi also found that the more involved a boy is in school and leisure activities, the less likely he was to become involved in delinquency. Or, to express this in another way, the more that a boy in the sample felt that he had nothing to do, the more likely he was to become involved in delinquent acts. Hirschi theorizes that lack of involvement and commitment to school releases a young person from a primary source of time structuring.[63]

Finally, in another confirmation of social control theory, Hirschi found that the less boys believed they should obey the law, the less likely they were to obey it. His self-report study also revealed that delinquents were relatively free of concern for the morality of their actions and that their values seemed to differ significantly from those of nondelinquents.[64] For example, more delinquent boys than nondelinquent boys agreed that:

- Most criminals shouldn't really be blamed for the things they have done.
- I can't seem to stay out of trouble no matter how hard I try.
- Most things that people call "delinquency" don't really hurt anyone.
- Policemen [do not] try to give kids an even break.
- It is alright [*sic*] to get around the law if you can get away with it.[65]

Evaluation of Social Control Theory   Social control theory has generated a considerable number of empirical studies, many of which have produced supportive results. Wiatrowski, Griswold, and Roberts explored the degree to which the four dimensions of the social bonds are mutually interdependent, as well as the direct and indirect effect of socioeconomic class. Using self-reports of 2213 tenth-grade boys, they concluded that items considered as indicators of attachment to school, parents, peers, future occupational commitment, and school involvement are mutually interdependent predictors of moderate delinquent acts.[66] Marvin D. Krohn and James L. Massey found a moderate relationship between a wide range of delinquent behaviors and social bond measures.[67] But both of these studies concluded that other factors as well as the social bond are needed to understand delinquent behavior.[68] Michael Hindelang, using subjects in the sixth through twelfth grades in a New York State school system, also found support for Hirschi's social control theory. The findings involving attachment to peers represented the major difference between his study and Hirschi's, for Hindelang found that identification with peers was directly related to delinquent involvements.[69]

Social control theory has several strengths or advantages. First, unlike many of the theories discussed in the past two chapters, it is well suited to empirical examination. Hirschi was able to test his theory with a population of adolescents because the basic theoretical constructs of control theory are clearly defined—for example, attachment to parents, involvement in school, and commitment to conventional activities.

Second, integrated theories have emerged recently, using the social control perspective to weave together the social settings of social control theory into a unified conceptualization of socialization processes.[70] Delbert S. Elliott and colleagues, as well as Richard E. Johnson, have used the concept of the social bond to synthesize other theories into a single explanatory paradigm.[71]

Third, social control theory has provided a number of insights into delinquent behavior. The importance of the intrafamily bond has been substantiated. The relationship between school and delinquency and peers and delinquency are other important areas addressed by control theory. Hirschi also examined the relationship between delinquency and such factors as aspirations, achievement, affection toward teachers, time spent on homework, use of the automobile, and leisure-time activities.

However, social control theory, which is widely regarded today as a valid explanation of delinquent behavior, does have limitations. First, several theoretical problems are found with the theory. Most importantly, it fails to describe the chain of events that weaken the social bond, and it divides delinquents into either socialized or unsocialized youths.

Second, Hirschi used a limited array of items in evaluating the dimensions of the social bond, and the questionnaire items he used to measure delinquency included only a few relatively minor behavior problems.[72] Third, the importance of other factors in the explanation of delinquency is indicated by the amount of delinquent behavior not explained by social control variables (usually 50 percent or more). Although this figure remains impressive compared with that for other explanations of delinquency, it still does not allow one to conclude that social control variables alone determine delinquent behavior.[73]

Fourth, perhaps the most critical flaw is that Hirschi's theory may adequately explain delinquency in juveniles who are involved only in relatively trivial offenses, but whether or not its findings apply as well to serious delinquents is questionable.

In sum, although social control theory has methodological and theoretical limitations, at present it has greater empirical support than any other explanation of delinquency. Researchers are increasingly using this theory to develop integrated explanations of delinquent behavior.

LABELING THEORY

The labeling perspective, sometimes called the "interactional theory of deviance" or the "social reaction" perspective, contends that society creates deviants by labeling those who are apprehended as "different" from other individuals, when in reality they are different only because they have been "tagged" with a deviant label.[74] Thus, labeling theorists zero in on the processes by which individuals become involved in deviant behavior and stress the part played by social audiences and their responses to the norm-violations of individuals.

The view that formal and informal social reactions to criminality can influence the subsequent attitudes and behaviors of criminals has been recognized for some time. Frank Tannenbaum, Edwin Lemert, and Howard Becker are three of the chief proponents of the labeling perspective.

Frank Tannenbaum: The Dramatization of Evil

In 1938, Frank Tannenbaum presented one of the earliest expressions of **labeling theory** in his book *Crime and the Community.* Tannenbaum examined the process whereby an individual came to the attention of the authorities and was "tagged" or labeled as different from other individuals. Tannenbaum theorized that this process produced a change in both the way these individuals were handled by the justice system and the way they came to view themselves:

> The process of making the criminal, therefore, is a process of tagging, defining, identifying, segregating, describing, emphasizing, making conscious and self-conscious; it becomes a way of stimulating, suggesting, emphasizing, and evoking the very traits that are complained of.
>
> The person becomes the thing he is described as being. . . . The way out is through a refusal to dramatize the evil. The less said about it the better.[75]

Criminals, according to Tannenbaum, are "made" by the way they are treated. He called the process of "making the criminal" the "dramatization of evil." He wrote that the process of tagging an individual resulted in the person becoming involved with other criminals, and he argued that such associations represented an attempt to escape the society responsible for negative labeling. The individual, then, became more and more involved in a deviant career and, regardless of the efforts of individuals in the community and justice system to stamp out his or her "evil" behavior, the negative behavior became "hardened" and resistant to positive values. Tannenbaum contended that the less the evil is dramatized, the less likely individuals are to become involved in deviant careers.[76]

Edwin M. Lemert: Primary and Secondary Deviation

The social reaction theory developed by Edwin M. Lemert provided a distinct alternative to the social disorganization theory of Shaw and McKay, the differential association notion of Sutherland, and the social structural approach of Merton. Lemert focused attention on the interaction between social control agents and rule violators and on how certain behaviors came to be labeled "criminal" or "delinquent" or "deviant."

Lemert's concept of **primary and secondary deviation** is regarded as one of the most important theoretical insights of the labeling perspective. According to Lemert, *primary deviation* refers to the behavior of the individual, and *secondary deviation* is society's response to that behavior. Society's reaction to the deviant, Lemert argues, forces a change in the status or role of the individual and, in effect, results in a transformation of the individual's identity.[77] Thus, the social reaction to the deviant, whether it be a disapproving glance or full-blown stigmatization, is critical in understanding the progressive commitment of a person to a deviant mode of life.

Lemert conceptualizes the process of becoming deviant as having the following stages:

> The sequence of interaction leading to secondary deviation is roughly as follows: (1) primary deviation; (2) social penalties; (3) further primary deviation; (4) stronger penalties and rejection; (5) further deviation, perhaps with hostilities and resentment beginning to focus upon those doing the penalizing; (6) crisis reached in the tolerance quotient, expressed in formal action by the community's stigmatizing of the deviant; (7) strengthening of the deviant conduct as a reaction to the stigmatizing and penalties; (8) ultimate acceptance of deviant social status and efforts at adjustment on the basis of the associated role.[78]

The social reaction theory of deviance also encompasses a social organizational perspective. As an organizational response, the concept of social reaction points to the capacity of control agents to impose such constraints upon the behavior of the deviant as are reflected in the terms "treat," "correct," and "punish."[79]

Howard Becker and the Outsider

Howard Becker aptly expresses the relationship between the rules of society and the process of being labeled as an outsider:

> Social groups create deviance by making the rules whose infraction constitutes deviance, and by applying those rules to particular people and labeling them as outsiders. From this point of view, deviance is not a quality of the act the person commits, but rather a consequence of the application by others of rules and sanctions to an "offender." The deviant is one to whom that label has successfully been applied; deviant behavior is behavior that people so label.[80]

Becker contends that once a person is caught and labeled, that person becomes an outsider and gains a new social status, with consequences for both self-image and his or her public identity. The individual is from then on regarded as a different kind of person.[81] In other words, before a person is labeled, he or she participates in a process of normal social interaction; once labeling has occurred, the individual is assigned a lowly status within the social structure.[82]

Evaluation of the Labeling Perspective

The labeling perspective has evoked mixed responses. Gary Jensen found that official labels are strongly related to the self-definition of delinquent youths and that white youths are more affected by official labels than are black youths.[83] Susan Ageton and Delbert Elliott also found that the self-concepts of white youths declined after they had police contacts.[84] But Jack Foster, Walter B. Reckless, and Simon Dinitz found that labeling by the juvenile justice system did not produce either changes in self-concept or increased delinquent behavior.[85] Stuart J. Miller, examining the effect of labeling during the institutional process, also concluded that such labels as "emotionally disturbed" or "aggressive behavior" had very little predictive power in the future behavior of hard-core delinquents.[86]

Labeling theory does have several strengths. First, its supporters have real sympathy for deviance. This sympathy is immediately evident in the labeling theorist's preference for speaking of "deviance" rather than "criminality." "Deviance," a sociological neologism, is found only in recent editions of English dictionaries. It is a term invented from the idea of "wandering from the way"; according to *Webster's New Collegiate Dictionary,* "wandering from the way" connotes sin or offense, a departure from a desirable course. Such ideas of wrong, of course, are less negative than the idea of crime. This shift in terminology also directs attention to the fact that in the "crime game," majorities are reacting to minorities. Thus, the translation of "crime" into "deviance" suggests that it may not be what one does that occasions arrest, censure, and punishment, but, rather, that what counts is the sense of being powerless or "socially disadvantaged."[87]

Second, the labeling perspective emphasizes the importance of rule making and power in the creation of deviant behavior. Considering the broader contexts of the labeling process lifts the focus of crime from the behavior of individual actors to the interactions of actors and their immediate and broader influences. Because society is looked upon as contributing to the process of becoming deviant, the rule making itself and the enforcement of those rules are acknowledged as critical processes in understanding the phenomenon of criminality.

Third, the emphasis upon role construction in labeling calls attention to the way behavior may be shaped by the expectations of those with whom individuals interact. It suggests a process in which both the self-concepts and the societal conceptions of individuals are reinforced by the early assignments of labels to certain of their acts. Thus, as part of a larger symbolic interactionist perspective, labeling theory suggests that individuals do take on the roles and self-concepts expected of them; that is, they are victims of self-fulfilling prophecies.

Fourth, such concepts as identity and career become meaningful when the criminal behavior of chronic offenders is examined. Individuals involved in one criminal act after the other do tend to see their lives largely in terms of criminal behavior. Crime is, in fact, a career to them, and they have internalized a deviant identity. This concept quickly becomes a reality in discussions with hard-core criminals who talk about "walking away from crime" and "starting a new life in the community."

The theoretical viability of labeling, however, has been questioned. Jack Gibbs argues that the labeling approach lacks clear-cut definitions and fails to produce a coherent set of interrelated propositions and testable hypotheses; therefore, it should not be considered a theory in any sense.[88] Gibbs states that the labeling approach raises major questions:

> ... the new conception has left at least four crucial questions unanswered. First, what elements in the scheme are intended to be definitions rather than substantive theory? Second, is the ultimate goal to explain deviant behavior or to explain reactions to deviation? Third, is deviant behavior to be identified exclusively in terms of reaction to it? Fourth, exactly what kind of reaction identifies behavior as deviant?[89]

Second, one reason why the labeling perspective has lost support in recent years is that it fails to answer a number of critical questions raised by the assumptions it makes: Are the conceptions we have of one another correct? Whose label really counts? When is a personal identity changed, and by whose stigmatizing effort? Does a "bad name" cause "bad action"? Is social response to crime generated more by the fact of the crime or by the legally irrelevant social characteristics of the offender?[90]

Third, the labeling perspective is criticized for denying the "badness" of the behavior of the criminal. Society is made the culprit, and the behavior of the criminal is excused. Thus, this perspective fails to take seriously the motivation of the criminal for his or her behavior; this failure becomes particularly important when dealing with actors who are aware of the high probability of apprehension for their behavior.[91]

In sum, although the popularity of the labeling perspective has dramatically declined in the 1970s and 1980s, it has had an enduring impact on the development of American criminology. (See Table 7.1 for a summary of social process theories and Box 7.1 for an application of structural and process theories to the female offender.)

ANALYSIS

This chapter suggests that disorder is generated in American society by the transmission of deviant individual patterns, by the development of deviant identity and career, and by the inability of criminals or delinquents to escape their deviant labels.

Transmission of Individual Patterns

The process of socialization involves learning individual patterns of behavior from parents, relatives, peers, school experience, and religious and other commu-

BOX 7.1

SOCIOLOGICAL THEORIES OF CRIME AND THE FEMALE OFFENDER

Considerable debate exists whether existing delinquency theories, which were developed to explain male delinquency, can be used to understand female delinquency as well. That is, will the "add women and stir" approach to delinquency theory be sufficient?

The field of delinquency research clearly focuses on lower-class male delinquency. Clifford R. Shaw and Henry D. McKay analyzed only the official arrest data on male delinquents in Chicago and repeatedly referred to these as "delinquency rates." In the early field work on delinquent gangs in Chicago, researchers confined their interest in talking to and following boys. The major theoretical approaches to delinquency also focus on the male subculture of lower-class communities as a generating milieu for delinquent behavior. Cohen states that the delinquency response "however it may be condemned by others on moral grounds, has at least one virtue; it incontestably confirms, in the eyes of all concerned, [the male's] essential masculinity." No mention of female delinquency can be found in Cloward and Ohlin's *Delinquency and Opportunity,* except that women are blamed for male delinquency. Edwin H. Sutherland was similarly male oriented, as much of his work was affected by case studies he conducted of male criminals. Indeed, when describing his notion of how differential association works, he used male examples. Finally, the work of Travis Hirschi on the social bonds that control delinquency was derived from research on male delinquents.

Some researchers contend that the male-oriented delinquency theories can also be used to explain female delinquency. Susan Datesman and colleagues and Steven Cernkovich and Peggy Giordano's studies show that the perception of blocked opportunity, or strain theory, may be even more strongly related to female involvement in delinquency than to male involvement. Proponents of social control theory contend that females are less involved in delinquency than males because sex-role socializations result in a greater tie to the social bond for females than for males. That is, girls may have less opportunity to engage in delinquent behavior because they are more closely supervised by parents. Furthermore, social control theorists claim that sex-role socialization results in a greater belief in the legitimacy of social rules for girls than for boys. Several studies of female delinquents have proposed a masculinity hypothesis. Freda Adler contends that as girls become more boy-like and acquire more "masculine" traits, they become more delinquent. F. T. Cullen, K. M. Golden, and B. Cullen found that the more adolescents (male and female) possessed "male" personality traits, the more likely they were to become involved in delinquency, but the relationship between masculinity and delinquency was stronger for males than for females. Peggy Giordano and Steven Cernkovich, pioneering the investigation of the importance of the peer group for delinquent girls, argue that peer associations must be given a central role in understanding changing patterns of delinquent involvement with girls.

In contrast to these "add women and stir" theories of juvenile delinquency, Media Chesney-Lind argues that a feminist theory of delinquency is needed. She notes that "it is increasingly clear that gender stratification in patriarchal society is as powerful a system as class." She proposes the construction of explanations of female behavior that are sensitive to its patriarchal context. A feminist analysis of delinquency would also examine ways in which agencies of social control act to reinforce the woman's place in a male society. She adds that efforts to construct a feminist model of delinquency must be sensitive to the situation of girls.

Chesney-Lind's theoretical assumptions about a feminist approach to delinquency were formulated by her studies of female criminals and female delinquents. In examining the backgrounds of adult women in prison, she found that virtually all had been the victims of physical and/or sexual abuse as youngsters, more than 60 percent had been sexually abused, and about half had been raped as young women. This situation had prompted these women to run away from home, where, once on the streets, they began engaging in prostitution and other forms of minor property crimes. They also began what became a lifetime problem with drugs. As adults possessing limited educational backgrounds and virtually no marketable occupational skills, these women continued criminal activities.

Source: Media Chesney-Lind, "Girls' Crime and Woman's Place: Toward a Feminist Model of Female Delinquency." Paper presented at the Annual Meeting of the American Society of Criminology, Montreal, Canada (November 10–14, 1987); and Clemens Bartollas, *Juvenile Delinquency* (New York: John Wiley, 1985), pp. 332–333.

nal experiences. With relatively few exceptions, parents attempt to teach children prosocial values and to encourage them to pursue crime-free lives. The patterns of behavior that children are exposed to in the school and in the community, however, are sometimes quite different from what their parents would wish for them. As Sutherland has suggested, the more intensely a person participates in a group and the more important the group is to that person, the more likely it is that he or she will acquire patterns of behavior from the group or, at the least, be influenced in the patterns of behavior he or she adopts. If a group adheres to antisocial attitudes, the individual is likely to learn criminogenic values and norms from them.

Table 7.1 SUMMARY OF SOCIAL PROCESS THEORIES OF CRIME

Theory	Cause of Crime Identified in the Theory	Supporting Research
Differential Association	Criminal behavior is expected of those individuals who have internalized a preponderance of definitions favorable to law violations	Moderate
Drift	Juvenile neutralizes himself or herself from the moral bounds of the law and drifts into delinquent behavior	Moderate
Containment	Strong inner and reinforcing external containment provide an insulation against criminal behavior	Moderate
Social Control	Criminal acts result when an individual's bond to society is weak or broken	Strong
Labeling	Society creates the deviant by labeling those who are apprehended as "different" from other juveniles, when in reality they are different only because they have been given a deviant label	Moderate

The significance of the individual patterns transmission argument is that the values and norms underlying disorder may be just as transmittable as those underlying order. Indeed, sometimes the values and norms underlying disorder appear to be more transmittable than those underlying order. The ghetto youth is frequently influenced more by successful crooks, pimps, and drug dealers than by successful prosocial individuals.

The power of individual patterns transmission can be seen in child abuse. For example, a girl who has been repeatedly beaten by her father may in turn physically abuse her own children. A mother reveals how the patterns of behavior she learned affect her behavior in the present:

> I was abused as a child. My father beat me all the time. I swore that when I had children it would be different, but I find myself doing the same thing. I keep telling myself that I won't do it again. But I get so angry that I lose control of myself. I just can't help what I do to the children.[92]

Development of Deviant Identity and Career

The criminological literature is full of autobiographical accounts of individuals pursuing a **deviant career**. The professional criminal sees himself or herself as separate and apart from the amateur and occasional criminal and looks down upon these "nonprofessionals":

> . . . the rest of them are on-again, off-again, hooligans, mulligans. . . . They're just not professional. I guess we frown on them as much as a doctor would a chiropractor. It's the same thing. A doctor, he's got a profession, and everything short of that . . . is not enough.[93]

A pertinent question, especially given the recent findings that a small group of offenders is committing a large proportion of the serious violent and property crimes in urban areas, is that of how these patterns of behavior are transmitted and stabilized. That is, what is the process of developing a deviant career?

In *Becoming Deviant,* Matza suggests that the process of developing a **deviant identity** consists of three stages.[94] The first stage is that of merely being around other deviants or career criminals. Matza defines this stage as affinity, and he sees the consequence of this stage as becoming receptive to deviant outlooks and behaviors. Affiliation, the second stage, is the process by which the individual's will is "converted to conduct novel for him but already established for others."[95] The significance of this second stage, according to Matza, is that the individual decides to become committed to criminal or deviant behavior. Signification, the third stage, means that the individual is willing to stand up for, in the sense of representing or exemplifying, criminal or deviant behavior. The individual has become committed to crime during affiliation and is willing to adopt criminal behavior and its accompanying values.

Matza's concept of the process of becoming committed to crime and standing up to that commitment offers a means of understanding the career or profes-

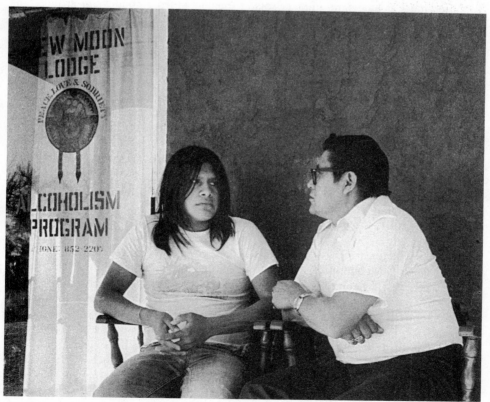

Escaping a deviant career. (*Source:* Michael D. Sullivan/TexaStock.)

sional criminal. The will, as well as an individual's commitment and conversion, are impossible to examine empirically; in fact, these terms are foreign to the scientific world view of the positivist. But conversations with career offenders do provide a glimpse of an abrupt change process in which they took on new values and sometimes a new world view.

The reality of the concept of deviant identity and career can be seen in the contacts of some offenders with the justice system. For example, a youth may become involved in minor delinquent acts from time to time, until one night when he and two companions are arrested during the break-in of a liquor store. The youth is referred to the juvenile court and adjudicated a delinquent by the court. Once labeled, the youth begins the process of interaction that leads him to pursue behaviors consistent with his new social identity. Before long, he has internalized the deviant label and become deeply involved in a delinquent career. Because he has accepted the role and status of his new career, he continues to commit delinquent acts and eventually goes on to adult crime.

Escape from a Deviant Label

The labeling perspective argues that the process of identifying and processing an individual as a deviant, in fact, isolates the person from nondeviant groups. The acceptance and internalization of a deviant label makes it difficult for an individual to return to a state of normalcy or nondeviancy. If an individual has been processed as a mental patient, an inmate of an adult correctional institution, or a resident of a juvenile correctional institution, it is even more difficult to reject the label. The chief reason for this, of course, is that society is reluctant to permit a person to shed certain labels. A prisoner is always an "ex-offender," and a mental patient is always an "ex-mental patient." Thus, a person who has refused to play by societal rules and has been officially sanctioned usually must carry the label of deviancy for a long time.

The criminal stigma goes with such an individual in seeking employment, applying for credit, running for public office, voting, meeting friends, and a thousand other social situations. What is clearly needed is a process or a ceremony whereby a deviant label can be removed. Ideally, this ceremony would erase the deficits of the past and permit the deviant to return to the fold of ordinary people.

In fact, a variety of relabeling ceremonies and communities are already in existence. The communal society is one of the best exemplifications of the relabeling process. The communal society represents an effort to establish an ideal social order apart from the perceived disorder of the larger society. The earliest communal societies in America were based on religious ideals; out of the religious utopian tradition came the Shaker communities, the Harmony Society, Amana or the Society of True Inspiration, Zoar, Oneida, and many others. The founders of these religious utopias criticized the evil and immorality of the society at large; instead of enduring life in this profane and evil environment, they attempted to create purified, spiritual societies based on fundamental Biblical truths. Rather than being resigned to a world that was filled with evil and immorality, the members of the communal society were assured harmony with nature, harmony among people, and harmony between the spirit and the flesh.[96]

Alcoholics Anonymous, Gamblers Anonymous, therapeutic communities for drug addicts, and even Weight Watchers are other examples of the numerous relabeling groups that have emerged to deal with deviant behavior. In the ceremonies that are part of these associations' activities, human failings are accepted with a more positive note. Participants are assured that they have the capacity to change their drinking, gambling, drug, or eating problem, thereby gaining self-confidence, self-acceptance, and group support.

Relabeling ceremonies are also starting to appear in the justice system. Former drug addicts and graduates of therapeutic communities are now being used as staff members of therapeutic communities. Ex-offenders are being employed in probation and parole agencies and in juvenile institutions. Criminals sometime receive a pardon for criminal offenses from the governor or even from the President; parolees or former parolees can also apply to have their criminal labels removed. Finally, probationers are frequently given deferred sentences that delay conviction on a guilty plea until the sentenced offender has served his or her probation term successfully; the offender then is given the opportunity to withdraw the plea and the court dismisses the charges.

POLICY IMPLICATIONS

The process of becoming deviant, the focus of this chapter, has particular relevance to social policy in American society at the present time. The current "get tough" crime control tactics pay little attention to the microanalysis of how individuals choose criminal or delinquent behavior.

Each of the social process theories in this chapter contributes to an understanding of how individuals become outsiders, separated from the social order. Differential association theory suggests that individuals learn from their association with small groups; if they are involved in antisocial groups, they are more likely to accept antisocial conduct norms or definitions. Social control theory adds that the more strongly attached individuals are to the social bond, the more likely it is that they will refrain from delinquent or criminal behavior. Containment theory states that positive experiences in the home, in the school, and in the community will lead to good self-concepts, thereby insulating individuals from crime and delinquency. Both drift and labeling theory propose that the key element in the process of becoming deviant is the societal reaction to unacceptable behavior.

The challenge of American society today is to ensure that citizens are exposed to positive processes rather than negative ones. Beginning with childhood and the family, and continuing with the community, schooling, and employment, individuals must have increased opportunities to realize their potential.

To provide for a more optimal development of individuals requires the following changes in American society: First, poor children especially must be provided with more positive role models. Second, everything possible must be done to reduce the stresses leading to family conflict and violence; dealing with unemployment, substandard housing, and inadequate medical care would be a good place to start. Third, the labeling of children, whether in school or in court, must be done cautiously.

Improvement in the quality of community life is also necessary in order for individuals to attain their optimal development. Differential association theory, drift, and control theories all are predicated on the idea of deviant patterns in culture being perpetuated through a process of learning. Youth gangs, prison gangs, and organized crime families show how individuals can be cast in a particular direction through their association with deviant groups. Participants tend to espouse any such group's deviant patterns, because they are attracted to its goals, cohesiveness, and intimacy of relationships.

The underclass particularly needs to become part of communal groups that provide positive experiences. Criminals and delinquents often have difficulty identifying with groups supporting positive goals. Yet countless deviants have had their lives turned around by such groups. The Shakers, an early communal society, took in waifs, or homeless children; Boys Town in Nebraska has a long history of reclaiming children in a reconstituted community, therapeutic communities are doing the same for drug addicts, and Alcoholics Anonymous and other self-help groups are serving the same function for their clientele. The task for policymakers is to expand these opportunities for the underclass and its children.

Finally, opening up economic opportunity for the underclass is a challenge for policymakers. The underclass, as suggested in Chapter 6, has real problems in the work realm. However, technological developments in the work place offer new economic opportunities for the poor. The assembly line is being replaced by robots, but a new assembly line of paper is emerging. (The processing of credit cards is one example of these emerging jobs.) Persistency and consistency are the key skills necessary in these new white-collar jobs. At present, no trade unions, nor any other organization or individual, has a monopoly on these emerging jobs; consequently, they represent a real opportunity to train the underclass to find meaningful employment within the new technological society.

SUMMARY

The social process theories discussed in this chapter provide additional pieces in the puzzle of why individuals become involved in criminal behavior. The disorders generating this behavior are evident in both primary and secondary social institutions. These findings of the social process theorists can be summarized as follows:

- The more individuals are exposed to antisocial definitions by peer groups, the more likely they are to become involved in criminal or delinquent behavior.
- The more individuals internalize negative feelings toward themselves, the more likely they are to become involved in criminal or delinquent behavior.

- The more individuals lack an attachment for the family, a desire to do well in school, and an involvement in community activities, the more likely they are to become involved in criminal or delinquent behavior.
- The more individuals experience unfairness in the way they are handled by the criminal justice system, the more likely they are to continue their involvement in criminal or delinquent behavior.
- The more negative labels individuals receive, the more likely they are to become involved in criminal behavior.

These findings, along with the ones discussed in the past three chapters, contribute to our understanding of what causes criminal or delinquent behavior. This particular chapter contributes the important insight that criminal behavior, like any other behavior, is part of the process of an individual's interaction with significant persons, groups, and institutions.

REFERENCES

Becker, Howard S. *Outsiders.* New York: Free Press, 1963.

Burgess, Robert L. "Differential Association Theory of Criminal Behavior." *Social Problems* 14 (Fall 1966), pp. 128–147.

Glaser, Daniel. "Criminality Theories and Behavioral Images." *American Journal of Sociology* 61 (March 1956), pp. 433–444.

Hirschi, Travis. *Causes of Delinquency and Its Origins.* Cambridge: Cambridge University Press, 1979.

Johnson, Richard E. *Juvenile Delinquency and Its Origins.* Cambridge: Cambridge University Press, 1979.

Lemert, Edwin M. *Social Pathology.* New York: McGraw-Hill, 1951.

Matza, David. *Delinquency and Drift.* New York: Wiley, 1964.

——. *Becoming Deviant.* Englewood Cliffs, N.J.: Prentice-Hall, 1969.

Pfohl, Stephen J. *Images of Deviance and Social Control.* New York: McGraw-Hill, 1985.

Reckless, Walter C. "A New Theory of Delinquency and Crime." *Federal Probation* 25 (December 1961), pp. 42–46.

Shoemaker, Donald J. *Theories of Delinquency: An Examination of Explanations of Delinquent Behavior.* New York: Oxford University Press, 1986.

Sutherland, Edwin H. "Development of a Theory." In *The Sutherland Papers,* edited by Albert K. Cohen, Alfred Lindensmith, and Karl Schuessler. Bloomington, Ind.: Indiana University Press, 1956.

——, and Cressey, Donald R. *Principles of Criminology.* 5th ed. Philadelphia: Lippincott, 1955.

Sykes, Gresham M., and Matza, David. "Techniques of Neutralization: A Theory of Delinquency." *American Sociological Review* 22 (September 1957), pp. 129–142.

NOTES

1. Interviewed in July 1984.
2. Harry King and William J. Chambliss, *Harry King: A Professional Thief's Journey* (New York: Wiley, 1984), p. 128.
3. Gabriel Tarde, *Penal Philosophy* (Boston: Little, Brown, 1912).

4. Ibid., p. 340.
5. Charles H. Cooley, *Human Nature and the Social Order* (New York: Schocken Books, 1964); George H. Mead, *Mind, Self and Society* (Chicago: University of Chicago Press, 1934).
6. Gwynn Nettler, *Explaining Crime,* 3d ed. (New York: McGraw-Hill, 1984), p. 254.
7. Edwin H. Sutherland, "A Statement of the Theory," in *The Sutherland Papers,* ed. Albert K. Cohen, Alfred Lindesmith, and Karl Schuessler (Bloomington, Ind.: Indiana University Press, 1956), p. 9.
8. Edwin H. Sutherland, *Principles of Criminology* (Philadelphia: Lippincott, 1947).
9. Ibid.
10. Harold Finestone, *Victims of Change: Juvenile Delinquents in American Society* (Westport, Conn.: Greenwood Press, 1976), p. 157.
11. Jack Henry Abbott, *In the Belly of the Beast: Letters from Prison* (New York: Vintage, 1981).
12. Stephen J. Pfohl, *Images of Deviance and Social Control* (New York: McGraw-Hill, 1985), pp. 241–242.
13. James S. Short, Jr., "Differential Association as a Hypothesis: Problems of Empirical Testing," *Social Problems* 8 (1960), pp. 14–25.
14. Albert Reiss and A. Lewis Rhodes, "The Distribution of Delinquency in the Social Class Structure," *American Sociological Review* 26 (1961), p. 732.
15. Brenda S. Griffin and Charles T. Griffin, "Marijuana Use Among Students and Peers," *Drug Forum* 7 (1978), pp. 155–165.
16. Melvin DeFleur and Richard Quinney, "A Reformulation of Sutherland's Differential Association Theory and a Strategy for Empirical Verification," *Journal of Research in Crime and Delinquency* 3 (January 1966), pp. 1–11.
17. Daniel Glaser, "Criminality Theory and Behavioral Images," *American Journal of Sociology* 61 (1956). pp. 433–444.
18. R. Burgess and R. Akers, "A Differential Association-Reinforcement Theory of Criminal Behavior," *Social Problems* 14 (1966), pp. 128–147.
19. Steven Box, *Deviance, Reality and Society* (New York: Holt, Rinehart and Winston, 1971), p. 21.
20. C. R. Jeffrey, "An Integrated Theory of Crime and Criminal Behavior," *Journal of Criminal Law, Criminology and Police Science* 49 (1959), pp. 533–552.
21. David Matza, *Delinquency and Drift* (New York: Wiley, 1964), p. 28.
22. Ibid., p. 49.
23. Ibid., p. 52.
24. Ibid., p. 69.
25. Ibid., p. 101.
26. Ibid., p. 88.
27. Ibid., p. 156.
28. Ibid., p. 181.
29. Ibid.
30. Ibid., p. 185.
31. Ibid., pp. 189.
32. Richard A. Ball, "An Empirical Exploration of Neutralization Theory," *Criminologia* 4 (1966), pp. 22–32. See also Richard Allen Ball, "A Report to the Ohio Youth Commission and Columbus Public Schools," based on Ph.D. dissertation, Ohio State University, 1965.
33. Robert Regoli and Eric Poole, "The Commitment of Delinquents to Their Misdeeds: A Reexamination," *Journal of Criminal Justice* 6 (1978), pp. 261–269.

34. Gresham M. Sykes and David Matza, "Techniques of Neutralization: A Theory of Delinquency," *American Sociogical Review* 22 (December 1957), pp. 664–666.
35. Travis Hirschi, *Causes of Delinquency and Its Origins* (Berkeley, Calif.: University of California Press, 1969), p. 24.
36. Ibid., p. 25.
37. Ian Taylor, Paul Walton, and Jack Young, *The New Criminology* (New York: Harper & Row, 1973), p. 186.
38. Walter C. Reckless, "A New Theory of Delinquency and Crime," *Federal Probation* 25 (December 1961), pp. 42–46; see also Reckless, *The Crime Problem,* 3d ed. New York: Appleton-Century-Crofts, 1961, pp. 335–359.
39. Nettler, *Explaining Crime,* p. 291.
40. Reckless, "A New Theory of Delinquency and Crime."
41. Simon Dinitz and Bettye A. Pfau-Vicent, "Self-Concept and Juvenile Delinquency: An Update," *Youth and Society* 14 (December 1982), pp. 133–158.
42. Walter C. Reckless and Simon Dinitz, *The Prevention of Juvenile Delinquency: An Experiment* (Columbus: Ohio State University Press, 1972).
43. G. F. Jensen, "Inner Containment and Delinquency," *Criminology* 64 (1973), pp. 464–470.
44. E. D. Lively, Simon Dinitz, and Walter C. Reckless, "Self-Concept as a Prediction of Juvenile Delinquency," *American Journal of Orthopsychiatry* 32 (1962), pp. 159–168.
45. H. B. Kaplan and A. D. Pokorny, "Self-Derogation and Childhood Broken Home," *Journal of Marriage and the Family* 33 (1971), pp. 328–337.
46. F. Ferracuti, Simon Dinitz, and E. Acosta de Brenes, *Delinquents and Nondelinquents in the Puerto Rican Slum Culture* (Columbus: Ohio State University Press, 1975).
47. H. B. Kaplan, *Deviant Behavior in Defense of Self* (New York: Academic Press, 1980).
48. Dinitz and Pfau-Vicent, "Self-Concept and Juvenile Delinquency," p. 155.
49. M. Schwartz and S. S. Tangri, "A Note on 'Self Concept as an Insulator Against Delinquency,'" *American Sociological Review* 30 (1965), pp. 922–926.
50. Reckless, *Crime Problem,* pp. 55–57.
51. Hirschi, *Causes of Delinquency,* p. 16.
52. Ibid., p. 31.
53. Ibid., p. 34.
54. Ibid., pp. 16–34.
55. Ibid., p. 83.
56. Ibid., p. 86.
57. Ibid., p. 20.
58. Ibid., p. 22.
59. Ibid., p. 200.
60. Ibid., p. 108.
61. Ibid., pp. 110–134.
62. Ibid., pp. 162–185.
63. Ibid., pp. 187–196.
64. Ibid., pp. 197–224.
65. Ibid., pp. 203–311.
66. Jerald Bachman, *Youth in Transition* (Ann Arbor, Mich.: Inter-University Consortium for Political and Social Research, University of Michigan, 1975).
67. Marvin D. Krohn and James L. Massey, "Social Control and Delinquent Behavior: An Examination of the Elements of the Social Bond" (unpublished paper, 1980).
68. Richard Salem, "Commitment and Delinquency: Social Attachments and Behavioral

Change in Group Homes" (Paper presented at the Annual Meeting of the Wisconsin Sociological Association, 22 October 1982), p. 5.

69. Michael J. Hindelang, "Causes of Delinquency: A Partial Replication and Extension," *Social Problems* 20 (Spring 1973), pp. 471–487.

70. Mark Colvin and John Pauly, "A Critique of Criminology: Toward an Integrated Structural-Marxist Theory of Delinquency Production," *American Journal of Sociology* (November 1983), p. 523.

71. Delbert S. Elliot, Suzanne S. Ageton, and Rachelle J. Canter, "An Integrated Theoretical Perspective on Delinquent Behavior," *Journal of Research in Crime and Delinquency* 16 (1979), pp. 3–27; and Richard E. Johnson, *Juvenile Delinquency and Its Origins* (Cambridge: Cambridge University Press, 1979).

72. Salem, "Commitment and Delinquency," p. 3.

73. Shoemaker, *Theories of Delinquency,* p. 175.

74. Nettler, *Explaining Crime,* p. 264.

75. Finestone, *Victims of Change,* p. 198.

76. Ibid.

77. Ibid., p. 198.

78. Edwin M. Lemert, *Social Pathology* (New York: McGraw-Hill, 1951), p. 16.

79. Ibid., p. 198.

80. Howard S. Becker, *Outsiders* (New York: Free Press, 1963), pp. 8–9.

81. Ibid., pp. 31–32.

82. Finestone, *Victims of Change,* p. 208.

83. Gary Jensen, "Labeling and Identity," *Criminology* 18 (1980), pp. 121–129.

84. Susan Ageton and Delbert Elliott, "The Effect of Legal Processing on Self-Concept" (Boulder, Colo.: Institute of Behavioral Sciences; University of Colorado, 1973).

85. Jack Foster, Simon Dinitz, and Walter C. Reckless, "Perceptions of Stigma Following Public Intervention for Delinquent Behavior," *Social Problems* 18 (1970), p. 202.

86. Stuart J. Miller, "Post-Institutional Adjustment of 443 Consecutive TICO Releases" (Ph.D. dissertation, The Ohio State University, 1971).

87. Nettler, *Explaining Crime,* p. 265.

88. Jack Gibbs, "Conceptions of Deviant Behavior: The Old and the New," *Pacific Sociological Review* 9 (Spring 1966), pp. 9–14.

89. Ibid., p. 13.

90. Nettler, *Explaining Crime,* p. 268.

91. Edwin M. Schur, *Labeling Deviant Behavior: Its Sociological Implications* (New York: Harper & Row, 1971), p. 14.

92. Interviewed in August 1985.

93. Bruce Jackson, *A Thief's Primer* (London: Macmillan, 1969), p. 144.

94. David Matza, *Becoming Deviant* (Englewood Cliffs, N.J.: Prentice-Hall, 1969), p. 90.

95. Ibid., p. 156.

96. Rosabeth Moss Kanter, *Commitment and Community: Communes and Utopias in Sociological Perspectives* (Cambridge, Mass.: Harvard University Press, 1972).

CHAPTER **8**

Conflict Theory and Crime

NATURE OF CONFLICT THEORY

DIMENSIONS OF CONFLICT THEORY

Socioeconomic Class and Marxist Criminology

Power and Authority Relationships

Group and Cultural Conflict

MARXIST CRIMINOLOGY AND EXPLANATIONS OF CRIMINAL BEHAVIOR

Oppressiveness of the Law

Alienation and Powerlessness in the Lower Class

Economic Exploitation of the Lower Class

Social Injustice

EVALUATION OF CONFLICT THEORY

ANALYSIS

Equality and Liberty

Social Cost of Upper-World Crime

Legitimacy of the State

POLICY IMPLICATIONS

SUMMARY

REFERENCES

NOTES

KEY TERMS

alienation	economic exploitation
capitalism	Instrumentalist Marxists
class struggles	lack of social justice
conduct norms	law as an oppressive force
conflict model	*lumpenproletariat*
Critical Theorists	Marxist criminologists
cultural conflict	power
dialectical thinking	Structural Marxists

Certainly, the newest and most dynamic factor in United States development during the Sixties was the sharp cleavage, indeed the class war situation which developed between the organized working classes and marginal lower classes. The combatants in this decade are not the historical enemies described by Marx but are more similar to enemies defined by fascist doctrines of the state. The working class has turned to the Leviathan with a vengeance. Not the liquidation of the state but its celebration has become of crucial importance. The working class demands legitimacy, law, order, and a ruling class willing and capable of exercising full authority. Social radicalism in American life has become the province of the reviled lumpenproletariat *and their intellectual underwriters. This development, shocking to classical ideologists, must rank as the most significant political event within the first world.*

—Irving Louis Horowitz[1]

The concept of order is an integral philosophical underpinning of conflict theory. Classical Marxist theorists contend that the present social order is fundamentally flawed and, therefore, that it must be replaced by a more humane social order. For this scenario to take place, the working class must unite in overthrowing the exploitative, capitalist ruling class. The new social order established following the revolution will be one in which all will share equally in the benefits of the means of production and in which each individual's needs will be met adequately by the larger social order.

A more humane social order is the vision of some **Marxist criminologists** of the 1980s.[2] The goals of this ideal society are reduced inequality, reduced reliance on formal institutions of justice, and reduced materialism. The social relations of this social order are committed to developing self-reliance, self-realization, and mutual aid.[3] This peaceful society can be attained by using compromise and negotiation on a community level to defuse violent social structures; communities must organize themselves in such a way to prevent crime and to help victims without punishing offenders when crime does occur.[4]

This chapter begins with an investigation of the nature of conflict theory, followed by an examination of the three dimensions of conflict theory. Then, Marxist criminology and its explanations of crime receive special attention.

NATURE OF CONFLICT THEORY

The development of the **conflict model** owes much to the concept of dialectics; this concept, like that of order, can be traced back to the philosophers of ancient Greece. Georg F. Hegel used the concept of **dialectical thinking** to explain human progress and social change. According to Hegel, a prevailing idea, or "thesis," eventually is challenged by an opposing idea, or "antithesis." The resultant conflict usually results in the merging of the two, or "synthesis."[5] Karl Marx applied the concept to the material world, rather than to ideas, as Hegel did. Marx called his approach the "materialist theory of history." He argued that the conflict was one of competing economic systems, in which the weak must ward off exploitation by the strong or powerful in society. Marx and Friedrich Engels identified the political state and its laws as: (1) a reflection of the kinds of social relations and imperatives generated by the economic organization of society; (2) a mechanism through which economically dominant classes seek to protect their interests and control subordinate classes; and (3) an institutional representation of the dominant ideology of social relations.[6]

George Simmel contended that unity and discord are inextricably intertwined and together act as an integrative force in society. Simmel added that "there probably exists no social unit in which convergent and divergent currents among its members are not inseparably interwoven."[7] Accordingly, Simmel's notion of dialectics acknowledged the existence of tendencies for order and disorder.

Lewis A. Coser and Ralf Dahrendorf further asserted that the functionalists misrepresented reality by being overly concerned with order and consensus.

Riots in an urban city. (*Source:* Michael D. Sullivan/TexaStock.)

Dahrendorf argued that the functionalist position presents a description of a utopian society—a society that never has existed and probably never will. Dahrendorf suggests that social researchers would be wise to opt for the conflict model because of its more realistic view, that society is held together by constraint and coercion rather than consensus.[8]

The conflict perspective also views social control as an outcome of the differential distribution of economic and political power in society; laws are seen as created by the powerful for their own benefit.[9] Richard Quinney, for example, contends that criminal law is a social control instrument of the state "organized to serve the interests of the dominant economic class, the capitalist ruling class."[10] Earlier, Willem Bonger in Holland made the same point: "In every society which is divided into a ruling class and a class ruled, penal law has been principally constituted according to the will of the former."[11]

DIMENSIONS OF CONFLICT THEORY

There is a great deal of variation in the ideas of conflict theorists, and, therefore, no single conflict theory can be identified. Some theories emphasize the importance of socioeconomic class, some focus more on power and authority relationships, and others examine group and cultural conflict.

Socioeconomic Class and Marxist Criminology

Karl Marx, who actually wrote very little on the subject of crime as the term is defined today, inspired a new school of criminology that emerged in the early 1970s. The school is variously described as "radical," "critical," "Marxist," "left wing," "socialist," or "new"; the term *Marxist* will be used throughout this chapter.

Marx was concerned both with deriving a theory of how societies change over time and with discovering how to go about changing society; he defined this forging of theory and practice as "praxis."[12] He saw the history of all societies as the history of **class struggles**, with crime acting as a consequence of those struggles.[13] He wrote in the *Communist Manifesto:*

> Freeman and slave, patrician and plebian, lord and serf, guildmaster and journeyman, in a word, oppressor and oppressed, stood in constant opposition to one another, carried on an uninterrupted, now hidden, now open fight, a reconstruction of society at large, or in the common ruin of the contending classes.[14]

According to Marx's theory, emerging with each historical period is a new class-based system of ranking. Marx argued that with **capitalism**, "society as a whole is more and more splitting up into two great classes directly facing each other—bourgeoisie [capitalist class] and proletariat [working class]."[15] The relations between the bourgeoisie and the proletariat become increasingly strained as the ruling class comes to control more and more of the society's wealth and the proletariat is increasingly pauperized. Marx contended that the seeds of the demise of capitalism lie in the relationship between the oppressive bourgeoisie and the pauperized proletariat.[16]

The Marxist perspective, especially the instrumentalist version, views the state and the law itself ultimately as tools of the ownership class, reflecting the economic interests of that class. It is capitalism, rather than human nature, that produces egocentric, greedy, and predatory human behavior. The ownership class is guilty of the crime of the brutal exploitation of the working class; revolution is a means to counter this violence and is both necessary and morally justifiable. Conventional crime, then, is caused by extreme poverty and economic disenfranchisement, products of the dehumanizing and demoralizing capitalist system.[17]

By the 1970s, the theorists Richard Quinney, William Chambliss, Tony Platt, Paul Takagi, Harold Pepinsky, Steven Spitzer, Herman Schwendinger and Julie Schwendinger, Raymond Michalowski, and Barry Krisberg, among others, were applying the Marxist perspective to the study of criminal law and criminology. Quinney, a leading radical theorist, summarizes this perspective:

1. American society is based on an advanced capitalist economy.
2. The state is organized to serve the interests of the dominant economic class, the capitalist ruling class.
3. Criminal law is an instrument of the state and ruling class to maintain and perpetuate the existing social and economic order.
4. Crime control in capitalist society is accomplished through a variety of institutions and agencies established and administered by a governmental elite, representing ruling-class interests, for the purpose of establishing domestic order.
5. The contradictions of advanced capitalism—the disjunction between existence and essence—require that the subordinate classes remain oppressed by whatever means necessary, especially through the coercion and violence of the legal system.
6. Only with the collapse of capitalist society and the creation of a new society, based on socialist principles, will there be a solution to the crime problem.[18]

Quinney adds that the natural products of and contradictions inherent in capitalism—such as alienation, inequality, poverty, unemployment, spiritual malaise, and economic crisis—can not be ignored in any attempt to understand crime in a capitalist society. He sees class as affecting the broad categories of crime—crimes of domination and repression and crimes of accommodation and resistance. Crimes of domination and repression are committed by the elite class and by their agents. Crimes of accommodation and resistance are committed by the *lumpenproletariat* (a term used by Marx to indicate those cast out of the productive work force) and by the working class, respectively.

Power and Authority Relationships

Max Weber's writings contain a theory of social stratification that has been applied to the study of crime.[19] Weber recognized the importance of the economic context in any analysis of social stratification, but he did not believe that a unidimensional approach could explain adequately the phenomenon of social stratification. He added power and prestige to the Marxist focus on poverty and held that these three variables were responsible for the development of hierarchies in society. Weber also proposed that property differences led to the development of classes, power differences to the creation of political parties, and prestige differences to the development of status groups.[20] Furthermore, Weber discussed the concept of "life chances" and argued that life chances were differentially related to social class. Thus, criminality exists in all societies and is the result of the political struggle among different groups attempting to promote or enhance their own life chances.[21]

Both Ralf Dahrendorf and Austin Turk have expanded upon the Weberian tradition by emphasizing the relationships between authorities and their subjects. Dahrendorf argues that **power** is the critical variable in explaining crime. He goes on to say that although Marx built his theory on only one form of power— property ownership—a more useful perspective could be constructed by incorporating a broader conception of power.[22]

Turk, utilizing the analyses of both Weber and Dahrendorf, postulates that every society is characterized by norms of deference and norms of domination within the authority structure.[23] An important variable in Turk's conflict theory is the distribution of power and prestige among individuals and groups in society. He lists ten "informal working premises":

1. Individuals diverge in their understanding and commitments.
2. Divergence leads, under specific conditions, to conflict.
3. Each conflicting party tries to promote his or her own understanding and commitments.
4. The result is a more or less conscious struggle over the available resources, and therefore of life chances.
5. People with similar understanding and commitments tend to join forces, and people who stay together tend to develop similar understandings and commitments.
6. Continuing conflicts tend to become routinized in the form of stratification systems.
7. Such systems (at least at the intergroup level) are characterized by economic exploitation sustained by political domination in all forms, from the most clearly violent to the most subtly ideological.
8. The relative power of conflicting parties determines their hierarchical position; changes in position only reflect changes in the distribution of power.
9. Convergence in understanding and commitment is generated by the (not necessarily voluntary) "outsiders," and the natural environment.
10. The relationship between divergence and convergence in human understanding and commitments is a dialectical one; ergo, the basic social process or dynamic is one of conflict.[24]

In sum, this version of conflict theory examines the power and authority relationships between the legal authorities who create, interpret, and enforce right/wrong standards for individuals in the political collectivity and for those who accept or resist but do not make such legal decisions.[25]

Group and Cultural Conflict

Group and **cultural conflict** is another dimension of the conflict perspective. Thorsten Sellin contends that to understand the cause of crime, it is necessary to understand the concept of **"conduct norms."** This concept refers to the ways members of a group should act under particular conditions. The violation of the rules guiding human behavior arouses a group reaction.[26] Individuals are members of many groups (family, work, political, religious, recreational), and each group adheres to its own conduct norms.[27] Sellin explains that "the more complex a culture becomes, . . . the greater is the chance that the norms of these groups will fail to agree.[28]

Sellin also states that an individual experiences a conflict of norms "when more or less divergent rules of conduct govern the specific life situation in which [he or she] may find himself."[29] The act of violating conduct norms is "abnormal behavior," and crime represents a particular kind of abnormal behavior distinguished by the fact that it is a violation of the conduct norms defined by criminal law.[30] In terms of criminal law, Sellin notes:

> The criminal law may be regarded as in part a body of rules, which prohibit specific forms of conduct and indicate punishments for violations. The character of these rules . . . depends upon the character and interests of those groups in the population which influence legislation. In some states these groups may comprise the majority, in others a minority, but the social values which receive the protection of criminal law are ultimately those which are treasured by the dominant interest groups.[31]

Sellin has also developed a theory of "primary and secondary culture conflict." Primary culture conflict takes place when one individual or group from one culture comes into contact with an individual or group from another culture with incompatible conduct norms. Secondary culture conflict refers to the conflict arising whenever society has diverging subcultures with different conduct norms.[32]

George B. Vold, following Sellin and Simmel, analyzes the dimension of group conflict. He views society "as a congeries [an aggregation] of groups held together in a shifting, but dynamic equilibrium of opposing group interests and efforts."[33] Vold formulates a theory of group conflict and applies it to particular types of crimes, but he does not attempt to explain all types of criminal behavior. He argues that group members are constantly engaged in defending and promoting their group's status. As groups move into one another's territory or sphere of influence and begin to compete in those areas, intergroup conflict is inevitable. The outcome of a group conflict results in a winner and a loser, unless a compromise is reached—but compromises never take place when one group is decidedly weaker than the other. Vold, like Simmel, believes that group loyalty develops and intensifies during group conflict.[34]

Vold further postulates that "the whole political process of law making, law breaking, and law enforcement directly reflects deep-seated and fundamental conflicts between interest groups and their more general struggles for the control of the police power of the state."[35] Vold addresses "crime as minority group behavior" and the "political nature of much criminal behavior."[36] Crime as minority group behavior is exhibited by those individuals who band together because they "are in some way at odds with organized society and with the police forces maintained by that society."[37] But "many kinds of criminal acts must be recognized as presenting primarily behavior in the front-line fringes of direct contact between groups struggling for the control of power in the political and cultural organization of society."[38] For example, crimes of a political nature are those resulting from a political protest movement, from conflict between company management and labor unions, and from attempts to overcome the caste system of racial segregation.[39] See Table 8.1 for a comparison of the three groups.

In sum, conflict criminologists can be divided into three groups—those emphasizing socioeconomic class, those emphasizing power and authority relationships, and those emphasizing group and cultural conflict. Those who emphasize socioeconomic class call themselves Marxist, radical, or critical criminologists and do not identify with the other two groups, because there are significant differences between their philosophy and those of the other two groups. The other two groups emphasize a plurality of interests and power and, unlike the Marxists, do not put a singular emphasis on capitalism. Nor do the non-Marxist criminologists reject the legal order as such, or the use of legal definitions of crime. Moreover, they favor reform over revolution.

MARXIST CRIMINOLOGY AND EXPLANATIONS OF CRIMINAL BEHAVIOR

Marxist criminology receives special attention in this section because a Marxist framework has been widely used to examine American criminology. Present-day Marxists see little to be gained by trying to understand the causes of criminal behavior. Instead, they believe that what must be examined is how the dominant or ruling classes use the law to oppress the subordinate classes, how the political economy and social structure create conditions generating feelings of powerlessness and alienation among lower-class individuals, how the economic system

Table 8.1 COMPARISON OF CONFLICT PERSPECTIVES

	Legal Definitions	Legal Order	Purpose of Conflict	Capitalism
Socioeconomic class (Marxists)	Rejection	Rejection	Revolution	Rejection
Power and authority relationships	Acceptance	Acceptance	Reform	Acceptance
Group and cultural conflict	Acceptance	Acceptance	Reform	Acceptance

exploits lower-class individuals, and how social justice for these individuals is lacking.

Oppressiveness of the Law

Marxist criminologists contend that certain acts are termed *criminal* because it is in the interest of the ruling class to so define them. Marxist theorists view **law as an oppressive force** that is used to promote and stabilize existing socioeconomic relations. The law maintains order, but it is an order imposed upon the powerless by the powerful.[40]

Law, according to Michalowski, emerges with the accumulation of surplus. The need to define property relations and to tax and regulate business requires a body of state-controlled law. The development of more complex forms of law and changes in substance are seen as attempts to maintain and increase the ability of owners of the means of production to acquire surplus or capital. The American system of state law, asserts Michalowski, was predicated on the principle of a two-class system of law that allowed economic elites to be essentially free from legal liability in their pursuit of profit while placing the working class under strict legal control.[41]

Anthony Platt, in describing the role played by wealthy "child-saving" reformers in creating the juvenile court, provides another explanation of how dominant classes use the law to control the subordinate classes:

> The juvenile court system was part of a general movement directed towards developing a specialized labor market and industrial discipline under corporate capitalism by creating new programs of adjudication and control for "delinquent," "dependent," and "neglected" youth. This, in turn, was related to augmenting the family and enforcing compulsory education in order to guarantee the proper reproduction of the labor force.[42]

Under the Wood Theft Law enacted in Germany in the nineteenth century, the state was entitled to sell public forests to corporate interests and wealthy individuals who wanted to sell lumber for profit. This practice interfered with the traditional practice of allowing peasants and small farmers free use of the trees in the public forests to build and heat their homes. Peasants who took wood from what had once been public lands were thus defined as criminals.[43]

E. P. Thompson agrees that law is clearly an instrument of the *de facto* ruling class that both defines and defends the rulers' claims upon resources and labor-power.[44] The law defines and defends "what shall be property and what shall be crime, and it mediates class relations with a set of appropriate rules and sanctions, all of which, ultimately, conform and consolidate existing class power." Thus, he argues, the rule of law is "only another mask for the rule of a class."[45]

However, Thompson adds that the Black Act in eighteenth-century England shows an example of how the ruling class itself is subject to the rule of law (see Box 8.1).[46] The English rulers played the "games of power according to rules that suited

BOX 8.1 **THE BLACK ACT**

E.P. Thompson's *Whigs and Hunters* examines early eighteenth-century English history, focusing particularly on the events behind the passage into law of 9 George I c.22, which came to be known as "The Waltham Black Act," or simply "The Black Act."

Enacted in four weeks in May 1723, without debate or serious division, the Black Act listed some 50 new capital offenses. The main category of offenders was of persons "armed with swords, fire-arms, or other offensive weapons, and having his or their faced blacked," who shall appear in any forest, chase, park, or enclosed ground "wherein any deer have been or shall be usually kept." It would appear that such persons must be engaged in one of the various offenses listed below, but the act was enlarged by successive judgments soon after its passage, so that merely arming and/or blacking one's face might constitute in themselves capital offenses.

The main group of offenses consisted of hunting, wounding or stealing red or fallow deer and poaching hares, conies, or fish. These were considered capital offenses if the persons involved were armed and disguised, or, in the case of deer, if the offenses were committed in the King's forest (whether the offenders were armed or not). Additional felonies included breaking down the head or mound of any fish pond; maliciously killing or maiming cattle; cutting down trees "planted in any avenue, or growing in any garden, orchard, or plantation"; setting fire to any house, barn, or haystack; maliciously shooting at any person; sending anonymous letters demanding "money, venison, or other valuable thing," and rescuing anyone from custody who was accused of any of these offenses. Sir Leon Radzinowicz comments on the severity of this act, which was to remain intact for a century:

> There is hardly a criminal act which did not come within the provision of the Black Act; offenses against public order, against the administration of criminal justice, against property, against the person, malicious injuries to property of varying degree—all came under this statute and all were punishable by death. Thus the act constituted in itself a complete and extremely severe criminal code.

The peasants who lived in the forest had reason to resent forest law because their economic survival was at stake. The economic screw had long been turned against the peasants in England, and they viewed the forest law as one more effort on the part of the elite to deprive them of what was rightfully theirs—food and wood from the forest. Venison was an important source of food, and wood was needed to provide warmth through the long cold winters.

Peasants also thought that deer stealing was too small a crime to be punished by death. Or, as one commentary put it, "They could scarcely be persuaded that the crime for which they suffered merited death. They said the deer were wild beasts, and that the poor, as well as the rich, might lawfully use them. . . ."

Source: E. P. Thompson, *Whigs and Hunters: The Origin of the Black Act* (New York: Pantheon Books, 1975), pp. 21–22, 37, 57–58, 77, 157, 162.

them, but, they could not break those rules or the whole game would be thrown away."[47] Thus, the law is oppressive, but, deviating from the traditional Marxist-structural critique of the law, Thompson contends that this oppression affects the rulers as well as the ruled.

Alienation and Powerlessness in the Lower Class

Marxist theorists argue that the problem of crime must be seen as part of the larger problem of class inequality, which leads to **alienation** and powerlessness in the lower class. This class inequality is reflected in the inferior status of women, minorities, and the young in American society.

Rape, wife battering, and forced sterilization, according to Marxist criminologists, constitute the most inhumane crimes against women. Although rape occurs in all social classes, it disproportionately victimizes poor and minority women. Rape victims, as with other violent street crimes, typically come from the most economically deprived segment of American society.

Herman Schwendinger and Julia Schwendinger, in their study of rape, concluded that the lower the family income, the greater the likelihood that a woman will be raped. They found that the vast majority of women who have experienced either rape or attempted rape come from families with annual incomes of less than $10,000. They also found that most rapes are planned, that nearly all involve the use of force, that many are extremely brutal, and that a majority of victims are passive during the attack.[48]

The alienation and powerlessness of minorities is illustrated by the consequences of the political activism of black gangs in Chicago in the late 1960s. In 1968, the three major supergangs in Chicago—the Vice Lords, the Blackstone Rangers, and the Disciples—campaigned against the reelection of Major Richard Daley's Democratic machine. This political activism resulted in immediate action from the Democratic machine following the election. Daley announced a crackdown on gang violence, and state's attorney Edward Hanrahan subsequently labeled the gang situation as the most serious crime problem in Chicago. Gang members charged at the time that they were being subjected to increased harassment from the police. Moreover, the courts began to increase dramatically the number of gang members sent to prison in Illinois.[49]

Richard Quinney has written that "violent gang activity may become a collective response of adolescents in slums to the problems of living in such areas of the city."[50] Balkan et al. have further noted that criminal street gang activity is most frequently found in those social settings where poverty, unemployment, drugs, and police encounters are commonplace. In such social contexts, gangs become both the source of a member's most meaningful social relationships and the source of protection where "life on the streets" has made survival an issue.[51]

In *The Children of Ishmael,* Barry Krisberg and James Austin assert that youth in a capitalist society typically are seen as a group of people who are in a sense expected to remain in a holding pattern until they can take their places in the work force.[52] The authors add that "young people form a subservient class, alienated, powerless, and prone to economic manipulation."[53] Young people are excluded from full participation in society's political institutions. They lack organized lobbies, have limited voting power, and hold few positions of authority. Furthermore, youths are subjected to controlling forces by the state, and, just like any other subordinate group in society, they find that their rights, privileges, and identities are defined by the "powers that be."[54]

Economic Exploitation of the Lower Class

Economic exploitation, according to Marxist criminologists, affects the poor in many ways. One result is higher rates of crime. The Marxists contend that three aspects of class inequality are strongly related to street crime: forced employment or unemployment, poverty, and income inequality.

A relationship between unemployment and crime is widely cited by Marxist criminologists. Harvey M. Brenner found that between 1920 and 1940 and between 1947 and 1973, there has been a positive relationship between unemployment and nearly every measure of criminal activity in California, Massachusetts, and New York (as well as in Canada, England, Wales, and Scotland). As unemployment goes up, so does the number of crimes known to the police; the number of arrests, trials, and convictions; and the number of imprisonments.[55] Other recent studies by I. Jankovic,[56] David Greenberg,[57] and M. G. Yeager,[58] also have found a strong relationship between unemployment and prison commitments. Moreover, A. D. Calvin has found a strong association between the unemployment of black youth and street crime.[59]

Income inequality, another aspect of class inequality in American society, may affect conventional street crimes even more than unemployment and poverty. John Braithwaite concluded from his extensive review and analysis of the available data that the widening of the income gap between rich and poor is the economic factor that most frequently leads to increases in street crime. Specifically, he found that those U.S. cities that have the widest income gaps between the low- and average-income earning parts of their populations consistently have the highest street crime rates.[60] This relationship between low- and average-income earning parts of their populations exists regardless of city size, geographic region, or the proportion of the city population made up of minority groups. Leo Carroll and Pamela I. Jackson's more recent study confirmed Braithwaite's findings. In their analysis of the *U.S. Census and Uniform Crime Report* data on 93 non–southern cities of over 50,000 population in 1960, they found that the level of income inequality is an important predictor of the level of violent crime.[61]

J. R. Blau and P. M. Blau's study also pointed out the importance of economic inequality—especially socioeconomic inequality between races—in explaining violent street crime, but they were unable to find any strong support for the "Southern tradition of violence" or the "subculture of violence" explanations. They concluded that if a "culture of violence" contributes to the incidence of violent crime, it too has its roots in pronounced economic inequalities.[62]

Moreover, victims, as well as street crime perpetrators, are likely to be poor, unemployed, or working in low-level, low-paying jobs. Thus, street crime tends to be an intra-class phenomenon: poor and working-class individuals tend to victimize other poor and working-class individuals.[63] Elliott Currie, in summarizing a series of victimization studies done by the Law Enforcement Assistance Administration of the U.S. Department of Justice during the 1970s, notes that:

> A woman whose family income is below $3,000 is roughly seven times as likely to be raped as a woman whose family income is between $15,000 and $25,000. A man with an annual income about $25,000 is only half as likely to be robbed as a man making less than $3,000, and less than one-third [times as likely to be] injured in a robbery. . . .[64]

J. Chapman found that most of the recent increases in female crime represent increases in petty property crimes, rather than increases in white-collar and occupational crime. She concludes that women commit more economic or property crimes when jobs are unavailable, not when they are more available.[65] N. Jurik, in another examination of the sex-role equality explanation, found that female offenders released from prison with either unemployment compensation or support from an employed male tended to be rearrested less often.[66]

The Marxist perspective also suggests that the relationship between business and government, especially during a period when the regulation of business is not viewed as a legitimate function of government, is directly related to corporate crime. Quinney, in this regard, says:

> As capitalism continues to develop, corporations must accumulate more capital and expand, raising profits by whatever means in order to survive. A consequence is increasing use of criminal operations—against the population, as well as against other corporations, the government, and the society. The capitalist economy becomes criminal in itself.[67]

Schwendinger and Schwendinger further argue that capitalism produces a marginal class of people who are superfluous from an economic standpoint. They also state that socialization agents within the social system, such as the school, tend to reinvent within each new generation the same class system: "The children of families that have more get more, because the public educational system converts human beings into potential commodities."[68] Schools, then, tend to be geared toward rewarding and assisting those youths who exhibit early indications of achieving the general potential success in institutions of higher learning and later in the job market. The selection is made at the expense of those who do not exhibit such potential in their early encounters with the educational system.[69]

Greenberg discusses juvenile theft in terms of structural obstacles to legiti-

From the kitchenette . . .
(*Source:* Library of Congress [LC-USF34-38777] with acknowledgment of *12 Million Black Voices* by Richard Wright, pp. 132–133. © 1941 Richard Wright.)

mate sources of funds. He states that the persistent decline in teenage employment, particularly among black teenagers, has left adolescents less and less capable of financing an increasingly costly social life, the importance of which is enhanced as the age segregation of society grows. Thus, adolescent theft is a response to the disjunction between the desire to participate in social activities with peers and the absence of legitimate means to finance this participation.[70]

Mark Colvin and John Pauly, in relating the Marxist perspective to juvenile delinquency, contend that delinquency is a latent outcome of the reproduction processes of capitalism. Using the empirical findings of others to support their model, they assert that parents' experiences of coerciveness in work-place control structures contribute to the development of coercive family control structures, which lead to alienated bonds with children. According to Colvin and Pauly, juveniles with alienated family bonds are more likely to be placed in coercive school control situations, which reinforce their alienated bonds. Their alienated bonds also lead these juveniles to greater association with alienated peers.[71]

. . . to the white folks' kitchen.
(*Source:* Library of Congress [LC-USF34-51738] with acknowledgment of *12 Million Black Voices* by Richard Wright, pp. 132–133. © 1941 Richard Wright.)

Colvin and Pauly conclude that these peer group control structures, along with the lack of distribution of economic opportunities, create two different paths of delinquent involvement. In the first path, the experience of coerciveness in peer group control relations mutually interacts with their alienated bonds to propel certain juveniles into serious, patterned, violent delinquent behavior. In the second path, the experience of remuneration from illegitimate sources creates an alternative utilitarian control structure that interacts with newly formed calculative bonds to propel other juveniles into serious, patterned, instrumental delinquent behavior.[72]

In sum, these studies conclude that the structural conditions of capitalist society lead to the exploitation of lower-class individuals. This exploitation, in turn, creates a marginal role for these lower-class individuals and influences their decision to pursue illegitimate means to satisfy their desires and needs.

Social Injustice

The thrust of the Marxist argument is that the criminal justice system is biased in favor of the middle and ruling classes so that by the time the end of the road is reached in prison, the vast majority of those found there come from the lower classes. This bias begins with the fact that the law excludes certain ruling class behaviors that do great harm, such as corporate pollution and the selling of dangerous products, and continues at every level of the criminal and juvenile justice processes. As Reiman so aptly expresses it:

> *For the same criminal behavior,* the poor are more likely to be arrested; if arrested, they are more likely to be charged; if charged, more likely to be convicted; if convicted, more likely to be sentenced to prison; and if sentenced, more likely to be given longer prison terms than members of the middle and upper classes. In other words, the image of the criminal population one sees in our nation's jails and prisons is an image distorted by the shape of the criminal justice system itself.[73]

The **lack of social justice** for the poor, Reiman points out, is particularly troublesome because white-collar crimes are more widespread and more expensive for society than street crimes (see Chapter 10). Yet, when the punishment of street offenders is compared with that of white-collar offenders, it is apparent that the latter receive far more lenient sentences. For example, banks lose six times as much money through embezzlement as through robbery, but only 17 percent of those convicted of embezzlement go to jail, while 91 percent of those convicted of bank robbery go to jail.[74]

Reiman goes on to argue that it is money that often determines guilt or innocence. The impoverished offender may not be able to afford bail, a situation that means jail unless he or she can be released on a pretrial release program. The jailed poor are handicapped in preparing their defense, are more susceptible to plea bargaining, and are limited in the quality of representation they will have. Furthermore, the system is biased against the poor when it comes to sentencing. The crimes of the poor not only carry harsher penalties, but, Reiman adds, "for *all* crimes, the poor receive less probation and more years of confinement than the better-heeled defendants convicted of the same offense, assuring us once again that the vast majority of those who are put behind bars are from the lowest social and economic classes in the nation."[75]

Reiman believes that the prison system is structured to fail. The prisons, filled disproportionately with the unemployed and underemployed, undereducated, the poor, and minorities, fail to deter, rehabilitate, and protect society. Reiman concludes that the actual goal of criminal justice policy is to maintain crime rather than reduce it.

The criminal justice system fails to reduce crime while making it look like crime is the work of the poor. And it does this in a way that conveys the image that the real danger to decent, law-abiding Americans comes from below them, rather than from above them, on the economic ladder. This image sanctifies the status quo with its disparities of wealth, privilege, and opportunity and thus serves the interests of the rich and powerful in America—the very ones who could change criminal justice policy if they were really unhappy with it.[76]

Marxist criminologists also argue that social justice is lacking for juveniles. Poor and disadvantaged youths tend to be disproportionately represented in the juvenile justice system despite the fact that research indicates that actual acts of delinquent behavior are more or less evenly distributed throughout the social spectrum.[77] Female status offenders are subjected to sexist treatment in the juvenile justice system.[78] Racism is present, and blacks and other minorities are dealt with more harshly than whites.[79] Thus, Marxist criminologists believe that the juvenile justice system administers different sorts of justice to the children of the "haves" and to the children of the "have-nots," to boys who commit delinquent offenses and to girls who commit "moral offenses," and to white youths and to nonwhite youths.

EVALUATION OF CONFLICT THEORY

An evaluation of conflict theory must recognize that the theoretical contributions of Marxist criminologists diverge from the assumptions, ideologies, and practices of other conflict theorists. Implementing the policies implied by Marxist criminologists would dramatically affect the way crime is defined, criminals are treated, theories are formulated and tested—and the way the sociopolitical-economic structure is run. However, Marxist criminologists themselves also differ in their interpretation of crime (see Box 8.2).

One of the strengths of conflict theory, especially Marxist criminology, is that it proposes a new social order, one based on equality and equity. Deprivation and scarcity are absent, and human need is provided for by the state. This proposed social order does not have slums, an underclass, or the debilitating effects of disorganized communities. Although only fragmentary descriptions of this new social order are found in the writings of Marx and his followers, Marxists are consistent in saying that as long as some are excluded from meaningful participation in the processes of economic distribution and consumption, there will be a "surplus population" that becomes alienated from society and responds with street crime.

Second, the conflict position is a reminder that it is necessary to use societal or more "macro" strategies to eliminate alienation, inequality, poverty, unemployment, and other such problems. Although the overriding concern of the past four chapters has been the offender and the question of whether or not he or she is responsible for criminal behavior, that preoccupation tends to excuse society from dealing with the social problems that result in crime.

BOX 8.2   **VARIATIONS IN MARXIST CRIMINOLOGY**

1. *Instrumentalist Marxists* view the entire apparatus of crime control—laws, courts, police, and prisons—as the tool or instrument of the ruling class (capitalists). These authors emphasize the benefits to the elite of the crime control structures in society. For example, in his book *Class, State, and Crime,* Richard Quinney points to the close correlation between the prison population and the unemployment rate. Quinney states that this correlation holds whether or not the amount of crime goes up because the prisons are used to warehouse surplus labor.

2. *Structural Marxists* tends to argue that the *form* of the legal system can work to reproduce capitalist social relations *without* the conscious deliberate use of the law and criminal justice system on the part of the ruling capitalists to repress workers. The state, as part of the superstructure, is said to operate in relative autonomy from the underlying class relations of capitalist society. The criminal law takes the form it does under capitalism because it is based on capitalist notions of private property and the exchange of commodities (including labor). Because of the partial autonomy of the state and the fact that the law as *ideology* must be based on claims of universal and not class interest, the legal system may not function directly in the interests of the ruling class. Indeed, it may occasionally "backfire" and allow gains to be made by the working class.

3. *Critical Theorists* often combine Marxist theory with the insights of later theorists, such as Sigmund Freud. They reject overly deterministic versions of Marxists (i.e., they do not see every social phenomenon as a direct expression of the class struggle). These authors tend to focus their critique on those aspects of modern culture that induce conformity and acceptance of domination, such as the ideology of mass consumption created by the advertising and entertainment industries. The potential of this strand of Marxism for the study of crime and criminal justice is largely undeveloped.

Source: Contributed to this volume by B. Keith Crew, University of Northern Iowa.

Third, conflict theorists have provided valuable insights for an understanding of crime and delinquency through their efforts to demystify the law and legal practices. These theorists have discussed how the meaning of crime, as defined by criminal law, is influenced by political, social, and economic factors. They also have helped clarify the importance of extralegal factors in juvenile and adult courts' decision making.

Fourth, the conflict position has greatly clarified the way power is used to make decisions in American society. Chambliss and Seidman state that "every detailed study of the emergence of legal norms has consistently shown the immense importance of interest-group activity, not 'the public interest,' as the critical variable in determining the content of legislation."[80] They add that "the higher a group's political and economic position, the greater is the probability that its views will be reflected in the laws."[81]

Fifth, the Marxist perspective advocates more power for women, all racial groups, and young people. Its proponents state that the subservient status of these groups in the past has resulted in their feeling alienated, powerless, and economically manipulated. They add that the poorer a person is, the most likely he or she is to be fitted into a subservient position in American society.

On the other hand, at least three major criticisms can be made about conflict theory, especially the Marxist perspective. First, Marxist theory tends to romanticize the criminal, embracing a deterministic viewpoint that, like labeling, minimizes the criminal act. This fascination with the "victimized offender" often ends with the portrayal of the lawbreaker as a political criminal no more responsible for his or her criminal behavior than positivism would have it. Significantly, some Marxist criminologists, such as David Greenberg and Elliott Currie, have recently moved away from this view.

Second, until recently, Marxist criminologists have had little interest in what they consider to be piecemeal reform of the criminal and juvenile justice systems. David Greenberg, disagreeing with this view, fears that a system not undergoing reform and change will become only more repressive:

> Some radicals have feared that successful campaigns to achieve short-run goals might make a socialist revolution hard to achieve. . . . If some concessions are won, this argument goes, militant opposition to the state will dry up. Behind this concern lies an implicit "big bang" model of how revolutions are made: conditions get worse and worse until the oppressed can't stand it anymore and one day explode. In the industrialized capitalist world such a model seems farfetched. In fact, it is a pernicious model, since it encourages socialists to sit back and do nothing while social conditions deteriorate. . . .[82]

Another criticism that can be made of those with little interest in "piecemeal reform" is that they are not advocating true Marxism. Marx himself argued that the struggle for freedom was where *praxis*, or practice, was formed.[83]

Finally, Marxist criminology has certain theoretical and empirical deficiencies. Logical deficiencies are apparent in the contention that the rules defining crime and delinquency in a capitalist society lead to the injuries or social harm caused by crime. All societies, whether capitalist or socialist, experience the injuries of crime and have seen fit to condemn the criminal.[84] Marxist criminology also overstates the evilness of the state and the goodness of the human being. Additionally, the claim that the Marxist perspective is a unique paradigm in American criminology is overstated, for this theoretical position has been shaped by such theories as social pathology, structural-functionalism, and labeling.[85]

ANALYSIS

The issues of equality and liberty, of the social cost of upper-world crime, and of the legitimacy of the state are fundamentally related to conflict theory and its perspective on social order in American society.

Equality and Liberty

John Rawls's *Theory of Justice* suggests that justice ultimately is based on the three principles of liberty, equality, and fraternity.[86] As both socialist and capitalist societies have discovered, the difficulty of achieving justice is the inevitable contradiction in these three principles. Those societies that grant liberty as a basic condition seem to have difficulty achieving equality among citizens. Similarly, those societies that are founded on equality and nonscarcity seem to result in the repression of liberty. Rawls's third principle, fraternity, is widely ignored, because of the inherent difficulty in achieving both liberty and equality.

The apparent contradictions in these principles become clearer when applied to the United States. This nation, founded on a constitutional order, values liberty as a top priority of its government. But, as social disruption has recently shaken the very foundations of society, liberty has been increasingly viewed as permitting licence. The principle of liberty still dominates the social policy of American society, but it is a principle that both conservatives and liberals say must be balanced with security and stability.

It has been obvious throughout most of the history of this nation that equality for the underclass is seriously lacking. Conflict theorists, particularly Marxist criminologists, are among the most vocal in charging that the prevailing social order of this society is exploitative toward the underclass.

Fraternity, the spirit of kinship or a sense of community, appears to be more feasible in homogeneous than in heterogeneous societies. American society—partly because of the fear of crime but for many other reasons as well—is increasingly characterized by the breakdown of community. This text repeatedly argues that supportive communal networks provide the best hope of dealing with social disruption, including crime.

In sum, the quality of life in a given society requires that justice be provided for its citizens. Justice itself involves a configuration of freedom of citizens, equality of classes, and development of community. American society, presently fractured by the problem of the control of crime, is increasingly experiencing a sense of loss of community. This loss is taking place at the same time that security is being emphasized at the expense of freedom and that social injustice of the underclass remains a serious problem.

Social Cost of Upper-World Crime

The criminological theories of the past four chapters clearly focus on lower-class crime. Marxist criminologists contend, however, that the social cost of upper-

A Franciscan Father distributes a small amount of food to a growing line of people on a cold morning in New York City. (*Source:* Jim Pozarik/Gamma-Liaison.)

world crime far exceeds that of lower-class crime. They are most critical of corporate-related crimes and crimes of the state.[87]

The categories of corporate crime include crimes against employees, crimes against consumers, and collective human jeopardy. Crimes against employees involve those instances when employers subject employees to dangers in the workplace, such as union busting, occupational health hazards, and discrimination against females and minorities. Crimes against consumers include excessive costs, unsafe products, and dangerous nutrition (e.g., the sale of adulterated products and the extensive use of chemical additives). Collective jeopardy takes place both when corporate decisions pollute the environment and when corporate practices have harmful effects on people in other nations. Examples of the international dimensions of human jeopardy are arms sales that heighten world tensions and colonial relationships that exploit natural resources and cheap labor from dependent nations (see Chapter 10 for a more extensive discussion of corporate crime).

Marxist criminologists also charge that the government commits two basic types of crimes against its citizens. First, there are the overt governmental decisions that benefit the powerful and at the same time do harm to the powerless. This bias of government is seen in the fact that whenever the interests of the powerful clash with those of the powerless, the decisions of government tend to benefit the powerful. For example, to stimulate the economy during an economic

BOX 8.3   **ABUSE OF POWER BY THE CIA AND FBI**

- The CIA opened and photographed nearly 250,000 first-class letters in the United States between 1953 and 1973.
- As director of the CIA, William Colby acknowledged to Congress that his organization had opened the mail of private citizens and accumulated secret files on more than 10,000 Americans.
- The FBI admitted to the Senate Intelligence Committee that it had committed 238 burglaries against 14 domestic organizations during a 26-year period ending in 1968.
- The FBI collected more than 500,000 dossiers between 1959 and 1971 on communists, black leaders, student radicals, and feminists. The FBI turned its arsenal of surveillance techniques on Martin Luther King, Jr. It was concerned with the political and personal activities of a man and a movement committed to nonviolence and democracy.

Source: D. Stanley Eitzen and Doug A. Timmer, *Criminology: Crime and Criminal Justice* (New York: John Wiley and Sons, 1985), pp. 346–347.

downturn, the government often provides subsidies to businesses rather than directly to needy individuals because of the assumption that private profit maximizes the public good. This practice reflects the general principle that business can conduct its affairs either undisturbed by or encouraged by government, whichever is of greater benefit to the business community. However, while capitalism profits from American government policy, Marxists assert that it is the powerless who bear the burden. Robert Hutchins characterized the basic principle guiding internal affairs: "Domestic policy is conducted according to one infallible rule: the costs and burdens of whatever is done must be borne by those least able to bear them."[88]

Second, the government, according to Marxist criminologists, is involved in five forms of lawlessness. These consist of three domestic crimes: (1) secrecy, lying, and deception; (2) the abuse of power by government agencies, especially the FBI and the CIA; and (3) the use of citizens as unwilling and unknowing guinea pigs. Watergate is a sad commentary on the first form of domestic crime, and the items in Box 8.3 illustrate well the second. The use of citizens as unwilling and unknowing guinea pigs is demonstrated by a recent declassification of government documents revealing that the American people had been subjects in 239 open-air bacteriological tests conducted by the Army between 1949 and 1969. During one of these tests, San Francisco was blanketed with poisonous bacteria known as serratia, which causes a type of pneumonia that can be fatal.

At the international level, Marxist criminologists claim that American intervention in the domestic affairs of other nations is a fourth level of government lawlessness and that war crimes represent a final form of government lawlessness. Evidence from Senate investigating committees, for example, has shown that over a 20-year period, the CIA was involved in more than 900 foreign interventions, including paramilitary operations, surreptitious manipulations of foreign governments, and assassinations. The war crimes of the United States, according to Marxist criminologists, began with the conquering of the American Indians but, most recently, are illustrated by the Vietnam experience. For example, the most infamous incident of the war was the March 1968 massacre at Song My (also known as My Lai), in which, under orders from their superiors, American soldiers killed more than 500 civilians.

Legitimacy of the State

In discussing upper-world criminality, Marxist criminologists raise serious questions about the trustworthiness of the state. They see the state as sanctioning decadent capitalism at the expense of the poor. Instead of being concerned that everyone has a stake in the system or is able to participate in the political and economic life of the society, Marxist theorists charge, the state is willing to sacrifice the well-being of the poor so that the rich can get richer. Perhaps they overstate the lawlessness of the state, especially in American interventions in the domestic affairs of other nations and war crimes. In this regard, there are few nations in the contemporary world, or even throughout history, that could escape this criticism. But the criticism that the state generates social injustice by ignoring the needs of the poor is much more difficult to refute.

Law is the institutionalization of conflict, and Marxist theorists claim that criminal law is created by rich or powerful interest groups to be used against the underclass. Law, then, represents a repressive vehicle of the dominant groups in American society used to control the poor. It is the poor whose crimes are most severely sanctioned and who make up the majority of the inmates in our overcrowded prisons.

Marxist criminologists charge that the failure of the modern state to integrate the needs of the various classes has resulted in a society that is on the verge of collapse, but they differ somewhat on what their role should be in dealing with this collapsing society. Traditionally, Marxist theorists have urged the proletariat to work for revolution—envisioning the great unity of workers against the decadent capitalist society—to create a just social order. That is, social reform cannot take place until the "big bang" or revolution. But a more recent position is that waiting for the revolution is a disservice to those who suffer at the hands of the current system.

However, Marxist criminologists have overstated the unity of the ruling elite. Conflict and competition often reflect the realities of decision-making at the upper levels of government, business, and politics. The assumption of a *unified* ruling elite pulling the strings of government and exploiting the working class is simply not true. As Thompson's *Whigs and Hunters* suggests, the members of the ruling class often are competing with each other for power.[89]

The Marxist criminologists' assertion of the repressiveness of the law has also overstated the case. Thompson points out that the law is used by the controlling classes to assert their will on the poor, but that they, in turn, are limited by the law they have created.[90] The convictions of those responsible for Watergate, of Vice President Spiro Agnew, and of various other politicians, judges, corporation executives, and influential members of the society are a reminder that the elite at least occasionally experiences criminal justice sanctions.

POLICY IMPLICATIONS

Conflict theory has much to teach advocacy groups about how power and domination affect the creation of policy. For example, conflict theory contends that control in American society is gained by those groups that wield the most power and resources; that once a group achieves dominance over others, it seeks to use the available societal mechanisms to maintain that dominance; that laws are formulated in the interests of the dominant group, with the result that those behaviors common to the less powerful groups may be restricted; and that the law enforcement and control systems operate to process disproportionately the less powerful members of society.

Marxist criminology's visions of a humanistic social order and of the plight of the marginal class also have important policy implications for this nation. The ideal social order, as previously indicated, is one in which equality is present, deprivation and scarcity are absent, and a genuine human community exists. Scott G. McNall, in a 1983 address to the Midwest Sociological Society, outlined the posture of individuals in this new order.[91] McNall cited Paul Ricoeur, who suggests that individuals realize themselves as people by recognizing that they are part of the larger entity, humanity. One's humanity, according to Ricoeur, is realized through participation in the act of speech. For Ricoeur, language has the power to call tyranny into question; not unlike George Herbert Mead or Marx, Ricoeur believes that a human being realizes humanness only through intersubjective acts (action between oneself and another). A person who becomes free has the power to call tyranny into question.[92]

McNall also cited Gilles Deleuze and Felix Guattari, who see the madness of modern civilization—which they call schizophrenia—as the product not just of one's personal or family history, but also of all the coercive forces in the environment: wars, racism, economic problems, status and class struggles. The task of the individual is to free himself or herself from the paranoia produced by this schizophrenic madness (which is not radically different from Marx's concept of alienation) and to challenge its power. A person challenges power by understanding it and how it controls him or her.[93]

McNall believes that human action can create more humane structures. He contends that "a system changes when old beliefs and ways of acting no longer suffice to explain the social world with which people are confronted."[94] He cites the rise of populism on the northern Great Plains in the late 1880s as an example of how the farmers were able to change the social order. McNall concluded his address by paraphrasing Marx's Eleventh Thesis on Feuerbach: "the purpose of philosophy, then, is not to interpret the world, but to change it," adding, "So it still is."[95]

In no other source is the plight of a marginal class so well documented as in the writings of Marxist criminologists. They examine what it has meant to racial minorities, women, and young people to be victimized by the larger society. They point out that the opportunity structure and economic exploitation of a society become key variables in understanding lower-class crime. Societies in which economic exploitation is extreme and in which opportunity is limited can be expected to have high rates of crime. Therefore, an adequate standard of living, as well as increased employment possibilities for all Americans, are critical issues in deterring adult and juvenile crime.

SUMMARY

The concept of conflict dates back to antiquity. Heraclitus of Ephesus, Herodotus, Aristotle, and Polybius are but a few of the classical thinkers who incorporated this concept into their discussions of the state. Today, the notion of conflict continues to be widely discussed in the analysis of society.

Marxist theorists are critical of the capitalist system. They claim that economic, social, and political equality can not be achieved under the present economic system. They also claim that crime in capitalist societies is caused by the efforts of the elite to maintain their power at all costs, through exploitation of the working class. Marxist criminology focuses primarily on how crime is generated by the social structure of advanced-capitalist societies. Marxist criminologists charge that the organization and operation of the American economy begins and ends with an elitist and racist society. Some in society are excluded from meaningful participation in economic production and, therefore, are unable to participate in the processes of economic distribution and consumption. The system, then, is structured to fail because it helps to maintain a large and visible, poor and minority criminal class that detracts attention from the problems that originate among the elite.

An examination of the past five chapters readily leads one to the conclusion that no one theory can be used to explain crime. Each of the main theories about the causes of crime provides but a small piece of the puzzle; combined, they are more helpful in understanding criminal behavior in the United States. The task is to increase the explanatory power of these theories by building on the strengths of each. The past chapters do provide some directions, or building blocks, that should be useful in providing a greater synthesis of the various explanations of criminal behavior.

First, as suggested by Shaw and McKay, an understanding of delinquent and criminal behavior requires a multilevel theoretical approach, with its offer of the promise of synthesis between sociobiological, psychological, and macro and micro sociological explanations.[96] Second, using the concept of the bonding processes in social control theory, juveniles and adults can be followed through life-cycle encounters with various socializing agencies.[97] That is, social control theory can be used to weave together the disconnected social settings into a unified conceptualization of socialization processes. Third, the androcentric, or male-focused, orientation of criminological theories must be balanced by more feminist theories of criminal behavior. Finally, the lower-class bias of criminological theories must be supplemented by more theories related to upper-world criminality.[98]

REFERENCES

Afanasyer, V. *Marxist Philosophy*. Moscow: Foreign Language Publishing House, n.d.

Beirne, Piers, and Quinney, Richard, eds. *Marxism and the Law*. New York: Wiley, 1982.

Colvin, Mark, and Pauly, John. "A Critique of Criminology: Toward an Integrated Structural-Marxist Theory of Delinquency Production." *American Journal of Sociology* 89 (November 1983), pp. 513–551.

Dahrendorf, Ralf. "Out of Utopia: Toward a Reorientation of Sociological Analysis." In *Sociological Theory: A Book of Readings,* edited by Lewis Coser and Bernard Rosenberg. New York: Macmillan, 1976.

Huff, C. Ronald. "Conflict Theory in Criminology." In *Radical Criminology,* edited by James Inciardi. Beverly Hills, Calif.: Sage, 1980.

Krisberg, Barry, and Austin, James, eds. *The Children of Ishmael: Critical Perspectives on Juvenile Justice.* Palo Alto, Calif.: Mayfield, 1978.

Marx, Karl, and Engels, Friedrich. *The Communist Manifesto.* Reprint. New York: International, 1979.

————. *Collected Works: Marx and Engels, 1851–1853.* Vol. II. New York: International, 1979.

Michalowski, Raymond J. *Order, Law, and Crime.* New York: Random House, 1985.

McNall, Scott G. "Variations on a Theme: Social Theory." *Sociological Quarterly* 24 (August 1983), pp. 471–487.

Platt, Anthony. *The Child Savers.* 2d ed. Chicago: University of Chicago Press, 1981.

Quinney, Richard. *Class, State, and Crime.* New York: Longman, 1980.

Sellin, Thorsten. *Culture, Conflict, and Crime.* New York: Social Science Research Council, 1938.

Taylor, Ian; Walton, Paul; and Young, Jock. *The New Criminology: For a Social Theory of Deviance.* London: Routledge & Kegan Paul, 1973.

Thompson, E. P. *Whigs and Hunters: The Origin of the Black Act.* New York: Pantheon Books, 1975.

Vold, George B. *Theoretical Criminology.* 2d ed. Prepared by Thomas J. Bernard. New York: Oxford University Press, 1979.

NOTES

1. Irving Louis Horowitz, *Three Worlds of Development,* 2d ed. (New York: Oxford University Press, 1972), p. xvii.

2. See Larry Tifft and Dennis Sullivan, *Crime, Criminology, and Anarchism: The Struggle To Be Human* (Great Britain: Cienfuegos Press, 1980); Raymond J. Michalowski, *Order, Law, and Crime: An Introduction to Criminology* (New York: Random House, 1985); and Harold E. Pepinsky, "A Sociology of Justice," *Annual Review of Sociology 1986* 12 (1986), pp. 93–108.

3. Tifft and Sullivan, *Crime, Criminology, and Anarchism,* p. 172, and Michalowski, *Order, Law, and Crime,* pp. 406–411.

4. Pepinsky, "A Sociology of Justice," pp. 102–105.

5. This traditional interpretation of Hegel's "thesis-antithesis-synthesis" is frequently questioned. See Ron E. Roberts and Robert Marsh Kloss, *Social Movements: Between the Balcony and the Barricade,* 2d ed. (St. Louis: Mosby, 1979), p. 16.

6. Stephen Spitzer, "Toward the Marxist Theory of Deviance," *Social Problems* 22 (1975), p. 638.

7. Georg Simmel, *Conflict,* trans. Kurt H. Wolf (Glencoe, Ill.: Free Press, 1955), pp. 15–30.

8. Ralf Dahrendorf, "Out of Utopia: Toward a Reorientation of Sociological Analysis," in *Sociological Theory: A Book of Readings,* ed. Lewis A. Coser and Bernard Rosenberg (New York: Macmillan, 1976), p. 198.

9. David Shichor, "The New Criminology: Some Critical Issues," *British Journal of Criminology* 20 (1980), p. 3.

10. Richard Quinney, *Critique of Legal Order: Crime Control in Capitalist Society* (Boston: Little, Brown, 1973), p. 16.

11. William Bonger, *Criminality and Economic Conditions,* abridged ed. (Bloomington, Ind.: Indiana University Press, 1969), p. 24.

12. Jonathan H. Turner, *The Structure of Sociological Theory* (Homewood, Ill.: Dorsey Press, 1978), p. 124.

13. Karl Marx and Friedrich Engels, *The Communist Manifesto* (reprinted, New York: International Publishers, 1979), p. 9.

14. Ibid.

15. Ibid.

16. Ibid., p. 9–21.

17. David O. Friedrichs, "Radical Criminology in the United States: An Interpretative Understanding," in *Radical Criminology,* ed. James Inciardi (Beverly Hills, Calif.: Sage, 1980), p. 38.

18. Richard Quinney, *Criminal Justice in America: A Critical Understanding* (Boston: Little, Brown, 1974), p. 24.

19. This section on power and authority relationships is largely derived from C. L. Ronald Huff, "Conflict Theory in Criminology," in *Radical Criminology,* ed. Inciardi, pp. 72–74.

20. Max Weber, "Class, Status, Party," in *Class, Status and Power,* ed. R. Bendix and S. M. Lipset (New York: Macmillan, 1953), pp. 63–75.

21. Ibid.

22. Ralf Dahrendorf, *Class and Class Conflict in Industrial Society* (Palo Alto: Stanford University Press, 1959).

23. A. T. Turk, "Class, Conflict, and Criminalization," *Sociological Focus* 10 (August 1977), pp. 209–220.

24. Austin T. Turk, "Analyzing Official Deviance: For Nonpartisan Conflict Analysis in Criminology," in *Radical Criminology,* ed. Inciardi, pp. 82–83.

25. Ian Taylor, Paul Walton, and Jock Young, *The New Criminology: For a Social Theory of Deviance* (Boston: Routledge & Kegan Paul, 1973), p. 241.

26. Thorsten Sellin, *Culture, Conflict, and Crime* (New York: Social Science Research Council, 1938), p. 28.

27. Ibid., p. 29.

28. Ibid.

29. Ibid.

30. Ibid., pp. 32, 57.

31. Ibid., p. 21.

32. Ibid., pp. 104–105.

33. George B. Vold, *Theoretical Criminology,* 2d ed., prepared by Thomas J. Bernard (New York: Oxford University Press, 1979), p. 283.

34. Ibid.

35. Ibid., p. 288.

36. Ibid., pp. 288–296.

37. Ibid., p. 289.

38. Ibid., p. 292.

39. Ibid., pp. 293–295.

40. J. R. Hepburn, "Social Control and the Legal Order: Legitimate Repression in a Capitalist State," *Contemporary Crisis* 1 (1977), p. 77.

41. Michalowski, *Order, Law, and Crime,* pp. 29–33.

42. Anthony M. Platt, "The Triumph of Benevolence: The Origins of the Juvenile Justice System in the United States," in *Criminal Justice in America,* edited by Richard Quinney (Boston: Little, Brown, 1974), p. 377.

43. D. Stanley Eitzen and Doug A. Timmer, *Criminology: Crime and Criminal Justice* (New York: Wiley, 1985), p. 45.

44. E. P. Thomson, *Whigs and Hunters: The Origin of the Black Act* (New York: Pantheon Books, 1975).

45. Ibid., p. 259.

46. Ibid., p. 263.

47. Ibid., p. 263.

48. J. R. Schwendinger and H. Schwendinger, *Rape and Inequality* (Beverly Hills, Calif.: Sage, 1983), p. 46.

49. See James Jacobs, *Stateville: Penitentiary in a Mass Society* (Chicago: University of Chicago Press, 1977).

50. Richard Quinney, *Criminology,* 2d ed. (Boston: Little, Brown, 1979), p. 227.

51. S. Balkan, R. J. Berger, and J. Schmidt, *Crime and Deviance in America: A Critical Approach* (Belmont, Calif.: Wadsworth, 1980).

52. Barry Krisberg and James Austin, eds., *The Children of Ishmael; Critical Perspectives on Juvenile Justice* (Palo Alto, Calif.: Mayfield, 1978), p. 219.

53. Ibid., p. 1.

54. Ibid., pp. 1–2.

55. H. M. Brenner, "Estimating the Social Costs of National Economic Policy: Implications for Mental and Physical Health and Criminal Aggression," Prepared for the Joint Economic Committee, U.S. Congress, Paper no. 5. (Washington, D.C.: U.S. Government Printing Office, 1976).

56. I. Jankovic, "Labor Market and Imprisonment," *Crime and Social Justice* 8 (Fall/ Winter 1977), pp. 17–31.

57. David F. Greenberg, "The Dynamics of Oscillatory Punishment Processes," *Journal of Criminal Law and Criminology* 68, no. 4 (1977), pp. 643–652.

58. M. G. Yeager, "Unemployment and Imprisonment," *Journal of Criminal Law and Criminology* (Winter 1979), pp. 586–588.

59. A. D. Calvin, "Unemployment Among Black Youths, Demographics and Crime," *Crime and Delinquency* 27 (April 1981), pp. 234–244.

60. J. Braithwaite, *Inequality, Crime, and Public Policy* (London: Routledge & Kegan Paul, 1979).

61. L. Carroll and P. I. Jackson, "Inequality, Opportunity, and Crime Rates in Central Cities," *Criminology* 21 (May 1983), pp. 178–194.

62. J. R. Blau and P. M. Blau, "The Cost of Inequality: Metropolitan Structure and Violent Crime," *American Sociological Review* 47 (February 1982), pp. 114–129.

63. Eitzen and Timmer, *Criminology,* p. 138.

64. E. Currie, "Crime: The Persuasive American Syndrome," *These Times* 1, no. 7 (1977), pp. 5–11.

65. J. Chapman, *Economic Realities and the Female Offender* (Lexington, Mass.: Addison-Wesley, 1971).

66. N. Jurik, "Women Ex-Offenders in the TARP Experiment," in *Money, Work, and Crime,* ed. P. Rossi, R. A. Berk, and K. Lenihan (New York: Academy Press, 1980), pp. 319–334.

67. Quinney, *Criminology,* pp. 202–208.

68. Herman Schwendinger and Julia R. Schwendinger, "Marginal Youth and Social Policy," *Social Problems* 24 (December 1976), p. 188.

69. Ibid., pp. 184–191.

70. David F. Greenberg, "Delinquency and the Age Structure of Society," *Contemporary Crisis* 1 (1977), p. 196–197.

71. Mark Colvin and John Pauly, "A Critique of Criminology: Toward an Integrated Structural-Marxist Theory of Delinquency Production," *American Journal of Sociology* 89 (November 1983), p. 543.

72. Ibid.

73. J. H. Reiman, *The Rich Get Richer and the Poor Get Prison: Ideology, Class and Criminal Justice* (New York: Wiley, 1979), p. 97.

74. J. Ruhl, "Employees Con Millions," *Rocky Mountain News* (31 March 1981), p. 815.

75. Reiman, *The Rich Get Richer,* p. 115.

76. Ibid., p. 5.

77. Krisberg and Austin, *Children of Ishmael,* p. 53.

78. Media Chesney-Lind, "Judicial Paternalism and the Female Status Offender: Training Women to Know Their Place," in *Children of Ishmael,* ed. Krisberg and Austin, p. 385.

79. Terrence P. Thornberry, "Race, Socioeconomic Status, and Sentencing in the Juvenile Justice System," *Journal of Criminal Law and Criminology* 64 (1973), pp. 90–98.

80. William J. Chambliss and Robert B. Seidman, *Law, Order, and Power* (Lexington, Mass.: Addison-Wesley, 1971), p. 73.

81. Ibid., pp. 473–474.

82. David F. Greenberg, *Crime and Capitalism: Readings in Marxist Criminology* (Palo Alto, Calif.: Mayfield, 1981), p. 489.

83. Karl Marx, "Theses on Feuerbach," *Collected Works* 5 (New York: International Publishers, 1976), pp. 3–6.

84. Lamar T. Empey, *American Delinquency: Its Meaning and Construction* (Homewood, Ill.: Dorsey Press, 1982), p. 436.

85. Robert F. Meier, "The New Criminology: Continuity in Criminological Theory," *Journal of Criminal Law and Criminology* 67 (1977), pp. 461–469.

86. John Rawls, *A Theory of Justice* (Cambridge, Mass.: Harvard University Press), 1971.

87. This section on the social costs of upper world crime is largely derived from Eitzen and Timmer, *Criminology,* pp. 189, 291–312, 330–354.

88. R. M. Hutchins, "Is Democracy Possible?" *The Center Magazine* 9 (January–February 1976), p. 4.

89. Thompson, *Whigs and Hunters.*

90. Ibid.
91. Scott G. McNall, "Variations on a Theme: Social Theory," *Sociological Quarterly* 24 (August 1983), pp. 471–487.
92. Ibid., p. 479.
93. Ibid., p. 480.
94. Ibid., p. 482.
95. Ibid., pp. 485–486.
96. See James F. Short, Jr., "Introduction," in *Delinquency, Crime and Society,* ed. Short (Chicago: University of Chicago Press, 1976), p. 3.
97. Colvin and Pauly, "A Critique of Criminology," pp. 513–551; Delbert S. Elliot, Suzanne S. Ageton, and Rachelle J. Carter, "An Integrated Theoretical Perspective on Delinquent Behavior," *Journal of Research in Crime and Delinquency* 16 (1979), pp. 3–27; and Richard E. Johnson, *Juvenile Delinquency and Its Origins* (Cambridge: Cambridge University Press, 1979).
98. For an example of one theory of upper-world crime, see Travis Hirschi and Michael Gottfredson, "Causes of White-Collar Crime," *Criminology* 25 (November 1987), pp. 949–974.

CHAPTER 9

Crimes of Violence

ADULT STREET CRIME

Murder and Nonnegligent Manslaughter

   Common Murderers
   Felony Homicides
   Simultaneous and Serial Murderers

Forcible Rape

   Rape Victims
   Characteristics of Rapists

Robbery

   Robbery Victims
   Characteristics of Robbers

Aggravated Assault

DOMESTIC VIOLENCE

Child Abuse and Neglect

   Neglect
   Physical Abuse
   Sexual Abuse

Spouse Abuse

   Female Battering
   Husband Abuse

Abuse of the Elderly

JUVENILE VIOLENCE

Delinquent Career

Violent Juvenile Gangs

TERRORISM

Trends Regarding Terrorism in the 1980s

ANALYSIS

Violence and the Social Order

Violence and Global Disorder

POLICY IMPLICATIONS

SUMMARY

REFERENCES

NOTES

KEY WORDS

aggravated assault	felony murderers	robbery
child abuse	female battering	serial murderers
cohort studies	husband abuse	sexual abuse
common murderers	mass murderers	simultaneous killers
date rape	neglect	terrorism
elder abuse	rape	youth gangs
family violence		

In major cities most of the violence is found in particular subcultures and in these subcultures violence is a way of life. I remember one incident that was typical in many ways to the violence that we dealt with on an ongoing basis. A lady was on her way from Frankfurt, Germany, to Frankfort, Kentucky. She hadn't seen her son for 36 years. She arrived at Dulles Airport, found a hotel for the night here in Washington, and then had supper. She was to meet her son and family the next day, and then spend the next two months with them.

She took a walk after supper and was confronted by this hood. He asked for money, and she responded in German because she knew no English. He shot her point-blank in the face, killing her. I had the task of meeting the family the next day and giving them the bad news. Several days later, I arrested a suspect, and he confessed that he shot her because she didn't give him the money. I said, "She didn't speak English." He answered, "That's not my fault." All he could understand was violence; he was immune to any other values.

—Homicide sergeant in the Washington, D.C., police department[1]

The failure to constrain violence, much less eradicate it, has been one of the saddest unrealized hopes of the twentieth century.[2] In the 1960s, violent crime struck down President John F. Kennedy, Robert Kennedy, and Martin Luther King, Jr. In the 1970s and early 1980s, attempts were made on the lives of two other presidents, Gerald Ford and Ronald Reagan. Americans, as previously stated, face seven to ten times the risk of death by homicide as the residents of most European countries and Japan.[3] The threat of violence, of course, is explicit in every robbery, rape, and assault, but it also is implicit in many property offenses. An incident that begins as a property crime can quickly escalate into a violent one.[4] Both liberals and conservatives readily agree that something must be done about violent crime in this nation. Indeed, the prevalence of violence calls the legitimacy of the social order into question.

ADULT STREET CRIME

Murder and nonnegligent manslaughter, forcible rape, robbery, and aggravated assault are the main types of violent crimes. The rates of violent crimes began to go up in the 1960s and early 1970s, and by the mid–1970s the public had become preoccupied with the danger of violent street crime.

In 1976 and 1977, the rates of violent crimes decreased for the first time since 1961, but by 1978, the rate of violent crime had again begun to increase. The rate continued to increase until 1983, when there was a 7 percent decrease over 1982; this decrease continued through 1984, but the rate of violent crime began to rise again in 1985 and 1986.[5] When the data for 1980 are compared with those of the 1960s, the increase in violent crime is readily apparent (see Table 9.1).

Murder and Nonnegligent Manslaughter

The *Uniform Crime Reports,* combining murder and nonnegligent manslaughter, defines these crimes as "the willful (nonnegligent) killing of one human being by another."[6] Murder, the most violent crime, has been on the upswing for the past 20 years. About 400 Americans are murdered each week. In 1986, 42 percent of

Table 9.1 VIOLENT CRIMES KNOWN TO AMERICAN POLICE, 1960–1986 (RATE PER 100,000 POPULATION)

Year	Murder	Aggravated Assault	"Murderous Attack"	Rape	Robbery
1960	5.1	86.1	91.2	9.6	60.1
1961	4.8	85.7	90.5	9.4	58.3
1962	4.6	88.6	93.2	9.4	59.7
1963	4.6	92.4	97.0	9.4	61.8
1964	4.9	106.2	111.1	11.2	68.2
1965	5.1	111.3	116.4	12.1	71.7
1966	5.6	120.3	125.9	13.2	80.8
1967	6.2	130.2	136.4	14.0	102.8
1968	6.9	143.8	150.7	15.9	131.8
1969	7.3	154.5	161.8	18.5	148.4
1970	7.9	164.8	172.7	18.7	172.1
1971	8.6	178.8	187.4	20.5	188.0
1972	9.2	188.8	198.0	22.5	180.7
1973	9.4	200.5	209.9	24.5	183.1
1974	9.8	215.8	225.6	26.2	209.3
1975	9.6	227.4	237.0	26.3	218.2
1976	8.8	228.7	237.5	26.4	195.8
1977	8.8	241.5	250.3	29.1	187.1
1978	9.0	255.9	264.9	30.8	191.3
1979	9.7	279.1	288.8	34.5	212.1
1980	10.2	290.6	300.8	36.4	243.5
1981	9.8	289.7	—[a]	36.0	258.7
1982	9.1	289.2	—[a]	34.0	238.9
1983	8.3	279.2	—[a]	33.7	216.5
1984	7.9	290.2	—[a]	35.7	205.4
1985	7.9	302.9	—[a]	36.6	205.5

[a]Material not available.

Source: Federal Bureau of Investigation, *Crime in the United States: Uniform Crime Reports* Washington, D.C.: U.S. Government Printing Office; Katherine M. Jamieson and T. J. Flanagan, *Sourcebook of Criminal Justice Statistics 1986* (Washington, D.C.: Department of Justice, 1987), p. 243.

the 20,613 murders occurred in the South, while the Western states recorded 22 percent; the Midwestern states, 19 percent; and the Northeastern states, 17 percent.[7] The main types of murderers are **common murderers, felony murderers,** and **mass** and **serial murderers.**

Common Murderers   The common slayer, statistically, is a young man in his twenties who kills another man only slightly older. This offender is likely to be acquainted with the victim and to use a gun.[8] Alcohol use, either by the victim or the offender, or both, is present in a significant proportion of violent deaths in the United States.[9] The common murderer does not generally evidence marked psychopathology. The homicide usually takes place during the process of interaction between two individuals; either the victim or the offender makes an offensive move toward the other, which results in a verbal or physical challenge. Violence, which is widely accepted in lower-class cultures as a means to "save face" or to handle problems, then ensues, leaving a victim dead or dying.[10] At other times, the homicide may be an act of revenge; even less frequently, the repressed hostility of an individual may explode in a homicidal encounter.

Felony Homicides   Mary Lorenz Dietz's *Killing for Profit: The Social Organization of Felony Homicide* is a fascinating book about felony homicide—that cold-blooded, impersonal, predatory murder that citizens fear the most. Felony homicides take place during robberies, executions, and sex killings and differ from other murders in a number of ways: (1) the killers in felony homicides are usually experienced, habitual, or career criminals; (2) planning and premeditation are a critical part of the murder; (3) there tend to be multiple victims and multiple offenders; (4) the victims are often forcibly/physically restrained; (5) a preceding argument is rare; and (6) the killer's role is hypothesized, tested, and then incorporated or rejected as part of the actor's self-concept.[11] Dietz contends that those who participate in felony homicides have learned to adhere to several norms of street violence, described in Box 9.1.

Robbery homicides generally have three discrete stages: the planning stage, the homicide encounter, and the post-homicide period. In the majority of the Detroit homicides Dietz examined, the planning time was short and the robbery usually took place within one or two days of the planning. In some robberies, the decision to kill is clearly part of the plan, but in other cases, Dietz found that not all the members of the group involved were informed of murder plans. Dietz found a pattern with robbery homicides in that at least two of the core members were willing to kill and the other members would go along with the killing. The victim was generally regarded as a disrespected and impersonal target. During the post-homicide period, the members of the robbery gang usually talked about what happened, often kidding one another about it.[12]

Executions, contracts, and revenge killings, according to Dietz, take place when a person has been judged by someone and sentenced to death. In a contract killing, a professional is hired to do the execution. The killer is called a "hit" man; in Detroit, the issuance of a contract is called "putting out a paper" on a person or persons. Dietz found that the price paid ranges from $50 to $10,000. Although

BOX 9.1 ## NORMS OF STREET VIOLENCE

Be first: Strike first and without warning: conceal your intentions.

Be fast: Hit as quickly and as hard as possible the first time. Do not wait to find out your victim's intentions. The more you hurt him initially the less likely he will be to hurt you. Don't hesitate.

Be final: Get the victim off his feet and immobilize him. Make sure he hasn't the inclination or the ability to get back at you. Kick him when he's down. If you don't put him at least temporarily out of commission, he's likely to come back not only angry but dangerous.

Be careful: Keep the odds in your favor. Stay in your own territory. Don't relax and get caught off guard. Keep your back to the wall. Locate the exits. Don't run your mouth.

Source: This material appears in Mary L. Dietz, "Violence and Control: A Study of Some Relationships of the Violent Subculture to the Control of Interpersonal Violence." (Ph.D. dissertation, Wayne State University, 1968), pp. 71–72.

some organizations, such as organized crime and drug groups, keep their own employed killers, most hit men hire out by the job to any employer.[13]

Sex-related killings are characterized by impersonal, predatory, and self-seeking behavior. As is the case in many robbery killings, the victim in most sex killings is someone who is in the wrong place at the wrong time. For example, sex offenders sometime decide ahead of time that if a woman is at a particular spot, "I will rape her." In this type of felony homicide, the offender is more likely to be a lone individual. The victim is usually killed to allow the killer to escape punishment. In most cases investigated by Dietz, victims had refused to cooperate with the perpetrator in some way.[14]

Simultaneous and Serial Murderers   There is a fundamental distinction between **simultaneous killers**—who murder their victims at the same time or in one episode—and serial killers—who slay their victims on different occasions.[15]

In recent decades, a number of simultaneous killings have taken place in the United States. The single worst mass slaying on a single day occurred in 1955, when an explosion on a passenger plane killed 44 people near Longmont, California. The son of one of the passengers was convicted of having planted the bomb in a plot to collect his mother's life insurance. In 1966, Richard F. Speck murdered eight student nurses in a Chicago dormitory. Also in 1966, Charles Whitman climbed atop the 307-foot tower on the campus of the University of Texas in Austin and opened fire; 91 bloody minutes later, 14 were dead or dying, and 30 more lay injured. On Easter Sunday, 1975, James Ruppert shot and killed ten family members in the family home at Hamilton, Ohio.[16] In 1984, a recently unemployed middle-aged man entered a McDonald's restaurant in San Ysidro, California, and shot everyone in sight. The toll of 21 dead and 19 wounded before

James Oliver Huberty was killed by police sharpshooters made this the largest single episode of mass shooting in this nation's history. Thirteen businessmen and gambling dealers were shot to death in a Seattle gambling club, on February 19, 1983. Then, on August 20, 1986, Patrick Henry Sherrill, a mail carrier in trouble with supervisors, opened fire in a crowded post office in Edmond, Oklahoma, killing 14 workers and injuring 7 others before killing himself.[17]

A serial murder occurs when one or more individuals commit a second murder that has no connection to the initial (or any subsequent) murder; this second murder is sometimes committed in a different geographic location from the first. In a serial murder, the motive is generally not material gain but is usually a compulsive act for gratification and based on fantasies. Victims may share common characteristics, such as being prestigeless, powerless, or from lower socioeconomic groups. Vagrants, prostitutes, migrant workers, homosexuals, children, and single and elderly women are often the targets of serial murders. But the key element in serial murderers is that the events surrounding them are not related.[18]

Serial murders, especially when they take place in a single community, strike terror in the hearts of citizens. Albert DeSalvo, the "Boston Strangler"; David Berkowitz, New York's "Son of Sam"; Kenneth Bianchi and Angelo Buono, Los Angeles' "Hillside Stranglers"; and Atlanta's Wayne Williams all created mass hysteria and nearly paralyzed their cities before they were arrested

Kenneth A. Bianchi: convicted, along with Angelo Buono Jr., his cousin, in slayings. (*Source:* AP–Wide World Photos.)

and convicted of their serial murders. Serial murderers sometimes are able to conceal their crimes either by traveling from one geographical area to another or by killing vagrants, hitchhikers, and runaways. Police believe that Ted Bundy may have been responsible for the deaths of up to 36 young women from Florida to the state of Washington before he was convicted in 1979 of murdering two Florida State University coeds and attempting to murder three others. Henry Lee Lucas initially confessed to having killed or assisted in killing at least 350 people between 1975 and 1983, although he has since recanted all his confessions. John Wayne Gacy, who sexually molested most of his victims, was convicted in Illinois of the slaying of 33 people.[19]

The National Crime Survey indicates that between 1982 and 1984 fewer than half of all violent crimes were committed by total strangers. This survey also revealed that among violent crimes, homicide was less likely to be committed by a stranger.[20] However, John Godwin has found a dramatic increase in stranger-to-stranger killings and argues that serial and multiple slayings are becoming more prevalent, quadrupling in the last decade.[21] James N. Gilbert, in his analysis of homicides in San Diego between 1970 and 1980, concludes that nearly 50 percent of all homicide victims did not know their killers.[22] Moreover, Margaret Zahn notes that a definite increase in stranger murders is taking place across the nation.[23]

Forcible Rape

Rape is defined legally as the sexual penetration of a woman's body without her consent; it always includes either the use or threat of force.[24] Forcible rapes numbered 90,434 in 1986, comprising 6 percent of the *Uniform Crime Reports'* violent crime volume and 1 percent of the crime index total. The South accounted for 37 percent of these offenses, the West for 24 percent, the Midwest for 23 percent, and the Northeast for 16 percent.[25]

Rape Victims A ten-year study of rape released by the Justice Department in 1985 revealed that between 1973 and 1982, 1,634,000 million rapes or attempted rapes took place in the United States. This study also reported that in 1983 one in every 600 women over 12 years of age was a rape victim. Other significant findings included:

- More than 70 percent of the victims were unmarried women.
- A woman was twice as likely to be attacked by a stranger as by someone she knew.
- Half the female victims reported a family income of less than $10,000; more than 90 percent reported income below $25,000.
- Two of every three cases involved victims from 16 to 24 years of age.
- About 15 percent of the incidents involved more than one assailant.
- Victims reported $72 million in medical expenses related to the attacks.
- An estimated 123,000 of the rapes involved male victims.[26]

Although rape occurs at all socioeconomic levels, it still disproportionately victimizes lower-class and minority women. Schwendinger and Schwendinger concluded that the lower the family income, the greater the likelihood of being raped.[27] However, **date rape** of college students is becoming increasingly well known among social scientists. The 1984 *Ms.* magazine Campus Project on Sexual Assault, in surveying 7000 students at 35 schools, found that:

- One-quarter of women in college today have been the victims of rape or attempted rape.
- Almost 90 percent of these victims knew their assailants.
- Fifty-two percent of all the women surveyed expressed some form of sexual victimization.
- One in every 12 men admitted to have fulfilled the prevailing definition of rape or attempted rape, yet virtually none of those men identified themselves as rapists.
- Forty-seven percent of the rapes were by first or casual dates, or by romantic acquaintances.
- The average age at the time of the rape was 18.
- More than 80 percent of the rapes occurred off-campus, with more than 50 percent on the man's turf: home, car, or other.
- More than one-third of the women raped did not discuss their experience with anyone; more than 90 percent did not tell the police.[28]

The Center for Rape Concern in Philadelphia sampled 1401 women who reported a rape or sexual assault to the police in Philadelphia. Interviews were conducted with the victims, generally within 48 hours of the rape, with a follow-up a year later. Data were also derived from police files, court reports, and hospital records. The results of this study indicated that rape victims suffered a variety of problems. Over one-half experienced problems related to their loss of feelings of self-worth. The majority had eating problems, with some nervously overeating and others not eating at all. Nearly one-half had sleeping problems, and some had nightmares. One-half had problems with social activities, especially those involving men. Two-fifths had difficulty with sexual adjustment. Those living with a husband had the greatest adjustment problems.[29]

The number of rapes increased more than any other violent crime during the 1970s, but rape still represents the most unreported of violent crimes. Rape victims are fearful of being stigmatized by friends, relatives, and husbands. They also are wary of insensitive police investigators. Moreover, victims are aware that reporting rape may do little or no good; rape still has the lowest conviction rate of violent crimes.

Characteristics of Rapists   Menachem Amir, who studied a sample of 646 forcible rape cases in Philadelphia in 1958 and 1960, found that the rapes were primarily intraracial. Offenders and victims were young, usually under 25; were unmarried; and knew each other. The majority of the offenders were unemployed individuals who committed most of their rapes on weekends.[30] A. Nicholas Groth, who conducted clinical studies of 500 rapists, found that rape is usually not an expression of sexual needs. One-third of his sample was made up of married men who had an active sex life with their wives, and the majority of the unmarried offenders had an active sex life with a consenting woman.[31]

Motivations for rape have been analyzed in terms of the categories of anger, power, and sadism. The angry rapist is expressing hostility, rage, contempt, and hatred toward the victim. The rape is typically impulsive, and the victim is usually brutalized more than is necessary to gain her submission. The power rapist uses his power to force the victim into submission. The control felt by the rapist is necessary to allow him to cope with his feelings of insecurity and inadequacy. He experiences anxiety, excitement, and anticipation, but little sexual satisfaction during the rape. The sadistic rapist stalks his victim, plans carefully, and waits for the right moment to attack. These rapists brutalize and torture their victims with instruments such as sticks or bottles.[32]

Robbery

Robbery, a violent form of theft, is distinguished from the crime of larceny because of the threat of violence involved. The FBI defines robbery as "the taking or attempting to take anything of value from the care, custody, or control of a person or persons by force or threat of force or violence and/or putting the victim in fear."[33] Whether called a stickup, holdup, mugging, or robbery, this crime is feared for both its actual and its potential violence. The use of or threat of force makes robbery a personal crime. Firearms or guns are the most frequently used weapon in robbery. The estimated 542,775 robbery offenses in 1986 comprised 4 percent of the Uniform Crime Reports' index crimes and 36 percent of the violent crimes (see Figure 9.1 for the trend in robberies since 1982).[34]

John E. Conklin's excellent study of robbery found that robbery is feared more by the public than any other crime. One reason for this fear is that robbery is generally committed by a stranger in an unexpected and potentially violent manner. The unpredictability, or chance-like nature of the offense, according to Conklin, makes it particularly threatening to the public. Another reason why the public fears robbery, of course, is that it incorporates both the threatening elements of the use of force and the theft of one's property.[35]

Robbery Victims The National Crime Survey reports that from 1973 through 1984, 14,681,100 robbery victimizations took place in the United States. Two-thirds of these robbery victims had property stolen, and a third were injured; nearly a fourth suffered both injury and property loss. Other major findings of this survey included:

- About 1 in 12 robbery victims experienced serious injuries.
- About half of all completed robberies involved losses of $82 or less.
- Offenders displayed weapons in almost half of all robberies and had guns in about one in five.
- Robbers were male in almost 9 out of 10 robbery victimizations.

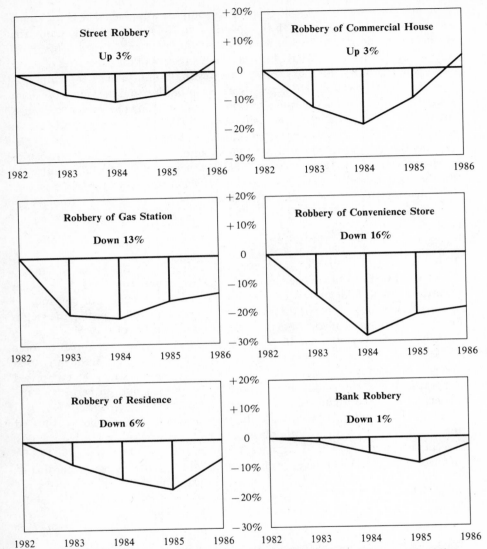

Figure 9.1 Trends in Types of Robberies, 1982–1986 [*Source:* Federal Bureau of Investigation, *Uniform Crime Reports* (Washington, D.C.: U.S. Government Printing Office, 1987), p. 19]

- Blacks experienced robberies at two and a half times the rate for whites.
- Robbery victims were more likely than rape or assault victims to encounter multiple offenders, strangers, or offenders with weapons.[36]

Characteristics of Robbers   Conklin, in interviewing 67 Massachusetts inmates, developed the following typology of robbers: professional, opportunist, addict, and alcoholic. He defines professionals "as those who manifest a long-term commitment to crime as a source of livelihood, who plan and organize their crimes prior to committing them, and who seek money to support a particular lifestyle that may be called hedonistic." Professional robbers tend to be white, in their mid-twenties, and from middle- or working-class backgrounds. These offenders are committed to robbery because it is direct, fast, and sometimes very profitable.[37]

Opportunist robbers, according to Conklin, are probably the most common type. They are usually black, in their teens or early twenties, and from lower-class backgrounds. He suggests that the term "petty materialist" describes this type of offender. Opportunist robbers generally choose accessible and vulnerable targets that net them small amounts of money, often less than $20. Elderly ladies with purses, drunks, cabdrivers, and people who walk alone on dark streets are favored victims.[38]

Conklin's addict robbers know before they rob that they must maintain a steady inflow of funds with which to buy drugs. Addicts try to choose targets intended to minimize risk, but their desperation for funds often results in carelessness in the selection of targets or the execution of the robberies.

Alcoholic robbers rarely consider how much money they will steal or what they will do with it once they have it. Instead, their intoxicated states sometimes lead them to assault others and then to take their money merely as an afterthought. Because their crimes are not planned, they are less likely to take precautions, and, therefore, alcoholic robbers are caught a higher proportion of the time than other robbery offenders.[39]

E.P. Fortune, M. Vega, and I.J. Silverman, in interviewing 33 women incarcerated for robbery in a Florida prison, found that the majority of the women were black, under 30 years old, and of average intelligence. The authors described these inmates as either situational robbers or career robbers. Situational robbers appeared to be influenced by a specific set of pressures or cues (distortion of judgment because of intoxicants, severe economic crisis, peer pressures). In contrast, career robbers committed their offenses as part of an internalized and continuing pattern of criminal activity. All of the 18 career robbers had extensive prior arrest records and histories of robbery.[40]

Interviews conducted by the Pretrial Services Branch of the Administration Office of U.S. Courts provide a profile of the typical bank robber prosecuted in Federal District Court. A young, male recidivist, he is likely to have a history of drug use, likely to be unemployed at the time of the crime, and slightly more likely to be black than white. Significantly, in a sample of convicted bank robbers, about half were rearrested within six years of their release from federal custody.[41]

Joan Petersilia's study of 49 imprisoned robbers estimated that the members of this group averaged about 20 crimes per year.[42] In a more recent Rand survey conducted by Peter Greenwood, convicted robbers in California reported committing, on the average, 53 robberies per year. Greenwood found that as a group, robbers are young, poor, and disproportionately minority group members. He also found that there are probably very few "pure" robbers—individuals who commit only this offense.[43]

Aggravated Assault

Aggravated assault is an unlawful attack by one person upon another for the purpose of inflicting severe or aggravated bodily harm. A weapon usually is used in this attempt to inflict great bodily harm or to cause death.[44] The more serious assaults, or felonies, are called aggravated assault, assault with a deadly weapon, or assault with intent to commit murder, while the less serious assaults, or misdemeanors, bear such labels as simple assault and fighting.

Aggravated assault is the most frequently committed violent crime in the United States. In 1986, an estimated 834,322 aggravated assaults took place, and upward trends in aggravated assault were evident throughout all regions and population groups. The increases over 1985 were 10 percent in the Northeast, 12 percent in the South, 14 percent in the Midwest, and 26 percent in the West. Nationally, the aggravated assault total rose 15 percent during the two-year period.[45]

Aggravated assaults are often initiated by a dare, a heated argument, a lack of money, a domestic quarrel, a jilted lover, or too much alcohol. Weapon distribution data for 1986 showed that 32 percent of the aggravated assaults reported were committed with blunt objects or other dangerous weapons; personal weapons such as hands, fists, and feet were used in 25 percent of the offenses; knives or cutting instruments in 22 percent; and firearms in 21 percent.[46]

The research on aggravated assaults outside the home is meager (the section following on family violence discusses some of the extensive research done on aggravated and simple assaults within the home). Pittman and Handy, in examining a 25-percent sample of 900 aggravated assault cases seen in 1961 by St. Louis police officers, found that the assailant and victim were typically male, black, and between the ages of 25 and 39 years. The peak hours of occurrence were Saturday evening between 5:00 P.M. and 2:00 A.M. The authors concluded that often the only difference between homicide and aggravated assault was the time it took to get the victim to the hospital.[47]

DOMESTIC VIOLENCE

The family represents the primary agent for the socialization of children and is the social group in which most children have their most enduring relationship. But within the family, considerable violence often takes place, between parents and children, between parents themselves, and sometimes between parents and grandparents. As the victims of family violence came out from behind the closed doors of the home in the late 1960s and early 1970s, **family violence** was transformed from a private issue into a social problem.[48] See Table 9.2 for the estimated family violence reported to the National Crime Survey from 1973 through 1981.

Table 9.2 ESTIMATED FAMILY VIOLENCE REPORTED TO NATIONAL
CRIME SURVEY, BY RELATIONSHIP OF OFFENDER TO
VICTIM

Relationship	1973–1981 Total	Yearly Average
Total by All Relatives	4,108,000[a]	456,000
Spouses or Ex-Spouses	2,333,000	259,000
Parents	263,000	29,000
Children	173,000	19,000
Brothers or Sisters	351,000	39,000
Other Relatives	988,000	110,000

[a]All estimates rounded to nearest thousand.
Source: Bureau of Justice Statistics, *Family Violence* (Washington, D.C.: U.S. Department of Justice, 1984), p. 3.

Child Abuse and Neglect

Child abuse and **neglect** has a profound influence on the behavior and attitudes of children and adolescents. The Federal Child Abuse Prevention and Treatment Act of 1974 defined child abuse and neglect as follows:

Child abuse and neglect means the physical or mental injury, sexual abuse, or maltreatment of a child under the age of 18 by a person who is responsible for the child's welfare under circumstances which indicate that the child's health or welfare is harmed or threatened thereby.[49]

Neglect   Neglect is generally defined as disregard of the physical, emotional, or moral needs of children or adolescents. Physical abuse and sexual abuse are far more violent than neglect, but the effects of neglect sometimes end in violence. For example, neglected children may starve to death, injure or kill themselves, or strike out at others (or themselves) later in life.

Physical Abuse   Physical abuse can be defined as intentional behavior directed toward a child by the parents or caretaker to cause pain, injury, or death. Douglas J. Besharov estimates that more than 2000 children die each year in circumstances that suggest abuse or neglect.[50]

Recent studies have found repeatedly that violent homes breed violent children. The most striking and troubling evidence comes from clinical studies of institutionalized violent delinquents and of children referred to child-abuse treatment programs. In a study of delinquent boys in a juvenile institution in Connecticut, Dorothy Lewis and colleagues compared the "extremely violent" youths with those who were less violent or aggressive. Of the more violent delinquents, 75 percent had a "history of abuse by parents or parent substitutes," versus 33 percent of the less violent.[51]

Lewis and her colleagues argue that the mechanisms by which child abuse breeds further violence are multiple and complex. The central nervous system

BOX 9.2   "I WANTED TO BLOT EVERYTHING OUT"

I was eleven years old when I first discovered that drugs could make the terrible world around me disappear. . . . When I was on drugs, I felt high, happy, and in control of my life. When I was high, I had peers; I finally belonged somewhere—in a group with other kids who took drugs. Whatever the others were taking, I took twice as much or more. I wasn't aware like the rest of them; I got high without worrying about how much I could handle or what it would do to me. It made me feel big and powerful because I didn't care what happened to me.

People said that taking too many drugs would burn out your brains. I used to think that I could become a vegetable if only I could succeed in burning out my brains. I wanted to be a vegetable. I used to picture myself as a head of lettuce. I used to look at mentally retarded people and think that they were so happy and didn't care about anything. I envied them because you could spit at them, and they would smile; they didn't seem to understand what hurt was.

Source: This material appears in "Incest: If You Think the Word Is Ugly, Take a Look at Its Effects" (Minneapolis: Christopher Street, Inc., 1979), pp. 11–12.

may be damaged by severe physical abuse, contributing to "impulsivity, attention disorders, and learning disabilities." This, in turn, can lead to delinquency through school failure and alienation. The abusive parent may provide a role model that children quickly learn to follow. Child abuse may also engender deep, long-lasting rage that children learn to displace onto others.[52]

Lewis et al. found that the single most important factor distinguishing the families of violent children from other families was the father's severe violence against the mother. Lewis and her colleagues conclude that this situation breeds violence because the children may model their own behavior on the pattern set by their fathers.[53]

Sexual Abuse   **Sexual abuse,** or incest, can be defined as any sexual activity that involves physical contact or sexual arousal between unmarried members of a family. The main expressions of incest within a family setting are oral-genital relations, the fondling of erogenous areas of the body, mutual masturbation, and intercourse.[54]

The reported cases of sexual abuse have recently experienced a dramatic rise, largely because states have passed more effective legislation on reporting of incest cases. According to Blair and Rita Justice, 50 to 500 percent increases in confirmed cases of incest are being reported both in urban areas and at the state level.[55] The Child Sexual Abuse Treatment Program in Santa Clara County, California, the best-known program in the nation, received 36 referrals in 1971, 180 in 1974, and 600 in 1977.[56]

Incest has been reported between fathers and daughters, fathers and sons, brothers and sisters, and mothers and sons, but incest between a father and daughter is reported most frequently. It is a devastating experience that sometimes has lifelong consequences.[57] In Box 9.2, Barbara A. Myers, former director of Christopher Street, Inc., and a victim of incest, tells what impact this experience had on her.

There is some evidence that sexual victims often become involved in deviant sexual behavior. The rates of promiscuity and prostitution appear to be high among female sexual abuse victims.[58] Sexual abuse is also frequently a part of the background of male prostitutes.[59] The self-destructive aspect of prostitution serves as another way of expressing rage at having been sexually and perhaps physically abused.

Spouse Abuse

The battering of wives first began to be acknowledged as a major social problem in the early 1970s; more recently some attention has been given to husband abuse.

Female Battering   **Female battering** takes place at the hands of husbands, former spouses, estranged spouses, and other men with whom women may live. The most recent data on female battering, based on the Justice Department's National Crime Survey for the last six months of 1983, reported that an average of 456,000

Domestic violence in action. (*Source:* Jill Freedman/Archive Pictures, Inc.)

cases of family violence take place each year, with the most common being the abuse by spouses or former spouses. This report went on to indicate that 57 percent of the total cases surveyed involved the battering of spouses or former spouses, and of this, 91 percent involved attacks on females by males.[60]

Other studies claim that these numbers seriously underestimate the extent of female battering. Richard J. Gelles found that one out of every six couples in America is involved in at least one incident of violence each year and that during the years of their marriage, one in four couples (28 percent) engages in physical violence.[61] From 2000 to 4000 women are beaten to death each year by their spouses, and battery is the "single major cause of injury to women, more significant than auto accidents, rapes, or muggings."[62]

Gelles concluded that the perception of alternatives was the major factor determining whether or not a woman decided to leave her battering spouse. Holding a job, according to Gelles, was the variable that best distinguished those who left from those who stayed. A job outside the home both enabled a wife to be less dependent on her spouse and contributed to her realization of the seriousness of spouse battering.[63]

The goal of "criminalizing" violence against women has been pursued in three class-action suits. In *Bruno* v. *Maguire* (1976), wives in New York City filed a class-action suit against the New York Police Department, probation officers, and family court employees for failing to prosecute abusive husbands. The police settled the case out of court. In 1977, a class action suit was filed against the Cleveland district attorney for failing to provide battered women equal protection under the law. The suit was settled by a consent decree ordering prosecutors to change their practices. The Oakland Police Department was accused of illegal conduct in discouraging arrests in cases of domestic violence. This case also was settled out of court.[64]

In a 1980 Kansas case, a jury acquitted a battered wife of killing her husband. At her trial, she testified that he had repeatedly tortured her mentally and sexually, stuck pins in her breasts, shocked her with a cattle prod, and shackled her in an underground tank. She decided to kill him when he informed her that he was planning to build a plywood coffin, wrap her in adhesive tape like a mummy, and keep her under the bed.[65]

Husband Abuse   In 1978, Susan Steinmetz wrote that contrary to some feminist and scholarly rhetoric, women are not the only victims of domestic violence. She went on to state that **husband abuse** is the most underreported form of family violence.[66] Murray Straus estimates that about 282,000 men are physically beaten by their wives each year.[67] Richard Gelles found that about as many women kill their husbands as men kill their wives, but he also found that women are seven times more likely than men to commit a violent act in self-defense.[68]

Abuse of the Elderly

Abuse of the elderly has become a topic of concern in the 1980s. Parental abuse has been called a "burgeoning national scandal." The discovery of a significant

---

BOX 9.3   **CATEGORIES OF ELDER ABUSE**

Physical Abuse.   Physical abuse is violence that results in bodily harm or mental distress. It includes assault, unjustified denial of another's rights, sexual abuse, restrictions on freedom of movement, and murder.

Negligence.   Negligence is the breach of duty or carelessness that results in injury or the violation of rights.

Financial Exploitation.   Financial exploitation involves the theft or conversion of money or objects of value belonging to an elderly person by a relative or caretaker. It can be accomplished by force or through misrepresentation.

Psychological Abuse.   Psychological abuse is the provoking of the fear of violence or isolation, including name calling and other forms of verbal assault and threats of placement in a nursing home. . . .

Violation of Rights.   The violation of rights is the breaching of rights that are guaranteed to all citizens by the Constitution, federal statutes, federal courts, and the states.

Self-neglect.   Self-neglect includes self-inflicted physical harm and the failure to take care of one's elderly person's diminished physical or mental abilities and is brought on by the attitudes and behavior of relatives.

Source: This material appears in Nan Hervig Giordano and Jeffrey A. Giordano, ''Elder Abuse: The Status of Current Knowledge,'' *Family Relations* 31 (1982), pp. 232–233.

---

number of elderly victims of family violence seems a natural outgrowth of the intensive research on the extent and patterns of domestic violence.[69]

Estimates of **elder abuse** range from 500,000 to 2.5 million cases a year.[70] Elizabeth Lau and Jordan Kosberg estimate that one of every ten elderly persons living with a family member is abused each year.[71] Marilyn R. Block and Jan D. Sinnott found that 4.1 percent of their elderly respondents in the urban areas of Maryland reported they were abused.[72] However, the extent of this problem remains unknown because available data generally have considerable methodological problems associated with them. The Select Committee on Aging cited the categories of elder abuse detailed in Box 9.3.

The typical abused person is a severely impaired woman, age 75 or over, white, widowed, and living with relatives.[73] The responsibility of caring for a dependent, aging parent can lead to a stressful situation for the caregiver as well as the entire family unit. The persons who find this caretaking role the most stressful appear to be those who are attempting to meet the needs of both a spouse and children and an older relative.[74]

JUVENILE VIOLENCE

The incidence of youth crime, especially in its more serious forms, appears to be considerably greater than the substantial proportions documented by official statistics. Franklin Zimring has noted that the extent and seriousness of violent juvenile delinquency is great enough that "since the early 1970s the violent young offender has moved steadily up the list of public concerns about crime until it is fair to characterize youth violence as a central theme of the politics of crime control."[75]

In response to the increased concern about violent youth crime, Congress in 1980 amended the Juvenile Justice and Delinquency Prevention Act of 1974 and directed the juvenile justice system to "give additional attention to the problem of juveniles who commit serious crimes."[76] In 1981 the Attorney General's Task Force on Violent Crime recommended that "any resources which are made available be directed toward the reduction of serious crime committed by juveniles, with particular emphasis on the serious, repeat offender."[77]

Delinquent Career

Marvin Wolfgang and colleagues conducted two important **cohort studies**. The first consisted of all males born in 1945 who resided in the city of Philadelphia from their tenth until their eighteenth birthdays. This study found several factors that were associated with chronic delinquency: race, and to a lesser extent, socioeconomic status; age at the current police contact; age at onset of delinquency; the average gravity of the delinquent career; the number of prior delinquent acts; and the severity of juvenile court dispositions.[78] The second study, which attempted to replicate the first study at a later time, examined boys and girls who were born in 1958 and resided in Philadelphia from their tenth until their eighteenth birthdays. The second study reached substantially the same findings as the first, but its main departures were found in the factors of race and social class, which were still noteworthy but less important than in the first study.[79]

David Farrington's Cambridge (England) Study of Delinquent Development is consistent in several ways with the two Philadelphia cohort studies. He found that those boys who were first adjudicated delinquent at the earliest ages were the most persistent and that the chances of sustaining another adjudication rose to a high level by the sixth delinquency adjudication.[80] In a companion study, Farrington concluded that one of the strongest indicators of delinquency adjudications and criminal convictions at ages 17 to 20 was prior adjudications between the ages of 14 and 16.[81]

N. Walker, W. Hammond, and D. Steer reviewed data on two large Scottish and English samples of juvenile and adult male offenders who had been convicted of first offenses in 1947 and 1959, respectively. They found that the number of prior convictions of any type—but especially the number of prior convictions for violence—was strongly related to subsequent convictions for violence.[82]

L. N. Robin's longitudinal analysis of four male samples also provides evidence of continuity across ages in assaultive behavior. Arrests, fighting, and institutional confinement during the adolescent years were related to adult antisocial behaviors such as violence, multiple serious arrests, and drug dependence.[83]

Finally, Donna Martin Hamparian and colleagues examined the records of those youths who were born in the years 1956 through 1960 and had been arrested for a violent offense in Columbus, Ohio. The analysis revealed several factors to be associated with recurrent juvenile violence: gender, social status, age at first arrest, age at first violent arrest, type of violent offense, and the severity of the court disposition. But, unlike the other cohort studies, the Columbus study did not reveal a progression of youth crime from less serious to more serious offenses.[84]

In sum, the cohort studies generally found that a few youths committed half or more of all juvenile offenses and an even higher percentage of violent juvenile offenses. More of these violent juvenile offenders were nonwhite than white. These studies also indicated that stricter punishments by the juvenile justice system are likely to encourage rather than to eliminate further delinquent behavior.

Violent Juvenile Gangs

From the late 1940s through the early 1960s, **youth gangs** in nearly every major urban area struck fear into the hearts of citizens. Then, when gangs began to reduce their activities or even to disappear from some urban areas in the mid- and late 1960s, some observers thought that the problem was coming to an end. However, as one city after another began to report serious problems with youth gangs in the early 1970s, it became apparent that the gangs had returned.

A gang member rides through the Los Angeles streets menacing people with a long knife. (*Source:* J. Ross Baughman–Visions.)

In the early 1970s, Walter B. Miller concluded that New York, Los Angeles, Chicago, Philadelphia, Detroit, and San Francisco were experiencing a dramatic rise in the number of gangs and gang crimes.[85] In 1975, Miller predicted that by the late 1970s and early 1980s, youth gang problems would worsen in Los Angeles, Detroit, and San Francisco; improve in Philadelphia; and remain stable in New York and Chicago. Failing to see any immediate relief from gang violence, he concluded his landmark study with these words:

> . . . the materials presented in this report appear amply to support the conclusion that youth gang violence is more lethal than ever before, that the security of a wider sector of the citizenry is threatened by gangs to a greater degree than ever before, and that violence and other illegal activities by members of youth gangs and groups in the United States of the mid-1970s represent a crime problem of the first magnitude which shows little prospect of early abatement.[86]

In the 1980s, there has been considerable documentation of Miller's prediction. Gang violence has indeed worsened noticeably in Los Angeles and Southern California, and gangs remain a serious problem in most major urban areas.[87] In Southern California, there has been a tremendous increase in gang-related killings, probably because of gang involvement in drug dealings. Significantly, some cities that have not had major problems with youth gangs in the past are now experiencing gang violence. The chief of police for the city of Phoenix observed in a newspaper interview:

> Youth gangs are not just bands of young people who take off their coats and have little scraps over a girl on a side street. They are armed. Vicious. Drunken. They rob and burglarize. They cruise the streets spoiling for blood. They kill. If the gangs grow, and their contempt for law deepens, they will rule the streets.[88]

TERRORISM

According to one definition, **terrorism** is political behavior in which symbolic violence is used in order to spread fear.[89] Jordan J. Paust defines terrorism as "a form of violent strategy, a form of coercion utilized to alter freedom of choice of others."[90] He adds:

> Terrorism, thus defined, involves the intentional use of violence or threat of violence by the precipitator(s) against an instrumental target in order to communicate to a primary target a threat of future violence. The object is to use intense fear or anxiety to coerce the primary target into behavior or to mold its attitudes in connection with a demanded power outcome.[91]

Terrorism is increasingly being viewed as a significant social problem. President Ronald Reagan, in a speech delivered in the presence of King Hussein of Jordan, referred to terrorism as "the new barbarism that threatens civilization."[92] Richard Clark, a St. John's University professor, argues, "In light of what terror-

BOX 9.4   ## SYMBIONESE LIBERATION ARMY

The reality of terrorism within the United States was brought to the attention of the public by the activities of the Symbionese Liberation Army. On November 6, 1973, while millions of Americans were busy at the polls, S.L.A. members voted by pulling triggers. On that autumn evening, Dr. Marcus Foster, superintendent of the Oakland, California, schools, and his chief assistant, Robert Blackburn, were met by small-arms fire as they walked from a school board meeting to Blackburn's parked car. Foster was killed in the attack; Blackburn, though critically injured, later recovered.

The Foster killing gained such national visibility because the guilty parties chose to advertise their involvement. The S.L.A., in defining their killing of Foster as a political act, sent their first communiqué to Radio Station KPFA in Berkeley. The members of the S.L.A. identified themselves and claimed credit for killing Foster. They also outlined the political reasons for which Foster had been killed and warned that more politically inspired killings would occur.

The Foster killing was only the first of a series of events engineered by the S.L.A. and intended to encourage others to embark on terrorist careers. The S.L.A. attained the most widespread media attention for its kidnapping of Patricia Hearst and the resulting Hearst food program. It is likely that Patricia Hearst was cast in the role of an instrumental target because of what she or her parents represented. In the eyes of S.L.A. members, her name stood for all that was wrong with the capitalist system.

Source: Robert Brainard Pearsall, *The Symbionese Liberation Army: Documents and Communication* (Amsterdam: Rodopi, 1974).

ists are willing to do and what their goal is (the destruction of the United States and Western civilization), it does not seem possible to survive without some form of crisis government."[93]

Brian M. Jenkins, in his impressive study of terrorism, points out that terrorism, like poverty, prejudice, and crime, is becoming another of society's chronic afflictions. He predicts that we are on the threshold of an era of armed conflict in which limited conventional warfare, guerrilla warfare, and international terrorism will coexist, with governments and subnational entities employing them "individually, interchangeably, sequentially, or simultaneously." Consequently, Jenkins notes, it will be necessary to develop capabilities to deal with all three modes of armed conflict, perhaps at the same time.[94]

Trends Regarding Terrorism in the 1980s

Terrorism in the United States during the 1980s can be characterized as "transnational," in contrast to the terrorism of the latter part of the 1970s, which had a

Table 9.3 **TERRORIST INCIDENTS IN THE UNITED STATES, 1980–1986**

Date	Total Incidents	Killed	Injured
1980	29	1	19
1981	42	1	4
1982	51	7	26
1983	31	6	4
1984	13	0	0
1985	7	—[a]	—[a]
1986[b]	0	0	0

[a]Information unavailable.
[b]As of May 5, 1986.
Source: Statistics of 1980–1984 are taken from *FBI Analysis of Terrorist Incidents and Terrorist Related Activities in the United States 1984,* prepared by Terrorist Research and Analytical Center, Terrorist Section, Criminal Investigative Division; statistics for 1985–1986 are from *USA Today,* "Webster Says FBI Beating Terrorism," 7 May 1986, p. 3.

more domestic favor. William H. Webster, director of the FBI, made this point when he testified in 1982:

> Most of the terrorist activities throughout the United States last year, numerically, were caused by groups that had foreign quarrels, foreign problems, foreign origins.[95]

Table 9.3 depicts terrorist incidents in the United States. During the time span covered here, domestic terrorist groups have gone from being the most active in 1981 and 1982 to being virtually inactive in 1985 and 1986. In recent years, the United States has experienced a steady decline in the frequency of terrorist incidents. It may be that the number of active terrorist groups operating in this nation are declining as well. For example, in 1984, 4 different groups were responsible for the 13 incidents that occurred that year; in 1983, 11 different groups were responsible for the 31 incidents.[96]

An examination of the data related to terrorism in the United States, including Puerto Rico, from 1977 to 1986 reveals that terrorist incidents were not isolated to any particular region of the United States. The northeastern region of the United States experienced by far the greatest number of incidents; Puerto Rico and the Western states ranked second and third respectively in number of incidents; Southern states ranked fourth; and north central states ranked a distant fifth.[97]

The most complete data on terrorism available are for the years 1981 and 1982. The following conclusions can be reached in comparing these two years:

1. Bombing was the most-used tactic during both years.
2. The number of persons injured or killed by terrorists rose dramatically in 1982.
3. Puerto Rican terrorist groups were the most active groups during 1981 and 1982 and increased in number in 1982.

4. Transnational terrorism is the most significant type of terrorism threatening United States' security.[98]

The importance of transnational terrorism became more pronounced during the mid–1980s when several events threatened United States' security. Several planes and a ship were hijacked, American citizens were kidnapped, and U.S. troops were attacked by terrorist groups.

ANALYSIS

Two of the critical issues relating to the preservation of order in society are violence and the legitimacy of the social order, and global violence and its potential for total disaster.

Violence and the Social Order

In a 1981 cover story, *Newsweek* deplored what it described as an epidemic of violent crime, while lamenting that we have lost "the old optimism proclaiming that we know what the problems are and that we have the solutions at hand."[99] The article suggested that we are helpless to do anything about violent crime in this nation.

Throughout the history of this nation, one violent response has generated a more violent response. This situation has sometimes been confined to the members of a violent subculture, but, at other times, it has occurred when authorities have resorted to violence to maintain social order. Further, the public has consistently taken the law into its own hands when it has become apparent that the forces of social control can no longer maintain order.

The high rates of violence in American society can be traced to many causes. Mass communication diffuses images of violence. Contemporary American society produces a technology that makes pervasive violence possible; urbanization, bureaucratization, and mobilization all contribute to an alienated and depersonalized society. The existence of an economically disenfranchised lower class, along with the failure to provide adequately for lower-class "losers," are other major factors leading to a violent society. Finally, in spite of overwhelming evidence that the lack of effective gun control contributes to urban violence, political leaders have refused to enact and enforce legislation on gun control.[100]

Violence may serve some productive ends for a social order, but ultimately the very nature of violence makes it the antithesis of harmonious social relations. The dependence on the use of force diminishes in relationship to the extent that the leadership of a state is regarded as authentically legitimate. Conversely, the extent to which a social order depends upon violence and force to maintain internal stability compromises its implicit or explicit claims to legitimacy.[101]

An inherently illegitimate social order produces an environment likely to foster various forms of violence. When the state is perceived to be illegitimate, a set of rationales for engaging in illegal and violent activity becomes available to citizens. Thus, no form of violence is more threatening to the survival of a social order than rationalized violence.[102] Rationalized violence in America is found on the streets, in the family, in corporations, and in terrorist activities.

Violence and Global Disorder

David O. Friedrichs contends that the escalating nuclear arms race, which had been essentially ignored by criminologists, is a matter that demands serious attention. He argues that the arms race puts the issue of street crime in proper perspective and shows the limitations of both mainstream and Marxist analyses.[103] Friedrichs quotes a speech that Richard Harding made during his tenure as president of the Australian and New Zealand Criminological Association:

> In the 1980s there is, in fact, only one important set of questions to ask: what can criminology and criminologists do to decrease the chances of the extinction of mankind and destruction of the planet? . . . [Criminology's] non-contribution to the most important issue facing civilization is shocking.[104]

Friedrichs speculates that a number of reasons may explain why criminology has largely ignored this issue: a denial of the reality of the threat; a perceived irrelevance of criminological training and expertise; a conviction that pursuit of the issue is not likely to pay off in terms of career goals; or a concern that attention to this issue will simply contribute to conservative initiatives.[105]

Harding went on to explain why criminologists have a real obligation to devote a great deal of attention to this issue:

> Surely, sentencing patterns in magistrates' courts in Wagga Wagga, or recidivism rates among female juvenile offenders convicted of car stealing in Whyalla, or police perception of porno shop users at Wollongong, or unreported domestic violence in Woolloomooloo are simply not worth bothering about in the 1980s. We know already that the circle is round and the square has four sides. To prove the criminological equivalent of this over and over again is a waste of time and talent. What might, perhaps, have been good stuff in the Forties and Fifties is irresponsible self-indulgence in the Eighties. There is no time left for mini-criminology.[106]

The nuclear arms issue has three implications for contemporary criminologists. First, it puts the street crime issue in its proper perspective; a nuclear "exchange" could cause more death and bodily harm in a matter of minutes than has been perpetrated by street criminals during the whole of history. Second, in terms of criminology's lack of unity, whereby proponents of conservative, liberal-cynical, and Marxist criminology are sometimes openly antagonistic toward each other, the nuclear arms race suggests the urgency of identifying points of reconciliation between mainstream, conservative, and Marxist perspectives.[107] Third, the issue of "ultimate" violence serves as a reminder to criminologists that the neglect of war and other macro issues, such as crimes against the poor and the environment, crimes against minorities and vulnerable groups (women, children, the aged, or the disabled), and criminal violations of human rights, can no longer be justified.

POLICY IMPLICATIONS

Violent crime poses a major threat to the American social order, but, unfortunately, no easy answers are available. We do know that murderers are usually caught. Silberman, who interviewed dozens of such offenders, reported that none knew or had even heard of active offenders who had escaped imprisonment, much less arrest.[108] We also know that violent offenders repeatedly appear in the criminal justice system. Anyone as active as those violent offenders contained in the Rand study provides many opportunities for arrest and prosecution. Indeed, as violent offenders become known, they become increasingly vulnerable to detection.[109] Moreover, we know that such offenders are dealt with harshly by the criminal justice system.[110]

The recurrent theme of this text is that to reduce the levels of crime, especially violent crime, requires a basic structural transformation of American society. The relevance of the following propositions to American society appears to provide an explanation of some of the reasons for the high rates of violent crime:

1. The greater the acceptability of violence in a culture, the higher the rates of violent crime.
2. The greater the economic inequality in a society, the higher the rates of violent crime.
3. The greater the silence on the issue of domestic violence, the higher the rates of violent crime.
4. The greater the acceptance of punitive and violent behavior within the family, the higher the rates of violent crime.
5. The greater the silence on the issue of gun control, the higher the rates of violent crime.
6. The greater the breakdown of communal bonds and the destruction of stable work roles, the higher the rates of violent crime.

SUMMARY

Violent crime has been a major problem throughout American history, as each new generation has felt itself threatened by some form of violent crime. Today, the basic forms of violent crimes are related to street crime, domestic violence, terrorist activity, and corporate crime (see Chapter 10 for a discussion of violence and corporate crime).

Although there is nothing as disruptive as the fear of random violence committed for political or ideological reasons, terrorist activities usually do not invade the daily lives of Americans. Similarly, the American public may read or hear about the explosions of the Ford Pinto's gas tank, about unsafe mines, or about unsafe drugs, but few individuals anticipate that the violent crimes of corporations or the government will affect the citizen on the streets. Juvenile and adult violent street crime, however, is a different matter. The fear of criminal victimization is something that citizens of most urban areas cannot ignore. Too many citizens feel unsafe and are unwilling to venture out at night. Unfortunately, their fears are too often realized.

The ultimate disorder of violent crime is that it brings into question the legitimacy of the state. The increasing frustrations the public feels concerning the criminal justice system have encouraged a return to popular, or vigilante, justice. But as various expressions of violent crimes continue to dominate the affairs of the state, the credibility of the state in controlling violence becomes more and more an issue.

REFERENCES

Browning, Frank and Gerassi, John. *The American Way of Crime.* New York: Putnam's, 1980.

Currie, Elliott. *Confronting Crime.* New York: Pantheon Books, 1985.

Dietz, Mary Lorenz. *Killing for Profit: The Social Organization of Felony Homicide.* Chicago: Nelson-Hall, 1983.

Friedrichs, David O. "Violence and the Politics of Crime." *Social Research* 48 (Spring 1981): 135–156.

Jenkins, Brian M. *International Terrorism: The Other World War.* Santa Monica, Ca.: Rand Corporation, 1985.

Justice, Blair, and Justice, Rita. *The Broken Taboo: Sex in the Family.* New York: Human Sciences Press, 1979.

Levin, Jack, and Fox, James Alan. *Mass Murder: America's Growing Menace.* New York: Plenum Press, 1985.

Moore, Mark H., et al. *Dangerous Offenders: The Elusive Target of Justice.* Cambridge, Mass.: Harvard University Press, 1984.

Wolfgang, Marvin E., and Weiner, Neil Alan. *Criminal Violence.* Beverly Hills: Sage, 1982.

NOTES

1. Interviewed in April 1987.
2. David O. Friedrichs, "Violence and the Politics of Crime," *Social Research* 48 (1981), p. 135.
3. Elliott Currie, *Confronting Crime: An American Challenge* (New York: Pantheon Books, 1985), p. 5.
4. Mark H. Moore et al., *Dangerous Offenders: The Elusive Target of Justice* (Cambridge, Mass.: Harvard University Press, 1984), p. 13.
5. Federal Bureau of Investigation, *Uniform Crime Reports* (Washington, D.C.: U.S. Government Printing Office, 1986), pp. 170, 172.
6. Ibid., p. 7.

7. Ibid., p. 8.

8. Charles E. Silberman, *Criminal Violence, Criminal Justice* (New York: Random House, 1978), p. 21.

9. Marvin E. Wolfgang, *Patterns in Criminal Homicide* (Philadelphia: University of Pennsylvania, 1958).

10. David F. Luckenbill, "Criminal Homicide as a Situated Transaction," *Social Problems* 25 (December 1977), pp. 176–186.

11. Mary Lorenz Dietz, *Killing for Profit: The Social Organization of Felony Homicide* (Chicago: Nelson-Hall, 1983), pp. 3–4.

12. Ibid., pp. 45–74.

13. Ibid., pp. 113–127.

14. Ibid., p. 197.

15. Jack Levin and James Alan Fox, *Mass Murder: America's Growing Menace* (New York: Plenum Press, 1985), p. 13.

16. "Mass Slayings, Many Sites," *New York Times* (August 8, 21, 1986), p. II 6:5.

17. Levin and Fox, *Mass Murder,* p. xi.

18. Steven A. Egger, "A Working Definition of Serial Murder and the Reduction of Linkage Blind," *Journal of Police Science and Administration* 12 (September 1984), p. 348.

19. Levin and Fox, *Mass Murder.*

20. Bureau of Justice Statistics, *Violent Crime by Strangers and Nonstrangers* (Washington, D.C.: U.S. Department of Justice, 1987), p. 1.

21. John Godwin, *Murder USA: The Ways We Kill Each Other* (New York: Ballantine Books, 1978), p. 7.

22. James N. Gilbert, "A Study of the Increased Rate of Unsolved Criminal Homicide in San Diego, California, and Its Relationship to Police Investigative Effectiveness," *American Journal of Police* 2 (1983), pp. 149–166.

23. Margaret A. Zahn, "Homicide in the Twentieth Century," in *History and Crime: Implications for Criminal Justice Policy,* ed. James A. Inciardi and Charles Faupel (Beverly Hills, Calif.: Sage, 1980), p. 124.

24. Federal Bureau of Investigation, *Uniform Crime Reports,* p. 13.

25. Ibid., p. 14.

26. Bureau of Justice Statistics, *The Crime of Rape* (Washington, D.C.: U.S. Department of Justice, 1985), pp. 1–3.

27. J. R. Schwendinger and H. Schwendinger, *Rape and Inequality* (Beverly Hills, Calif.: Sage, 1983).

28. Ellen Sweet, "Date Rape: The Story of an Epidemic and Those Who Deny It," *Ms.* 14 (October 1985), p. 58.

29. Thomas W. McCahill et. al., *The Aftermath of Rape* (Lexington, Mass.: Heath, 1979), p. 4.

30. Menachem Amir, *Patterns in Forcible Rape* (Chicago: University of Chicago Press, 1971).

31. A. Nicholas Groth, *Men Who Rape: The Psychology of the Offender* (New York: Plenum Press, 1979).

32. Ibid., pp. 13–58.

33. Federal Bureau of Investigation, *Uniform Crime Reports,* p. 15.

34. Ibid., p. 16.

35. John E. Conklin, *Robbery and the Criminal Justice System* (Philadelphia: Lippincott, 1972), pp. 4–5.

36. Bureau of Justice Statistics, *Robbery Victims* (Washington, D.C.: U.S. Department of Justice, 1987), p. 1.
37. Conklin, *Robbery and the Criminal Justice System,* pp. 63–64.
38. Ibid., pp. 68–69.
39. Ibid., pp. 71–72, 76.
40. E. P. Fortune, M. Vega, and I. J. Silberman, "A Study of Female Robbers in a Southern Correctional Institution," *Journal of Criminal Justice* 8 (1980), pp. 317–325.
41. Bureau of Justice Statistics, *Bank Robbery* (Washington, D.C.: U.S. Department of Justice, 1984), p. 2.
42. Joan Petersilia and Peter W. Greenwood, with Marvin Lavin, *Criminal Careers of Habitual Felons* (Santa Monica, Calif.: Rand Corporation, August 1977).
43. Peter W. Greenwood with Alan Abrahamse, *Selective Incapacitation* (Santa Monica, Calif.: Rand Corporation, August 1982), pp. 41, 43.
44. Federal Bureau of Investigation, *Uniform Crime Reports,* p. 21.
45. Ibid., p. 22.
46. Ibid. For a discussion of weapons used during assaults, see also Stuart J. Miller, Simon Dinitz, and John P. Conrad, *Careers of the Violent* (Lexington, Mass.: Lexington Books, 1982), p. 63.
47. D. J. Pittman, and W. J. Handy, "Patterns in Criminal Aggravated Assault," in *Crime in America,* ed. B. Cohen (Itasca, Ill.: Peacock, 1970.
48. Richard J. Gelles, "Domestic Criminal Violence," in *Criminal Violence,* ed. Marvin E. Wolfgang and Neil Alan Weiner (Beverly Hills, Calif.: Sage, 1982), p. 201.
49. Ibid., p. 203.
50. Douglas J. Besharov, "The Legal Aspects of Reporting Known and Suspected Child Abuse and Neglect," *Villanova Law Review* 23 (1978), p. 458.
51. Dorothy O. Lewis et al., "Violent Juvenile Delinquents: Psychiatric, Neurological, Psychological, and Abuse Factors," *American Journal of Psychiatry* 137 (1980), pp. 1211–1216.
52. Ibid.
53. Dorothy O. Lewis et al., "Homicidally Aggressive Young Children: Neuropsychiatric and Experienced Correlates," *American Journal of Psychiatry* 140 (February 1983).
54. Blair Justice and Rita Justice, *The Broken Taboo: Sex in the Family* (New York: Human Sciences Press, 1979), p. 25.
55. Ibid., p. 16.
56. Ibid.
57. K. C. Meiselman, *Incest: A Psychological Study of Causes and Effects with Treatment Recommendations* (San Francisco: Josey-Bass, 1978).
58. David Finkelhor, *Sexually Victimized Children* (New York: Free Press, 1979), p. 214.
59. J. James and J. Meyerding, "Early Sexual Experiences as a Factor in Prostitution," *Archives of Sexual Behavior* 7 (1977), pp. 31–42; and Justice and Justice, *Broken Taboo,* p. 197.
60. "Study Details Family Violence," *New York Times,* 23 April 1984, p. 5.
61. See Richard J. Gelles, *Family Violence* (Beverly Hills, Calif.: Sage, 1979), p. 92; Straus, Gelles, and Steinmetz, *Behind Closed Doors* (New York: Doubleday, 1980).
62. "Wife Beating: The Silent Crime," *Time,* 5 September 1983, p. 23.
63. Gelles, "Domestic Criminal Violence."
64. Ibid., p. 207.

65. "Jury Acquits Woman Who Admits Slaying, Hiding Mate," *Tulsa World,* 9 March 1983, p. CI.

66. Susan Steinmetz, "The Battered Husband Syndrome," *Victimology* 2 (1978), pp. 499–509.

67. Cited in "Wife Beating: The Silent Crime," p. 23.

68. Gelles, *Family Violence,* p. 137.

69. Claire Pedrick-Cornell and Richard J. Gelles, "Elder Abuse: The Status of Current Knowledge," *Family Relations* 31 (1982), p. 457.

70. Nan Hervig Giordano and Jeffrey A. Giordano, "Elder Abuse: A Review of the Literature," *Social Work* 29 (1984), p. 233.

71. Elizabeth Lau and Jordan Kosberg, "Abuse of the Elderly in Informal Care Providers: Practice and Research Issues" (Paper presented at the 31st Annual Meeting of the Gerontological Society, Dallas, Texas, 20 November 1978).

72. Marilyn R. Block and Jan D. Sinnott, eds., "The Battered Elder Syndrome: An Exploratory Study" (Unpublished manuscript, University of Maryland Center on Aging, 1979).

73. Giordano and Giordano, "Elder Abuse," pp. 232–233.

74. Ibid., p. 236.

75. Franklin E. Zimring, "The Serious Juvenile offender: Notes on an Unknown Quality," in *The Serious Juvenile Offender: Proceedings of a National Symposium* (Washington, D.C.: U.S. Government Printing Office, 1978).

76. Neil Alan Weiner, "The Challenge of Violent Juvenile Delinquency" (Unpublished paper, Center for Studies in Criminology and Criminal Law, University of Pennsylvania, n.d.).

77. Quoted in Weiner, "Challenge," p. 6.

78. Paul E. Tracy, Marvin E. Wolfgang, and Robert M. Figlio, *Delinquency in Two Birth Cohorts: Executive Summary* (Washington, D.C.: U.S. Department of Justice, 1985).

79. Ibid.

80. D. P. Farrington, "Longitudinal Research on Crime and Delinquency," in *Crime and Justice,* vol. 1, ed. N. Morris and M. Tonry (Chicago: University of Chicago Press, 1979).

81. Ibid.

82. N. Walker, W. Hammond, and D. Steer, "Repeated Violence," *Criminal Law Review* (1947), pp. 465–472.

83. L. N. Robins, "Aetiological Implications in Studies of Childhood Histories Relating to Antisocial Personality," in *Psychopathic Behavior,* ed. R. D. Hare and D. Schaling (New York: Wiley, 1978).

84. Donna Martin Hamparian, *The Violent Few: A Study of Dangerous Juveniles* (Lexington, Mass.: Lexington Books, 1980).

85. Walter B. Miller, *Violence by Youth Gangs and Youth Groups as a Crime Problem in Major American Cities* (Washington, D.C.: U.S. Government Printing Office, 1975).

86. Ibid., p. 205.

87. See James Diego Vigil, "The Gang Subculture and Locura: Variations in Acts and Actors" (Paper presented at the Annual Meeting of the American Society of Criminology, San Diego, California, 19 November 1985).

88. *Arizona Republic,* 18 June 1980.

89. Kurt L. Mielke, *"Understanding Political Terrorism: A Sociological Exploration,"* (M.A. thesis, University of Northern Iowa, May 1984), p. 6.

90. Quoted in Yonah Alexander and Seymour Maxwell Finger, eds., *Terrorism: Interdisciplinary Perspectives* (New York: John Jay Press, 1977), pp. 20–21.

91. Ibid.

92. Cable Network News, CNN, 13 February 1984.

93. Quoted in Kurt Finsterbush and George McKenna, eds., *Taking Sides: Views on Controversial Social Issues,* 2d ed. (Guilford, Conn.: Dushkin, 1982), pp. 291–292.

94. Brian M. Jenkins, *International Terrorism: The Other World War* (Santa Monica, Calif.: Rand 1985).

95. *F.B.I. Oversight Hearing,* 4 February 1982.

96. Mielke, *Understanding Political Terrorism.*

97. Ibid.

98. Ibid.

99. Quoted in Elliott Currie, *Confronting Crime: An American Challenge* (New York: Pantheon Books, 1985), p. 10.

100. David O. Friedrichs, "Violence and the Politics of Crime," *Social Research* 48 (Spring 1981), pp. 149–150.

101. For various perspectives on the legitimation of violence, see R. M. Fogelson, *Violence as Protest* (Garden City, N.Y.: Doubleday, 1971); M. A. Weinstein, *The Ideology of Violence* (Columbus, Ohio: Merrill, 1974); and Ted Honderich, *Political Violence* (Ithaca, N.Y.: Cornell University Press, 1977).

102. David O. Friedrichs, "Violent Crime and the Radical Critique: Past Trends and Future Prospects" (Paper presented to the Annual Meeting of the American Society of Criminology, Cincinnati, November 7–11, 1984), p. 9.

103. Ibid.

104. Richard Harding, "Nuclear Energy and the Destiny of Mankind—Some Important Criminological Perspectives," *Australian and New Zealand Journal of Criminology* 16 (1983), pp. 81–92.

105. Friedrichs, "Violent Crime and the Radical Critique," p. 9.

106. Harding, "Nuclear Energy and the Destiny of Mankind," pp. 90–91.

107. Friedrichs, "Violent Crime and the Radical Critique," p. 10.

108. Charles E. Silberman, *Criminal Violence, Criminal Justice* (New York: Random House, 1978).

109. Moore, *Dangerous Offenders,* p. 47.

110. Samuel Walker, *Sense and Nonsense About Crime: A Policy Guide* (Belmont, Calif.: Brooks/Cole, 1985), p. 31.

CHAPTER 10

Property Crimes

TRADITIONAL PROPERTY CRIMES
Burglary
Larceny-Theft
  Pickpocketing
  Shoplifting
Motor Vehicle Theft
Fraud
Arson
WHITE-COLLAR CRIME
Occupational White-Collar Crime
  Forgery and Counterfeiting
  Embezzlement
  Computer Crime
Corporate Crime
  Extent of Corporate Crime

ORGANIZED CRIME
Structural Versus Process Views of Organized Crime
The Mafia
Services
ANALYSIS
Property Offenders Differentiated
  Professional Offenders
  Occasional Offenders
  Career Offenders
Social Disorder of Property Crimes
POLICY IMPLICATIONS
SUMMARY
REFERENCES
NOTES

KEY TERMS

arson
burglary
career offenders
computer crimes
confidence games
corporate crimes
counterfeiting
embezzlement
fence

forgery
fraud
La Cosa Nostra
larceny
lush workers
Mafia
organized crimes
motor vehicle theft

occasional offenders
occupational white-collar crime
pickpocketing
professional criminals
shoplifting
street crimes
target-hardening devices
white-collar crimes

One thing that you must understand is that professional criminals trust one another, to the extent that Bad-Eye and I used to argue about who was going to take the money home. Each one of us was insistent that the other guy take it home. That meant that the guy that took it home had to roll the coins up and take them down to the bank, changing them for paper. We would always argue about who would take the money home. We trusted one another completely for an honest split, which we got from one another. I never gave it a thought to beat Bad-Eye, and I'm sure he never thought to beat me anytime.

—Harry King, ex–safe cracker[1]

This chapter examines such diverse property offenses as **street crime, white-collar crime, corporate crime,** and **organized crime.** Property crimes occur nearly four times as frequently as violent crimes. In the opening quotation to this chapter, Harry King, a professional box-man (safe cracker) from 1910 to 1960, talks about the rules that guided the behavior of property offenders in the past. But no longer do traditional, or street, property offenders trust one another; no longer do rules guide their behavior. The structured criminal behavior of past decades has been transformed by drugs and alcohol abuse, by ever-present informers, by improved technology of law enforcement, and by the increasing lack of specialization in criminal activity. The day of the professional has largely passed. Ours is the time of the opportunistic, jack-of-all-trades property offender.

In contrast, corporate and organized criminals typically have order in their criminal activities. The skill level is such in corporate crime that outsiders frequently have considerable difficulty even determining that the law has been broken. Order is equally characteristic of organized crime. Membership frequently requires a certain ethnic background and an invitation, and there are prescribed rules and clear sanctions. In Box 10.1, Joseph Bonanno, former leader of the Maranzano family in New York City, speaks about the rules of the family and how these rules provide order to their criminal activities.

<table>
<tr><td>BOX 10.1</td><td colspan="2">RULES TO LIVE BY</td></tr>
</table>

BOX 10.1   **RULES TO LIVE BY**

The code of conduct prescribed by the Family is not written in any book. Our Tradition is mightier than any book. We pass down the knowledge personally from generation to generation. . . .

This is how I presided over my Family. . . . I did not tolerate any dealings in prostitution or narcotics. I was against extortion as an arbitrary instrument of collecting money from people. Perhaps other Families didn't adhere to my strict guidelines, but this was my way. . . . All societies, whether the unit of cooperation be that of the family, the tribe, the city or the nation, use force, at some level, to enforce the rules of that society. No well-ordered society tolerates indiscriminate and arbitrary violence. My world was no exception.

In discussing the role of violence in my world I don't expect outsiders to condone or approve of the rules by which we lived. I would only ask the outsiders to appreciate the context of our lives. The first step is to recognize that traditionally a Sicilian has a personal sense of justice. If a "man of honor" is wronged it is up to him to redress that wrong personally. He does not go to the judicial machinery of the state. For this to work, everyone clearly must understand what is wrong and what is right. . . .

Contrary to popular belief, business disputes rarely rose to the level of violence. If two Family members disagreed over a business arrangement between them, the matter was usually resolved at a hearing by their group leader, whose decisions were binding. . . . Our entire system of cooperation and connections depended on trust. A handshake often closed a deal; a nod of the head indicated assent. . . .

A Family member's behavior toward outsiders was his own responsibility. . . . if outsiders tampered with a Family member the outsiders became enemies of us all. . . . One of the strictest rules we had toward outsiders was the injunction against killing a policeman or a reporter. . . . He merely had a job to do. We understood that, and very often ways could be found so that he would not interfere with us and we wouldn't interfere with him.

Source: This material appears in Joseph Bonanno with Sergio Latti, *A Man of Honor: The Autobiography of Joseph Bonanno* (New York: Simon and Schuster, 1983), pp. 154–159.

TRADITIONAL PROPERTY CRIMES

Burglary, larceny-theft, motor vehicle theft, and arson are the index property crimes tracked in the FBI's *Uniform Crime Reports.* Fraud is also a property crime in the *Uniform Crime Reports.*

Burglary

Burglary, the most common property offense, is defined as the unlawful entry into a structure to commit a felony or theft. The *Uniform Crime Reports* divides burglary into three categories: forcible entry, unlawful entry without force, and attempted forcible entry.[2] Based on reported crimes from nearly all police jurisdictions in this country, the 1986 estimated burglary total was 3,241,410. Up 4.5 percent from 1985 but 10 percent below the rate in 1982, the 1986 burglary rate was 1,345 per 100,000 inhabitants nationwide. This offense accounted for 25 percent of all Index crimes reported to law enforcement agencies and 28 percent of all property crimes.[3] See Figure 10.1 for the trends in burglaries since 1982.

The highest burglary rate occurred in the Southern states, which had 39 percent. The Western states followed with 25 percent; the Midwestern states, 20 percent; and the Northeastern states, 16 percent. About two-thirds of all burglaries were residential burglaries. Seventy percent of all burglaries involved forcible entry, 22 percent were unlawful entry without force, and the remainder were forcible entry attempts.[4]

Target-hardening devices—(alarms, lights, private security)—help, but they are more likely to displace the burglary to another time, a different location

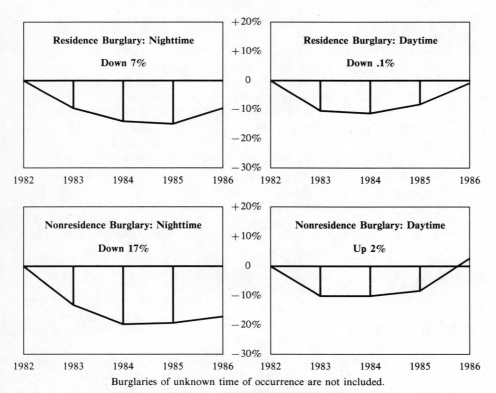

Burglaries of unknown time of occurrence are not included.

Figure 10.1   Trends in Burglary, 1982–1986 [*Source:* Federal Bureau of Investigation, *Uniform Crime Reports, 1986* (Washington, D.C.: U.S. Government Printing Office, 1987), p. 26]

BOX 10.2

THE FENCE: OVERLAPPING NATURE
OF ORDER AND DISORDER

A **"fence,"** a criminal receiver of stolen merchandise, is crucial if the professional burglar or shoplifter expects to make a real profit from his or her crimes. The significance of the fence has been recognized since the notorious Jonathan Wild elevated criminal receivership to nearly an art form before he was hanged in early eighteenth-century England.

Darrell J. Steffensmeier's *The Fence: In the Shadow of Two Worlds* describes the experiences of "Sam Goodman." The main character, he reveals how he became involved in fencing operations and how he dealt stolen goods before he was arrested and convicted.

Sam lived in two worlds, the law-abiding and the law-violating. Although he was a legitimate and successful businessman, he also happened to peddle stolen property. When business was slow or the opportunity arose, he knew how to pull a good "heist" or con a sucker into buying worthless goods. Sam possessed all the qualities of a true entrepreneur, but he straddled the boundary between legal and illegal. He was in business to make a profit, but, as he puts it, "It's very hard to do well in business unless you chisel or clip in one way or another." The notion of honor among thieves is a pervasive theme in Steffensmeier's study. Merchandise stolen the night before could be deposited in the alley behind Sam's shop and be left unprotected.

Another theme is the need for a fence to be "well connected." This means that, at times, the fence provides a service for upstanding citizens or even members of the law enforcement profession, and that at other times that the fence knows how to contract out a job that involves burglary or fraud. This interconnectedness among the fence, the conventional community, and the underworld enables the fence to have ties to all levels of society and to emerge as a broker in mediating contact between the deviant and the conformist.

Source: Darrell J. Steffensmeier, *The Fence: In the Shadow of Two Worlds* (Totowa, N.J.: Rowman & Littlefield, 1986).

in the same area, or a different area than to prevent the crime entirely. Rural break-ins, hitherto uncommon, have become a problem recently, because our improved and expanded highway system makes small towns and open spaces more accessible.

The FBI estimates that the total annual loss from burglaries is about $3.1 billion, an average of $960 per burglary.[5] This figure is probably exaggerated; victims sometimes overreport the amount taken for insurance and tax purposes. The stolen items in burglaries generally are saleable merchandise, such as televisions or stereo sets. Cash, jewelry, furs, clothing, guns, credit cards, checks, and stocks and bonds are other items that are frequently taken.

House burglary, or housebreaking, has a long history. As long ago as nineteenth-century England, the manufacture and use of skeleton keys had become a fine art, and the more experienced burglars bragged that they could open any lock. Modern burglars rely less upon skeleton keys and mechanical devices and more on stealth. They may work on observation or tips as to the location of accessible homes with valuable contents, as well as when occupants will be gone.[6]

The Bureau of Justice Statistics (BJS) found that a substantial proportion of violent crimes occur during household burglaries. For example, 60 percent of all rapes in the home, 60 percent of all home robberies (use or the threat of force), and about a third of home aggravated and simple assaults are committed by burglars. During the 10-year period 1972–1983, 2.8 million such violent crimes occurred in conjunction with burglaries.[7]

Mike Maguire, in a British study of 322 victims of burglary, found that the most common reaction to the crime was anger or annoyance (30 percent). Although only 9 percent of the victims indicated that fear was their first reaction, at least 6 percent suffered acute distress shortly after discovering the crime. Their reactions included severe shock, trembling, panic, and uncontrolled weeping.[8] One individual recalled, "I was hysterical. I ran screaming to my neighbor and hammered on her door. Then I went icy cold and shivered for hours."[9] A common reaction is the feeling of having been violated, of sharing one's dwelling and possessions with a stranger.

Larceny-Theft

Larceny can be defined as the unlawful taking, carrying, or leading away of property from the possession of another without the use of force or fear. It includes such crimes as shoplifting, thefts of parts and accessories for and from motor vehicles, boat theft, and the theft of agricultural products, livestock, and farm machinery.[10] An estimated 7,257,153 larceny-theft offenses were reported in 1986. This high-volume crime made up 55 percent of the Crime Index total and 62 percent of all property crimes. (See Figure 10.2 for the distribution of the various larceny offenses.)[11]

The Southern states recorded 36 percent of the total larceny offenses; the Western states registered 25 percent; Midwestern states, 23 percent; and Northeastern states, 17 percent. A comparison of 1985 and 1986 figures shows that larceny-theft increased 5 percent nationally. The five-year and ten-year volume trends show a 2 percent increase over 1982 and a 23 percent increase over the 1977 figures.[12]

Pickpocketing   **Pickpocketing,** an ancient form of sneak theft, involves the surreptitious theft of money from an individual's person without his or her cooperation or knowledge. Although this form of larceny-theft has a long history, it constitutes only 1 percent of the *Uniform Crime Reports* totals for larceny-theft. It seems to be taking place less frequently in recent years.[13] The process of pickpocketing generally includes: (1) the selection of a victim, (2) the locating of the money on the victim's person, (3) the maneuvering of the victim into the

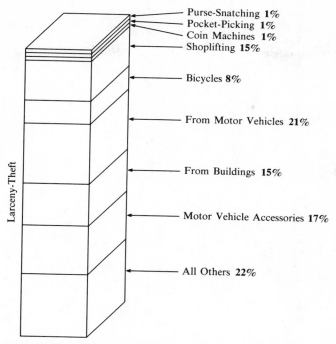

Purse-Snatching **1%**
Pocket-Picking **1%**
Coin Machines **1%**
Shoplifting **15%**

Bicycles **8%**

From Motor Vehicles **21%**

From Buildings **15%**

Motor Vehicle Accessories **17%**

All Others **22%**

Larceny-Theft

Figure 10.2 Larceny Analysis, 1986 [*Source:* Federal Bureau of Investigation, *Uniform Crime Reports, 1986* (Washington, D.C.: U.S. Government Printing Office, 1987), p. 31]

proper position, (4) the act of theft, and (5) the passing of the stolen property to a confederate. Professional pickpockets generally work in groups of two or more, with each member playing a specific and defined role in the total operation.[14]

Lush workers are low-status pickpockets who prowl dark halls and alleys in order to steal from sleeping drunks or who frequent public places and rob sleepers. This crime generally is resorted to by criminals only when they are in desperate need of money or when working without the protection of a pickpocket mob. Lush workers, sometimes called jack rollers, work alone or in twos and threes in subways, railroad and bus terminals, and public parks.[15]

Shoplifting It is estimated that 12 cents of every dollar spent by consumers represents an incremental cost caused by **shoplifting.** Shoplifting accounts for 11 percent of all larceny crimes, and it produces losses exceeding $3.5 billion annually.[16] Shoplifters can be classified into two groups on the basis of the merchandise they steal: the booster, or commercial shoplifter, who steals merchandise for resale; the pilferer, who takes merchandise for private use.[17]

Professional shoplifters, not surprisingly, not only are apprehended much less frequently than amateurs, but they also take more per theft. Frequently members of highly skilled and well-organized groups, they generally wear special clothing to conceal and carry stolen merchandise. They are often equipped with

A youth is taken into custody by police after stealing a purse. (*Source:* Tom Kelly.)

scissors or razor blades for snipping price tags from stolen merchandise, carry lists of items they intend to steal, and plan their offenses in advance. Professional shoplifters must use the services of a fence to peddle their stolen property.

Mary Owens Cameron examined a sample of shoplifters apprehended in a Chicago department store between 1943 and 1950 and a sample of women charged with petty larceny and shoplifting in Chicago courts between 1948 and 1950. She found that "normal" and "respectable" people participated in shoplifting, although the lower class was somewhat overrepresented. She also concluded that shoplifting was not a form of compulsive, neurotic, or irrational behavior. When shoplifters were arrested and interrogated, they felt humiliated and tended to stop pilfering. The rate of recidivism, according to Cameron, was extremely low, for the rewards of shoplifting were apparently not worth the cost in reputation and self-esteem.[18]

Gerald Robin examined shoplifting patterns in three of the five largest department stores in Philadelphia in 1958. He found that nearly half the shoplifters in the Philadelphia stores were black and that women shoplifters outnumbered males. In addition, his study concluded that juvenile shoplifting was commonly a group activity, whereas adults were more frequently loners.[19]

Motor Vehicle Theft

Motor vehicle theft is defined as the actual or attempted theft of a motor vehicle. This offense category includes the stealing of automobiles, trucks, buses, motorcycles, motorscooters, and snowmobiles.[20] In 1986, according to the *Uniform Crime Reports,* there were 1,224,137 motor vehicle thefts: 462 per 100,000 people, a 6 percent increase over 1985. About three-quarters of the vehicles stolen were passenger cars. Nationwide, an estimated average of 1 of every 159 registered motor vehicles was stolen.[21]

Motor vehicle thefts are grouped into four categories: (1) joyriding, (2) thefts of vehicles for use in other crimes, (3) thefts for transportation, and (4) professional thefts. Joyriding thefts constitute the majority of motor vehicle thefts. The perpetrator is generally a teenager, 15 to 19 years of age, who steals a car on a dare. Adult criminals most frequently steal cars for use in other crimes and then abandon the stolen vehicles. Thefts for transportation are committed by transients, hitchhikers, and runaways. The stolen car is usually abandoned when the thief reaches his or her destination or runs out of gas. Finally, the professional auto thief steals with the specific intent of making a profit, either by altering the car for resale or dismantling the vehicle for parts. A byproduct of motor vehicle theft is the fact that garages are offered a source of auto parts—the "chop shop"—which is faster and much cheaper in providing car parts than car manufacturers or auto parts dealers. Chop shops are able, with pit-stop efficiency, to dismantle a car in a number of hours. The FBI considers the chop shop one of the most lucrative illegal businesses today.[22]

In 1986, 91 percent of the persons arrested for auto theft were males. Sixty-four percent of the arrestees were white, 35 percent were black, and 16 percent were Hispanic. Arrestees for auto theft tended to be young: 58 percent were under 21 years of age, and 39 percent were under 18 years of age.[23] Interestingly, juvenile car thieves tend to be more intelligent and advanced in reading skills than other delinquent youths.[24] A white, 17-year-old, institutionalized auto thief explained why he repeatedly committed this crime:

> I suppose I stole 150 cars. It was a real thrill, and I had it down to a science. I could wire it and get it going in a few seconds. Man, when you take off, nothing describes this "high." It was a lark when I started. I would drive the car a while, and it was always an Eldorado, or something like that, and then I would park it somewhere. But by the time I got caught and sent here, I was selling the cars. I was even taking orders for certain types of cars.[25]

In comparing federal prisoners charged with auto theft with those charged with other offenses, Larry Karacki found that the car thieves showed greater residential mobility, were more likely to have been in military service or confinement prior to their offense, and had poorer work records. In addition, car thieves tended to have a more problematic adjustment to institutional life and to have higher rates of recidivism than other prisoners.[26]

Fraud

The *Uniform Crime Reports* documents that 276,169 individuals were arrested by the police for **fraud** in 1986.[27] Frauds are committed either by businessmen during the course of their occupations or by professional criminals.

In the maintenance and repair business, home-repair frauds occur in chimney repair, furnace repair, painting, termite control, basement waterproofing, and roofing. Homeowners are sometimes charged for work undone, shoddy workmanship and materials, and promises that go unfilled. Another practice common to the auto and other repair industries is the use of flat-rate labor costs. This means that labor for repair is charged according to the standard amount of time a given job is supposed to take, not the time actually taken. Thus, customers may pay for shop and mechanic time that is never used.

Fraud takes place in health care in such forms as unnecessary surgery, fee splitting among doctors (a practice whereby doctors pay those who refer patients to them), and Medicaid and Medicare double billing schemes.

Fraud in land sales takes place through deceptive sales techniques, delay or default on development practices, multiple sale of the same property, and misrepresenting the value and amenities of the land.[28]

The professional criminal has traditionally been associated with various methods of fraud. The term **professional criminal** is applied to property offenders who have the highest status and skill level. James A. Inciardi further defines the professional criminal:

> Professional crime traditionally refers to the nonviolent forms of criminal behavior that are undertaken with a high degree of skill for monetary gain, and that exploit interests which tend to maximize financial opportunities and minimize the possibilities of apprehension. It is a specialized variety of career crime, reflecting an occupational structure similar to many of the "learned" professions and other vocational pursuits, and as noted . . ., typical forms of professional crime include pickpocketing, burglary, shoplifting, forgery and counterfeiting, extortion, sneak theft, and confidence swindling.[29]

Swindling, or **confidence games,** refers to any operation that takes advantage of the confidence placed by the victim in the swindler or confidence person. The "big con" and the "short con" are differentiated by the amount of preparation needed and the quantity of benefits reaped. All confidence games generally involve the following steps:

1. Locating and investigating the victim (putting up the mark);
2. Gaining the victim's confidence (playing the con);
3. Steering him to meet the inside man (roping the mark);
4. Showing the victim how he can make a large amount of money, most often dishonestly (telling the tale);
5. Allowing the victim to earn a profit (the convicter)—this is not always part of "short-con" games;
6. Determining how much the victim will invest (the breakdown);

   7. Sending the victim for his money (putting him on the send);
   8. Fleecing him (the touch);
   9. Getting rid of him (the blowoff); and
   10. Forestalling action by the law (putting in the fix).[30]

Arson

Arson is a recent addition to the *Uniform Crime Reports* crime index. Arson is defined as any willful or malicious burning or attempt to burn, with or without intent to defraud, a dwelling house, public building, motor vehicle or aircraft, and personal property of another.[31] Only fires determined through investigation to have been willfully or maliciously set are classified as arson. During 1986, 110,732 arson offenses were reported to the police.[32]

The number of arson offenses rose 6 percent in 1986 over the 1985 total. Regionally, arson increased 10 percent in the Midwest and 8 percent in the South, but it declined 3 percent in the West and 2 percent in the Northeast. In 1986, structures such as dwellings and businesses were the most frequent target of arsonists and were involved in 55 percent of the reported incidents. Twenty-eight percent of the arsons were directed at mobile property, such as motor vehicles and trailers, while property such as crops and timber accounted for 17 percent.[33]

Police made an estimated 18,700 arrests for arson during 1986. As with auto theft, a high proportion of arrestees were young (40 percent under 18), male (86 percent), and white (75 percent).[34] Young arsonists frequently commit the crime for a thrill or out of boredom. An adult probation officer recalls an experience he had during his teenage years:

> We were bored one night and didn't have anything to do. One of the guys got the idea, "Let's go burn Jones's barn down." Mr. Jones was a next-door neighbor. He owned a big farm and wasn't very popular with any of us. None of us had ever done anything wrong before, but there we marched, like experienced arsonists, to do a job. And we really did a job; there wasn't anything left of his barn when the fire quit smoking. Shit, if we had been caught, it would have been all over.[35]

WHITE-COLLAR CRIME

In his 1939 presidential address to the American Sociological Association, Edwin H. Sutherland introduced the concept of white-collar crime. Sutherland defined *white-collar crime* as "crime committed by a person of respectability and high social status in the course of his occupation."[36] Herbert Edelhertz, in developing an expanded definition of the term, defines it as "an illegal act or series of illegal acts committed by nonphysical means and by concealment or guile, to obtain money or property, to avoid the payment or loss of money or property, or to obtain business or personal advantage."[37]

Sutherland believed that white-collar crimes were very costly to American society:

> The financial cost of white-collar crime is probably several times as great as the financial cost of all the crimes which are customarily regarded as the "crime problem." . . . the financial loss from white-collar crime, great as it is, is less important than the damage to social relations. White-collar crimes violate trust and therefore create distrust, which lowers social morale and produces disorganization on a large scale. Other crimes produce relatively little effect on social institutions or social organization.[38]

There have been many recent estimates of the financial and social costs of white-collar crime. A 1979 *Newsweek* article, "Crime in the Suites," reported that white-collar crime costs the nation "staggering billions" of dollars every year.[39] Ralph Nader, the consumer advocate, has suggested that even in the matter of deaths, corporate crimes are more costly to American society than street crimes.[40]

In addition to the social disorder resulting from financial losses, violations of trust, the lowering of social morale, and even deaths, white-collar crime also produces physical and environmental harm, a moral climate in society that encourages deceit, and frustration, anger, and general displeasure with "the system."[41] August Bequi contends that upper-world crimes have a far greater impact than traditional crimes and may even signal the decay of our democratic form of government.[42]

Public concern about white-collar criminality and corporate crime has recently increased. Studies reveal that the public views white-collar criminality as more serious than in the past, that it has lost confidence in those running major companies, and that it believes that most corporate executives are dishonest. In this context, it is not surprising that the public sees the law as an appropriate means to establish order in the business community and that the public supports attempts by the courts to "get tough" in dealing with the occupational crimes of the rich.[43]

Stanton Wheeler and colleagues found, surprisingly, that higher-status white-collar offenders received more severe sanctions than lower-status white-collar offenders.[44] In contrast, however, John Hagan and Patricia Parker's study of securities violators in Ontario, Canada, over a 17-year period revealed that "punishment of white-collar crime is not only a function of class position, but also of the kinds of organized white-collar criminal behavior that certain class positions make possible."[45] Managers were treated with disproportionate severity and employers with disproportionate leniency. "Employers," they concluded, "are in positions of power that allow them to be distanced from criminal events and that can obscure their involvement in them."[46]

Occupational White-Collar Crime

Herbert Edelhertz has identified the basic elements of **occupational white-collar crime:**

- Intent to commit a wrongful act or to achieve a purpose inconsistent with law or public policy.

- Disguise of purpose or intent.
- Reliance by [the] perpetrator on ignorance or carelessness of [the] victim.
- Acquiescence by [the] victim in what he believes to be the true nature and content of the transaction.
- Concealment of the crime by
  1. preventing the victim from realizing that he has been victimized, or
  2. relying on the fact that only a small percentage of victims will react to what has happened, and making provisions for restitution to or other handling of the disgruntled victims, or
  3. creation of a deceptive paper, organization, or transactional façade to disguise the true nature of what has occurred.[47]

The occupational category of white-collar crimes involves crimes committed by persons operating as individuals. These offenses are perpetrated by persons pursuing some individual objective and generally do not involve face-to-face contact with the victims. These crimes are a violation of duty, loyalty, or fidelity to an employer or client.

Examples of such crimes are employee embezzlement, the acceptance of bribes or other favors by government or corporate agents, the misuse of labor pension funds, employee theft, securities fraud, payroll and expense account padding, conspiracy to defraud in restraint of trade, "insider" trading on the markets, false advertising and selling (e.g., "bait and switch" tactics), corruption and bribery, misapplication of funds, violations of health and safety standards, vendor fraud (as in Medicare claims), and insurer fraud (as in car theft claims).

In sum, white-collar crime often mimics legitimate business transactions. White-collar crime may be as prevalent at the upper reaches of society as street crime is at the lower end. White-collar crime often is not reported as crime but rather is covered in the pages of financial sections in the *Wall Street Journal* and the *New York Times*. Its hallmarks are misrepresentation and duplicity, and, like street crime, it takes a dreadful toll on social trust.

Forgery and Counterfeiting The *Uniform Crime Reports* documents that 73,205 individuals were arrested for **forgery** and **counterfeiting** offenses in 1986.[48] These crimes are varieties of fraud, but they differ from confidence operations, since the thief is not necessarily in a face-to-face relationship with the victim. Forgery and counterfeiting both are frauds in that the act of forging a name or note carries an intent to deceive. Nineteenth-century forgeries involved imitations of handwriting, duplications of corporate bonds and securities, printing of false currency, and raising the value of bank checks. But the acts of counterfeiting and check forgery in large denominations have increasingly disappeared from the domain of the professional criminal since the advent of the twentieth century. One informant, paroled after a three-year incarceration for forgery, suggests that few professional forgers exist today:

I have been arrested over fifty times, almost always for forgery. And I think I'm one of a kind. There are few good forgers any more, and they don't work in mobs as they did fifty years ago. I've worked alone so long that I only see familiar faces on the T.V. set—and I don't even know these people.[49]

Apparently, modern forgery is undertaken primarily by solitary thieves with blank checks stolen from individuals or corporations. Check kiting, a swindle related to forgery, is directed against banks. This fraudulent operation involves the covering of bad checks with other bad checks. Double-pledging, which is similar to kiting, is undertaken using false collateral on loans. Most frequently, this crime involves selling a mortgage to several different banks, or securing loans based on fraudulent insurance policies. Travelers' checks also provide an opportunity for the forger's operations, as well as the theft or illicit production of credit cards.

Counterfeiting is related to forgery in that it represents an alternative method of producing illegal tender. Counterfeit operations range from those involving solitary entrepreneurs who produce and distribute only a few bills at a time to those run by large organizations undertaking currency fraud running into millions of dollars. Because of technological advances in duplicating machines that make counterfeiting easier, the government has embarked on a program to "harden" our currency and prevent counterfeiting; new bills will be circulated within the next five years.

Embezzlement   Jerome Hall wrote in 1932 that **embezzlement** was a white-collar crime that infested all strata of American society.[50] The *Uniform Crime Reports* documents that 10,032 offenders were arrested for embezzlement in 1986.[51] Donald Cressey's *Other People's Money* was the first systematic and analytic investigation of embezzlement.[52] In interviewing 133 male embezzlers at three prisons, Cressey concluded that a three-stage process was involved in "becoming" a trust violator:

> Trusted persons become trust violators when they conceive of themselves as having a financial problem which is nonshareable, are aware that this problem can be secretly resolved by violation of the position of financial trust, and are able to apply to their own conduct in that situation verbalizations which enable them to adjust their conceptions of themselves as trusted persons with their conceptions of themselves as users of the entrusted funds or property.[53]

Three studies on embezzlement have elaborated on or challenged Cressey's main thesis. Gwynn Nettler, basing his research on a small sample of six embezzlers in Canada, concluded that the "detective theory" and the "auditor hypothesis" are better explanations for embezzlement than that suggested by Cressey. The "detective theory" looks for individuals with gambling debts, excessive use of alcohol, and extensive involvement with women. The police contend that most embezzlers are involved in all three of these areas. The "auditor hypothesis" explains theft by a person of trust as stemming from two factors, desire and opportunity.[54]

Charles McCaghy believes that Cressey's theory needs two modifications. First, Cressey did not account for individuals who sought employment in a position of trust with the specific intent of embezzling once the job was obtained, and, second, he did not consider those instances where employees act together for the purpose of embezzling.[55]

Mark Pogrebin, Eric Poole, and Robert Regoli examined 62 offenders convicted by federal courts of embezzling in Denver and concluded that the typical embezzler was a 26-year-old white female with a high school education. These embezzlers usually worked in a low, entry-level position (72 percent), such as bank teller, bookkeeper, or mailroom clerk. They tended to commit their crimes alone (82 percent), and over 50 percent of them had held their position for less than 12 months before their discovery. These embezzlers reported that they had committed the crime because of a need for money (to pay personal debts, 66.1 percent; for extravagant purchases, 43.5 percent; to pay relatives' debts, 9.7 percent; to buy illegal drugs, 8.1 percent; for financial investments, 4.8 percent; and to gamble, 3.2 percent).[56]

Alice Franklin, in examining the differences between male and female employees who stole from employers, found that the men were more likely to be young and single, while the women tended to be older and married. The women were primarily employed in sales and clerical positions, and their thefts were relatively petty; 81 percent of them were valued at between $1 and $150. Franklin concluded that the petty nature of female theft might reflect both a lack of opportunity and a lack of skill in financial manipulations.[57]

In 1983, the Bureau of Justice Statistics examined the white-collar crimes of forgery-counterfeiting, fraud, and embezzlement in six jurisdictions. It found that just half of the 28,012 white-collar dispositions were for forgery/counterfeiting, 38 percent for fraud, and 8 percent were for embezzlement.[58] Other findings included:

1. Eighty percent of those arrested for white-collar felonies were prosecuted.
2. Seventy-four percent of those arrested for white-collar crimes were subsequently convicted.
3. Sixty percent of those arrested and convicted for white-collar crimes were sentenced to incarceration.
4. Those convicted for white-collar crimes were much less likely to be sentenced to incarceration for more than a year (18 percent) than were violent offenders (39 percent) or property offenders (26 percent).
5. Females made up a much higher proportion of those arrested for white-collar crimes than for other types of crimes.
6. Almost half of those arrested for white-collar felonies were at least 30 years old, making them older on average than violent and property offenders and about the same age as public-order offenders.[59]

Computer Crime   According to reported data, the computer criminal steals more than $100 million a year, but experts think that losses may actually run as high as $40 billion a year. Only about 1 percent of **computer crimes** are ever detected; indeed, only 1 in 22,000 of the detected computer crimes will be successfully prosecuted. The average loss per incident of computer crime theft is estimated to be $621,000.[60]

Computer crime has a number of unique features. First, the offender and the victim are removed from each other. Second, computer criminals utilize new methods, some of which avoid detention or prevention with present technology. Third, computer crimes can be set up to occur after the offender leaves an organization, so that he or she need not be present at the scene of the crime. Fourth, a computer crime can be repeated automatically at periodic intervals. Finally, legal complexities make computer crime particularly difficult to prosecute.[61] See Box 10.3 for the various categories into which computer theft, or electronic data processing (EDP) crimes, can be divided.

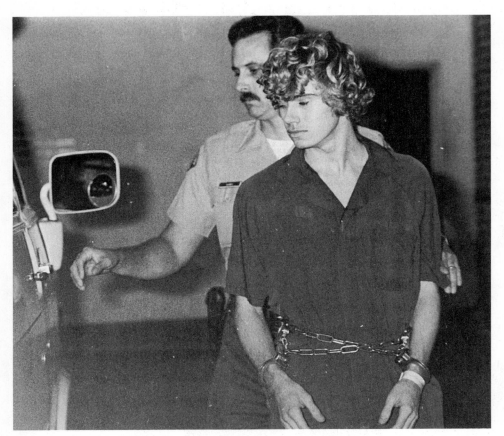

Nineteen-year-old UCLA student is led manacled from Los Angeles Municipal Court after pleading innocent to charges of using his home computer to break into a U.S. Department of Defense communications system. (*Source:* AP–Wide World Photos.)

BOX 10.3   **THE CATEGORIES OF COMPUTER CRIME**

Data diddling: The unauthorized modification, replacement, insertion, or deletion of data before or during their input to a computer system.

Superzapping: The unauthorized use of utility computer programs to modify, destroy, disclose, or use data or computer programs in a computer system.

Impersonation: Taking and using the identity of an authorized computer user to use the computer in his stead.

Piggybacking: The unauthorized interdiction of a communication circuit to covertly replace an authorized user.

Wire tapping: Covertly tapping into a communication circuit but the circuit carries digitized data instead of voice data.

Trojan horse: Covertly inserting computer instructions into a computer program that is authorized for use in a computer.

Asynchronous attack: Compromising a computer system by taking advantage of weaknesses in its asynchronous functions.

Trap door: A weakness or error introduced into or left in a computer program that can be exploited at a later time to compromise a computer system.

Salami methods: Transferring small amounts of assets (slices of salami) from a large number of accounts into a favored account which then can be converted to a fraudulent gain.

Logic bomb: A computer program or part of a program that is automatically repeatedly executed to test the state and contents of a computer system.

Data leakage: A method for covertly obtaining data from a computer system by leaking it out in small amounts.

Simulation: A common computer application that can be used to simulate a fraud for planning purposes or as an aid in regulating, monitoring, or accounting in the perpetration of an ongoing complex fraud.

Source: This material appears in Donn B. Parker, "Computer-Related White-Collar Crime," in *White-Collar Crime: Theory and Research,* ed. Gilbert Geis and Ezra Stotland (Beverly Hills, Calif: Sage, 1980), pp. 203–205.

Corporate Crime

Marshall B. Clinard and Peter C. Yeager define corporate crime as a particular type of white-collar crime:

> . . . Corporate crime actually is organizational crime occurring in the context of complex relationships and expectations among boards of directors, executives,

and managers, on the one hand, and among parent corporations, corporate divisions, and subsidiaries, on the other. This concept of corporate crime has developed rather gradually, and it is only natural that it should often be confused with the broader area of crime in the so-called white-collar occupations.[62]

Occupational crime, according to Clinard and Yeager, is committed largely by individuals and small groups of individuals in connection with their occupation, but corporate crime is "enacted by collectivities or aggregates of discrete individuals; it is hardly comparable to the action of a lone individual."[63]

Extent of Corporate Crime   In the late 1940s, Sutherland examined the life history, an average of 45 years, of 70 of the largest manufacturing, mining, and mercantile corporations in the United States. His basic sources were the official records of violations of laws governing restraint of trade; misrepresentation in advertising; infringement of patents, trademarks, and copyrights; unfair labor practices; rebates; financial fraud; and violations of wartime (World War II) regulations. His methodology actually minimized the incidence of socially harmful acts by corporations because it: (1) limited the analysis to a narrow range of crimes; (2) considered only violations of the law, so that it ignored many legal but nevertheless harmful acts; and (3) used official records, which omitted the approximately 50 percent of cases that were settled out of court.[64]

Despite these limitations, Sutherland found that criminal behavior by large corporations was "normal," persistent, organized, and much more extensive than existing data suggested. In addition to actual convictions, there were a total of 980 negative decisions against the 70 corporations, an average of 14 against each, with one company receiving 50. Sutherland also found that 97 percent of these 70 corporations were recidivists (having two or more adverse decisions against them). Furthermore, he found, corporate officials who violated the law on behalf of their companies did not lose status among their business associates. Although corporate officials, like professional thieves, customarily felt contempt for the law and the government because these institutions impeded profitable behaviors, the officials employed experts in law, public relations, and advertising to build up and maintain the corporation's public image as law-abiding and community-oriented.[65]

Fortune magazine compiled a list of major corporations found guilty of crimes during the 1970s. The crimes were domestic bribery, fraud, illegal political contributions, tax evasion, and antitrust violations. Of the 1043 corporations examined, *Fortune* found that 11 percent had been involved in at least one major crime in the ten-year period. Of the 163 separate crimes recorded, 60 percent were antitrust violations. *Fortune* even noted that a subsidiary of Time, Inc., the publisher of *Fortune,* was 1 of 22 companies convicted in antitrust cases.[66]

Marshall B. Clinard and Peter C. Yeager investigated the number of criminal, civil, and administrative actions either initiated or completed by 25 federal agencies against the 477 largest publicly owned manufacturing corporations in the United States during 1975 and 1976.[67] They discovered that during these two years:

BEFORE AFTER

Drawing by Cheney. © *1988 The New Yorker Magazine, Inc.*

- More than 60 percent of the corporations had at least one legal action instituted against them.
- One-fourth of these corporations had multiple cases of nonminor violations.
- Eight percent of these corporations accounted for 52 percent of all violations.
- The larger the corporation, the greater the likelihood of being involved in a violation.
- Corporations with annual sales exceeding $1 billion had twice the expected number of violations (given their number in the sample). They also were more likely to commit the more serious offenses.
- The automobile, oil refining, and drug industries accounted for almost one-half of all violations. About 90 percent of the corporations in these industries violated the law at least once.[68]

More recently, the *Academy of Management Journal* analyzed violations of antitrust laws and the Federal Trade Commission Act by Fortune 500 companies between 1980 and 1984. Corporate illegality was measured by the "total number of instances in which firms were found guilty in litigated cases, were parties to nonlitigated consent decrees, or were involved in unsettled cases in which the court found substantial merit to the charges against them." Although the researchers examined only a limited area of corporate conduct, they found that these companies averaged nearly one violation each and "that the mean for those firms which were involved in some type of illegal activity was three acts."[69]

Criminologists are now beginning to assert that unsafe work conditions, defective products, air and water pollution, and food and drug adulteration can lead to violent outcomes and that, therefore, corporations ought to be held responsible for the consequences of their actions. As Box 10.4 shows, the infamous Ford Pinto is a dramatic case in point.

BOX 10.4 **THE FORD PINTO**

From its beginning, the Ford Pinto was flawed by a fuel system that ruptured easily in rear-end collisions. Ford owned the patent on a much safer gas tank, but decided to continue to manufacture the car as it was, even though preproduction crash tests established the existence of the problem. This decision was made chiefly because the Pinto was on a tight production schedule, and Ford wanted to enter the subcompact market, then dominated by Volkswagen, as quickly as possible.

Ford calculated that a repair costing $11 per car would make the car safe, but it decided that this was too costly. The company reasoned that 180 burn deaths, 180 serious burn injuries, and 2100 burned vehicles would cost $49 million (each death was figured at $200,000), but that a recall of all Pintos and the $11 repair would amount to $137 million.

Following publication of an exposé charging Ford Motor Company with deliberately endangering the public, the U.S. Transportation Department investigated all subcompacts for the possibility of gasoline tank fires. Their survey initially revealed that since 1975, 26 Pintos had been involved in fatal fires that had taken 35 lives. Ralph Nader brought further public attention to this controversy as he charged Ford with "corporate callousness" and demanded that the Pinto be recalled immediately. In May 1978, the National Traffic Highway Safety Administration concurred that a safety defect did exist in the fuel system of the 1.9 million Pintos produced from 1970 through 1976 and Ford was ordered to recall the car for corrective repairs in June 1978.

At the same time, civil actions were being brought against Ford. An estimated 20 to 50 civil suits were reportedly pending against Ford for damages suffered by Pinto owners. The largest and most publicized of court settlements involved the case of a 13-year-old boy who suffered burns over 95 percent of his body when the Pinto in which he was a passenger was struck from behind and exploded. The court awarded the litigant $2.841 million for personal compensation and an unsolicited $125 million in punitive damages. The punitive damages were significant because it is necessary to establish intentional negligence so gross as to amount to intentional injury before awarding such damages.

Source: Francis T. Cullen et al., *Corporate Crime Under Attack* (Cincinnati: Anderson, 1987); M. Dowie, "Pinto Madness," in *Crisis in American Institutions,* ed. J. H. Skolnick and E. Currie, 4th ed. (Boston: Little, Brown); and Victoria Lynn Swinger and Ronald A. Farrell, "Corporate Homicide: Definitional Processes in the Creation of Deviance," *Law and Society Review* 15 (1980/1981), pp. 161–181.

Irwin Ross, the author of the *Fortune* study, notes four rationalizations for corporate crimes:

1. The common perception within the business community is that activities such as fixing prices are not crimes.
2. Within certain industries (e.g., trucking, construction, and on the loading docks), it is customary to bribe in order to achieve competitive advantage.
3. In regulated industries companies sometimes violate the law by doing acts that are legal in other industries. In the beer industry, for example, the federal and state governments prohibit some otherwise normal sales techniques such as discounts and rebates.
4. There are extensive pressures on corporate executives to "produce or perish." The competitive climate, then, drives some individuals outside the law for an edge.[70]

Gilbert Geis's examination of the heavy electrical equipment antitrust cases of 1961 offers one of the best examples of how large corporations are, for the most part, able to escape criminal sanctions. Geis notes that this antitrust conspiracy was characterized by its willful and blatant nature. The criminal offenses involved were openly in contradiction to the letter and the spirit of the Sherman Antitrust Act of 1890, which forbids price-fixing arrangements as restraints upon free trade. Forty-five persons representing 29 companies were indicted. They were accused of price fixing by rigging bids and dividing the available market through a secret cartel. To effect the conspiracy, the defendants used secret codes and clandestine meetings. The major fines were set against General Electric and Westinghouse, the two largest companies involved in the conspiracy. Seven executives received jail terms of 30 days, but good behavior earned the men a 5-day reduction in their sentences.[71]

Clinard and Yeager also found that despite the costs of corporate crime, both to individuals and society, corporations and corporate executives have gone relatively unpunished. For example, in only 1.5 percent of all enforcement actions was a corporate officer convicted of a crime. Equally significant is the fact that of those convicted, 63 percent received probation, 21 percent had their sentences suspended, and only 29 percent were incarcerated.[72]

Diane Vaughan's study of the Revco Drug Store, Inc., one of the nation's largest retail drug chains and a Medicaid provider, shows how difficult it is to prove criminal violations by a corporation. Although Revco was found guilty in July 1977 of a computer-generated double-billing scheme that resulted in the loss of over a half million dollars in Medicaid funds to the Ohio Department of Public Welfare, the intricacies of the case and the use of computer technology required five separate state agencies to discover, investigate, and prosecute the case. The complexities of the case were such that the offense would not have been discovered at all, Vaughan concluded, if it were not for a serendipitous series of events.[73]

ORGANIZED CRIME

Francis A. J. Ianni has defined organized crime "as an integral part of the American social system that brings together a public that demands certain goods and services that are defined as illegal, an organization of individuals who produce or supply those goods and services, and corrupt public officials who protect such individuals for their own profit or gain."[74] Peter A. Lupsha adds that organized crime brings together a group of individuals who develop "task roles and specializations, patterns of interaction, statuses and relationships, spheres of accountability, and responsibility." With continuity over time, they "engage in acts legal and illegal usually involving (1) large amounts of capital, (2) buffets (nonmember associates), (3) the use of violence or the threat of violence (actual or perceived), (4) the corruption of public officials, their agents, or those in position of responsibility and trust."[75]

Organized crime has existed in one form or another since the early history of this nation. The roots of organized crime go back to the ethnic street gangs that appeared in New York City, New Orleans, and elsewhere in the late eighteenth century. A number of crime histories have traced modern syndicates, those that have arisen since 1900, to two traditions. One is the Jewish gangster tradition, best exemplified by Murder, Incorporated, which traces its roots to Arnold Rothstein, Lewis "Lepke" Buchalter, Jacob "Gurrah" Shapiro, Meyer Lansky,

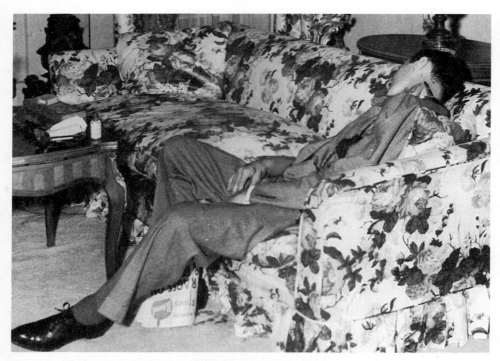

The end of Buggsy Siegel. (*Source:* AP–Wide World Photos.)

and a Cleveland bootleg ring called the Mayfield Road Gang, whereby Moe Dalitz rose to power. The Jewish mobsters diversified quickly into labor racketeering and invested their money in legal and illegal gambling resorts. Italian gangsters, in the other tradition, first became involved in bootlegging and remained closely connected to their own neighborhoods. With the end of bootlegging, Italian mobsters used their control of vice—backroom gambling, the numbers rackets, prostitution, pornography, and narcotics—and the payoffs that went with them to lay the foundation for the control of city political machines, especially the corrupt political machines in old Northern cities.[76]

Organized crime has flourished for several reasons. First, organized activity and organization provides increased profits and reduced risks for those involved in crime. Second, the provision of illegal but desirable goods and services generally has not been viewed by the public as a serious crime. Third, the presence of an organized criminal group frequently reduces the amount of other crimes in the neighborhood; that is, organized groups tend to "police" their own territory to eliminate competition. Fourth, organized crime provides a protective umbrella similar to a political patronage system for community residents who need assistance of different types; for example, the organization may intervene on behalf of people seeking legitimate jobs, contribute to local political campaigns, and obtain political favors. Finally, organized crime flourishes because it provides a channel of social mobility to groups excluded from legitimate routes to economic success.[77]

Structural Versus Process Views of Organized Crime

The two basic approaches to an analysis of organized crime are the structural view and the process view. The structural approach usually argues that the criminal syndicate is a highly structured network of sustained relationships. It has such bureaucratic dimensions as a division of labor, differentiated status and power, channels of communication, and a chain of command. The network is sustained both by a collection of normative forces originating in the culture in which the syndicate is grounded and by the formal rules and procedures, including sanctions, that are incumbent on all participants. Structuralists tend to emphasize ethnic conformity, common socialization and values, and the secret nature of criminal syndicates (rituals, vows, pledges, and ceremonies).[78]

The structure and organization of the Italian criminal syndicate known as La Cosa Nostra exemplifies qualities defined in the structural view. The La Cosa Nostra emerged from a bloody struggle in 1930 and 1931 known as the "Castellamarese War," which started between Italian and Sicilian gangs in New York and eventually spread throughout the nation. After the fighting ended, a meeting was held among the leaders of all the syndicates, at which it was decided to form a national cartel. In a later meeting at the Waldorf Astoria Hotel in New York, non-Italians—including such groups as the Bugs and Meyer Mob and the Cleveland syndicate headed by Moe Dalitz became part of the cartel. But the term *La Cosa Nostra,* which Joseph Valachi popularized in his Senate testimony before the McClellan Committee, is not a correct label for the Italian syndicate outside the New York metropolitan area. In New England, the Italian syndicate is known as "the Office"; in Chicago, it is called "the Outfit"; and in Buffalo, it is called "the Arm." The social organization of Italian syndicates has not changed much since the 1930s. These syndicates currently consist of about 25 "families" located primarily in the Northeast and Midwest, but they have members and operations in other states. A "family" is organized as a hierarchy, with a set of rules demanding loyalty and silence (see Figure 10.3).[79]

Since the mid–1960s, a number of studies have proposed a process view to replace the structural position.[80] Using a variety of approaches, they have attacked the structural position as factually inaccurate, based more on myths, preconceptions, folklore, and imagination than on empirical data. As a competing point of view, the process of interaction patterns among participants has been

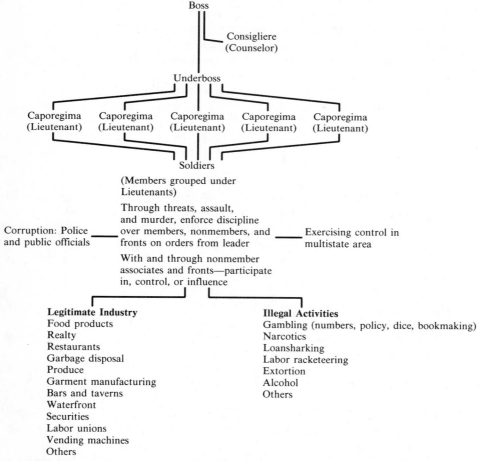

Figure 10.3 An Organized Crime Family [*Source:* President's Commission on Law Enforcement and Administration of Justice, *Task Force Report: Organized Crime* (Washington, D.C.: U.S. Government Printing Office, 1967), p. 9]

suggested as the most fruitful approach for understanding syndicate crime. This view argues that group relation networks labeled "The Mafia" are best understood as an extension of the interaction and exchange processes inherent in social life. Instead of being rigid and highly formalized, these networks are plastic, rife with change, and not amenable to bureaucratic models. For process theorists, organized crime is seen as a relationship system that is concerned with the exchange of things and governed by pragmatism and utility that is relevant to the goals of the actors.[81] Table 10.1 summarizes the distinctions between the two models.

Ianni's work *Black Mafia* is based on the process view. He contends that in some areas the Italians were moving or being forced out of organized crime, and, in turn, were being replaced by networks of black and Hispanic organized criminals. He describes two networks—a loosely organized network in the Central Harlem area of New York City and a more structured network in Paterson, New Jersey. Ianni argues that when the more developed structured network of black crime in Paterson was compared with the loosely structured one in Harlem, a vivid picture emerged showing the process of black crime operations becoming organized into a true black Mafia.[82]

The Mafia

Organized crime was given national coverage in 1950, when the U.S. Senate Special Committee to Investigate Crime in Interstate Commerce—better known as the Kefauver Committee—held meetings with such organized crime figures as Frank Costello, Joe Adonis, and Charles Fischetti. Organized crime gained more public exposure in 1957 when 75 alleged organized crime leaders were discovered at a meeting in Joseph Barbara's home in Appalachin, New York. They had come from all parts of the United States and three other countries.

Americans have always seemed to think that some individual or group is pulling all the complicated strings to which this jumbled world dances. In politics,

Table 10.1 COMPARISON OF THE STRUCTURAL AND PROCESS MODELS OF SYNDICATES

Mechanism	Typology of Syndicate Model	
	Structuralist	**Process**
Organization	rigid, bureaucratic, formal	loose, shifting, coalitional
Cohesion	overarching cultural norms and values; values precede utility	utility and pragmatism; utility precedes value
Membership	ethnicity, race, homogeneity of types, especially ethnicity and race	expediency and propinquity; ethnic and racial heterogeneity
Motivation	group persistence for its own sake; the goal is subordinate to the group	pragmatic achievement of goals; the group is subordinate to the goal

Source: Tom Mieczkowski, "Syndicated Crime in the Caribbean: A Case Study," in *Career Criminals*, ed. Gordon P. Waldo (Beverly Hills, Calif.: Sage, 1983), p. 93.

workers have typically seen "Big Business" or "Wall Street" as the cause of problems, while the business segment has blamed the "Roosevelt New Dealers" and their successors. In the field of crime, the group to blame has been "the Mafia." The Kefauver Committee gave credence to an omnipotent Mafia, as its report indicated:

> There is a nationwide crime syndicate known as the Mafia. . . . Its leaders are usually found in control of the most lucrative rackets in their cities. There are indications of a centralized direction and control of these rackets. . . . The Mafia is the cement that helps to bind the Costello-Adonis-Lansky syndicate of New York and the Accarado-Guzik-Fischetti syndicate of Chicago. . . . These groups have kept in touch with Luciano since his deportation from the country.[83]

Joseph Valachi's 1963 testimony before a Senate subcommittee investigating organized crime also lent support to the idea of the **Mafia's** control over a national crime syndicate.[84] Valachi's testimony was collaborated in part in 1980 by another criminal-turned-government-informant, Jimmy Fratianno. Unlike Valachi, Fratianno was said to be a high-ranking member of an organized criminal group, and his testimony contributed to the conviction of a number of suspected organized criminals. But his testimony, like Valachi's, failed to prove the existence of a national conspiracy of organized criminals.[85]

The accuracy of the Mafia hypothesis has increasingly been questioned. Joseph Albini contends that the claims about a national commission in charge of a criminal conspiracy are defective, because they attribute more formal structure to organized crime than actually exists.[86] Gordon Hawkins notes that much of the Mafia myth is based on the testimony of a "dubious character" and "petty gangster," Joseph Valachi.[87] Dwight Smith adds that *mafia* stands for a state of mind or attitude on the part of Italian-Americans that involves family loyalty and similar values, rather than a highly organized criminal hierarchy.[88] In 1985, Governor Mario Cuomo of New York said in a speech, "I believe you [the press] use 'Mafia' as equated with organized crime. It is an ugly stereotype that gets used over and over again against Italians. . . . All organized crime is not all Italian."[89] Even more to the point, Joseph Bonanno, a former New York City organized crime leader, dismisses the Mafia hypothesis with these words: "In any case, what Americans call 'Mafia' never was an institution, an organization, a corporate body. As best as I can figure out, this fallacy continues to receive its strongest acceptance not in the minds of ordinary people but in the minds of law-enforcement agents."[90]

Services

In addition to such old "standbys" as narcotics, gambling, prostitution, and pornography, organized crime has now diversified into fields involving financial institutions; food industries; automobile sales; travel agencies; scavenger services; pinball machines; cigarette vending machines; beer and liquor sales; service industries (such as those providing linen to hotels and restaurants and paper towels to restaurants); boxing; and union racketeering.[91] Significantly, the diversity of organized crime, as well as the influence organized crime has over politicians and law enforcement officials in some urban communities, has given it enormous control over some areas of the American economy.[92]

ANALYSIS

The order and disorder thesis is helpful in examining the criminal activities of property offenders and in appraising the cost of property crimes.

Property Offenders Differentiated

The professional offender, the occasional offender, and the career offender are the three basic types of property offenders. Each type can be examined in terms of five variables: rates of offending, expressive or instrumental explanation for the crime, skills in criminal behavior, rules governing criminality, and ability to avoid prosecution and conviction.

Professional Offenders   Professional property offenders of old were guided by specific rules governing their behavior. They had *modus operandi* (M.O.) that made their behavior predictable to law enforcement officials. In a real sense, they were skilled workers, usually specializing in one form of property crime, such as safecracking. They took pride in what they did, and, although they knew that sooner or later they would "take a vacation" at the state's expense, this eventuality did not deter their commitment to or development of their criminal specialty.

Today, the professional of the past has been replaced by a sophisticated criminal who utilizes the latest in technology. The activities of the professional criminal now include such crimes as computer fraud, counterfeiting, and the forging of documents, passports, and legal status identification papers. The professional criminal today tends to commit crimes for instrumental (pertaining to some basic goal, objective, or means) rather than expressive (arising from some pressing need or emotion) reasons.[93] This offender may be a high producer or a low producer in terms of rates of criminal activity, but he or she lacks the subcultural rules that guided the professional in the past. The skill level of this new professional tends to be sophisticated, and many of these criminals, especially computer criminals, are able to avoid prosecution and conviction.

Occasional Offenders   The bulk of thefts are committed by "opportunity criminals," individuals who from time to time commit a property offense. Their crimes involve such sundry behaviors as shoplifting, taking a towel from a motel, joyriding, employee theft, tax cheating, and small-scale, naive check forgery. These individuals tend to be amateurs whose decision to steal is spontaneous and whose acts are typically unplanned, unskilled, and haphazard.

Occasional offenders do not normally perceive of themselves as criminals. They are more likely to become involved in crime when opportunity or situational inducements arise. Situational inducements, according to John Hepburn, are short-run influences on an individual's behavior that increase the likelihood of risk taking. Examples of such inducements are stress; physiological factors, such as drug addiction; economic factors, such as financial problems; and social factors, including peer pressure.[94] Thus, the sporadic criminal behavior of occasional property offenders, whether street offenders or white-collar criminals, is usually intended to meet some pressing need. The skill level of occasional criminals is generally low, and few rules guide their criminal behavior. The expressive nature of their criminal activity, the lack of rules, and the low skill level all contribute to high rates of apprehension and prosecution.

Career Offenders   The **career offender** may be either a street offender or a corporate or organized criminal. The Rand studies of street career offenders have suggested that a common world view characterizes these individuals. They found that "high-rate offenders tended to share a set of beliefs that were consistent with their criminal lifestyle—e.g., that they could beat the odds, that they were better than the average criminal, that crime was exciting, and that regular work was boring."[95] They also found that "younger offenders were more likely than older offenders to have extensive juvenile records, to use drugs, and to have criminal attitudes and self-identities," characteristics that are strongly related to criminal behavior.[96]

Thus, a street career offender is committed to crime as a way of life, accepts it as an identity, and frequently belongs to a criminal subculture. The criminal activities of these high-rate producers are in no way characterized by rules. The behavior of recidivist property offenders, who sometimes commit several hundred crimes a year, may be spurred on by addiction to drugs and alcohol, by educational deficiencies, or by the inability to find a job. The overlapping nature of their criminal activity refers to the fact that property crimes, such as burglary, may end up with a violent rape or assault. The criminal activities of recidivist property offenders today seem to be characterized more by desperation than by order, and it is this inherent disorder that results in their eventual apprehension and conviction for their crimes.

The criminal behavior of many corporate criminals and most organized criminals, however, is more instrumental than expressive in nature. Viewing crime as a goal or means to attain some other objective, such as power or success in sales, corporate criminals, especially, tend not to see themselves as criminals. The organization socializes them into accepting deviant values and teaches them the means by which these values can be attained.

There are many reasons why the disorder of corporate crime goes relatively unpunished. Some of these are that the law is weak and ambiguous when it comes to corporate crimes, that corporations carry political clout, and that it is difficult to know when a corporation has actually committed a crime. The most important of these reasons appears to be the fact that corporate crime adapts to a set of rules that are understood by those involved, that provide a sense of consistency and predictability, and that are difficult for outsiders to understand. The rules vary from corporation to corporation, and corporate executives appear able to maintain a bond of secrecy that is similar to that found in organized crime families.

Social Disorder of Property Crimes

Violent crime is indeed a serious problem in America, exceeding by large proportions the amounts of violent crime found in other Western societies. But even more so than violent crime, property crime is intruding upon the quality of American life and is generating fear and distrust among our citizens. One of the serious consequences of property crimes is that Americans have become afraid that the very fabric of the American society is so soiled by crime that no one can be trusted and that everyone is trying to cheat one another. White-collar crimes, including occupational and corporate crimes, are far more expensive to American society than street crimes. In fact, the costs of white-collar crime, especially corporate crime, exceed the total costs of all other types of crime.

However, despite the costs of property crime to society, the sanctions for these offenses are relatively lenient. For example, only about one burglary in seven results in an arrest and conviction. The rates for arrest and conviction of larceny and theft are even less. Equally as serious, corporate and organized criminals are dramatically less likely to receive criminal sanctions. Thus, it seems, the more serious the disorder that property offenders pose to society, the less punishment they receive for their illegal behavior.

POLICY IMPLICATIONS

The social control of both corporate and organized criminality is a major issue facing policymakers. The control of organized crime will be examined in Chapter 11, while this policy section investigates the control of corporate crime.

Clinard and Yeager have suggested that efforts to control corporate crime have taken one of three approaches: voluntary change in both corporate attitudes and structure; the intervention of the political state to force changes in corporate structure, along with legal measures to deter or to punish; and consumer action.[97]

These researchers advocate that the inculcation of ethical principles forms the basis of crime prevention and control, for it is impossible to control complex corporate violations solely by enforcement measures. Corporate management and boards of directors must be made to recognize the basic importance to society of avoiding illegal behavior.[98]

The strengthening of business ethics, according to Clinard and Yeager, begins with the efforts of individual corporations. Companies must take steps to avoid price fixing, producing or selling unsafe products, dealing in kickbacks and bribes, polluting the environment, and discriminating against, or endangering the health of, employees. Second, it is necessary to develop more effective general corporate business codes; the ethical behavior of corporate executives should be influenced by such influential business organizations as the U.S. Chamber of Commerce, the National Association of Manufacturers, the Conference Board, the Committee for Economic Development, and the Business Roundtable. Third, it is necessary for corporate executives to censure other executives who have violated ethical and legal codes. Finally, schools of business administration must instill a more effective and realistic sense of business ethics in their graduates.[99]

SUMMARY

Property crimes, by far the most common criminal activity in the United States, have been the subject of this chapter. The most frequent traditional, or street, crimes are burglaries, larceny-thefts, and auto thefts. Such crimes are terrifying to the American public. But far more costly to society are organized and white-collar crimes, including occupational and corporate crimes. White-collar workers who commit criminal violations during the course of their occupations are more likely to receive punishment than are corporations themselves, and high-ranked organized criminals tend to be more immune from criminal sanctions than are lower-ranked ones.

This chapter has discussed a number of themes relating to order and disorder. First, the more personal crimes are, the more terrified the public becomes by crime. Second, the more visible crimes are, the more the public insists upon their enforcement. Third, the more orderly the rules governing them, the more acceptable crimes are and the less likely they are to receive strong law enforcement. Fourth, the more complex the rules, the more likely they are to go unpunished. Finally, the more property crimes go unpunished, the more criminogenic the American society will become.

REFERENCES

Abadinsky, Howard. *Organized Crime.* 2d ed. Chicago: Nelson-Hall, 1985.

Albanese, Jay S. "God and the Mafia Revisited: From Valachi to Fratianno." In *Career Criminals,* edited by Gordon P. Waldo. Beverly Hills, Calif.: Sage, 1983.

Bonanno, Joseph, with Lalli, Sergio. *A Man of Honor.* New York: Simon and Schuster, 1983.

Cameron, M. O. *The Booster and the Snitch.* Glencoe, Ill.: Free Press, 1964.

Clinard, M. B., and Yeager, P. C. *Corporate Crime.* New York: Free Press, 1980.

Cullen, Francis T.; Maakestad, William J.; and Cavender, Gray. *Corporate Crime Under Attack.* Cincinnati: Anderson, 1987.

Edelhertz, H. *The Nature, Impact, and Prosecution of White-Collar Crime.* Washington, D.C.: U.S. Government Printing Office, 1970.

———. White Collar and Professional Crime: Challenge for the 1980s. Paper presented at the Annual Meeting of the American Association for the Advancement of Science, 7 January 1982.

Ianni, Francis A. *Black Mafia.* New York: Simon and Schuster, 1974.

Lupsha, Peter A. "Networks Versus Networking: Analysis of an Organized Crime Group." In *Career Criminals,* edited by Gordon P. Waldo. Beverly Hills, Calif.: Sage, 1983.

Ross, I. "How Lawless Are Big Companies?" *Fortune,* 1 December 1980. pp. 56–64.

Steffensmeier, Darrell J. *The Fence: In the Shadow of Two Worlds.* Totowa, N.J.: Rowman and Littlefield, 1986.

Sutherland, E. H. "White-Collar Criminality." *American Sociological Review* 5 (February 1940), pp. 1–12.

——. *White Collar Crime.* New York: Dryden, 1949.

Vaughan, Diane. *Controlling Unlawful Organizational Behavior: Social Structure and Corporate Misconduct.* Chicago: University of Chicago Press, 1983.

NOTES

1. Harry King and William J. Chambliss, *Harry King: A Professional Thief's Journey* (New York: Wiley, 1984).
2. Federal Bureau of Investigation, *Uniform Crime Reports, 1986* (Washington, D.C.: U.S. Government Printing Office, 1987), p. 24.
3. Ibid., p. 25.
4. Ibid.
5. Ibid.
6. James Inciardi, *Careers in Crime* (Chicago: Rand-McNally, 1975), p. 5.
7. Bureau of Justice Statistics, *Household Burglary* (Washington, D.C.: U.S. Department of Justice, 1985), p. 1.
8. Mike Maguire, "The Impact of Burglary upon Victims," *British Journal of Criminology* 20 (July 1980), p. 263.
9. Ibid.
10. Federal Bureau of Investigation, *Uniform Crime Reports, 1986,* p. 28.
11. Ibid., p. 29.
12. Ibid.
13. Ibid.
14. Inciardi, *Careers in Crime,* p. 20.
15. Ibid., p. 21.
16. Harold J. Vetter and Ira J. Silverman, *Criminology and Crime: An Introduction* (New York: Harper & Row, 1986), p. 119.
17. Ibid., p. 120.
18. M. O. Cameron, *The Booster and the Snitch* (Glencoe, Ill.: Free Press, 1964).
19. Gerald D. Robin, "Patterns of Department Store Shoplifting," *Crime and Delinquency* 9 (April 1963), pp. 163–172.
20. Federal Bureau of Investigation, *Uniform Crime Reports, 1986,* p. 33.
21. Ibid., p. 34.
22. Vetter and Silverman, *Criminology and Crime,* p. 125.
23. Federal Bureau of Investigation, *Uniform Crime Reports, 1986,* pp. 36–37.
24. Don C. Gibbons, *Society, Crime, and Criminal Behavior,* 4th ed. (Englewood Cliffs, N.J.: Prentice-Hall, 1982), p. 263.
25. Interviewed in April 1973.
26. Larry Karacki, "Youthful Auto Theft Offender Study," Federal Bureau of Prisons, 1966. Unpublished.
27. Federal Bureau of Investigation, *Uniform Crime Reports, 1986,* p. 114.
28. D. Stanley Eitzen and Doug A. Timmer, *Criminology: Crime and Criminal Justice* (New York: John Wiley, 1985), pp. 189–194.

29. Inciardi, *Careers in Crime*, p. 5.
30. Ibid., p. 22.
31. Federal Bureau of Investigation, *Uniform Crime Reports, 1986,* p. 36.
32. Ibid., p. 37.
33. Ibid.
34. Ibid., p. 39.
35. Interviewed in February 1985.
36. Edwin H. Sutherland, *White Collar Crime* (New York: Holt, 1949), p. 9.
37. Herbert Edelhertz, *The Nature, Impact and Prosecution of White Collar Crime* (Washington, D.C.: U.S. Government Printing Office, 1970), p. 3.
38. Edwin Sutherland, "White-Collar Criminality," *American Sociological Review* 5 (1940), pp. 2–10.
39. Crime in the Suites: On the Rise," *Newsweek,* 3 December 1979, p. 114.
40. Ibid.
41. President's Commission on Law Enforcement and Administration of Justice, *Crime and Its Impact—Task Force Report* (Washington, D.C.: U.S. Government Printing Office, 1967).
42. August Bequai, *White-Collar Crime: A 20th Century Crisis* (Lexington, Mass.: Heath, 1978).
43. Francis T. Cullen et al., *Corporate Crime Under Attack: The Ford Pinto Case and Beyond* (Cincinnati: Anderson, 1987), p. 43. See also Cullen, "The Seriousness of Crime Revisited: Have Attitudes Toward White-Collar Crime Changed?," *Criminology* 20 (May 1982), pp. 82–102.
44. Stanton Wheeler and Mitchell Lewis Rothman, "The Organization as a Weapon In White-Collar Crime," *Michigan Law Review* 80, pp. 1403–1426.
45. John Hagan, and Patricia Parker, "White-Collar Crime and Punishment: The Class Structure and Legal Sanctioning of Securities Violations," *American Sociological Review* 50 (June 1985), pp. 302–316.
46. Ibid., p. 313.
47. Edelhertz, *White Collar Crime.*
48. Federal Bureau of Investigation, *Uniform Crime Reports, 1986,* p. 172.
49. Inciardi, *Careers in Crime*, pp. 26–27.
50. Jerome Hall, *Theft, Law and Society* (New York: Bobbs-Merrill, 1932).
51. Federal Bureau of Investigation, *Uniform Crime Reports, 1986,* p. 27.
52. Donald R. Cressey, *Other People's Money* (New York: Free Press, 1953).
53. Ibid., p. 172.
54. Gwynn Nettler, *Explaining Crime,* 3rd ed. (New York: McGraw-Hill, 1984).
55. Charles McCaghy, *Crime in American Society* (New York: Macmillan, 1980).
56. Mark Pogrebin, Eric Poole, and Robert Regoli, *Stealing Money: An Assessment of Bank Embezzlers* (Paper presented at the Annual Meeting of the American Society of Criminology, Denver, Colorado, November 1984), pp. 8–9.
57. Alice Franklin, "Criminality in the Work Place: A Comparison of Male and Female Offenders," in *Criminology of Deviant Women,* ed. Freda Adler and Rita Simon (Boston: Houghton Mifflin, 1979), p. 169.
58. Bureau of Justice Statistics, *Tracking Offenders: White-Collar Crime,* (November 1986) p. 1.
59. Ibid.
60. August Bequai, *Computer Crime* (Lexington, Mass.: Heath, 1978), p. xii.
61. Robert L. Bonn, *Criminology* (New York: McGraw-Hill, 1984), p. 276.

62. Marshall B. Clinard and Peter C. Yeager, *Corporate Crime* (New York: Free Press, 1980), p. 19.

63. Susan Shapiro, "A Background Paper on White Collar Crime" (Paper presented at the Faculty Seminar on White Collar Crime, Yale Law School, February 1976).

64. Sutherland, *White Collar Crime.*

65. Ibid., pp. 217–233.

66. I. Ross, "How Lawless Are Big Companies?" *Fortune* 102 (December 1980), pp. 62–63.

67. Clinard and Yeager, *Corporate Crime.*

68. Ibid., p. 64.

69. Idalene F. Kesner, Bart Victor, and Bruce Y. Lamont, "Board Composition and the Commission of Illegal Acts: An Investigation of Fortune 500 Companies," *Academy of Management Journal* 29 (December 1986), p. 794.

70. Ross, "How Lawless Are Big Companies?"

71. Gilbert Geis, "Heavy Electrical Equipment Antitrust Cases of 1961," in *Corporate and Governmental Deviance,* ed. M. David Ermann and Richard J. Lundman (New York: Oxford University Press, 1987), pp. 124–144.

72. Clinard and Yeager, *Corporate Crime,* pp. 119–120.

73. Diane Vaughan, *Controlling Unlawful Organizational Behavior: Social Structure and Corporate Misconduct* (Chicago: University of Chicago Press, 1983), p. 12.

74. Francis A. J. Ianni, *Black Mafia: Ethnic Succession in Organized Crime* (New York: Simon and Schuster, 1974), p. 15.

75. Peter A. Lupsha, "Networks Versus Networking: Analysis of an Organized Crime Group," in *Career Criminals,* ed. Gordon P. Waldo (Beverly Hills, Calif.: Sage, 1983), pp. 59–86.

76. Frank Browning and John Gerassi, *The American Way of Crime* (New York: Putnam's, 1980), pp. 438–439.

77. Charles W. Thomas and John R. Hepburn, *Crime, Criminal Law, and Criminology* (Dubuque, Ia.: Brown, 1983), p. 314.

78. Tom Mieczkowski, "Syndicated Crime in the Caribbean: A Case Study," in *Career Criminals,* ed. Gordon P. Waldo (Beverly Hills, Calif.: Sage, 1983), pp. 89–101.

79. Vetter and Silverman, *Criminology and Crime,* p. 157.

80. J. Albini, "Reactions to the Questioning of the Mafia Myth," *The Mad, The Bad, and the Different* (Lexington, Mass.: Heath, 1981); G. Hawkins, "God and the Mafia," *Public Interest* 14 (Winter); H. Hess, *Mafia and Mafiosi: The Structure of Power* (Lexington, Mass.: Heath, 1973); D. Smith, *The Mafia Mystique,* (New York: Basic Books, 1975).

81. Mieczkowski, "Syndicated Crime in the Caribbean," pp. 89–101.

82. Ianni, *Black Mafia,* p. 20.

83. U.S. Congress, Senate Special Committee to Investigate Crime in Interstate Commerce, 81st Cong., 2d Sess., and 82d Cong., 1st Sess., 1951.

84. U.S. Congress, Senate Permanent Subcommittee on Investigations of Government Operations, 88 Cong., 1st Sess., 1963.

85. Jay S. Albanese, "God and the Mafia Revisited: From Valachi to Fratianno," in *Career Criminals,* ed. Gordon P. Waldo (Beverly Hills, Calif.: Sage, 1983), p. 44.

86. Joseph L. Albini, *The American Mafia: Genesis of a Legend* (Englewood Cliffs, N.J.: Prentice-Hall, 1971).

87. Hawkins, "God and the Mafia," pp. 24–51.

88. Smith, *The Mafia Myth.*

89. "Cuomo Denies Mafia Affiliation," *New Yorker* (November 2, 1987), pp. 44–48.

90. Joseph Bonanno with Sergio Lalli, *A Man of Honor* (New York: Simon and Schuster, 1983), pp. 404–405.
91. See Howard Abadinsky, *Organized Crime,* 2d ed. (Chicago: Nelson-Hall, 1985).
92. U.S. Congress, Senate Select Committee on Improper Activities in the Labor and Management Field, 85 Cong., 2d Sess., 1958.
93. See Marshall B. Clinard and Richard Quinney, "A Typology of Criminal Behavior," in *Criminal Justice: Allies and Adversaries* (Pacific Palisades, Calif.: Palisades, 1978), pp. 65–72.
94. John Hepburn, "Occasional Criminals," in *Major Forms of Crime,* ed. Robert Meier (Beverly Hills, Calif.: Sage, 1984), pp. 73–94.
95. Jan Chaiken and Marcia Chaiken, with Joyce Peterson, *Varieties of Criminal Behavior: Summary and Policy Implications* (Santa Monica, Calif.: Rand Corporation, 1982); and Joan Petersilia and Paul Honig, with Charles Hubay, *The Prison Experience of Career Criminals* (Santa Monica, Calif.: Rand Corporation, 1977).
96. Peter W. Greenwood with Allan Abrahams, *Selective Incapacitation,* prepared for the National Institute of Justice, U.S. Department of Justice (Santa Monica, Calif.: Rand Corporation, 1982), p. 19.
97. Clinard and Yeager, *Corporate Crime,* p. 9.
98. Ibid., p. 300.
99. Ibid., pp. 302–304.

CHAPTER 11

Crimes Against
the Public Order

SUBSTANCE ABUSE
Alcohol
Marijuana
Cocaine
The Opiates
Enforcement and Drugs
PROSTITUTION
Varieties of Prostitutes
Legality and Prostitution
HOMOSEXUALITY
GAMBLING
Illegal Markets

Bookmaking
Numbers
Legality and Gambling
VAGRANCY
ANALYSIS
Disorder of Choosing Safety over Freedom
Disorder of Becoming a Victim
Disorder of Enforcing Public Order Laws
POLICY IMPLICATIONS
SUMMARY
REFERENCES
NOTES

KEY TERMS

AIDS

alcohol and drug dependency

bookmaking

call girl

Call Off Your Old Tired Ethics (COYOTE)

Centers for Disease Control

cocaine

gambling

heroin

homosexuality

legislating morality

marijuana

money laundering

numbers

opium

pimp

prostitution

streetwalker

vagrancy

> *Drugs are considered a victimless crime, but the drug user's family, friends, people who live around them, and even strangers all end up victims. When you are strung-out on heroin, you are married body and soul to it. It becomes your whole life. You'll lie, cheat, steal, and sometimes kill people for it. Nothing will stop a heroin user when he really needs a fix. Addicts end up the biggest victim of all. To best describe a heroin user, and I know because I've been one, this person is a snake who is deadly and gives no warning.*
> —Former California heroin addict[1]

The discord between morality and legality is nowhere more apparent in American criminal law than in public order crimes (also called victimless crimes, transactional crimes, or consensual crimes). Prostitution, gambling, substance abuse, public drunkenness, pornography, and homosexuality are the most obvious examples of those crimes that entail "the attempt to control, by criminal law, the willing exchange of socially disapproved but widely demanded goods or services."[2]

The dilemma of **legislating morality** was a major theme of the 1970s. Proponents of deinstitutionalizing victimless, or public order, crimes argued that a substantial amount of criminal law in the United States was created for the express intention of publicly enforcing moral principles.[3] Kenneth A. Johnson explains: "Since the conduct in question is not injurious to other persons or property, it can be considered as an attempt by society to regulate the kinds of behavior that disturbs its sense of public morality."[4]

However, public acceptance of public order crimes is experiencing a change. The fear of AIDS, herpes, and gonorrhea is generating a serious backlash against prostitution and homosexuality. The use of intravenous drugs not only speeds the spread of **AIDS** but also leads to addicted babies, fetal damage, fetal brain damage, and fetal hyperactivity. The sudden deaths in 1986 of such major sports performers as Len Bias and Don Rogers have alerted the public to the dangers

The assistance of Bruce A. Elkema was invaluable in the research and development of this chapter.

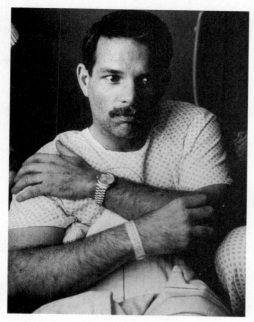

An AIDS patient in Hollywood Community Hospital.
(*Source:* Erich Hartmann/Magnum Photos, Inc.)

of cocaine use. First Lady Nancy Reagan's campaign against drug use has further contributed to an increased public consciousness about the perils of drug use. Moreover, the relationship between drug use and increased rates of violent and property crimes is becoming public knowledge. Finally, pornography is being blamed, especially by Protestant fundamentalists and other religious groups, for contributing to the moral decline of the nation. They are concerned, for example, about the increased popularity and availability of X-rated movies.

Thus health, rather than morality or the overreach of the criminal law, has become the central issue related to public order crimes in the 1980s. The disorder of public order crimes is defined in terms of a health hazard, and this interpretation, in fact, affects the legitimacy of governmental controls. The **Centers for Disease Control** is displacing the Drug Enforcement Administration as the hand-wringing agency.

SUBSTANCE ABUSE

Alcohol and drug dependency create a heavy social cost. The *Uniform Crime Reports* shows that over 30 percent of all arrests in 1986 were related to alcohol or drugs. Out of 9,944,411 arrests in 1986, 666,132 were for drug abuse violations, 1,390,597 for driving under the influence, 469,317 for liquor laws violations, and 750,887 were for public drunkenness.[5]

Sixty percent or more of all incoming prison inmates are alcohol or drug dependent.[6] But abuse is no longer a marginal lower-class, minority group phenomenon. Cocaine use among high-school students, for example, quadrupled between 1972 and 1982. With coke, speed, tranquilizers, and antidepressants, abuse crosses socioeconomic and racial barriers. Furthermore, one out of two Americans will be involved in an alcohol-related auto accident in his or her lifetime. One-half of all traffic fatalities involve alcohol, and 20 percent, or 5000, of these fatalities are teenagers. Drug use costs the American economy at least $26 billion annually.[7]

Alcohol

The reaction to Prohibition served to foster the view of alcohol use as acceptable behavior that should largely be free from legal controls. Alcohol was not perceived as a dangerous drug by the public; the illicit use of "hard drugs" was seen as a serious problem by the same individuals who had urged repeal of Prohibition.[8]

Yet, in spite of the greater tolerance for alcohol use, alcohol-related arrests far outnumber other drug arrests. About 80 percent of all drug arrests can be linked to alcohol, whether the offense involves public drunkenness (the number-one drug offense), the violation of liquor laws governing sale and consumption, or driving while intoxicated. The burgeoning health hazards of alcohol can be seen in the numerous crimes committed by those under the influence of alcohol, by the abuse of alcohol while driving, and by the increased tendency of teenagers to develop drinking problems.

The National Council on Alcoholism reports that approximately 64 percent of murders, 41 percent of assaults, 34 percent of rapes, 29 percent of other sex crimes, 30 percent of suicides, 56 percent of assaults in the home, and 60 percent of cases of child abuse may be linked to alcohol abuse. The council goes on to claim that when alcoholism is treated, violent behavior is known to decrease.[9] The Bureau of Justice Statistics survey of prisoners found that almost one-half of the inmates reported they had been drinking just before the commission of the criminal act for which they were incarcerated, with more than three-fifths stating that they had been drinking heavily.[10]

The abuse of alcohol while driving has also recently become a public concern. MADD (Mothers Against Drunk Drivers), started by a California mother whose son was killed by a drunk driver; RID (Remove Intoxicated Drivers); and SADD (Students Against Drunk Drivers) are movements typical of the 1980s. This emphasis on deterring drunk driving has resulted in more than 30 states' passing statutes stiffening their DUI (driving under the influence) or DWI (driving while intoxicated) laws and raising the age at which it is lawful to drink. For example, in California, a drunk driver now faces up to six months in jail, a $500 fine, suspension of operator's license for six months, and impounding of the vehicle.

Finally, the increased number of adolescents who are abusing alcohol is becoming a matter of grave public concern. The U.S. Government Report on Alcohol and Health found that by the senior year of high school, 89.9 percent of boys and 83.2 percent of girls have taken a drink at least once.[11] Television programs portraying teenage alcoholics, television commercials with teenagers saying that "it is not cool" to drink, and talk shows on teenage alcoholics all are expressions of this growing concern.

Marijuana

After alcohol, **marijuana** is the most frequently used drug. The National Institute of Drug Abuse of the U.S. Department of Health and Human Services has found that between 1962 and 1980, the proportion of persons 18 to 25 years of age who have used marijuana increased from 4 to 68 percent. The 1979 National Survey on Drug Abuse, conducted by the same agency, reported that between 1972 and 1979, experience with marijuana and cocaine doubled among 12- to 17-year-olds and among those over 25 years of age.[12] A juvenile probation officer noted: "We are finding an awful lot of young people who are using marijuana on a daily basis. There also seems to be an increased number of 'heads,' kids whose drug use dominates their lives. It is hard to keep your life together when you're using 'pot' on a daily basis."[13]

Marijuana was first introduced into the United States in 1920. The passage by Congress of the Marijuana Tax in 1937 outlawed its general use. Subsequently, every state enacted laws forbidding its use. But in recent years, six states—Alaska, California, Colorado, Maine, Ohio, and Oregon—have decriminalized marijuana for personal use, reducing penalties to a moderate fine for possession of a small amount of the drug and making possession a misdemeanor instead of a criminal act.

Heated debates about the hazards of using marijuana have been waged for some time. Recent research has documented more ill effects of long-term marijuana use than have been suggested in the past. For example, several studies in the 1970s showed lowered male hormone levels, brain damage, and various other effects—but most of these studies have been challenged on the grounds of poor research techniques and methodology.[14]

Cocaine

Cocaine, the powdered derivative of the South American coca plant, is currently replacing other illegal drugs in popularity. Two million Americans are estimated to spend $20 million each year to buy the 60,000 pounds of the substance smuggled into this country.[15] The major source of "coke" is Colombia, and its distribution has become a major diplomatic issue in Central America.

Cocaine is so expensive ($125 or more per gram on the streets) that it is generally used in very sparing quantities; until recently, it was believed to be less addicting than other illegal hard drugs. Cocaine soon soared to popularity in the mid- to late 1970s among the "jet set," the entertainment crowd, young executives, highly paid athletes, and many others. Patricia A. Adler, who studied an upper-level drug-dealing and -smuggling community, concluded that as an intoxicating substance, cocaine offers several advantages over marijuana:

First, it [cocaine] produced a warm and sociable high, characterized by feelings of friendship and euphoria. Second, it could be snorted quickly and without odor, making it handier and more discreet. Third, when snorted in moderation, it appeared to have few harmful physical consequences. Fourth, it was much less bulky, enabling people to carry it inconspicuously.[16]

But the 1986 deaths of a University of Maryland star basketball player and of an outstanding defensive back for the Cleveland Browns professional football team serve as tragic reminders of the dangers of the drug. Recently, a less expensive, more potent version of cocaine has achieved great popularity. Called "crack," this dangerous substance has generated great concern among law enforcement and health professionals.

The Opiates

Opium, which is derived from certain species of the poppy, is the source of heroin, morphine, paragoric, and codeine, some of which are still used medically. **Heroin**, a refined form of morphine, was introduced about the turn of the twentieth century. In the 1960s, most heroin reaching the United States was from poppies grown in Turkey and was processed and distributed from Marseilles, France. In

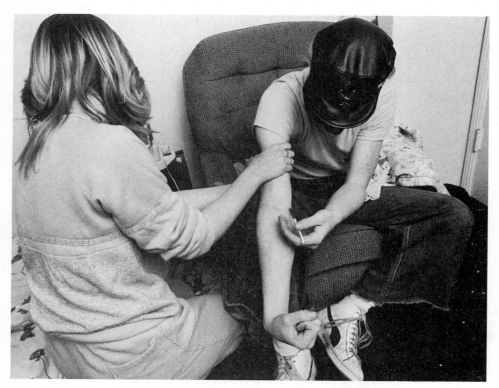

A heroin user shoots up. (*Source:* Mark Ellen Mark/Archive Pictures, Inc.)

1971, "the French Connection" was disrupted by a joint French-American campaign, and an agreement between the United States and Turkey resulted in a ban on the growing of opium poppies in that country.

The shortage of heroin created panic among addicts, many of whom enrolled in addiction treatment programs. It was estimated at the time that the number of heroin addicts dropped from about 600,000 in 1970 to 300,000 or less in 1974. In 1975, when officials were predicting that addiction rates would be permanently lowered, heroin from Mexico and Southeast Asia became available on the New York market; within a year, Mexico was reputedly supplying 90 percent of all heroin shipped to America. The Mexican government then took tough measures to stop the flow of illegal drugs across the border. Poppy fields were sprayed with powerful herbicides, which so limited the supply that the street price of heroin rose in New York City from $1.18 per milligram in 1975 to $1.75 per milligram in 1978.[17]

Enforcement and Drugs

The United States is once again waging a war on drugs. The argument is repeatedly made that violations of drug laws do not fit the category of victimless crimes. Users are victims of their own behavior; they also are victims of the pusher and others who directly or indirectly supply them with drugs. Moreover, there are the victims whose property is stolen by addicts seeking money for drug purchases, and, of course, society is victimized because it must spend millions of dollars and police hours dealing with the drug problem.[18]

The failure to curb the flow of drugs is illustrated by the ill-fated "Operation Intercept." Initiated on September 21, 1969, this federal program used thousands of police agents and cost millions of dollars. Its basic purpose was to stem the flow of drugs across the Mexico–United States border. It proved to be a disaster, for within a few days, it tied up border traffic for miles, as hundreds of angered individuals were forced to submit to strip searches. The Mexican government became so irritated that it requested the operation be immediately terminated. Its long-term effect was to encourage the importation of stronger marijuana than the Mexican variety from North Africa and Viet Nam. Operation Intercept also encouraged the growth and harvest of a domestic crop in the United States.[19] Norval Morris and Gordon Hawkins state:

> There seems to be no doubt, . . . that the policy of criminalization and the operations of criminal justice agencies in this field have in themselves been criminogenic without measurably diminishing the extent of the drug problem or reducing the supply of narcotics entering the country. There is substantial evidence that organized criminals engaged in drug traffic have made and continue to make high profits. There is evidence, too, that criminalization of the distribution of drugs has caused much collateral crime with drug addicts, "to support their habits," as the President's Crime Commission put it, "stealing millions of dollars worth of property every year and contributing to the public's fear of robbery and burglary."[20]

BOX 11.1   **NARRATION FROM A DRUG ADDICT**

I was busted for [heroin] possession at twenty-three. I'll never forget that judge. He was the first judge of the Narcotic Court in Chicago. He put his glasses down, and he talked like he was right out of a Western movie. He said, "Boy, you haven't got a bad record. Do you use drugs?" I said, "No, your honor, I swear I don't use drugs." I was very convincing because I was still high; I had smuggled some dope in the jail with me. He looked down at me, and said, "I'm going to give you six months in the house of corrections. How's that?" And everybody else is telling me, take it. Don't get the man mad.

They locked me up, and I thought six months is nothing. But I was still high and in a world of fantasy. The first night wasn't so bad because I was still mellow. At that time, they didn't give a dope fiend nothing—not even an aspirin. For three days I wanted to die. If you've never slept on prison sheets, they're like canvas. I wore the skin off my body. You're supposed to beat the straw mattress to get the lumps out and soften it up. But all I wanted to do was beat myself. The worse part of kicking the habit is you become a zombie. The first week went by, and I still wasn't sleeping. To get a good night's sleep, it takes ninety days, maybe longer. If you went to sleep for fifteen minutes, you felt worse or you'd be dripping wet from slobbering.

Finally, I started feeling better, blending in and learning the ins and outs of prison. You couldn't learn anything there, except how to burglarize something, or how to stick somebody up, or how to be a pimp. At that time, dope dealers were respected in prison. I wasn't intimidated by anyone. I had been on the streets for years. I knew how to protect myself. I got out in February, and I wondered if I would stay off drugs.

About a block from my house, I saw an old friend, and he yelled, "Hi, Joe, you want to get high?" I said, "Yeah." And I was off and running. After that first high, I forgot all about prison. That was yesterday. I forgot about how I was sick, and how I had to listen to the police [prison guards] telling me what to do. I was arrested one month later. I was selling dope to this guy right on the corner. The cops busted us and found a syringe in my pocket.

Source: Interviewed in August 1985.

The Harvard economist Thomas C. Schelling adds, "If narcotics were not illegal, there could be no black market and no monopoly profits, and the interest in 'pushing' it would probably be not much greater than pharmaceutical interest in pills to reduce the symptoms of common colds."[21] Furthermore, the brunt of law enforcement falls heavily on the user and the addict rather than on traffickers, thereby creating a persecuted minority with its own self-sustaining myths and

---

BOX 11.2   **HANDLING THE ISSUE OF DRUG ABUSE**

Not only are we clogging the justice system, but we are corrupting foreign policy, are corrupting police officers, and are wasting resources. I just don't think the law enforcement approach is likely to succeed in cutting down either supply or demand. I'm not saying that there is no deterrent effect. There obviously is, but I think the costs in the way we are doing it now are greater than the benefits.

What I would be inclined to suggest is a decriminalization of certain drugs as an experiment. I would start with those that seem least dangerous. For instance, among the drugs that are considered the major hitters—marijuana, cocaine, and heroin—I would start with marijuana and decriminalize it. What I mean by decriminalizing it is that adults, not kids, could get it at will. If it works reasonably well and doesn't lead to social horrors that people claim will occur, I would then consider the next most dangerous drug, which is heroin. Ultimately, I can imagine a society where virtually all of the currently controlled drugs would be available.

Source: Interviewed in June 1987.

---

ideology.[22] In Box 11.2, a law professor gives his opinion of how society can better handle the issue of drug abuse.

However, the decriminalization of drugs is no longer a popular issue in the late 1980s. Instead, the predominant concern now is the health hazards of using drugs. The fear of AIDS alone has made the use of intravenous drugs a serious health matter. In addition, drug addiction is associated with high rates of violent and property crimes, with reduced longevity, poor diets, fetus damage and addicted babies, increased conflict within the home, problematic performance on the job, and irregular attendance and poor performance at school.

PROSTITUTION

Prostitution is known as "the oldest profession." The term itself derives from the Latin *prostituere,* which means "to cause to stand in front of." *Prostitution* can be defined as the delivery of sexual stimulation and gratification for profit. This definition omits the requirement of sexual intercourse, because the act of prostitution does not always require physical contact between two or more persons. It is estimated that there may be as many as one-quarter to one-half million full- or part-time prostitutes in the United States.[23] In 1986, the *Uniform Crime Reports* show, 94,415 arrests were made for prostitution and commercialized vice.[24] The form of prostitution appears to have changed to some extent:

Working the streets. (*Source:* Bob Daemmrich.)

The business of prostitution, embracing modern marketing techniques and skirting the law, is branching out from its downtown closet into Middle America. Like its cousin the blue movie, today's brothel is likely to be around the corner—in the form of a massage parlor, lotion studio, nude photo club, sexual intercourse school, escort service, dial-a-message, sauna bath house, or some other thinly disguised supermarket for sexual services.[25]

The earliest record of prostitution dates back to the Mesopotamian River Valley, one of the several sources of civilization, where priests engaged in sex to promote fertility in the community. In the earliest legal codes, few sexual activities were singled out for legal repression. But with the spread of Christianity, an ever-increasing number of sexual prohibitions became part of the law. At the heart of Christian theology was the belief that pleasure in sex was evil and damnable. It was not so much the act that was condemned but the pleasure that was connected with it.[26]

During the settling of the American West, the "house of ill repute"—known variously as the "bordello," "whorehouse," "cathouse," and "brothel"—became popular. These businesses frequently were located in a section of town called the "red-light district," so named because of the practice of advertising by means of a red lantern or light. Folklore and such television shows as "Bonanza" and "Gunsmoke" testify to such Western legends as the "whore with a heart of gold."

However, while the Western whorehouse was being romanticized, citizens on the East Coast were beginning to have second thoughts. The 1910 Mann Act and the Federal White Slave Act heralded the beginning of the end for the red-light districts. The purpose of the Mann Act was to prevent the recruitment of young women across state lines. Still, individual houses of prostitution continued to thrive even with the decline of red-light districts.[27]

In the 1970s, prostitution policies became part of a reform agenda. Liberal attitudes toward noncommercial sex and changing views of female sexuality influenced the reappraisal of prostitution laws. How could one prosecute a prostitute for peddling sex, it was asked, when on the same street one could legally purchase admission to peep shows and X-rated films? Civil liberties lawyers, feminist activists, and prostitute groups mounted legal challenges, published articles, and held public protests against social injustice toward the prostitute. Prostitutes appeared on talk shows, and filmmakers portrayed the brutal world of sexual abuse and danger in the prostitute's life.[28]

A prostitute union movement was launched in France in 1975, and in the United States, the first and best-known of the prostitute groups—**Call Off Your Old Tired Ethics (COYOTE)**—began in San Francisco. Margo St. James, its founder and master tactician, is responsible for its success and endurance. COYOTE, along with other prostitute organizations, protested police harassment and the lack of social benefits such as pensions and unemployment insurance. St. James rejected the feminist argument that prostitution was degrading work and harmful to women; instead, she insisted that prostitution was merely a job for most women, and a lucrative one compared with most women's work.[29]

However, Eleanor M. Miller's *Street Woman,* which is based on intensive interviews with 64 prostitutes in Milwaukee, contends that prostitution evolves out of the profound social and economic problems confronting teenage girls, especially young women of color.[30] For black women, constituting over half of Miller's sample, movement into prostitution occurred as a consequence of exposure to deviant street networks. Generally recruited by older black males with lengthy criminal records, these women organized themselves into "pseudo families" and engaged chiefly, but not exclusively, in prostitution. Faced with the burdens of pregnancy and single motherhood (the young women interviewed had a total of 81 children), the women viewed prostitution as an alternative to boring and low-paying jobs. Attracted by the excitement and money involved in prostitution, they soon found that the life was not nearly as glamorous and remunerative as they had anticipated.[31]

For whites, Miller found, street prostitution was not so much a hustle into which one drifted as it was a survival strategy. For this group, there was often a direct link between prostitution and difficulties with parents, runaway behavior, and contact with the juvenile justice system. Interviewees described family lives characterized by disorganization, extremely high levels of violence, and abuse. But running away from these chaotic settings resulted in arrest and lengthy detention as status offenders.[32]

Virtually all the street women had some experience with drugs, but Miller found that drug dependency, except for Hispanic women, was not the factor motivating participation in street hustling. Their relationships with men were characterized by violence and exploitation, and, as the women aged, they increasingly came into contact with the criminal justice system.[33]

A youth service bureau counselor who works primarily with runaways explains how the need for money, or survival, has led to increased prostitution among teenage girls:

> A lot more girls are selling their bodies. There's more younger hookers, 13 or 14 years old. They just don't care. It's a way they can have all the clothes they want, all the blue jeans and shoes they want. All the drugs they want. It's an easy way to make money. If it was legal and had a tax on it, they would find something else. The mindset of society is that money is great and you can have anything you want if you have money. So, kids will do anything they can to get money.[34]

Varieties of Prostitutes

The process of becoming a prostitute involves more than a decision to suspend traditional morality and "do what comes naturally" for money. Rules and techniques must be learned through a process known as "being turned out." Although most prostitutes are female, there is a small but growing number of male prostitutes, especially young boys. Both female and male prostitutes cater to a male clientele.

A prostitute's sexual career appears to have three stages. The first stage is characterized by a pattern of "pick-up" sex. This pattern is often reinforced by peer group expectation as the way to attain excitement and male attention. The idea of adding the incentive of money develops, as any "kicks" such experiences provide begin to fade. The second stage is the transitional one between the straight world and the world of prostitution. During this stage, the individual usually engages in prostitution as a part-time activity; at the same time, she (or he) may continue to work at a conventional job and maintain social ties with the straight world. It is during the transitional stage that an individual discovers whether she (or he) is willing to satisfy a broad range of client requests, can learn to adapt to police surveillance and entrapment procedures, can handle clients who are unwilling to pay, and can substitute a business ethic for previous motivations. During the final stage, the prostitute acquires the deviant identity and fully accepts identification of self with the identity of a prostitute.[35]

The twentieth century has seen the diversification of the varieties of prostitutes. The **streetwalker**, an individual who approaches men on the street and indicates a willingness to exchange sexual activity for money, occupies the lowest rung. The approach must be made carefully in case the man is a police officer who could make an arrest for soliciting. The streetwalker is also the most active, serving perhaps 10 to 20 clients, or "johns," in a particular evening. Streetwalkers often are organized into groups or "stables," each of which is handled by a **pimp** or "main man." Streetwalkers are frequently abused by their pimps. The financial arrangement between the prostitute and her pimp requires that the prostitute give all her earnings to the pimp; in turn, she receives expense money, clothing, medical, and legal expenses. (See Box 11.3 for more details about the relationship between the pimp and prostitute.)

The middle rung in the status hierarchy is occupied by the part-time or house prostitute. Such individuals usually work out of houses or share an apartment. A pimp or a madam may not be necessary, because many of the women freelance, getting their customers by referral. The services of these prostitutes are usually more expensive than those of streetwalkers. Recently, this category of prostitution has come to be populated in part by students and housewives. The full-timers who operate from massage parlors, model studios, and escort services also occupy this level.

The **call girl** is on the top rung of her profession. There are almost no pimps or madams at this level, and these prostitutes usually depend on referrals from their customers. They receive premium prices and usually service a fairly wealthy clientele, adjusting the price according to the client's ability to pay. These prostitutes may have a room reserved at a local hotel or operate out of their own apartments or the apartment of a friend.

Legality and Prostitution

Most states have laws that prohibit promiscuous sexual intercourse for hire; other states simply define prostitution as promiscuous sexual intercourse and make no mention of money. Still other states prohibit any kind of sexual conduct for hire. In addition, every state has laws against inducing minors to engage in prostitution. But this public order crime almost seems to be designed to thwart police efforts to bring it under control. In the majority of states, prostitution is treated as a misdemeanor, punishable by a short sentence and minimal fine. Significantly, even in the few states that treat prostitution as a felony, judges usually mete out only probation and small fines. Thus, because the courts throughout the nation do not regard prostitution as a serious problem, any police effort to clean up the situation seems doomed from the outset.[36]

Morris and Hawkins contend that "the use of law enforcement resources in this way [to arrest prostitutes], is a fruitless effort to promote moral virtue, is wasteful and socially injurious."[37] Herbert Packer adds:

There seems little reason to believe that the incidence of prostitution has been seriously reduced by criminal law enforcement, although the forms in which it is conducted have altered. . . .

As the courts become increasingly strict about the evidence that will satisfy a charge of prostitution or solicitation, the brunt of enforcement falls ever more

BOX 11.3   **INTERVIEW WITH A TEENAGE PROSTITUTE**

Question: Why does a teenage girl become a prostitute?

Answer: If you're working for yourself, the money is pretty good. If you are working regular, you make $1,000 or more a week if you work every night. You can either work in a massage parlor or on the streets.

Question: How old are teenage prostitutes and how do they learn what to do?

Answer: They are usually fifteen and up. Older women have a lot of influence and power over younger ones. Most street prostitutes have pimps, who have a lot of control over their girls.

Question: What are the advantages of having a pimp?

Answer: Some girls feel that pimps help you as much as you can help them. They feel that their pimps care about them. When you are new to a territory, it is nice to have a man who knows the territory and will take care of you. They furnish a room over your head, provide you with all the necessities that you need, and make certain you eat well. The pimp is there to bail you out when you go to jail. He'll make certain that none of the other pimps hassle or rob you.

As far as I'm concerned, there ain't no advantages in having a pimp. They would like you to believe that they will take care of you, but after they get you, you might see clothes but that's about it. Some will give you a little spending money, but the majority take it all. If you need something, they will either take you out to buy it or give you money to buy it. A lot of prostitutes are into drugs, and as long as they are getting their drugs, they're happy. Coke, heroin, and weed are the drugs most widely used. . . .

Source: Interviewed in a Midwestern city by Linda Bartollas in June 1981.

heavily on those women who are so desperate that they will take the greatest risk. . . . The law is caught between unrealistic severity and triviality, with triviality winning the day. The whole tedious, expensive, degrading process of enforcement activity produces no results: no deterrence, very little incapacitation, and certainly no reform.[38]

In the 1970s, there was some debate over whether or not prostitution should be decriminalized. Several counties of Nevada, with its two state meccas of gambling in Las Vegas and Reno, decriminalized prostitution. Oregon has enacted legislation that legalizes houses of prostitution in an indirect way. Since January 1977, these houses have been licensed as "relaxation treatment businesses," to allow the state to exercise some control without unconstitutional interference. In Box 11.4, Joseph P. Lentini summarizes the views of the proponents and opponents of legalization.

In sum, although the social control of prostitution poses enormous problems, the current public health scare over AIDS, herpes, and a penicillin-resistant strain of gonorrhea makes it unlikely that the public or policymakers in most jurisdictions will support the decriminalization of prostitution. The health hazards involved simply make the decriminalization of prostitution too risky.

HOMOSEXUALITY

A homosexual can be defined as an individual who has a preferential erotic attraction to members of the same sex.[39] Homosexual behavior has been found throughout history. In some cultures such behavior has been subjected to severe punishment, including death; yet, even when homosexual behavior has been banned, it has continued to exist.

Evelyn Hooker, in a study of 30 male homosexuals, observed that these homosexuals engaged in varied and changeable forms of sexual activity. Thus, characterizations of such persons as "fellators," "insertees," "passive," or "active" oversimplify the real world. She also concluded that this group of homosexuals did not vary in psychological well-being from a sample of heterosexuals.[40]

Morton Hunt has estimated that in the United States about three million men are mainly or exclusively homosexual and that two million women are mainly or exclusively lesbian.[41] Although homosexuals, or "gays," in this nation have faced a continued negative public response, public hostility was defused somewhat during the 1970s. The fact that increasing numbers of homosexuals were willing to "come out of the closet" and take their stand on "gay rights" contributed to this reduction of public stigma. The public activities of gay citizens, including marches and demonstrations, also contributed to greater public exposure and acceptance. Still, studies during the 1970s indicated that a majority of people viewed homosexuals as sick, sinful, or dangerous.[42]

Homosexuals also have faced prosecution in the courts and discrimination on the job and elsewhere. Homosexuality is no longer a crime, except when force is involved, but homosexuals continue to face legal liabilities. Oral and anal sex and other forms of nongenital heterosexual intercourse are banned in some jurisdictions under statutes prohibiting sodomy, deviant sexuality, or buggery. The penalties for such sexual activity range from three years to life imprisonment. Known homosexuals are still considered security risks and are not allowed to work in the CIA and the FBI; they also are barred from military service. Furthermore, known homosexuals are not permitted to live together in public housing, and public employers in some jurisdictions may discriminate against homosexuals.[43]

The few gains homosexuals made in the 1970s are rapidly disappearing because the fear of AIDS is causing a backlash against homosexual behavior. Medical epidemiologists inform the public that AIDS may cause a worldwide epidemic that will threaten the very existence of society, and the sexual practices

BOX 11.4   # LEGALIZED PROSTITUTION POLICY

Proponents

1. The function of criminal law is not to coerce citizens toward virtue by imposing public standards on private morality.
2. The resources of the criminal justice system are limited while the incidence of serious crime is high. We cannot justify the hundreds of thousands of police man hours used in the abortive attempt to eliminate prostitution.
3. For centuries we have been trying to eliminate prostitution and failed. Legalization and control will at least put society in control.
4. Legalization and control will eliminate the pimp and middleman who live off the earnings of the prostitute.
5. Legalization and control will eliminate the peripheral crimes which attain to prostitution. Drunk rolling, robbery, and extortion will become things of the past in relation to prostitution.
6. Legalized houses of prostitution would provide weekly medical examinations of prostitutes, thus reducing the incidence of venereal disease.
7. Most prostitutes enter the business voluntarily and so legalization will merely be the recognition of this fact. . . .

Opponents

1. Prostitution exploits women unconscionably.
2. Licensed houses of prostitution are disseminators of VD, to as full an extent as an unregulated system of prostitution.
3. No system of prostitution has been able to eliminate the pimps, who take so much of the prostitute's earnings.
4. Legalization would require an elaborate retirement system to take care of the prostitute as she gets older and unable to work.
5. Many prostitutes are members of minority groups. Licensing black, Puerto Rican, and Chicano women as prostitutes for white customers would only increase racial tensions.
6. Wherever prostitution has been legalized there have always been a greater number of unlicensed, illegal prostitutes.
7. We have no experience with decriminalization and cannot tell in advance if it could work.

Source: This material appears in Joseph P. Lentini, *Vice and Narcotics Control* (Beverly Hills, Calif.: Glencoe Press, 1977), pp. 72–73.

''Back room'' gambling. (*Source:* Michael D. Sullivan/TexaStock.)

of homosexuals are being blamed for this ever-spreading disease. Miami's repeal of its gay-rights ordinance stands as evidence of this rapidly increasing hostility toward homosexuals. In 1985, Houston voters rejected by a four-to-one margin a proposal to eliminate sexual preference in hiring, firing, and promoting city employees.

GAMBLING

Gambling, one of the vice crimes, poses little or no direct threat to the health or moral character of the bettor, unless he or she becomes a compulsive gambler. Definitions of gambling usually involve the exchange of money without any equivalent value, material or personal; the possession of money determined solely by chance; the winner's gain by the loss of losers; and the taking of an avoidable risk.[44] Gambling generally attaches little or no stigma to the bettor, and any financial injury incurred affects only the bettor and his or her family. In 1986, the *Uniform Crime Reports* show, 24,860 gambling arrests took place.[45]

Joseph P. Lentini explains Americans' ambivalent attitude toward gambling:

The American people are fond of gambling. In fact, roughly 60 percent of the population of this country has at one time or another gambled on some game of chance. Despite the fact that we take pride in our reputation as hardworking people who achieve by doing, we tend to believe in luck, and all have within us the desire to get something for nothing. For this reason most Americans have extremely ambivalent attitudes toward gambling and the existing antigambling laws. These attitudes have been manifested in a number of ways in recent years.[46]

Illegal Markets

Bookmaking and **numbers** are two forms of gambling that are typically associated with the underworld.

Bookmaking   Wagering on athletic and racing events has a long history in the United States. Many major political figures in the nineteenth century were known for their interest in horses and wagering. Indeed, a racing meet between the best Northern horse and the best Southern horse attracted 65,000 spectators in 1823; bets as large as $50,000 were supposedly wagered.[47]

By the turn of the twentieth century, bookmakers had become highly organized and extremely prominent in city politics. With a national circuit of over one hundred tracks, operating during different periods of time throughout the year, and a substantial Irish working-class population with a real interest in horses, a large off-track betting industry grew up in a number of major cities.[48] The focus of much of the Kefauver (Senate Committee on Organized Crime) Committee's inquiry into illegal gambling was the monopoly of racing information. The committee was concerned with whether or not the national monopoly in information was used to control local bookmaking in various cities. Perhaps the most important finding of the Kefauver Committee was the pervasiveness of gambling corruption among the police.[49]

Today, both horse and sports betting—which has replaced horse betting as the major source of business—are handled by bookmakers. Some of the larger operators take sports bets only. Sports wagering is restricted to such team sports as football (college and professional), basketball (college and professional), and baseball (professional only). Little wagering is done on hockey, the other major professional sport, and almost none on any individual sports, except for a few special events such as the world heavyweight boxing title.[50]

Most sports bets are made on the outcome of a single game. For example, in basketball or football, one team is generally given a handicap of a certain number of points, called the "spread." If the New York Giants were a three-point favorite over the Denver Broncos, the person who bet on the Giants would win only if the Giants won by more than three points. If the Broncos won, or lost by less, then the bettor would lose. If the Giants won by exactly three points, then all bets would be returned to the bettors; in order to avoid that situation, the spread frequently is given a half-point value, such as three-and-a-half.

Bookmaking enterprises are known to be extremely unstable. Among the reasons for their instability is poor entrepreneurial performance, either in management of risk or in control of agents. The impact of law enforcement, in terms of both incarceration and disruption, is another source of instability. Bookmakers also have difficulty in obtaining capital on reasonable terms. Thus, many bookmakers lose control of their own operations and move to subordinate roles in other operations. Few bookmakers retain their operations over a long period of time.[51]

Numbers Both legal and illegal lotteries have long been popular in American cities. But during the last half of the nineteenth century, many states outlawed lotteries. As dependence on state lotteries withered, local operators began to draw their own numbers. In the early part of the twentieth century, numbers, as the practice is currently known, began to be played among the growing number of poor blacks in New York and Detroit. During the Prohibition era, bootleggers operating in the poor areas of the city recognized the profit to be gained from these lotteries. They used the capital they had accumulated from bootlegging, along with their local political connections, to move into the numbers business. They forced the experienced black operators to either join them or withdraw from the business. For example, in Harlem, the major black neighborhood in New York City in the 1920s and 1930s, the infamous Dutch Schultz took over the numbers rackets from black operators with the assistance of politicians.[52]

The numbers game is an active form of lottery, in which the bettor is permitted to choose any number between 000 and 999. The numbers operator runs the risk of losing money on any given day, for a disproportionately large number of bettors may choose the winning number (in conventional lotteries, only a fixed number of tickets is sold). Bettors can choose the amount of money they wish to bet, another practice that differs from those of the conventional lottery with its fixed-price tickets. Any dispute between the bettor and the bank concerning the bet can be settled with the bettor's copy of the transaction. The bettor is paid a fixed multiple ("pay-out rate") of the amount he or she bets. The pay-off is generally lower for certain predesignated numbers ("cut numbers").[53]

"Straight betting" means placing bets on three digits; two-digit betting is known as "bolita"; and single-digit bets are called "single action." The pay-out on single action is typically 8 to 1; on bolita it is about 60 to 1. The bulk of bets seem to be placed on three digits. The bets pass from the collector to a "pick-up man," who usually is the salaried agent of a person known as a "controller." The controller is a middle manager in the numbers operation, with responsibilities to both the collectors and the bank. Collectors and controllers do not generally meet every day; routine transactions can be handled through the pick-up man.[54]

Legality and Gambling

Gambling may be this nation's largest and most profitable illegal industry. Yet criminal justice experts are in total agreement that the criminal sanction is ineffective in preventing individuals from engaging in gambling. Gambling is a consensual transaction; it is easily concealed and involves conduct about which none of the parties involved is likely to complain. The criminal sanction exerts little deterrent force because the public does not regard gambling as wrongful behavior. Laws against private social gambling are unenforceable; laws against public social gambling and commercial gambling can be enforced to a degree, but enforcement must be a continuous, on-going process.[55] The Committee on Gambling Law Enforcement drew the following conclusions:

1. The laws against gambling in private are a symbolic gesture on the part of legislators; they are neither enforced [nor] enforceable in any reasonable sense of the word.
2. Legislators have given police a relatively unattractive job, for which police can get little credit if they do a good job and considerable abuse if they fail.
3. The laws against public social gambling and commercial gambling are enforceable to the extent that other comparable laws are enforceable. The resources devoted to gambling law enforcement are very modest and the results, with a few notable exceptions, are modest as well. Most departments realistically strive for one of several models of limited enforcement.
4. Regional, multi-service criminal organizations were reported to directly control all or a substantial portion of illegal gambling operations. . . . These cities were much more likely than others to have had publicly disclosed gambling-related corruption in the past.[56]

Even more serious than the difficulty of enforcing gambling laws is the relationship between gambling and organized crime. Morris and Hawkins have noted that "gambling is the greatest source of revenue for organized crime."[57] The participation of organized crime in gambling is also encouraged by the fact that the penalties for gambling, in most jurisdictions, are relatively slight. Indeed, more often than not, those arrested and brought to trial are required only to pay a small fine or serve a short sentence.[58]

However, the involvement of organized crime in gambling has decreased with the decriminalization of gambling. Indeed, gambling has become a major source of revenue in many states. The majority of states, at least in the Northeast, now have state lotteries. A winning six-digit number has been known to return $40 million. In Ohio, a recent constitutional amendment channels all state lottery profits into the support of public education.

VAGRANCY

Vagrancy laws, as mentioned earlier, have a long history. In the past, they were used as a means to force the lower class to be employed in the factories and mills of the rising industrial state. Today, such laws are more likely to be enforced against the homeless, the outsider, or the troublemaker. Vagrants are typically seen as those who bring disorder or those who violate community expectations of what constitutes appropriate civil behavior. In 1986, the *Uniform Crime Reports* documented 32,615 arrests for **vagrancy**.[59]

"Skid Row" alcoholics have long been of interest to criminologists. Most

"Skid Rowees" come from humble backgrounds and have been isolated from conventional patterns of social life and social ties for most of their adult lives.[60] For example, David Pittman and C. Wayne Gordon, who gathered data on 187 male chronic inebriates in the Monroe County Penitentiary in Rochester, New York, found that nearly 60 percent of the alcoholics had been married at some time, but almost none were living with their wives, that 70 percent had not gone beyond grammar school, that 68 percent were unskilled workers, and that the majority of these individuals had backgrounds of great residential instability. They went on to report that the alcoholics were products of early family backgrounds marked by inadequate socialization. Thus, these individuals were ill equipped by virtue of their backgrounds to embark on stable adult lives and successful occupational endeavors.[61]

The fact is that there appears to be an increasing number of the homeless (many of whom were once hospitalized in mental hospitals), the alienated, and the downtrodden in our cities. Such individuals have no stake in the system. Some have been released prematurely from mental institutions, many have felony records, and most have withdrawn from constructive social activities. Their behavior would be offensive in suburban and rural communities and is barely tolerable in urban settings. At a time in which a perceptual transition is taking place from the idea of badness to a preoccupation with injurious behavior to the physical, mental, and moral well-being of society, these individuals may increasingly be viewed as a threat to the social order (see Box 11.5).

George L. Kelling raises the question, "Do we want police officers to develop a 'What the hell' attitude toward disorderly or dangerous behavior, even if it is not technically illegal?"[62] Kelling argues that the maintenance of order requires the police to keep the streets clean of those who are linked in citizens' minds to personal danger and serious crime. He has in mind "drunks, gangs, prostitutes, obstreperous youth, as well as panhandling and other behaviors considered disorderly."[63] Kelling contends that "just as unrepaired windows in buildings may signal that nobody cares and lead to additional vandalism and damage, so unintended disorderly behavior may also communicate that nobody cares (or that nobody can or will do anything about disorder) and thus lead to increasingly aggressive criminal and dangerous predatory behavior."[64]

Kelling admits that because disorder is a condition rather than an act, there is no clear and consistent definition of the problem. For example, disorder depends on the number of persons or events involved. One prostitute or one person drinking on the street may not create disorder, but two such individuals may; it depends on each community's perceptual thresholds of what threatens basic order. The time that a behavior takes place is also an important factor. The kinds of revelry and noisemaking appropriate on New Year's Eve generally are not appropriate at other times. Location is of further importance in determining order; what is acceptable in some neighborhoods may be far from unacceptable in others.[65] Kelling states:

Disorder, then, is a condition resulting from behavior that, depending on location, time, and local traditions, is offensive in its violation of local expectations

BOX 11.5 **THE HOMELESS**

There are at least 350,000 homeless people in the United States, perhaps as many as 3 million. The word *homelessness* is a catch phrase describing a condition of life into which pour all of those marginalized or scared off by processes beyond their control. Here are the groups that can be packed into the single category of "the homeless":

- Veterans, mainly from the Vietnam War, who constitute nearly 50 percent of all homeless males in some American cities.
- Mentally ill who, in some parts of the nation, make up about 25 percent of the homeless.
- Physically disabled or chronically ill who either do not receive any benefits or whose benefits do not enable them to afford permanent shelter.
- Elderly on fixed income whose funds are no longer adequate for their needs.
- Men, women, and whole families who are made destitute by the loss of a job.
- Single parents, usually women, without the resources or skills to establish new lives.
- Runaway children, many of whom have been sexually and physically abused.
- Alcoholics and drug addicts whose troubles often begin with one of the other conditions listed here.
- Tramps, hobos, and transients who have taken to the streets for a variety of reasons and who prefer to be there.

The homeless tell a variety of sad stories. Max, a homeless male in California, describes his life:

> You've got to have a buddy, for one thing. If you lay here on the river, you've got to sleep with one eye open and one hand on your knife in your bag. People would just as soon kick your head in as to look at you. And you've got enough adversities. . . . I picked up a guy a couple months ago. He was about 22 and he couldn't make it on the street. I was showing him how to make it, just to survive. I caught him going through my bag when I was down at the river washin' up. When I left him, he wasn't moving. It's just the survival of the asphalt jungle. 'Cause I know one thing he's got a broken hand and a couple of broken ribs. I just packed up my stuff and left. It might sound barbaric, but it's just a matter of survival.

Sam, one of the organizers of a tent city for the homeless in California, talks about his motivation for participation:

> Somebody's got to make a stand. There's roughly 80,000 homeless in California. . . . This has been going on so long. This ain't but a drop in

the bucket. There's 50 people on the river for every person you see here. They're scared—tired of rejection. They just give up. [When they give up] they hit the wine bottle to where they can't do nothin'. Just like me. That's what got me into this situation in the first place. I haven't touched a bottle in 6 years. We've got people trying to get in the Halfway House. That's filled up.

Alice, foraging in a dumpster outside a McDonald's restaurant, tells that she is a college graduate who went to Chicago to teach school. Then one night she was raped. She had a nervous breakdown, went to a mental institution for three months, lost her job, and slipped into a long depression. She stayed with friends until she could save enough money to come to Los Angeles, where she has lived on the streets since 1980. Charles, a 26-year-old homeless man, has been on the road for four months. He was married with two children and employed. After his breakup with his wife, his life fell apart. "I left the car with her. I got ripped off on my way up here [to Sacramento] at a rest stop, from my wallet and everything I owned. With no ID, I can't get assistance. With no housing I can't get a job, with no job I can't get no housing. I didn't know where to turn."

The homeless reduce their world to a small area and try to protect themselves from a world that might otherwise be too much to bear. But to the larger society, the homeless represent a threat to the social order. The homeless tend to be viewed as strangers, aliens; and their presence, in itself, constitutes a kind of violence. It deprives us of our sense of safety. The homeless also rob the public of its sense of decency. Public drinking, doping, loitering, panhandling, stealing, molesting, defecating, and urinating are all signs of their disorderly and unmanageable behavior. The homeless strike the fear that the barbarian hordes are at the gates, and civilization is soon to be ended.

Source: Peter Marin, "Helping and Hating the Homeless: The Struggle at the Margins of America," *Harper* 274 (January 1987), pp. 39–49; and Ron E. Roberts, "Lumpen Communards: The Stirring of Communal Consciousness Among the Homeless." Paper presented to the XXVII World Congress of the International Institute of Sociology, University of Washington (5 September 1984).

for normalcy and peace in a community. Whether malevolent or innocent in intent, disorderly behavior powerfully shapes the quality of urban life and citizens' views both of their own safety and the ability of government to ensure it.[66]

Kelling has no problem with giving the police the authority to determine when a citizen is violating community traditions and creating disorder. But others balk at the thought of giving the "guardians of order" so much authority in maintaining order. Critics contend that giving the police the authority to control order maintenance activities only generates disorder for minorities, the poor, and the downtrodden. Whether or not vagrancy and other disorderly activities make people feel unsafe, as Kelling suggests, they certainly make people feel uncomfortable.

ANALYSIS

The order and disorder theme of this text can be applied to the disorders of emphasizing safety over freedom, of becoming a victim, and of enforcing public order laws.

Disorder of Choosing Safety over Freedom

A basic principle of constitutional order is that sanctions inflicting both stigma and loss of liberty should be used only sparingly in a society that regards itself as free and open.[67] In his essay "On Liberty," John Stuart Mill, the British philosopher, wrote:

> The sole end for which mankind are warranted, individually or collectively, in interfering with the liberty of action of any of their number, is self-protection. That the only purpose for which power can be rightfully exercised over any member of civilized community, against his will, is to prevent harm to others.[68]

Jeremy Bentham, the classical criminologist, had earlier warned about the negative consequences of morally defining legality: "With what chance of success . . . would a legislature go about to extirpate drunkenness and fornication by dint of legal punishment?" Bentham questioned whether all the tortures that human ingenuity could invent would prevent these behaviors. The end result of such an effort, Bentham felt, would be that "such a mass of evil would be produced by the punishment, as would exceed, a thousandfold, the utmost possible mischief of the offense."[69]

H. L. A. Hart, a highly esteemed British jurist, built on the works of Bentham and Mill to develop a philosophy of legal sanctions and morality. A central question in Hart's inquiry is, "Ought immorality [to] be a crime?"[70] His writings express a deep and abiding concern for individual rights and freedoms inherent in a democratic society. He continuously points out the necessity of guarding against any infringements by the law on individual or group morality.

The argument can be raised that the overreach of the law, even in matters relating to the public's health, seriously intrudes upon the freedom of the individual. The state, in effect, takes responsibility away from the individual and imposes controls that appear to be inappropriate in a free and democratic society. There are certain activities, continues the argument, that are not the business of the state. They are totally contained within the sphere of the family or social group, and, therefore, involve acts that are personal and require only the consent of those involved.

However, in the 1980s the factor of health has replaced the 1970s debates on morality as the chief justification for the public's scapegoating of public order crimes. The announcements of public health agencies, as well as extensive media coverage, have made the public acutely aware of the hazards of AIDS, herpes, gonorrhea, and other diseases associated with prostitution, homosexuality, and drug use. Current estimates are that there are some 40,000 diagnosed AIDS patients and many more who are not as yet visible. The AIDS "epidemic" has been particularly troublesome in the schools, where parents are vehemently opposed to the possibility of AIDS "carriers" in the classroom. Medical personnel have also been caught up in the dilemmas associated with the treatment of AIDS patients.

Furthermore, the public appears to be fed up with allowing victimizers to "get away with it," and, therefore, is receptive to "get tough" policies on drunken driving and dope addiction. Public sentiment tends to support the status quo, and the current tendency is to divert attention from more "sensitive" crimes, such as white-collar, governmental, environmental, and industrial crimes. Finally, "moral majority" and social agenda advocates have become strong interest groups and are successfully lobbying for more punitive legislation against public order crimes.

Prostitution, homosexuality, drug addiction, pornography, vagrancy, gambling, and the ancillary component of organized crime do, in fact, threaten social order. Whether in fact all the perceived threats are real or not, they create patterns of disorder in the social fabric. Some of these acts pose real health hazards; others create victims among public order offenders. Furthermore, they provide an opportunity for organized crime to flourish, and this situation, in turn, encourages the expansion of public order crimes.

There are two dilemmas at hand. First, there is the dilemma of choosing between collective well-being and the individual freedom of citizens to pursue behaviors that may be harmful to them. Unquestionably, considerable problems are involved in granting individual freedom in areas that the public cannot manage and, even more seriously, in areas that generate health risks for others. But, on the other hand, loss of individual freedoms is a spectre feared by this society ever since its founding.

Second, there is the dilemma of dealing with all the implications of the recent concern and focus on the health arena. To perceive what has traditionally been viewed in moral or criminal terms as health matters means that much must be rethought; perhaps some cherished concepts must be discarded. The Centers for Disease Control is even defining such crimes as murder as health matters. The medicalization of deviance, as Conrad and Schneider put it, is not new.[71] In the recent past, the medicalization of deviance involved treating, rather than punishing, deviants, but this approach eventually was discarded with "real" criminals because it was regarded as an ineffective and "soft" approach to the disorder of crime. Still, even with the emphasis on health, the social control issues remain. For example, what should be done with those who are addicted, are involved in sex crimes, have no home, choose to engage in homosexual sex, and so forth?

Disorder of Becoming a Victim

Public order crimes have also been called victimless crimes. In the past these crimes were assumed to lack "direct victims," either because of consensual participation or because of their assumed harmlessness.[72] But the actual life experiences of participants in public order crimes challenges the idea of these crimes as victimless. Drug addicts, alcoholics, and prostitutes not only experience a variety of victimizing experiences themselves, but they also victimize their families, friends, neighbors, and strangers. A drug addict reports:

> There are a lot of victims left over after the dust settles. Take the time we boosted this house to get our drug money. It was in a middle-class area. We busted the door in, pulled up with our truck, and emptied the house of everything that wasn't tied to the floor. You can imagine what those victims felt like when they came home and found everything they owned and that meant something to them was gone—never to be seen again.[73]

The study of victimology, focusing on the victims of crime, regained popularity in the 1940s, primarily because of the work of Hans von Hentig and, later, of Stephen Schafer.[74] The major victimization programs that exist today serve raped women, beaten or molested children, battered wives, the elderly, and certain other victims of violence. The vulnerability and suffering of these people are leading citizens to push for programs to meet their needs. No longer must victims rely solely upon those police and prosecutors who may happen to be caring individuals. Concern for the victim is now becoming a matter of public policy, and both criminal justice agencies and citizens' groups, including police, prosecutors, hospitals, county commissioners, religious organizations, private agencies, and volunteer agencies, are working to help solve long-standing problems of victimization.

The truth is that some of the most victimized members of the American society are those who victimize themselves and their families through public order crimes. These victims are largely ignored because it is generally thought that they bring their troubles upon themselves. Some are eventually able to help themselves (e.g., they quit drinking or taking drugs), and some are able to find help in supportive social networks and therapeutic settings, but too many squander their lives and, in the process, create countless other victims.

Disorder of Enforcing Public Order Laws

The attempt to curb public order crimes has resulted in considerable disorder. First, public order laws have generally been unenforceable. In fact, the difficulty of enforcing these laws has encouraged the police to become involved in utilizing entrapment techniques as well as engaging in widespread corruption. Second, these laws have led to a pervasive disrespect for the law on the part of the public. This reaction is especially apparent when the law is designed to regulate behavior in which large numbers of people are engaged but is only selectively enforced—if enforced at all. Third, laws designed to regulate morality have left the criminal justice system wide open for discrimination. For example, sex discrimination is the rule in the enforcement of laws against prostitution; laws regulating sodomy are generally enforced only against male homosexuals; other public order laws may be used for deporting aliens for "immoral behavior"; and such laws may be selectively enforced on the basis of social class or variables such as race. Finally, these laws constitute a deleterious invasion of personal freedoms and liberties.[75]

The "revolving door" practice, which is exemplified by arrests for prostitution and public intoxication, demonstrates the futility of enforcing public morality. For example, streetwalkers are routinely hauled into court, but then are bailed out, fined, and let back on the job in short order. This practice typifies the aura of hypocrisy and futility that surrounds the attempt to enforce legislation curbing public order crimes.[76]

The enforcement of public order laws has clearly provided an opportunity for the development of organized crime. When the law denied the public the right to drink, the gangsters of the 1920s made alcohol available to a willing clientele. When the law denied citizens the escape of "getting high," the public bought illegal drugs from whatever sources were available: the French Connection, the Mexican Connection, the South American Connection, and even the Backyard Connection. When the law denied access to prostitution and pornography, the public continued to turn to the streetwalkers, massage parlors, and call girls as well as local pornographic movies and book stores. When the law denied the right to gamble, the bookmaker and numbers operations thrived.

POLICY IMPLICATIONS

The social control of organized crime poses a major problem for the American society. President Ronald Reagan indicated his concern for the need to combat organized crime by naming a 20-person Organized Crime Commission in July 1983. The commission, headed by Judge Irving R. Kaufman of the U.S. Court of Appeals for the Second Circuit, first reported its findings to President Reagan in 1986 (the final report was published in 1987).[77]

Unlike the 1967 report issued by the President's Commission,[78] which proposed new tools to combat organized crime, the 1986 President's Commission generally found existing tools to be adequate. Still, they were not seen as the answer to wiping out organized crime over the long run. The 1986 report made recommendations for each of its identified problem areas: drugs, labor racketeering, money laundering, and gambling.[79]

The report on drugs made 13 recommendations arguing that drug policy "must emphasize more strongly efforts to reduce the demand for drugs."[80] It recommended that the cost of drug enforcement be subsidized by seizure and forfeiture of traffickers' assets, and that the United Nations should sponsor a model "International Controlled Substance Act" to assist in eradicating narcotics distribution at its source.

With regard to labor-management racketeering, it was found that the 1970 Racketeer Influenced and Corrupt Organization (RICO) provisions and union decertification laws "have been underutilized."[81] Prosecution efforts to remove racketeer influence over unions and legitimate businesses were also seen as "largely ineffective." The need for a national strategy to combat labor racketeering, as well as better organization of prosecution efforts, was recognized. Moreover, it was suggested that antitrust offenses become eligible for electronic surveillance under Title III.

The commission defined *money laundering* as "the due process by which one conceals the existence, illegal source, or illegal application of income, and then disguises that income to make it appear legitimate."[82] The commission concluded that the Bank Secrecy Act is not sufficient for adequate prosecutions; the penalties are too light and the act does not allow needed government surveillance to detect money-laundering schemes.

Finally, there was less consensus concerning strategies to fight gambling, chiefly because of the disagreement over the priority that gambling enforcement should have in a strategy to reduce organized crime. The commission stated:

> The extent to which illegal gambling should be targeted, either as unacceptable per se or as a revenue source for other . . . organized criminal activities, and the priority to be given to any such targeting, is one of the more challenging subjects facing policy makers and law enforcement officials in the near future.[83]

However, the recent commission and its reports will probably not have any greater success in controlling organized crime than did those commissions that preceded it. The reason for this, as suggested in this chapter, is that organized crime thrives because it provides for the satisfaction of widely demanded, but legally prohibited, activities or products. Gus Tyler noted that American attempts to suppress immorality have provided the seed bed out of which organized crime has developed. He went on to add:

> Our puritanism creates a whole range of illegal commodities and services for which there is a widespread demand. Into the gap between what people want and what people can legally get leaps the underworld as purveyor and pimp, with gambling tables, narcotics, and women. Puritanism gives the underworld a monopoly on a market with an almost unsatiable demand.[84]

Three groups of citizens are bound together in the organized crime complex: the criminals who engage in organized crime, the police and city officials with whom they may be in collusion, and those citizens who purchase the services of racketeers, drug pushers, gamblers, and other related types.[85] Thus, the control of organized crime ultimately depends upon citizens' refusal to purchase the services of criminals who engage in organized crime and upon stricter punishments of the police and politicians who cooperate with organized crime.

SUMMARY

The present criminal code is a result of a series of historical accidents, emotional overreaction, and the political habit of adding a punishment to every legislative proposition.[85] The legislation of crimes of the public order in this nation—prostitution, homosexuality, pornography, gambling, and the use of drugs and alcohol—has resulted in one of the most moralistic approaches to the law in Western society.

However, the 1980s have added a new dimension to these crimes—the matter of health and community safety. On the one hand, it may be wise to exercise constraint in the use of the criminal law in dealing with these behaviors. Indeed, there is good evidence that the unintended consequences of criminalizing these acts take on greater significance than the intended ones. But, on the other hand, the increasing health hazards related to many of these crimes are justifiably frightening to society. The central issue of the present is how these crimes can be controlled without infringing upon the freedoms of the individual.

REFERENCES

Adler, Patricia A. *Wheeling and Dealing: An Ethnography of an Upper-Level Drug Dealing and Smuggling Community.* New York: Columbia University Press, 1985.

Committee on Homosexual Offenses and Prostitution. *Report.* London: Her Majesty's Stationery Office, 1957.

Conrad, Peter, and Schneider, Joseph W. *Deviance and Medicalization: From Badness to Sickness.* St. Louis: Mosby, 1980.

Hart, H. L. A. *Law, Liberty, and Morality.* Stanford, Calif.: Stanford University Press, 1963.

Hobson, Barbara Meil. *Uneasy Virtue: The Politics of Prostitution and the American Reform Tradition.* New York: Basic Books, 1987.

Johnson, Kenneth A. *Public Order Criminal Behavior and Criminal Laws: The Question of Legal Decriminalization.* San Francisco: R & E Research Associates, 1977.

Lentini, Joseph P. *Vice and Narcotics Control.* Beverly Hills, Calif.: Glencoe Press, 1977.

Miller, Eleanor M. *Street Women.* Philadelphia: Temple University Press, 1986.

Mill, John Stuart. *Utilitarianism: On Liberty, Essay on Bentham,* edited by Mary Warnock. Cleveland: World Publishing Company, 1962.

Morris, Norval, and Hawkins, Gordon. *The Honest Politician's Guide to Crime Control.* Chicago: University of Chicago Press, 1969.

Packer, Herbert L. *The Limits of the Criminal Sanction.* Stanford, Calif.: Stanford University Press, 1968.

Reuter, Peter. *Disorganized Crime.* Cambridge, Mass.: Massachusetts Institute of Technology Press, 1983.

Schur, Edwin. *Crimes Without Victims.* Englewood Cliffs, N.J.: Prentice-Hall, 1965.

Schur, Edwin M., and Bedau, Hugo Adam. *Victimless Crimes, Two Sides of a Controversy.* Englewood Cliffs, N.J.: Prentice-Hall, 1974.

The Report of the Commission on Obscenity and Pornography. New York: Bantam Books, 1970.

NOTES

1. Interviewed in June 1987.
2. Edwin M. Schur and Hugo Adam Bedau, *Victimless Crimes, Two Sides of a Controversy* (Englewood Cliffs, N.J.: Prentice-Hall, 1974), p. 8.

3. Richard Quinney, *The Problem of Crime* (New York: Dodd, Mead, 1970).

4. Kenneth A. Johnson, *Public Order Criminal Behavior and Criminal Laws: The Question of Legal Decriminalization* (San Francisco: R & E Research Associates, 1977), p. 4.

5. Federal Bureau of Investigation, *Uniform Crime Reports, 1986* (Washington, D.C.: U.S. Government Printing Office, 1987), p. 172.

6. Bureau of Justice Statistics, *Prisoners and Drugs* (Washington, D.C.: U.S. Department of Justice, 1983), p. 1.

7. Vincent N. Parrillo, John Stimson, and Ardyth Stimson, *Contemporary Social Problems* (New York: Wiley, 1985), p. 71.

8. Hugh D. Barlow, *Introduction to Criminology,* 2d ed. (Boston: Little, Brown, 1981).

9. Sue Titus Reid, *Crime and Criminology,* 4th ed. (New York: Holt, Rinehart & Winston, 1985), p. 24.

10. Bureau of Justice Statistics, *Prisoners and Drugs,* p. 1.

11. U.S. Department of Health, Education and Welfare, *The Special Report to the U.S. Congress on Alcohol and Health* (Washington, D.C.: U.S. Government Printing Office, 1978).

12. U.S. Department of Health and Human Services, *ADAMHA News* 6 (July 1980), pp. 1–6.

13. Interviewed in March 1986.

14. Joseph Julian, *Social Problems,* 3d ed. (Englewood Cliffs, N.J.: Prentice-Hall, 1980), p. 136.

15. "The Colombia Connection," *Time,* 29 January 1979, pp. 22–29.

16. Patricia A. Adler, *Wheeling and Dealing: An Ethnography of an Upper-Level Drug Dealing and Smuggling Community* (New York: Columbia University Press, 1985), p. 8.

17. "Mexican Connection," *Newsweek,* 10 April 1978.

18. Barlow, *Introduction to Criminology,* p. 304.

19. Ibid., p. 304.

20. Norval Morris and Gordon Hawkins, *The Honest Politician's Guide to Crime Control* (Chicago: University of Chicago Press, 1969), p. 10.

21. Ibid., p. 9.

22. Ibid., p. 10.

23. S. Rathus, *Human Sexuality* (New York: Holt, Rinehart & Winston, 1983), p. 463.

24. Federal Bureau of Investigation, *Uniform Crime Reports,* p. 172.

25. The *New York Times,* 9 June 1974.

26. Barlow, *Introduction to Criminology.*

27. Harold J. Vetter and Ira J. Silverman, *Criminology and Crime: An Introduction* (New York: Harper & Row, 1986), p. 195.

28. Barbara Meil Hobson, *Uneasy Virtue: The Politics of Prostitution and the American Reform Tradition* (New York: Basic Books, Inc., 1987), pp. 209–210.

29. Ibid., pp. 216–217.

30. Eleanor M. Miller, *Street Women* (Philadelphia: Temple University Press, 1986).

31. Ibid.

32. Ibid.

33. Ibid.

34. Interviewed in December 1985.

35. Vetter and Silverman, *Criminology and Crime,* p. 195.

36. Howard S. Becker, *The Outsiders: Studies in the Sociology of Deviance* (New York: Free Press, 1963), pp. 63–65.

37. Norval Morris and Gordon Hawkins, *Honest Politician's Guide,* p. 4.

38. Herbert L. Packer, *The Limits of the Criminal Sanction* (Stanford, Calif.: Stanford University Press, 1968), pp. 436, 437, 439.

39. Judd Marmor, "The Multiple Roots of Homosexual Behavior," in *Homosexual Behavior,* ed. J. Marmor (New York: Basic Books, 1980), p. 5.

40. Evelyn Hooker, "Male Homosexuality," in *Taboo Topics,* ed. Norman L. Farberow (New York: Atherton Press, 1963), pp. 44–55.

41. C. S. Ford and F. A. Beach, *Patterns of Sexual Behavior* (New York: Harper & Bros., 1951).

42. Rathus, *Human Sexuality,* p. 395.

43. Larry J. Siegel, *Criminology,* (St. Paul, Minn.: West, 1983).

44. Joseph R. Lentini, *Vice and Narcotics Control* (Beverly Hills, Calif.: Glencoe Press, 1977), pp. 8–9.

45. Federal Bureau of Investigation, *Uniform Crime Reports,* p. 172.

46. Lentini, *Vice and Narcotics Control,* pp. 25–26.

47. Henry Chafetz, *Play the Devil: A History of Gambling in the United States from 1692 to 1955* (New York: Potter, 1960).

48. Mark Haller, *Bootlegging in Chicago: The Structure of An Illegal Enterprise* (Paper presented at American Historical Association Convention, 28 December 1974).

49. Peter Reuter, *Disorganized Crime* (Cambridge, Mass.: Massachusetts Institute of Technology Press, 1984), pp. 15–16.

50. Ibid., p. 17.

51. Ibid., pp. 45–46.

52. Ibid.

53. Ibid., pp. 47–48.

54. Ibid., pp. 48–49.

55. Packer, *Limits of the Criminal Sanction,* p. 442.

56. Floyd J. Fowler, Jr., Thomas W. Mangione, and Fredrick E. Pratter, *Gambling Law Enforcement In Major American Cities* (Washington, D.C.: U.S. Government Printing Office, 1978).

57. Morris and Hawkins, *Honest Politician's Guide,* p. 10.

58. Lentini, *Vice and Narcotics Control,* p. 27.

59. Federal Bureau of Investigation, *Uniform Crime Reports,* p. 172.

60. Don C. Gibbons, *Society, Crime, and Criminal Behavior* (Englewood Cliffs, N.J.: Prentice-Hall, 1982), p. 367.

61. David J. Pittman and C. Wayne Gordon, *Revolving Door* (New York: Free Press, 1958), pp. 16–58.

62. George L. Kelling, "Aquiring a Taste for Order: The Community and Police," *Crime & Delinquency* 33 (January 1982), p. 91.

63. Ibid., p. 93.

64. Ibid.

65. Ibid., pp. 94–95.

66. Ibid.

67. Packer, *Limits of the Criminal Sanction,* pp. 249–250.

68. John Stuart Mill, *Ultilitarianism: On Liberty, Essay on Bentham,* edited by Mary Warnock (Cleveland: World Publishing Company, 1962). p. 135.

69. Jeremy Bentham, *An Introduction to the Principles of Morals and Legislation* (New York: Hafner, 1948), p. 320.

70. H. L. A. Hart, *Law, Liberty, and Morality* (Stanford, Calif.: Stanford University Press), p. 4.

71. Peter Conrad and Joseph W. Schneider, *Deviance and Medicalization: From Badness to Sickness* (St. Louis: Mosby, 1980).

72. Schur, *Victimless Crimes,* p. 171.

73. Interviewed in July 1987.

74. Hans Von Hentig, *The Criminal and His Victim* (New York: Schocken, 1979); and Stephen Schafer, *The Victim and His Criminal: A Study in Functional Responsibility* (New York: Random House, 1968).

75. See Morris and Hawkins, *Honest Politician's Guide.*

76. Ibid.

77. President's Commission on Organized Crime, *The Impact: Organized Crime Today* (Washington, D.C.: U.S. Government Printing Office, 1987).

78. President's Commission on Law Enforcement and Administration of Justice, *Task Force Report: Organized Crime* (Washington, D.C.: U.S. Government Printing Office, 1967).

79. President's Commission on Law Enforcement and Administration of Justice, *The Impact.*

80. President's Commission on Organized Crime, *America's Habit: Drug Abuse, Drug Trafficking and Organized Crime,* Interim Report (Washington, D.C.: U.S. Government Printing Office, 1986), p. 463.

81. President's Commission on Organized Crime, *The Edge: Organized Crime, Business, and Labor Unions,* Interim Report (Washington, D.C.: U.S. Government Printing Office, 1986), p. 5.

82. President's Commission on Organized Crime, *Organized Crime and Money Laundering,* Record of Hearing II (Washington, D.C.: U.S. Government Printing Office, 1984).

83. President's Commission on Organized Crime, *Organized Crime and Gambling,* Record of Hearing VII. (Washington, D.C.: U.S. Government Printing Office, 1985), p. 637.

84. Gus Tyler, ed., *Organized Crime in America* (Ann Arbor; University of Michigan Press, 1962), p. 48.

85. Gibbons, *Society, Crime, and Criminal Behavior,* p. 336.

86. Morris and Hawkins, *Honest Politician's Guide,* p. 27.

CHAPTER **12**

The Criminal Justice System

DEVELOPMENT OF SOCIAL CONTROL IN AMERICAN SOCIETY

Early American Practices

Social Control in the Nineteenth Century

Social Disorder in American Society
Law Enforcement
The Courts
Corrections

The Twentieth Century: A Time of Change

Changing Ideologies
Institution Building
Professionalization

CRIMINAL JUSTICE: A SEARCH FOR ORDER

Structure of the Criminal Justice System

Functions of the Criminal Justice System

Components of Criminal Justice
Systemic Nature of Criminal Justice
The Process of Justice

CRIMINAL JUSTICE: A SYSTEM IN CHAOS

Fragmentation

Overload

Limited Capacity

POLICY IMPLICATIONS

SUMMARY

REFERENCES

NOTES

KEY TERMS

arraignment   *parens patria* philosophy
Auburn Penitentiary   plea bargaining
Eastern Penitentiary   Panopticon
Elmira Reformatory   preliminary hearing
house of refuge   Quakers
fragmentation   system of watchmen
jail   systems approach
medical model   Walnut Street Jail in Philadelphia
overload

It's time for honest talk, for plain talk. There has been a breakdown in the criminal justice system in America. It just plain isn't working. All too often repeat offenders, habitual lawbreakers, career criminals, call them what you will, are robbing, raping, and beating with impunity and, as I said, quite literally getting away with murder. The people are sickened and outraged. They demand that we put a stop to it.

—Ronald Reagan, 1981[1]

The criminal justice system currently is being bombarded with criticism. Indeed, no one, regardless of political persuasion, seems to be happy with the justice process. Conservatives charge that "crime pays" because the justice system is totally inefficient in catching, convicting, and punishing criminals.[2] The courts, they say, act scandalously, letting too many criminals go "scot-free." Nor does the system care for victims.[3] Meanwhile, liberals accuse the criminal justice system of being repressive.[4] They contend that the elimination of poverty, inequality, and racial discrimination is needed before America can deal with crime.[5] They accuse police departments of being riddled with inefficiency, corruption, and brutality.[6] Lower-class minorities, according to liberals, are likely to have their due process rights violated at all levels of the justice system.[7] Liberals, like conservatives, have little confidence in the corrections system.

Thus, from both the right and the left, the justice system is being charged with failing to bring order to American society. In the 1980s, the dissatisfaction with the disorderly justice system has become so intense that increased numbers of citizens are turning to various expressions of popular justice. The increased tendency of public officials to turn to the private sector (private security agencies, privately administered community-based corrections agencies, and private prisons) is another indication of dissatisfaction with the public sector criminal justice system.

Beginning with an examination of the history of social control in American society, this chapter compares the way the justice system is supposed to function as opposed to the disorderly way it actually does its business.

DEVELOPMENT OF SOCIAL CONTROL IN AMERICAN SOCIETY

Until recently, American scholars have ignored their criminal justice heritage. Over the past two decades, most published works on criminal justice have been ahistorical in structure, content, and perspective.[8] Yet any understanding of the social control of crime today requires an understanding of such questions as: Is the quality of justice better or worse today than it used to be? How does the role of the police today differ from that of fifty or one hundred years ago? Has there ever been a "golden age" of law, order, and justice in the United States?

Early American Practices

The history of American dealings with crime begins with the transplanting of European institutions to the new world. The colonists were influenced by their various cultural and legal heritages in developing criminal codes, law enforcement systems, and methods of punishment. Early American systems of control and sanction resembled those of England, Holland, and France, depending upon the particular colony. Yet their new environment influenced the colonists to borrow selectively, leaving behind elements they did not like.[9]

The county sheriff was the most important law enforcement official in colonial society. The sheriff performed such tasks as enforcing the law, collecting taxes, supervising elections, and handling much of the legal business of county government. The mayor, who was the chief law enforcement officer in villages and cities, appointed the high constable and various lesser constables and marshals to assist him.

The criminal codes that developed in the colonies differed from English law in that they showed a much stronger Biblical influence. Colonial criminal codes also were more lenient than those of England, especially when it came to the death penalty. For example, the colonies had 11 crimes punishable by death compared to more than 200 in England. Finally, governmental authority was often weak in the colonies because each colony had to deal with the problem of establishing stable communities on the frontier. It was this weakness of official authority that gave rise to the American tradition of vigilantism.

The colonial courts played an important role in the social and economic life of the county and often served as the legislative, executive, and judicial branches of county government. The justice of the peace, in an office that could be traced far back into English history, handled the bulk of the court cases. But the more serious cases were heard by courts composed of several judges. The district attorney, usually appointed by the governor of the colony, handled the prosecution of cases. Defendants had representation of defense counsel when they could afford it.

The concept of the **jail** was brought to the colonies from England. Virginia established the first colonial jail, but the Pennsylvania jails became the models for other states. Prisoners in each county were placed under the jurisdiction of the sheriff, who fed and lodged them. Colonial jails were less places of punishment than holding facilities for those awaiting trial. They resembled houses and had no distinctive architectural features. Prisoners were placed in ordinary rooms (sometimes there was only one), and no attempt was made to classify and segregate them; escapes were common.

The **Quakers** in Pennsylvania had a great deal of influence in improving the jails and later in developing the American version of the penitentiary. In 1776, a number of Quakers formed the Philadelphia Society for Assisting Distressed Prisoners, which led two years later to the formation of the Philadelphia Society for Alleviating the Miseries of Public Prisons. In 1787, this society gathered at the home of Benjamin Franklin to hear Dr. Benjamin Rush read a paper on new methods for treating criminals. Rush proposed a prison program that would:

1. Classify prisoners for housing.
2. Provide prison labor, which would make the institutions self-supportive.
3. Include gardens to provide food and outdoor areas for recreation.
4. Classify convicts according to the nature of their crime—whether it arose out of passion, habit, temptation, or mental illness.[10]

Rush's proposal led to the renovation in 1790 of the Old **Walnut Street Jail in Philadelphia** to include a cell house of 36 solitary cells. This first American prison paid each male prisoner almost the same wages as were paid for similar work in the community. Guards were forbidden to use corporal punishment, and inmates could be pardoned by the governor for good conduct. The program at Walnut Street Jail, like those established at several other prisons at the time, worked well for a few years, but the reform effort eventually collapsed "due to overcrowding, idleness, and incompetent personnel."[11]

Social Control in the Nineteenth Century

American society experienced a major transformation in the second decade of the nineteenth century as a result of westward expansion, industrialization, immigration, urbanization, and the slavery controversy. When it became clear that the existing institutions were inadequate to meet the social control needs of this emerging society, the modern police, court system, juvenile and adult correctional institutions were developed. In the final decades of the nineteenth century, probation and parole also were created to deal with the disorder of crime.

Social Disorder in American Society   Expansion westward was a particularly lawless process. Individuals with a vested interest in "law and order" often took the law into their own hands, and vigilante groups took the opportunity to impose their own ideas of law and order in the absence of a law-oriented society. Racist acts, often directed toward the American Indian, were further evidence of the lawlessness of the frontier.[12]

Riotous disorder in the cities matched the anarchy of the frontier. In the 1830s, a frightening wave of riots swept through urban areas; in 1838 Abraham Lincoln warned the populace about the "increasing disregard for the law which pervades the country."[13] The source of much of this violence was immigration, which brought an increasing mixture of religions, languages, and lifestyles to America. Contrary to popular folklore, the wave of immigration led to a "boiling caldron of ethnic suspicion and hatred," rather than a harmonious "melting pot."[14]

Economic problems also contributed to violent disorder. Depositors and investors destroyed banks that failed. Workers retaliated with violence against the injustices of the new industrialists. By the second half of the century, industrial violence had become class warfare. The worst episode took place in 1877, when angry workers attacked and destroyed railroad properties in dozens of cities across the nation.

Finally, the struggle over slavery gave birth to new forms of lawlessness and violence. As early as the 1830s, the anti-slavery movement had provoked violent actions in both the North and the South. In Boston, Cincinnati, and Philadelphia, mobs provoked riots, attacking white abolitionists as well as free black citizens. The Civil War and Reconstruction unleashed other expressions of violence. In Southern and border states, the war divided communities, and sometimes families, into pro-South and pro-Union factions, a division that often generated violence. Then, during Reconstruction, the Ku Klux Klan arose to reestablish white supremacy. Along with disenfranchisement, segregation, and institutional inequality, lynching and violence against blacks became the norm.

Law Enforcement   The demands for order and tranquility in the growing cities, as well as the need for consolidating urban governments, led to the creation of the modern police. As mass immigration from European countries swelled American cities, tensions grew among various cultural, religious, and political groups. By the middle of the 1830s, Boston, New York, and Philadelphia were finding it difficult to deal with riots and civil disorder, because they had no form of social control available other than the military.

In 1833, the city of Philadelphia modified its watch system—which had been adapted from the English **system of watchmen** and constables—to include a paid day watch and night watch, but New York is credited with organizing the first police force. In 1844, the New York State legislature gave cities and towns the power to organize police forces, and the city of New York then consolidated its day and night watches under the leadership of an appointed chief of police. Similar police systems were soon adopted in Baltimore, Boston, Chicago, Cincinnati, Newark, New Orleans, and Philadelphia.[15]

These early police departments borrowed selectively from the organization of the London Metropolitan Police. The most striking difference between the English and American models was in the area of control. In England, the strong central leadership in the Metropolitan Police was able to deal immediately with police problems. The English police also had clear lines of authority up to the commissioner, who, in turn, was responsible to the home secretary in Parliament.

In contrast, the American system was very disorganized, with unclear lines of authority. A police officer in any given city could be at the command of either the chief of police, the mayor, an elected alderman—or all three. Police officers were hired and fired at the will of the elected city officials. Favors were rewarded and scores settled by the hiring and firing of police officers.

The police in nineteenth-century America were primarily tools of local politicians; according to Robert Fogelson, the police departments became "adjuncts of the political machine."[16] This political control led to widespread corruption and brutality and made the police ineffective in preventing crime or providing services.

The Courts   During the nineteenth century, the industrial revolution and skyrocketing population growth in urban areas made it impossible for courts to continue to be administered by a traveling judge and local jurors. To meet the needs of the changing society, a resident court was developed, with a full-time judge who sat and heard a high volume of cases initiated by police officers and processed by a district attorney.

During the late nineteenth century, many other changes took place in the court structure. The part-time justice of the peace in urban areas was largely replaced by a full-time magistrate. The practice of releasing the accused on a bail bond promised by family or friend was replaced by release on a bond insured by a corporation and administered by a professional bail bondsman. The first attempts were made by legislators to develop a rational and comprehensive criminal code. Moreover, the use of the jury, which symbolizes the important role of ordinary citizens in the justice process, began to decline. Finally, plea bargaining became acceptable in some jurisdictions.

Corrections   By the 1820s, the penitentiary had emerged as the basic means of punishing criminals. David J. Rothman claims that Americans saw their traditional society and values disintegrating under the pressure of immigration and industrialization, and they therefore turned to institutionalization as a model for social order.[17] The purpose of the penitentiary was to make up for a "bad" environment by providing offenders with a properly structured, or ordered, environment that would enable them to repent of their wrongdoings and become useful citizens upon their return to the community. The penitentiary was in part a product of the idealism of the Jacksonian period, which saw the young American nation as having an unlimited capacity to solve its social problems.

The Pennsylvania and Auburn penitentiaries, the two major systems of prison discipline, used solitude and work to attain moral reformation. The system at the **Eastern Penitentiary,** the more renowned of the two Pennsylvania institutions, was based on Quaker ideology. Extreme measures were used to keep prisoners from each other. Each prisoner had his own cell (12 feet long, 7½ feet wide, and 16 feet high), work area, and exercise yard; prisoners were even prevented from seeing each other at Sunday worship services. Rothman describes how the process of reform was intended to work in the Pennsylvania penitentiaries:

Thrown upon his own innate sentiments, with no evil example to lead him astray, and with kindness and proper instruction at hand to bolster his resolu-

Eastern Penitentiary, Philadelphia, Pennsylvania. (*Source:* Warshaw Collection/Archive Center, Smithsonian Institution.)

tion, the criminal would start his rehabilitation. Then after a period of total isolation, without companions, books, or tools, officials would allow the inmate to work in his cell. . . . The convict would sit in his cell and work with his tools daily, so that during the course of his sentence regularity and discipline would become habitual. He would return to the community cured of vice and idleness, to take his place as a responsible citizen.[18]

The "silent" or "congregate" **Auburn** system developed in New York isolated prisoners at night in their own cells but permitted them to work and eat together in groups during the day. While the Auburn system permitted visual contact, it allowed no conversation among prisoners. Because prisoners could work and exercise together in communal areas, they required much smaller cells than the ones in the Pennsylvania institutions. It was this fact that explains why the Auburn system emerged victorious over the Pennsylvania system. However, in contrast to the moral environment envisioned by reformers, the Auburn system in practice required prisoners to work long hours, subjected them to a variety of humiliations, and used corporal punishment liberally. The punitive discipline of the Auburn system was shaped by Warden Elam Lynds, who often informed visitors that the first step in the reform of criminals was to break their spirits.

The **house of refuge**, the first juvenile institution, was also established during the 1820s. Reformers believed that such institutions provided an orderly, disciplined environment similar to that of the "ideal" Puritan family.[19] By the middle of the nineteenth century, houses of refuge had taken on many of the characteristics of modern-day training schools. They were isolated from urban areas; youths lived in cottages; and inmates were supervised by cottage "parents."

In 1870, another attempt was made to reform the prison. At the National Congress of Penitentiary and Reformatory Discipline, the idea of the reformatory, a correctional institution for youthful offenders from 18 to 30 years of age, was proposed.[20] Rothman notes that penal reformers at this time believed that "the appropriate task was to reform incarceration, not to launch a fundamental attack on it."[21] Reformers were afraid that abolition of prison would lead to the restoration of such penal practices as whipping posts and the gallows. Furthermore, they remained committed to the idea that prisons could accomplish rehabilitation.

In 1876, the **Elmira Reformatory**, representing the first and most ambitious attempt to fulfill the vision of reformers, was opened in New York State. The basic reforms put into effect were: (1) a "mark system," by which prisoners could receive marks or rewards for satisfactory behavior; (2) the use of graded levels of accommodation and privilege; (3) programs of educational and vocational training, moral and religious instruction, military drill, gymnastics, and other forms of athletics; (4) the indeterminate sentence and parole; and (5) aftercare supervision. Zebulon Brockway, the superintendent for 20 years, was responsible for deciding when a prisoner was ready for release, so that he could retain anyone who was not responding appropriately to the reformatory's programs.

Reformatories were built in 12 states over the next two decades, but the lofty principles of Elmira and the other reformatories fell far short in practice. Reformers soon realized that the reformatories were still violent, stone-walled, multitiered fortresses, no more conducive to reform than the old Auburn-type penitentiaries.

In the 1870s, a reform movement sought to improve the plight of women in prison. Up until that time, the only prisons available for women offenders were men's prisons, where female inmates suffered from neglect and inferior care as well as from the threat of rape and forced prostitution at the hands of male prisoners and guards. The new reformatories for women were intended to imitate a familial setting, housing women in "cottages" where they were supervised by houseparents and trained to be domestics and homemakers.

Nicole Hahn Rafter argues that although reformatories improved the lot of women, the legislation that established the reformatories also permitted lengthy incarceration for petty offenses. Women were both punished more severely than men for the same offenses and punished for behavior that was considered acceptable for a man. By the 1930s, reformatories for women had ceased to exist, but Rafter contends that women prisoners continue to receive partial justice in that their treatment is simultaneously less harsh and less adequate. Thus, although the reformatory for women led in some respects to a softening of the punitive process, at the same time it cast women prisoners into a situation of dependency from which they still have not recovered.[22]

Probation and parole also first appeared during the mid- to latter part of the nineteenth century. John Augustus, a Boston shoemaker who volunteered his time to supervise offenders in the 1830s and 1840s, is credited with being the father of probation. In the late 1870s and 1880s, paid probation officers were appointed first in Boston and then throughout Massachusetts. Parole, as previ-

BOX 12.1   **FOUCAULT'S VISION**

The French philosopher Michel Foucault was attracted to that aspect of the nineteenth-century prison that attempted to control both the freedom of movement and the minds of those confined. He focused on Jeremy Bentham's proposal that prisoners be confined in a structure arranged so that a guard could be in the center of the building and see into each cell without being seen. The prisoner, then, would have the impression that he was always being watched by an omnipresent representative of the state. Bentham called the prison he envisioned and the principle it encompassed "the Panopticon."

The importance of the concept of the **Panopticon**, according to Foucault, was the potential ability to have total power over selected populations. He saw the prison of the nineteenth century as a system of power and domination transferable beyond the prison to other areas of life. Foucault reasoned that if one is under the impression of always being under surveillance, an automatic functioning of power is assured. Eventually, there is no need for the physical presence of an actual enforcer because the individual incorporates the power to control himself or herself.

Today, increasingly, we are watched by omnipresent video cameras, and all types of personal information about us is stored in research and data banks. The computer has become the new omnipresent power. In the electronic age, spatial limitations are bypassed. Using such traces of behavior as credit card applications, traffic tickets, telephone bills, loan applications, welfare files, fingerprints, income transactions, and so forth, the computer can put together information yielding a full picture of an individual's life. Thus, using Foucault's analysis, the wider structure of control is an outgrowth of mechanisms and concepts used to manage confined populations.

Source: This section is based on Neal Shover and Werner J. Einstadter's analysis of Michel Foucault's *Discipline and Punishment: The Birth of the Prison* in their *Analyzing American Corrections* (Belmont, Calif.: Wadsworth, 1988), pp. 202–204.

ously indicated, was instituted at the Elmira Reformatory; prisoners released early would receive supervision in the community.

The Twentieth Century: A Time of Change

Changing ideologies, institution building, and professionalism have been the main themes in the development of the criminal justice system in the twentieth century.

Changing Ideologies   Throughout the twentieth century, reform and repression have alternatively been viewed as the means to attain crime control in American society. The Progressive Era, that period from about 1890 to 1920, introduced a wave of reform. This mood of optimism led to the development of individualized treatment of offenders. The development of community-based corrections, the use of the medical model to rehabilitate offenders, experimentation with inmate self-government, and the expanded use of indeterminate sentencing all resulted from the emphasis on individualized treatment.[23]

As proponents of the **medical model**, psychiatrists contended that criminals were sick rather than bad and that it was sickness that drove them to crime. These founders of the therapeutic state had little patience with the concept of the personal responsibility, or culpability, of offenders, because they were more concerned with finding cures than assigning moral blame. They promised that they could cure the disease of criminality by dealing with offenders on an individual basis, by prescribing the proper kind of treatment, and by implementing the ideal treatment plan.

Under the leadership of psychiatrists, whose presence in prisons was well established by the 1920s, the medical model was implemented in correctional institutions throughout the nation. The basic goal was to make the prison into a hospital, or treatment center. One supporter of the medical model explained how it could transform the prison:

> We have to treat [inmates] as sick people, which in every respect they are. . . . It is the hope of the more progressive elements in psychopathology and criminality that the guard and the jailer will be replaced by the nurse, and the judge by the psychiatrist, whose sole attempt will be to treat and cure the individual instead of merely to punish him. Then and only then can we hope to lessen, even if not entirely to abolish, crime, the most costly burden that society has today.[24]

The juvenile courts, the first of which was established in Cook County (Chicago) in 1899, were also based on the rehabilitative ideal. The state, according to the *parens patriae* philosophy of the juvenile court system, was established as a surrogate parent for children in trouble. The informal setting of this court and the parental demeanor of the judge was intended to enable wayward youth to be "saved" or "rescued" from their lives of crime. Juvenile probation officers, who were under the auspices of the juvenile court, quickly accepted the treatment philosophy, and, within a decade, adult probation officers accepted the rehabilitation, or medical model.

However, in the late 1960s and early 1970s, a criticism mounted against the rehabilitative ideal. In 1974, Robert Martinson startled corrections personnel, as well as the public, with the pronouncement that "with few and isolated exceptions, the rehabilitative efforts that have been reported so far have had no appreciable effect on recidivism."[25] Some of its proponents came to the defense of rehabilitation, but the general mood concerning offender rehabilitation continues to be one of pessimism and discouragement. In Box 12.2, David Shichor argues that rehabilitation as an ideal, as well as a correctional practice, will gain renewed impetus in the near future.

BOX 12.2   **THE FUTURE OF REHABILITATION**

It is suggested that some of the major reasons for the return to the rehabilitative ideal and rehabilitative policies will be the following:

First, future orientation, which is based on an optimistic *weltanschauung* [world view], is a fundamental characteristic of the American ethos. The currently popular penological principles—retribution, deterrence and incapacitation—are basically the expression of . . . "brutal pessimism." . . . This pessimistic public view probably will not prevail very long; people generally need to feel that there is hope. As Conrad states, "the foundation of rehabilitation is hope. It is also the foundation of order." . . . Support for the idea of rehabilitation involves also a measure of confidence in the social institutions. Thus, if the American public will not lose completely its confidence in the viability of its institutions, somewhere along the line certain measures of rehabilitation will have to be returned.

Second, rehabilitation, with all the possible abuses that it may contain or generate, is strongly rooted in humanitarian reform . . . In fact, rehabilitation is the only penological principle which has any connection with humanitarian values. . . .

Third, the prevailing utilitarian approach, which claims that rehabilitative policies are not effective in reducing crime rates, does not seem to offer a more successful alternative in this respect. . . .

Fourth, another major reason for the survival of the rehabilitative ideal and some rehabilitative programs is connected with the fact that in spite of the generally conservative social atmosphere, many people still believe in the importance of rehabilitation as a major goal of corrections. . . .

Fifth, the fact that American society is extremely individualistic, and the value of individualism is held very high, will encourage the maintenance of a measure of individual treatment in penology. . . .

Source: This material appears in David Shichor, "Penal Policies: Some Recent Trends," *Legal Studies Forum* 11 (1987), pp. 68–70.

In the mid–1970s, a concern with crime control arose as part of a political backlash by a public frightened by street riots, student unrest, militant rhetoric, and the assault on middle-class values by the counterculture. The stance was referred to as "law and order," "getting tough" on crime, or a "war on crime"; its emphasis was on punishing offenders for their behavior. The two basic positions, as previously discussed, were retribution, or the justice model, and utilitarianism, or the utilitarianism punishment model.

The basic idea of retributionist principles is to mete out punishment according to the past behavior of offenders.[26] The only reason to punish an offender is because he or she deserves it, but the punishment given the offender must be proportionate to the social harm inflicted upon society.[27] In contrast, the utilitarianism principles suggest that the major policy in dealing with offenders should be deterrence and/or incapacitation. That is, punishment should have some social benefit, either the protection of the social order or the deterrence of crime.[28]

Institution Building   Law enforcement, the courts, and corrections have all been involved in institution building in the twentieth century. Federal police, state police, county police, municipal police, and private police have expanded to the point that some 40,000 police departments currently exist. A dual court system developed early in the twentieth century: one system of separate state courts, which were charged to prosecute and try crimes defined by state legislatures, and another system of federal courts, whose jurisdiction was restricted to federal crimes defined by the acts of Congress.

Those in corrections also embarked on an immense program of institution building. The Federal Bureau of Prisons, formed in the 1930s, today maintains over 60 correctional institutions, ranging from large maximum-security fortresses to small, minimum-security corrections "showplaces." State departments of corrections were established following World War II and built many correctional facilities. Private corrections, long a leader in community-based corrections, also became involved in the prison business in the 1970s and 1980s.[29]

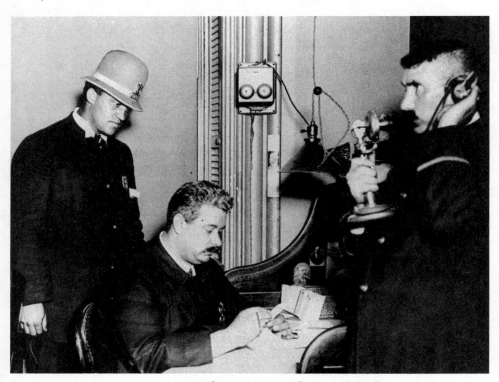

New York police headquarters, c. 1910. (*Source:* Library of Congress [LC-USZ62-50070].)

The fear of crime has led to a concern with greater efficiency in apprehending, convicting, and punishing criminals. This concern has, in turn, encouraged the development of a "systems" perspective toward criminal justice. The growth of a vast criminal justice bureaucracy was also influenced by the popularity of systems analysis in the decades following World War II. Proponents of systems analysis forcefully argued that the complexity of today's systems make it necessary to use systems analysis to make informed decisions.

Professionalization   The police professionalism movement among law enforcement agencies has gathered momentum with each decade of the twentieth century. Reformers have claimed that the key to professionalism is the elimination of political influence. Proponents have further argued that a professional police department is an efficient and nonpartisan agency committed to the highest standards of public service. Increased training and education, elevation of standards, and the achievement of accreditation have become goals of professional police departments. The quest for professionalism has also guided the development of corrections throughout the twentieth century. Corrections administrators, most noticeably in the decades following the Second World War, have abandoned autocratic managerial practices and pursued participatory or democratic management techniques, upgraded standards, and accreditation of correctional agencies.

In sum, a historical review of social control in American society reveals certain persistent motifs: a cycle of reform and a reactive repressiveness after the failure of reform; a continued belief in the efficacy of imprisonment; the influence of social, political, and economic factors; and unreal expectations toward the justice system. The external pressures and constraints facing the justice system, as well as the overwhelming tasks it is given, mean that the quest for order in criminal justice frequently gives birth to systemic disorder. The untidiness of the justice system, of course, ultimately mirrors the frustrations of dealing with an intractable crime problem.

CRIMINAL JUSTICE: A SEARCH FOR ORDER

The structure, purposes, functions, and means of processing offenders are intended to enable the criminal justice system to maintain an orderly society. Unfortunately, as discussed later in this chapter, the system's actual structure, functions, and procedures are so untidy that the system itself is chaotic.

Structure of the Criminal Justice System

The criminal justice system is divided into three components, or subsystems: the police; the courts, including prosecution and defense; and corrections, including probation, parole, residential programs in the community, and short- and long-term institutions.

Political control of the justice system is evident at all levels. State legislatures, as well as Congress, define criminal behavior and establish criminal penalties. They also pass laws defining criminal procedures, including rules and regulations regarding search warrants, bail, trial court procedures, and sentencing. Legislatures are also responsible for providing financial support for statewide criminal justice agencies and programs. The executive branch, the power of which is vested in such public officials as the president, governors, mayors, and county commissioners, appoints and dismisses executive directors or heads of criminal justice agencies. The president and state governors also have the power to grant pardons for crimes and to commute sentences.

The criminal justice system is further made up of two distinct systems, federal and state. Both the federal and state justice systems have enforcement, adjudication, and correctional functions, but they have widely different authority and scope of activities. Federal agencies are authorized to enforce only those laws prescribed under the powers granted by Congress; in recent years, however, Congress has expanded the scope of federal law.

The criminal justice system currently consists of 73,000 public agencies, which have an annual budget of over $10 billion and a staff of almost 12 million individuals. There are approximately 40,000 police agencies, 17,000 courts, 4,600 correctional institutions, and 3,200 probation and parole departments.[30] The agencies of the justice system annually arrest 12 million persons and prosecute 2 million defendants.[31] The daily population of state and federal correctional institutions is approaching 550,000 prisoners, and, at the end of 1985, nearly 1,900,000 individuals were on probation, and 280,000 were on parole.[32]

Today, some 50 federal agencies involved in some type of law enforcement responsibility employ 25,000 full-time personnel. Local police agencies make up the largest portion of law enforcement personnel in the United States. New York City employs over 26,000 full-time officers, and Los Angeles employs some 7,000 officers. Yet police agencies for the most part are still small. It is estimated that more than 90 percent of all police agencies in this nation employ fewer than 10 persons. Furthermore, there are more than one million private police, far exceeding the number of public police.[33] Private security guards or police can be found guarding shopping centers, apartment buildings, office buildings, factories, sports centers, college campuses, and hospitals.

The court system's organization is even more complex than that of police departments. Most states divide their criminal court systems into three tiers: courts of limited jurisdiction, courts of general jurisdiction, and courts of appellate jurisdiction. The lower or inferior courts are at the bottom of the judicial hierarchy; they are frequently called municipal or magistrates' courts. The second tier consists of trial courts, which may be called county courts, district courts, superior courts, and courts of common pleas. The third tier consists of appellate courts, which include both the state and federal forums that hear all challenges to the decisions of the lower courts. Appellate courts are further divided into intermediate and final appellate courts (see Figure 12.1 for an example of a state court system).

The federal government has also established a three-tiered court system,

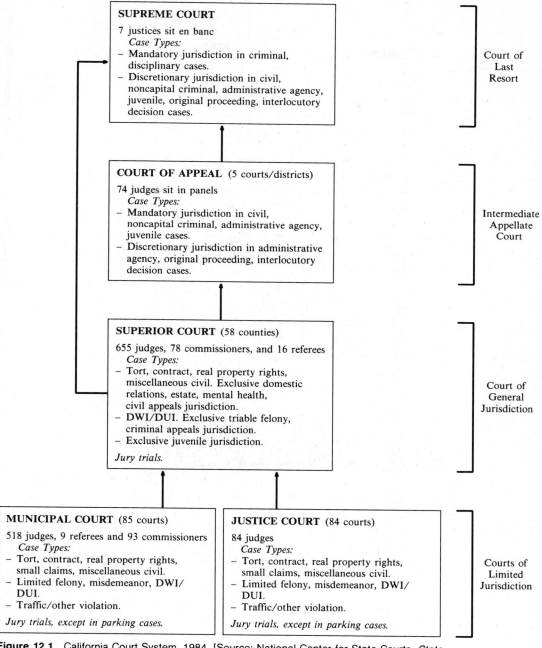

Figure 12.1 California Court System, 1984. [Source: National Center for State Courts, *State Court Caseload Statistics: Annual Report 1984* (Williamsburg, Va.: National Center for State Courts 1986), p. 200]

consisting of the U.S. District Courts, the U.S. Courts of Appeals, and the U.S. Supreme Court (see Figure 12.2). There are 92 federal district courts; each state has at least one. The 11 federal courts of appeals hear all appeals from federal district courts as well as the appeals of the decisions of certain administrative and regulatory agencies. The U.S. Supreme Court is the final appellate court for both the state and federal court systems, and its justices hear only cases that they have decided involve a new or important point of constitutional law. The Supreme Court hears only about 200 cases a year, a small fraction of those brought to its attention.

The nearly eight thousand correctional agencies are made up of local jails and police lockups, state and federal correctional institutions, state departments of corrections, state and county probation and parole departments, halfway houses, and reception centers. These agencies provide nine correctional services: juvenile detention; juvenile probation; administration of juvenile institutions; juvenile aftercare (parole); adult misdemeanor and felony probation; administration of adult institutions for detention, of adult short-term institutions, and of adult felony institutions; and parole.

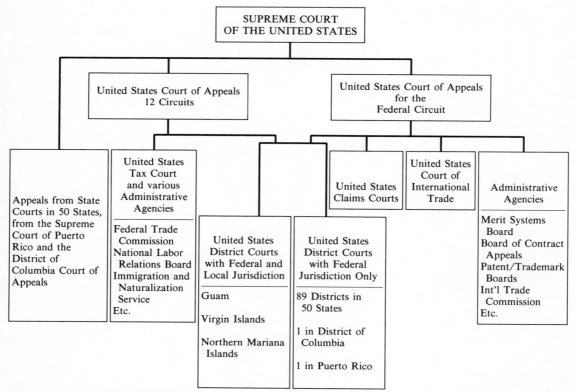

Figure 12.2   The United States Court System. [Source: American Bar Association, *Law and the Courts* (Chicago, Ill.: ABA, 1988)]

Functions of the Criminal Justice System

Each of the main components of the criminal justice system has specific functions of its own; yet the components of criminal justice overall are supposed to function as a system.

Components of Criminal Justice The functions of law enforcement, courts, and corrections differ significantly. Law enforcement is charged with clearing crimes by arresting law violators who are prosecuted and convicted in the court system. The task of corrections is to provide control and correction of those sentenced by the courts.

The three main functions of the police are law enforcement, order maintenance, and crime prevention. Law enforcement involves making "good" arrests (i.e., those that are based on sufficient evidence and that do not violate an individual's constitutional rights); obtaining confessions; building strong cases that result in convictions; and increasing crime clearance rates. The order maintenance responsibilities, which are so demanding on a police officer's time, include assignments such as settling family disputes, furnishing information to citizens, providing emergency ambulance services, preventing suicides, assisting disaster victims, aiding the physically disabled and mentally ill, and giving shelter to drunks.

Crime prevention responsibilities consist both of delinquency prevention programs in the schools and crime prevention activities in the community, such as checking the homes of families on vacation, checking commercial dwellings after work hours, and engaging in proactive means of deterring crime before it occurs. In addition to the time-honored responsibilities of law enforcement, order maintenance, and crime prevention, the police also are called to regulate traffic and parking, issue various permits, and guard public morals through the enforcement of community standards regarding books, movies, and plays.

The main functions of the courts are to dispose of criminal cases and to supervise juvenile probation and some adult probation departments. The courts of limited jurisdiction generally handle all cases as they move from arrest to the adjudicative stages of the criminal justice process. These courts are charged to deal with all of the less serious cases, the misdemeanors, petty offenses, and local ordinance violations. They also handle the more serious cases that require bail and appointment of counsel for indigents before transfer to the trial court. The courts of general jurisdiction, or the trial courts, dispose of serious cases through dismissal, guilty pleas, or trials. Dismissals and guilty pleas are the most frequent outcomes, for only 5 to 10 percent of all defendants arrested eventually go to trial. The state and federal appellate courts are primarily concerned with the issues of law, and only when new evidence is uncovered do they deal with the issues of fact that are significant to the trial court.

The prosecutor—or district attorney, county attorney, or state attorney—represents the state and seeks conviction, while the defense attorney—who may be privately retained, court appointed, or a public defender—tries to gain acquittal or dismissal of the charges against his or her client. If the client is willing to plead guilty, the defense attorney is expected to enter into plea negotiations and obtain for the defendant the best bargain possible in terms of sentencing disposition.

Corrections is charged with providing care of those offenders sent to this subsystem. Departments of corrections formerly were charged to rehabilitate offenders sentenced by the courts, but today in most states the courts require that these agencies provide safe, secure, and humane care and grant prisoners all the constitutional rights not expressly denied by the nature of their incarceration. Departments of corrections also are required to protect society against escapees from correctional facilities. Both probation and parole officers have assigned caseloads and must report to the court on those who violate the law. If parolees violate the conditions of parole or commit additional crimes, it may be necessary to revoke them or return them to prison.

Seven states now claim integrated corrections departments that bring together all or most of the nine correctional functions. Another expression of the integrated services concept is found in the community corrections acts passed in Minnesota, Oregon, and Kansas in the 1970s. In addition, model comprehensive community-based programs have been developed in Polk County, Iowa, and Montgomery County, Maryland.

Systemic Nature of Criminal Justice   Although criminal justice, as previously noted, had begun to be viewed as a system by the end of the nineteenth century, the emphasis placed by the President's Crime Commission on the systemic nature of criminal justice did not become widely accepted until the late 1960s. The **systems approach** advocated by the President's Crime Commission focuses on the interrelationships among the components of criminal justice.

Criminal justice, according to the systems approach, is made up of complex interacting elements. Cooperation takes place among the components of criminal justice system as they share in mutual goal setting, sharing of resources, and coordinated planning. The primary goals of the systemic approach are efficiency and cost-effectiveness. The system is internally interdependent and to some degree externally autonomous; change in one part of the system affects the other subsystems.

The systems approach, which is widely used in such diverse fields as national defense, medicine, and business management, is based on several elements. First, the approach is grounded on the principle that it is impossible to get an accurate picture of a phenomenon without examining the relationships among the separate parts and the whole. Second, the systems approach requires a clear understanding of goals and objectives, both of the entire system and of its component parts. Third, the systems approach requires that goals be stated in such a way that they can be measured.[34]

The Process of Justice   The means by which a case is processed through the criminal justice system is an essential part of bringing order to the disorder of crime. The criminal justice process usually encompasses the following crucial steps (see Figure 12.3).

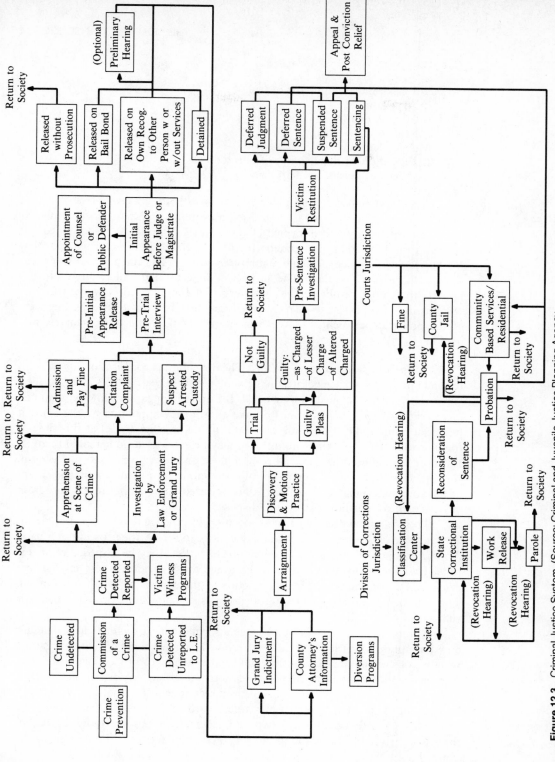

Figure 12.3 Criminal Justice System. (Source: Criminal and Juvenile Justice Planning Agency, Des Moines, Ohio, May 23, 1983)

1. Investigation
2. Arrest and booking
3. Initial and preliminary hearing
4. Arraignment
5. Plea bargaining or trial
6. Sentencing hearing
7. Appellate review
8. Probation or department of corrections
9. Parole or release on supervision

Arrest and booking   If a police officer investigating a crime feels probable cause exists that an individual committed a criminal act, that person generally is taken into custody and informed of the charges. The major exception to this procedure is that some police departments, especially in California and New York, permit the officer to issue a summons that directs the accused to appear in court on a specified date. The suspect is fingerprinted and photographed, a process that often results in the discovery that the accused is wanted for the commission of other crimes. The accused may also be interrogated by members of the police department and the prosecutor's staff at the time of arrest and booking.

Initial and preliminary hearing   The defendant is constitutionally guaranteed an initial appearance before a judicial officer shortly after arrest. The accused is read the charges against him or her at this initial appearance and is reminded of the right to remain silent and to have an attorney appointed by the court if he or she cannot afford to retain one. Bail, if any, is officially set at this time; if the defendant can raise the amount of money or is released on personal recognizance or into some other pretrial program, he or she is given pretrial freedom. But the defendant who is unable to raise the money required (about 10 percent of the amount stipulated as bail) or is not released on a pretrial release program must return to jail until the case is disposed at trial.

The **preliminary hearing** usually occurs within seven to ten days after arrest. The purpose of this hearing is to allow the judge to review the prosecution's case. A misdemeanor offense, such as public drunkenness, may be disposed of at this time. If the case involves a felony, the judge must decide if there is sufficient evidence for an indictment, for a reduction of the charge, or even for dismissal. The role of the prosecutor at this hearing is to show that probable cause is sufficient for an indictment.

The prosecution generally initiates a formal charge against the defendant about a month after the preliminary hearing. The court must decide at this time whether or not the prosecution has sufficient evidence to proceed with the case. The prosecution then can present the case to the grand jury for an indictment. The grand jury usually goes along with the recommendations of the prosecutor; indeed, the grand jury is sometimes referred to as "the rubber stamp" of the prosecutor. A defendant charged with a misdemeanor can waive these proceedings; if a jurisdiction uses the grand jury system, a felony case must go to the grand jury.

Arraignment   The arraignment hearing follows shortly after an indictment has been handed down, and it is then that the defendant must plead guilty or not guilty. If the plea is guilty, the court usually asks for a presentence investigation report from the probation department. If the defendant pleads not guilty, he or she usually has two or three months following **arraignment** to prepare a defense. The defendant also has the choice of having the case tried before a jury or judge and jury. However, only 5 to 10 percent of all cases ever go to trial, because of the wide use of **plea bargaining.**

Plea bargaining or trial   Plea bargaining may be initiated by either the prosecuting attorney or the defense attorney. This procedure depends on the willingness of the prosecution to recommend a reduction of the charge in exchange for a guilty plea. Plea bargaining is advantageous to the prosecutor because it guarantees a conviction, which might not have taken place if the case came to trial. Defendants who are guilty of the crime charged against them also profit from plea bargaining, because they receive a reduction in the charge, thereby resulting in a lighter sentence. It is estimated that up to 90 percent of court cases are resolved by plea bargaining. This "negotiated justice" prevents the system from falling apart; were every eligible case to go to trial, the glut would paralyze the courts.

Sentencing hearing   For those defendants who have either pleaded guilty or been found guilty during a trial, the judge must decide upon the appropriate sentence during a sentencing hearing. The presentence investigation report from a probation officer assists the judge in making a decision at this time. This presentence investigation generally includes a sentencing recommendation, and research suggests that judges follow these recommendations about 95 percent of the time. The chief penalties imposed for minor offenders consist of fines, short periods in jail, and suspended sentences; for serious offenses, defendants may receive probation, placement in a residential program, jail sentences, prison sentences of up to life, or for aggravated murder, the death sentence.

Appellate review   Following the determination of guilt and the pronouncement of sentence, the defendant has the right to appeal the case. About one case in five is appealed. Appeals are based on disagreement over points of law or charges of judicial misconduct; a defendant is not allowed to challenge the appropriateness of the sentence. The court may be petitioned to set bail so that the defendant can be released during the appeals process.

Probation or department of corrections   Probation is a service run by the local courts. Probation permits the convicted offender to remain in the community under the supervision of a probation officer and the conditions set by the court. An offender who completes probation without further incident is discharged from the supervision of the judicial system. If a probationer violates probation or commits another criminal act, a court hearing may be held to determine if probation should be revoked or its conditions modified.

The offender who is sentenced to the department of corrections may be sent to a separate reception facility, but he or she is more likely to be sent to an orientation unit at a state prison. A decision concerning the proper security level and programs needs of the inmate is made during this classification process. Inmates who have received the death penalty are sequestered in a separate unit.

Parole or release or supervision   Parole or release at the expiration of the sentence concludes the inmate's imprisonment. The jurisdiction of the justice system ends with the successful completion of the parole period.

CRIMINAL JUSTICE: A SYSTEM IN CHAOS

The thesis of this chapter is that the justice system is characterized more by chaos than by order. This thesis can be supported by an examination of the sources of systemic disorder—fragmentation, overload, and limited capacity.

Chaos in prison: mattress discarded from cell after an inmate decided to burn it. (*Source:* Marino Colman/EKM–Nepenthe.)

Fragmentation

In the twentieth century, criminal justice has increasingly come to be viewed in terms of a systemic model. A criminal justice flowchart points out efficiency and cost-effectiveness as primary goals of the justice system (see Figure 12.3). The process of conceptualizing the flow of cases shows the importance of inputs and outputs, with the ultimate objective being the efficient management of workload and improved productivity.

The systemic approach is based on the assumption that to be effective in dealing with the disorder of crime, all the components of the justice system must cooperate and work together. However, the interdependence and cooperation needed among the police, courts, and corrections is sometimes so far from reality that critics accuse the criminal justice process of being a nonsystem. The National Advisory Report on Criminal Justice Standards and Goals has described this **fragmentation**:

> The American criminal justice system is so complex and the interrelationships among its components are so varied that even its supporters view it as a kind of crazy quilt. There are wide variations in the way in which federal, state, and local governments administer, finance, and operate correctional services. These services may be centralized at the state level, decentralized in municipalities and counties, or shared by the state, counties, and cities in an almost infinite number of ways. In their attempts to create more hopeful alternatives to incarceration, legislatures created reformatories, probation, parole, and a host of services for delinquent children. These alternatives evolved without central control or direction. The correctional system became a nonsystem.[35]

Several factors contribute to the fragmentation of the system. First, the interrelationships among its components are often characterized by conflict and even hostility as a result of competition for attention and funds outside the system. Second, the police, courts, and corrections are independent jurisdictions, each administered by separate agencies, and each with separate powers or authority, lines of communication, and accountability. Third, each component sets its own goals. Fourth, the laws and philosophies of justice vary from state to state and even from jurisdiction to jurisdiction within a state. Finally, each of the subsystems tends to attract individuals with differences in personality, social background, training and education, values, and attitudes. These factors lead to different ideologies about the law, crime, and criminals and contribute to strained relations and distrust among criminal justice actors.[36]

Among the consequences of fragmentation are misunderstandings and lack of cooperation among the police, courts, and corrections. Fragmentation also leads to conflict between federal and state justice agencies, between county and municipal justice agencies, and between the juvenile and adult justice systems. In addition, fragmentation contributes to misinformation.[37] Offenders are sometimes the only ones who know what is taking place during their progress through the system. Furthermore, fragmentation results in the duplication of services, as similar programs and services are offered by two or more agencies, sometimes at the same time.

Overload

Losing the war on crime has not discouraged Americans from trying harder. They continue to beseech legal and political policymakers to arrest, prosecute, and imprison more offenders. Law enforcement does not have sufficient resources today to deal with rampant crime. Even so, too many suspects are arrested, and the clogging of cases in court makes the actors feel pressured to plea bargain most of the cases appearing before them. The mammoth case loads handled by criminal justice practitioners, in turn, typically lead to an assembly-line system of justice. Corrections also struggles with **overload**; the disorder arising from overcrowding makes it nearly impossible for correctional administrators to meet minimum standards of humane confinement for prisoners. Indeed, 36 states are presently under court order to reduce overcrowding in their prisons.

Furthermore, overload is one of the contributing factors leading to burnout and high turnover among criminal justice practitioners. The ongoing stress of dealing with large case loads affects nearly all criminal justice staff who have direct contact with offenders. High levels of stress also result from the fact that overcrowded prisons are dangerous places in which to work.

Limited Capacity

The capacity limitations of the criminal justice system are evident in its inability to impose sufficient costs on lawbreakers. For example, the criminal justice system is sometimes compared to a funnel. At the top are the numerous suspects who are arrested; at the bottom are the few who are convicted. For some suspects, prosecutors refuse to file charges; for others, charges are eventually dropped or the prosecution is unable to produce convincing evidence of guilt. Nationally, about one-half of all felony arrests fail to result in a conviction.[38] Todd R. Clear and George F. Cole add an even more gloomy picture: of every 1000 felonies committed, only 540 are reported to the police, and only 65 suspects are arrested. Of those arrested, 36 are convicted, 17 are sentenced to custody, and only 3 are sentenced to prison over one year.[39]

The criminal justice system is also limited because it does not often impose severe sanctions on white-collar and corporate criminals. The charge that the criminal justice system "ignores" a great deal of white-collar criminality or cannot successfully prosecute it leaves us with a system where crime pays for middle- and upper-class offenders. As previously suggested, white-collar and corporate crimes cost the American society far more than does street crime.

Moreover, the criminal justice system is limited because it cannot affect the larger social problems affecting American society. Most of the clients of the justice process are the poor—those individuals whose potential has been restricted because of the lack of social equality, racial discrimination, and inequalities of education and vocational opportunities.

In a 1974 keynote address at the American Correctional Association Annual Meeting, Norval Morris defined why the criminal justice system has such limited capacity:

> Let dogmatism substitute for argument: the fact of the matter is that in every country—including this country—the criminal justice system is of limited capacity. . . . It could and should catch and convict more criminals (in particular, those guilty of serious crimes of violence or threats of violence to the person, major depredations to property, and substantial interference with governmental processes); it should, with more principle, impose deterrent and community protective punishment; it should better help those convicted criminals who wish to conform to a reasonably lawabiding life. It should be a better containment of crime. It could in my view measurably reduce crime. But it cannot grapple at all preventively with the deep-seated problem of social inequality, racial discrimination, inequalities of education and vocational opportunity, an underclass locked in by poverty amidst conspicuous luxury that overwhelms our still exiguously funded efforts at crime control.[40]

POLICY IMPLICATIONS

Today, as in the past, the American public is disillusioned with the crime reduction strategies of the criminal justice system. But to design effective crime control strategies is no easy matter. There are 50 separate state criminal justice systems, each with its own criminal code, and one federal system.

Still, a number of changes in the criminal justice subsystems promise overall improvement to the system. First, consolidation and integration of services are needed in all of the justice components. The courts have made the greatest strides in consolidation of court services, but the diversity of court services across the nation shows that they have taken only the first steps in a long journey. In corrections, seven states now have integrated departments, but fragmentation, rather than integration, best characterizes the corrections systems in most states. Law enforcement officials also are concerned about the need for consolidation, but they have made even less progress in integrating law enforcement services. Do we really need 40,000 separate law enforcement agencies?

Second, the reduction of discretionary justice promises to bring improvement to the justice process. Too many decisions are made through a series of informal and largely hidden procedures (i.e., police-citizen encounters, plea bargaining, correctional officer–inmate encounters). Such unregulated decisions can lead to excessive use of force by police officers, to discriminatory treatment of minority groups at all points in the justice process, to unfair discriminatory decisions about inmates, and to capricious and arbitrary decisions by a parole board. David Fogel asserts that "if we cannot treat with reliability, we can at least be fair, reasonable, humane, and constitutional in practice."[41]

Third, upgrading standards offers another means of systemwide change. A number of professional organizations, national and state commissions, and other groups have proposed standards, models, and guidelines to improve the fairness and efficiency of the juvenile and adult justice systems. The often-conflicting standards of the various agencies show two points of consensus: first, there is agreement that there is a need to upgrade the procedures and practices of the justice system, and second, standards are viewed as an effective means to accomplish this goal. Unfortunately, because existing standards are often the reflection of the varying ideologies of criminal justice and because writers of these standards rarely attempt to conform with existing standards, their impact is reduced.

Fourth, the vestiges of unfairness in the justice process must be reduced. Among those subjected to this unfairness are unconvicted and innocent defendants who must stay in jail because they are too poor to raise bond; defendants whose court-appointed attorney or public defender counsel gives them an inadequate defense because of his or her own case overload; citizens who are treated brutally while under arrest and prisoners who are badly treated during confinement; property offenders who are sent to prison when both their needs and those of society could be better served by community-based programs; first-time offenders who are sexually violated in jail or prison; vulnerable prisoners who must stay in lockup or protective custody for 23 hours a day because they cannot protect themselves; prisoners who are confined in inadequate living space and who do not receive their constitutionally guaranteed services and rights; and criminals who are put to death by the state while others equally guilty of a vicious crime are spared.

Finally, as long as the criminal justice system continues to be so overloaded, it will have limited capacity to handle the crime problem any more effectively. On the one hand, until society provides more effectively for the needs of the poor, especially the very poor, crime will continue to be a major problem of American society. On the other hand, decriminalization of some of the public order crimes, as well as the administrative regulation of undesirable business practices instead of criminal code regulations, would reduce the numbers of those caught up in the net of the criminal justice system.

SUMMARY

The United States is preoccupied and frustrated by the crime problem, which is consistently listed in national opinion polls as one of the top three social problems. The fear that this nation is losing the war on crime and the enormous personal and financial costs of crime make it imperative that some means be found to reduce crime.

This chapter, a preface to the four that follow, has suggested that the criminal justice system is chaotic, so much so that it is barely functional in some jurisdictions. In the larger context, the criminal justice system reflects the confusion and impotence of dealing with crime in American society. Within the system itself, there are too many actors, too many stages, and too many options. The individual actors of the justice system are faced with conflicting mandates, roles,

pressures, and expectations, which lead to a general sense of distrust and alienation. There are so many impediments to their proper functioning that the rates
of burnout and turnover are excessive. Indeed, it is amazing that the justice
system survives as well as it does.

REFERENCES

Conley, John A. "Criminal Justice History as a Field of Research: A Review of the
Literature, 1960–1975." *Journal of Criminal Justice* 5 (1977) pp. 13–28.

Foucault, Michel. *Discipline and Punishment: The Birth of the Prison.* New York: Vintage,
1979.

Friedman, Lawrence M. "The Devil Is Not Dead: Exploring the History of Criminal
Justice." *Georgia Law Review* 11 (Winter 1977), pp. 257–274.

Lane, R. *Policing the City: Boston, 1822–1885.* Cambridge: Harvard University Press,
1967.

Rafter, Nicole Hahn. *Partial Justice: Women in State Prisons, 1800–1935.* Boston: Northeastern University Press, 1985.

Richardson, J. F. *The New York City Police: Colonial Times to 1901.* New York: Oxford
University Press, 1970.

Rossum, Ralph A. *The Politics of the Criminal Justice System: An Organizational Analysis.*
New York: Marcel Dekker, 1978.

Rothman, David J. *The Discovery of the Asylum: Social Order and Disorder in the New
Republic.* Boston: Little, Brown, 1971.

Shover, Neal, and Einstadter, Werner J. *Analyzing American Corrections.* Belmont, Calif.:
Wadsworth, 1988.

Silberman, Charles E. *Criminal Justice, Criminal Violence.* New York: Random House,
1978.

Walker, Samuel. *Popular Justice: A History of American Criminal Justice.* New York:
Oxford University Press, 1980.

Walker, Samuel. *Sense and Nonsense About Crime.* Monterey, Calif.: Brooks/Cole, 1985.

NOTES

1. Speech before the International Association of Chiefs of Police, New Orleans, September 1981.

2. See James Q. Wilson, *Thinking About Crime,* 2d ed. (New York: Basic Books, 1983),
and Ernest van den Haag, *Punishing Criminals* (New York: Basic Books, 1975), for
the development of this position.

3. David Fogel has used the disregard of victims as one of the key areas for reform in
his justice model; see David Fogel and Joe Hudson, eds., *Justice as Fairness: Perspectives on the Justice Model for Corrections* (Cincinnati: Anderson, 1981).

4. See, for example, Francis T. Cullen and Karen E. Gilbert, *Reaffirming Rehabilitation*
(Cincinnati: Anderson, 1982).

5. See Ramsey Clark, *Crime in America* (New York: Simon and Schuster, 1970), for a
classic statement of this liberal position.

6. Samuel Walker, *Popular Justice: A History of American Criminal Justice* (New York:
Oxford University Press, 1980).

7. Jeffrey H. Reiman, *The Rich Get Richer and the Poor Get Prison* (New York: Random House, 1979), pp. 199–308.

8. John A. Conley, "Criminal Justice History as a Field of Research: A Review of the Literature, 1960–1975," *Journal of Criminal Justice* 5 (1977), p. 13.

9. Walker, *Popular Justice*, pp. 1–52.

10. Wayne Morris, ed., "The Attorney General's Survey of Release Procedures," in *Penology: The Evolution of Corrections in America*, ed. George C. Killinger and Paul F. Cromwell, Jr. (St. Paul: West, 1973), p. 23.

11. Ibid., p. 33.

12. Walker, *Popular Justice*.

13. Richard Maxwell Brown, *Strain of Violence: Historical Studies of American Violence and Vigilantism* (New York: Oxford University Press, 1975), pp. 3–36.

14. Walker, *Popular Justice*, p. 57.

15. James F. Richardson, *Urban Police in the United States* (Port Washington, N.Y.: Kennikat Press, 1974), pp. 19–34. See also J. F. Richardson, *The New York Police: Colonial Times to 1901* (New York: Oxford University Press, 1970), and R. Lane, *Policing the City: Boston, 1822–1885* (Cambridge: Harvard University Press, 1967).

16. Robert M. Fogelson, *Big City Police* (Cambridge: Harvard University Press, 1977).

17. David J. Rothman, *The Discovery of the Asylum: Social Order and Disorder in the Republic* (Boston: Little, Brown, 1971). John A. Conley claims, however, that Rothman's thesis is too simplistic to explain such a phenomenon as the impact of immigration, industrialism, individualism, and emerging capitalism on the stability of society; see Conley, "Criminal Justice History," p. 17.

18. Rothman, *Discovery of the Asylum*, pp. 85–86.

19. Ibid., pp. 213–214.

20. *Transactions of the National Congress on Penitentiary and Reformatory Discipline*, cited in David Fogel, "*. . . We Are the Living Proof . . .*": The Justice Model for Corrections (Cincinnati: Anderson, 1975), p. 32.

21. David J. Rothman, *Conscience and Convenience* (Boston: Little, Brown, 1980), p. 29.

22. Nicole Hahn Rafter, *Partial Justice: Women in State Prisons, 1800–1935* (Boston: Northeastern University Press, 1985).

23. Rothman, *Conscience and Convenience*, pp. 32–60.

24. Benjamin Kaysman, citied in Edwin Sutherland and Donald Cressey, *Criminology*, 9th ed. (Philadelphia: Lippincott, 1973), p. 605.

25. R. Martinson, "What Works? Questions and Answers About Prison Reform," *Public Interest* 35 (1974), pp. 22–54.

26. D. F. Greenberg and D. Humphries, "The Cooptation of Fixed Sentencing Reform," *Crime and Delinquency* (April 1980), pp. 206–225.

27. Fogel, ". . . We are The Living Proof. . . ."

28. James O. Wilson and Ernest Van den Haag are the main spokespersons for this position.

29. For discussion of the development of private prisons, see Joan Mullen, *Corrections and the Private Sector* (Washington, D.C.: National Institute of Justice; U.S. Department of Justice, 1985), and Craig Becker and Amy Dreu Stanley, "Incarceration Inc.: The Downside of Private Prisons," *The Nation*, 15 June 1985, pp. 728–729.

30. Bureau of Justice Statistics, *Justice Agencies in the United States, Summary Report* (Washington, D.C.: U.S. Government Printing Office, 1980), p. vii.

31. U.S. Department of Justice, *Crime in the United States* (Washington, D.C.: U.S. Government Printing Office, 1981), p. 7.

32. Bureau of Justice Statistics, *Probation and Parole 1985* (Washington, D.C.: U.S. Government Printing Office, 1987), p. 1.

33. U.S. Department of Justice, *Criminal Justice Sourcebook* (Washington, D.C.: U.S. Government Printing Office, 1985), p. 29.

34. Ronald J. Waldron, *et al., The Criminal Justice System: An Introduction,* 3rd ed. (Boston: Houghton Mifflin Company, 1984), pp. 4–59.

35. National Advisory Commission on Criminal Justice Standards and Goals, Correction, p. 598.

36. Gerald D. Robin, *Introduction to the Criminal Justice System* (New York: Harper & Row, 1980), pp. 46–47.

37. Ralph A. Rossum, in *The Politics of the Criminal Justice System: An Organizational Analysis* (New York: Marcel Dekker, 1978), uses compliance analysis, or the influence of power, to analyze the intercompliance, or interrelationship, problems that exist among the criminal justice components.

38. Joan Petersilia, *The Influence of Criminal Justice Research* (Santa Monica, Calif.: Rand Corporation, 1987), p. 25.

39. Todd R. Clear and George F. Cole, *American Corrections* (Monterey, Calif.: Brooks/Cole, 1986), p. 158.

40. Norval Morris, "Keynote Address," *Proceedings of the One Hundred and Fifth Annual Congress of Correction* (College Park: American Correctional Association, 1976), p. 3.

41. David Fogel and Joe Hudson, eds., *Justice as Fairness: Perspectives on the Justice Model* (Cincinnati: Anderson, 1981), p. viii.

The Police

GUARDIANS OF THE SOCIAL ORDER

DIVERGENT CULTURES WITHIN THE POLICE

Professionalism: The Bureaucratization of
  Policing

The Police Culture

  Socialization into the Police Culture
  The Police Working Personality
  The Police Culture and the Informal System

CRIME REDUCTION

Community-Oriented Policing

Policing Repeat Offenders

Arresting Spousal Assaulters

POLICE DISCRETION

Constitutional Protections and the Police

  Investigative and Arrest Powers
  Custodial Interrogation

Police Corruption

Police Brutality

INTEGRATION OF WOMEN AND MINORITY
  GROUPS INTO POLICING

Women as Police Officers

Minority Police Officers

ANALYSIS

Freedom and Order

Order and the Police

POLICY IMPLICATIONS

Community-Oriented Policing

  Police-Community Reciprocity
  Areal Decentralization of Command
  Reorientation of Patrol
  Civilianization

Resolution of Conflict Between Management
  and Police Cultures

Reduction of Stress

SUMMARY

REFERENCES

NOTES

KEY TERMS

Carroll doctrine

civilianization

community-oriented policing

deadly force

Exclusionary Rule

guardians of the social order

inevitable discovery exception

informal rules

informal system

plain view doctrine

police brutality

police corruption

police culture

police discretion

policing repeat offenders

proactive tactics

professionalism

prompt arraignment rule

public safety exception

reactive tactics

search and seizure

socialization

spousal assault

stop-and-frisk

wing span search

The police in democratic societies are required to maintain order and to do so under the rule of law. As functionaries charged with maintaining order, they are part of the bureaucracy. The ideology of democratic bureaucracy emphasizes initiative rather than disciplined adherence to rules and regulations. By contrast the rule of law emphasizes rights of the individual citizen and constraints upon the initiative of legal officials. This tension between the operational consequences of the idea of order, efficiency, and initiative, on the one hand, and legality, on the other hand, constitutes the principal problem of police as a democratic, legal organization.

—Jerome H. Skolnick[1]

The police are the most visible front-line agents for ordering society. According to Richard V. Ericson, the police have the mandate "to use a system of rules and authoritative commands to transform troublesome, fragile situations back into a normal or efficient state."[2] Ericson adds that it is not the function of the police to produce a new order, but instead, "their everyday actions are directed at reproducing the existing order (the 'normal or efficient state') and the order (system of rules) by which this is accomplished."[3] The actions of the police, then, are designed to keep the existing order in its original state.

One of the ways the police have maintained order in American society is by mediating social conflict.[4] In attempting to quell discontent over the Vietnam War, the police became involved in openly controlling antiwar demonstrations and in infiltrating the antiwar movement. In student protests on college campuses across the nation and in riots in 100 American cities, the police were called to restrain demonstrators and rioters and to prevent further destruction of property.

Loras A. Jaeger contributed an early draft of this chapter.

In the civil rights movement of the 1960s, the police role was that of defusing racial violence and of seeing that the law was enforced.

However, while the police have become "the long thin line" that separates American society from anarchy, they also have contributed to the social disorder of the larger society. The early history of policing in America is filled with scandal; political control, corruption, and brutality were characteristic of nineteenth-century police. The public, not surprisingly, lacked respect for the police, and open conflict with the public has been an enduring characteristic of policing in this nation. The alienation between the public and the police became particularly evident in the 1960s. In police interactions with minorities in the slums and with students on college campuses, open conflicts erupted time after time. Indeed, the police were looked upon as symbols of the deteriorating relationship between blacks and whites in the cities.

GUARDIANS OF THE SOCIAL ORDER

The police serve as the **guardians of the social order** in several ways. The police maintain public order by catching criminals. The public calls the police when crimes are taking place or have taken place; the public also turns to the police for protection from possible criminal acts.

The police maintain public order by keeping the streets safe. They are charged to take over when a community emergency occurs; examples of such emergencies are the blackout in New York City in 1977 and natural disasters such as floods, hurricanes, and tornadoes. The public also turns to the police to preserve order at times of both peaceful or violent demonstrations, suicide attempts, and domestic squabbles. The maintenance of order further includes the protection against drunken drivers, the investigation of reported child abuse, and the apprehension of runaway and kidnapped children. Moreover, the public expects the police to control such crimes as prostitution, intoxication in public places, disorderly conduct, and nuisance behavior such as boisterous parties. In addition, the social order relies on the police to maintain traffic control on the streets, provide security at public schools, and patrol athletic contests to prevent the violence which sometimes occurs. Finally, the public depends on the police to perform a legion of service tasks—helping a citizen get in his or her locked vehicle, providing escort service for a funeral procession, checking businesses at night and the homes of citizens on vacation, rescuing cats from trees, and picking up the remains of dead animals from the streets.

Herman Goldstein's *Policing a Free Society* summarizes eight responsibilities of the police in maintaining order in American society:

1. To prevent and control conduct widely recognized as threatening to life and property (serious crime).
2. To aid individuals who are in danger of physical harm, such as the victim of a criminal attack.

3. To protect constitutional guarantees such as the right of free speech and assembly.
4. To facilitate the movement of people and vehicles.
5. To assist those who cannot care for themselves: the intoxicated, the addicted, the mentally ill, the physically disabled, the old, and the young.
6. To resolve conflict, whether it be between individuals, groups of individuals, or individuals and government.
7. To identify problems that have the potential for becoming more serious problems for the individual citizen, for the police, or for the government.
8. To create and maintain a feeling of security in the community.[5]

This chapter analyzes how successful the police are in fulfilling these responsibilities. The most important factors determining the success of the police are the emerging conflict between the management and the police culture, the effectiveness of crime reduction techniques, the adequacy of constitutional protections of suspects, the degree to which the police achieve gender and racial integration, and the ability of the police to control brutality and corruption.

DIVERGENT CULTURES WITHIN THE POLICE

The tightly knit and unified police departments of the past have been replaced by those characterized by conflict between the management culture and the street culture. Over the past two decades, several movements in policing have resulted in the emergence of the two cultures within policing.

First, federally funded programs in the 1960s and 1970s led to increased numbers of college-educated police officers. This "young guard" brought new ideas and skills to policing, such as professionalism, proactive policing, and interest in accreditation, and within a few years these young officers had assumed the leadership of departments across the nation.

Second, local units of government began to recruit chiefs from outside the department. Line officers often found it difficult to identify with the new chiefs who had not risen through the ranks. Patrol officers also frequently resented these leaders who introduced new ideas that affected existing power structures, job responsibilities, and previously taken-for-granted privileges.

Third, as much as new chiefs might want to be apolitical, they quickly discovered that they had to win respect and support from locally elected officials to survive in the job. But their own officers accused administrators of disloyalty when they made decisions that seemed to be more concerned about satisfying local leaders than in looking out for their officers.

Professionalism: The Bureaucratization of Policing

At the beginning of the twentieth century, a reform movement emerged in the United States. Progressive-minded individuals pursued reforms in the economic

August Vollmer working in his Berkeley home. (*Source:* Courtesy Bancroft Library of the University of California, Berkeley.)

arena, attacked social injustice, and demanded accountability from local units of government. Police administrators began to advocate the philosophy that the reform of the police through **professionalism** is the basic means by which the police can be made more effective, more efficient, and more accountable to the public. August Vollmer, O. W. Wilson, and William H. Parker, three of the most noted police reformers, all believed strongly that police officers must be carefully selected, well trained, free from political interference, and provided with the most up-to-date technology and hardware. In the past several decades, the goal of professionalism has guided many of the changes made in police departments across the nation (see Box 13.1).

Professionalism is usually viewed as including three related elements. Professionals can be described as experts who apply the results of theoretical knowledge acquired during an extended period of training to a specialized area of human endeavor. The authority of professionals is based on the claim that they are qualified to apply a particular body of knowledge. Second, professionals are expected to be devoted to an ideal of community service rather than to the attainment of material well-being. Finally, professionals rely on their own code of conduct and the close scrutiny of peers to monitor their behavior, and, therefore, they claim autonomy from external controls.[6]

However, the achievement of professionalism in policing is questionable when analyzed in terms of only these criteria. First, there is considerable doubt about the claim to expertise that is characteristic of the professional. The skills demanded and the training received for police work fall far short of the extensive

BOX 13.1   # THE MOVE TOWARD A PROFESSIONALIZED POLICE

1920–1930   The Wickersham Commission is established to investigate police abuses and procedures.

1930–1940   Improvements are made in police communication systems. The Uniform Crime Reporting system becomes widely accepted. The F.B.I. Laboratory and the National Academy are established to train local county and state officers.

1940–1950   Following World War II, new techniques in private sector management orientation are implemented. Operational techniques in personnel utilization based on military experience are also drawn up.

1950–1960   With the increased use of the patrol vehicle, foot patrol becomes almost nonexistent. The law enforcement code of ethics is drawn up.

1960–1970   In 1965, the President's Commission on Law Enforcement and Administration of Justice is established. The Law Enforcement Assistance Administration (LEAA) is mandated by Congress to provide state, county, and local law enforcement agencies with funds in the areas of education, research, and the purchase of equipment. The U.S. Supreme Court hands down court decisions that assure constitutional safeguards for individuals taken into custody by the police.

1970–today   The establishment of police community relations units increases dramatically. Police recruiting also crosses gender and racial lines. Court suits lead to affirmative action hiring and promotion policies. The increase in black population of the cities also gives this nation its first black chiefs, such as Lee Brown and Reuben M. Greenberg, and black security cabinet members. Telecommunication and data processing become an integral part of law enforcement. Training is established as the number one priority in most police agencies. Specialized services are developed, such as tactical units, team policing, and juvenile divisions. Standards are implemented, and a nationwide process of accreditation is initiated.

training and specialized skills demanded of the professional. Second, because police departments are characterized by a high degree of bureaucratization, they are more oriented toward the chain of command and the values of the peer group than toward the ideals of professionalism. Finally, the uncertainties of police work demand deviations from the universalistic and formalistic values embedded in professionalism.[7]

The Police Culture

The **police culture** helps the officer to deal with conflict with the management culture and the indifference and sometimes hostility of the public. One of the key functions of the police culture is to convey honor, which is too often denied to police officers by police administrators and the public.[8] As one patrol officer noted, "You take all the crap, you are not trusted, you are expected to behave like a robot and never make mistakes. . . ."[9]

Loyalty is another characteristic of the police culture. A patrol officer put it this way: "I'm for the guys in blue! Anyone criticizes a fellow copper, that's like criticizing someone in my family; we have to stick together."[10] The police culture demands unstinting loyalty to fellow officers; and officers, in turn, have an environment that provides a place to relieve real and imagined wrongs inflicted by the public, safety from punitive and nonsupportive supervisors and administrators, and the emotional support required to perform difficult tasks.[11]

The police officer is introduced to the police culture through a process of socialization; during this process, commitment to the working personality of the police and the informal code takes place.

Socialization into the Police Culture   James W. Sterling defines *socialization* as "a formal or informal learning process by which an individual becomes aware of and committed to behavioral norms which are seen as appropriate and right for specific role performance."[12]

The informal code in action. (*Source:* Jill Freedman/Archive Pictures, Inc.)

John Van Maanen studied the process of the recruit's initiation into a police organization and found that it occurred in four stages: choice, introduction, encounter, and metamorphosis (transformation).[13] The process begins when an individual decides to become a police officer. The second stage extends from the early days on the force to the time the rookie completes the academy training. As part of the academy experience, recruits are informed that the police share experiences different from those of most citizens.

During the encounter stage, rookies are informed by their training officers and later by peers that the police are expected to do society's "dirty work" and that the help they offer the community will go largely unappreciated. The daily experiences of rookies reinforce this "us–them" attitude, as they meet the public mainly "in their sorrow, their degradation, their evil, and their defeat."[14] Consequently, the officers' feelings of isolation from the community lead them to share their world with only a privileged few—their friends on the force and a limited number of outsiders.

In the final stage, or metamorphosis, the officer realizes that police work is not all fun and excitement, but in fact is rather routine and boring. Conflict with administrators, especially in large departments, often develops at this time. Totally disenchanted with the general public, the officer also may develop a general cynicism toward police work.[15]

The Police Working Personality   Jerome Skolnick lists three factors that contribute to the police "working personality": danger, authority, and efficiency.[16] The elements of danger and authority, both of which are conveyed by the academy and by the training officer, are especially important in understanding the police personality. The rookie is taught to sense danger and to be aware of potentially dangerous situations. This approach makes the police officer constantly suspicious of any situation, particularly one that appears to be out of the ordinary. According to Skolnick, "the element of danger isolates the policeman socially from the segment of the citizenry which he regards as symbolically dangerous and also from the conventional citizenry with whom he identifies."[17]

The police officer is unquestionably an authority figure. He or she has the power to detain, to question, to arrest, and to regulate the movements and liberties of citizens. Although Mary Jeanette C. Hageman contends that police are in reality less authoritarian than they are traditionally perceived,[18] Arthur Niederhoffer argues that a tendency toward authoritarianism develops during the day-by-day socialization of police officers. Yet Niederhoffer describes two groups within the police occupation that vary significantly in terms of authoritarianism. He regards the "old-timer" street cop as authoritarian and tough-minded, but he asserts that police officers who are part of the professional movement advocate education, public relations, nonaggressive policing, and adherence to strict legality in doing their jobs.[19]

Efficiency is another important aspect of the working personality of the police. Police departments commonly emphasize "activity," "batting averages," "quotas," and "collars" as yardsticks to measure performance on the job. Skolnick contends that the demand for efficiency requires the police to become craftsmen in order to meet the yardsticks for performance placed upon them by the department.[20]

Niederhoffer considers cynicism to be a fundamental characteristic of the working personality of the police. From his own police experiences and those of others, Niederhoffer found that cynicism originates during a police officer's initial training in the academy, continues to increase for about the first eight years, and then decreases slightly thereafter.[21] Algernon Black, in examining police cynicism, further notes:

> The police are exposed to the ultimate inhuman foolishness, human madness, human crookedness, and cruelty. There is not a behavior which men have thought of in their worst moments that the police officer has not faced . . . inevitably, it takes its toll in the loss of sensitivity and compassion and faith. . . . The result is a tough shield, a protective cynicism perhaps that is necessary to survival on the job.[22]

The Police Culture and the Informal System   The use of **informal rules**, especially among street officers, fills the gaps not covered by formal rules and provides the status and social satisfaction the formal system does not provide. Thus, the **informal system** and its norms arise because the formal system does not adequately take care of the needs of police officers. The violation of an informal rule often causes extreme peer reaction, which in some cases is far more damaging to the individual officer than any formal discipline (such as written warnings or suspensions). See Box 13.2 for examples of these informal rules.[23]

In summary, the conflict between the values of the police culture and the hierarchical control demanded by the values of police professionalism is the root of tensions and alienation within police departments. The key to understanding the exercise of discretion by police officers lies in the interaction between the values and beliefs of line officers and the goals, incentives, and pressures of the management culture.[24]

CRIME REDUCTION

Enforcement of the law, or crime reduction, is a difficult task for the police today. Research done over the past 20 years has indicated that there are several reasons why traditional police approaches are not working in reducing crime. First, as pointed out throughout this text, crime is part of American culture and requires societal, as well as individual, means of intervention. Second, many street crimes and, probably, most white-collar and organized crimes do not come to the attention of the police. Third, crime has become so varied and complicated in the twentieth century that it requires more effective forms of police services than are typically found in most departments. See Box 13.3 (page 390) for Jerome H. Skolnick and David H. Bayley's summary of the relevant research.

Community-oriented policing, the policing of repeat offenders, and the

BOX 13.2 **THE INFORMAL CODE**

"An officer must never let another officer be hurt or killed." This is probably the most important informal rule in police work. An officer should do everything possible, including risking personal injury, to assist another officer in trouble.

"Keep your sergeant happy." Even in the academy, recruits are likely to hear: "Fellas, don't mess around with your sergeant or you'll have a hard road to travel. If he or she gives you an order to do something you don't like, do it. If you don't, good luck."

"Don't push us too far." Officers, according to the code, establish work norms they consider to be fair. If they feel superiors are being unfair, they find ways indirectly to put pressure on supervisors.

"Cover your ass." Another informal rule is that if officers have serious doubts about how to handle a situation, they are to "cover their ass." The best way to do this is to call the sergeant or field commander.

"Be as threatening as it is wise to be." The officer must learn who can and cannot be threatened. To threaten important people is considered stupid.

"Keep your nose clean." If officers want to be promoted, the informal code advises, it is necessary to avoid drinking on duty, getting the department into a lawsuit because of inappropriate behavior, or placing another officer in danger because of "cooping" (sleeping on duty).

"Get to know your neighborhood." This rule means officers must get to know the boundaries of their sectors as well as the types of people within them; this information helps them avoid trouble with local citizens.

"Maintain the edge." The police officer must always stay in control. One way to do this is to keep citizens off balance by having the first and last words.

"Protect your own." Officers should not write tickets for law enforcement or quasi–law enforcement officers or for close family members.

"Show smarts." This tenet means officers should avoid "putting themselves on front street," in situations in which they can look bad. They also should make certain that citizens do not catch them doing anything improper.

"Stay with your own." Social contacts with civilians should be avoided because citizens do not understand police officers. Letting off steam, then, should be done with other officers. In addition, "choir

practice" (drinking after duty) should be done in bars frequented by police officers.

Source: These tenets were constructed from interviews conducted with police officers and are listed in Clemens Bartollas, Stuart J. Miller, and Paul B. Wice, *Participants in American Criminal Justice: The Promise and the Performance* (Englewood Cliffs, N.J.: Prentice-Hall, 1983), pp. 101–102.

practice of arresting spousal assaulters are three relatively new and promising approaches to crime reduction.

Community-Oriented Policing

In conducting studies of police departments in Denver, Colorado; Detroit, Michigan; Houston, Texas; Newark, New Jersey; Oakland, California; and Santa Ana, California, Skolnick and Bayley concluded that **community-oriented policing** is the wave of the future and represents the best hope that the police have for reducing crime.[25] The policy implications section of this chapter discusses four strategies they recommend to improve community-oriented policing.

Policing Repeat Offenders

The fact that a small proportion of criminals commits a disproportionately large number of crimes is a major issue in crime control policies and has led to a broad interest in programs that deal with career criminals. The programs currently used for repeat offenders rely on various combinations of reactive and proactive tactics. **Reactive tactics** include prioritized service of warrants against identified "career" criminals; notification of the prosecutor when an identified career criminal is arrested; and more active case supplementation through development of additional witnesses, evidence, or information about the other cases against the offender. **Proactive tactics** include the use of decoys, surveillance, buy-bust schemes, and phony fencing operations.[26]

The most comprehensive and perhaps the most effective strategy to date for **policing repeat offenders** is the Repeat Offender Project (ROR), a specialized unit set up in Washington, D.C. In their 1986 evaluation of this program, Susan E. Martin and Lawrence W. Sherman found that ROR substantially increased the likelihood of arrest for persons targeted. ROR arrestees had longer and more serious histories of prior arrests than a comparison sample of arrestees in other police units. The ROR arrestees were also more likely to be prosecuted and convicted on felony charges and more likely to be incarcerated. Martin and Sherman concluded that the creation of selective apprehension units provides a promising new strategy for major urban police departments.[27]

Arresting Spousal Assaulters

Police have long found **spousal assault** calls among the most problematic to handle. Officers typically attempt to restore some semblance of order and then leave.[28] However, in a study Richard Berk and Lawrence Sherman conducted in

BOX 13.3 **TRADITIONAL APPROACHES ARE NOT WORKING**

Specifically, this is what [previous research] has found out:

First, increasing the number of police does not necessarily reduce crime rates or raise the proportion of crimes solved. The same is true for budgetary expenditures on the police. . . .

Second, random motorized patrolling neither reduces crime nor improves chances of catching suspects. Moreover, it does not reassure citizens enough to affect their fear of crime, nor does it engender trust in the police. Regular patrols by police officers on foot, on the other hand, were shown to reduce citizens' fear of crime, although they have no demonstrable impact on the crime rate.

Third, two-person patrol cars are not more effective than one-person cars in reducing crime or catching criminals. Furthermore, injuries to police officers are not more likely to occur in one-person cars.

Fourth, saturation patrolling does reduce crime, but only temporarily, largely by displacing it to other areas.

Fifth, the kind of crime that terrifies Americans most—mugging, robbery, burglary, rape, homicide—is rarely encountered by police on patrol. . . .

Sixth, improving response time to emergency calls has no effect on the likelihood of catching criminals or even in satisfying involved citizens. One recent and very large study showed that the chances of making an arrest on the spot drop below 10 percent if even one minute elapses from the time the crime is committed. . . .

Seventh, crimes are not solved—in the sense of offenders arrested and prosecuted—through criminal investigations conducted by police departments. Generally, crimes are solved because offenders are immediately apprehended or someone identifies them specifically—a name, an address, a license plate number. If neither of those things happen, the studies show, the chances that any crime will be solved fall to less than one in ten.

Source: This material appears in Jerome H. Skolnick and David H. Bayley, *The New Blue Line* (New York: The Free Press, 1986), pp. 4–6. See Skolnick and Bayley for specific references to the studies mentioned in this box.

Minneapolis, they found that arresting spousal assailants resulted in the lowest rate of repeated incidents over the following six months. They concluded: "The arrest treatment is clearly an improvement over sending the suspect away, which produced two and a half times as many repeat incidents as arrest"; the low rate holds "regardless of the race, employment status, educational level, criminal history of the suspect, or how long the suspect was in jail when arrested."[29] In replicating this study in a California county, Richard Beck and Phyllis J. Newton found that arrests substantially reduce the number of new incidents of wife

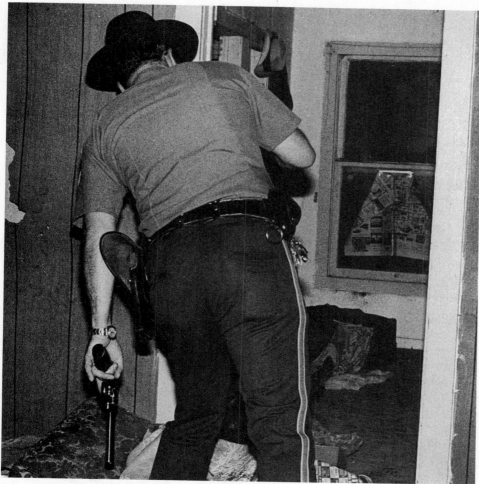

The danger of police work. (*Source:* Patrick Chauvel/Sygma.)

battery; the reductions are greatest for those whom the police would ordinarily be inclined to arrest.[30] These findings led police departments in Dallas, Denver, Houston, Minneapolis, New York, and Phoenix to use arrest more frequently in cases of spousal assault, and ten states have enacted laws making spouse abuse a separate criminal offense.[31]

POLICE DISCRETION

K. Davis refers to **police discretion** as existing "whenever the effective limits on [the officer's] power leave him free to make a choice among possible courses of action or inaction."[32] Discretion is an inescapable element of police work for two main reasons. Instead of telling a police officer exactly what to do, the law defines only the outer limits of discretion and what the police officer may not do.[33] Discretion is also an ever-present reality because of scarce resources. Administrators frequently lack sufficient resources to deploy specialized units and, therefore, the most important decisions often are made by the officers assigned to the streets.

The police have been charged with the misuse of discretion in infringing on the individual freedoms guaranteed by the Constitution. Failure to grant an individual's due process rights at the time of arrest can result in dismissal of the case by the courts. The public is shocked when citizens are informed by the media that the perpetrator of a rape or murder will go "scot-free" because police failed to grant the criminal his constitutional rights.

The abuse of discretion in corruption and the excessive use of force have also brought wide criticism on the police. Politicians do not want the media coverage that goes with evidence of abuse and excessive force by the local police. Nor do they want an outcry from the minority community concerning police brutality, particularly in cases involving the killing or maiming of teenage criminals in which officers claim self-defense.

Constitutional Protections and the Police

Police powers can be divided into two broad areas: investigation and arrest, and custodial interrogation.

Investigative and Arrest Powers   The investigative and arrest powers of the police include the right in certain situations to frisk, to search vehicles and property, to exercise seizure, to question, to detain, to restrain, and to use force. The Exclusionary Rule, which excludes any illegally seized evidence from use in a criminal trial, sets the standard for citizen protection against police misconduct and clarifies the investigative and arrest powers of the police. The Fourth Amendment defines the "right of the people to be secure in their persons, papers, and effects, against unreasonable searches and seizures."

In the landmark case *Mapp* v. *Ohio* (1961), the Supreme Court ruled "that all evidence obtained by searches and seizures in violation of the constitution is, by same authority, inadmissible in a state court."[34] Thus, the Court applied the same constitutional standards for searches and seizures to both the federal and state systems (see Box 13.4 for the main facts of this case).

A tightening of the **Exclusionary Rule** took place after Warren Burger became chief justice in 1969. Several Supreme Court decisions in the 1970s limited the use of the Exclusionary Rule. In *Brewer* v. *Williams* (1977), a divided Court narrowly held that the defendant's right to counsel under the Sixth Amendment had been violated, and his conviction for murder was overturned.[35] Williams was again tried and convicted. On appeal to the Supreme Court, Williams asked that the convictions be overturned because evidence introduced at the time of the second trial was derived from the finding of the dead girl's body. But the Court ruled that evidence found when Williams led police to the body was admissible, using the **"inevitable discovery exception"** to the Exclusionary Rule. The Court

BOX 13.4   **MAPP V. OHIO**

Cleveland police, acting on information that a suspect in a bombing incident was hiding in Darlee Mapp's residence, asked Mapp for permission to search. She consulted her attorney and then refused to grant permission for entry. The police left but soon returned, again seeking permission for admittance. The police forced entry when she failed to answer the door. As the police officers started to walk upstairs, they were confronted by Mapp, who demanded to see a search warrant. A paper that was not a search warrant was shown. Mapp grabbed the paper, and a search took place after officers retrieved the paper. During the search, police found "four little pamphlets, a couple of photographs, and a little pencil doodle—all of which were alleged to be pornographic." On the basis of the seized items, Mapp was convicted of knowingly having "in her possession and under her control certain lewd and lascivious books, pictures, and photographs."

Source: Mapp v. *Ohio,* 367 U.S. 643 (1961).

reasoned that since some two hundred persons were searching that area, the body would have inevitably been found (see Box 13.5 for the main facts of this case).[36]

In *New York* v. *Quarles* (1984), the Supreme Court announced the **"public safety exception"** to the Exclusionary Rule. Benjamin Quarles, a rape suspect, was arrested and handcuffed. He was questioned about the whereabouts of a gun the victim of the rape had indicated her attacker was carrying at the time of the assault. Quarles, who was not given his rights under the *Miranda* ruling, told police the location of the gun, which was later recovered. The Court ruled that the "overriding considerations of public safety justified the officer's failure to provide *Miranda* warnings before he asked questions devoted to locating the abandoned weapon."[37]

The Supreme Court then developed what is known as the "good faith exception" to the Exclusionary Rule. In *U.S.* v. *Leon* (1984), the search warrant was held by the trial court to have been issued without sufficient probable cause,[38] and in *Massachusetts* v. *Sheppard* (1984), the search warrant was held by the trial court to be deficient because it had not sufficiently identified the items to be seized.[39] On appeal, the Supreme Court ruled in both cases that the evidence seized would serve no valid purpose if excluded because the police had acted on good faith and had used what they believed to be valid search warrants.

In summary, the Warren Court's sweeping decisions in the 1960s on the excluding of evidence obtained without regard to constitutional rights have been partially attenuated by the Burger and Rehnquist courts in the 1970s and 1980s.

Search and seizure   The searching of persons, vehicles, and property are the three areas involved in **search and seizure**. Legal searches of persons include those authorized by search warrant, consent from the person to be searched,

BOX 13.5   *BREWER* V. *WILLIAMS*

> The case involved Robert Anthony Williams, charged in the state of
> Iowa with the Christmas Eve 1968 murder of a ten-year-old girl who had
> disappeared from a YMCA building in Des Moines. Williams was later
> arrested in Davenport, Iowa. Before Williams was transported from
> Davenport to Des Moines, his lawyer told police personnel not to ques-
> tion him on the trip. The police agreed, but during the trip a detective
> played on Williams's emotions and got him to talk.
>
> The detective told Williams that several inches of snow was pre-
> dicted that night and the snow would cover the body. He went on to say,
> "And since we will be going right past the area on the way into Des
> Moines, I feel that we could stop and locate the body, that the parents
> of this little girl should be entitled to a Christian burial for the little girl
> who was snatched away from them on Christmas Eve and murdered."
> This prompted Williams to lead the police to a culvert along a gravel
> road, where the body was found.
>
> Source: Brewer v. Williams, 430 U.S. 387 (1977).

search incident to a lawful arrest, and the stop-and-frisk of a suspect for the police
officer's protection.

The use of a search warrant, which is issued by a judicial officer when there
is probable cause that a crime has been committed, is the preferable means of
conducting the search of a person. A search may also be conducted with the
consent of the person, if consent is voluntary and not obtained under duress.
Police in most cases are permitted to search a person at the time of or immediately
after an arrest. Finally, the courts have given the police permission to stop, detain,
and subject a person to a "pat down" if they have reasonable suspicion that a
crime has just been, is being, or is about to be committed.

Terry v. *Ohio* is the landmark **stop-and-frisk** case. (Box 13.6 describes the
background of the case.[40])

The Supreme Court ruled that "the revolver seized from Terry was properly
admitted in evidence against him at the time he seized petitioner and searched
him for weapons." The Court also stated: "Officer McFadden had reasonable
grounds to believe that petitioner was armed and dangerous, and it was necessary
for the protection of himself and others to take swift measures to discover the true
facts and neutralize the threat of harm if it materialized."[41]

The most widely used legal means to search vehicles involve authorization
based on the search warrant, consent, incident to arrest, automobile exception,
plain view searches, and emergency searches. The **"Carroll doctrine"** and the
"plain view doctrine" are two guidelines provided by the Supreme Court for
vehicle searches.

In a 1925 case, *Carroll* v. *United States,* federal officers who believed that
contraband was being transported in an automobile had stopped the vehicle and

seized the illegal liquor. They then arrested George Carroll and another person. On appeal, the Court ruled that the seizure was justified and established two rules. First, in order to invoke the Carroll doctrine, police needed to have enough evidence of probable cause so that if time permitted, they could secure a search warrant. Second, in order to invoke the doctrine, urgent circumstances must exist that call for immediate action. In the case of a moving vehicle, the urgent circumstances would be the mobility of the vehicle.[42]

The plain view doctrine essentially means that objects in plain view of a police officer can be subject to seizure and may later be introduced in court as evidence. In *Harris* v. *United States* (1947), the Supreme Court ruled that anything a police officer sees in plain view when the officer has a right to be where he or she is and is not the product of a search is admissible as evidence.[43]

The legal means to search premises involve search warrant, consent, enter to arrest, incident to arrest, and urgent circumstances. The courts require the use of a search warrant for the search of premises more often than for any other type of search. The Supreme Court has been reluctant to relax the rules concerning search of premises because of the idea that "one's home is one's castle."

For example, police went to Ted Steven Chimel's home in Santa Ana, California with a warrant charging him with burglary. The police asked permission to look around, but Chimel objected. The police conducted a search, claiming that a search could be conducted based on the lawful arrest. The search took about an hour, and property was seized. Chimel was convicted, but on appeal to the U.S. Supreme Court, his conviction was reversed. The Court ruled that "the search here went far beyond the petitioner's person and the area from within which he might have obtained either a weapon or something that could have been

| BOX 13.7 | *MIRANDA V. ARIZONA* |

Ernesto Miranda was arrested on March 13, 1963, and taken to a local police station for questioning. He was suspected of having kidnapped and raped an 18-year-old woman. Miranda was placed in a lineup and was identified by the victim. He was then interrogated by the police for two hours, at which time he signed a written confession. Over Miranda's objections, the confession was admitted at the trial, and he was convicted of kidnapping and rape. He was given a 20- to 30-year sentence on each count.

The U.S. Supreme Court reversed Miranda's conviction, because the interrogation was defined as inherently coercive and because the procedures violated the constitutional rights of suspects as found in the Fourth, Fifth, Sixth, and Fourteenth amendments.

Source: Miranda v. Arizona, 384 U.S. (1966).

used as evidence against him."[44] As defined by this decision, the **"wing span search"** area is strictly limited to the area reachable by the suspect, and any such search must be made immediately after the arrest.

Custodial Interrogation   The protections against self-incrimination, the prompt arraignment rule, and the improper use of lineups limit the powers of the police once a person has been taken into custody.

The protections against a person's being compelled to be a witness against himself or herself are inherent in the Fifth Amendment. *Miranda* v. *Arizona* (1966) is the landmark case in self-incrimination (see Box 13.7).[45] In *Miranda*, the Court held that whenever a person who is about to be interrogated by the police "has been taken into custody or otherwise deprived of his freedom of action in any significant way," he or she must be given the following warnings:

1. That he/she has the right to remain silent, and that he/she may choose not to answer any questions;
2. That if the person does answer questions, these answers can be used as evidence against himself or herself;
3. That he/she has a right to consult with a lawyer before or during the questioning of the police; and
4. That if he/she cannot afford to hire a lawyer, one will be provided without costs.[46]

These warnings are to be given in such a way that the suspect clearly understands them. The *Miranda* decision also directed that police are to invoke the warnings when two elements are present: (1) custody—the suspect is not free to leave the area where he or she is being questioned; and (2) interrogation—The police plan to ask questions with the express purpose of soliciting an admission of wrongdoing. Thus, it is not necessary to give Miranda warnings to an arrested suspect unless the police plan to interrogate this person.

The **prompt arraignment rule**, as stated in *McNabb* v. *United States,* ordered that confessions obtained after unreasonable delay before arraignment could not be used as evidence in a federal court.[47] However, this rule was never accepted by state courts and eventually was modified at the federal government level, because it was generally agreed that misconduct by the police did not warrant dismissing such crucial evidence as a confession, especially when the suspect had committed a heinous crime.

The Supreme Court has usually permitted the use of police lineups prior to trial for the purpose of identification, but the police must use care to insure that the persons in the lineups are of similar size, race, age, and appearance.

Police Corruption

Herman Goldstein defines **corruption** as "the misuse of authority by a police officer in a manner designed to provide personal gain for the officer or for others."[48] There are various types of police corruption, from using political favoritism for personal gain, ignoring crime, and accepting gifts for favors to outright theft and extortion.[49]

The 1973 report of the Knapp Commission, the most famous of the commissions that have been formed over the years to investigate police corruption, portrayed a picture of widespread corruption throughout the New York City Police Department. The report indicated that both uniformed and plain clothes officers were:

- Keeping money and/or narcotics confiscated at the time of an arrest or a raid;
- Selling narcotics to addict-informants in exchange for stolen goods;
- Passing confiscated drugs to police informants for sale to addicts;
- Storing narcotics, needles, and other drug paraphernalia in police lockers;
- Accepting money or narcotics from suspected narcotics violators as payment for the disclosure of official information;
- Introducing potential customers to narcotics pushers;
- Revealing the identity of a government informant to narcotics criminals;
- Providing armed protection for narcotics dealers.[50]

New officers usually are not sufficiently familiar with their precincts and the people in them to do much more than observe what is going on. But even if they have the opportunity to make extra money or engage in any of the other expressions of corruption, either idealistic beliefs or the fear of getting caught usually causes them to turn it down. Eventually, however, new officers are led into corruption by corrupt fellow officers.

Lawrence W. Sherman has divided the process of becoming corrupt into five stages. The first stage consists of accepting "perks"—coffee, cigarettes, drinks, theater tickets, or meals from managers of bars and restaurants. These offers may come as early as the first few days on the job. The second stage involves taking free drinks or five or ten dollars in exchange for allowing a bar to stay open "another hour" after closing hours. The third stage includes such behaviors as taking twenty dollars handed over with a driver's license when a citizen is stopped for speeding or accepting merchandise from drivers who are unloading trucks in no parking zones. The fourth stage is when the police officer begins to accept payoffs from gamblers; accepting such an offer means the officer is solidly entrenched with other corrupt officers. Finally, the transition from clean to corrupt is completed when the officer accepts money obtained from the sale of narcotics. This is a major step because the money from drug use is regarded as "dirty," since drug use involves harm to others.[51]

The Knapp Commission made eight recommendations aimed at curtailing future corrupt activities. As one of its most effective recommendations, the Commission urged that within the New York City Police Department, there should be established a bureau whose sole responsibility would be the detection of illegal or criminal wrongdoing on the part of the police.[52] This concept of an internal affairs unit has been adopted in police departments across the nation.

In New York City, the internal affairs bureau at one point went so far as to begin what is called "integrity testing." An integrity test might follow this general course of events: an undercover member of the Internal Affairs Bureau, acting in the role of a citizen, supposedly finds a wallet or purse containing money. The item is given to a police officer, and the officer is watched to see if he or she will turn the item into the proper location with all the contents or will attempt to find the owner.

In summary, corruption emerges out of the values and norms of the social order, the criminal justice system, and the local police departments. Faced with corruption in the political community, in the local court system, and within the department, the police officer finds it easier to justify a moral shift in his or her own standards. Once minor forms of corruption become acceptable behavior, and an officer changes status from "clean" to "dirty," then more serious and illegal expressions of corruption become acceptable. Yet police corruption does considerable damage to the police, undermining the confidence of the public, destroying the respect for law, and harming police morale.

Police Brutality

The police are given the power to use reasonable force in order to control a situation or to make an arrest. Lawmakers and the courts do not expect the police to place their lives in jeopardy or to withstand physical abuse without defending themselves or using some degree of force in order to repel the attack or abuse. Drunks, wifebeaters, hostile juveniles, fleeing felons, persons stopped for speeding on highways, and individuals caught in criminal acts all may decide to resist arrest or attack police officers. Most such attacks are unprovoked and are the actions of individuals who are extremely angry, high on drugs, or too upset to know what they are doing. In other instances, citizens are hostile to anyone in authority or may regard being stopped by the police as a personal affront.

The complaints of intimidation, excessive force, and **police brutality** have been a burden for law enforcement since policing developed into its present form in the mid-nineteenth century. Most police officers are against excessive force. Veterans often warn rookies to watch out for "the guy with all the RAs [resisting arrests] and DCs [disorderly conducts]." A few "bad eggs" gain reputations for being unable to make "quiet" arrests and, in fact, these officers may actually incite citizens to violence. If citizens fail to respond aggressively, these officers may find some pretext for initiating violence themselves.

Excessive force, or police brutality, typically falls into three categories:

1. Situations in which the emotions of both the police and the participants are high, such as riots or mass demonstrations. Tempers flare on both sides, and police sometimes find it difficult to control their emotions.
2. Situations in which a police group or organization systematically and, as part of a regular pattern, inflicts excessive force, or brutality, on citizens. This is most common in areas where racial hostility between police and citizens exists (e.g., during the civil rights marches in the South).
3. Situations in which the police during their day-to-day activities infrequently use force beyond that which is necessary to control the situation or make an arrest. In most of these situations, the police officer has been subjected to verbal abuse and some physical resistance.

The inappropriate use of deadly force, especially in situations involving minorities, has become a controversial issue. James J. Fyfe, in examining nearly 3000 police shooting incidents in New York City from January 1971 to December 1975, found that a positive relationship, or correlation, existed between a neighborhood's violent arrest rate and the frequency of police shootings. He also discovered that both black and Hispanic officers were about twice as likely to kill civilians of their own race as white officers were. Furthermore, in examining the most hazardous precincts, where the highest incidents of police shootings took place, Fyfe again found no evidence of discriminatory employment of deadly force; black, Hispanic, and white officers assigned to these dangerous areas shot at civilians at about the same rate.[53]

The use of **deadly force** is traditionally considered to be justified only when a person can not be captured any other way and either the person has used or threatened to use deadly force in committing a felony, or the peace officer reasonably believes the person would use deadly force unless immediately apprehended. Criticism of this policy, however, has led many police departments to justify lethal force only as a matter of self-protection. But the definition of what constitutes a threat to a police officer's life remains ambiguous. Does it mean that an officer can not shoot until a suspect shoots first? Or does it mean that a suspect only needs to make a "furtive movement," a vague term indicating that the individual might use a weapon?[54]

Proponents of police professionalism claim that brutality has been significantly reduced in the past decade because of the fear of civil suits, the presence of internal affairs officers, the greater willingness of the police to suspend one of their own, the more extensive training provided to police officers, and the integration of minority officers into police departments. But the late 1970s brutality of Houston patrol officers, two shootings by the Los Angeles Police Department, and the death of a black businessman at the hands of the Miami police are grim reminders that excessive force is still a serious problem in American policing.[55] These incidents and others raise the question anew concerning the ability of bureaucratic structures to control street-level officers' use of discretion.

INTEGRATION OF WOMEN AND MINORITY GROUPS INTO POLICING

Police departments have recently received increased pressure to hire more women and minorities as sworn officers. Ellen Hochstedler and associates examined recruitment of women and minorities in 20 large police departments in the United States and found impressive increases between 1967 and 1981; the number of minority and women officers increased 330 percent during this period.[56] Yet women at present represent only 6 percent of the police officers in the United States, and numbers of minority officers are still below satisfactory levels in most departments.

Women as Police Officers

The 1964 Civil Rights Act and the 1972 Equal Employment Opportunity Commission (EEOC) made it illegal to discriminate in employment. Peter Horne offers one explanation for why women continue to make few inroads in policing:

> In policing, a man is "all right" until he proves himself unacceptable but a woman is unacceptable until she proves herself "all right." But then [when she proves herself] policemen say that she's the exception to the rule, and that most policewomen are not "all right."[57]

Researchers have demonstrated that women can handle the crime fighting, combat, rescue, peacekeeping, and social service duties of police work as well as men, regardless of differences in biological constitution and socialization patterns.[58] Male officers may question whether or not female officers can handle patrol as well as males, but several empirical evaluations of women police officers have found that women perform patrol in a similar and equally effective manner as do men.[59]

Susan E. Martin, in her study of women in policing, found that women are considered mere tokens by male police officers, and "they face performance pressures, isolation from co-workers, tests of loyalty, and entrapment in sterotypic roles."[60] The solution to this problem would appear to be the hiring of more women police officers, but increasing the percentage of women on a police force may not necessarily bring about a change in the attitudes of male officers or a greater acceptance of female officers. Martin is not optimistic about the future: "It is likely that the dynamics of tokenism will continue to operate, leaving policewomen with a number of difficult choices in the face of the expectation that they think like men, work like dogs, and act like ladies."[61]

Minority Police Officers

The race riots of the 1960s and the resulting civil rights laws of the federal government placed pressure on local police departments to hire more minority officers. Black male police officers have been better received than members of other minority groups and women, but acceptance has not come easily. The history of blacks in policing has been one of continued discriminatory treatment by both the white officers and the public, involving discrimination in appointments, entrance and promotion testing, assignments, evaluations, treatment by supervisors, and salaries.

Nicholas Alex, in studying the roles of black police officers in the New York City Police Department, found that white police officers were often accepting of the black officer at the work place but typically excluded him or her in social settings. He also found that the black officer faced the problem of "double marginality"—that is, not being accepted either by whites or by members of his or her own race.[62]

Atlanta police officer on duty in patrol car with computer terminal. (*Source:* Randy Taylor/ Sygma.)

More recently, Stephen Leinen, drawing on intensive interviews with 46 black New York City police officers, concluded that outright institutional discrimination has been eliminated in that department. Blacks not only are actively encouraged to join the department, but, once hired, they are assigned the same basic duties as whites, promoted through civil service without regard to race, often occupy command positions over whites, and have available avenues of grievance redress both within and outside the police agency. Blacks can also expect to be assigned to precincts on a more-or-less random basis. Consistent with Alex's earlier study, Leinen found that black officers, as a rule, do not fraternize with white officers after work.[63]

ANALYSIS

An examination of how the police contribute to order and disorder is helpful in understanding policing in American society.

Freedom and Order

One of the central issues facing the criminal justice system is that of achieving a balance between the rights of the individual and the collective well-being of the society. The delicate balancing of these two considerations becomes a pivotal matter in terms of the constitutional protections of suspects accused of a crime. The writers of the Constitution faced this balancing problem. They borrowed from the social philosophies that decried the lack of freedom in European societies in the eighteen century, and they sought to ensure that oppressive governments would never dominate the American colonies. Thus, the freedom of the individual citizen is a central theme of the Constitution, and its amendments.

The courts require the police to make lawful arrests of suspects and to provide them with their constitutionally guaranteed rights, but arresting criminals, especially those who commit property and narcotic offenses, is not an easy task. The challenge of arresting suspects lawfully is made more complicated by the ever-changing rules of the courts. The Warren Court used one interpretation of the rights of law-violating individuals, but decisions of the Burger Court have resulted in a retreat from the Exclusionary Rule, the erosion of *Miranda,* the expansion of stop-and-frisk, and omnibus decisions that seem more compatible with police needs and interests.

Some patrol officers do react to the pressure put on them to make "good busts" by using illegal means, such as committing perjury on the stand or falsifying evidence, but cynicism toward the legal process is a much more common response. Such cynicism has led to the development of what might be called a "gamester attitude." Thus, patrol officers frequently say that sometimes they "won" and sometimes they "lost" the case, and the ever-shifting rules of the game make it hard to predict what will happen. They also argue that whatever happens after an arrest has been made has little to do with justice.

Order and the Police

The mandate of the police is to provide a feeling of security and order in the community.[64] In dealing with any situation, the police officer must decide what, if anything, is out of order and then use the various tools at his or her disposal to reconstruct order.[65] The police maintain order in a variety of ways. They are repeatedly used as an "advance guard" of municipal reform, especially in the maintenance of public order and the protection of property.[66] The police also impose social discipline in the name of public propriety. They are responsible for establishing a fixed presence in the community for systematic surveillance. Therefore, they patrol with a suspicious eye for the wrong people in the wrong places at the wrong times.[67] Furthermore, the police serve as the guardians of the social order by mediating social conflict, by providing a variety of social and public safety services, by catching criminals, and by aiding victims of crime.

The task of the police is to show that they can "keep the lid on crime" and "keep the streets clean," but, at the same time, they must convince the public that they need more resources to fight crime. The police, then, must make the community believe that things will be more orderly if they are supplied with better cars, better-trained officers, better crime laboratories, and higher pay.[68]

However, while the police claim to be the guardians of order, they themselves do contribute to disorder. Mutual disrespect, especially with minorities, has long characterized relations between the police and the public. "Curbside justice" administered with a nightstick has sometimes been the police response to the public's lack of respect and compliance. The police organization was initially opposed to the acceptance of minorities and has remained resistant to the integration of women.

Departmental conflict has led to disorder within the police organization. For the past several decades, professionalism has been the "holy grail" of American policing, the preferred solution to corruption, to hostility toward and by the public, and to the rising crime rates. Yet the conflict between organizational elites and street officers has resulted in a continuous struggle over the prerogatives and autonomy of police officers and is at the root of tensions and alienation within police bureaucracies.[69]

Finally, the high stress of police work, especially in urban departments, has contributed to a wide range of problems among police officers, including family conflicts, divorce, physical illnesses, depression, alcoholism, cynicism, and job "burnout."

POLICY IMPLICATIONS

The improvement of community-based policing, the resolution of conflict between management and the police culture, and the reduction of stress on police officers are three important ways to improve police services.

Community-Oriented Policing

Skolnick and Bayley's *The New Blue Line* recommends four crime control strategies, all of which can be used to improve community-based policing.[70]

Police-Community Reciprocity   The concept of police-community reciprocity implies that police serve, learn from, and are accountable to the community. Such reciprocity is necessary if citizens are to become participants in crime prevention. Citizens must become motivated to work with and alongside police officers. Without the reciprocity of community feedback and participation, the police are in no position to locate community needs in an optimal fashion.

Areal Decentralization of Command   A reciprocal understanding of community crime prevention will usually be linked closely with a strategy of areal decentralization of command. Areal decentralization makes it easier for neighborhood groups or block organizations to work directly with the police. This sort of commitment, in turn, serves to heighten the community's trust in the police.

Reorientation of Patrol   Skolnick and Bayley recommend the return of foot patrol, because foot patrol is proactive, not reactive, and appears to generate the positive effects of increasing the chances of preventing crime before it occurs, of generating goodwill in the neighborhood, of reducing the public's fear of crime, and of raising officers' morale.

Civilianization   *Civilianization,* or the increased use of civilians, suggests a system of stratification that exists alongside of or in addition to the ranking structure found in police departments. A far-reaching and controversial innovation, **civilianization** offers a number of advantages. First, it is attractive in part because police officers have become so costly. Second, the wider use of civilians enables sworn officers to concentrate on rapid response to emergency situations; more officers are available to handle true emergencies. Finally, civilians drawn from within the inner-city communities that are being policed are likely to possess specialized linguistic skills and cultural understandings useful in dealing with other citizens of the community.

Resolution of Conflict Between Management and Police Cultures

The following strategies promise to reduce some of the conflict between management and police cultures:

1. Give more organizational decision-making responsibility to line officers, which should promote greater unity between the divergent management and street cultures.
2. Increase salaries, as well as upgrade the status and prestige of city and county police officers, to match the levels of state and federal police officers.
3. Lobby for federally funded programs that permit law enforcement of-

ficers to have their college tuition and expenses paid. At the same time, improve standards of police departments by raising the educational requirements of police work.

Reduction of Stress

The serious problem of stress requires that stress management techniques be emphasized in police departments across the nation. Some promising techniques currently being used to help police officers manage stress include the following:

- The development of technical skills to support officers in critical incident situations;
- Human relations training programs and encounter groups and sensitivity training;
- Police identity workshops, utilizing role playing, cognitive input, simulation of critical incidents, and personality management feedback;
- A team-building format that trains a unit of police officers to counter tension and stress and to provide group support;
- Crisis intervention training and interpersonal conflict management training;
- Participative management and team policing;
- Biofeedback techniques.[71]

SUMMARY

The police have immense power in American society. Day in and day out, they must deal with the most important political issues—justice, equality, and liberty. Police decisions have momentous consequences for the fate of groups and individuals. The danger is that the police will abuse the power entrusted to them, and the history of American policing shows that this has sometimes happened.

The issues discussed in this chapter—constitutional protections, corruption, and brutality—are critical in determining the quality of law enforcement in a free and democratic society. Police discretion cannot be eliminated because the police are a unique organization in the sense that lower-level members (patrol officers) have a very wide range of discretion, and, in fact, are the "gate keepers" of the criminal justice system. Illegal arrests, corruption, and brutality, which are more likely to be found in urban than in suburban and rural departments, are matters that professionalized departments are attempting to control.

The increased conflict between street-level officers and administrators has encouraged the development of the police culture. This culture is transmitted to young recruits through a variety of socializing experiences—at the academy, while riding with a training officer, and through daily interaction with peers. Loyalty to the police culture, or informal system, is reinforced because of the feeling that the formal system does not adequately provide for the needs of patrol officers. Moreover, the use of informal rules fills the gap not covered by formal rules and provides the status and acceptance the formal system does not provide.

The police must function within the prevailing moral consensus of society. Thus, they must operate within the bounds of prevailing values in order to maintain their moral authority. The improvement of the police ultimately depends upon greater coordination between the police and the community. This means that police officers must have more positive contact with those whom they serve. But, at the same time, grass-root community groups must take responsibility for dealing with their own problems to a much greater degree than has been the case in urban settings.

REFERENCES

Brown, Michael K. *Working the Street: Police Discretion and the Dilemmas of Reform.* New York: Russell Sage Foundation, 1981.

Ericson, Richard V. *Reproducing Order: A Study of Police Patrol Work.* Toronto: University of Toronto Press, 1982.

Fyfe, James J. "Geographic Correlates of Police Shootings: A Micro Analysis." *Journal of Research in Crime and Delinquency* (January 1980), pp. 108–109.

Goldstein, Herman. *Policing a Free Society.* Cambridge, Mass.: Ballinger, 1977.

Leinen, Stephen. *Black Police, White Society.* New York: New York University Press, 1984.

Martin, Susan. *Breaking and Entering: Policewomen on Patrol.* Berkeley, Calif.: University of California Press, 1980.

Niederhoffer, Arthur. *Behind the Shield: The Police in Urban Society.* Garden City, N.Y.: Doubleday, 1967.

Reuss-Ianni, Elizabeth. *Two Cultures of Policing: Street Cops and Management Cops.* New Brunswick, N.J.: Transaction Books, 1984.

Rubenstein, Jonathan. *City Police.* New York: Farrar, Straus, & Giroux, 1973.

Sherman, Lawrence W. "Becoming Bent: Moral Careers of Corrupt Policemen." In *Police Corruption: A Sociological Perspective,* edited by Lawrence W. Sherman. Garden City, N.Y.: Anchor Books, 1974: pp. 191–208.

Sherman, Lawrence W., and Berk, Richard A. "The Specific Deterrent Effects of Arrest for Domestic Assault." *American Sociological Review* 49 (1984), pp. 261–271.

Skolnick, Jerome H. *Justice Without Trial.* 2d ed. New York: Wiley, 1972.

———, and Bayley, David H. *The New Blue Line: Police Innovation in Six American Cities.* New York: Free Press, 1986.

Van Maanen, John. "Observation on the Making of Policemen." In *The Ambivalent Force: Perspective on the Police,* edited by Abraham S. Blumberg and Elaine Niederhoffer. 3rd ed. New York: Holt, Rinehart & Winston, 1985, pp. 91–102.

NOTES

1. Jerome H. Skolnick, *Justice Without Trial,* 2d ed. (New York: Wiley, 1979).
2. Richard V. Ericson, *Reproducing Order: A Study of Police Patrol Work* (Toronto: University of Toronto Press, 1982), p. 7.
3. Ibid.
4. For a discussion of the police and social disorder in the nineteenth century, see Samuel

Walker, *Popular Justice: A History of American Criminal Justice* (New York: Oxford University Press, 1980), pp. 56–59.

5. Herman Goldstein, *Policing a Free Society* (Cambridge, Mass.: Ballinger, 1977), p. 35.
6. Michael K. Brown, *Working the Street: Police Discretion and the Dilemmas of Reform* (New York: Russell Sage Foundation, 1981), pp. 39–40.
7. Ibid., pp. 41, 50.
8. Ibid., pp. 81–82.
9. Ibid.
10. Ibid., pp. 82–83.
11. Ibid., pp. 84–85.
12. James W. Sterling, *Changes in Role Concepts of Police Officers* (Gaithersburg, Md.: International Association of Chiefs of Police, 1977), pp. 8–9.
13. John Van Maanen, "Observation on the Making of Policemen," in *The Ambivalent Force: Perspective on the Police,* ed. Abraham S. Blumberg and Elaine Niederhoffer, 3d ed. (New York: Holt, Rinehart, & Winston, 1985), pp. 91–102.
14. Ruben G. Rumbart and Egon Bittner, "Changing Conceptions of the Police Role: A Sociological Review," in *Crime and Justice: An Annual Review of Research, Volume I,* ed. Norval Morris and Michael Torny (Chicago: University of Chicago Press, 1979), p. 254.
15. Van Maanen, "Observation on the Making of Policemen," pp. 91–102.
16. Skolnick, *Justice Without Trial,* p. 102.
17. Ibid., p. 103.
18. Mary Jeanette C. Hageman, "Who Joins the Force for What Reasons: An Argument for 'The New Breed,' " *Journal of Police Science and Administration* 7 (1979), pp. 6–7.
19. Arthur Niederhoffer, *Behind the Shield: The Police in Urban Society* (Garden City, N.Y.: Doubleday, 1967), pp. 131–132.
20. Skolnick, *Justice Without Trial,* pp. 169–199.
21. Niederhoffer, *Behind the Shield,* p. 104.
22. Algernon Black, *The People and the Police* (New York: McGraw-Hill, 1968), pp. 6–7.
23. For the informal code of police officers in the New York Police Department, see Elizabeth Reussi-Ianni, *Two Cultures of Policing: Street Cops and Management Cops* (New Brunswick, N.J.: Transaction Books, 1984), pp. 13–16.
24. Brown, *Working the Street,* pp. 31, 91.
25. Jerome H. Skolnick and David H. Bayley, *The New Blue Line: Police Innovations in Six American Cities* (New York: Free Press, 1986).
26. Susan E. Martin and Lawrence W. Sherman, "Selective Apprehension: A Police Strategy For Repeat Offenders," *Criminology* 24 (1986), pp. 155–173.
27. Ibid.
28. Lawrence W. Sherman and Richard A. Berk, "The Specific Deterrent Effects of Arrest for Domestic Assault," *American Sociological Review* 49 (1984), pp. 261–262.
29. Lawrence W. Sherman and Richard A. Berk, *The Minneapolis Domestic Violence Experiment* (Washington, D.C.: Police Foundation, 1984).
30. Richard A. Berk and Phyllis J. Newton, "Does Arrest Really Deter Wife Battery? An Effort to Replicate the Findings of the Minneapolis Spouse Abuse Experiment," *American Sociological Review* 50 (April 1985), pp. 253–262.
31. Joan Petersilia, *The Influence of Criminal Justice Research,* (Santa Monica, Calif.: Rand Corporation, June 1987), p. 22.
32. K. Davis, *Discretionary Justice* (Baton Rouge: Louisiana State University Press, 1969), p. 4.
33. Brown, *Working the Street,* pp. 4–5.

34. *Mapp* v. *Ohio,* 367 U.S. 643 (1961).
35. *Brewer* v. *Williams,* 430 U.S. 387 (1977).
36. *Nix* v. *Williams,* 8 LOB 133 (1984).
37. *New York* v. *Quarles,* 8 LOB 133 (1984).
38. *United States* v. *Leon,* 8 LOB 145 (1984).
39. *Massachusetts* v. *Sheppard,* 8 LOB 150 (1984).
40. *Terry* v. *Ohio,* 392 U.S. 1 (1968).
41. Ibid.
42. *Carroll* v. *United States,* 267 U.S. 132 (1925).
43. *Harris* v. *United States,* 390 U.S. 234 (1968).
44. *Chimel* v. *California,* 395 U.S. 752 (1969).
45. *Miranda* v. *Arizona,* 384 U.S. 436 (1966).
46. Ibid.
47. *McNabb* v. *United States,* 318 U.S. 332 (1943).
48. Goldstein, *Policing a Free Society,* pp. 93–94.
49. Patrick V. Murphy, "Corruptive Influences," *Local Government Police Management* (1982), p. 53.
50. Commission to Investigate Allegations of Police Corruption and the City's Anti-Corruption Procedures, *Report* (New York: Braziller, 1973), pp. 91–115.
51. Lawrence W. Sherman, "Becoming Bent: Moral Careers of Corrupt Policemen," in *Police Corruption: A Sociological Perspective,* ed. Sherman (Garden City, N.Y.: Anchor Books, 1974), pp. 191–208.
52. Murphy, "Corruptive Influences," pp. 60–65.
53. James J. Fyfe, "Geographic Correlates of Police Shootings: A Micro Analysis," *Journal of Research in Crime and Delinquency* (January 1980), pp. 108–109.
54. Brown, *Working the Street,* pp. 151–152.
55. On the violence in the Houston Police Department, see Tom Curtis, "Police in Houston Pictured as Brutal and Unchecked," *Washington Post,* 13 June 1977, Section A, p. 1; on the shootings in Los Angeles, see "Los Angeles County Attorney to Probe Slaying of Nude Man," *Los Angeles Times,* 13 August 1977, Section I, p. 1; for an account of Arthur McDuffie's death and the actions of the Miami police, see George Lardner, Jr., "McDuffie Death: It Seemed to Be Open-Shut Case," *Washington Post,* 21 May 1978, p. 1.
56. Ellen Hochstedler, Robert M. Regoli, and Eric D. Poole, "Changing the Guard in American Cities: A Current Empirical Assessment of Integration in Twenty Municipal Police Departments," *Criminal Justice Review* 9 (1984), pp. 8–14.
57. Peter Horne, *Women in Law Enforcement,* 2d ed. (Springfield, Ill.: Thomas, 1980), p. 209.
58. Jennifer Hunt, "Feminization and Cultural Change: The Introduction of Women into Policing" (Paper presented at the American Society of Criminology Annual Meeting, Toronto, Canada, November 1985).
59. Horne, *Women in Law Enforcement.*
60. Susan E. Martin, "*Police*women and Police*women:* Occupational Role Dilemmas and Choices of Female Officers," *Journal of Police Science and Administration* 7, no.3 (1979), pp. 314–323.
61. Ibid., p. 323.
62. Nicholas Alex, *Black in Blue* (New York: Appleton-Century-Crofts, 1969).
63. Stephen Leinen, *Black Police, White Society* (New York: New York University Press, 1984), p. 244.
64. Goldstein, *Policing a Free Society,* p. 35.

65. Ericson, *Reproducing Order,* p. 9.
66. George L. Kelling, "Acquiring a Taste for Order: The Community and the Police," *Crime and Delinquency* 33 (January 1987), pp. 90–102.
67. Ericson, *Reproducing Order,* pp. 8, 206–207.
68. Ibid., p. 8.
69. Brown, *Working the Street,* p. 60.
70. Skolnick and Bayley, *New Blue Line,* p. 4.
71. John Blackman, "Police Stress" in *Policing Society,* ed. W. Clinton Terry III (New York: Wiley, 1985), pp. 393–399.

CHAPTER **14**

The Courts

STRUCTURE OF THE CRIMINAL COURTS

The State Court System

Lower Courts

Courts of General Jurisdiction

State Appellate Courts

The Federal Court System

U.S. District Courts

U.S. Courts of Appeals

The U.S. Supreme Court

PRETRIAL PROCESSES

The Charging Decision

Pretrial Release

Pretrial Diversion

Plea Bargaining

CRIMINAL TRIAL

Steps in the Criminal Trial Process

Opening Statements

Evidence

Directed Verdict

Closing Argument

Judge's Instruction to the Jury

Verdict of the Jury

SENTENCING

Indeterminate or Determinate Sentencing

Sentencing Hearing

ANALYSIS

Order and Disorder

Structured Order Within the Courthouse

POLICY IMPLICATIONS

Plea Bargaining Reform

Sentencing Reform

SUMMARY

REFERENCES

NOTES

KEY TERMS

allocution

bail

Career Criminal Prosecution (CCP)
  programs

charging decision

circumstantial evidence

closing argument

courthouse work team

courts of general jurisdiction

directed evidence

directed verdict

expert testimony

federal courts

flat-time sentencing

judicial activism

jury

lower courts

mandatory sentencing

percentage bail programs

per curiam decision

plea bargaining

presumptive sentencing

pretrial diversion programs

pretrial release

preventive detention statutes

real evidence

release on recognizance
  (ROR)

sentencing

sentencing hearing

state appellate courts

state courts

supervised release

testimonial evidence

trial

U.S. Courts of Appeals

U.S. District Courts

U.S. Supreme Court

writ of certiorari

. . . the history of liberty has largely been the observance of procedural safeguards. . . . Safeguards must be provided against the dangers of the overzealous as well as the despotic.

—Justice Felix Frankfurter[1]

It is time for some honest talk about the problem of order in the United States. Let us always respect our courts and those who serve on them. But let us also recognize that some of our courts in their decisions have gone too far in weakening the peace forces against the criminal forces and we must act to restore the balance. . . .

—Richard M. Nixon[2]

The United States is governed by the rule of law. But the difference between the law of the statute books and the living law, or the law in action, can be understood only by viewing the court officials who apply the law. The law can be compared to the stage of a theater, for it provides boundaries for the actors. It is like the script of a play because it provides the parts, but it also differs from a script for the important reason that the dialogue is not predetermined. The law creates a decision-making apparatus and provides cues for justice actors to make their decisions. Yet the law still leaves ample opportunity for these officials to decide

---

BOX 14.1   **ORDER IN THE COURT**

> Despite the prevalence of dishonesty, I have learned that the American system of criminal justice generally produces fairly accurate results: few defendants who are innocent are convicted. Some who are guilty are, of course, acquitted. And a large number are never brought to trial. But that is part of a system that boasts "better ten guilty go free than even one innocent be wrongly convicted." The corruption lies not so much in the *results* of the justice system as in its *processes.*
>
> . . . The American criminal justice system is corrupt to its core: it depends on a pervasive dishonesty by its participants. It is unfair: it discriminates against the poor, the uneducated, the members of minority groups. But it is *not* grossly inaccurate: large numbers of innocent defendants do not populate our prisons. Nor can our system fairly be characterized as "repressive." There is more freedom to speak, write, organize, and advocate in America today than there is or has ever been in any country in the history of the world. . . . This does not mean that I believe there is *enough* justice here. There is not. But a comparison with other times and places lends perspective to our situation.
>
> Part of the reason why we are as free as we are, and why our criminal justice system retains a modicum of rough justice despite its corruption and unfairness, is our adversary process: the process by which every defendant may challenge the government. . . . Imagine a system where the guilty and the despised—or at least those so regarded by the powers that be—were not entitled to representation!
>
> *Source:* This material appears in Alan M. Dershowitz, *The Best Defense* (New York: Random House, 1982), pp. xviii–ix.

on the basis of discretion, judgment, reasoned opinion, or even prejudice. Court actors are assisted in the decision-making process by informal policies and norms that guide their actions. These policies and norms are usually developed by the **courthouse work team**.[3]

"Order in the court" is the way bailiffs usually announce the arrival of the judge. The question of how much order actually exists in the court is one of the more fascinating in the examination of the social control of crime. In Box 14.1, Alan M. Dershowitz examines the issue of order in the courts of this nation.

STRUCTURE OF THE CRIMINAL COURTS

The United States has developed a dual court system: one system of separate **state courts** that are charged to prosecute and try crimes defined by state legislatures, and another system of **federal courts** whose jurisdiction is restricted to the federal crimes defined by the acts of Congress, the Constitution, and other case law.

Table 14.1 FILINGS IN COURTS OF GENERAL AND LIMITED JURISDICTION BY CASE TYPE, CALENDAR YEAR 1983 OR FISCAL YEAR 1982–1983

State	Civil	Criminal	Juvenile	Total excluding traffic	Traffic	Total including traffic
Total	12,839,400	10,511,116	1,142,271	24,074,511	57,287,920	80,580,851[a]
Alabama	210,626	136,986	45,173	392,785	208,030	600,815
Alaska[b]	30,065	30,697	1,497	62,259	89,281	151,540
Arizona	151,293	290,080	8,489	449,862	943,181	1,393,043
Arkansas[d]	153,176	141,737	10,318	305,231	383,236	688,467
California[c]	1,637,247	961,769	100,656	2,699,672	15,219,611	17,919,283
Colorado	194,727	56,396	18,055	269,178	170,703	439,281
Connecticut	199,912	116,633	11,328	327,873	355,473	683,346
Delaware[c]	52,975	74,312	(e)	127,287	153,899	281,186
District of Columbia[d]	133,377	31,846	10,091	175,314	13,645	188,959
Florida	565,367	486,361	89,395	1,141,123	2,876,747	4,017,870
Georgia[c,f]	322,765	383,157	32,350	738,272	178,173	916,445
Hawaii[c]	50,902	30,687	9,006	90,595	900,741	991,336
Idaho	54,209	40,965	6,291	101,465	199,894	301,359
Illinois[c]	590,790	640,239	27,127	1,258,156	6,643,531	7,901,687
Iowa[c]	143,007	23,925	6,469	173,401	653,579	826,980
Kansas[c]	115,426	23,371	10,455	149,252	267,988	417,240
Kentucky	183,970	221,832	35,182	440,984	265,434	706,418
Louisiana[c,f]	256,660	471,528	50,489	778,677	438,326	1,217,003
Maine	58,563	37,128	3,240	98,931	146,214	245,145
Maryland[c]	610,718	159,508	33,804	804,030	723,737	1,527,767
Massachusetts[h]	461,922	235,675	43,105	740,702	326,591	1,067,293
Michigan	509,818	272,456	25,036	807,310	1,855,823	2,663,133
Minnesota[b,c]	236,933	130,203	33,582	400,718	1,483,886	1,884,604
Missouri[b,d]	208,304	79,186	20,451	307,941	371,719	679,660
Montana	25,072	2,933	1,111	29,116	—	—
Nebraska[c,f]	75,551	171,698	4,652	251,901	157,541	409,442
New Hampshire	84,959	79,487	7,131	171,577	194,965	366,542
New Jersey[c]	575,962	462,191	102,481	1,140,634	4,595,758	5,736,392
New Mexico[c]	72,390	21,484	5,422	99,296	252,615	351,911
New York[c]	1,217,035	717,907	(i)	1,934,942	452,414	2,387,356
North Carolina[j]	401,457	472,104	21,442	895,003	728,517	1,623,520
North Dakota	29,979	19,236	1,463	50,678	125,454	176,132
Oklahoma	223,289	67,890	—	—	243,263	—
Oregon	124,920	143,374	12,326	280,620	546,885	827,505
Pennsylvania[b,k,l,m]	403,641	578,500	51,108	1,033,249	3,674,054	4,707,303
Rhode Island[f]	42,601	42,967	6,282	91,850	—	—

South Carolina[f,g]	104,444	36,646	8,795	149,885	—	—
South Dakota[b,g]	38,621	16,322	1,257	56,200	122,359	178,559
Tennessee[b]	99,437	40,116	41,725	181,278	—	
Texas[c]	665,175	1,480,519	11,978	2,157,672	7,256,865	9,414,537
Utah[c]	104,136	103,956	34,843	242,935	835,205	1,078,140
Vermont[b,c]	28,046	19,749	1,600	49,395	100,878	150,273
Virginia[c,n]	732,290	445,898	128,567	1,306,755	1,152,699	2,459,454
Washington[c]	204,677	160,939	21,074	386,690	1,546,950	1,933,640
West Virginia[c]	126,981	101,050	8,148	236,179	129,718	365,897
Wisconsin[o]	293,913	154,448	39,277	487,638	216,750	704,388
Wyoming	32,072	95,025		85,588		

Note: These figures represent virtually all cases filed in general jurisdiction courts and between 70 and 80 percent of cases filed in limited jurisdiction courts for those states reporting. The following courts reported no data: **Alabama** (Probate Court, Municipal Court), **Arkansas** (Justice of the Peace Court), **Georgia** (Municipal Courts of Savannah and Columbus, Civil Court, Small Claims Court, Justice of the Peace Courts, County Recorder's Courts, Municipal Courts—includes Mayor's, Recorder's, Police, and City Council Courts), **Kansas** (Municipal Court), **Louisiana** (Justice of the Peace Court, Mayor's Court), **Maine** (Probate Court, Municipal Court), **Maryland** (Orphan's Court), **Montana** (Justice of the Peace Court, City Court, Municipal Court), **Nebraska** (Workmen's Compensation Court), **New Mexico** (Municipal Court, Probate Court), **New York** (Town and Village Justice Court), **Rhode Island** (Municipal Court, Probate Court), **Tennessee** (General Sessions Court, Municipal Court, Trial Justice Court), **West Virginia** (Municipal Court, Justice of the Peace Court, District Court), and **Wisconsin** (54 of the 211 Municipal Courts reported no data).

—Data not reported.

[a] Total excludes those states that did not report filings for all categories.

[b] Criminal caseload includes driving while intoxicated (DWI) cases.

[c] Traffic caseload includes parking cases. In Virginia, however, only contested parking cases are included.

[d] Juvenile caseload includes paternity cases in Arkansas, adoption cases in Missouri, and 5,956 neglect cases in the District of Columbia.

[e] Criminal caseload in Delaware includes all juvenile cases and traffic cases in the Court of Common Pleas.

[f] Criminal caseload includes some general jurisdiction court traffic cases.

[g] Traffic caseload in South Dakota includes minor nontraffic cases. Traffic case totals from magistrates and municipal courts in South Carolina are unavailable, but are estimated to be at 600,000.

[h] Does not include 235,254 decriminalized motor vehicle complaints.

[i] Civil caseload in New York includes juvenile cases. In addition to the civil caseload reported here, 16,344 filings were reported for the mandatory arbitration program for cases involving damages of $6,000 or less, and 1,879 filings for the Small Claims Assessment Review Program for appeals of real property assessments.

[j] Number of juvenile hearings in North Carolina was used to represent the number of filings.

[k] The data reported were recently submitted to the Administrative Office of Pennsylvania Courts by the separate courts of Pennsylvania. Consequently, the Administrative Office cannot confirm, at this time, the accuracy of the data.

[l] Tort figures are 97 percent complete.

[m] Felony figures are 98 percent complete.

[n] Juvenile caseload in Virginia includes juvenile traffic cases.

[o] Includes only contested Circuit Court traffic cases.

Source: Bureau of Justice Statistics, *Case Filings in State Courts* (Washington, D.C.: U.S. Department of Justice, 1984), p. 2.

The State Court System

There are 51 separate court systems because each state is a sovereign government. For 1983, 46 states and the District of Columbia reported more than 80 million cases filed in state courts of general and limited jurisdiction (see Table 14.1).[4] The variation among the states in terms of court organization and personnel makes the state court system the least coordinated component of the criminal justice process. This extensive variation makes it impossible to identify the different types of state courts by their names alone. However, by describing the court's jurisdiction—which involves the court's legal authority to preside over, handle, and take action in specific cases—it is possible to identify three levels of state courts:

1. The courts of limited jurisdiction, which consist of lower, inferior, municipal, district, misdemeanor, police, justice of the peace, or the courts of first instance;
2. The courts of general jurisdiction, which are the trial or felony courts; and
3. The courts of appellate jurisdiction, whose task it is to review the decisions of lower courts.

Lower Courts   The **lower courts** bear little resemblance to trial or appellate courts. Their jurisdiction usually encompasses petty offenses, serious misdemeanors, lesser felonies, and, in some states, felonies punishable by five years imprisonment or more. These courts play an important role in major felony cases by setting bail and determining whether adequate probable cause exists to try a defendant.

The argument can be made that lower courts, along with the police, play the most important role in creating citizen impressions of the criminal justice system. Several million persons are drawn into contact with these courts each year as defendants, complainants, or witnesses. In fact, about 90 to 95 percent of all cases are handled in the lower courts.[5]

In exercising their extensive responsibilities, the lower court judges are relatively unaccountable to legal authority. Job security is no problem, as these positions are frequently attained through political appointments. The judge may feel free to draw on extralegal criteria, and the actual decision-making process of the lower court often is a mere shadow of the adversarial procedure of reasoned adjudication. Although the U.S. Supreme Court's ruling in *Argersinger* v. *Hamlin* (1972) held that those who are unable to afford counsel in lower courts and are charged with any type of criminal offenses that might result in a jail term have a right to appointed counsel,[6] the disposition of most cases continues to follow the same well-developed routines. Guilty pleas predominate and are swiftly dealt with; the right of counsel is slighted or discouraged. Defendants also are often persuaded into giving up their rights to trial, appeal, discovery, or confrontation of witnesses; sentencing is determined more by rough rules of thumb than by an orderly exploration of individual cases.[7]

In sum, lower courts have overwhelming case loads, and the means by which defendants are rapidly processed through this court system has been compared to an assembly line.[8] Adversarial procedures are too cumbersome and

---

BOX 14.2   ## THE SETTING OF THE LOWER COURTS

Lower criminal courts are a world apart. They bear little resemblance either to the popular image of trial courts or to actual practices of higher trial courts, which handle far fewer cases. In the lower courts trials are rare events, and even protracted plea bargaining is an exception. Jammed every morning with a new mass of arrestees who have been picked up the night before, lower courts rapidly process what the police consider "routine" problems—barroom brawls, neighborhood squabbles, domestic disputes, welfare cheating, shoplifting, drug possession, and prostitution—not "real" crimes. Those courts are chaotic and confusing; officials communicate in a verbal shorthand wholly unintelligible to accused and accuser alike, and they seem to make arbitrary decisions, sending one person to jail and freeing the next. But for the most part they are lenient; they sentence few people to jail and impose few large fines. Their facilities are terrible. Courtrooms are crowded, chambers are dingy, and libraries are virtually nonexistent. Even the newer courtrooms age quickly, worn down by hard use and constant abuse.

Source: This material appears in Malcolm M. Feeley, *The Process Is the Punishment: Handling Cases in a Lower Criminal Court* (New York: Russell Sage Foundation, 1979), pp. 3–4.

time-consuming for these overcrowded courtrooms, where defendants are sometimes processed en masse. According to Malcolm M. Feeley's study of a lower court in New Haven, Connecticut, lower courts function the way they do because officials in these courts realize that the real punishment is the pretrial cost rather than any penalties that may be meted out. He adds that "whereas rapid and perfunctory practices foster error and caprice, they do reduce pretrial costs and in the aggregate may render rough justice."[9] However, John P. Ryan's study of the Columbus (Ohio) Municipal Court found that this lower court was much more severe in the sanctions imposed upon convicted defendants than the New Haven court. With the Columbus court, the outcome, as well as the process, was the punishment.[10]

Courts of General Jurisdiction   Of the approximately 3656 courts of general jurisdiction, about 90 percent are state administered, while the remainder are controlled by local counties or municipalites.[11] These felony courts hear cases where defendants may be sentenced to long prison terms or even receive the death penalty, as well as civil suits that usually involve more than $1000.

These courts are usually located at the county seat; in some states several counties share a single court. Judges of these courts are always lawyers, and they generally remain on the bench for relatively long terms. Nearly all jury trials are heard in these courts, but 90 to 95 percent of the cases are heard by the judge alone.

Most courtrooms seem full of history. An elevated judge's bench dominates the strictly ordered room, flanked by a flag and seal, the ultimate symbols of governmental authority. The jury box, counsel table, and witness stand represent the specialized activities and organizations that have evolved over the years. The open area between the bench, counsel table, and the jury box is available for movement but is usually avoided, like a magic circle reserved for special ceremonies. The bar cutting across the middle of the room is perhaps the most striking furnishing; it serves the important function of separating all the official participants from the mere spectators—the public for whom the justice is to be done.[12]

Describing state courts of general jurisdiction is difficult because no two states possess identical court structures and the jurisdictions of lower and higher trial courts frequently overlap. But the majority of trial courts have a certain number of characteristics in common. First, they normally have an overload of cases. Like the lower courts, trial courts must find ways of circumventing the judicial process to deal with their heavy case loads. Second, guilty pleas are used in the vast majority of cases in these courts. Third, the process of court proceedings is often shaped by the social network of three legal actors—the judge, the prosecutor, and the defense attorney—and the court actors have developed a number of rules to expedite the court process (see Box 14.3).[13] Fourth, lengthy delays generally characterize the proceedings in these courts.[14]

However, a number of studies have found that the untidy court process nevertheless usually produces results that are surprisingly rational and just. Charles E. Silberman, in his five-year study of the criminal justice process, came to the conclusion that "prosecutors and judges generally use their discretion . . . to prosecute, convict, and punish 'real criminals,' " while at the same time showing "appropriate leniency to those whose crimes are not serious, or who seem to pose no real danger to the community."[15] Stuart A. Scheingold adds that:

> . . . it seems that sentencing practices are in no sense of the term irrational— that is, without rhyme nor reason and disparate almost by definition. Sentences are, instead, based on reasoned decisions rooted in understandings of right and wrong that are widely shared by criminal court professionals working in their respective jurisdictions. And these understandings become rather like unwritten rules for the criminal courts.[16]

State Appellate Courts   The state supreme court, also known as the court of appeals, supreme judicial court, supreme court of appeals, or court of last resort, represents the final decision point within state courts. The main task of these approximately two hundred state-administered courts is to hear appeals from lower state courts. Thirty-six states have established intermediate appellate courts, whose decisions are usually reviewable by the state supreme, or **appellate, court**. In those states with intermediate appellate courts, most appeals go to the intermediate courts.

Studies of appellate case loads in the states for which data are available show a steady increase up until the early 1930s, followed by a rapid drop during the remaining years of the Depression and World War II. By the late 1940s, appellate case loads were at less than half their previous high, but after several years of gradual growth, case loads began to increase rapidly in the mid-1960s.

BOX 14.3   **RULES IN TRIAL COURTS**

In the process of litigating these cases, writing this book, and teaching my classes, I have discerned a series of "rules" that seem—in practice—to govern the justice game in America today. Most of the participants in the criminal justice system understand them. Although these rules never appear in print, they seem to control the realities of the process. Like all rules, they are necessarily stated in oversimplified terms. But they tell an important part of how the system operates in practice. Here are some of the key rules of the justice game:

Rule I: Almost all criminal defendants are, in fact, guilty.

Rule II: All criminal defense lawyers, prosecutors, and judges understand and believe Rule I.

Rule III: It is easier to convict guilty defendants by violating the Constitution than by complying with it, and in some cases it is impossible to convict guilty defendants without violating the Constitution.

Rule IV: Almost all police lie about whether they violated the Constitution in order to convict guilty defendants.

Rule V: All prosecutors, judges, and defense attorneys are aware of Rule IV.

Rule VI: Many prosecutors implicitly encourage police to lie about whether they violated the Constitution in order to convict guilty defendants.

Rule VII: All judges are aware of Rule VI.

Rule VIII: Most trial judges pretend to believe police officers who they know are lying.

Rule IX: All appellate judges are aware of Rule VIII, yet many pretend to believe the trial judges who pretend to believe the lying police officers.

Rule X: Most judges disbelieve defendants about whether their constitutional rights have been violated, even if they are telling the truth.

Rule XI: Most judges and prosecutors would not knowingly convict a defendant who they believe to be innocent of the crime charged (or a closely related crime).

Rule XII: Rule XI does not apply to members of organized crime, drug dealers, career criminals, or potential informers.

Rule XIII: Nobody really wants justice.

Source: This material appears in Alan M. Dershowitz, *The Best Defense* (New York: Random House, 1982), pp. xxi–xxii.

Supreme Court justices pose in the courtroom of the Supreme Court of Texas in Austin. (*Source:* Bob Daemmrich.)

This growth has continued to the present; indeed, the case loads of state appellate courts have grown faster than the growing work loads of most other components of the justice system throughout the past decade.[17]

The primary responsibility of the state supreme court is to review the procedures used in appealed cases to establish whether or not an error was made by the lower courts. Judicial error includes such acts as admitting into evidence illegally seized materials, charging a jury improperly, permitting a prosecutor to ask witnesses improper questions, and showing prejudice toward the defendant. The state supreme courts usually cling more closely to established legal tradition and tend to be less innovative than federal appeals courts and the U.S. Supreme Court. The majority of judges in state supreme courts regard themselves as law interpreters rather than law makers.[18]

The Federal Court System

The federal government also has established a three-tiered court system: the U.S. District Courts, the U.S. Courts of Appeals, and the U.S. Supreme Court.

U.S. District Courts   Federal trial courts, or **U.S. District Courts**, are more simply organized than state courts. Ninety-two federal district courts exist, and each state has at least one. District courts usually have several judges, each presiding over his or her own branch of the court.

Criminal matters involving the violation of a federal law are brought to these courts. Among such violations are counterfeiting, taking a stolen car across state boundaries, robbing a bank, dealing in illegal narcotics, engaging in subversive activity or draft evasion, and being involved in organized crime. Civil matters brought to these courts include large suits involving the citizens of two states and complicated antitrust complaints filed by the federal government. Criminal cases are more likely to involve juries than are civil cases.

Federal district courts have ruled on some of the most important decisions regarding prisoners' rights. In fact, because of the failure of state courts to rule on these issues, the federal district courts have been flooded with petitions from state prisoners.[19] Federal district courts have also become involved in some of the most sensational cases of the twentieth century. The Watergate trials of the 1970s, as well as the plea bargaining of former Vice President Spiro Agnew, brought increased publicity—and criticism—to the federal courts. Their handling of the political trials of the late 1960s and early 1970s (the Chicago Seven, Dr. Benjamin Spock, Daniel Ellsberg, and the Berrigan brothers) resulted in more criticism directed at federal trial courts.[20]

U.S. Courts of Appeals   The 11 federal **courts of appeals** hear all appeals from federal district courts as well as the decisions of specified administrative and regulatory agencies. In addition, they occasionally exercise original jurisdiction over a case. These courts must also deal with the problem of case overload, as the work loads of these courts have quadrupled in the past two decades.[21]

The largest federal court of appeals has 15 judges and the smallest has 3. Judges meet in groups of 3 to hear cases, as all appeals are heard by panels of judges. There are no juries in appellate proceedings. Litigants generally have no way of knowing which judges will hear their cases; the chief judge of the court routinely changes the composition of the panels. Justices work from the briefs, the records of the trial, and the oral arguments presented before the court. Each side is allotted a certain period of time to argue the case before the justices. However, appellate justices have long complained about the quality of oral arguments, and they tend to depend less and less on them.[22]

The federal courts of appeals have 11 intermediate appellate courts. Appeals normally must be directed to these courts before being taken to the federal courts of appeals. In most instances, the court of appeals decision is final. If the court affirms the trial court decision, the trial court is ordered to execute it. If it reverses the trial court's decision, a new trial must be held. A few cases are appealed, or carried, to the U.S. Supreme Court.[23]

The U.S. Supreme Court   The final court of appeals is the **U.S. Supreme Court**. Cases reach this court through a variety of routes: from federal courts of appeals, from the special three-judge federal courts, from petition by paupers (generally state and federal prisoners), and from a small number of cases involving disputes between states.[24]

Certiorari and appeal are the most important means by which the Supreme Court grants a review. A **writ of certiorari** requires a favorable vote by four justices to order a lower court to send up the records of a case. The Supreme Court has total discretionary authority to grant a writ of certiorari, and it does not need to justify its refusal to grant this writ; only about 5 percent of those cases in the certiorari jurisdiction are accepted. Although the Court was originally meant to take all cases in the appeals category, the Court has made the review of appeals cases discretionary by dismissing those that lack a "substantial federal question." About one-half of those cases falling in the appeals category are accepted.[25]

Each request for a hearing goes to the Chief Justice. The other eight justices or their law clerks then examine the petition. A conference is held, and a vote is taken. When four justices vote in favor of review, the case is docketed; if fewer than four support the petition, the case is rejected and the decision of the lower court stands.

The attorneys of a case accepted for review have the opportunity to submit whatever additional briefs and materials they desire. It is also possible for interest groups who have received permission of the litigants and the Court to file what are called *amicus* briefs. Most cases are decided without oral review. The justices confer on the cases and decide with a brief opinion called a *per curiam* **decision**; these decisions merely state the decision of the Court and cite other cases that supplied some basis for the Court's action.[26]

Cases scheduled for oral argument are handled very differently. The Court allows each side to speak for a specified period of time, generally an hour, during which time each attorney is expected to emphasize what he or she believes is relevant to the case. He or she must also be prepared to answer whatever questions one or more of the justices may ask. Following oral arguments, the Court reserves its decision until it goes into conference to discuss the cases that have been argued. Only the chief justice and the eight associate justices may attend the conferences at which the justices decide how to rule on the argued cases and which new cases to hear.[27]

Throughout most of the nineteenth century, the Supreme Court generally confined its role to keeping the activities of the federal government within clearly defined constitutional boundaries. But during the middle of the twentieth century, the Warren Court changed that role to one of **"judicial activism,"** whereby justices actually set policy according to their own beliefs. The greatest contribution of the Warren Court was its philosophical advancement of a broad-based equalitarianism.[28] Glendon Schubert, a widely respected authority on the Supreme Court, has noted:

> In relation to its predecessors, the Warren Court was the most activist court not only in America, but with a high degree of probability, also in world history, in regard alike to the number and the diversity of the civil libertarian causes that it sponsored, and the degree of favorable support that it gave to such causes.[29]

Conservatives in the 1960s reacted strongly to the decisions of the Warren Court, and the Court's posture became a major issue in the 1968 presidential campaign. Candidate Richard Nixon stated that he wanted judges who would be "strict constructionists" of the Constitution and who would not encroach on areas belonging to Congress and the president. After his nomination, Nixon added, "I think some of our judges have gone too far in assuming for themselves a mandate which is not there, and that is, to put their social and economic ideas into their decisions.[30]

President Richard Nixon had four of his nominees confirmed by the Senate and appointed to the Supreme Court. Nixon first had nominated and received confirmation of Warren Earl Burger as Chief Justice. Then, after two of Nixon's nominees failed to receive confirmation, Harry Blackmun was nominated and unanimously confirmed by the Senate. The president later said, in nominating Lewis Powell and William Rehnquist, that the type of judge he wanted was a judicial conservative who would "not twist or bend the Constitution in order to perpetuate his personal, political, and social values.[31]

However, conservatives in the 1970s still were not happy with the decisions of the Burger Court. David Forte, a Cleveland State University law professor, stated, "The Burger Court is becoming as activist as was the Court under Chief Justice Earl Warren. It is taking the view that it will decide what is good for everybody else."[32] Terry Eastland, a special assistant to the U.S. Attorney General, added:

Not only has the Burger Court failed to overturn, or even to modify substantially, the principal decisions of the Warren Court. It has also compiled a record of judicial activism that rivals its predecessor. Specifically, it is the Burger Court, not the Warren Court, that has approved busing as a remedy for segregation, announced a woman's right to abortion, extended procedural due process to public-school children charged with misbehavior, and effectively rewritten the Civil Rights Act of 1964.[33]

But in the 1980s, liberals have become concerned about the increasingly conservative decisions of the Burger Court. The confirmations of Justice Sandra Day O'Connor—the first female justice of the Supreme Court—of Chief Justice William Rehnquist, of Justice Antonin Scalia, and of Justice Anthony Kennedy may weight the Court firmly in a conservative position. The area of criminal procedure safeguards is one in which the decisions of the current Supreme Court are likely to be much more conservative than the decisions of the Burger Court.

In summary, although the U.S. Supreme Court is the most orderly court in the United States and its rulings are designed to be faithful to the due process protections of the Constitution, the influence of politics does create untidiness in this high court. Presidents nominate judges with particular political persuasions, and, once confirmed by the Senate, justices do usually "stick to the party line" in their decision making.

PRETRIAL PROCESSES

The prosecutor is generally responsible for making or recommending four major decisions during the legal processes that take place prior to trial: whether or not a defendant will be charged and with what offenses; whether a defendant will receive pretrial release or detention; whether or not a defendant will receive pretrial diversion; and whether a defendant's case will be plea bargained or go to trial.

The Charging Decision

The first pretrial procedure is the formal charging of the arrested person with a crime. Although state statutes generally provide no specific guidelines on how the **charging decision** should be handled or who is responsible for making it, local courts usually adopt procedures that allow some criminal justice actors more influence than others. Clearly, whoever controls the charging decision is the gatekeeper of the criminal courts.[34]

The prosecutor dominates in most courtrooms. David Neubauer's study of the court system in Prairie City, Illinois, revealed that prosecutors, when presented with a case, would ask, "Is the case prosecutable?" But the notion of a prosecutable case required more than probable cause, the normal standard for arrest; it required that the case be sufficient for a conviction at a jury trial. The state attorney's office in Prairie City, as well as those in most other jurisdictions, saw no advantage in filing on a legally weak case that might survive a preliminary hearing but would lose at trial.[35]

As long as they can secure a conviction, prosecutors generally want to be fair in applying the criminal law. Although prosecutors do presume the guilt of defendants, they typically try to balance the presumption of guilt with what W. Boyd Littrell calls the "operational morality of fairness."[36] Littrell found that prosecutors usually tried to be fair to defendants and not overcharge them.[37] But there are certainly exceptions to this general rule. For example, Jerome Skolnick found in his study of West Coast jurisdictions that the police frequently were able to pressure prosecutors into overcharging defendants.[38] The prosecution of career criminals represents another exception to this general rule of fairness (see Box 14.4).

Pretrial Release

Pretrial release is another important decision made at the pretrial stage because those who receive it are spared the weeks or months of waiting in jails or pretrial detention centers. On June 30, 1985, an estimated 256,615 inmates were held in local jails throughout the nation. About half the adult inmates were unconvicted; that is, they were on trial or awaiting arraignment or trial. During the fiscal year ending June 30, 1985, an estimated 16.6 million were admitted and released from local jails, about half of whom were unconvicted.[39]

BOX 14.4 **SELECTIVE PROSECUTION OF CAREER CRIMINALS**

Dealing with the career criminal, as previously discussed, is one of the most difficult challenges facing criminal justice agencies today. Early studies of recidivism generally revealed that habitual offenders often managed to "beat the system," receiving relatively lenient treatment from prosecutors in exchange for guilty pleas or from judges who were optimistic about the rehabilitative ideal.

Even when deterrence and "just deserts" replaced rehabilitation as a sentencing objective, many habitual offenders continued to beat the system. In urban areas, especially, prosecution procedures were often responsible for letting career criminals slip through the net. Heavy case flows forced most big-city prosecution offices to handle cases on an assembly-line model. Individual deputies specialized in particular aspects of the court process, which meant that the deputy who actually appeared in court frequently knew little more about the case than the information provided in the court documents or notes from deputies who had handled the earlier steps. This situation often resulted in dismissal of the case because the prosecuting attorney was not prepared for testimony given in hearings or trials, a witness failed to appear, or some other administrative foul-up took place.

In an effort to eliminate the "revolving door" treatment of criminal repeaters, **Career Criminal Prosecution (CCP) programs** were established in over 50 jurisdictions across the nation. Charles Work, who spearheaded this movement, used the Bronx Major Offense Unit as an exemplary model. By the 1980s, CCPs had been established in more than 100 prosecutors' offices. Although programs varied from site to site, the following elements were usually evident:

- A special unit of experienced deputies devoted exclusively to prosecuting career cases.
- Some case-selector criteria based on prior record, current offense, and other subjective factors (e.g., weapons, presence of drugs).
- Early involvement by the prosecutor in potential CCP cases to ensure an adequate police investigation.
- Vertical representation, whereby a single deputy is assigned to handle each case at the time of filing, retaining responsibility for all subsequent actions through to sentencing.
- A concentrated effort to see that CCP defendants receive long prison terms, generally precluding plea bargaining.

Source: Joan Petersilia, *The Influence of Criminal Justice Research* (Santa Monica, Calif.: Rand Corporation, 1987), pp. 35–37.

| *BOX 14.5* | **THE RABBLE** |

In my own research, I found that beyond poverty and its correlates—undereducation, unemployment, and minority status—jail prisoners share two essential characteristics: detachment and disrepute. They are detached because they are not well integrated into conventional society, they are not members of conventional social organizations, they have few ties to conventional social networks, and they are carriers of unconventional values and beliefs. They are disreputable because they are perceived as irksome, offensive, threatening, capable of arousal, even protorevolutionary. In this book, I shall refer to them as the *rabble,* meaning the disorganized and disorderly, the lowest class of people.

I found that it is these two features—detachment and disrepute—that lead the police to watch and arrest the rabble so frequently, regardless of whether or not they are engaged in crime, or at least in serious crime. (Most of the rabble commit petty crimes, such as drinking on the street, and are usually vulnerable to arrest.)

These findings suggest that the basic purpose of the jail differs radically from the purpose ascribed to it by government officials and academicians. It is this: the jail was invented, and continues to be operated, in order to manage society's rabble. Society's impulse to manage the rabble has many sources, but the subjectively perceived "offensiveness" of the rabble is at least as important as any real threat it poses to society.

Source: This material appears in John Irwin, *The Jail: Managing the Underclass in American Society* (Berkeley, Calif.: University of California Press, 1985), p. 2.

Jails are one of the most widely criticized institutions in American society. The jail has no constituency and few supporters. Richard W. Velde, former administrator of the Law Enforcement Assistance Administration (LEAA), considers jails to be "brutal, filthy cesspools of crime—institutions which serve to brutalize and embitter men to prevent them from returning to a useful role in society."[40] John Irwin, in his recent study of San Francisco jails, found that "instead of 'criminals,' the jail receives and confines mostly detached and disreputable persons who are arrested more because they are offensive than because they have committed crimes."[41] Irwin concluded that the primary purpose of the jail is to manage these persons, whom he calls "rabble" (see Box 14.5).

In addition to sparing them the jail or detention center, pretrial release grants defendants the opportunity to continue their jobs, the freedom to collect evidence in the community, the financial and emotional support of their families, and the right to come into court as free citizens rather than in handcuffs and in custody. Furthermore, judges appear to be more reluctant to imprison defendants who stand before them as free men and women in civilian dress than they are to sentence to imprisonment defendants who are already in jail and appear in the uniform of the jail.[42]

Pretrial release programs have their roots in the English legal tradition. Under common law, it was possible to issue a summons to a misdemeanant or a felon to appear in court at a later date if the judge was satisfied that the person summoned would appear. In the United States, the procedure eventually developed into the bail system, by which a defendant can be released from jail until trial by paying an amount set by the judge as surety of appearance.

The system of **bail** in the United States gave rise to the commercial bail bondsman. This courtroom actor would post bail for the defendant for a fee that usually amounted to 10 percent of the required bail. Commercial bail received considerable criticism for the scandal and corruption associated with it. For example, bail bondsmen often paid kickbacks to other courtroom actors for referrals or special considerations; judges sometimes would not collect forfeited bails from professional bondsmen.

In 1961, the Manhattan Bail Project, the brainchild of Louis Schweitzer and Herbert Sturz, was set up in order to persuade judges to release without bail defendants who appeared to have stable ties in the community. The basis for this project of **release on recognizance (ROR)** was the development of a point scale to determine who was a good risk to appear for trial. Similar ROR projects, as well as other pretrial release programs, were developed throughout the nation in the late 1960s and early 1970s.

Release on recognizance is the most widely used means of pretrial release. The court puts defendants on their own honor to report when scheduled. The most typical procedure is for a ROR staff member to interview an arrestee and to verify certain data about him or her. If a defendant scores the required number of verified points, according to the preestablished criteria, he or she is recommended for ROR. If the presiding judge of the criminal court agrees with the recommendation and the district attorney decides not to contest it in court, the defendant is released.

Under the **percentage bail program**, the defendant deposits a percentage (usually 10 percent) of the bail amount with the court clerk. The defendant is released from custody once the specified percent is paid; when the defendant appears in court, 90 percent of the original 10 percent is refunded. In Illinois, where percentage bail is the most frequent form of pretrial release, only the defendant is permitted to execute the bond. No professional bondsman, surety, or fidelity company may pay the bond. In Kentucky and Oregon, defendants who have not received ROR or any other means of conditional release have a right to be released under percentage bail.

Supervised release is a pretrial release program that requires frequent contacts between the defendant and a pretrial officer, including phone calls and office interviews. The main purpose of such supervision is to enforce the conditions imposed, but defendants are also helped with housing, finances, medical care, employment, and alcohol- or drug-related problems. In high-risk cases, intensive supervision may be used, requiring several contacts a week with a pretrial release officer.

Pretrial agencies play a valued role in releasing defendants from jail, but they now are facing a difficult time. Shrinking sources of funding make their economic survival precarious. Many pretrial agencies have had to close their doors because they were unable to attain funding from local communities. Of even greater consequence to the pretrial projects is the backlash from the public. Today, most people would like to see arrestees remain in jail or lockup until trial. Heavily publicized cases of violent crimes committed by persons awaiting trial has led to the introduction of legislation to toughen pretrial release standards (**preventive detention statutes**).[43] This movement has the support of law enforcement officials, victims groups, and many others.

Pretrial Diversion

In many jurisdictions, minor offenders often have the opportunity to be diverted to **pretrial diversion programs**. The emphasis on diversion began in 1967 when the President's Commission on Law Enforcement and Administration of Justice recommended the establishment of alternatives to the justice system.[44]

Resolution of citizens' disputes, deferred prosecution, Treatment Alternatives to Street Crime, and therapeutic communities for drug offenders have been the most widely used diversionary programs for adults. While such alternative programs have been helpful in resolving disputes informally, in enabling eligible defendants to avoid the stigma of prosecution and conviction, and in providing

"They're offering a deal—you pay court costs and damages, they drop charges of breaking and entering."

Drawing by Maslin. © 1988 *The New Yorker Magazine, Inc.*

special services for drug abusers, they have experienced hard times during the 1980s. The decline of federal funding has meant that many agencies have had to close because they were unable to secure sufficient funding from local and private sources. Further, these programs have encountered the criticism that they widen the net of jurisdiction of the justice system as they involve individuals who otherwise would have merely been fined and released.[45]

Plea Bargaining

Plea bargaining can be defined as a process by which the defendant in a criminal case relinquishes his or her right to go to trial in exchange for a reduction in charge and/or sentence.[46] The prosecutor, normally the dominant actor in plea bargaining, generally has considerable bargaining power, as he or she can choose any of the following alternatives: (1) reduction of the original charge; (2) dismissal of other charges; (3) recommendation of probation or other leniency; (4) agreement to make no recommendation as to sentence or not to oppose a defense plea of leniency; (5) agreement to dismiss charges against a codefendant; and (6) specific sentence such as restitution or incarceration at a particular prison.[47]

The defense counsel may be a privately retained attorney, a court-appointed counsel, a public defender, or a lawyer provided by the contract system (individual attorneys, bar associations, or private law firms contract to provide services for a specified dollar amount).[48] Public defenders, who represent the majority of criminal defendants, are generally initially resistant to plea bargaining; they bring to the court expectations of doing battle with the prosecutor. However, the majority of defense attorneys typically become convinced over time to plea bargain most of their cases. First, it does not take defense attorneys long to realize that most of their clients are indeed factually guilty. Second, defense attorneys learn that all too frequently they have no legal grounds to challenge the state's evidence. Third, defense attorneys, especially public defenders, find that many of their clients are the misfits of society, the societal "losers"; dealing with such a clientele encourages defense attorneys to negotiate a plea. Finally, defense attorneys discover that punitive sanctions are imposed on those who refuse to plea bargain. For example, prosecutors may use sanctions ranging from simple harassment to an unwillingness to show the defense attorney any files to a refusal to plea bargain on any cases to the threat of going to trial in every case.[49]

Some judges are actively involved in the plea negotiation process, while others merely ratify the plea worked out by the prosecutor and the defense counsel. James A. Cramer et al., in examining the judicial role in plea bargaining in six jurisdictions, found that while judicial participation was common in most jurisdictions, the overall trend was for judges to play a less direct role in the plea bargaining process.[50]

One of the strongest reasons for the continued use of plea bargaining is that many experts believe it would be impossible for criminal courts to permit every defendant to claim the right to a jury trial.[51] That is, if more defendants demanded a full-length trial, the crushing backlog of cases would bring the court system to a grinding halt. The U.S. Supreme Court appears to have been influenced by the argument for the administrative necessity of plea bargaining. In several decisions, the Court has sanctioned plea bargaining as long as the guilty plea is entered voluntarily and as long as the defendant enters the plea bargain agreement knowingly and intelligently.[52]

Plea bargaining can also be justified by the fact that the state benefits from it in a number of ways. First, court calendars are cleared. Second, each guilty plea saves the state the considerable cost of going to trial. Third, guilty pleas save time for court actors and for citizens who would otherwise appear in court as witnesses and jurors. Finally, the state sometimes gets a bargain on weak cases—a fact that violates the ideals of due process protections guaranteed by the Constitution.[53]

Moreover, the argument can be made that plea bargaining is needed to alleviate the severity of the criminal law. Arthur Rosett and Donald R. Cressey see criminal law as so severe "that its full application in all but an occasional aggravated case would be unthinkably cruel, expensive, and socially destructive."[54]

However, the use of plea bargaining has come under extensive criticism in recent years. The New York State Special Commission on Attica, set up to examine one of the bloodiest prison riots in history (43 inmates and guards died when the New York State National Guard was called in to quell the inmate rebellion), concluded:

> What makes inmates most cynical about their preprison experience is the plea-bargaining system. . . .
> Even though an inmate may receive the benefit of a shorter sentence, the plea-bargaining system is characterized by deception and hypocrisy which divorce the inmate from the reality of his crime. . . . The Hughes Committee [the Joint Legislative Committee on Crime] made a study of prisoner attitudes towards plea bargaining . . . and found that almost 99 percent of the inmates surveyed had been solicited to enter a plea bargain. Most were bitter, believing that they did not receive effective legal representation or that the judge did not keep the state's promise of a sentence which had induced them to enter guilty pleas.[55]

Critics of plea bargaining also contend that once arrested, those accused of crimes are presumed to be guilty and are subjected to nearly irresistible pressures to plead guilty.[56] The charges are further made that defense counsels typically become part of a bureaucratic justice system, and, therefore, their organizational roles require them to place pressure on their clients to negotiate a guilty plea[57]; unquestionably, the courthouse work group is generally committed to employing plea bargaining to keep the court case load current.[58] Hard-line critics assert that plea bargaining permits serious criminals to "get off easy," but others argue that plea bargaining leads to undue harshness for some defendants.[59]

The difficulty of evaluating plea bargaining is found in the fact that considerable variation exists among cities in terms of the pattern of plea bargaining and the proportion of cases disposed of through guilty pleas.[60] Malcolm M. Feeley states that "reliance on a single term such as *plea bargaining* imposes a blanket of uniformity on a process in which great diversity and intensity in combativeness—short of trial—does in fact exist."[61] Lynn Mather, in her study of Los Angeles courts, also agrees; she found that criminal courts vary from one jurisdiction to the next in frequency of plea bargaining, the dominance of prosecutor or judge over plea bargaining, the stage at which plea negotiations are likely to take place, and whether the bargaining focuses on the charge or on the sentence.[62]

CRIMINAL TRIAL

The **trial** is the culmination of a number of events in the court process. However, the percentage of criminal cases that reach the trial stage is very small even though the right to a trial is guaranteed under the Constitution. Indeed, only about 5 percent of criminal cases go to trial, and fewer than half of those cases are tried before a jury. Yet the due process or adversarial goal of the court process is more fully achieved during a trial.

Steps in the Criminal Trial Process

The criminal trial is made up of a number of steps, as shown in Figure 14.1.

Opening Statements   The prosecutor is the first to present an opening statement, which is followed by the statement of the defense. The opening statement of the prosecutor usually outlines the case and states that the government will prove beyond a reasonable doubt that the defendant committed the crime with which he or she is charged.

Evidence   The burden is on the prosecution to present evidence showing guilt, as the legal assumption in a criminal trial is that the defendant is innocent until proven guilty. Evidence may be presented to the jury in several ways: testimony under oath by eyewitnesses or witnesses with any knowledge of the case; testimony by expert witnesses; property seized during the arrest; the results of the police investigation, photographs, and reports; and sworn statements or depositions.

There are four basic types of evidence: real evidence, testimonial evidence, direct evidence, and circumstantial evidence. *Real evidence* refers to such concrete objects as weapons, photographs, recovered property, fingerprints, and casts of tire tracks or shoe prints. The gathering of real evidence is governed by the Fourth Amendment to the Constitution; if such evidence is found to have been seized illegally, the Court can rule that the evidence is not admissible in the trial. **Testimonial evidence** is the testimony of witnesses who, under oath, address the facts of the case. All witnesses may be examined or questioned by the prosecution and cross-examined by the defense. **Directed evidence** is that which was observed firsthand. For example, directed evidence might be the testimony of an eyewitness who observed the crime and can identify the suspect. **Circumstantial evidence** is

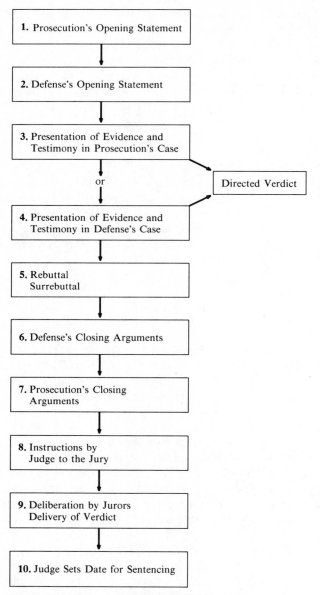

Figure 14.1 Steps in the Criminal Trial Process.

evidence that is introduced into court and is material or applies to the criminal case being tried. For example, a witness may testify that he saw the defendant wearing a brown jacket and running two blocks from the scene of a robbery.

Expert testimony is given by an expert witness—a person who has specific expertise in a certain area. Coroners, medical examiners, and psychiatrists are commonly used as expert witnesses. The usual role of the coroner or medical examiner is to give an opinion on the cause of a person's death.

Directed Verdict   Following the presentation of its evidence, the prosecution rests its case and allows the defense to present its evidence. The defense frequently moves for a **directed verdict** at this stage of the trial. Such a request means that the defense attorney is asking the judge to order the jury to return a verdict of not guilty. If the judge sustains the motion, or agrees, he or she will instruct the jury to acquit, or find the defendant not guilty. If the judge overrules the motion, the trial continues. Judges also can direct acquittal at this stage without a motion by the defense, but this is done very infrequently.

Closing Argument   When both the prosecution and the defense have presented their evidence, each side has an opportunity to make one final plea to the jury, the **closing argument**. The burden to prove the crime is on the prosecution, and, therefore, the prosecutor makes the final argument. The prosecutor typically reviews the evidence and attempts to convince the jury that proof beyond a reasonable doubt has been presented.

Judge's Instruction to the Jury   The judge's instructions, or charge, to the jury inform the jurors of the elements of the offense charged or those of any lesser

Judge confers with defense attorney and prosecutor during a criminal trial. (*Source:* Michael O'Brien/Archive Pictures, Inc.)

offenses, the type of evidence needed to prove each element of the offense or lesser offenses, and the evidence needed to prove guilt beyond a reasonable doubt.

Verdict of the Jury   After instructions from the judge, the **jury** retires to the jury room to decide the verdict. Each jury has a foreman or forewoman as a leader; and in most states, this leader is elected by the jurors. The jurors discuss the evidence presented and take successive votes until they agree on a verdict.

In all but two states, the vote by the jurors must be unanimous. If the jurors cannot reach a unanimous verdict, the trial is considered a hung jury, and the prosecutor may bring the defendant to trial again. If the verdict is not guilty, the judge releases the defendant unless other charges are pending (or the defendant is already incarcerated for another crime). If the verdict is guilty, the judge usually orders a presentence investigation.

SENTENCING

The **sentencing** of convicted offenders is at the hub of the criminal justice process. As many states have experimented with one or more types of sentencing reform—guidelines, determinate sentencing, mandatory sentences, and alternative forms of punishment—the discretion in dispositions available to judges has decreased over the past decade. The stated purposes of sentencing have shifted from an emphasis on utilitarian aims, particularly rehabilitation, toward a greater focus on deserved punishment, on the proportionality of sanctions to harm done, and on equity.[63]

Criminal sentencing and the sanctions it imposes represent society's most powerful means to deter criminal behavior. Society expects sentences that are proportionate to the seriousness of the criminal behavior, that incapacitate violent criminals, and that protect innocent people from becoming victims of crime.[64]

Indeterminate or Determinate Sentencing

The indeterminate sentencing model is based on the assumption that criminals should be imprisoned until they are "cured" of criminality. Although the range of indeterminate sentencing ideally would be from one day to life imprisonment, as California decreed in its sentencing statutes for forty years, nearly all jurisdictions at present limit these sentences by establishing statutory minimums and maximums.

The first states to enact determinate sentencing statutes were Alaska, Arizona, California, Connecticut, Colorado, Illinois, Indiana, Maine, Minnesota, North Carolina, Pennsylvania, and Washington; by 1985, at least 15 states in all had enacted determinate sentencing statutes. Ten states had abolished their parole boards, and 35 states had established mandatory minimum sentences for specified crimes.[65] The U.S. Sentencing Commission currently recommends that a point system be used in judicial decision making.

The main forms of determinate sentencing are flat-time sentences, mandatory sentences, and presumptive sentences. In **flat-time sentencing**, the judge may choose between probation and imprisonment but has limited discretion in setting the length of any prison sentence. The gravity of the crime determines the actual incarceration time. There is no possibility under flat-time sentencing for reduction or increase of the sentence once an offender is incarcerated.

The **presumptive sentence** is based upon the concept of "just deserts," which, as was discussed earlier, has been proposed by David Fogel, Andrew von Hirsch, and the Twentieth Century Fund in *Fair and Certain Punishment*.[66] Richard Singer explains how presumptive sentencing allows the judge some flexibility in determining the sentence:

> Presumptive sentencing would require a judge to impose a selected sentence, which is the "normal" sentence to be imposed for "normal" crimes upon "normal" offenders in all cases, but would allow the judge to vary from the presumptive sentence where there were aggravating or mitigating circumstances which could be articulated and which would be placed in writing, subject to appellate review.[67]

Mandatory sentencing sets a required number of years of incarceration for specific crimes. The Rockefeller Drug Law, the Bartley-Fox Gun Law, and the Michigan Mandatory Minimum Sentence for the sale of narcotics all carry set terms of imprisonment. The law establishing a mandatory sentence may state, for example, that armed robbery shall be punishable by a term of imprisonment between 6 and 20 years and that every judge must impose a specific sentence within that range. A mandatory sentence still allows credit for "good time," which can reduce a mandatory sentence by a third or more.

Indeterminate sentencing has lost favor because of the wide disparities in sentencing practices, the adverse effects of release uncertainty, and the coercive nature of requiring participation in rehabilitative programs to attain release. In defense of indeterminate sentencing, Charles E. Silberman states that judges usually use their discretion to punish those who should be punished, while showing appropriate leniency to those who have committed minor crimes.[68] Proponents of indeterminate sentencing also charge that the uniform rules of determinate sentencing cannot work in the real world of criminal justice because the failure to individualize sentences will create a more harsh justice system. It has already been shown that determinate sentences are largely responsible for prison overcrowding. Finally, according to supporters of indeterminate sentencing, determinate sentences have been used by politicians to create a more repressive criminal justice system because of the increased length of sentences.[69]

In short, determinate sentencing has been widely recognized as a reform whose time has come.[70] N. Gatz and F.G. Vito even define it as "the major correctional reform of this decade."[71] Over one-quarter of state legislatures have adopted a determinate sentencing structure. But, as this section has suggested, there is both wide support and sharp criticism of this sentencing practice. An increasingly popular viewpoint is that indeterminate sentencing should be retained, but that judges need some guidelines in making the sentencing decision.

Sentencing Hearing

At the **sentencing hearing,** the judge considers recommendations by the prosecutor, the defense attorney, and, sometimes, by the probation officer. The convicted offender also has the right to address the court at this time, in a speech known as an *allocution.* In jurisdictions where sentence bargaining takes place, the judge generally imposes the sentence agreed on by the prosecutor and the defense attorney.

In most state jurisdictions and in the federal system, a presentence investigation is usually conducted prior to the sentencing hearing. The responsibility of the probation officer or presentence investigator is to provide in the presentence investigation (PSI) report information that will help the judge make an appropriate sentencing decision.

Whether the judge or the jury should sentence is an issue that has received some debate. Most jurisdictions in the United States place the responsibility for

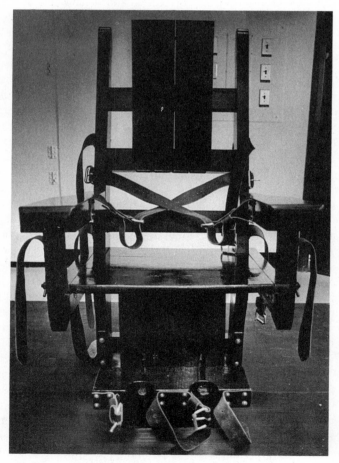

The chair. (*Source:* Tom Kelly.)

sentencing exclusively with the trial judge, except in capital cases. Although a dozen or so states leave the sentencing decision to the jury for noncapital crimes, there has been recent opposition to jury sentencing in noncapital cases because the jury is seen as lacking the necessary expertise to make a proper sentencing decision.[72]

The sentencing options available to judges vary from jurisdiction to jurisdiction, but, according to the crime charged, they typically include diversionary programs, fines, probation, jail confinement, incarceration in a state or federal institution, and the death penalty.

Capital punishment represents the most extreme—and controversial—punishment a state can administer. Seven states executed a total of 18 prisoners during 1986, bringing the total number of executions to 68 since 1976, the year that the U.S. Supreme Court upheld the death penalty in three separate cases. During 1986, 297 prisoners were received under sentence of death; at year-end, 32 states reported a total of 1781 prisoners under sentence of death, all for murder. The majority of those under sentence of death (1006) were white; 750 were black; 16 were American Indians; and 9 were Asian (see Table 14.2 for the number of persons executed by jurisdiction from 1930 to 1985).[73]

ANALYSIS

In analyzing the structure and functions of the criminal courts, overlapping relationships between order and disorder make the decision making of the courts appear simultaneously rational and irrational.

Order and Disorder

Lower courts are clearly chaotic. Defendants are sometimes processed en masse in an obviously disorderly and untidy environment. State trial courts have much smaller case loads than the lower courts, but they still lack adequate resources to stage full-length trials with many defendants. It is generally agreed that a percentage much larger than the 5 to 10 percent of all defendants receiving full-length trials at present would bring the trial courts to a state of gridlock. The lengthy delays are further evidence of the disorder within trial courts.

Plea bargaining, or plea negotiations, is used by most lower and trial courts to maintain an orderly environment. Considerable controversy exists as to whether this means of attaining the court's organizational goals is fair to defendants. Many of the trappings of the due process, or adversarial, model are missing in this procedure. Defendants are presumed to be guilty, coercion is sometimes used to obtain a guilty plea, the defense counsel often seems to be more committed to the courthouse work group and its organizational goals than to the defense of his or her client, and a good part of the negotiations takes place in secret. Sometimes plea bargaining works to the advantage of the defendant and sometimes it does not. Those who plead guilty because they are afraid of going to trial are most likely to be victimized by this process.

Anti–death penalty demonstrator. (*Source:* Robert V. Eckert Jr./
EKM–Nepenthe.)

Judges also are frequently accused of disparity in their sentencing practices. Indeed, studies have shown that offenders who have similar conviction crimes and criminal records frequently receive very dissimilar sentences.[74] The differences in some instances appear to reflect differences in the philosophical orientations of judges or to the locale, but in others, the differences seem to be related to nonlegal defendant characteristics, such as race or socioeconomic status.[75] Petersilia summarizes the findings of this research: "Although offense and offender characteristics accounted for much of the total variation in sentencing, judicial discretion was evidently responsible for a significant proportion of the rest."[76]

Thus, it can not be denied that the process of justice in American courtrooms is untidy, disorderly, and somewhat chaotic. But while the procedures or process of justice may be disorderly, there appears to be substantial evidence that the outcome is usually rational and represents in the aggregate "rough justice." Malcolm M. Feeley found that the end results of the lower courts may be more orderly than the disordered environment would lead one to expect; the process

Table 14.2 NUMBER OF PERSONS EXECUTED, BY JURISDICTION IN RANK ORDER, 1930–1985

State	Number Executed	
	Since 1930	Since 1977
U.S. total	3,909	50
Georgia	372	6
New York	329	
Texas	307	10
California	292	
North Carolina	265	2
Florida	183	13
Ohio	172	
South Carolina	163	1
Mississippi	155	1
Pennsylvania	152	
Louisiana	140	7
Alabama	136	1
Arkansas	118	
Kentucky	103	
Virginia	96	4
Tennessee	93	
Illinois	90	
New Jersey	74	
Maryland	68	
Missouri	62	
Oklahoma	60	
Washington	47	
Colorado	47	
Indiana	43	2
West Virginia	40	
District of Columbia	40	
Arizona	38	
Federal system	33	
Nevada	31	2
Massachusetts	27	
Connecticut	21	
Oregon	19	
Iowa	18	
Kansas	15	
Utah	14	1
Delaware	12	
New Mexico	8	
Wyoming	7	
Montana	6	
Vermont	4	
Nebraska	4	
Idaho	3	
South Dakota	1	
New Hampshire	1	
Wisconsin	0	
Rhode Island	0	
North Dakota	0	
Minnesota	0	

Table 14.2 (*Continued*)

State	Number Executed	
	Since 1930	**Since 1977**
Michigan	0	
Maine	0	
Hawaii	0	
Alaska	0	

Source: Bureau of Justice Statistics, *Capital Punishment, 1985* (Washington, D.C.: U.S. Department of Justice, 1986), p. 7.

itself provides sufficient punishment in most cases.[77] Charles Silberman, in analyzing the decision making of trial courts, adds:

> I have been arguing a heretical and paradoxical thesis: That a seemingly irrational and unjust adult judicial process produces results that are surprisingly rational and just. Exceptions—too many of them—do occur, but for the most part, prosecutors and judges use their discretion to carry out the intent, if not the precise letter, of the law, i.e., to prosecute, convict, and punish "real criminals," while showing appropriate leniency to those whose crimes are not serious or who seem to pose no real danger to the community.[78]

Structured Order Within the Courthouse

The courtroom setting of the 1980s is characterized by the attempt to rationalize the justice process for the purpose of attaining efficiency and productivity. The decade of the 1980s is the decade of the manager; nobody can stand an untidy system. At an organizational level, the appointment of court administrators across the nation and the introduction of the management information system (MIS) approach have contributed to bringing administrative order to a disorderly system.

The commonality among the individuals who make up the courthouse work group also brings order to the courthouse. First, most are lawyers, and they have learned a particular way of problem solving (the legal paradigm) in law school. Legal training teaches lawyers a concern for precedent while sensitizing them to the procedural implications of current judgments. Specifically, legal reasoning focuses attention on three areas: rules, facts, and analogy. For example, the judge's job is to look at a given set of facts and to decide on the basis of analogy whether these facts call for the application of one rule or another. Thus, the legal paradigm greatly shapes how court actors define their jobs and fulfill their responsibilities.[79]

Second, the individual traits of these various actors are largely overshadowed by the goals of courthouse work group, as these actors learn the advantages of cooperating with each other. The judge, the prosecutor, and the defense attorney perform quite specialized functions, but their activities are constrained by the incentives and shared goals motivating the members of the work group. They operate in a common task environment that provides common resources and imposes common constraints on their behaviors.[80]

In short, rules, roles, and relationships contribute to structured order within the courtroom. If one breaks one of these courtroom rules, one must suffer the consequences. In a real sense, structure and ritualism sometimes become more important to the functioning of the courtroom work group than its formal function in the justice system.

POLICY IMPLICATIONS

Much of the criticism the courts receive is undeserved. The courts alone can not solve the problem of crime or even make a significant dent in it. Nor can they rehabilitate defendants or prevent recidivism. In dealing with society's failures, the courts fail far more than they succeed. They obviously can not do what the family, the church, the workplace, and the school could not do.[81]

Yet, as previously discussed, the courts can and should work better. The reform of plea bargaining and the achievement of sentencing reform are two promising areas for improvement in the performance of the criminal courts.

Plea Bargaining Reform

Plea bargaining must be reformed so that the due process rights and constitutional safeguards of defendants are not violated during this process. This reform process should include several areas:

1. Legislatures must reduce the statutory maximum punishments for crime. Discretionary decision making could then be restricted to cases in which the punishment must be adjusted to the particular circumstances of defendants in the interests of justice, rather than being used to soften the punishment of almost every defendant brought into the courthouse.
2. The quality of public defenders' offices across the nation must be upgraded so that the quality of services are equal or superior to those provided by privately retained attorneys.
3. The criminal laws establish a commitment to punish offenders at levels well beyond our current administrative capacity.[82] If the severity of the criminal law were reduced, it is likely that the incidence of acquiscence to a guilty plea through threat would also be reduced.
4. The presumption of guilt must always be tempered by the morality of fairness. The aim of fairness provides a reassurance that court officials are behaving in a responsible way.[83]
5. The plea bargaining process must be open and take place in the presence of all participants. Such openness would better ensure that the defendant no longer feels like a nonperson, used and manipulated by the justice system.

Sentencing Reform

Sentencing guidelines, the major innovation of the 1980s, appear to offer the best hope of sentencing reform. Such guidelines provide each judge with an empirically derived sentence specifically tailored to the individual case. Sentencing guidelines, which are intended to be merely a statistical guide, indicate what the judges in the particular jurisdiction have done in similar situations. Thus, the guidelines are intended to serve as benchmarks, or reference points, against which a judge may measure the sentence he or she plans to impose.[84]

Minnesota was one of the first states to adopt formal sentencing guidelines, and several states followed Minnesota in implementing statewide sentencing guidelines. In addition, sentencing guidelines were implemented in Denver, Chicago, Newark, and Phoenix. Petersilia summarizes the research that has been done on sentencing guidelines:

1. Researchers can produce effective guidelines—that is, guidelines that promote consistency—which can be implemented without dislocations in the system, and reduce discretion without compromising judicial integrity.
2. The sentences generated by the guidelines fall within a range and are considered as recommendations allowing some judicial discretion where circumstances warrant it.
3. Researchers have highlighted the implementation difficulties, and pinpointed the pivotal points where resistance might negate the impact of guidelines.[85]

SUMMARY

The theory, rationale, and underlying ideologies of the law, as noted in this chapter and elsewhere, drive the criminal justice system and provide the justifications for what happens in court. The most important decisions during the pretrial stage are: what to charge defendants with, whether or not to grant them pretrial release, whether or not to grant them diversion, and whether or not to offer them a guilty plea to a lesser charge or sentence. In the court process, a decision must be made about the guilt of a defendant for the crime or crimes with which he or she has been charged; if the defendant is found guilty, he or she must be sentenced at the time of the sentencing hearing.

These decisions have serious implications for defendants. For example, arrestees who are denied pretrial release and must wait unconvicted for the legal process to deal with their cases are denied freedom. This decision may provide security for society and its need for order, but it may needlessly take away the freedom of some defendants. These arrestees may be exposed to rape or assault from predatory prisoners, and those who have been confined face a greater likelihood of their being convicted at the time of trial and of receiving a prison sentence.

The decisions made during the court process are political decisions, in that they allocate values and freedom; these decisions, as countless critics have remarked, have an impact on the issues of order and disorder in the larger society and on defendants and their families. It is reassuring that the untidy and often chaotic procedures and processes of criminal courts generally result in orderly and rational outcomes. Yet this "rough justice" in the aggregate often violates the due process rights of defendants when individual cases are considered. For this reason alone, the courts in this free and democratic society can and must do better.

REFERENCES

Blumberg, Abraham S. *Criminal Justice: Issues and Ironies.* 2d ed. New York: New Viewpoints, 1979.

Eisenstein, James. *Political and the Legal Process.* New York: Harper & Row, 1973.

Feeley, Malcolm M. *The Process Is the Punishment: Handling Cases in a Lower Criminal Court.* New York: Russell Sage Foundation, 1979.

———. *Court Reform on Trial.* New York: Basic Books, 1983.

Jacob, Herbert. *Justice in America: Courts, Lawyers, and the Judicial Process.* 3d ed. Boston: Little, Brown, 1979.

Levin, Martin A. *Urban Politics and the Criminal Court.* Chicago: University of Chicago Press, 1977.

Littrell, W. Boyd. *Bureaucratic Justice.* Beverly Hills, Calif.: Sage, 1977.

Moore, Mark H.; Estrich, Susan R.; McGillis, Daniel; and Spelman, William. *Dangerous Offenders: The Elusive Target of Justice.* Cambridge, Mass.: Harvard University Press, 1984.

Neubauer, David W. *Criminal Justice in Middle America.* Morristown, N.J.: General Learning Press, 1974.

Petersilia, Joan. *The Influence of Criminal Justice Research.* Santa Monica, Calif.: Rand Corporation, 1987.

Ryan, John Paul. "Adjudication and Sentencing in a Misdemeanor Court: The Outcome is the Punishment." *Law and Society Review* 15 (1980–1981) pp. 79–107.

Silberman, Charles E. *Criminal Violence, Criminal Justice.* New York: Random House, 1978.

"Special Issue on Plea Bargaining." *Law and Society Review* 13 (Winter 1979), pp. 189–687.

NOTES

1. Jerome Hall, *General Principles of Criminal Law,* 2d ed. (Indianapolis: Bobbs Merrill, 1947).
2. Thomas E. Cronin, Tania Z. Cronin, and Michael E. Milakovich, *U.S. v. Crime in the Streets* (Bloomington, Ind.: Indiana University Press, 1981).
3. David W. Neubauer, *Criminal Justice in Middle America* (Morristown, N.J.: General Learning Pres, 1974), p. 251.
4. Bureau of Justice Statistics, *Case Filings in State Courts, 1983* (Washington, D.C.: U.S. Department of Justice), p. 1.
5. Malcolm M. Feeley, *The Process Is the Punishment: Handling Cases in a Lower Criminal Court* (New York: Russell Sage Foundation, 1979), p. xv.
6. *Argersinger* v. *Hamlin,* 407 U.S. 25 (1972).
7. John A. Robertson, *Rough Justice: Perspectives on Lower Criminal Courts* (Boston: Little, Brown, 1974), pp. xvii–xviii.

8. See Jonathan D. Casper, *American Criminal Justice: The Defendant's Perspective* (Englewood Cliffs, N.J.: Prentice-Hall, 1972, and Abraham S. Blumberg, *Criminal Justice: Issues and Ironies,* 2d ed. (New York: New Viewpoints, 1979).

9. Feeley, *The Process Is the Punishment,* pp. 241–242.

10. John Paul Ryan, "Adjudication and Sentencing In a Misdemeanor Court: The Outcome Is the Punishment," *Law and Society Review,* 15 (1980–1981), p. 79.

11. A statistical summary of state court organization can be found in *State Court Systems* (Chicago: Council of State Governments, 1976).

12. Arthur Rosett and Donald R. Cressey, *Justice by Consent: Plea Bargains in the American Courthouse* (Philadelphia: Lippincott, 1976), pp. 47–48.

13. Ibid., pp. 90–91. See also James Eisenstein and Herbert Jacob, *Felony Justice: An Organizational Analysis of Criminal Courts* (Boston: Little, Brown, 1977); W. Boyd Littrell, *Bureaucratic Justice* (Beverly Hills, Calif.: Sage, 1979); and Neubauer, *Criminal Justice in Middle America.*

14. Martin A. Levin, *Urban Politics and the Criminal Courts* (Chicago: University of Chicago Press, 1977), pp. 231–233.

15. Charles E. Silberman, *Criminal Violence, Criminal Justice* (New York: Random House, 1978), p. 285.

16. Stuart A. Scheingold, *The Politics of Law and Order: Street Crime and Public Policy* (New York: Longman, 1984), p. 193.

17. Bureau of Justice Statistics Bulletin, *The Growth of Appeals* (Washington, D.C.: U.S. Department of Justice), p. 1.

18. Herbert Jacob, *Justice in America: Courts, Lawyers, and the Judicial Process,* 3d ed. (Boston: Little, Brown, 1978), p. 218.

19. The 1978 state court decision in Tennessee, in which six state prison facilities were found to be in violation of prisoners' constitutional rights, was one of the first major state court decisions against state corrections officials.

20. See Francis A. Allen, *The Crimes of Politics: Political Dimensions of Criminal Justice* (Cambridge, Mass.: Harvard University Press, 1974), pp. 53–62.

21. Jacob, *Justice in America,* pp. 213.

22. "The Second Circuit: Federal Judicial Administration in Microcosm," *Columbia Law Review,* 63 (1963), p. 890.

23. Jacob, *Justice in America,* pp. 213–215.

24. Ibid., p. 216.

25. Henry J. Abraham, *The Judicial Process,* 3d ed. (New York: Oxford University Press, 1975), pp. 169–188.

26. Stephen L. Wasby, *Continuity and Change: From the Warren Court to the Burger Court* (Pacific Palisades, Calif.: Goodyear, 1976), p. 33.

27. Jacob, *Justice in America,* p. 221.

28. Ibid., pp. 221–222.

29. Glendon Schubert, *The Constitutional Polity* (Boston: Boston University Press, 1970), p. 71.

30. James Simon, *In His Own Image: The Supreme Court in Richard Nixon's America* (New York: McKay, 1973), p. 8.

31. Ibid., p. 227.

32. Quoted in Robert W. Lee, "Looking at the Reagan High Court," *Public Opinion* (November 1984), p. 34.

33. Quoted in Lee, "Looking at the Reagan High Court," p. 38.

34. Neubauer, *Criminal Justice in Middle America,* p. 251.

35. Ibid., pp. 117–118.

36. Littrell, *Bureaucratic Justice,* p. 151.

37. Ibid., p. 152.

38. Jerome Skolnick; *Justice Without Trial,* 2d ed. (New York: Wiley, 1972).

39. Bureau of Justice Statistics, *Jail Inmates, 1985* (Washington, D.C.: U.S. Department of Justice, 1987), p. 1.

40. *The Correctional Trainer* (Newsletter for Illinois Correctional Staff Training, Fall 1970), p. 109.

41. John Irwin, *Managing the Underclass in American Society* (Berkeley, Calif.: University of California Press, 1985), p. xiii.

42. Ann Rankin, "Effects of Pretrial Detention," *New York University Law Review* 39 (1964), p. 642; Daniel Freed and Patricia Wald, *Bail in the United States: 1964,* Report to the National Conference on Bail and Criminal Justice (Washington, D.C.: U.S. Government Printing Office, 1964), pp. 46–47.

43. Alaska, Delaware, Hawaii, Maryland, Michigan, Nebraska, North Carolina, Pennsylvania, and South Carolina are among the states that recognize community safety as a factor to be considered in setting pretrial release conditions.

44. The President's Commission on Law Enforcement and Administration of Justice, *Task Force Report: Corrections* (Washington, D.C.: U.S. Government Printing Office, 1967).

45. For a recent expression of this position, see James Austin and Barry Krisberg, "Wider, Stronger, and Different Nets: The Dialectics of Criminal Justice Reform," *Journal of Research in Crime and Delinquency* 18 (January 1981), p. 165.

46. Milton Heumann, *Plea Bargaining: The Experience of Prosecutors, Judges, and Defense Attorneys* (Chicago: University of Chicago Press, 1978), p. 1.

47. Nicholas N. Kittrie and Elyce H. Zenoff, *Sanctions, Sentencing, and Corrections* (Mineola, N.Y.: Foundation Press, 1981), p. 167.

48. Bureau of Justice Statistics, *Criminal Defense Systems* (Washington, D.C.: U.S. Department of Justice, 1984), p. 2.

49. Heumann, *Plea Bargaining,* p. 69.

50. James A. Cramer, Henry H. Rossman, and William F. McDonald, "The Judicial Role in Plea-Bargaining," in *Plea Bargaining,* ed. William F. McDonald and James A. Cramer (Lexington, Mass.: Heath, 1980), p. 142.

51. Neubauer, *Criminal Justice in Middle America,* p. 194.

52. *Brady* v. *United States,* 397 U.S. 742 (1969); *McMann* v. *Richardson,* 397 U.S. 759 (1969); *North Carolina* v. *Alford,* 400 U.S. 25 (1970); and *Santobello* v. *New York,* 404 U.S. 259 (1971).

53. Littrell, *Bureaucratic Justice,* p. 214.

54. Rosett and Cressey, *Justice by Consent,* pp. 22–24.

55. New York Special Commission on Attica, *Attica* (New York: Praeger, 1972), pp. 30–31.

56. National Advisory Commission on Criminal Justice Standards and Goals, *Report on Courts* (Washington, D.C.: U.S. Government Printing Office, 1973), pp. 42–45; David Sudnow, "Normal Crimes: Sociological Features of the Penal Code in a Public Defender Office," *Social Problems* 12 (1965), p. 255: David Newman, *Conviction: The Determination of Guilt or Innocence* (Boston: Little, Brown, Donald Newman, "Pleading Guilty for Considerations: A Study of Bargain Justice," *Journal of Criminal Law, Criminology, and Police Science* 46 (March–April 1956), pp. 780–790; and Dominick Vetri, "Guilty Pleas Bargaining: Compromises by Prosecutors to Secure Guilty Please," *University of Pennsylvania Law Review* 112 (1964), pp. 865–895.

57. Blumberg, *Criminal Justice,* p. 21.

58. Eisenstein and Jacob, *Felony Justice.*
59. Blumberg, *Criminal Justice,* p. 242–246.
60. Levin, *Urban Politics,* p. 85.
61. Feeley, *The Process Is the Punishment,* p. 29.
62. Lynn M. Mather, *Plea Bargaining or Trial?* (Lexington, Mass.: Lexington Books; Heath, 1979), p. 1.
63. Don M. Gottfredson, "Criminal Sentencing in Transition," *Judicature* 68 (October–November 1984), p. 125.
64. James K. Stewart, "Introduction," *Judicature* 68 (October–November 1984), p. 124.
65. Joan Petersilia, *The Influence of Criminal Justice Research* (Santa Monica, Calif.: Rand Corporation, 1987), p. 53.
66. Andrew von Hirsch, *Doing Justice* (New York: Hill & Wang, 1975); The Twentieth Century Fund, *Fair and Certain Punishment* (New York: McGraw-Hill, 1976); and David Fogel, " . . . *We Are the Living Proof": The Justice Model of Corrections* (Cincinnati: Anderson, 1975).
67. Richard Singer, "In Favor of 'Presumptive Sentences' Set by the Sentencing Commission," *Crime and Delinquency* 24 (October 1978), pp. 401–427.
68. Charles E. Silberman, *Criminal Violence, Criminal Justice* (New York: Random House, 1978), p. 285.
69. Francis T. Cullen and Karen E. Gilbert, *Reaffirming Rehabilitation* (Cincinnati: Anderson, 1982).
70. M. S. Serrill, "Determinate Sentencing—The History, the Theory, the Debate," *Corrections Magazine* (September 1977), pp. 3–13.
71. N. Gatz and F. G. Vito, "The Use of the Determinate Sentence—A Historical Perspective: A Research Note," *Journal of Criminal Justice* 10 (1982), pp. 323–329.
72. Kaplan, *Criminal Justice.*
73. Bureau of Justice Statistics, *Capital Punishment, 1986* (Washington, D.C.: U.S. Department of Justice, 1987), p. 1.
74. Gary Kleck, "Life Support for Ailing Hypotheses: Summarizing the Evidence on Racial Discrimination in Sentencing," *Law and Human Behavior* 9 (1985).
75. Petersilia, *Influence of Criminal Justice Research,* p. 50.
76. Ibid.
77. Feeley, *The Process Is the Punishment,* p. 281.
78. Silberman, *Criminal Violence, Criminal Justice,* p. 285.
79. Stuart A. Scheingold, *The Politics of Rights: Lawyers, Public Policy and the Judicial Process,* 3d ed. (Boston: Little, Brown, 1978), p. 287.
80. Eisenstadt and Jacob, *Felony Justice,* p. 35. See also Peter Nardulli, *The Courtroom Elite: An Organizational Perspective on Criminal Justice* (Cambridge, Mass.: Ballinger, 1978).
81. Jacob, *Justice in America,* pp. 164–165.
82. Mark H. Moore, *Dangerous Offenders: The Elusive Target of Justice* (Cambridge, Mass.: Harvard University Press, 1984), p. 97.
83. Malcolm M. Feeley, *Court Reform on Trial: Why Simple Solutions Fail* (New York: Basic Books, 1983), p. 9.
84. Leslie T. Wilkins et al., *Sentencing Guidelines: Structuring Judicial Decisions: Report on the Feasibility Study* (Washington, D.C.: U.S. Government Printing Office, LEAA, 1978), p. 2.
85. Petersilia, *Influence of Criminal Justice Research,* p. 53.

CHAPTER **15**

The Prison

A SOCIOLOGICAL ANALYSIS OF THE PRISON

The Changing Administration of the Prison

Charismatic or Autocratic Leadership
The Bureaucratization of Prison Administration

Services and Programs

The Inmate World

The Big House
The Correctional Institution
The Contemporary Prison

Problems of American Prisons

Overcrowding
Increased Violence
Deterioration of Staff Morale

The Invasion of the Courts

Prisoners' Rights in U.S. Corrections

ANALYSIS OF THE PRISON

Perseverance of the Prison

Microcosm of the Larger Society

Freedom Versus Order

POLICY IMPLICATIONS

Reduction of Overcrowded Prisons

Humane Prisons

The Lawful Prison
The Safe Prison
The Industrious Prison
The Hopeful Prison

SUMMARY

REFERENCES

NOTES

KEY TERMS

autocratic warden

Big House

building tenders (B.T.s)

contemporary prison

contraband markets

correctional institution

deprivation model

deterioration of staff morale

"hands off" doctrine

importation model

inmate code

institutional violence

management information systems (MIS)

maximum-security prisons

overcrowding

prison abolitionists

prison gangs

prisonization

prison riots

Stateville Penitentiary

> *I am finding prison a curious combination of unrelenting tension and acute
> boredom. The boredom comes from the lack of stimulating things to do, of
> course; the tension rises out of the collective tension of more than a thousand
> convicts. On the surface, life here appears to run almost placidly but one needs
> to go only a little beneath the surface to find the whirlpools and eddies of anger
> and frustration. The muttering of discontent and rebellion goes on constantly:
> the* sotto voce *sneer whenever we pass an official or guard, the glare carefully
> calculated to express contempt without arousing overt retaliation, the tempers
> that rise so swiftly to the breaking point.*
>
> —Alfred Hassler, imprisoned as a conscientious objector[1]

Imprisonment represents a desperate attempt to create order from disorder. In
a futile effort to cope with the crime problem, the United States sends more people
to prison for longer periods than any Western nation.[2] Times change, and so do
correctional goals, managerial philosophies, and problems of prisons, but what
is constant is the difficulty of inmates' "doing time." Alfred Hassler, imprisoned
as a conscientious objector during World War II, portrays the boredom and
tensions of life within the walls. Other more recent commentaries on the prison
have focused on racial unrest, the intimidating presence of inmate gangs, the
violent atmosphere, loss of staff control, and ever-expanding contraband markets.[3]

Long a national disgrace, the prison system is an out-of-control dumping
grounds for lower-class "losers." Now, with the new federal and state commitment to mandatory minimum sentences and to stronger penalties for crimes
involving the possession of weapons, the penal system is near the breaking point.
Riots, disturbances, and disorders, as well as ever-present abuses and indignities,
are simply the overt manifestation of anomie inside the walls. Like seismologists,
Americans are aware of the internal rumbling and the occasional belching of
fumes, but seem powerless to prevent the periodic "blowouts" and violent erup-
tions.[4]

A SOCIOLOGICAL ANALYSIS OF THE PRISON

James Jacobs's analysis of **Stateville Penitentiary,** commonly acknowledged as one of the world's toughest prisons, presents an excellent portrayal of the problems and characteristics of **maximum-security prisons.** Building on the thesis first expressed in Donald Clemmer's *The Prison Community,* that prisons are a microcosm of the larger society, Jacobs shows how Stateville reflects the social organization and moral values of the larger society.[5]

The Changing Administration of the Prison

Jacobs begins his work by tracing the movement from charismatic or autocratic leadership to rational-legal forms of authority to ever-increasing bureaucratic structures.

Charismatic or Autocratic Leadership   Joseph Ragen, who is no doubt the best-known **autocratic warden** in the history of U.S. corrections, ruled Stateville Penitentiary from 1936 to 1965. He was appointed to establish a stable social order at Stateville, which had been plagued in the preceding ten years by one crisis after the other. Jacobs describes Ragen's rule in this way:

> Joe Ragen's 30-year "rule" of Stateville was based upon the patriarchal authority that he achieved. In the vocabulary of both employees and inmates, "he ran it." The "old boss" devoted his life to perfecting the world's most orderly prison regime. He exercised personal control over every detail, no matter how insignificant. He tolerated challenges neither by inmates nor by employees nor by outside interest groups. He cultivated an image which made him seem invincible to his subordinates as well as to the prisoners.[6]

Autocratic wardens like Joe Ragen ran orderly prisons. Ragen had such control that there were no riots or escapes from within the walls during his years as warden; in contrast to earlier years, only two guards and three inmates were killed during this time.[7] Autocratic wardens were sovereign as long as they kept in favor with the governor's office. Believing that no one else could run their prisons, they took total responsibility for planning, staffing, and controlling. They refused to accept either staff or inmate resistance; indeed, the prisoners, like slaves, were denied nearly every human right beyond survival. Autocratic wardens used the "snitch system" to ensure that they had informants among both inmates and staff. They mixed terror, incentives, and favoritism in order to keep their subjects "fearful but not desperate, hopeful but always uncertain."[8]

For decades, the Texas Department of Corrections (T.D.C.) used autocratic principles to maintain safe, productive, clean, and disciplined prison operations.[9] Then, in the *Ruiz* v. *Estelle* (1980) decision, a federal judge declared unconstitutional such T.D.C. policies as compulsory field labor and the "snitch system."[10] James W. Marquart and Julian B. Roebuck examined the snitch system at the Johnson Unit in Texas (see Box 15.1).

BOX 15.1   **SOCIAL CONTROL IN A MAXIMUM-SECURITY PRISON**

To facilitate control and order, staff members enlisted the "official" aid of inmates as informers and surrogate guards. These snitches, called **building tenders (B.T.s)** and turnkeys, in turn cultivated their own inmate snitches. In contrast to many prison systems in which snitches are perceived as the weakest, despicable, and pitiful creatures in the prisoner society, the B.T.s and turnkeys at the Johnston Unit were physically and mentally superior inmates. Typically, they were also more violent and criminally sophisticated than the ordinary inmates.

B.T.s were given the authority by prison administrators to discipline erring inmates who disturbed the social order. For example, an inmate found stealing another's property was likely to receive a slap across the face, a punch in the stomach, or both. If the erring inmate continued to steal, he was summarily beaten and, with the staff's approval, was moved to another cellblock. But the B.T.s were much more effective in controlling inmates' behavior in the cellblock by preventing incidents. They spent much of their time talking with other inmates, especially the runners. Runners, who had much more contact with ordinary inmates than B.T.s, secured and relayed information on work strikes, loansharking, stealing of state property, the distilling of liquor, homosexual acts, revenge plans, and escapes.

In sum, the day-to-day maintenance of order depended on the cooptation of elites, a snitching system, and the terrorization of ordinary inmates. In this regimented and predictable environment, the staff's power, authority, and presence permeated the prison. But almost immediately after the B.T. system was purged from all the Texas prisons, there was an escalation in violence. In 1984, the T.D.C. prisons had 24 inmate-inmate homicides and nearly 400 stabbings, representing a new level of violence.

Source: James W. Marquart and Julian B. Roebuck "Prison Guards and Snitches: Social Control in a Maximum Security Institution," in *The Dilemmas of Punishment,* ed. Kenneth C. Haas and Geoffrey P. Alpert (Prospect Heights, Ill.: Waveland Press, 1986), pp. 158–176.

The Bureaucratization of Prison Administration   Following World War II, prison absolutism collapsed in nearly every state when governors and legislators demanded the creation of management systems that would assure the control of prisons through chains of accountability. Their demands led to the development of correctional systems in which the absolute authority of autocratic wardens was replaced by specific, limited, and delegated power. Set up in the bureaucratic tradition, correctional systems worked toward greater efficiency, higher performance standards, clearer accountability, more flexible programming, and better allocation of resources.[11]

The head of the corrections department, whether he or she is called director, commissioner, secretary, or administrator, runs the department from the state capital. As an appointee of the governor, he or she is responsible for supervising wardens of state institutions, as well as for public relations, political contracts with the legislature, fiscal management, policy implementation, and long-range planning. Directors may supervise wardens directly, or they may turn that responsibility over to a subordinate, who then reports back to the director.

The years from 1970 to 1975, according to Jacobs, represented the "emergence of a professional administration" in Illinois. However, the new bureaucrats had enormous problems with both inmates and staff. On one hand, inspired by a rehabilitative ideal, the bureaucrats attempted to enhance the "respect," "dignity," and "status" of the prisoner; but, on the other hand, they rapidly lost control of the prison to the inmates. Meanwhile, line staff (correctional officers) thought that the bureaucrats' human relations model was "giving away the store" to the prisoners. Inmate gangs took advantage of the lack of staff leadership and gained greater control inside the prison.[12]

In the 1970s, corrections officials throughout the nation, like those at Stateville, turned to private sector management theory in their attempt to administer correctional institutions. But they soon discovered that the new management theory did not solve the problems in American prisons. By the early 1980s, most correctional administrators had come to agree that contemporary prisons had more violence, worse living conditions, and fewer programmatic opportunities than those under the autocratic rule of old.

Today, innovations within the prison combined with external supervision are enabling federal and some state corrections officials to shape a new environment based on accountability, functional integration, risk assessment, and institutional differentiation. **Management information systems (MIS)** have led to system-wide changes; for example, inefficient wardens have been demoted, inmates are tracked more effectively throughout the system, personnel have been upgraded, and population needs can be projected. Smaller and newer prisons, better classification systems, and unit management have helped to defuse institutional violence.[13] Institutional security has been improved through new technology.

Improved means of supervising correctional institutions have also been developed. Legislative task forces exam everything from free time (recreation) on death row to T.I.E.—Training, Industry, and Education vocational programs. Ombudsmen are more widely used in correctional institutions. There is more court supervision of prisons than ever before, and all kinds of legal people are daily within the prison.

In some states, the determinate sentence is acting to "cool" the prison. For example, 55 percent of all new admissions in Ohio's prisons are on 6-month, 12-month, or 18-month fixed terms; the relatively short terms for most minor felony inmates have influenced these offenders to want *no* action. Yet Lynne Goodstein and John Hepburn, in examining the impact of determinate sentencing in Connecticut, Illinois, and Minnesota prisons, concluded that "determinate sentencing has had essentially no impact on inmate adjustment or institutional climate."[14]

| BOX 15.2 | **AIDS IN PRISONS AND JAILS** |

Acquired Immune Deficiency Syndrome (AIDS) has rapidly become one of the most difficult and complex public health issues facing the United States. The rapid increase in cases in recent years, as well as the continued uncertainty as to the future course of the disease's spread, led President Reagan to term AIDS "the nation's number one health priority."

In the correctional context, it is believed that dealing with the problem of AIDS poses particularly difficult problems because inmate populations may include high proportions of individuals in AIDS risk groups, particularly intravenous drug users. A recent national study conducted by the National Institute of Justice and the American Correctional Association found that since 1981, there have been 455 confirmed AIDS cases in 25 state and federal prison systems. Twenty large city and county jail systems reported 311 cases of AIDS among inmates.

Only four state correctional systems (Nevada, Colorado, Iowa, and Missouri) have implemented or plan to implement mass screening programs for inmates. But almost 90 percent of the responding jurisdictions do employ testing for more limited purposes. The highest priority in the correctional response is providing timely, professional, and compassionate medical care to inmates who become ill with the disease.

Source: Theodore M. Hammett, *AIDS in Prisons and Jails: Issues and Options* (Washington, D.C.: U.S. Department of Justice, 1986), pp. 1–3.

Services and Programs

As a result of class action suits, prisons now are required by the courts to offer certain basic services. Medical care is provided for those who are ill. A nurse is usually on duty during the day, and a physician is present in the clinic on designated days each week. Box 15.2 discusses the care of AIDS patients in prison. Dental care is generally available at most larger prisons.

The modern prison also must provide for the visitation rights of prisoners. Most states now permit contact visitation (whereby a prisoner and his or her visitor are permitted to have some physical contact, such as holding hands). An inmate commissary is available where inmates can buy articles such as tobacco, candy, instant coffee, prepared foods, and toilet articles. In addition, the prison is required to provide a library, including a law library, for prisoners.

Recreational programs receive heavy emphasis in prison. Popular recreational activities include weight lifting, softball, baseball, football, volleyball, handball, horseshoes, shuffleboard, jogging, table tennis, and movies. Organizational sports are also popular, as cell blocks compete against each other. Religious activities also figure in prison life. Protestant, Catholic, and Muslim services are conducted each week. The institution also generally employs a full- or part-time Protestant and Catholic chaplain.

Prisoners can become involved in education or vocational training. Adult basic education (ABC) programs, preparation for the general education diploma (GED), and sometimes even postsecondary college courses are available at most larger correctional institutions. Vocational education for men consists of such programs as barbering, printing, welding, machine shop, automotive body and fender repair, and auto-mechanics. In larger prisons, many other vocational programs are available as well. Vocational programs for women generally include beauty culture, secretarial training, data processing, business machine operations, and baking and food preparation, but women's prisons are beginning to offer nontraditional programs. For example, the women's prison in Nebraska offers a course in truck driving, and that at Bedford Hills in New York provides courses in auto mechanics, electronics, and video technology, along with more traditional courses.

Psychotherapy, transactional analysis (TA), reality therapy, behavior modification, and the therapeutic community are the most widely used treatment modalities. However, self-help programs are much more popular in prison now than the traditional rehabilitative programs. Self-help programs focus on one or more of the following areas: ethnic and cultural studies, skill development, personal insight, attitude improvement, or consciousness raising. Among the self-help programs found most frequently in prison are Jaycees, Lifers, Dale Carnegie, Checks Anonymous, Native American Spiritual and Cultural Awareness Group,

Compulsory field labor in Texas Department of Corrections, banned by federal court in 1980. (*Source:* Danny Lyon/Magnum Photos, Inc.)

yoga, Y'ai Chi Ch'uan, transcendental meditation (TM), Erhard's Seminars Training (EST), Positive Mental Attitude (P.M.A.), assertiveness training, moral development, and Emotional Maturity Instruction.

Joe Ragen looked upon treatment as a means of control, and during his rule, Stateville had one of the largest educational enrollments of any prison in the nation. But as rehabilitative philosophy came under increased attack in the 1970s, it was deemphasized as an element necessary for prison order. Significantly, at the same time that the formal role of treatment was minimized, the federal courts began to require that prisons deliver a minimum standard of services to prisoners.

The Inmate World

John Irwin's division of the recent history of the prison into three eras—those of the Big House, the correctional institution, and the contemporary prison—provides a helpful outline in examining the inmate world.[15]

The Big House   The **"Big House,"** which conjures up an image of the prison that still prevails in the minds of many, dominated American corrections from the early twentieth century through the 1950s. In the Big House, prison populations showed considerable homogeneity. Inmates usually were white, were thieves (and not very good ones at that), and had spent several stints in prison during the course of their criminal careers.[16]

New prisoners were informed by both staff and other inmates that they could do "easy time" or "hard time." The staff assured prisoners that to disturb the order within the walls would bring them "hard time." Old "cons" reaffirmed the message that the "keepers" were in control and prisoners had to make the best of it. To make their time easier in the Big House, convicts developed their own informal rules, language, and social roles. As described by Gresham M. Sykes and Sheldon L. Messinger, the informal code, or norms, was based on the following tenets:

1. Don't interfere with inmate interests.
2. Never rat on a con.
3. Do your own time.
4. Don't exploit fellow inmates.
5. Be tough; be a man; never back down from a fight.
6. Don't trust the hacks [guards] or the things they stand for.[17]

The **inmate code** had a special role in the system that developed, for it was ultimately functional to both prison administrators and prisoners.[18] In the eyes of prison staff, the code promoted order, for it encouraged just doing one's time rather than creating problems. Disorder within the walls could mean that the informal arrangements between leaders and staff would be set aside, and prisoners would lose privileges it had sometimes taken years to attain. But the code also protected the self-respect of inmates because the cons knew they were maintaining order, not for the staff, but for themselves. "Hacks" or "screws" [guards] were the enemy, and a convict who was worthy of his role within the prison would make his animosity toward the enemy very clear.

Donald Clemmer, who studied the Big House in his seminal study of Menard Prison in southern Illinois, claimed that the solidarity of the inmate world caused prisoners to become more criminalized. Clemmer coined the concept of **prisonization**, defining it as the "taking on in greater or less degree of the folkways, customs, and general culture of the penitentiary."[19] "Prisonization," he added, "is a process of assimilation, in which prisoners adopt a subordinate status, learn prison argot [language], take on the habits of other prisoners, engage in various forms of deviant behavior such as homosexual behavior and gambling, develop antagonistic attitudes toward guards, and become acquainted with inmate dogmas and mores."[20]

The Correctional Institution   After World War II, **correctional institutions** replaced Big Houses in many states. The use of indeterminate sentencing, classification, and treatment represented the realization of the rehabilitative ideal in correctional institutions.[21] But as most staff knew and new prisoners quickly learned, the primary purpose of the correctional institution was to punish, control, and restrain prisoners, and treatment played only a minor role.

Michel Foucault has argued that the rehabilitative ideal is the ultimate means of promoting order within the correctional institution.[22] The fact that most prisoners were busy at work or at school, whether or not they believed in the rehabilitative ideal, promoted peace and stability. The indeterminate sentence and the parole board represented a more direct means of promoting order, or control, because they communicated the clear message to the inmate that conformity was necessary for release.

As black prisoners began to increase in numbers in the late 1950s, racial unrest and hostility became the major source of disruption within the correctional institution. Racial unrest followed the desegregation of housing units, jobs, classrooms, and recreational programs in the prison. Racial unrest toppled the social order in many prisons, but when it fell, inmates tried to stop the disintegration, mend the cracks, and pull the pieces back together.[23]

The social reintegration of prisoners began in the late 1960s, as inmates began to redefine their relationships with one another, the prison administration, the criminal justice system, and society in a more political fashion. The politicization of prisoners contributed to the outbreak of a series of prison riots totally different from those of past eras. The riots were more organized, supported from the outside, led by prisoners who defined themselves as political activists, and intended to make far-reaching changes in the prison and justice system, if not in society itself.[24]

During the early 1970s, women prisoners also began to be influenced by the political and social events of the day. In 1972 and 1973, female prisoners in five institutions—Alderson Federal Reformatory for Women in West Virginia, Muncy Correctional Institution in Pennsylvania, Ohio Reformatory for Women, Philadelphia House of Corrections, and Niantic Women's Prison in Connecticut—staged hunger strikes, destroyed institutional property, took hostages, in-

Women in prison. (*Source:* David E. Kennedy/TexaStock.)

jured staff, and tried to escape from prison. In these and other women's prisons, women gave vent to their frustrations and began to demand more rights.

The inmate's response to imprisonment received some examination during the era of the correctional institution. Stanton Wheeler, in a study of the Washington State Reformatory, found strong support for Clemmer's concept of prisonization. But Wheeler found that the degree of prisonization varied according to the phase of an inmate's institutional stay; the inmate was most strongly influenced by the norms of the inmate subculture during the middle stage of his or her prison stay (with more than six months remaining).[25]

Further examination of the process of prisonization led to the development of the **deprivation model** and the **importation model**. The deprivation model, according to Gresham Sykes, describes the prisoner's attempt to adapt to the deprivations imposed by incarceration.[26] But John Irwin and Donald R. Cressey, among others, contended that patterns of behavior are brought to, or imported into prison, rather than developed within the walls.[27] Charles W. Thomas, in a study of a maximum-security prison in a southeastern state, concluded that the integration of both the deprivation and importations models was needed to understand the impact of the prison culture upon an inmate. Thomas found that the greater the degree of similarity between preprison activities and the norms of the prison subculture, the greater the receptivity to the influences of prisonization. He also found that those inmates who had the greatest degree of contact with the outside world had the lowest degree of prisonization.[28]

The Contemporary Prison The setting of the 1980s inmate world remains one of violence, but now the mood is one of disillusionment. The hopelessness experienced by many inmates can be explained by the ever-increasing problem of idleness, by longer sentences, by tighter controls imposed by staff, by overcrowded institutions, by the decline of political ideology, by the reduced possibility of relief through the judicial process, and by problems with drug and alcohol abuse.

In the **contemporary prison**, the social order often verges on total collapse; in fact, at times, the social order does collapse, but over the long term, this fragmented, tense, and violent setting remains intact because inmates ultimately prefer order to disorder. As one gang leader stated, "We're in control around here. If we wanted to, we could take the prison apart, but we choose not to. We've too much to lose."[29]

Increased administrative control and stiffer penalties for criminal behavior also have curbed some of the violence in prisons. The increased number of habitual offender statutes has led to the "greying" of the prison population (i.e., the average inmate is older now), and these offenders realize that they must make peace because they may be imprisoned for the rest of their lives.

Personal survival and involvement in the contraband market are two major preoccupations of inmates today. While order prevails in the larger social order, disorder is apparent in the daily existence of the inmate society. A misspoken word, a slight bump of another inmate, an unpaid gambling debt, a racial slur, or an invasion of the "turf" of another can bring a violent attack. Prisoners who escape physical assaults and sexual victimization are able to accomplish this feat because they follow these rules:

- Never show weakness to anybody.
- Never take anything from another inmate, unless you are certain you can pay it back.
- Never go into another inmate's cell, unless you know him or her very well.
- Never get into a threatening position, unless you have some lethal means to protect yourself.[30]

First-timers sometimes learn these lessons too late, and they may find themselves the sexual victim of their cellmate or other inmates. But even those inmates who are able to protect themselves from other prisoners cannot ignore the social networks of prison life. They must stick to their own racial groups and, in a gang-controlled prison, must decide if they want to go it alone or join a gang organization. New inmates have a particularly difficult time remaining independent in a gang-controlled prison. One gang leader said, "In here, you can't fly alone. You've got to fly with someone."[31]

David B. Kalinich, in examining the **contraband market** at the State Prison Southern Michigan (SPSM), found that the flow of contraband throughout the prison was extensive. *Contraband* can be defined as "any unauthorized substance or material" possessed by inmates: e.g., weapons, drugs, alcoholic beverages, gambling, prohibited appliances, and clothing. Gambling, institutional privileges, special food and canteen services, and prostitution also can be acquired through the contraband market. Although contraband has always been found in American prisons, the drug appetites and addictions of today's prisoners have encouraged the expansion of this market. Kalinich found that the most visible and widely used drug was marijuana, but large amounts of heroin, some cocaine, and an assortment of amphetamines and tranquilizers were also available.[32] The Bureau of Justice Statistics, in examining the use of drugs by prison inmates, found that half had taken drugs during the month just prior to the crime for which they were sent to prison, about half were under the influence of drugs at the time of their offense, and more than three-fourths had used drugs at some time during their lives.[33]

Lynne Goodstein's study of three adult male state correctional institutions in two northeastern states provides a serious critique of this nation's policy of imprisonment. She found that the inmates who adjusted most successfuly to a prison environment encountered more difficulty making the transition from institutional life to freedom. She concluded that the inmates who were least able to adjust to the formal institutional culture seemed to make the smoothest transition to community life. She adds that "it is ironic that . . . inmates who accepted the basic structure of the prison, who were well adjusted to the routine, and who held more desirable prison jobs . . . had the most difficulty adjusting to the outside world."[34]

Problems of American Prisons

James Jacobs's *Stateville* identified three problems that megaprisons faced in the 1970s: **overcrowding,** control of **institutional violence,** and **deterioration of staff morale**. These problems continue to present major crises in correctional institutions today.

Overcrowding The soaring prison popultion first began to affect American corrections in the mid-1970s. According to the Bureau of Justice Statistics, the number of inmates has risen more than 150 percent since 1974—from 200,000 to over 500,000; on January 1, 1987, 546,659 inmates were confined in state and federal correctional institutions.[35] The upward trend continues largely because of the increase in the length of sentences imposed and served in many states. Between 1980 and 1986 the prison population grew by nearly 217,000 inmates—an increase of about 66 percent (see Table 15.1).[36]

The number of sentenced federal prisoners grew at a faster rate than that of state prisoners in 1986 (11.7 percent versus 8.6 percent). The growth in the sentenced prisoner population in the Western states (14.5 percent) was higher than in the other regions of the United States; the Northeast increased 8.8 percent,

Table 15.1 **CHANGES IN THE STATE AND FEDERAL PRISON POPULATION, 1980–1986**

Year	Number of Inmates	Annual Percent Change	Total Percent Change Since 1980
1980	329,821		
1981	369,930	12.2%	12.2%
1982	413,806	11.9	25.5
1983	437,248	5.7	32.6
1984	464,567	6.2	40.9
1985	503,271	8.3	52.6
1986	546,659	8.6	65.7

Source: Bureau of Justice Statistics, *Prisoners in 1986* (Washington, D.C.: U.S. Department of Justice, 1987), p. 1.

the Midwest 7.8 percent, and Southern states by 6.4 percent. Sentenced state prison populations in Western states more than doubled (up nearly 116 percent), compared to a growth of 83 percent in the Northeast, 59 percent in the Midwest, and 46 percent in the South.[37]

The state prison populations rose most rapidly during 1986 in Nevada (19.5 percent), California (18.7 percent), Michigan and New Mexico (16.8 percent), and Oklahoma (15.2 percent). Women prisoners numbered 26,610 at the end of 1986, an increase during the year of 15.1 percent, compared with an 8.3 percent increase in the male population; in fact, the female prison population has grown at a faster rate than the male population in each year since 1981. Finally, at the end of 1986, 17 states reported a total of 13,770 state prisoners held in local jails because of crowding in state facilities.[38]

The runaway growth of prison populations has caused prisoners to be double- and triple-celled and to be forced to sleep in shower rooms, corridors, dayrooms, infirmaries, gymnasiums, and vocational shops. Florida, Texas, and other states have bought army tents and placed prisoners in prison yards. Arkansas purchased 65 house trailers to house 400 prisoners. Louisiana considered converting a ship into a floating prison, but gave the idea up when the state could not raise the necessary funds.[39]

John Conrad, in an eloquent denunciation of the overcrowded prison, says that fortresses like Jackson (Michigan), San Quentin (California), and Attica (New York) are:

> . . . areas of social violence in which order is precarious and life itself is increasingly perilous for all. The megaprison is an unnatural condition for life. In no other context are people expected to live like ants in a hill, thousands of men kept in continuous proximity to one another. In these pathogenic circumstances the system controllers are justified in always expecting and preparing for the worst—murder, riot, and chaos.[40]

Overcrowded prisons result in increased idleness among inmates and contribute to a rise in institutional violence. Overpopulated prisons also mean inhumane settings for confinement: two or three prisoners may be housed in a cell that was intended for one, basic services (medical care, for example) may be denied, and due process rights may be overlooked.[41] Overcrowding also contributes to lowered job satisfaction and morale among staff.

Corrections officials hoped that prison construction across the nation would ease the problem of overpopulation, but such has not been the case. Prisons continue to be overcrowded because of the overuse of maximum-security facilities and because of mandatory sentencing provisions.[42] Furthermore, prison populations tend to expand to fill the available space, and it usually does not take long when a state opens a new prison to fill the beds. Even after the current prison building boom is finished, the discrepancy between design capacity and actual population is likely to be as great as it was before the building program began.[43]

Increased Violence   **Riots** and major disturbances, inmate aggression toward other inmates, and inmate and staff conflict constitute the main forms of prison violence.

Prison disturbances can be nonviolent, violent, or both. Nonviolent disturbances consist of hunger strikes, work stoppages, sitdown strikes, and the mass filing of grievances. Violent inmate disturbances include assaults on prison staff; the burning or destroying of institutional property; and the taking control of a cell block, a yard, or an entire prison, with or without hostages.

Collective violence has always been endemic in prison life. Since 1951, there has been, on the average, at least one major prison riot a year in the United States. These riots have occurred in all areas of the country, have more often than not involved the taking of guards as hostages, and have nearly always featured widespread arson and vandalism. The targets of destruction consistently have been the school, shops, and infirmaries inside the walls. Counseling centers, chapels, and recreational facilities have been torched with regularity. The message delivered by the inmates is that punishment and therapy do not mix; the only reality is the pain of punishment—all else is cosmetic.

The 1980 riot at the Penitentiary of New Mexico at Santa Fe shows the callous disregard for life and property that accompanies a prison disturbance. During a 36-hour rampage of burning and destruction, 33 inmates were killed, many of them horribly mutilated, and 57 inmates and 9 staff members were seriously injured.[44]

In the wake of the tragedies of the New Mexico riot, the Kingston and Archambault riots in Canada (the latter taking the lives of three guards and two prisoners), the torching of the Idaho prison, and the uprisings in Holmesburg and Sing Sing, prison administrators must be particularly concerned about the eruption of a violent riot. The McKay Commission, investigating the 1971 Attica riot, with its 43 dead and 80 wounded, concluded that "Attica is every prison and every prison is Attica."[45] Today, it would appear that every prison is Santa Fe and Santa Fe is every prison.[46]

Violence directed toward staff must also be a critical concern of correctional administrators. In the autocratic model of prison administration, prisoners would not dare strike a staff member. But correctional officers at the present time daily experience the hostility of inmates. In fact, tower positions, long the most undesir-

The clean-up at the Penitentiary of New Mexico, Santa Fe. (*Source:* Norman Bergsma/Sygma.)

able jobs in the prison, are now sought after because they require no contact with the inmate.

James Jacobs claims that the most important of the factors contributing to violence at Stateville was the presence of four Chicago street gangs—the Blackstone Rangers (who later renamed themselves the Black P Stone Nation), the Devil's Disciples, the Conservative Vice Lords, and the Latin Kings.[47] A 1985 national study of **prison gangs** found gangs in 33 states. The most gangs were reported by Pennsylvania (15) and Illinois (14); the largest number of gang members were found in Illinois (5300), Pennsylvania (2400), and California (2050). Gang members made up 3 percent of all inmates in state and federal prisons.[48]

Prison gangs vary from loosely organized to highly organized and structured groups. The gangs that are imported from the streets are particularly highly organized. For example, the Conservative Vice Lords, a Chicago-based street gang, has 21 divisions. This gang, as well as the other Chicago "supergangs," has a well-established leadership structure and clearly defined social norms. Violations of these social norms bring punishment ranging from a beating to death.

Prison gangs spread from one state to another in several ways. Gang members may be sometimes transferred to a federal or another state correctional institution, and they spread the teachings of the mother gang. Gang members may move to another state and, when imprisoned for criminal activities, start a gang organization in the correctional facility. Or gang members may be traveling through a state and be imprisoned in that state because of a crime they commit. Finally, some street gang leaders send gang members to other states specifically to establish a gang organization. One chief of a Chicago street gang reported, "We want a national organization of the Unknown Vice Lords, and so we have sent our people to Wisconsin, Minnesota, and Michigan. It won't be long before we are coast to coast."[49]

Inmate gangs usually specialize in economic victimization. Typically, they force all independent operators out of business and either divide the spoils of drugs, gambling rackets, and prostitution rings among themselves or fight to the death to determine who will establish a monopoly within the prison.[50] High levels of violence may occur when gangs are in conflict with each other. Interracial conflict also disrupts institutional life when such conflict is made a deliberate policy of large gangs organized along racial and ethnic dimensions.

At present, however, institutional violence appears to be tapering off as administrators recapture some of the control they once had. For example, the summers of 1986 and 1987 were quiet despite expectations to the contrary.

Deterioration of Staff Morale   Jacobs found at Stateville that in the 1970s the guards became demoralized and alienated in the face of escalating violence and loss of control.[51] Studies of prison guards in the 1980s continue to find them to be isolated workers caught in an environment fraught with tension and uncertainty. Guards are characterized as "imprisoned,"[52] as "society's professional prisoners,"[53] and as individuals who feel "rejected, shunned, and even despised."[54]

Ben M. Crouch contends that the realities of danger and loss of control are the chief factors leading to the **deterioration of morale** among prison guards. Fear and uncertainty, according to Crouch, are daily realities for many guards. They observe inmate–inmate violence and know that it could at any time be directed at them.[55] "If the inmates want you, they can get you" is one of the most often repeated sayings among correctional officers. One gang member spoke to this danger: "We've this gang member. He is only five feet or so tall. One Friday, this lieutenant worked him over real good. The next Monday we took [stabbed] two lieutenants. One was dead for hours before they found him."[56]

Guards, according to Crouch, are also concerned about the diminished control over inmates.[57] They long for the "good old days" of order, peace, and tranquillity, when they were in control and inmates were dependent on them. John R. Hepburn and Ann E. Crepin found that while prisoners are becoming less dependent on guards, it appears that guards' dependence on prisoners has increased because of overcrowded prisons and the violent and unstable nature of the inmate society. Hepburn and Crepin concluded that "the greater the dependence on prisoners, either for the performance of one's job or for one's personal safety, the greater the role strain and the lower the job satisfaction."[58]

The Invasion of the Courts

Correctional law—the accumulated body of constitutional case law; federal, state, and local regulatory law; and standards and legal opinions—defines the rights of prisoners during confinement.

Prisoners' Rights in U.S. Corrections   Throughout the history of American corrections, the prisoner had been a slave of the state. The 1871 case *Ruffin* v. *The Commonwealth of Virginia* ruled:

> [The prisoner] has, as a consequence of his crime, not only forfeited his liberty, but all his personal rights except those which the law in its humanity accords to him. He is for the time being the slave of the state.[59]

The courts maintained this hands-off doctrine until the mid-1960s for several reasons: (1) judges felt that the administration of prisons was an executive rather than a judicial function; (2) judges acknowledged their lack of expertise in corrections; and (3) judges feared their intervention would have an adverse affect on prison discipline.[60] However, during the period from 1966 to 1976, federal judges, especially, became extensively involved in ruling on prisoners' rights within correctional institutions. In the *Coleman* v. *Peyton* and *Johnson* v. *Avery* cases, the U.S. Supreme Court ruled that access to the courts is a fundamental right which correctional officials cannot deny or obstruct.[61]

Jacobs documents how the federal court of Illinois became increasingly involved in the life and affairs of Stateville Penitentiary. In the mid-1960s, the Muslims in the prison petitioned the courts for the right to practice their religion, including the right to observe their food taboos. The administration fought the court action, but slowly and surely the Muslims were given more and more rights within the prison. Jacobs aptly expresses the impact of legal intervention:

> While the impact of the federal courts on the prison has been profound, the means by which this impact has been made are subtle and indirect. It has been the threat of lawsuits, the dislike for court appearances, the fear of personal liability, and the requirement of rational rules rather than revolutionary judicial decisions that have led to the greatest change in the Stateville organization. While the precise holdings of the court decisions have often been quite modest and even conservative, the indirect ramifications of judicial intervention into the prison have been farreaching.[62]

The rights of prisoners in the following areas have been litigated and upheld: conditions of confinement, first Amendment religious rights, mail, access to the media, due process, and rights of access to the courts.

In terms of First Amendment religious rights, the federal courts have consistently held that the religious rights granted to one religious group within correctional facilities must be given to all such groups. Yet the courts have been reluctant to permit the free exercise of religion to a degree that might infringe upon institutional security.

The censorship of personal correspondence has been litigated more than any other correctional procedure. A chief reason for this frequency, as the U.S. Supreme Court ruled in *Procunier* v. *Martinez,* is that "censorship of prison mail works a consequential restriction on the First and Fourteenth Amendment rights of those who are not prisoners."[63] The impact of this and other such cases has essentially been to eliminate the censorship of outgoing correspondence; incoming correspondence may still be checked for contraband, but not for content.

Another critical concern of inmates is the censorship of publications and manuscripts. The courts have generally advised a broadening of the rights of prisoners to publish articles and books. In the federal prison system, confidential access to the media is assured via the "prisoner mailbox," through which correspondence to media personnel is transmitted unopened.[64]

A major area of litigation concerning due process rights in prison involves disciplinary meetings. In the landmark *Wolff* v. *McDonnell* decision, the U.S. Supreme Court defined the due process rights of prisoners in disciplinary meetings:

1. The inmate must receive advance written notice of the alleged rules infraction;
2. The prisoner must be allowed sufficient time to present a defense against the charges;
3. The prisoner must be allowed to present disciplinary evidence on his or her behalf and therefore may call witness, as long as the security of the institution is not jeopardized;
4. The prisoner is permitted to seek counsel from another inmate or a staff member when the circumstances of the disciplinary infraction are complex or the prisoner is illiterate;
5. The prisoner is to be provided with a written statement of the findings of the committee, the evidence relied upon, and the rationale for the action. A written record of the proceedings must also be maintained.[65]

The significance of this case is that it standardized certain rights and freedoms in correctional institutions. Although prisoners received some procedural safeguards to protect themselves against disciplinary abuses, they did not receive all the due process rights of a criminal trial. Nor did the Supreme Court deny the right of correctional officials to revoke "good time" of prisoners (the practice by which acceptable behavior of prisoners during confinement results in reduced length of imprisonment).

The question of what constitutes "cruel and unusual punishment" (in violation of the Eighth Amendment) has been widely litigated in the courts. The decisions in *Talley* v. *Stephens* and *Jackson* v. *Bishop* found that whippings of prisoners constitutes cruel and unusual punishment, and flogging of prisoners has now been outlawed in nearly every state.[66] But the courts have generally supported the solitary confinement of troublesome prisoners, unless the conditions are clearly "shocking" or "debasing." For example, one decision held the punishment was cruel and unusual when the inmate in solitary confinement was denuded, exposed to winter cold, and deprived of such basic elements of hygiene as soap and toilet paper.[67] The intervention of the courts has made solitary confinement a far different experience than in the past, when prisoners were thrown into dark and damp cells and given a bread-and-water diet, sometimes for extended periods of time. Today, prisoners in solitary confinement must be fed the same diet as those not in solitary confinement, must be adequately clothed, must be placed in a cell that has light and warmth, and cannot be physically harmed.

Inmates have sometimes sought damages from prison administration for physical and sexual attacks by other prisoners. They have done this by suing the individual responsible in a civil tort suit for negligence. If a staff member, too, is deemed culpable and is employed by the federal government, the Federal Tort Claim Act can be used, or an action for violation of civil rights under section 1983 of the Civil Rights Act can be brought.[68] Although the courts have generally agreed that inmates deserve protection against predatory prisoners, officials are not likely to be held responsible, unless the inmate can prove that repeated attempts were made to warn officials of an impending assault.

Finally, at one time or another, the courts have ruled that the overall conditions of confinement of certain prisons in 36 states and of all the major prisons of Alabama, Arkansas, Florida, Louisiana, Mississippi, Nevada, New Hampshire, Texas, Wyoming, and Rhode Island inflict cruel and unusual punishment upon prisoners.

However, by 1976, court decisions had shifted toward favoring institutional concerns over prisoners' rights. During the spring of 1976, this more restrained approach was expressed in four U.S. Supreme Court decisions: *Bexter* v. *Palmigiano,* [69] *Enomoto* v. *Clutchette,* [70] *Meachum* v. *Haymes,* [71] and the most clearly, in *Meachum* v. *Fano:*

> Give a valid condition, the criminal defendant has been constitutionally deprived of his liberty to the extent that the state may confine him and subject him to the rules of its prison system so long as the conditions of confinement do not otherwise violate the Constitution.[72]

The retreat of judicial intervention continued as the U.S. Supreme court ruled eight to one in 1981 that "double celling" in the maximum-security Ohio prison at Lucasville does not violate "constitutional standards of decency" under the Eighth Amendment. In overturning the lower court's decision, the Court ruled that "cruel and unusual punishment" does not necessarily forbid more than one person in a cell but is more involved with the "totality of circumstances" in prison.[73] The tone of this decision was particularly discouraging to those who had looked to the courts for relief in concerns related to the Eighth Amendment.[74]

In sum, prisoners have made the greatest gains in the right to send and receive letters, but they also have made strides regarding their right to communicate with lawyers and the courts. Further, the courts have permitted the right of religious freedom as long as it does not jeopardize institutional security. Courts have additionally been willing to rule on the totality of conditions in a prison setting when prisoners appeared to be undergoing severe dehumanization and deterioration in their mental and physical well-being.[75] Thus, prisoners retain basic human rights, but they are not entitled to the same degree of constitutional protections that they enjoyed before conviction.

ANALYSIS OF THE PRISON

Several questions pertain to the relationship between order and the prison: What is the relationship between order and the prison's continued existence? Is the prison a microcosm of the larger society? What is the relationship between freedom and order in the prison?

Perseverance of the Prison

A recurring proposal made by prison reformers is to abolish the prison. Reformers who advocate abolition usually insist that prisons, regardless of how new, professionally staffed, or well-equipped, are profoundly harmful; that they embitter all those within their walls, staff as well as prisoners; and that they ultimately cause inmates to become more criminogenic.[76]

Prison abolitionists are obviously fighting a rear-guard action, as pressures for more use of imprisonment are coming from every quarter. The prison clearly continues to be accepted in American society because it fulfills the need for order of the larger society. Michael Ignatieff, in explaining the persistent support given the penitentiary in England from 1750 to 1850, says:

> The persistent support for the penitentiary is inexplicable so long as we assume that its appeal rested on its functional capacity to control crime. Instead, its support rested on a larger social need. It had appeal because the reformers succeeded in presenting it as a response, not merely to crime, but to the whole social crisis of a period, and as part of a larger strategy of political, social, and legal reform designed to reestablish order on a new foundation.[77]

As David Rothman has pointed out, Americans also have maintained a commitment to the prison because of the belief that it brings order. In the post–Civil War decades, penal reformers believed that "the appropriate task was to reform incarceration, not to launch a fundamental attack on it."[78] They were afraid that the abolition of the prison would lead to the restoration of brutal practices such as the whipping post and the gallows. Reformers were further committed to the idea that prisons could rehabilitate. According to Rothman, "The prospect of doing good, not merely the desire to avoid greater harm, ultimately bound another generation of well-meaning observers to the practice of incarceration."[79]

The prison continues to exist today in the United States because the public and the policymakers believe that it is needed in order to deal with the disorder of crime. In a law-and-order environment, imprisonment is used with increasing frequency so that law-abiding citizens do not feel cheated by impunity for the law-breaker. Michael Sherman and Gordon Hawkins have rightly contended that imprisonment is overused because legislatures, prosecutors, and judges do not know what else to do. They add that the "legalist needs for retribution cannot be met in other ways, so they have to be met by imprisonment."[80]

Yet it may be argued that the order of the favored classes is the social order the prison is protecting. George Rusche and Otto Kirchheimer, in their analysis of the evolution of punishment in Europe from the twelfth century to the nine-teenth century, showed the integral relationship between the institutions of pun-ishment and a society's economic system. They stressed that the wide acceptance of the principle of "less eligibility" had crucial implications for penal practices and conditions. This principle holds that prison conditions must always be worse than those of the working poor; otherwise, the working poor would not be encouraged to remain in the work force.[81]

Microcosm of the Larger Society

James Jacobs's analysis of Stateville concludes that the prison is a microcosm of the larger society; that is, the social organization and moral values, as well as the major societal changes, of the larger society are found in the micro society within the walls.[82] Donald Clemmer also notes the existence of numerous parallels between the prison and free world. He writes, "In a sense the prison culture reflects the American culture, for it is a culture within it."[83] Furthermore, James Fox observes that "the same civil rights issues, religious issues, and other social issues appear in prison as also appear in the city. The prison reflects the society it serves."[84]

However, while the argument can be made that the prison is a microcosm of the larger society, it is a distorted image of the larger society that is found within the prison walls. In its analysis of the 1971 Attica rebellion, the New York State Special Commission on Attica stated: "While it is a microcosm reflecting the forces and emotions of the larger society, the prison actually magnifies and intensifies these forces, because it is so enclosed."[85] Raymond Michalowski, in comparing the class diversions, organizational conflicts, sexual subjugation, and racial conflict in the prison and in free society, states:

> Prisons in America exist as a kind of distorted mirror image of American Society. Like the mirrors in a carnival fun-house, prisons exaggerate and expand some of the characteristics of the society they reflect. Yet, like fun-house mirrors, what they show is based on the very real object they are reflecting. The parallel between free society and prisons exists at both the organizational and the social level.[86]

To take this comparison between the prison and society a step further, the disorders of society—especially poverty, breakdown of community, racial and gender discrimination, violent crime, and mental illness—are found in more exaggerated form within the prison. The vast majority of prisoners come from pockets of poverty. They have grown up in disorganized communities, have been victims of racial and sexual discrimination, have varying degrees of emotional disturbance, and have victimized others. As these individuals come into the prison, they must deal with the deprivations of confinement in an environment full of racial unrest and division. Predators in the outside world may well become the victims in this enclosed world. For those who have emotional problems, the world of the prison is even more chaotic.

Freedom Versus Order

The question of the relationship between individual freedom and order would arise even if American prisons were acknowledged to be effective. The suspicion is spreading that most of the years spent in confinement do not serve any constructive function for the prisoner. Disorder continues both inside and outside the walls of our prisons. The crucial problem lies with society's practice of taking away a great deal of personal liberty without getting increased order in return.[87]

The preservation of order within the penitentiary has always been the chief responsibility of prison administrators. Although some headway has been made in regaining control of the prison, it is clear that maximum-security prisons are still out of control. If the prison must continue to exist, then the task is to regain control, or to reconstitute order.

The intervention of the courts has been the most important factor in expanding the freedoms of prisoners and improving their quality of life. Ensuring inmates' constitutionally guaranteed due process rights, the courts have mandated, is a critical responsibility of corrections officials. Prisoners are now spared the autocratic and old-style disciplinarian who intimidated both staff and inmates and threw recalcitrant prisoners into the "hole." Significantly, however, prisoners have gained more freedoms at the same time that they have lost the sense of safety they once had.

The issue is how to gain control of the prison without depriving inmates of their recently gained freedoms. The horn of the dilemma is that it appears to be a choice between two undesirable outcomes: either a controlled and punitive environment or a freer, unsafe environment. Certainly, the prison of the past has little to recommend it. Inmates were perhaps safer and prison life was probably more consistent in terms of the expected behavioral responses of staff and prisoners, but the inhumane and brutal measures inflicted on prisoners have no place in a free and democratic society. Yet the freedoms of the present are granted in overcrowded facilities filled with violence, idleness, and fear. The prudent prisoner simply checks into protective custody—if he can. Prisoners may have greater freedom, but more and more prisoners are willing to trade some of this freedom for 24-hour lockup in protective custody.

POLICY IMPLICATIONS

Humanitarian reform requires many changes in the structure, administration, and operations of the prison. Imprisonment in and of itself is sufficient punishment, without being exposed to further penalties and brutalities inflicted by other prisoners or by staff.[88] In achieving humanitarian reform, the issues of overcrowding and the necessary dimensions of a humane institution cannot be ignored.

Reduction of Overcrowded Prisons

Empirical research indicates that prison crowding has an adverse effect on both institutional management and maintenance and on employee satisfaction and stress. Prison crowding also promotes rule infractions by inmates, transmission of diseases, mental health problems, and collective and interpersonal violence.[89] Moreover, prison crowding has resulted in lawsuits in many states; for example, in 1987, 36 states and the District of Columbia were under court order or involved in litigation concerning conditions of confinement in their prison systems.[90] There is little disagreement concerning the reality of overcrowded prisons, but sharp disagreement exists over what should be done about it.

Michael Sherman and Gordon Hawkins's *Imprisonment in America* proposes a strategy that has the promise of accomplishing significant reductions in prison overcrowding.[91] They recommend that imprisonment be used primarily where it seems necessary to meet the threat of physical violence. They contend that if such a policy were enacted, a substantial proportion of those now incarcerated would not be imprisoned. To illustrate their point, they state that only about 47 percent of the prisoners in this nation have been sent to prison for crimes against the person (homicide, arson, rape, robbery, and assault; over one-third are incarcerated for property crimes, principally burglary and auto theft, and the remaining 20 percent have been convicted of crimes against public order, most of which are drug offenses.[92]

In the area of prison construction, Sherman and Hawkins recommend that "new prison space should be built to replace existing facilities or to bring them up to humane and constitutional standards." They add, "in most states, the effect

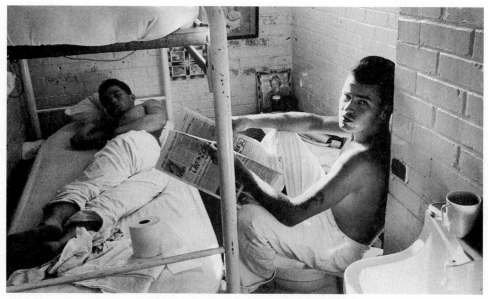

Life in a contemporary prison. (*Source:* Danny Lyon/Magnum Photos, Inc.)

of construction programs, indeed the conditions of funding them, should be that they do not increase capacity."[93] This recommendation takes seriously the argument that building new prisons generates only an increased number of prisoners, because the prison population expands to fill the available beds.

Mandatory sentencing acts and the overuse of maximum-security institutions are two other causes of crowded facilities. A 1982 Bureau of Justice report stated that 37 states had enacted some form of mandatory sentencing during the immediately preceding years—including mandatory prison terms for repeat offenders, for illegal drug sale or possession, and for crimes committed with firearms. Literally thousands of bills are introduced each year in state legislatures to increase prison terms for specific crimes.[94] Furthermore, although 30 to 40 percent of inmates are housed in maximum-security facilities, experts agree that only 10 to 15 percent actually require maximum-security imprisonment.[95]

Clearly, each state must develop its own overcrowding control measures, based on its history and current political climate, as well as on the values and philosophies of its policymakers.[96] Seven states—Colorado, Louisiana, Michigan, Ohio, Oregon, South Carolina, and Tennessee—have turned to the National Prison and Jail Overcrowding Project of the Center of Effective Public Policy for help in reducing overcrowding.[97] The staff of this project has won a number of legislative battles in several states; in other states, it has been less successful (see Box 15.3).

Until a state can achieve the long-term objectives of reforming the criminal law, on reclassifying who is sent to maximum security prisons, and on replacing existing facilities, short-term strategies to reduce prison crowding offer some solutions:

- intensive probation supervision, which would divert designated felons from prison population to probation services;
- "capping" legislation, which would establish a population limit and provide for emergency release measures to maintain a desired population level;
- extended parole, which would direct the parole board to use risk assessments in establishing length of parole supervision;
- community corrections acts, which would keep certain offenders in the community who would otherwise be sent to prison;
- emergency powers act, which would permit the governor to release state inmates up to 90 days early when prison populations exceed operating capacity.[98]

Humane Prisons

In attempting to improve the quality of institutional life for inmates, a worthwhile goal is to create humane institutions that simulate as much as possible the conditions of the real world. This simulation of the real world can be accomplished only when prisons are lawful, safe, industrious, and hopeful.[99]

BOX 15.3 **NATIONAL PRISON AND JAIL OVERCROWDING PROJECT**

- In South Carolina, the project successfully lobbied the legislature for an emergency prison overcrowding release act in 1983.
- The Louisiana legislature passed a law backed by the project authorizing the hiring of more than one hundred additional probation officers. The purpose of this law was to encourage the use of probation as an alternative to imprisonment.
- In Tennessee, the project worked with the governor's office to fashion a package of reform bills. The package, including a statewide community corrections act, was presented to the legislature during an emergency session on prison overcrowding in 1985.
- In Colorado, an innovative bill that would have capped the state's prison population at 600 inmates per 100,000 population at risk was rejected by the governor.
- After some initial legislative successes in Michigan, the prison overcrowding project there failed to gain consensus on a proposal for $200 million in new prison construction.
- In Oregon, an emergency prison release bill backed by the project died in the legislature in 1983, and an emergency jail release bill was vetoed in 1985. But the project was able to establish a statewide council of criminal justice officials and private citizens authorized to draft a new sentencing plan.
- In Ohio, a "good time" credit bill and an emergency release bill recommended by project staff passed the legislature and were signed by the governor in 1987.

Source: Bruce Cory, "Shaping Policy to Ease Crowding," *Corrections Compendium* X (January 1986), pp. 6–7, and *Interim Report of the Governor's Committee on Prison Crowding,* State of Ohio, January 1986, pp. 4–9.

The Lawful Prison   The purpose of the lawful prison is to prevent proscribed actions and conduct and to provide inmates with all the rights granted by case law. Violators within the prison must be punished appropriately under conditions in which due process procedures prevail. If the administration tolerates unlawful conduct by staff or prisoners, such as freely flowing drugs, thriving gambling rackets, and prostitution rings, nothing else that it attempts will succeed.[100]

The Safe Prison   Both prisoners and staff must be assured of their safety in prison. Although physical attacks on staff and inmates do take place in minimum-security institutions, medium- and maximum-security prisons are the most likely settings for physical and sexual victimization, stabbings, and homicides. Guards across the nation express a common complaint—that they have neither the control nor the respect they used to have. Nor do inmates feel any safer. The new breed of inmates brings with it the criminal expertise of street gang sophistication, the mechanics of narcotics distribution, and a toleration for mayhem at a level hitherto unknown in American prisons.

To insure inmate and staff safety, changes are needed in the design and administration of prisons. Small prisons holding no more than four hundred inmates should be built. The physical design of the prison and its operations must ensure that adequately trained guards are in close contact with inmates in living quarters and at work assignments. Guards can best serve the interests of order and safety when they are competent in human relations, so that information can flow freely between prisoners and guard without fear that it will be misused, without expectation of special favor, and under conditions of respect and responsibility.[101] All of Ohio's newly built prisons attempt to implement these policies. Furthermore, its state correctional academy, as well as those in a number of other states, train newcomers and old-timers alike in interpersonal relations and the management of people without resorting to force and violence.

The Industrious Prison   Idleness is one of the real problems of prison life today. Because of overcrowded prisons, what work there is to be done is spread so thin that it is no longer work. The yards and cell blocks are full of inmates trying to cope with their ennui. Some inmates engage in physical activities, such as lifting weights, but too many inmates scheme during idle hours about drug drop-offs, prostitution rings, and "hitting" (stabbing) inmates in competing gangs.

As a step toward easing the idleness, inmates need to be provided with more work and to have the work they do valued. Inmates must be paid for their work. Workers in prison are denied the value of their labor when they are paid at the low rates allowed in most correctional systems; although to pay inmates the rates prevailing in the free market may be unrealistic, higher pay will produce benefits more than commensurate with the increased cost. Finally, work that is more marketable must be found. The useless and menial work characteristic of most prison industries is inappropriate because it fails to equip inmates for employment in the free community.[102]

Fortunately, the 1980s have seen the revival of prison industries. This trend has emerged as a result of the pioneering involvement of a few private corporations and the driving force of former Chief Justice Warren E. Burger. Burger formulated the "factories with fences" concept and began promoting it with great energy. One of Burger's widely quoted sayings is "To put people behind walls and bars and do little or nothing to change them is to win a battle but lose a war. It is wrong. It is expensive. It is stupid."[103]

The Hopeful Prison   Finally, prisons should provide renewed hope. The loss of hope is one of the consequences of a criminal career. To provide renewed hope, prisons should offer inmates such programs as remedial elementary education, vocational training, individual and group therapy, and self-help techniques. No penalty should be levied against an inmate for failure to participate in a program, but there must be some incentive to engage in treatment. In the hopeful prison, inmates must feel that they have say in their own lives. There is strong evidence that the freedom to make some decisions is needed to build a sense of responsibility. Finally, in the hopeful prison, prisoners must feel that they have acceptance in the outside community. Without such contact, the only reality for the inmate is the cell blocks, the yard, and the prison industrial plant.[104]

SUMMARY

Who is sentenced to prison, the deprivations that are imposed, and the authority invested in the custodians tell much about a society's values, its distribution of power, and its system of legal rights and obligations. It can also be argued that the extent to which currently accepted humanitarian norms and values apply to the lives of prisoners, the most peripheral members of society, reveals a great deal about the overall moral order. Thus, the true character of a society can be inferred from an examination of its prisons.[105]

Such an examination of our prisons would result in a grave indictment of federal and state policies. Our prisons are very punitive, and prisoners are sent there *for* punishment rather than *as* punishment. Prison overcrowding, institutional violence, and deterioration of staff morale are all reminders that America's policy of imprisonment needs major overhauling. Judicial intervention has influenced many positive changes within the walls, including more progressive corrections officials, upgraded standards and accreditation, better trained staff, and more humane conditions for prisoners. But existing disorder within the walls, especially in the lives of guards and inmates, demonstrates quite clearly that judicial intervention is not enough. One of the major challenges facing this nation is to shape and implement a new philosophy of imprisonment.

There was a time when Americans believed in the possibility of personal redemption. The public's perception was the cozy and optimistic view of a growing, self-assertive, optimistic nation, and this optimistic view still finds expression in the hundreds of voluntary associations of deviants and in the pop psychologies that rocket across the horizon and disappear. But today's climate is closer to one of pessimism and hopelessness. Dante's inscription of hell is equally appropriate for a maximum-security prison: "Abandon all hope, ye who enter here." Until we find new approaches for dealing with our prisons, we will confine prisoners without much hope. John Conrad has noted, "To restore hope, protracted confinement must be restricted to those relatively few criminals who present a clear and present danger. To do otherwise is to mock history, experience, and knowledge."[106]

REFERENCES

Bowker, Lee. *Prison Victimization.* New York: Elsevier, 1980.

Camp, George M., and Camp, Camille Graham. *Prison Gangs: Their Extent, Nature and Impact on Prisons.* Washington, D.C.: U.S. Government Printing Office, 1985.

Carroll, Lee. *Hacks, Blacks, and Cons.* Lexington, Mass.: Heath, 1974.

Clemmer, Donald. *The Prison Community.* New York: Holt, Rinehart & Winston, 1958.

Haas, Kenneth C., and Alpert, Geoffrey P., eds. *The Dilemmas of Punishment: Readings in Contemporary Corrections.* Prospect Heights, Ill.: Waveland Press, 1986.

Ignatieff, Michael. *A Just Measure of Pain: The Penitentiary in the Industrial Revolution, 1750–1850.* New York: Pantheon Books, 1978.

Irwin, John. *Prisons in Turmoil.* Boston: Little, Brown, 1980.

Jacobs, James B. *Stateville: The Penitentiary in Mass Society.* Chicago: University of Chicago Press, 1977.

Jacobs, James B. *New Perspectives on Prisons and Imprisonment.* Ithaca, N.Y.: Cornell University Press, 1983.

Kalinich, David B. *Power, Stability, and Contraband: The Inmate Economy.* Prospect Heights, Ill.: Waveland Press, 1986.

Marquart, James W., and Roebuck, Julian B. "Prison Guards and 'Snitches': Deviance Within a Total Institution." *British Journal of Criminology* 25 (July 1985) pp. 217–233.

Petersilia, Joan. *The Influence of Criminal Justice Research.* Santa Monica, Calif.: Rand Corporation, 1987.

Rothman, David J. *Conscience and Convenience.* Boston: Little, Brown, 1980.

Rusche, Georg, and Kirchheimer, Otto. *Punishment and Social Structure.* New York: Russel & Russel, 1939.

Sherman, Michael, and Hawkins, Gordon. *Imprisonment in America: Choosing the Future.* Chicago: University of Chicago Press, 1981.

Stastny, Charles, and Tyrnauer, Gabrielle. *Who Rules the Joint? The Changing Political Culture of Maximum-Security Prisons in America.* Lexington, Mass.: Heath, 1981.

Sykes, Richard. *The Society of Captives.* Princeton, N.J.: Princeton University Press, 1958.

NOTES

1. Alfred Hassler, *Diary of a Self-Made Convict* (Chicago: Regnery, 1954), pp. 70–71.

2. See Bureau of Justice Statistics, *Imprisonment in Four Countries* (Washington, D.C.: U.S. Department of Justice, 1987).

3. See James Jacobs, *Stateville: The Penitentiary in Mass Society* (Chicago: University of Chicago Press, 1977); Lee Bowker, *Prison Victimization* (New York: Elsevier, 1980); Lee Carroll, *Hacks, Blacks, and Cons* (Lexington, Mass.: Heath, 1974); Erik Olin Wright, *The Politics of Punishment: A Critical Analysis of Prisons in America* (New York: Harper & Row, Colophon Books, 1973); Ben M. Crouch, "Prison Guards on the Line," in *The Dilemmas Of Punishment: Readings in Contemporary Corrections,* ed. Kenneth C. Haas and Geoffrey P. Alpert (Prospect Heights, Ill.: Waveland Press, 1986), pp. 177–206; and David B. Kalinich, *Power, Stability, and Contraband: The Inmate Economy* (Prospect Heights, Ill.: Waveland Press, 1986).

4. See Bert Useem, "Disorganization and the New Mexico Prison Riot of 1980," *American Sociological Review* 50 (October 1985), pp. 677–688.

5. James B. Jacobs, *Stateville,* p. 2.

6. Ibid., p. 29.

7. Ibid., pp. 29–33.

8. John Conrad and Simon Dinitz, "Position Paper for the Seminar on the Isolated Prisoner" (Paper presented at the Academy for Contemporary Problems, National Institute of Corrections, Columbus, Ohio, 8–9 December 1977), pp. 4–11.

9. For an articulate statement of the mission of the Texas Department of Corrections, see the interview with George Beto, former director of the T.D.C., in Clemens Bartollas, *Introduction to Corrections* (New York: Harper & Row, 1981), pp. 306–309.

10. *Ruiz* v. *Estelle,* 503 F. Supp. 1265 (S. D. Texas) 1980.

11. Conrad and Dinitz, "Position Paper," pp. 4–11.

12. Jacobs, *Stateville,* pp. 57, 85–86.

13. For a discussion of the new classification systems, see Joan Petersilia, *The Influence of Criminal Justice Research* (Santa Monica, Calif.: Rand Corporation, 1987), pp. 60–61.

14. Lynne Goodstein and John Hepburn, *Determinate Sentencing and Imprisonment* (Cincinnati: Anderson, 1985), p. 165.

15. John Irwin, *Prisons in Turmoil* (Boston: Little, Brown, 1980).

16. Ibid., p. 20.

17. Adapted from Gresham M. Sykes and Sheldon L. Messinger, "The Inmate Social System," in *Theoretical Studies in the Social Organization of the Prison,* ed. Richard A. Cloward, Donald R. Cressey, George H. Grosser, Richard McCleery, Lloyd E. Ohlin, Gresham M. Sykes, and Sheldon L. Messinger (New York: Social Science Research Council, 1960), pp. 6–8.

18. Gresham Sykes, *The Society of Captives* (Princeton, N.J.: Princeton University Press, 1958), and Sykes and Messinger, "Inmate Social System."

19. Clemmer, *Prison Community,* p. 299.

20. Ibid., pp. 299–300.

21. Irwin, *Prisons in Turmoil,* pp. 37, 40.

22. Michel Foucault, *Discipline and Punishment: The Birth of the Prison* (New York: Pantheon Books, 1977).

23. Irwin, *Prisons in Turmoil,* p. 75.

24. Ibid., pp. 76–77.

25. Stanton Wheeler, "Socialization in Correctional Communities," *American Sociological Review* 26 (October 1961), pp. 697–712.

26. Sykes, *Society of Captives.*

27. John Irwin and Donald R. Cressey, "Theieves, Convicts and the Inmate Culture," *Social Problems* 10 (Fall 1962), p. 143.

28. Charles W. Thomas, "Prisonization or Resocialization: A Study of External Factors Associated with the Impact of Imprisonment," *Journal of Research in Crime and Delinquency* 10 (January 1975), pp. 13–21; and Charles W. Thomas, "Toward a More Inclusive Model of the Inmate Contraculture," *Criminology* 8 (November 1970), pp. 251–262.

29. Interviewed in May 1981.

30. These survival lessons were described by various ex-offenders.

31. Interviewed in March 1978.

32. Kalinich, *Power, Stability, and Contraband,* p. 42.

33. Bureau of Justice Statistics, *Prisoners and Drugs* (Washington, D.C.: U.S. Government Printing Office, 1983), pp. 1–2.

34. Lynne Goodstein, "Prisonization and the Transition to Community Life," *Journal of Research in Crime and Delinquency* 16 (July 1979), pp. 265–266.

35. Bureau of Justice Statistics, *Prisoners in 1986* (Washington, D.C.: U.S. Government Printing Office, 1987), p. 1.

36. Ibid.

37. Ibid., p. 2.

476   THE PRISON

38. Ibid., pp. 2, 4.
39. Steve Gettinger, "U.S. Prison Populations Hit All-Time High," *Corrections Magazine* 2 (March 1976), pp. 13–16.
40. John P. Conrad, "Which Way Is the Revolution?" in *Should We Build More Prisons,* ed. Matthew Matlin (Hackensack, N.J.: National Council on Crime and Delinquency, 1977), pp. 10, 14.
41. For the negative effects of crowding on inmate behavior, see Paul B. Paulus et al., "The Effects of Crowding in Prisons and Jails," in *Reactions to Crime: The Public, the Police, Courts, and Prisons,* ed. David P. Farrington and John Gunn (New York: J Wiley, 1986).
42. Petersilia, *Influence of Criminal Justice Research,* p. 58.
43. J. Mullen, K. Carlson, and B. Smith, *American Prisons and Jails, Vol. 1, Summary and Policy Implications of a National Survey,* Abt Associates, Inc., for National Institute of Justice, U.S. Department of Justice, 1980.
44. For an examination of the riot at the New Mexico State Penitentiary, see Bert Useem, "Disorganization and the New Mexico Prison Riot of 1980," *American Sociological Review* 50 (1985), pp. 677–688; and Mark Colvin, "The 1980 New Mexico Prison Riot," *Social Problems* 29 (June 1982), pp. 459–463.
45. *Attica: The Official Report of the New York State Special Commission on Attica* (New York: Praeger, 1972).
46. Charles Stastny and Gabrielle Tyrnauer, *Who Rules the Joint? The Changing Political Culture of Maximum-Security Prisons in America* (Lexington Mass.: Lexington Books, Heath, 1981), p. 5.
47. Jacobs, *Stateville,* p. 146.
48. George M. Camp and Camille Graham Camp, *Prison Gangs: Their Extent, Nature and Impact on Prisons* (Washington, D.C.: U.S. Government Printing Office, 1985), p. vii.
49. Interviewed in March 1984.
50. Jacobs, *Stateville,* and Bowker, *Prison Victimization.*
51. Jacobs, *Stateville,* p. 179.
52. L. Lombardo, *Guards Imprisoned* (New York: Elsevier, 1981).
53. R. J. Wicks, *Guard: Society's Professional Prisoner* (Houston: Gulf, 1980).
54. J. Jacobs and L. Zimmer, "Collective Bargaining and Labor Unrest," in *New Perspectives in Prisons and Imprisonment,* ed. J. Jacobs (Ithaca, N.Y.: Cornell University Press, 1983), pp. 145–159.
55. Ben Crouch, "Prison Guards on the Line," p. 181.
56. Interviewed in June 1981.
57. Crouch, "Prison Guards on the Line," pp. 184–185.
58. John R. Hepburn and Ann E. Crepin, "Dependence Relations in a Coercive Organization: A Study of the Strategies of Accommodation and Repression by Prison Guards" (unpublished, n.d.), pp. 4, 12.
59. *Rufflin* v. *The Commonwealth of Virginia,* 62 Va (21Gratt.) 790, 796 (1871).
60. John W. Palmer, *Constitutional Rights of Prisoner,* 2d ed. (Cincinnati: Anderson, 1977), p. 174.
61. *Coleman* v. *Peyton,* 302 2bd (4th Cir. 1966), and *Johnson* v. *Avery* 89 S. Ct. 747 (1969).
62. Jacobs, *Stateville,* pp. 106–107.
63. *Procunier* v. *Martinez,* 416 U.S. 396 (1974).
64. *Washington Post Company* v. *Kleindienst,* 494 F. 2d 994, 997 (D.C. Cir. 1974).

65. "Prison Discipline Must Include Notice," *Prisoner Law Reporter* 3 (July 1975), pp. 51–53.

66. *Talley* v. *Stephens,* 247 F. Supp. 683 (E.D. Ark, 1965), and *Jackson* v. *Bishop,* 404 F. 2d 571 (8th Cir. 1968).

67. 387 F. 2d 519 (2d Cir. 1967).

68. David Fogel, ". . . *We Are the Living Proof" The Justice Model for Corrections* (Cincinnati: Anderson, 1975), p. 135.

69. *Baxter* v. *Palmigiano,* 96 S. Ct. 1551 (1976).

70. *Enomoto* v. *Clutchette,* 96 S. Ct. 1551 (1976).

71. *Meachum* v. *Haymes,* 96 S. Ct. 2543 (1976).

72. *Meachum* v. *Fano,* 96 S. Ct. 2543 (1976).

73. *Rhodes* v. *Chapman,* 29 *Criminal Law Review* 3061 (1981).

74. Stastny and Tyrnauer, *Who Rules the Joint?,* p. 39.

75. Conclusions of Nan Aron, contained in Bartollas, *Introduction to Corrections,* p. 349.

76. President's Commission on Crime and the Administration of Justice," *Corrections* (Washington, D.C.: U.S. Government Printing Office), p. 99.

77. Michael Ignatieff, *A Just Measure of Pain: The Penitentiary in The Industrial Revolution, 1750–1850* (New York: Pantheon Books, 1978), p. 210.

78. David J. Rothman, *Conscience and Convenience* (Boston: Little, Brown, 1980), p. 29.

79. Ibid., p. 31.

80. Michael Sherman and Gordon Hawkins, *Imprisonment in America: Choosing the Future* (Chicago: University of Chicago Press, 1981), p. 100.

81. Georg Rusche and Otto Kirchheimer, *Punishment and Social Structure* (New York: Russel & Russel, 1939).

82. Jacobs, *Stateville.*

83. Donald Clemmer, *The Prison Community* (New York: Holt, Rinehart & Winston, 1966), p. 298.

84. Cited in Charles Reasons, "Racism, Prison, and Prisoners' Rights," *Issues in Criminology* 9 (1974), p. 7.

85. New York State Special Commission on Attica, *Attica* (New York: Praeger, 1972), p. 82.

86. Raymond Michalowski, *Order, Law and Crime* (New York: Random House, 1984).

87. Sherman and Hawkins, *Imprisonment in America,* pp. 1–2.

88. Norval Morris and James Jacobs, *Proposals for Prison Reform,* Public Affairs Pamphlet 510; University of Chicago, July 1974, p. 4.

89. Paulus et al., "Effects of Crowding in Prisons and Jails."

90. Petersilia, *Influence of Criminal Justice Research,* p. 58.

91. Sherman and Hawkins, *Imprisonment in America,* pp. 101–122.

92. Abt Associates, *Prison Population and Policy Changes,* p. 172.

93. Sherman and Hawkins, *Imprisonment in America,* p. 101.

94. Cited in Petersilia, *Influence of Criminal Justice Research,* p. 55.

95. Ibid., p. 58.

96. Gerald Kaufman, "The National Prison Overcrowding Project: Policy Analysis and Policies: A New Approach" (Paper presented at the Annual Meeting of the American Society of Criminology (November 1984).

97. Ibid., p. 25.

98. Ibid., pp. 21–25.

99. This section on policy is adapted from John P. Conrad and Simon Dinitz, "The State's Strongest Medicine," in *Justice and Consequences,* ed. John P. Conrad (Lexington, Mass.; Lexington Books; Heath, 1981), pp. 51–70; and Simon Dinitz, "Are

Safe and Humane Prisons Possible?" *Australia and New Zealand Journal of Criminology* 14 (March 1981), pp. 11–16.

100. Dinitz, "Are Safe and Humane Prisons Possible?" p. 11.

101. Ibid., p. 13.

102. Ibid., p. 14.

103. Quoted in Gail S. Funke, ed., *National Conference on Prison Industries: Discussion and Recommendations* (Washington, D.C.: National Center for Innovation in Corrections, 1986).

104. To add another dimension of hope, John P. Conrad says that the prison should be a school of citizenship; see Conrad, "Where There's Hope There's Life," in *Justice as Fairness,* ed. David Fogel and Joe Hudson (Cincinnati: Anderson, 1981), pp. 16–19.

105. James B. Jacobs, *New Perspective on Prisons and Imprisonment* (Ithaca N.Y.: Cornell University Press, 1983), p. 17.

106. Conrad and Dinitz, "The State's Strongest Medicine," in Cleon Faust and D. Robert Webster, *An Anatomy of Criminal Justice* (Lexington, Mass.: Lexington Books, 1980), p. 257.

CHAPTER **16**

Probation, Parole, and Community-Based Corrections

OVERVIEW OF COMMUNITY-BASED CORRECTIONS

Social Context of the 1960s and Early 1970s

Philosophical Underpinnings

Anti-Institutionalization
Reintegrative Philosophy

Administrative Strategies

"Get-Tough" Policies

Trends in the Late 1980s

PROBATION

Changing Goals of Probation Services

Reintegrative Philosophy
The Justice Model
Reduced Risk and Increased Surveillance
    Models

Risk Assessment

Classification
Intensive Supervision

The Probation Officer

Casework Management and Other
    Administrative Duties

Supervision of Probationers
Reports to the Courts

PAROLE

Parole Under Attack

Parole Guidelines

Supervision of Ex-offenders

EVALUATION OF PROBATION AND PAROLE

RESIDENTIAL PROGRAMS

ANALYSIS

The Quest for Order

Disorder in Community-Based Programs

POLICY IMPLICATIONS

Reconstruction of Urban Communities

**Coordinated Administration of
    Community-Based Corrections**

SUMMARY

REFERENCES

NOTES

KEY TERMS

California Community Treatment
   Project (CTP)
classification systems
community corrections act
Community Resource Management
   Team (CRMT)
community resource manager
community restitution programs
electronic monitoring
halfway house
home furlough program
house arrest
intensive parole projects
internalization

intensive supervision
parole
parole guidelines
presentence investigation reports
   (PSI)
probation
re-entry shock
reintegrative philosophy
risk assessment scales
residential programs
social disorganization/social control
   model
victimization/deterrence model
work-release programs

The individuals being granted probation today are more firmly entrenched in a criminal lifestyle than even four years ago. They have less education, less skills, fewer support systems or intact marriages. The client of today is probably an abuser of drugs or alcohol. Basically, the typical probation client has more long-term problems of a serious nature than previously seen. In addition, the probation officer of today has a larger case load and fewer resources available with which to address these problems.

Probation is also becoming more of a dollars and cents issue. Economics and our overcrowded prisons are clearly taking precedence over risk to community in the sentencing process. This has had a direct effect on probation in two ways. First, individuals are receiving probation for more serious offenses than ever before. Second, probation is frequently not being revoked in light of a new arrest.

—Probation officer in the midwest[1]

Probation, parole, and residential facilities are the basic forms of community-based corrections. These programs provide an alternative to institutionalization, offer services for reintegration of offenders into community life, and strengthen the ability of a community to accept responsibility for its problems. Supporters of community-based corrections also assert that community programs are the best hope that corrections has of bringing order from the disorder of the crime, because they are more humane to offenders, less costly to the state or county, and at least as effective as institutionalization for eligible offenders who pose no risk for violence. However, as the opening quotation for this chapter indicates, community-based corrections faces several challenges today—large case loads, more dangerous clients, problem-besieged clients, lack of resources, and continued community opposition.

This chapter begins with an overview of community-based corrections, then describes and evaluates the basic forms of community programs, and concludes with policy recommendations.

OVERVIEW OF COMMUNITY-BASED CORRECTIONS

Theoretical support for community-based corrections is set down in the reports of the President's Commission on Law Enforcement and Administration of Justice, *Task Force Report: Corrections,* [2] and of the National Advisory Commission on Criminal Justice Standards and Goals, *Corrections.* [3] The social setting in which these documents were published led to their rapid acceptance as guidelines for corrections in the community.

Social Context of the 1960s and Early 1970s

Community-based corrections had its origins in the nineteenth century and experienced a period of growth at the turn of the twentieth century. Then, in the early 1960s, Richard McGee, Milton Burdman, Douglass Grant, Marguerite Warren, and John Conrad, all California prison administrators and researchers, began working on the concept of community corrections. This group concluded that community-based programs are far more therapeutic than debilitating prison environments.

This group, which also knew that the public would resist community-based corrections, set up an experiment, the **California Community Treatment Project (CTP)**, in which wards in California Youth Authority institutions were randomly assigned to control and experimental groups. Those in the experimental group were immediately released to community supervision, while the controls were released after serving normal sentences. The initial evaluation of this project found that the overall success rate of those assigned to the experimental group was higher than of those in the control group. [4] With the apparent success of rehabilitation in the community, community corrections supporters persuaded the California legislature to embark on a large probation subsidy program in which the state paid counties to place offenders on probation rather than sending them to the state's prisons.

At the same time, crime was emerging as a major social problem, and President Lyndon B. Johnson appointed the President's Commission on Law Enforcement and Administration of Justice to study the problem and make recommendations. Californians dominated the Task Force on Corrections: 8 of the 63 consultants were employees of the California Department of Corrections or Youth Authority, and 7 more were California academicians who had worked closely with the CTP and probation subsidy programs.

The recommendations of the Corrections Task Force captured the imagination and support of the American public in the late 1960s and early 1970s. The spirit of the times was one of reform. The area of mental health had gone through a period of deinstitutionalization in the 1960s, in which more and more mental health patients were kept in the community rather than placed in large institutions. The turbulence brought on by the Vietnam War, urban riots and disturbances on college campuses, and the widespread questioning of traditional values by the counterculture fostered a receptivity to new solutions. The bloody prison riots that erupted between 1971 and 1973 helped support the inevitable conclusion that there must be a better way.

But it was federal funding that provided the catalyst linking correctional ideology with social and political realities and thereby created a huge array of community-based programs throughout the nation. For example, from the inception of the Law Enforcement Assistance Administration (LEAA) in 1967 to July 1975, $23,837,512 of the Safe Street Act federal monies were matched with $12,300,710 from state and local funds for grants devoted solely to residential aftercare programs for adults.

Philosophical Underpinnings

The new mission for community-based corrections focused on the criticism of correctional institutions and on the role of correctional programs in the community.

Anti-Institutionalization   The Corrections Task Force of the President's Commission on Law Enforcement and Administration of Justice stressed the need for alternatives to prisons because too many of these long-term institutions were understaffed and underequipped and had problems with overcrowding, brutality, and corruption.[5] The commission's report also charged that the fortress-like prison was usually remote from urban communities and that this inaccessibility interfered with efforts to reintegrate inmates into community settings and made it difficult to recruit correctional staff, especially professionals.[6]

The National Advisory Commission on Criminal Justice Standards and Goals also explained why it was necessary to keep offenders out of correctional institutions:

> Prisons tend to dehumanize people. . . . Their weaknesses are made worse, and their capacity for responsibility and self-government is eroded by regimentation. Add to these facts the physical and mental conditions resulting from overcrowding and from the various ways in which institutions ignore the rights of offenders, and the riots of the present time are hardly to be wondered at. Safety for society may be achieved for a limited time if offenders are kept out of circulation, but no real public protection is provided if confinement serves mainly to prepare men for more, and more skilled, criminality.[7]

In short, both the President's Crime Commission and the National Advisory Commission established their case for community-based corrections by showing the failure of correctional institutions. The National Advisory Commission report went so far as to advise that "states should refrain from building any more state institutions for juveniles" and "should also refrain from building more state institutions for adults for the next ten years, except where total institution planning shows that the need is imperative."[8]

Reintegrative Philosophy   A major contribution of the reports of the President's Crime Commission and the National Advisory Commission is that they developed the basic assumptions of **reintegrative philosophy**. First, these reports claimed that offenders' problems must be solved in the community where they began. Second, society has a responsibility for dealing with its own problems, and it can partly fulfill this responsibility by helping law violators reintegrate themselves into community living. Third, meaningful community contacts are required to achieve the objectives of reintegration. Offenders must be offered opportunities to assume the normal roles of family member, employee, and citizen. Offenders also need opportunities for personal growth in accepting environments. Finally, advocates of the reintegration model recommended community-based corrections for all but hard-core criminals, and they would offer those offenders who had to be institutionalized a wide variety of reentry programs, permit inmates to be brought into the decision-making process so that they could choose their prison programs, and provide the necessary services so that offenders could restore family ties and obtain employment and education.[9]

The process by which change takes place in the reintegration model is known as **internalization**. To achieve internalization, offenders must be presented with such options as employment, education, recreation, and any other activities needed to provide direct or indirect alternatives to criminal behavior. Advocates of this model reason that through a process of experimentation, offenders can learn how to meet their needs in law-abiding ways so that they will alter socially unacceptable values and behaviors.

Administrative Strategies

The early 1970s, the "Golden Age of Community-Based Corrections," saw the rise of several new approaches to administering corrections programs in the community. First, three states—Minnesota, Oregon, and Kansas—indicated support of community-based corrections by passing innovative **community corrections acts**. The Minnesota Community Corrections Act (CCA), a broad and comprehensive act, served as the model for other community corrections acts. The CCA had four major purposes: (1) the reduction of commitments to state prisons; (2) encouragement of local units of government to maintain responsibility for offenders whose crimes were not serious (those who would receive a sentence of less than five years in a state facility); (3) the promotion of community corrections planning at the local level; and (4) improved coordination among local components of the criminal justice system.[10]

Second, a few counties developed coordinated services that involved several subsystems of the correctional system. For example, a model comprehensive program was developed in Polk County (Des Moines), Iowa. The Des Moines program, which was later replicated throughout Iowa and elsewhere, included pretrial screening and release, supervised pretrial release, presentence investigation and probation, and a community-based corrections facility.[11]

Third, some 30 states began to provide both probation and parole services through the same agency, making it possible for officers to supervise combined case loads.[12] It was argued that the combined system requires only one office, one set of directives, and one supervisory hierarchy; that the same goals are sought; and that the same skills are required for supervision of offenders on both probation and parole.[13]

"Get-Tough" Policies

In the mid–1970s, public acceptance of community-based corrections declined. The rise of crime convinced the public that a "get-tough" approach was needed. Hard-liners were quick to recommend incarceration as a more fitting way of dealing with crime. Moreover, too many poorly planned and inadequately operated programs, along with the publicity given to crimes committed by offenders placed in these programs, also contributed to the change in public opinion of community-based corrections. The following news item indicates the questionable management typical of many community-based programs:

> WASHINGTON (AP)—For three years, convicts Willie Bell and John Irby regularly left prison for the workaday world of a job-release program. Police now say that while commuting from their cells the pair worked at becoming kings of a major drug network. Police say the two inmates at the District of Columbia prison in nearby Lorton, Virginia, used their work-release jobs "as a front for a well-planned narcotics conspiracy." Both were arrested on narcotics law violations.[14]

The courts continued to place on probation nearly 60 percent of convicted offenders, or over one million offenders each year, but this most widely used judicial disposition came under increased pressure from proponents of the "get-tough" approach. Residential facilities came under even greater criticism, so much so that it became difficult both to establish new programs and to sustain those already functioning in the community. Political pressure on departments of corrections resulted in the assignment of far fewer offenders to work-release and home furloughs. Finally, parole was so extensively criticized that some states and the federal system even abolished it, at least on paper.

Then, in the 1980s, overcrowded prisons had a dramatic impact on the mission of community-based corrections. Federal court orders to relieve prison overcrowded conditions in 36 states meant that the states had to do something. Although a possible long-term solution was prison construction, a more immediate solution was needed. Probation and parole suddenly regained the favor of judges and political policymakers, and the numbers, especially of those on probation, soon skyrocketed.

Trends in the Late 1980s

In the late 1980s, a new mission in community-based corrections is being defined, based upon expansion rather than retrenchment. The new mission has a number of emerging themes. First, **intensive supervision** is being proposed as the means by which more offenders can be left in the community without jeopardizing the protection of society. Second, more attention is being given substance abusers, primarily because so many offenders have histories of substance abuse. Third, more emphasis is being placed on **community restitution programs** and work orders. Indeed, in some court systems, restitution is almost an inevitable condition of probation status. Fourth, conflict resolution approaches in the community are receiving greater emphasis. Fifth, bureaucratic efficiency and accountability is now demanded of community-based programs. Sixth, **electronic monitoring** is again being proposed as a means by which the supervision of offenders can be improved. Finally, there appears to be a trend of returning responsibility to the counties while, at the same time, permitting privately operated programs to play a major role in administering community-based programs.

PROBATION

Probation can be defined as a court service by which the defendant's freedom in the community continues or is only briefly interrupted, but under which the person is subject to supervision by a probation officer and to the conditions imposed by the court. The sentencing court retains the authority to modify the conditions of the sentence or to resentence the offender if he or she violates the conditions of probation or commits a new crime.

Probation is the most widely used judicial disposition. On January 1, 1986, 1,870,132 adult offenders—64.4 percent of the 2.9 million adults under the care or custody of a correctional agency—were on probation. This record population grew by 159,000 or 7.4 percent, during 1985; since 1979, the number on probation has increased by nearly 800,000, a 65 percent increase.[15] See Table 16.1 for the numbers of adults on probation at the end of 1985.

The most common conditions of probation include fines, restitution to victims, community service, payment of court-appointed attorney fees or state-imposed fees, participation in drug or alcohol abuse programs, and gainful employment. These conditions satisfy the desire both to consider the needs of victims and to teach offenders responsible behavior. Financial restitution and community service are particularly widely used today. The use of restitution actually predates both incarceration and modern forms of community treatment; the current trend is toward a more purposeful and imaginative use of restitution. At times, the victim is even involved with the offender in the development of restitution agreements.[16]

Probationers and parolees in many states are now required to pay a monthly fee to the state while they are under supervision. In 1984, at least 18 states permitted or actually imposed these fees.[17] The states claim that the purposes of

Table 16.1 ADULTS ON PROBATION, 1985

Regions and jurisdictions	Probation population, 12/31/84	1985[a]		Probation population, 12/31/85	Percent change in probation population, 1984-85	1985 probationers per 100,000 adult residents
		Entries	Exits			
U.S., total	1,740,948	1,174,832	1,046,383	1,870,132	7.4%	1,064
Federal	52,351	24,293	21,427	55,217	5.5	31
State	1,688,597	1,150,539	1,024,956	1,814,915	7.5	1,033
Northeast	287,728	182,169	173,506	296,391	3.0	786
Connecticut[b]	46,681	37,486	47,362	36,805		1,522
Maine	4,368	3,124	3,041	4,451	1.9	518
Massachusetts	23,141	18,005	16,509	24,637	6.5	553
New Hampshire	3,126	2,338	2,368	3,096	−1.0	416
New Jersey	44,208	26,704	22,446	48,466	9.6	850
New York	90,011	39,360	28,555	100,816	12.0	752
Pennsylvania	64,310	47,830	46,854	65,286	1.5	727
Rhode Island	7,147	3,946	3,557	7,536	5.4	1,014
Vermont	4,736	3,376	2,814	5,298	11.9	1,341
Midwest	347,357	257,300	229,380	376,012	8.2	869
Illinois	63,477	40,990	30,311	74,156	16.8	879
Indiana	36,004	37,167	34,050	39,121	8.7	980
Iowa	11,924	12,693	12,554	12,063	1.2	571
Kansas	15,576	8,235	8,338	15,473	−.7	867
Michigan	70,948	54,456	50,242	75,162	5.9	1,138
Minnesota	31,440	29,101	27,555	32,986	4.9	1,080
Missouri	23,574	17,063	13,877	26,760	13.5	723
Nebraska	10,763	12,200	12,243	10,720	−.4	926
North Dakota	1,517	822	770	1,569	3.4	322
Ohio	58,194	33,734	30,463	61,465	5.6	781
South Dakota	1,514	—		2,249	48.5	448
Wisconsin	22,426	10,839	8,977	24,288	8.3	696
South	730,682	513,211	448,519	795,374	8.9	1,327
Alabama	16,338	5,399	5,217	16,520	1.1	569
Arkansas	8,238	2,049	1,019	9,268	12.5	541
Delaware	6,373	4,316	3,856	7,103	11.5	1,528
District of Columbia	10,319	10,455	8,997	11,777	14.1	2,384
Florida	118,318	142,021	129,572	130,767	10.5	1,481

State				
Georgia	90,057	52,820	48,416	94,461	4.9
Kentucky	15,004	4,493	4,610	14,887	-.8
Louisiana	26,733	12,779	12,874	26,638	-.4
Maryland	64,827	39,297	36,986	67,138	3.6
Mississippi	6,570	2,647	2,581	6,636	1.0
North Carolina	52,600	31,874	28,267	56,207	6.9
Oklahoma	18,809	9,445	7,944	20,310	8.0
South Carolina	17,043	9,606	8,685	17,964	5.4
Tennessee	23,598	16,464	15,414	24,648	4.5
Texas	235,568	160,267	125,926	269,909	14.6
Virginia	16,690	7,000	6,454	17,236	3.3
West Virginia	3,597	2,279	1,971	3,905	8.6
West	322,830	197,859	173,551	347,138	7.5
Alaska	2,064	1,196	654	2,606	26.3
Arizona	16,687	7,911	6,422	18,176	8.9
California	195,864	108,979	94,394	210,449	7.4
Colorado	16,693	10,462	9,543	17,612	5.5
Hawaii	6,686	5,252	3,952	7,986	19.4
Idaho	3,151	2,135	1,872	3,414	8.3
Montana	2,471	1,172	931	2,712	9.8
Nevada	5,226	2,351	2,212	5,365	2.7
New Mexico	3,926	3,151	2,892	4,185	6.6
Oregon	21,452	13,961	13,036	22,377	4.3
Utah	7,721	3,541	4,932	6,330	-18.0
Washington	39,181	36,674	31,607	44,248	12.9
Wyoming	1,708	1,074	1,104	1,678	-1.8

—Data not available.

[a]Totals do not include South Dakota's entries and exits. . . .

[b]Connecticut transferred jurisdiction of 12,990 pretrial alcohol cases from the probation staff to the Pre-Trial Bail Commission. Thus, yearend counts were not comparable.

Source: Bureau of Justice Statistics, *Probation and Parole, 1985* (Washington, D.C.: U.S. Department of Justice, 1987), p. 2.

these fees include offsetting the costs of probation and parole supervision, helping pay for drug testing for those under supervision, and supplementing the state's victim-compensation fund.[18]

Many forms of probation exist today. Standard probation means a probationer is supervised by a probation officer for a specified period. Informal probation, or probation without adjudication, is a highly debated form of probation by which an offender is supervised without placing him or her under the jurisdiction of the formal justice system. Bench, or unsupervised, probation is another form of probation, used especially with misdemeanants.

The deferred sentence delays conviction on a guilty plea until the sentenced offender has successfully served his or her probation term. The offender is then given the opportunity to withdraw the plea, and the court dismisses the charges. Some jurisdictions also suspend a prison sentence order after formal conviction, permitting the defendant to serve the sentence in the community while on probation.

Shock probation is used in Ohio, Idaho, Indiana, Kentucky, Tennessee, Iowa, and Texas. In Ohio, which developed the first shock probation statute, the offender, his or her attorney, or the sentencing judge can submit a motion to suspend the remainder of the sentence after a felon has served at least 30, but fewer than 60, days of his or her sentence and to release the inmate on probation. Within 60 days of the filing of the motion, the judge who heard the case must hold a hearing on the motion; he or she is permitted another 10 days in which to rule on the motion.[19] Ohio is also combining intensive supervision and shock probation to improve the community adjustment of probationers after they are released from prison.[20]

Changing Goals of Probation Services

In the past two decades, three goals have been advocated for probation services: the rehabilitative goal of reintegration, the due process principles of the justice model, and the reduced risk and increased surveillance models. The role of the probation officer changes significantly with each of these goals.

Reintegrative Philosophy   As previously discussed, the social context was one of reform in the late 1960s and early 1970s, and, supported by blue ribbon commissions and funded by federal dollars, the reintegrative philosophy was widely accepted by probation officers across the nation. Elliott Studt makes clear the need for community involvement in the task of reintegration:

> It is too seldom recognized that reintegration is a two-way relationship requiring open doors and support from the community as well as responsible performance by the parolee [or the probationer]. No one can reintegrate in vacuo.[21]

Adopting the reintegrative philosophy required changes in probation and parole services, such as team approaches, pooled case loads, service brokerage, referred services, and job placement development.[22] In the mid-1970s, as the rehabilitation model came under increasing attack, a number of probation administrators adopted the concept of the **Community Resource Management Team (CRMT)**. Under this approach to probation services, officers are divided into teams, and each team takes responsibility for a case load and makes decisions on what community resources are needed by clients. Team members are usually specialists in "needs subsystems," and the specialist links the probationer with whatever services in the community are necessary.[23]

The Justice Model   David Fogel argues that probation lacks direction, has low status, and is experiencing a decline in public confidence.[24] Fogel, P. McAnany, and D. Thompson have offered the following suggestions to provide direction for probation:

1. Probation is a penal sanction whose main characteristic is punitive.
2. Probation should be a sentence, not a substitute for a real sentence that is threatened after future violation—it should not be subject to reduction or addition.
3. Probation should be part of a single graduated range of penal sanctions and should be available as the sentence for all levels of crime, except the most serious felonies.
4. The gravity of the probation sentence should be determined by both the length of term and the quality and quantity of the conditions.
5. Conditions should be justified in terms of the seriousness of the offense, though other purposes may be served by such conditions, such as incapacitation.[25]

Fogel also wants to reduce the discretionary authority of probation officers, and, therefore, recommends that the standard of proof for the revocation of probation be as strong as the original finding that resulted in the sentence of probation (i.e., beyond a reasonable doubt). Furthermore, the presentence investigation report should be regarded as a legal document, and defendants have the right to know the contents of this report. Fogel and other advocates of the justice model recommend increasing restitution programs, because they believe it is only fair for offenders to pay for the social harm they have inflicted. Fogel emphasizes that probation should be as concerned with the victim of crime as it is with the offender.[26]

Reduced Risk and Increased Surveillance Models   In the late 1970s, probation came under criticism as a lenient measure that allowed offenders to escape their just punishment. R. L. Thomas explains why probation suffers from this "soft on criminals" image:

> Probation lacks the forceful imagery which other occupations in criminal justice can claim. Police catch criminals, prosecutors try to get them locked up, judges put them in prison, guards and wardens keep them there, [but] probation, in the public view, offers crime and the criminal a second chance.[27]

In an attempt to convince the public, as well as policymakers, that probation could be "tougher" on criminals, probation administrators began to emphasize strategies that would better ensure public protection. The combination of protection and incarceration takes several forms. The "split sentence" combines incarceration with probation as a separate sentence. Intermittent confinement means weekend, night, or vacation confinement in jail during the time a person is on probation. The diagnostic study followed by probation, an option in a number of jurisdictions (California, Kansas, North Dakota, and Pennsylvania, and the federal system), permits the judge to confine an offender for a limited period of time before sentencing him or her to probation.[28]

Intensive supervision, a new but already widely used program, seems especially useful with high-risk probationers. This type of program, initiated in Georgia, is based on the belief that increased contact and referral result in more positive adjustment, as evidenced, for example, by a higher employment rate and a lower rate of involvement in crime. The typical pattern is for one or more probation officers to assume a small case load made up of probationers who require intensive supervision. These probationers are contacted several times a week, through unannounced home visits and other means.[29]

Risk Assessment

The public demands community safety from potentially dangerous probationers and parolees, but, at the same time, the numbers of those on probation are skyrocketing and more serious offenders are being sentenced to probation. For example, Joan Petersilia and colleagues discovered that in 1984, close to 1 percent of all Californians were on probation and that about one-third of these probationers had been convicted of felony crimes. In a recidivism study of felony probationers in Los Angeles and Alameda counties, they found that 65 percent of the total sample had been rearrested and 53 percent had official charges filed against them. Of those charges, 75 percent involved burglary/theft, robbery, or other violent crimes—the crimes most threatening to public order.[30]

Classification   Considerations of public safety have led most probation departments to develop **classification systems** for placing offenders under intensive, medium, or minimum supervision. Most of these instruments are modeled after the Wisconsin system, or the NIC Model Probation Client Classification and Case Management System.[31] The Wisconsin system is currently used in at least 100 jurisdictions throughout the United States.[32]

Under the Wisconsin system, a risk/needs assessment evaluation is made of each probationer at regular intervals. The risk scale was derived from empirical studies that showed certain factors to be good predictors of recidivism—such as prior arrest record, age at first conviction, the nature of the offense for which the probationer was convicted, and employment patterns.

The needs assessment focuses on such indicators as emotional stability, financial management, family relationships, and health. The scores derived from the risk/needs assessment are used to classify probationers by required level of supervision—intensive, medium, or minimum. These levels, in turn, impose corresponding restrictions on liberty and requirements for contact between offenders and probation staff. Reassessment of cases takes place at regular intervals, and the level of supervision may be increased or reduced.[33]

Intensive Supervision   Intensive supervision of high-risk probationers has been used by jurisdictions to meet the challenge of probation services. Such programs reassure conservative policymakers by promising intensive surveillance of high-risk offenders, satisfy federal judges that official discretion is being properly used, and reduce the need to commit new funds for prison construction.[34] John Conrad has suggested that intensive supervision programs "offer realistic prospects for a wide-ranging renovation of American penology."[35]

The Georgia Intensive Probation Supervision (IPS) program is the strictest form of intensive probation in the United States. Thirteen teams across the state—each composed of a probation officer and a "surveillance officer"—watch over no more than 25 probationers at a time. They see their clients at least five times a week, sometimes more often. Probationers have a curfew, which is checked on frequently.[36] A 1987 evaluation showed that offenders placed in IPS had lower rates of recidivism than comparison groups of offenders released from prison and supervised on regular probation, and that the majority who committed new crimes were involved in less serious forms of criminal behavior.[37] The positive evaluation of Georgia's project has encouraged New York, Texas, Washington State and New Jersey to develop their own intensive probation projects. Some large county probation offices have also set up similar intensive programs.

A probation officer meeting with a client. (*Source:* Bob Daemmrich.)

Probation staffs, overburdened with mammoth case loads and challenged to provide adequate supervision to protect public safety, have sought new options to deal with certain types of offenders. In some jurisdictions, the search has led to the use of electronic and computer technology to monitor offenders placed on **house arrest** or in community corrections programs. Through electronic monitoring devices, corrections staffs can verify that an offender is at home or in a community correctional center during specified hours.[38]

The device used in these programs is typically an electronic transmitter worn on the wrist or ankle that emits a signal received by another device connected to the telephone in the probationer's home. The signal is then relayed to a central computer in the probation office. If the probationer moves beyond a specified distance from the phone or tampers with the device, the interruption of the signal is recorded by the computer, and an alert is sounded. Adjustments are made for different times of day; for example, to allow a person to go to work but to be at home by a specified time.[39]

Richard Ball and Robert Lilly, in examining home arrests, concluded that the use of surveillance technology reduces the involvement of the community with the offender. They add that "the rapid development of electronic monitoring now suggests that the system . . . may be more interested in maintaining bureaucratic control . . . than involving the community in the monitoring of compliance."[40]

The Probation Officer

The three basic functions of an adult probation officer are to manage a case load and perform certain other administrative responsibilities, to supervise probationers, and to make reports to the courts.

Casework Management and Other Administrative Duties   Probation agencies, as discussed above, commonly divide probationers into various categories, based upon their needs and the risk they present to the community. Using these needs/risk assessments, the probation officer keeps an up-to-date casework file, carries out periodic reviews, devises a system for ensuring that reports will be ready when due, keeps up with the necessary paperwork, and compiles the required statistical reports.

Supervision of Probationers   The probation officer of the past wore two hats—that of law enforcement, or supervision, and that of treatment. In the 1970s, treatment was emphasized, as officers were expected to be resource managers, or brokers. The role of **community resource manager** was based on the premise that "the probation officer will have primary responsibility for meshing a probationer's needs with a range of available services and for supervising the delivery of these services."[41]

More recently, the law enforcement, or surveillance, role has greatly increased in importance. With one-third of probationers across the nation convicted felons and with society's hard-line mood, probation officers are aware that they must closely supervise their case loads.[42] The task of supervision is made even more difficult because of the increasing sizes of probation case loads.

The influence of bureaucratic structures and processes is causing much greater constraints to be placed on probationers.[43] All too frequently, probation officers are informed that the first commandment of working in an office is not to embarass the agency. This "play-it-safe" posture has led to a bureaucratic rigidity that has caused job burnout with staff.[44] A probation officer charged:

> I used to enjoy my job, but I don't anymore. Administrators are more interested in controlling us than in providing services to clients. The way they control us is to create one crisis after another. We're always in a state of uncertainty what will happen next.[45]

Reports to the Courts   The probation officer must also write reports to the court. The **presentence investigation (PSI)** is the major such report, but the officer must file others as well, such as a notice of violations and a full violation-of-probation report before revocation hearings are held.

The primary purpose of the presentence investigation is to help the court decide whether or not to grant probation, to determine the conditions of probation, to determine the length of the sentence, and to decide upon community-based or institutional placement for the defendant.[46]

A PSI typically involves six categories. First, information about the offense is included, specifying the exact nature of the offense; a section may be included that permits the defendant to report his or her version of what happened. Second, the individual's prior record is listed; some jurisdictions also permit the listing of juvenile adjudications. Third, the personal background of the individual is examined: upbringing, education, marital situation, employment, physical and emotional health, military service, and financial situation. Fourth, the prosecution is given an opportunity to enter into the report its opinion of the appropriate disposition. Fifth, a concise review of the foregoing information is drawn together and presented along with the possible sentencing alternatives available to the court. Finally, the probation officer submits to the court what he or she believes to be the most appropriate sentence based upon the information in the report.[47] The importance of this final category is evident in the fact that studies show that judges' sentencing decisions follow the probation officer's recommendation about 95 percent of the time.[48]

The revocation of probation is highly important to probationers, because it can result in a prison sentence. This judicial procedure takes place when a probation officer recommends to the court that probation should be revoked because a probationer has committed a new crime or violated the conditions of his or her probation.

The U.S. Supreme Court has ruled on three important cases concerning probation revocation: *Mempa* v. *Rhay* (1968), *Gagnon* v. *Scarpelli* (1973), and *Bearden* v. *Georgia* (1983).[49] In *Mempa,* the Court held that the Sixth Amend-

BOX 16.1   **RIGHTS OF PROBATIONERS IN
               PRESENTENCE INVESTIGATION**

Disclosure of the contents of the presentence investigation has been the major issue concerning the PSI to be litigated by the courts. Counsels for the defense advocate disclosure because they want the opportunity to challenge any disputable statements in this report. Probation officers, not surprisingly, dislike disclosure because it is more difficult to secure information from potential witnesses and informants if they know the defendants will learn what was said.

The most important case dealing with presentence disclosure is *Williams* v. *New York State* (1949). The jury had convicted Williams of murder and recommended a life sentence, but when the judge imposed the death sentence on the basis of the presentence report, Williams appealed, arguing that the sentencing violated his process rights "in that the sentence of death was based upon information supplied by witnesses with whom the accused had not been confronted and as to whom he had no opportunity for cross-examination or rebuttal." The U.S. Supreme Court court rejected Williams's appeal, concluding that the disclosure to the defendant of the presentence report would prevent judges from obtaining information they need to make a sentencing decision. Nevertheless, the present trend among state courts is toward disclosure of the PSI.

Source: Williams v. *New York State,* 339, U.S. 128, 2d Cir. 3023 (1949).

ment's right to counsel applies to the sentencing hearing because it is a crucial state of criminal prosecution. In *Gagnon* v. *Scarpelli,* the Court ruled that both probationers and parolees have a constitutionally limited right to counsel in revocation proceedings. The Court also held that the right to counsel should be decided on a case-by-case basis and that considerable discretion must be given the responsible agency in making the decision. In *Bearden* v. *Georgia,* the Court decided that a judge can not properly revoke a defendant's probation for failure to pay a fine and make restitution, unless there is evidence and finding that the probationer was somehow responsible for the failure and that alternative forms of punishment are inadequate to meet the state's interest in punishment and deterrence.

In sum, because of overcrowded prisons, probation services are currently flooded with probationers, many of whom would have been sent to prison if there were space for them. Society's hard-line mood mandates that better surveillance be given to these more serious and more problem-oriented probationers. Meanwhile, bureaucratic controls have increased, and the treatment ideologies of the past have declined in importance, resulting in less job involvement and higher rates of burnout among probation officers.

PAROLE

Those on **parole** numbered 277,438 on January 1, 1986—a new record population. Thirty-one states had increases in parole populations during 1985 (see Table 16.2). Parole populations grew most rapidly in the Western states, with California accounting for nearly two-thirds of the region's increase. In contrast, the number of offenders under parole supervision declined by nearly 10 percent in the Midwestern states.[50]

From its first use in American corrections in the 1870s up until the 1970s, parole was largely spared critical evaluation because it was regarded as functional, or necessary, in maintaining the smooth operation of the justice system. Franklin E. Zimring has identified three functions of the parole board that give it a valued role in maintaining order in the criminal justice system. First, a parole board permits the courts to advertise heavy criminal sanctions at the time of sentencing but to reduce sentences quietly later. Second, a parole board distributes the power in the justice system. Third, a parole board is able to even out disparities in sentencing in different jurisdictions.[51]

The administration of parole has five basic characteristics that are shared by all jurisdictions: (1) parole is a form of release from incarceration; (2) selection for parole release is discretionary; (3) authority to release rests with an administrative agency in the executive branch; (4) parole release involves the supervision of those released; and (5) release is conditional and the parole authority retains the power to revoke liberty.[52]

Parole Under Attack

The value of parole has been debated for more than a decade. The first major work to focus on the detrimental effects of parole discretion was the American Friends Service Committee's 1971 *Struggle for Justice.* The authors argued that the exercise of parole boards' discretionary power to release is repeatedly abused, for the parole decision is often based on reasons unrelated to risk or rehabilitation.[53] In 1974, the Citizen's Inquiry on Parole and Criminal Justice, chaired by former U.S. Attorney General Ramsey Clark, published a *Report on New York Parole,* which was an even more severe indictment of parole. The New York report criticized parole and the indeterminate sentence as based on faulty theory and as abusive, unfair, cruel, and a camouflage for other activities in the criminal justice system. The report argued for the abolition of the broad discretionary power of the parole board.[54]

In addition, three important works on sentencing were published in the 1970s, by Judge Marvin E. Frankel,[55] by the Committee for Study of Incarceration,[56] and by the Twentieth Century Fund Task Force on Criminal Sentencing.[57] All agreed that fairness and certainty in punishment should be the goals of sentencing reform. These highly respected works also attacked the wide discretion granted to parole boards. The Committee for the Study of Incarceration suggested a sentencing system based on the theory that punishment should be commensurate to the offense committed.[58]

Table 16.2 ADULTS ON PAROLE, 1985

Regions and jurisdictions	Parole population 12/31/84	1985 Entries	1985 Exits	Parole population 12/31/85	Percent change in parole population, 1984–85	1985 parolees per 100,000 adult residents
U.S., total	266,992	183,422	172,976	277,438	3.9%	158
Federal	16,854	7,932	7,926	16,860	—	10
State	250,138	175,490	165,050	260,578	4.2	148
Northeast	54,419	29,631	26,934	57,116	5.0	152
Connecticut	868	300	571	597	−31.2	25
Maine	122	0	54	68	−44.3	8
Massachusetts	4,447	3,382	3,333	4,496	1.1	101
New Hampshire	455	147	149	453	−.4	61
New Jersey	12,206	7,849	6,670	13,385	9.7	235
New York	24,212	12,458	11,391	25,279	4.4	189
Pennsylvania	11,371	5,017	4,188	12,200	7.3	136
Rhode Island	394	347	339	402	2.0	54
Vermont	344	131	239	236	−31.4	60
Midwest	46,967	30,485	35,140	42,312	−9.9	98
Illinois	11,383	8,268	8,230	11,421	.3	135
Indiana	2,900	3,208	3,311	2,797	−3.6	70
Iowa	1,662	1,932	1,623	1,971	18.6	93
Kansas	1,997	1,207	922	2,282	14.3	128
Michigan	9,365	3,698	6,424	6,639	−29.1	101
Minnesota	1,418	1,327	1,381	1,364	−3.8	45
Missouri	4,366	2,507	2,339	4,534	3.8	123
Nebraska	361	396	393	364	.8	31
North Dakota	159	156	149	166	4.4	34
Ohio	9,065	4,792	7,348	6,509	−28.2	83
South Dakota	438	375	398	415	−5.3	83
Wisconsin	3,853	2,619	2,622	3,850	—	110
South	102,128	65,269	57,978	109,419	7.1	183
Alabama	2,194	1,459	1,228	2,425	10.5	84
Arkansas	3,463	1,673	1,306	3,830	10.6	224
Delaware	830	520	486	864	4.1	186
District of Columbia	2,696	1,256	1,612	2,340	−13.2	474
Florida	5,661	3,947	5,394	4,214	−25.6	48

Georgia	7,246	7,964	6,672	8,538	17.8	198
Kentucky	3,567	2,482	2,578	3,471	-2.7	128
Louisiana	3,087	2,137	1,506	3,718	20.4	119
Maryland	7,046	4,885	4,623	7,308	3.7	222
Mississippi	3,108	1,798	1,514	3,392	9.1	186
North Carolina	3,892	4,575	5,283	3,184	-18.2	68
Oklahoma	1,880	619	874	1,625	-13.6	68
South Carolina	3,441	1,076	1,256	3,261	-5.2	135
Tennessee	6,524	4,530	3,555	7,499	14.9	212
Texas	40,783	21,291	14,603	47,471	16.4	410
Virginia	5,986	4,690	5,035	5,641	-5.8	132
West Virginia	724	367	453	638	-11.9	45
West	46,624	50,105	44,998	51,731	11.0	148
Alaska	147	114	106	155	5.4	44
Arizona	1,660	2,433	2,376	1,717	3.4	74
California	30,645	36,900	33,562	33,983	10.9	174
Colorado	1,709	2,002	1,708	2,003	17.2	85
Hawaii	526	304	114	716	36.1	94
Idaho	381	302	200	483	26.8	71
Montana	691	291	288	694	.4	117
Nevada	1,187	1,242	1,116	1,313	10.6	183
New Mexico	1,194	894	973	1,115	-6.6	111
Oregon	1,764	2,527	2,281	2,010	13.9	102
Utah	1,115	663	604	1,174	5.3	114
Washington	5,253	2,234	1,448	6,039	15.0	187
Wyoming	352	199	222	329	-6.5	94

—Less than 0.1%.

Source: Bureau of Justice Statistics, *Probation and Parole, 1985* (Washington, D.C.: U.S. Department of Justice, 1987), p. 3.

A parole board hearing. (*Source:* Ethan Hoffman/Archive Pictures, Inc.)

As of 1983, 33 states had modified their sentencing codes to make parole procedures more restrictive. Of the 36 states retaining elements of indeterminate sentencing, 19, or 52.8 percent, had adopted more severe parole policies. Of the 15 states adopting determinate sentencing codes, 14, or 93 percent, had developed more severe parole policies. Eight states totally eliminated parole.[59] But parole boards began to fight back by adopting **parole guidelines** that set, early in inmates' terms, the exact time they will serve.

Parole Guidelines

The federal probation system, Florida, Georgia, Hawaii, Louisiana, Minnesota, Missouri, New Jersey, New York, North Carolina, Oregon, Virginia, and Washington all have adopted parole release guidelines. The guidelines of the Federal Parole Commission, which have been in effect since 1973, influenced the development of many of the state guidelines.[60]

In October 1973, the U.S. Board of Parole put into operation a reorganization and regionalization plan. Case decision making authority is delegated to panels of hearing examiners. There is a two-level administrative appeal process for prisoners who contest the decision. The plan also provides a written explanation to those prisoners who are denied parole.[61]

A three-step process was created by the new policy guidelines. First, upon reviewing a prisoner's case, the examiner panel gives the case a *salient factor score,* ranging from zero to 11. The higher the score, the more likely a candidate the prisoner is for successful completion of parole. Second, the case is given an *offense severity rating* on a scale of 1 to 8. As an aid in this process, examiners are given a chart listing offense categories under each severity rating. Finally, equipped with the salient factor score and the offense severity rating, the examiners refer to another chart, which reveals the amount of time a prisoner should serve, assuming good prison performance. Table 16.3 shows how a prisoner's salient factor score and offense severity rating are cross-classified to arrive at the average amount of time to be served before release on parole.[62]

Parole guidelines have their critics. Opponents charge that guidelines should be applied by judges, not parole boards, and that guidelines fail to attack judicial discretion, the principal source of sentencing disparity. But, on balance, these widely accepted guidelines represent a major advancement over the traditional process of decision making by most parole boards.

Supervision of Ex-offenders

A significant issue in the ongoing debate about the abolition of parole concerns the supervision of ex-offenders. Many policymakers in those states that have

Table 16.3 GUIDELINES FOR DECISION MAKING, U.S. PAROLE COMMISSION

Offense Characteristics: Severity of Offense Behavior	Offender Characteristics: Parole Prognosis (Salient Factor Score 1981)			
	Very Good (10–8)	Good (7–6)	Fair (5–4)	Poor (3–0)
Category One (for example, possession of small amount of marijuana, communicating threats to kill)	Guideline Range			
	< =4 months	< =8 months	8–12 months	12–16 months
Category Two (for example, obtaining drugs for personal use by fraudulent means, unlawfully entering the U.S.)	< =6 months	< =10 months	12–16 months	16–22 months
Category Three (for example, perjury, escape)	< =10 months	12–16 months	18–24 months	24–32 months
Category Four (for example, involuntary manslaughter, communicating threats to kill)	12–18 months	20–26 months	26–34 months	34–44 months
Category Five (for example, robbery, extortion, safecracking)	24–36 months	36–48 months	48–60 months	60–72 months
Category Six (for example, illegal disposal of hazardous waste, assault with bodily injury)	40–52 months	52–64 months	64–78 months	78–100 months
Category Seven (for example, voluntary manslaughter, rape, arson)	52–80 months	64–92 months	78–110 months	100–148 months
Category Eight (for example, murder, treason, espionage)	100+ months	120+ months	150+ months	180+ months

Source: U.S. Parole Commission (Washington, D.C.: U.S. Government Printing Office: 1985), p. 12.

passed determinate sentencing acts want to retain parole supervision, for different reasons. Some policymakers support community supervision of ex-offenders in order to cushion the **"re-entry shock."** The process of providing assistance and control to ex-offenders is viewed as a means of simultaneously protecting public safety and promoting the reintegration of the offender into the community. Eliot Studt, in an often-quoted statement, explains the need for gradual re-entry to the community:

> The parolee moves directly from the subservient, deprived, and highly structured life of the prison into a world that bombards him with stimuli, expects behavior to which he has long been unaccustomed, and presents him with multitudinous problems about which he must make decisions. Food does not taste right, and often does not "sit well" after a meal; making change in a restaurant or on a bus proves unexpectedly troublesome; people and traffic seem to move with unsettling speed; and small events, anticipated with pleasure, result in exhaustion. Coming from a setting in which all time is structured for him, the parolee suddenly has no schedule except that which he can create for himself, often without the benefit of a timepiece to mark the hours.[63]

Law-and-order decision makers in those states adopting determinate sentencing laws do not want inmates released from prison without supervision because they are fearful that ex-offenders will prey upon the social order. These decision makers also are sensitive to the fact that some inmates are being released early in order to meet court-ordered prison population "caps."[64]

Risk assessment scales and **intensive parole projects** have been developed to reduce the risk of parolees committing more crimes. See Table 16.4 for the parole risk assessment instrument that was developed in Tennessee. Intensive parole, like probation, is sometimes combined with such strategies as home incarceration or electronic monitoring.[65]

The parole officer must see to it that parolees receive their constitutional rights. In the decision in *Morrisey* v. *Brewer,* the most important case concerning parole revocation, the U.S. Supreme Court ruled that the protection and due process rights of the Fourteenth Amendment apply to parole revocation.[66] Since *Morrisey,* federal courts have also held that parolees have no legal right to bail pending a revocation hearing[67] and that all that is needed to satisfy the parole board at the revocation hearing is a demonstration that the parolee has failed to meet the conditions of parole.[68] In terms of this second issue, the ruling means that the standard of proof does not need to go beyond a reasonable doubt.

The organizational constraints appear to be as strong in parole as they are in probation departments. Both Richard McCleary, in an examination of a large district parole office in Illinois, and Robert C. Prus and John R. Stratton, in their study of parole agents in a Midwestern state, found that bureaucratic, or organizational, constraints were extremely influential on officers' supervision of parolees.[69]

Table 16.4   PAROLE RISK ASSESSMENT INSTRUMENT

Risk Factor	Category	Score	
Number of previous paroles on this sentence	None	0	___
	One or more	5	
Maximum sentence length at time of release	5 years or less	0	___
	6–9 years	2	
	10 years or more	5	
Age at first juvenile adjudication	No juvenile record	0	___
	13 or younger	1	
	14 or over	3	
Number of previous felony incarcerations	None	0	___
	1 or more	4	
Instant offense was burglary, forgery, or fraud	No	0	___
	Yes	3	
Living arrangement with spouse or parents	Yes	0	___
	No	3	
Age at incarceration on current offense	32 or older	0	___
	22–31	1	
	21 or younger	3	
Employment status at first parole contact	Employed	0	___
	Unemployed	2	
Parole officer assessment of attitude	Positive	0	___
	Generally positive	2	
	Generally negative	5	
	Negative	7	
Parole officer assessment of risk	Minimum	0	___
	Medium	1	
	Maximum	2	
		Total Score:	___

Score Ranges: 0–10 minimum, 11–17 medium, 18–24 maximum, 25+ intensive supervision

Source: Department of Corrections: Tennessee, 1986.

EVALUATION OF PROBATION AND PAROLE

The purpose of community-based corrections is to bring order to the disorder of crime. Proponents have promised that it would accomplish this purpose because its programs are much more humane and economical and somewhat more effective in reducing recidivism than imprisonment. Some supporters of community-based corrections even predicted in the early 1970s that the effectiveness of community-based programs would eventually result in the closing of most prisons.

Most studies of probation and parole show that the majority of offenders complete these programs successfully. In fact, of the more than one-half million adults discharged from probation in 1984, 80.9 percent had completed their terms successfully.[70] Lawrence A. Bennett, a highly respected corrections researcher, draws the following conclusions about the effectiveness of probation and parole:[71]

- A fair proportion (25 to 30 percent) of those under supervision need only minimal supervision for a short period.[72]
- Carefully planned and executed intensive supervision programs can be effective in reducing failure rates with selected kinds of offenders.[73]
- Some special types of well-executed service delivery programs are associated with improved adjustment.[74]
- Volunteers can augment probation and parole services without a decrease in effectiveness.[75]
- Ex-offenders can make a valuable contribution as aides to parole or probation officers and function at a level of impact comparable to that of regular officers.[76]

However, Petersilia's study of 1672 felony probationers in two California counties showed that 65 percent of the entire probation sample were arrested during the 40-month follow-up period and 51 percent were formally charged and convicted.[77] She found that offenders originally convicted of burglary, theft, or forgery were the most likely to become recidivists, followed by those who were convicted of violent and drug offenses. Hence, she contends, felony probationers, much more so than other probationers, present a serious threat to public safety.[78] Moreover, within 6 years after their release from prison in 1978, an estimated 69 percent of 3995 young parolees had been rearrested; 53 percent had been reconvicted; and 49 percent were reincarcerated.[79]

The largest percentage of parolees returned to prison in the 1970s study were returned for technical violations of parole rules (such as frequenting bars or taverns).[80] The criminologist and ex-offender John Irwin argues that parole success would be higher if the system itself did not set parolees up for failure (see Box 16.2).

Probation and parole have been hailed as effective in reducing the disorder of crime, with less cost to the governmental unit and with far less trauma to the offender. Yet, the recent tendency of placing offenders with more serious criminal histories on parole or probation may result in higher rates of recidivism for such offenders. Intensive supervision of more of these high-risk offenders may be needed to reduce the threat they pose to public safety.

RESIDENTIAL PROGRAMS

Probation centers, work-release centers, restitution centers, pre-release centers, and halfway houses are the main residential programs for adult offenders. These facilities are reserved either for probationers who are making marginal adjustments to community supervision or for parolees who are assigned to them as a condition of their release from prison.

Nearly all these facilities provide for **home furlough programs**. Home furloughs, which are also called home visits, temporary leaves, and temporary community release, permit offenders to spend time, usually 24 to 72 hours, with their families at home.

| *BOX 16.2* | **PAROLE SETS A PAROLEE UP FOR FAILURE** |

The way parole sets a person up for failure is twofold. First, it places more restrictions upon parolees than are contained in the law. They even have more restrictions than are required of ordinary citizens. These are persons who have not been very skilled in the past of living within stringent regulations. The parolee usually finds it hard enough to live within a loose interpretation of the law, but certainly almost impossible to live within the conditions of parole.

Second, parole sets a person up for failure because of the surveillance of the parole agent. The relationship with the parole agent makes parolees' lives more visible. They hide their deviance from the parole agent and very often get away with it. But there is the possibility the parole agent will discover them. They play a game which has high costs and, if they lose, they go back to prison.

I think this criticism of parole is still true. In California, one of the manifestations of this now is that parolees who have any history of drug use are required to give urine samples on a regular basis. A very high percent of them are showing up with some illegal drug and are being returned to prison. Some people are now estimating that the recidivism rate in California for the first year is 75 percent. Ordinary citizens do not have to take drug testing, and, if they gave drug testing to the general population, a very high percentage would fail.

Source: Interviewed in June 1987.

Most residential programs also offer **work-release programs**, in which residents leave the facility in the morning, generally with lunch and enough money for transportation, and return at the end of the workday. Some pre-release and work-release centers offer information and instruction on such topics as job opportunities, legal problems and contracts, and the purpose and function of the law.

However, Michael Sherman and Gordon Hawkins report that a 1978 federal survey found only 8000 individuals in **residential programs**. This low figure was not a result of lack of space, because most jurisdictions reported that they had empty community-based facilities. Sherman and Hawkins conclude that the reason for the underuse of residential facilities is that these programs do not meet the crime control requirements of a broad-based criminal justice policy. That is, these facilities are deemed irrelevant to that pool of serious violent offenders against whom society demands protection. Residential programs also focus so much on the interests of the prisoner and on reducing institutional populations that they have become suspect from the perspective of much of the political spectrum.[81]

On top of this, residential programs must be located somewhere in the community, preferably in a residential area. But all too frequently, residential programs end up in old warehouses, grocery stores, and railroad stations. Ellis MacDougall, former head of five state corrections departments, says that "trying to get into residential areas is a battle you can't win. They just don't want you."[82] Yet, as a probation officer indicates, there is a strong need for **halfway houses:**

> The concept of the halfway house is an excellent one. It is primarily appropriate for individuals who do not yet possess a lengthy criminal record, but because of their actions or attitudes toward society, require a close level of supervision. The halfway house is a setting where responsible behavior can be required, monitored, and reinforced. This setting can lessen the negative influence of family or friends, which, in many instances, seem to be factors in their criminal behavior.[83]

Some exemplary residential programs do exist. The PORT Corrections Center in Rochester, Minnesota, is a nationally recognized halfway house for probationers. This facility, which provides treatment for high-risk probationers, has several striking features. First, the local community strongly endorses the program. Dr. Francis A. Tyce, medical director of the Rochester State Hospital and a strong supporter of PORT, has noted: "The community is behind us 100 percent. The program wouldn't last another 24 hours if the important people in the community weren't behind it."[84] Second, the facility has a tradition of strong staff leadership. Indeed, the first director of PORT was Kenneth Schoen, who

Sharing chores in a halfway house. (*Source:* David E. Kennedy/TexaStock.)

later became commissioner of corrections in Minnesota. Third, a problem-solving model developed by the staff seems to be effective in helping residents make more responsible decisions about their lives. A resident explains: "PORT is helpful to us because it teaches us problem solving and how to survive on the streets. It helps a person to think of the consequences of his behavior."[85] Fourth, residents must negotiate a treatment contract with staff, as well as with members of their group, and gain release from the facility by completing the terms of the contract.

In summary, while a need exists for residential settings to bring order to the lives of offenders in the community, residential care remains underutilized. That the community is so resistant to these programs—especially when they have an actual street address—is the major hurdle to be overcome.

ANALYSIS

The order and disorder thesis is helpful in understanding the impact of community-based corrections.

The Quest for Order

In the mid- and late 1970s, probation came under intense criticism from all quarters. The charge was increasingly voiced that probation was too soft on crime and that the lax supervision given to probationers permitted them to continue committing criminal behavior. Throughout the 1980s, as probation services have attempted to regain credibility with policymakers and the public by developing more intensive means of supervision, the numbers of those placed on probation have skyrocketed. Economic and political factors appear to offer the best explanation of why probation has grown so much during a time of widespread criticism of community-based programs. Andrew T. Scull concluded that the "drive for control of soaring costs" of overcrowded prisons was the primary factor underlying the move toward probation.[86] Politicians concluded that unless other means of social control could be found, prison construction would place a heavy burden upon state budgets.

In the 1970s, a movement to abolish parole gained momentum. Liberals were concerned about the inequities that parole brought to the lives of prisoners. David Fogel and others claimed that the capricious and arbitrary decisions made by parole boards were inhumane, unfair, and discriminatory.[87] Meanwhile, conservatives charged that parole boards were "soft" on crime, claiming that they released dangerous criminals to prey upon innocent victims.

The movement to abolish parole largely subsided in the late 1970s, but in the 1980s, parole has become the focus of controversy over early releases from prison. Federal court orders to reduce prison overcrowding forced many states to release prisoners early. Not surprisingly, "get-tough-with-crime" advocates have been incensed about early releases from prison.

To bring order to the sentencing and parole processes, conservatives and liberals in 15 states joined together to design determinate sentencing legislation.

It was believed that determinate sentencing would be more humane to offenders—who would know when they would be released—and to society—as inappropriate decisions would not be made by an inept parole board. But only 8 of these 15 states eliminated parole and only 1 of these states failed to provide for mandatory supervision of prison releases.

Overall, community-based corrections is more humane to offenders, less costly, and at least as effective as institutionalization. But it cannot be denied that these programs have fallen far short of the hopes of reformers in the early 1970s. They have not ushered in a "Golden Age of Corrections." They have not infused corrections with a new spirit. Nor have they replaced the fortress-like prison. With pressures from federal courts to relieve the problem of prison overcrowding and with the inability of states to afford more prison construction, record numbers have been placed on probation and parole. Society may be uncomfortable with the increased risks of expanded probation and parole, but the fact of the matter is that crime control in this nation is currently unable to function without these community-based programs.

Disorder in Community-Based Programs

The dramatic rise in case loads and the loss of idealism have made probation and parole officers frustrated and increasingly dissatisfied with their jobs. While they still must contend with lack of public acceptance, low salaries, and sometimes hostile clients, they now are faced as well with greater responsibilities, reduced community resources, lack of a treatment orientation, and increased bureaucratic constraints. As a result, officers often feel alienated from clients, administrators, the courts, and even the state legislature. One probation officer noted:

> The public is beginning to demand to know what we are doing with "those people." This, along with the shrinking tax dollars available, has created a push for greater accountability. I certainly do not argue against that. However, when the emphasis begins to be placed on generating numbers or designing forms to reduce people to categories, probation agencies are on the wrong track. These new tools are frequently of more use to the administration and legislature than to the probation officer or the client.[88]

Much of the problem is that too much was expected of community-based corrections. Indeed, the key presumptions upon which community-based programs were based have proven to be inaccurate. First, it was claimed that the community would be willing to become involved in and to provide constructive experiences for offenders. Instead, opposition has been the main public response over the past decade. Second, it was promised that the relationships found in community programs would bring order to participants' lives. In fact, few positive relationships are developed in the typically impersonal contacts between officers and clients in probation and parole and in the security-oriented settings of residential facilities. Finally, it was assumed that the accepting environments of community programs would encourage change in correctional clients. Today, restraint rather than acceptance best characterizes the mission of community-based corrections, and resistance is the most frequent response of correctional clients.

POLICY IMPLICATIONS

The most distinguishing feature of community-based corrections is the nature of the linkages between correctional programs and the community. The programs become more entrenched in the community as the frequency and duration of community relationships increase. But the quality of community relationships is even more important than their frequency and duration.[89]

This chapter has suggested that the quality of these community relationships is not good at the present time. To improve the quality of community relationships, as well as the quality of the programs themselves, two changes are needed: (1) the reconstruction of urban communities, and (2) the coordinated administration of community-based programs.

Reconstruction of Urban Communities

One of the serious flaws of community-based corrections today is that communities are not taking responsibility for their social problems, including crime. Urban communities, especially, are atomized and disorganized. A number of steps are needed in order for urban communities to develop greater resources for dealing with crime. First, a **victimization/deterrence model** provides a helpful means for establishing community crime control. In this model, widely used in middle-class communities, the neighborhood cooperates with the police in developing crime prevention strategies. For this model to be more fully implemented in urban communities, the alienation that frequently exists between citizens and the police must be resolved.[90]

Second, the **social disorganization/social control model** suggests another means of community crime control. Initially utilized by Shaw and McKay in the Chicago Area Project, the social disorganization/social control model is now used in La Playa de Ponce (Puerto Rico), in mediation with youth gangs in a half dozen urban areas, and in the House of Umoja (Philadelphia).[91] In these and other projects, grass-roots community groups provide a network of youth services. This network must be extended to those marginal individuals who seem unable to "make it" in socially acceptable ways—the "lower-class losers," "the "rabble," and the homeless. (In this regard, 40 percent of the homeless have felony arrests.[92])

Third, the community control/social change model requires that residents join together to gain increasing control over basic institutions in order to provide for their collective and individual needs. Core urban communities are economically and socially depressed, and therefore, community organization is necessary for them to gain control over their immediate environment and to deal with their problems.[93]

Coordinated Administration of Community-Based Corrections

Programs administered by the state and locally coordinated by a corrections advisory board appear to be the most effective way to operate community-based corrections. Community corrections acts, as enacted in Minnesota, Oregon, and Kansas, are examples of such organizational strategies. These acts are designed so that the state provides a financial subsidy for participating counties. As part of the process of becoming eligible for the state subsidy, county commissioners must establish a local corrections advisory board. This board is responsible for developing a comprehensive plan that identifies correctional needs and defines the programs and services required to meet these needs. The hoped for consequence of such a strategy is greater support in the community for community-based corrections, the development of a wide array of programs, and the decreased use of state institutions.

SUMMARY

Community-based corrections is made up of probation, parole, and residential programs. Its theoretical underpinnings are found in the President's Crime Commission reports and in the National Advisory Commission report. The rise of community-based corrections took place in a social context that was condusive to reform; when the social context changed to a "no-nonsense" approach to crime, public acceptance waned. Yet although residential programs have lost much of their public support, skyrocketing prison populations have forced a return to probation and parole in the 1980s.

Today, community-based corrections is rethinking its mission in a social context unwilling to accept the permissiveness of the past era. Retrenchment and defensiveness are currently guiding the development of a new mission. The emerging characteristics of this new mission appear to be intensive supervision, restitution and community work programs, bureaucratic efficiency and accountability, greater attention to substance abusers, conflict resolution among citizens, experimentation with electronic monitoring, and returning responsibility to the counties.

There is good reason to support the expansion of community-based corrections. Crime is a community problem, and the community is a more appropriate setting in which to deal with this disorder than an isolated long-term correctional institution. Participants in community programs are spared the degradation, deprivation, violence, and victimization characteristic of prison life. Probation, parole, and residential programs also have a more normalizing atmosphere than that found in prison settings. As a result of this more normalizing atmosphere, properly supervised offenders are more likely to have lower rates of recidivism and more positive life experiences.

REFERENCES

Ball, Richard A., and Lilly, J. Robert. "The Phenomenology of Privacy and the Power of the State: Home Incarceration with Electronic Monitoring." In *Issues in Criminology and Criminal Justice,* edited by J. E. Scott and Travis Hirschi. Beverly Hills, Calif.: Sage, 1987.

Carter, Robert M.; Glaser, Daniel; and Wilkins, Leslie T.; eds. *Probation, Parole and Community Corrections.* 3d ed. New York: Wiley, 1984.

Clear, Todd R., and Gallagher, Kenneth W. "Probation and Parole Supervision: A Review of Current Classification Practices." *Crime and Delinquency* 31 (1985), pp. 423–443.

Conrad, John P. "The Penal Dilemma and Its Emerging Solution." *Crime and Delinquency* 31 (1985), pp. 411–422.

Cullen, Francis T., and Wonziak, John F. "Fighting the Appeal of Repression." *Crime and Social Justice* 18 (Winter 1982), pp. 23–33.

Erwin, Billie S. *Evaluation of Intensive Probation Supervision in Georgia,* Atlanta: Georgia Department of Offender Rehabilitation, Office of Evaluation, 1984.

Gettinger, Stephen. "Community Corrections Begins to Pay Off." *Corrections Magazine* 5 (June 1979), pp. 11–13

Nelson, E. K.; Ohmart, Howard; and Harlow, Nora; eds. *Promising Strategies for Probation and Parole.* Washington, D.C.: U.S. Government Printing Office, 1978.

O'Leary, Vincent. "Reshaping Community Corrections." *Crime and Delinquency* 31 (July 1985), pp. 349–366.

Petersilia, Joan. "Community Supervision: Trends and Critical Issues." *Crime and Delinquency* 31 (July 1985), pp. 339–347.

———. *Probation and Felony Offenders.* Washington, D.C.: U.S. Department of Justice, 1985.

Shover, Neal, and Einstadter, Werner J. *Analyzing American Corrections.* Belmont, Calif: Wadsworth, 1988.

Travis, Lawrence F., ed. *Probation, Parole, and Community Corrections: A Reader.* Prospect Heights, Ill.: Waveland Press, 1985.

NOTES

1. Interviewed in March 1985.
2. President's Commission on Law Enforcement and Administration of Justice, *Task Force Report: Corrections* (Washington, D.C.: U.S. Government Printing Office, 1967).
3. National Advisory Commission on Criminal Justice Standards and Goals, *Corrections* (Washington, D.C.: U.S. Government Printing Office, 1973).
4. For a history of the Community Treatment Project, see Edwin M. Lemert and Forest Dill, *Offenders in the Community* (Lexington, Mass.: Heath, 1978).
5. President's Commission, *Task Force Report: Corrections.*
6. Ibid.
7. National Advisory Commission, *Corrections,* p. 121.
8. National Advisory Commission on Criminal Justice Standards and Goals, *A National Strategy to Reduce Crime* (Washington, D.C.: U.S. Government Printing Office, 1973), p. 187.

9. President's Commission, *Task Force Report: Corrections,* p. 7.

10. For a description of the Minnesota Community Corrections Act, see Stephen Gettinger, "Community Corrections Begins to Pay Off," *Corrections Magazine* 5 (June 1979), pp. 11–13.

11. For a description of the Des Moines Project, see David Boorkman et al., *An Exemplary Project: Community-Based Corrections in Des Moines* (Washington, D.C.: U.S. Department of Justice, 1976).

12. David T. Stanley, *Prisoners Among Us* (Washington, D.C.: Brookings, 1976), pp. 87–88.

13. National Advisory Commission, *Corrections,* pp. 313–316.

14. This item was published in a small-town newspaper in Illinois the first week of November 1976.

15. Bureau of Justice Statistics, *Probation and Parole, 1985* (Washington, D.C.: U.S. Government Printing Office, 1987), p. 1.

16. E. K. Nelson, Jr., Howard Ohmart, and Nora Harlow, "Promising Strategies for Probation and Parole," in *Probation, Parole, and Community Corrections: A Reader,* ed. Robert M. Carter, Daniel Glaser, and Leslie T. Wilkins, 3d ed. (New York: Wiley, 1984), p. 410.

17. Timothy J. Flanagan and Edmund F. McGarrell, eds., *Sourcebook of Criminal Justice Statistics* (Washington, D.C.: U.S. Government Printing Office, 1986), Table 1.44.

18. Neal Shover and Werner J. Einstadter, *Analyzing American Corrections* (Belmont, Calif.: Wadsworth, 1988), p. 121.

19. John R. Faine and Edward Bohlander, Jr., *Shock Probation: The Kentucky Experience* (Bowling Green, Ky.: Western Kentucky University Press, 1973), pp. 7, 9.

20. Edward J. Latessa and Gennaro F. Vito, "The Effects of Intensive Supervision on Shock Probationers" (Paper presented at the Annual Meeting of the Academy of Criminal Justice Sciences, 29 March 1984).

21. Elliot Studt, *Surveillance and Service in Parole* (Los Angeles: University of California Institute of Government and Public Affairs, 1972).

22. Harry E. Allen, "The Organization and Effectiveness of Community Corrections," in *Probation, Parole, and Community Corrections,* ed. Carter, Glaser, and Wilkins, p. 189.

23. Rob Wilson, "Probation/Parole Officers as 'Resource Brokers,' " *Corrections Magazine* 5 (June 1978), p. 48.

24. David Fogel, "Probation in Search of an Advocate" (Paper presented at the 13th Annual John Jay Criminal Justice Institute, New York, 15 May 1981), pp. 2–6.

25. P. McAnany, D. Thompson, and D. Fogel, "Probation Mission: Practice in Search of Principle" (Paper presented at the National Forum on Criminal Justice, Cherry Hill, N.J., 1981).

26. For Fogel's thoughts on probation, see the interview in Clemens Bartollas, *Correctional Treatment: Theory and Practice* (Englewood Cliffs, N.J.: Prentice-Hall, 1985), pp. 45–46.

27. William P. Adams, Paul M. Chandler, and M. G. Neithercutt, "The San Francisco Project: A Critique," *Federal Probation* 35 (1971), pp. 45–53.

28. Nicolette Prisi, "Combining Incarceration and Probation," in *Probation, Parole, and Community Corrections,* ed. Carter, Glaser, and Wilkins, pp. 68–70.

29. Billie S. Erwin, *Evaluation of Intensive Probation Supervision in Georgia* (Atlanta: Georgia Department of Offender Rehabilitation, Office of Evaluation, 1984); Joan Petersilia, "Community Supervision: Trends and Critical Issues," *Crime and Delinquency* 31 (1985), pp. 339–347; John P. Conrad, "The Penal Dilemma and Its Emerg-

ing Solution," *Crime and Delinquency* 31 (1985), pp. 411–422; Frank S. Pearson, "New Jersey's Intensive Supervision Program: A Progress Report," *Crime and Delinquency* 31 (1985), pp. 393–410.

30. Joan Petersilia, *Probation and Felony Offenders* (Washington, D.C.: U.S. Department of Justice, 1985), p. 2.

31. Todd R. Clear and Kenneth W. Gallagher, "Probation and Parole Supervision: A Review of Current Classification Practices," *Crime and Delinquency* 31 (July 1985).

32. Joan Petersilia, *The Influence of Criminal Justice Research* (Santa Monica, Calif.: Rand Corporation, 1987), p. 72.

33. Ibid.

34. Shover and Einstadter, *Analyzing American Corrections,* p. 137.

35. Conrad, "The Penal Dilemma," p. 411.

36. Stephen Gettinger, "Intensive Supervision: Can It Rehabilitate Probation?" *Corrections Magazine* (April 1983), p. 8.

37. Billie Erwin and Lawrence Bennett, "New Dimensions in Probation: Georgia's Experience with Intensive Probation Supervision (IPS)," *Research in Brief* (Washington, D.C.: National Institute of Justice, 1987).

38. Daniel Ford and Annesley K. Schmidt, "Electronically Monitored Home Confinement," *NIJ Reports* (Washington, D.C.: National Institute of Justice, 1985), p. 2.

39. Shover and Einstadter, *Analyzing American Corrections,* p. 152.

40. Richard A. Ball and J. Robert Lilly, "The Phenomenology of Privacy and the Power of the State: Home Incarceration with Electronic Monitoring," in *Issues in Criminology and Criminal Justice,* ed. J. E. Scott and Travis Hirschi (Beverly Hills, Calif.: Sage, 1987).

41. National Advisory Commission, *Corrections,* p. 322.

42. Petersilia, *Probation and Felony Offenders,* p. 2.

43. Shover and Einstadter, *Analyzing American Corrections,* p. 134.

44. See John T. Whitehead, "Job Burnout in Probation and Parole: Its Extent and Intervention Implications," *Criminal Justice Behavior* 12 (March 1985), pp. 91–110.

45. Interviewed in October 1987.

46. Howard Abadinsky, *Probation and Parole: Theory and Practice* (Englewood Cliffs, N.J.: Prentice-Hall, 1977), p. 92.

47. "The Presentence Investigation, Publication 105," Division of Probation, Administrative Office of the United States Courts, Vol. X/A (Washington, D.C.: U.S. Government Printing Office, vol. X/A), pp. 1–3, 4.

48. Eugene H. Czajkoski, "Exposing the Quasi-Judicial Role of the Probation Officer," *Federal Probation* 37 (September 1973), pp. 9–10.

49. *Mempa* v. *Rhay,* 339, U.S. 128, 2d Cir. 3023 (1968); *Gagnon* v. *Scarpelli,* 411, U.S. 778 (1973); *Bearden* v. *Georgia,* 433 Crl 3103 (1983).

50. Bureau of Justice Statistics, *Probation and Parole, 1985,* p. 1. Parole populations included those released from prison by a parole board as well as those released to a term of supervision after completion of a determinate, or fixed, sentence (mandatory release).

51. Franklin E. Zimring, "Making the Punishment Fit the Crime: A Consumers' Guide to Sentencing Reform," *Occasional Papers* (Chicago: University of Chicago Law School, 1977), pp. 7–8.

52. *Attorney General's Survey of Release Procedures* (Washington, D.C.: U.S. Government Printing Office, 1936), p. 4.

53. American Friends Service Committee, *Struggle for Justice: A Report on Crime and Punishment in America* (New York: Hill & Wang, 1971), p. 26.

54. Citizen's Inquiry on Parole and Criminal Justice, *Report on New York Parole* (New York: Citizen's Inquiry, 1974).

55. Marvin E. Frankel, *Criminal Sentences* (New York: Hill & Wang, 1972).

56. Andrew von Hirsch, *Doing Justice* (New York: Hill & Wang, 1976).

57. Twentieth-Century Fund Task Force on Criminal Sentencing, *Fair and Certain Punishment* (New York: McGraw-Hill, 1976).

58. Von Hirsch, *Doing Justice.*

59. Shover and Einstadter, *Analyzing American Corrections,* p. 135.

60. Kevin Krajick, "Parole: Discretion Is Out, Guidelines Are In," *Corrections Magazine* 4 (December 1978), pp. 39–49.

61. Shover and Einstadter, *Analyzing American Corrections,* p. 135.

62. Ibid., pp. 135–136.

63. Eliot Studt, *Surveillance and Service in Parole* (Los Angeles: UCLA Institute of Government, 1972), pp. 16–17.

64. James Austin, "Using Early Release to Relieve Prison Crowding," *Crime and Delinquency* 32 (1986), pp. 404–452.

65. Ford and Schmidt, "Electronically Monitored Home Confinement," pp. 2–6.

66. *Morrisey* v. *Brewer,* 408, U.S. 1971, 92 S. (1972).

67. *In re Whitney,* 421 F. 2d 337, 1st, Cir. (1970).

68. *United States* v. *Strada,* 503 F. 2d 1081, 8th Cir. (1974).

69. Richard McCleery, *Dangerous Men* (Beverly Hills, Calif.: Sage, 1978); and Robert C. Prus and John R. Stratton, "Parole Revocation Decisionmaking: Private Typings and Official Designations," *Federal Probation* 40 (1976), pp. 48–53.

70. Bureau of Justice Statistics, *Probation and Parole, 1985.*

71. Lawrence A. Bennett, "Evaluation of Probation, Parole, and Correctional Programs," in *Probation, Parole and Community Corrections,* ed. Carter, Glaser, and Wilkins, p. 400.

72. Douglas Lipton, Robert Martinson, and Judith Wolkes, *The Effectiveness of Correctional Treatment* (New York: Praeger, 1975).

73. Robert M. Carter and Cameron R. Dightman, *Washington and Evaluation of the Minimum Service Caseloads in the Diversion of Probation and Parole,* Research Report 5 (Olympia, Wash.: Washington Department of Institutions, 1969); James Robinson et al., *The San Francisco Project: A Study of Federal Probation: Final Report, Research Report 14* (Berkeley, Calif.: University of California School of Criminology, April 1969).

74. California Youth Authority, *Increased Parole Effectiveness: Program Final Report* (Sacramento, Calif.: California Council on Criminal Justice, 1974); Perlman, *Deferred Prosecution on Criminal Justice—A Case Study of the Genesee County (MI) Citizens Probation Authority* (Lansing, Mich.: Michigan Office of Criminal Justice Programs, 1972).

75. Richard Ku, Richard Moore, and Keith Griffiths, *Volunteer Probation Counselor Program—An Exemplary Project* (Washington, D.C.: NILECJ, 1975).

76. Joseph H. Scott, *Ex-Offenders as Parole Officers—An Evaluation of the Parole Aide Program in Ohio* (Lexington, Mass.: Heath, 1975); Harry E. Allen and Ramon R. Priestino, *Parole Officer Aid Program in Ohio: An Exemplary Project* (Columbus, Ohio: Ohio State University, Program for the Study of Crime and Delinquency, 1975).

77. Petersilia, *Granting Felons Probation,* p. 21.

78. Petersilia, *Probation and Felony Offenders,* p. 3.

79. Bureau of Justice Statistics, *Recidivism of Young Parolees* (Washington, D.C.: U.S. Department of Justice, 1987), p. 1.

80. Shover and Einstadter, *Analyzing American Corrections,* p. 123.
81. Michael Sherman and Gordon Hawkins, *Imprisonment in Ameria: Choosing the Future* (Chicago: University of Chicago Press, 1981), pp. 101–102.
82. Quoted in Kevin Krajick, "Not on My Block," *Corrections Magazine* 6 (October 1980), p. 20.
83. Interviewed in March 1985.
84. Interviewed in August 1981.
85. Interviewed in August 1981.
86. Andrew T. Scull, *Decarceration: Community Treatment and the Deviant: A Radical View* (Englewood Cliffs, N.J.: Prentice-Hall, 1977) p. 140.
87. David Fogel, *". . . We are the Living Proof": The Justice Model For Corrections,* 2d ed. (Cincinnati: Anderson, 1979) p. 204.
88. Interviewed in March 1985.
89. Robert M. Coates, "A Working Paper on Community-Based Corrections: Concept, Historical Development, Impact, and Potential Dangers" (Paper presented at the Massachusetts Standards and Goals Conference, 18 November 1974), pp. 3–4.
90. Peter Iadicola, "Community Crime Control Strategies" (Paper presented at the Annual Meeting of the American Society of Criminology, Cincinnati, Ohio, 11 November 1984), pp. 1–7.
91. See Bartollas, *Correctional Treatment,* pp. 77–119, for a description of these programs.
92. Iadicola, "Community Crime Control Strategies," pp. 9–12.
93. Ibid., pp. 12–13.

CHAPTER 17

Coping with Criminal Behavior Through Technology

THE AMERICAN CONTRIBUTION
TARGET HARDENING
BIOMEDICAL INTERVENTION
Critical Organ Surgery
  Castration
  Psychosurgery
Drug Treatment
  Direct Forms

  Indirect Forms
ETHICAL PROBLEMS
Intrusion
Irreversibility
Involuntary Administration
Overcontrol
SUMMARY
NOTES

KEY TERMS

biomedical intervention   psychotropic drugs
critical organ surgery   target hardening
psychosurgery

Where there is no vision, the people perish.

—Proverbs 29:18

The American belief in progress has been dashed by international crises and internal conflict. With it has also died the rehabilitation ideal in criminology, corrections, and the treatment of deviance. Intellectually, the rehabilitation philosophy was made respectable by the victory of positivism over classicism, empiricism over speculative philosophy, the clinical over the legal perspective, causal ambiguity over legal certainty—and by the acceptance of the viewpoint elevating the actor over his act.[1] On the policy level, this movement focused on humanizing our total institutions and on rehabilitating the inmates. To these lofty ends, a mixed bag of legal and medical crusaders, civil libertarians, crusty institutional administrators, and other worldly academic types, supported by a cast of moral entrepreneurs, humanists, clergy, concerned laity, and cause-oriented persons of all descriptions, changed the treatment of "outsiders" in big and little ways—from the creation of the juvenile court system in 1899 and the introduction of probation and parole to the less dramatic introduction of small amenities into the drab and unstimulating lives of the institutionalized. A full recital is long and impressive. The list, in recent years, includes: the revision of state penal codes and the medieval conceptions they harbored; the introduction of legal and due process procedures into the total institutions; using volunteers as agents of reform; the abolition of corporal and capital punishment; and the development of a great variety of prevention and treatment programs, including the emergence of the voluntary associations of deviants starting with Alcoholics Anonymous.[2]

The great triumphs of the reform movement, however, center on decriminalization, community-based care, deinstitutionalization, and more equitable and accountable police, and court processes.[3] Despite these improvements, any reasonable review might fairly conclude that the criminal justice and correctional systems, both juvenile and adult, are probably in poorer shape today than at any time in this century. For somewhat different reasons, so are the mental health and mental retardation services. Giving the reformer the edge, they are marginally better. One must ask, however, whether they would be tolerable at all were it not for the quiet but persistent agitation on behalf of deviant, disruptive, and dependent citizens.[4] That the same evidence of failure to alter these systems for the

---

This chapter has been adapted from Simon Dinitz's paper "Coping with Deviant Behavior Through Technology," published by Sam Houston State University in *Criminal Justice Research Bulletin* 3 (1987).

better is true of nearly every other aspect of the health, education and welfare complex is little consolation. Ideas, and the practices that flow from them, are rooted in the material and organizational climate of the times. Such is the present climate that faith in rehabilitation, in the traditional sense, has run its course. The question is, Why?

First, success breeds failure. The therapeutic ideology was destroyed by its own modest successes as much as by the upheavals of the civil rights, anti-war, urban, and student revolts that shook American society to its very foundations in the twenty years after the 1954 *Brown* v. *Board of Education* desegregation decision of the Supreme Court. For the moment, at least, the treatment philosophy is under siege by both radical and the resurgent neoclassical perspectives. The critical perspective has called attention, again, to the systemic rather than individual nature of our problems[5]; neoclassicism to the need for redress of the social defense–deviant treatment balance.[6] The radical—that is, the critical—view surfaced in response to the inequities of a social system that produces some winners but all too many losers; neoclassicism experienced rebirth as a response to this radical challenge and to the increasingly justifiable fear about crime in the streets—in the 1980s the primary concern of the citizenry—committed by socially processed losers.

Second, the sympathy for deviants was a response to the technological revolution that destroyed the old social order—the "cake of custom" so cherished by Sumner, the *gemeinschaft* of Tonnies, and the social integration theory of Durkheim. Reformism flowered as masses of rootless and uprooted people, immigrants and migrants, seeking to reconstruct their lives, descended on America's cities and towns. When private philanthropy proved both inadequate and patronizing, the preconditions were established for the eventual adoption of major reforms in education, in health, in employment, and in criminal justice.[7]

Third, dissatisfaction with the traditional social order received yet another irreversible jolt—the ascendancy of Freudian, neo-Freudian, and pseudo-Freudian doctrines as the explanatory framework for the massive personal disorganization and pathology during much of this century. Overlooking, for the moment at least, the cool reception accorded Freudian dogma for several decades after the introduction of psychoanalysis to a stunned and unbelieving medical profession, the psychodynamic perspective coupled with the decay of historic social institutions may be said to constitute the basis of the modern therapeutic model.[8]

Fourth, the postindustrial society gave rise to a quasi-welfare state—the "Swedenization" of America. This social welfare tradition is now so deeply embedded in American life that even political swings are unlikely to alter public involvement in private troubles. In truth, private troubles are public matters. But, as C. Wright Mills warned, it is easier to help poor "unfortunates" than to eliminate the causes that produce and sustain them. Hence, social problems are reduced to the treatment of personal pathologies.

In corrections, for example, there is no recommendation in the 1870 Declaration of Principles of the American Correctional Association that has not been enacted. Such, however, is the peculiar nature of the discipline that many of the glories attained in the reformist struggle—indeterminate sentences; education, psychological, and classification services; various iterations of psychotherapeutic intervention; the special handling of juveniles—are now under fire. Some, like the parole system, are in the process of being dismantled in favor of mandatory sentences. Yesterday's humaneness is today's patronization of the defenseless. The historic fight for the right to treatment has become today's struggle for the right to be left alone. Yesteryear's belief in rehabilitation has been undercut by the reintroduction of the belief in the efficacy of "just deserts," deterrence, and incapacitation.[9]

In short, even while new standards and goals are being set for the treatment of children, delinquents, addicts, depressives, and other social deviants, by everyone from the United Nations to the various national advisory groups and commissions, the cutting edge of reform has been dulled. Ameliorative efforts will continue to alleviate some of the grosser inadequacies of the human services systems. Piecemeal efforts at reform will be successful in minor ways. Most reformers are discouraged and disenchanted by their failure to create a just, fair, and humane treatment system. In corrections, for example, the questions now are not whether to fight the new death penalty laws in the 35 or so states in which they have been enacted, to replace the megaprisons, or to abolish parole. These are still open questions, to be sure, but all seem rather unimportant to that exhausted band of aging dreamers. The central issue, now, has little to do with nostrums and panaceas. The overarching concern now is whether criminal and mental health institutions are to function as the ultimate repository for the social misfits and the déclassé whose productivity is redundant in our postindustrial world.[10] If the state facility is to be the ultimate warehouse, then no amount of conjugal visiting, work, educational and home furloughs; fixed net sentences; lowered age of adult responsibility; or other reforms in the prison or in the subsystems of law enforcement, prosecution, and courts will promote the return of such superfluous persons to the mainstream of American life. The time has come to confront the basic temporal reality; unless drastic alterations occur in postmodern society, the health, welfare, and educational sectors will fail to reform, to educate, and to provide the decent health services that many societies such as Japan, the Scandinavian bloc, and the Benelux nations seem much better able to furnish. The dilemma is this: either we lower our expectations and accept social inequality, stratification, and deprivation as inevitable or we recast present society radically and dramatically. The social Darwinists and neoclassicists argue the inevitability of the former; the critical criminologists, the latter. In the meantime, a very fearful public looks to its experts for guidance—experts who, lacking a new paradigm, can offer only the most prosaic recommendations for reshaping the human services systems. Improving the lot of inmates, mental patients, retardates, addicts, and sexual deviants is no small matter, of course. But the many specific recommendations for reform are not going to fundamentally alter our treatment of the disvalued and stigmatized.

In the absence of such a verified body of knowledge, criminology-corrections-deviance has consisted of one etiological and treatment bandwagon after another. Most such theories, chiefly the organic, have mercifully departed the scene quietly after a rapid rise and slow burn-out.[11] We refer, by way of illustration, to the Dugdale and Goddard abominations stemming from their respective work on the Jukes and Kallikaks; the rise and fall of the EEG fad, which produced so many tracings and so little substance; and, most recently, to the tumult and great expectations arising from the discovery of the XYY chromosome. Indeed, this faddism may be traced back to the phrenologists, the constitutional inferiority writers, the earlier "juicers" or hormonal researchers, the "heredity as destiny" European school, the Glueck type of eclectics, and the various brands of other determinists.[12]

One principle defies refutation in the history of the search for the "deviant" individual. This principle is that any perspective, no matter how outlandish, tends to surface over and over again in the guise and terminology appropriate to its temporal resurrection. Thus, sociobiology is back in the person of Edward O. Wilson. The earlier "juicers" are back; the Pavlovians and Skinnerians now parade under the banner of behavior modifiers, and the bell that produced salivation in the dog is now called "the reinforcer." An in-depth review of this cyclicity of ideas dressed in the newest verbal fashions has been explored by Ysabel Rennie in her volume *The Dangerous Offender: Science and Mythos in the Making of Public Policy*.[13] But Rennie is by no means the first to document the ebb and flow of theories in criminology and, more importantly, their incorporation in penal law and treatment programs.

THE AMERICAN CONTRIBUTION

The Chicago school, the first authentic U.S. philosophy concerning social deviance, was a derivation of the social gospel movement among white, small town, Protestant reformers responding to the hordes of immigrants and to the accelerating process of urbanization. The Chicagoans wanted to return to the *gemeinschaft* of the small Midwestern or New England communities from which they came. Origins aside, these scholars, especially Robert Park, Louis Wirth, and Ernest Burgess and their students, paved the way for the emergence of nearly all non-Marxist sociological perspectives. Drawing on a variety of European social-political theorists—Weber, Durkheim, Spencer, Tarde—the Chicago school evolved a perspective that, above all, focused on consensus and integration as the "normal" state of social organization and, within this cohesive context, a limited amount of deviant behavior was necessary and functional to the social system.[14]

The Chicagoans' emphasis on cohesion found in these unassimilated millions the naïve human resources for Israel Zangwill's unfulfilled and probably unfulfillable dream of the "melting pot"; for universal public education; for the emergence of the juvenile court. The Chicagoans pushed social welfare beyond Hull House and the Educational Alliance. They rejected the old country rigidities of class and caste. They placed their bets on social mobility and meritocracy as the basis for progress and the amelioration of social problems. Above all, the Chicago view was optimistic. There were ends to be achieved, problems to be solved, progress to be made. Technology, according to Ogburn, was the key. It would create an unimagined and unimaginable range of problems (and in this he was surely correct). But this same key would also provide the solutions. The time discrepancy between the appearance of the technical blockbuster and its containment was dubbed "culture lag"—a concept that, unfortunately, is now out of vogue.[15]

The Chicago school came to focus on social disorganization as the key element in deviance. By *social disorganization,* Clifford Shaw meant the attenuation of the consensual norms and standards in the ethnic and national ghettos of the largest American cities. This process of the attenuation of earlier norms proved to be the basis for differential association and differential identification, as Sutherland and Glaser were to argue.[16]

Meanwhile, Sellin was dealing with much the same problem of normative disintegration in his justly famous statement on culture conflict and its significance for crime.[17] This position is nowhere more definitively observed than in the Middle East, where clashes of religious, cultural, Western–non-Western, modern-traditional groups are recapitulating, in a much more virulent way, the U.S. experience of the period from 1890 to 1940. As in the United States, far from assimilating this diversity and creating a new society, these conflicts threaten the internal fabric of countries in the region.

The point of this discussion, to repeat, is that the American ethos and cultural universals emphasized optimism, modernism, progress, and consensus. Conflict afflicted only the Old World, with its silly national, religious, and ethnic antagonisms. There was nothing inherent in society that a lot of goodwill and a pinch of technical know-how could not set straight.

Similarly, the American ethos rejected the cold-blooded rationality of utilitarianism.[18] Ours was, after all, a compassionate society. An examination of the social commentary during the period 1890 to 1940 demonstrates convincingly a preoccupation not with class and ideology, but with such basic and prosaic problems as alcoholism, crime, poverty, racial injustice, mental retardation, and prostitution. In short, dependent, disruptive, and deviant people were the problem. Major institutional change was neither necessary nor warranted. This bias was substantially true of all areas—from the legal and economic to the family and educational institutions. The system was assumed to be fair—but no system is perfect; crime, mental illness, and chronic drunkenness are, after all, perfectly normal no matter what the social organization is like.[19] The prescription: leave the system alone and treat the personal pathologies. Rehabilitate, educate, provide insight. Above all, make it possible for the lowliest and most humble of men and women to climb to the top or, at least, to rise.

In practice, the reformers did improve the facilities and care given the three d's—the dependent, disruptive, and delinquent—if only very modestly. Dix, Beers, and Deutsch took on the mental hospitals; the Wickersham Commission took on crime; Gompers, Hillman, Mitchell, and Lewis, the appalling conditions of labor; the Anti-Saloon League, Demon Rum; the Child Savers, the deplorable treatment of delinquent, neglected, and abused children; the Federal Bureau of Narcotics, the narcotics problem.[20] Under the New Deal, in the period from 1932 to 1944, alphabet agencies proliferated. The coalition put together by the New

Dealers consisted of the underprivileged, populists, academics, ethnics, urban blue-collar workers, and some farmers. It survived long enough to move the United States into the age of the quasi-welfare state—a direction that appears irreversible. One need not be prophetic to predict the rise of national employment, income, health, and housing standards to replace the present chaos in these areas. If nothing else, the near fiscal bankruptcy of America's major cities and counties may accelerate the federalization of social services, especially criminal justice. Revenue sharing, contrary to its stated goals, will be the forerunner of various federalization policies. The liberal impulse, spent in criminology-corrections, is still very much a factor in the formulation of policies in other social and economic areas.

Certain events become benchmarks in human affairs. Often these events are so "silent" that their significance becomes evident only in historical perspective. Such an event was the closing of the American frontier in the 1890s. If the eminent historian Frederick Jackson Turner is to be believed, this closing profoundly altered the American dream. It damped the unbridled optimism of the times, circumscribed future growth, changed migration patterns, and, eventually, forced the sovereign states to become a sovereign nation.[21]

With all due respect to Turner's thesis, an even more notable landmark in the American experience was the successful structural and, to a lesser degree, interpersonal assimilation of the nearly 60 million immigrants who were admitted, if not warmly welcomed, to this country in the short span of about half a century. By the end of World War II, the etiology of deviant, disruptive, and dependent conduct could no longer be attributed to social pathology, social disorganization, and culture conflict—shorthand concepts for the acculturation experience and consequences. A profound shift had occurred in the lay and professional construction of social reality.

It became evident, though usually unsaid, that many of the unassimilated had become the unassimilable. No amount of social intervention could or would melt the "unmeltable" millions in our midst. In consequence, and in contradiction to the intensely professed and much admired American ethos, a two-tiered social and economic system took shape. Warner, and then Hollingshead, began to look at the constituent elements of social class; Hunter initiated the search for community elites, Mills for the power elite. The dam had burst, the unthinkable had become speakable.[22]

The realization of the existence and persistence of a semi-permanent underclass of "losers" with its own ethics, values, goals, and expectations startled the social science community and fragmented it politically. Disenchanted New Dealers and New Frontiersmen spread the word to the lay community in their syndicated columns. Respected political sociologists agitated the intellectual community by challenging traditional liberal assumptions about the nature of human nature and the role of the state. A new form of social Darwinism emerged. In criminology, etiological concerns rapidly lost popularity to the neoclassical doctrines focusing once again on punishment, deterrence, and incapacitation.

A social historian might date the origin of the "unmeltable" assumption to a most influential book: William I. Whyte's *Street Corner Society.*[23] In discussing the divergent paths taken by street-corner and college groups in a working-class area, Whyte's theory was the forerunner of some of the sub-cultural and limited opportunity themes later pursued by Cohen and by Cloward and Ohlin, as well as by Wolfgang and Ferracuti and by Liebow. As Walter Miller elaborated, the underclass has internalized a coherent set of values—trouble, toughness, smartness, expressive goals—conducive to deviant conduct. For Walter Miller it is not position discontent or limited opportunity, though both are real, but rather the lifestyle of segments of the underclass that makes street crimes like robbery and burglary a virtual underclass monopoly.[24]

This more or less permanent underclass is very different from previous underclass groups in two respects: first, it is different qualitatively, and second, the social system seems indisposed to develop new methods to permit the upward circulation of this underclass. On the first count, the new underclass consists of the socioeconomic failures, some four generations deep now, of previous rural migrations to the city. Included, too, are the remnants of earlier immigrant groups. To these must be added the personally disorganized—alcoholics, drug addicts, and the ambulatory mentally ill. The socially created and processed unmeltables consist of ghetto blacks and Hispanics and, in some parts of the country, of native Americans. This more or less permanent underclass has no voice and no vote. This makes blacks, Hispanics, and the personally disorganized prime targets for economic and political exploitation. More and more isolated in central cities, cut off from community life by inner belts and by the provincialism inherent in their status, these individuals are evidence that the line between class and caste is fading. Few of the poverty and welfare programs have actually touched this sizeable underclass. Nothing on the horizon is likely to be more effective.

On the second count, social reformers premised their activities on some variation of the Protestant ethic. They assumed an inherent and universal desire for self-improvement. The will was there; the tools lacking. Provide the tools, and upward social mobility must and will follow. Current disillusionment with reform is consequently related to the shift in public perception of the values of the underclass. If one rejects upward social mobility as an attainable goal and is preoccupied with just "getting by," these prescriptions seem odd indeed. Education and vocational training offer little to people who have already failed repeatedly in our schools. One can afford the luxury of the latest therapeutic games only after other needs have been met. Even behavior modification programs work less effectively with the underclass. In short, individually oriented rehabilitation programs do not and cannot reach the caste-like underclass.

Even more depressing has been the collapse of consensus on what constitutes a desirable and normative lifestyle. What was "sinful" and "immoral" conduct in the early part of the century gave way to "abnormal," "pathological," "aberrant," "criminal," and "disorganized" behavior in the 1930s, to "deviant" behavior in the 1950s, and merely "variant" behavior in the late 1960s and early 1970s. Public tolerance has markedly increased for variant lifestyles, however outlandish. We now accept as normal that which we only recently abhorred as sinful. We are fearful of being perceived as square and straight—the new outsiders of our time. With Erasmus it is possible to conclude that when everything is possible, nothing is true. Many reformers have unfortunately concluded that little or no special education is required to remain a loser, a never-will-be, a permanent outsider with a variant lifestyle. More than any other development, it seems that the American acceptance and even celebration of deviance has mortally undercut the idea of rehabilitation.

The failure of a century of crime and deviance prevention and treatment programs predicated on traditional conceptions of etiology—family disorganization, poverty, intrapsychic disabilities and sociocultural deprivation—has stimulated the search for innovative and harder approaches to the social defense.[25] If nothing conventional now works, then something must be found that will or at least might. Worldwide hysteria about crime on the streets, some of it justified; the visceral feeling that Spengler may have been correct after all and that Western society is in decline;[26] the soaring crime rate; and the sudden emergence of international terror has convinced even some civil libertarians that cherished freedoms may have to be sacrificed to preserve the fragile social fabric.

The new "down with reform" backlash is daily fueled by disconcerting news from every quarter. In Italy, civil servants, politicians, and business executives and their families live in dread of the knee-capping Red Brigades and the nonideological ransom abductors. Elsewhere in Europe the problem is less intense but just as real.[27] In much of Latin America violence is endemic and, in some countries, seriously out of control.[28] In London, hoodlum gangs attack each other as well as victims of opportunity in the underground and at football contests. In New York City, at least 1800 persons were murdered in 1979—just 100 fewer than in all of Japan. Twelve other U.S. cities including Dallas, Houston, Atlanta, and Chicago had even more murders per capita than New York.[29] In 1980, Tel Aviv recorded its first ransom kidnapping-murder in the history of the state of Israel.[30] In the same city, more than 100 residential and 60 commercial burglaries are reported to the police each day. In Columbus, Ohio, the prototypical middle American city, celebrated as such by politicians of all ideological coloration, there were over 70 armed bank robberies in the first seven months of 1980. All told, there are about 4000 major personal crimes committed annually in the Columbus metropolitan area, with a population of just about a million people.[31] In the Eastern bloc, reports persist that violence and theft are on the increase; in the Soviet Union drunkenness and hooliganism are a national disgrace.[32] Even tranquil nations are under the gun, so to speak, with their long histories of public civility under great stress. Public attitudes toward street crime are hardening in Switzerland, Holland, and in Scandinavia.[33] In Australia, a 1978 public opinion poll found that crimes of violence and high unemployment were the two issues that most concerned citizens.[34] Of all the modern countries, only Japan seems to have the crime problem under control, thanks largely to an integrated network of institutional arrangements that tie family, school, neighborhood, and work place together.[35]

In Western Europe and, especially, in the United States, the failure of the criminal justice system to rehabilitate, to reform, to deter, and even to punish fairly has led to consideration and implementation of options that would have been unthinkable in the 1940s, 1950s, and even 1960s. These options are more intrusive, sometimes irreversible, and designed to prevent and control disruptive and deviant behavior. It is a sign of the times when anything less than overcontrolling measures is thought to reflect a mollycoddling attitude toward malefactors.[36]

As a response, two general approaches will dominate crime and deviance prevention and treatment in decades to come. These are target hardening and biomedical intervention, which transfer technology from engineering, architecture, and the biological sciences into social engineering and individual treatment activities.

TARGET HARDENING

One of the great growth industries in the United States is the personal and property security business. Disenchanted with the law enforcement apparatus and the functioning of the criminal justice system, citizens are retreating to "safe" houses, safe streets, safe neighborhoods. Like the residents of medieval cities, affluent Americans are creating sheltered environments using age-old methods in combination with the new higher technology.[37] For example, there are now many more persons (estimates range from two to four times as many) engaged in private security than in public policing.[38] On nightly walks in many neighborhoods, we invariably encounter a small car with a mounted spotlight and side-door identification as a private security vehicle, driven by a man who exhibits all the suspiciousness and paranoia of a trained police officer. House to house goes this car, searchlighting doors, windows, grounds. It is altogether eerie and yet reassuring, although there is no evidence that such patrols make much difference.

Many neighbors have burglarproofed their homes with all manner of electronic gadgetry. A stray dog will cause an alarm to sound, Klaxons to blare, and the police, on a direct line, to be alerted. Local locksmiths are unable to meet the demand for installation of dead bolts; security experts for window, roof, and basement wiring. Peephole manufacturers are bullish on business; automatic garage door openers and closers are everywhere in evidence; and the omnipresent television camera, hidden alarm buttons, and anti–car theft devices are part of the increasing use of hardware by a citizenry scared to death of intruders and robbers and larcenists.

There are now 60 to 80 million handguns, at least, in the hands of the general population; chemical Mace is readily available in cans; fierce-looking dogs stand guard and gentler ones are kept around to bark the alarm. In multi-unit middle- to upper-income dwellings, tenants are greeted by doormen, escorted to elevators, taken to their residence floor, and deposited safely at their doors.[39] Huge flare lights on tall stanchions illuminate the night; civilian crime alert watchmen walk high-crime density areas, two by two, whistles at the ready.

Parking meters and vending machines are fitted with anti-slug devices; cabs and transit buses contain exact coin change boxes to protect the drivers from robbery; helicopters, light beams searching the night, seek out suspects; metal detectors protect against hijacking; special detectors, at exit points, aid libraries and shops in preventing books and goods from disappearing.[40] And now computer information systems, in the blink of an eye, can call up information on lost and stolen vehicles nationwide. Communication systems are so ubiquitous that police departments feel deprived if they are not part of some information network like LEEDS or CLEAR.[41]

Much of this software-hardware revolution in crime prevention is a spinoff of the high technology developments—especially information processing—in other fields. But a substantial part of the reason for the utilization of this costly machinery is public determination to achieve security at almost any cost.

Target hardening has always been the prudent thing to do—whether in building the stone and mortar shield of medieval fortress cities or shuttering a store at the close of a day's business—but the turbulence of the 1960s elevated the level of fear, facilitating the rapid technology transfer. Presidential candidate Barry Goldwater gave the crime in the streets issue centrality in his campaign; President Lyndon Johnson eventually captured it as his own. Jane Jacobs talked about how to make central cities safe by attracting more people to them;[42] Oscar Newman, by providing defensible space.[43]

The concept of target hardening was bought by the Law Enforcement Assistance Administration (LEAA) soon after the sorry spectacle of the deliberate destruction of the Pruitt-Igoe low-income, high-rise housing project in St. Louis and the conversion to housing for the aged of similar housing projects elsewhere. Pruitt-Igoe, a ten-year-old, reasonably decent high-rise complex was leveled by the city because juvenile gangs terrorized, robbed, and raped residents; destroyed property; set fires; openly peddled drugs; jammed the elevators; and made it impossible for tenants to park their cars in the neighborhood or walk alone in safety. Terror exceeded control potential;[44] thus, the decision to raze Pruitt-Igoe. Differing only in magnitude, similar tales can be recounted of the fate of high-rise complexes elsewhere. In Columbus, for example, Bolivar Arms was converted from apartments for low-income families to housing for the aged—and the problems, in lesser degree, still make life hazardous for the residents in the high rise and in the surrounding low-rise buildings. The entire area bears a stigma that may make renewal difficult.

Pruitt-Igoe ignited an interest in hard architecture and defensible space that has been consistently reinforced by experiences in areas such as the South Bronx, Bedford-Stuyvesant, and, indeed, in cities large and small. Oscar Newman sketched the dimensions of the application of the principle of defensible space: low-rise houses, optimum surveillance potential, partitioned buildings so that only a few tenants share an entrance, semiprivate and private versus public space, common lobbies and playgrounds for a few families, parking lots under play decks. Newman offers a long list of components enhancing defensible space, and many have been incorporated in both low-income and middle-upper projects.[45] Sad to relate, however, many, even most, evaluations of the effectiveness of this approach have been inconclusive or even negative. Robert Sommer, C. Ray Jeffery, and others have concluded that hard architecture and target hardening approaches are simply overwhelmed by the human elements in the equation.[46]

Reppetto and Gabor have called attention to crime displacement.[47] As we target harden the subways, crime is driven into the streets and onto buses. As bigger shops are better protected, robbers go for the Mom-and-Pop store operations. If you flood one area with patrol officers, in cruisers and on foot, some other neighborhood becomes vulnerable. Rural areas, the last bastions of safety, are now routinely vandalized by marauding groups of car-borne juveniles. Valuable machinery can easily be taken by professional thieves and farm homes burglarized as a result of the new accessibility to rural areas.[48]

With all its problems and failures to date, the target-hardening approach nevertheless commends itself as a rational and fear-reducing method of regaining some small measure of personal control over one's safety and property.

BIOMEDICAL INTERVENTION

More fundamental than measures of physical control is the burgeoning field of **biomedical intervention.**[49] It is a matter of record that modern, that is, positivist, criminology began with a distinctly medical-biological bias. This perspective has long dominated the Italian school and almost all of Western European and Latin American criminology, though to a lesser extent today. Only in the United States and Canada did criminology acquire a sociocultural perspective, derived from the unique American experience with the acculturation process.

Most early biomedical theory and research on the etiology of crime, delinquency, alcoholism, and other personal deviancies seems peculiar, indeed, in retrospect.[50] Terms like *born criminal, atavism* (or regression to a lower level of evolutionary development), *natural criminals, constitutionally inferior persons, criminal morons* and *imbeciles,* and *asthenics* and *mesomorphs* dotted the early literature and ended only with the rise and fall of Hitler. While lay memory of that unspeakable period has dimmed (there are now over 100 books denying that the Holocaust occurred), biologists have not forgotten and many are rightly reluctant to initiate research with humans.[51] Nevertheless, the biomedical revolution is slowly penetrating the field of deviance. Sociobiology is enjoying increasing popularity as Edward Wilson, Desmond Morris, Konrad Lorenz, Lionel Tiger, and Robin Fox spread the doctrine that nature takes precedence over nurture in everything from obedience and aggression to social organization.[52] The continuing conflict over educational and intellectual potential is more strident than ever in the pronouncements and denunciations of the research and conclusions of Jensen, Shockley, and Herrnstein regarding black-white IQ differences. Twin studies are back in vogue, and these are more sophisticated than the pioneering research of Lange and Rosanoff and of the fraudulent studies of a former president of the British Psychological Society, Cyril Burt. The new twin studies, by Mednick and Christiansen in particular, are models of first-class work. The general conclusion, however, is the same. Genetic material outweighs environmental influences in the criminality of identical twins reared by criminal and noncriminal adoptive fathers.[53] Finally, the greatest splash recently was made by the report in 1961 of the XYY chromosomal abnormality by Sandberg in *Lancet.*

After considerable work, however, the most that can now be said is that, except for the tiniest minority of males 71 inches or taller, there is nothing to suggest that aggressivity and violence is related to the XYY syndrome. One newborn male in 1000 is likely to have an XYY defect; in maximum-security prisons the ratio among tall males is one in 150, and in prison hospitals for the criminally insane the ratio may be as low as one in 50. In fact, genital deformities, low IQ, or no known defects at all—especially the last—are more common than is aggressive or violent criminality. Still, the XYY argument played some part in the defense of murderers Daniel Hugon in France, Lawrence Hannel in Australia, and Richard Speck in the United States.[54]

The desire for a biomedical explanation, for the medicalization of deviance, is so great that cohort studies are in progress to determine the influence of reproductive casualty as reflected in minimal brain damage on deviant behavior; other studies are concerned with the link between poor maternal nutrition, or smoking and drinking while pregnant, and subsequent behavioral impairment of offspring.[55] There is also research on nutrition and hyperkinesis and related disorders and on neurotransmitter and hormonal abnormalities and problems in chronic antisocial conduct. For our purpose, it is enough to focus on biomedical interventions and not on explanations per se. Thus, we will discuss two biomedical interventions: critical organ surgery and drug treatment.

Critical Organ Surgery

Castration   In the decade prior to World War I, for reasons better left for historians to research, panic swept the United States about the rising and intolerable problems created by assaultive sex offenders, drug addicts, habitual criminals, and excessive drinkers and alcoholics. Part of the generalized fear and revulsion focused on prostitutes, chronic offenders, and mental incompetents. Moral indignation soon gave way to punitive legislation. The Volstead Act ushered in the era of prohibition in January of 1920.[56] Prohibition was repealed in 1933, but not before syndicated crime emerged as an unanticipated and still uncontrolled consequence. The Harrison Act of 1914 made drug possession illegal and called for heavy penalties for physicians who prescribed narcotic substances. The Baumes Law, passed in New York in 1926, ushered in the life sentence for habitual offenders. Habitual offender statutes still exist in 43 states and LEAA, before its demise, financially supported career criminal offender sections in prosecutors' offices all over the country.[57]

Most important of all for the acceptance of **critical organ surgery** was the Briggs Act in Massachusetts in 1911, which singled out the violent sex offender as being in need of special legal attention. This approach was pushed to the extreme by Maryland, which enacted a defective delinquent law with an indefinite sentence that led to the development of an institution called Patuxent to treat and warehouse these "defective delinquents."[58] This general climate of opinion pushed the use of castration as a method for the control of sexually aggressive males— violent rapists to be exact. The law allowing castration was passed in 1907; not until 1921 did the Supreme Court hold involuntary castration to be unconstitutional.[59] No one knows how many men were castrated during this 14-year period, but it is a safe bet that mandatory castrations were not uncommon, particularly in the South. Parenthetically, the parallel to castration in males was the wholesale sterilization of mentally defective women following the Supreme Court decision in *Buck* v. *Bell* rendered by Justice Oliver Wendell Holmes: "Three generations of imbeciles are enough."[60] Since no one studied the lives of the castrated offenders subsequent to their surgery, it is impossible to determine their postsurgical adjustment. In Denmark, however, Dr. G. K. Sturup performed castrations, technically voluntary, on a considerable number of sex offenders for the better part of three decades in a prison hospital (Herstedvester). The post-hospital experience of these individuals, mostly violent rapists, was excellent.[61] Only about 2 percent committed later crimes—none sexual—after castration. Dr. Sturup's successor at Herstedvester has since abandoned the use of castration. In Holland, too, castration was used for a time with sex offenders but apparently it has also been discontinued there.[62] In any event, the need for castration no longer exists; anti-androgen drugs do a better job in reducing libido.

Psychosurgery   Psychosurgery is a dreaded, intrusive, and irreversible procedure. Unfortunately, like so many other highly touted biomedical approaches, the damage done far exceeds the benefits accrued when there are no compelling medical reasons for **psychosurgery.**

The rather naïve belief in organicity as the basis of madness and badness has encouraged the exploration of surgical intervention in providing relief.[63] Many neurosurgeons have performed surgery on patients suffering from otherwise intractable psychiatric or neurological illness who also displayed uncontrollable aggression. Improved knowledge of the interrelationships of parts of the limbic system in the expression of aggressive behavior initially led to the extensive use of the removal of prefrontal cortical tissue and interruption of neural tracts to this brain region. Subsequently, as techniques have been refined, and in attempts to reduce morbidity, mortality, and unwanted impairment of other behavior, neurosurgical treatments have become more selective and discrete: they now involve highly localized lesions in specific regions of the amygdala and cingulate portions of the cerebral cortex. There are thousands of amygdalotomies reported throughout the world for the treatment of a variety of clinical indications, many of which include aggressive symptoms. Neurosurgeons performing hypothalotomies have claimed a marked calming effect in most acting-out patients. Similarly, surgical destruction of parts of the thalamus or cingulate cortex has been performed in patients both suffering from a variety of illnesses and exhibiting aggressive behavior; results have been mixed.[64]

The success of early work with animals—e.g., stimulation experiments in cats and monkeys suggesting a hypothalamic component to the expression of aggression, or the ablation of prefrontal areas in chimpanzees as a cure for temper tantrums—led to psychosurgery in human patients. Success with psychosurgery was sufficient to win Moniz a Nobel Prize in 1949.[65] As many as 50,000 lobotomies were performed in the United States in the 1950s before they became less fashionable.[66] As methods of lesioning have become more precise, employing stereotaxic machines for accurate lesion placements, a high rate of surgical intervention continued; as many as 12,000 were performed from 1965 to 1968. The goals of such intervention were numerous: to reduce otherwise intractable pain, tremor, spasticity, and seizures, but also to reduce emotional disturbances including aggression, hyperkinesis, and psychosis.

In 1951, a researcher reported some success in the treatment of aggressive, assaultive patients with temporal lobe epilepsy by surgery in the amygdala. Eventually, such surgery was performed in the absence of temporal lobe epilepsy, with only abnormal EEG and behavior disturbances as the required criteria. By 1963 psychosurgery was employed on selected mentally defective subjects to ameliorate hyperactive and destructive conduct.[67]

Although psychosurgery is not a casual undertaking, many thousands of severely troubled patients were treated with psychosurgery during the Fifties and Sixties. Even now, many responsible neurosurgeons believe that to withhold such therapy from individuals with otherwise uncontrollably violent and aggressive behavior is to deprive them of their only significant chance for assistance and relief.[68] However, the outcomes of such surgical procedures are often poorly reported. The results of those that have been reported have been mixed. Moreover, there are major problems in evaluating such subjects. In the past, crude surgical extirpation and major tractotomy in the central nervous system produced gross personality changes in individuals. More sophisticated treatment of precisely located lesions now produces less general brain damage. Nevertheless, even though lesions are used to treat difficult behavioral problems, the consequences of lesions—even those that are very circumscribed—of highly interconnected structures in the brain have proved to be global rather than specific in terms of selected behavior patterns.

Most of the surgical procedures reported in the literature are usually described as successful, but the unreported attempts are probably less than successful. Furthermore, estimation of a successful outcome has been difficult for several reasons, including the diversity of symptoms used for patient selection, unsystematic follow-up, and incomplete descriptions or evaluations of other treatments administered to the patients studied.[69]

Still, over the years, evidence has been accumulating that some pathologic irritability and acting out is related to brain pathology, thereby justifying surgical intervention. Tumors or other irritants in certain brain regions, especially the limbic lobe and associated structure, often facilitate aggressive behavior. And even in the absence of specific lesions, individuals manifesting the "behavioral dyscontrol syndrome" often have disturbed EEG patterns originating in the limbic system. Surgical removal of parts of such regions may result in the alleviation of the pathologic behavior—but not without danger to the individual. Psychosurgery is a serious, irreversible intervention; the fact that it is still used indicates the desperation of those who must cope with these serious behavioral problems.

The general frustration with the ineffectiveness of conventional psychological-psychiatric treatment has stimulated a growing scientific interest in nonmedically defined deviant individuals and has led to pressure for the application of psychosurgery in prisons. Some are so convinced that there are brain regions specifically dedicated to regulating the expression of violence that they have proposed surgery, even in the absence of pathology, to excise the regions of the brain that supposedly regulate undesirable behavior.[70]

There is also a growing feeling in some circles that there are people who "have so much spontaneous activity in the neural systems which underlie aggressive behavior that they are a constant threat to themselves and to those around them."[71] In the absence of data drawn from experimentation with human subjects, arbitrary and sometimes inappropriate extrapolations from animal data have led to the impression that a great deal of human violence is probably triggered by abnormality in the brain and that brain disease may be implicated even in collective actions such as prison riots and urban violence. Such thinking has resulted in a call for wider testing of limbic system function to locate individuals in the general population who are easily triggered to impulsive violence.[72]

The work and views of Mark and Ervin and of Delgado deserve special attention. Mark and Ervin believe that predispositions to violence due to brain dysfunction are a reality and were a significant factor in the urban racial turmoil of the 1960s. According to Mark and Ervin, violence is associated with a "dyscontrol syndrome," a cluster of symptoms consisting of various behavioral facts that include a history of physical assault, a problem with alcohol, a history of impulsive and sometimes violent or assaultive sexuality, and a history of reckless driving and serious motor accidents. Individuals suffering from this syndrome are the people who will also be drawn, as though by a magnet, to group violence and rioting because of "low violence thresholds." According to Mark and Ervin, such persons must be found and treated, surgically if necessary, for both their welfare and ours since they suffer from some specific, but unlocated, type of temporal lobe disease. Their propensity to violence can be stopped (or, indeed, enhanced) by stimulating different sites in the amygdala and hippocampus.[73]

Little wonder, then, that the black community reacted to the Mark-Ervin call for brain surgery as a direct threat to blacks.[74] What is surprising is that the general theme of a "dyscontrol syndrome" should come as a shock to anyone. With no fanfare at all, Glusman had described an uncontrollably violent type as suffering from "the hypothalamic 'Savage' syndrome," and more recently, there has been a resurgence of interest in the "criminal personality."[75] Neither Glusman nor Yochelson and Samenow, however, suggest brain surgery as a preferred or recommended treatment.

Delgado, on the other hand, is quite radical in his philosophy about the need for and utility of brain control. His ideas about biotechnology involve experimentation to determine the exact sites of brain dysfunction. This can be achieved, he argues, by implanting electrodes into the brain and stimulating each of the various potential sites until the exact location of the undesirable behavior is determined. Once this is accomplished, stereotaxic surgery will obliterate the offending site and the behavior—once and for all—without causing gross functional deficits.[76] The audacity of this seriously proffered recommendation is simply stunning: Tinker until you find the right spot and then obliterate it with "state of the art" precision. Delgado sees his approach as an adventure comparable to the exploration of outer space.[77] He asks for a mass media blitz to enlist public understanding and support for this effort, which will be promoted by neurobiological institutes.[78] In truth, as Goldman relates in some detail, neurobiologists have been stimulating and ablating structures in the limbic lobe in laboratory animals for years with occasionally solid but mostly equivocal results. Thus, lesions in the hypothalamus of animals ordinarily induce symptoms of rage; cysts in a comparable area of the human brain will do likewise, as postmortems of uncontrollably violent humans have revealed. Furthermore, the emotional symptoms associated with rabies have been linked to lesions in the hippocampus or ram's horn–like structure in the limbic lobe.[79] But Delgado's bravado goes beyond any reasonable body of supporting data and is both philosophically repugnant and theoretically premature. Psychosurgery may yet achieve acceptance as a legitimate procedure in the treatment of certain behaviorally deviant humans who cannot be contained or managed by other less intrusive means. But we sincerely hope that more is known before psychosurgery achieves such legitimacy.

Drug Treatment

Direct Forms   Knowledge of the chemistry of the brain and its functional dependence on various endogenous substances, including hormones and neurotransmitters, has increased rapidly in recent years. Some behavioral abnormalities have been found to be associated with specific chemical defects and many more such relationships have been proposed. Whether or not it is correct, this point of view has generated great activity among pharmacologists aimed at developing drugs that modify nervous system mechanisms. A considerable number of these drugs have proved sufficiently potent and safe to permit their use to control human behavior. In recent years, therefore, psychosurgery has been replaced by drug treatment, the effects of which usually can be adjusted or reversed.

A number of **psychotropic drugs** have the ability to ameliorate some deviant activities. According to Resnick, "psychotropic drugs now available may help individuals who are aggressive, irritable, unstable, egocentric, easily offended, obsessive, compulsive, and dependent, who demonstrate such symptoms as anxiety, depression, hysteria, agony, unexplainable and motiveless behavior, [and] recurrent violent emotional upset including temper tantrums and violent rages."[80]

The introduction of antipsychotic drugs, such as the phenothiazines, into psychiatry dramatically altered institutions and psychiatry itself.[81] Management of acting-out patients by means of drugs quickly replaced management by surgery or even by heavy sedation and mechanical restraints. Over and above their sedative actions, antipsychotic drugs such as chlorpromazine decrease acting out, reduce ward noise, and ameliorate psychotic symptoms.[82] Newer and more potent phenothiazines and butyrophenones have even fewer sedative side effects. Such agents have also been employed in a variety of conditions in which aggression is displayed in mental defectives, certain types of depressives, sexual deviants, alcoholics, and disturbed adolescents and hyperactive children.[83]

The association of acting-out aggressive behavior with possible subcortical EEG abnormalities has led to the use of antiseizure drugs to control hyperexcitability and hostility in children with severe behavior disorders as well as in psychiatric patients displaying, among other symptoms, anger, irritability, and tension. Other treatable symptoms include explosiveness, low frustration tolerance, irritability, impulsive behavior, compulsive behavior, erratic behavior, inability to delay gratification, mood swings, short attention spans, and undirected activity.[84]

Treatment of hyperkinetic children by drugs that cause mood arousal often reduces symptoms that include aggressiveness, temper tantrums, and impulsiveness. This result is a startling paradox that is not yet well understood. These drugs may sometimes also be useful in treating adults with immature personalities who display outbursts of spontaneous aggression, such as sociopaths.[85]

Lithium chloride, an agent used to forestall episodic mania and depression, has been reported to decrease combative behavior in subjects who did not suffer from affective disorders.[86] Minor tranquilizers that are especially nontoxic can control the symptoms of tension and anxiety. The more effective of these drugs, Valium and Librium, reduce aggressive excitability, hostility, and irritability at dose levels that cause only minimal sedation and ataxia.

In another area, the effects of therapeutic castration can now be duplicated by chemical means. Such treatments today have been applied most often to the aggressive sexual offender. Estrogens have been used to depress sexuality in men for more than 20 years.[87] Although animal experiments have suggested that estrogens can reduce acting out, unpleasant and potentially serious side effects have precluded further use of such hormones in humans. For a time, progestins were employed because they inhibited testicular functions without the feminizing effects of estrogens. However, since chronic administration of progesterone may lead to testicular atrophy, a new compound developed in the late 1960s, cyproterone, which acts effectively yet reversibly, is applied increasingly in the treatment of sexually aggressive offenders.[88] This compound is one of several anti-androgens that control libido, sex drive, and sexual performance and that reduce or eliminate sexual behavior in the human male. The actions are reversible; harmful side effects, such as general feminization and obesity, appear to be minimal. Under such circumstances, a therapeutic approach involving anti-androgens is likely to be accepted as a legitimate form of medical intervention. Ferracuti and Bartilotti confirm this conclusion in their recent review of some of the complex social, methodological, and legal problems involved with the utilization of anti-androgens in the treatment of the sex offender.[89]

Antabuse is a widely used drug in treating alcoholics and excessive drinkers who want to remain sober. Antabuse causes physical intolerance even to very small amounts of alcohol and consequently compels abstinence. Methadone is often used as a substitute agent with heroin addicts. Unfortunately, experience has indicated that addicts often supplement the methadone with heroin, thereby nullifying its effectiveness. Furthermore, an unanticipated consequence of methadone maintenance programs has been the development of a black market for this rather potent, but not euphoria-producing, narcotic agent. It is now clear that methadone maintenance is a flawed technique of treatment.[90]

A promising new approach to the treatment of heroin addiction is suggested by the exploration of the narcotic antagonists or opiate-blocking agents. Cyclazocine and naloxene were mentioned in the President's Commission Report by the LEAA Task Force on Drugs in 1967 as possible treatment agents. However, for various reasons connected with their administration and their toxicity, neither substance has been widely employed. More recently, a similar agent, naltrexone, has been used to maintain addicts in a drug-free state in the hope that their dependence will disappear during their "sobriety." So far, naltrexone has been administered to over 1000 addicts and has been found to be well tolerated, physically safe, and to produce a highly effective blockade against opiates. The results have been favorable: addicts rarely challenge the blockade with opiates and some addicts claim a reduction in craving for heroin. Since treatment outcome depends on the voluntary taking of naltrexone on a regular basis, the desire of the addict to be abstinent is the key to the success of the intervention. For this reason, the re-addiction rate is likely to be very high.[91]

In treating drug addiction, the most promising recent development concerns the endorphins, endogenous hormone-like substances that have the same analgesic and anaesthetic properties as the opiates. To date, however, these substances have been used only with laboratory animals and, as noted, it is difficult to project laboratory findings to street addicts who have options to take or reject any drug, however therapeutic.

Finally, the utility of drug treatment for specific classes of deviants is difficult to dispute. In a three-year experimental study followed by five years of follow-up, our research group demonstrated the superiority of a drug home care program for schizophrenics over both a placebo home care program and over ordinary hospital care. When all patients were returned to the ordinary care regimens available to schizophrenics, all three groups—drug and placebo home care and hospital controls—showed rehospitalization rates on the order of 60 to 70 percent in a five-year period subsequent to the program.[92] In another long-term experimental study, a research group showed that imipramine (Tofranil), a mild anti-depressive, had a positive effect on the physical, psychological, and institutional adjustment of chronically antisocial offenders in prison.[93]

Drug treatment remains the promise of the next few decades. Laboratories are experimenting with hormones and new hormone-like substances in a variety of contexts. Such experimentation has focused on the motivation, acquisition, retrieval, and extinction of learning; on arousal states; and on the perception of pain, as well as on clinical depression and other behavioral problems, including schizophrenia.

This new class of substances consists of chains of relatively few (3 to 14) amino acids called polypeptides. The polypeptides most intensively studied are those normally secreted by the pituitary glands, the adrenocorticotrophic hormone (ACTH), the melanocyte-stimulating hormone (MSH), and the anti-diuretic hormone (ADH) as well as fragments of these hormones. As the names imply, each has some easily characterized regulatory action on peripheral organs. In addition, however, it appears that these substances, carried in the blood, exert profound effects on various behavioral mechanisms. Thus, in animals, several of these substances that are secreted during stressful situations (i.e., fright, flight, or fight), by acting back on the brain independently of their other actions, can facilitate learning, focusing of attention, and retaining and retrieving learned responses. There are still relatively few studies on the effects of these peptides in humans, but there are indications that they act in the same way. The effects of fragments of these hormones, often polypeptides of no more than five amino acids, as well as more potent synthetic analogs, are being cautiously investigated in humans, particularly in the areas of amnesia and learning disabilities.[94]

The growing list of other relatively simple endogenous substances that can alter arousal states, modify perceptions of pain, and affect attention, recall, and other aspects of learning has immediate medical utility. The recent discovery of these substances has already reshaped the way we think about the biologic substrates of normal and abnormal behavior. Substances of this nature, produced normally in the body and now easily synthesized in the laboratory, seem to be essential for the translation of experiential input into the biologic codes with which human brains organize the business of living. Body functions that produce or respond to these substances are newly recognized not only as possible sources of pathologic behavior but also as points that are accessible to current biochemical and medical intervention. So far there has been little discussion, publicly at least, of the possibility of using the agents to improve, for example, the memories of normal people, but it is an idea that cannot help but occur to anyone who has ever forgotten anything. There is also the far-reaching possibility of such substances being used to facilitate learning and conditioning programs, programs that can be designed not only to treat behaviors of deficient or retarded individuals but also to help them cope in socially acceptable ways.

Marx's reviews in *Science* describe several experiments with human subjects. In 1971, Kastin and his associates found that MSH (the first 13 amino acids of the 39 acid molecule of ACTH) can improve a male's visual memory under drug and placebo injection conditions. MSH has also been found to enhance attention, or rather, to focus it more directly. The same substance also appears to reduce anxiety. So does ACTH, indicating there may be polypeptides that have such special action. Other research with humans shows that ACTH increases auditory attention in females, and some Dutch researchers have presented data that show that ACTH also increases motivation. On the behavioral level, a peptide, TRH, was administered to patients suffering from depression. Prompt, but brief, relief of symptoms occurred after a single injection of this peptide. In nondepressive women, TRH produced relaxation, mild euphoria, and a sense of increased energy.

The most startling finding to date has been the discovery of the existence of two related brain proteins, now called enkephalins and endorphins, that act at the morphine nerve receptor sites in the brain. These substances are, in fact, pain-relieving peptides. As David de Wied, a major figure in peptide studies, says of the status of the field, "A number of these peptides will be used in the future to improve mental performance of people, primarily in those who have deficiencies in this respect like the elderly or children with minimal brain damage." Adds another forefront researcher, "These peptides will be used to modify behavior in a specific manner and will open a new field of cognitive psychopharmacology."[95] Obviously, peptide research is in its infancy. Much more work will have to be done to determine how the peptides produce their behavioral effects and to locate the target neurons.

Who knows what major behavioral changes will be accomplished with relative ease by mimicking normal endogenous processes? We can only be sure that we are still at the beginning of an understanding of the brain protein revolution.

Indirect Forms   It is one thing to use drugs and electric shock as treatment modalities and a very different matter to use the same techniques in classical conditioning and aversive suppression experiments.[96] And yet, until a recent series of court rulings ended their use in such situations, these methods were applied to alcoholics, addicts, and sex offenders in an effort to extinguish the compulsive-obsessive and addictive behaviors.[97] Emetics—nausea-producing agents, chiefly emetine hydrochloride and apomorphine—have been used extensively with alcoholics, excessive drinkers, and opiate addicts to decondition the addiction.[98] The usual procedure is to give the patient the emetic and then, just before the onset of the nausea, give him a shot of alcohol in whatever manner and in whatever amount he or she is accustomed to imbibing it. Theoretically, the patient pairs his or her dreadful reaction with the alcohol and after a prescribed series of such pairings will avoid the alcohol at all costs. There are clinics in the United States that specialize in such procedures with an outcome no better or worse than less dramatic interventions. This aversive technique has sometimes been augmented by a clever setting; thus, one medical center constructed a barroom setting so that the patron-patient would associate the place, the alcohol, and the unpleasant reaction. The results were no better with the barroom than without it.

In the case of homosexuals, pedophiles, and aggressive sex offenders such as rapists, the emetic is administered shortly before an erotic stimulus is projected on a screen. The drug-induced illness and retching follows and the pairing continues for a prescribed series of sessions, after which the formerly erotic stimulus is likely to have lost its appeal—at least temporarily.

In addition to the emetics, a curare-like substance has been used in much the same way. Called succinylchoine chloride (Anectine), this agent causes muscle paralysis, including cessation of breathing. The administration of the succinycholine is followed by the presentation of the alcohol or sexual stimulus. Paralysis occurs; the patient feels that he or she is suffocating and will die.[99] The patient is resuscitated in 30 seconds, but the fear persists for many months. Anyone who has ever experienced heart or breathing cessation knows the terror induced by the paralysis. So intrusive is this method, and similar methods involving the injection of other drugs, that the courts have uniformly held them to be cruel and unusual punishments, violations of due process, and unfair and overreaching procedures. Furthermore, not even this paralysis-inducing technique has been found to be more effective than such nonintrusive methods as desensitization.

As late as the 1960s, the Tucker Prison in Arkansas was still punishing prisoners for major infractions by administering an electric shock to the testes. Electric shock had been used as early as 1930 as an unconditioned stimulus with alcoholics, by 1935 with homosexuals, and still later with transvestites, fetishists, sadists, and voyeurs. It has also been used with rapists: penile erection is induced by object presentation; the ensuing shock produces memorable pain. A course of such treatments would seem to be sufficient reason for substituting another deviant behavior for the one being deconditioned.[100]

A number of experimenters and inventors have come up with shock- or pulse-producing gadgets to combat cigarette use (e.g., a cigarette case that emits a shock whenever opened), a rythmical pulse device to be worn by stutterers to regulate the cadence of speech, and a gadget that beeps when a person with "round shoulders" slouches.

The biomedical revolution is still in its infancy in the treatment and control, or at least management, of deviancy. Nevertheless, Valium is already the most widely prescribed of all drugs and other mood-altering agents are in common use. Most importantly, the pharmacologic agents are becoming more specific and better targeted to the disability being treated. The behavior modification approach has lost favor, but it is unlikely to disappear completely in the coming two decades.

ETHICAL PROBLEMS

Despite its promise, however, most criminologists are as one in their opposition to the biomedical management and control of deviance. Drugs, genetic engineering, and behavior modification raise anew the specter of totalitarian control of human society, of *1984,* of *Clockwork Orange,* and of the "Brave New World." Never have we been closer to achieving the management and control of conduct, to altering forever the human species. The Nazi concentration camp medical experiments, the classification of political dissidents as psychiatric cases in the Soviet Union, the tales of brainwashing of United States POWs by the North Koreans in the 1950s and North Vietnamese in the 1960s and 1970s, as well as all the physical and bio-medical tortures and controls visited on enemies of the state in various parts of the globe, are sufficient cause for concern. The biomedical revolution is susceptible to and invites perversion and use in a political context for political ends. But the nightmare begins even closer to home. Even the most benign and therapeutic use of biomedical interventions raises serious ethical issues. In this sense, the crime problem has made victims and hostages of all of us.

The ethical problems raised by some of the new surveillance measures and by the latest biomedical interventions lie in the fact that they are intrusive, irreversible, involuntary, and overcontrolling. They also violate the fundamental principle of medical ethics: Do no harm, but be a healer.[101]

Intrusion

In the nature of things, modification by external means of one's physical and psychological state is inherently intrusive.[102] Up to a point, the success of medicine in this century may be attributed to its increasingly specific intrusion for the purpose of healing. But it is one thing to radiate a patient or extirpate a tumor or bypass an arterial blockage and quite another to intrude radically to reduce aggression or libido as a method of social control. Intrusion is justifiable in the first instance because it is life preserving; it probably is unjustifiable in the second because it heals nothing, preserves nothing, even in a purely medical sense. The aim is social control, easier management, societal protection. The patient is violated for reasons other than to make him or her whole again. It is for this reason that courts have ruled that prisoners and others under state control cannot give informed consent in biomedical experiments.[103]

Irreversibility

As a general principle, no procedure should be allowed that cannot be reversed. This proscription would automatically eliminate the use of castration, sterilization, and psychosurgery for nonmedical purposes. It should be noted that within ten years of the introduction of lobotomies, the phenothiazines made them unnecessary. The drug cyproterone will probably make castration a needlessly cruel and barbaric "treatment" for violent sex offenders. There are persons who would ban all shock therapy, even for depressives who fail to respond to psychoactive drugs. The argument is that many millions of neurons are destroyed with each shock—neurons that can never be replaced. The cumulative damage to cognition is irreversible.

Involuntary Administration

Two major projects in Ohio illustrate both the problem of informed consent and the conception of prisoners as guinea pigs historically held by experimental scientists. A number of long-term prisoners at the old Ohio Penitentiary (population 4800 then) "volunteered" to accept injections of live cancer cells in order to test the hypothesis that the immune system of normal persons would reject the malignant cells. While the inmates were never openly promised early parole or commutation for participation, they never doubted that early release or special privileges would inevitably follow. Voluntary? Involuntary? Who is to say that possible death by injection of cancer is not preferable to life inside the walls—the choice these inmates made.

The second "voluntary" subject study concerned the testing of various types of IUDs using women prisoner volunteers in the Ohio Reformatory for Women. We can verify that the project took place; we cannot address all the rumors and stories that naturally flowed from this experiment. But confined subjects are not wholly free to give their consent. Many were trading participation for reduced time.

Biomedical interventions lend themselves to use by volunteers as escapes from the "pain of punishment" that is the common lot of the prisoner. We have deliberately used extreme illustrations to highlight the problems that must be addressed to insure that prisons never become for prisoners what laboratories are for rats. The worst case in memory, and it is a dreadfully depressing one, is the experiment of the 1930s in which prisoners were infected with venereal disease and left untreated, partly by design, partly by neglect, for the remainder of their lives. A few were located and treated in the 1970s, some 40 years too late to undo the damage done them.[104]

Overcontrol

Nothing pleases us more than living and working in a tranquil environment. From years of experience as a researcher in a teaching mental hospital, we can verify that the reduction of the ward noise level is a number one priority. A day in a calm, antiseptic environment free of aggressive outbursts, shrieking, and "patient upsets," as they are delicately known, is a day to be cherished. Until quite recently, it was impossible to achieve this modest goal. Patients had to be subdued, restrained, isolated, and prevented from harming themselves and others. But tranquilizers put an end to all that. The modern soma changed a madhouse into a hospital, burly attendants into treatment staff, crazy people into placid residents. The phenothiazines and tricyclics and all the other agents may cure nothing and nobody, but they help managers manage.

What we observed in mental hospitals is true of most total institutions for the dependent, disruptive, and deviant. Drugs are used to control, not to treat; to ease the burden of idleness; to achieve some sort of psychic well-being. Institutional dispensaries are little more than pill centers. Name your symptoms—sleeplessness, nervousness, irritability or drowsiness, lethargy, fatigue—and get your pills. The new institutional discipline is predicated on tranquilization and sedation, on permitting, even tacitly encouraging, feelings of well-being. No need for counseling, preparation for release, learning to cope, job training, education. Licit drugs are the agents of managers, of parents, and of school teachers.[105]

As in private life, it is also the case that if mild substances work well, stronger substances work better. Hence the tendency to escalate product, dosage, and frequency of administration and to look with benign neglect on the illicit substances that add spice to the volatile mix of institutional life. Living better chemically promotes institutional survival and tranquility. Just imagine what the turmoil would be like if we didn't rely on these medically prescribed agents, when, even with them, institutions are neither safe, secure, nor therapeutic.

SUMMARY

That the problem of street crime is out of control is a widely accepted belief. When other and more costly criminal behaviors, such as white-collar, corporate, organized, and public order crimes, are added to the total picture, then the matter of crime becomes one of the most serious social problems facing American society today. The health risks posed by AIDS and the gloomy forecast of a worldwide epidemic comparable to the plagues in the Middle Ages are even more pressing matters related to crime in the minds of the American public. In short, crime is a crippling disorder to the American society, one that affects every citizen in some way.

The problem of crime, as this text has repeatedly stated, is tied up with the wider social, economic, and political order, and, accordingly, it eludes quick cure-alls. Rehabilitative strategies have given way to "get-tough" approaches, and now technology and medicine are increasingly being used to handle the disorder of crime. The social control methods of the future—expanded use of technology, of voluntary associations, and of medicalization—will fail, as countless measures have failed before, unless effective measures are employed to overcome unemployment, slums, abusive treatment of children, and the marginality of lower-class losers.

It is claimed that a major law of the universe is entropy, in that everything is moving toward disorder. In any closed system, or institution, it can be argued, entropy is the inevitable result of social existence. Crime is toxic. It is undeniably toxic to victims, but it is also toxic to offenders and those who work with them. However, efforts to reduce crime, according to the law of entropy, will fail because this disorder is an inevitable and normal part of the social order.

Perhaps! But where do we go from here? Is freedom to give way to the need for an orderly society? Is conformity to replace individuality and creativity? Is equality to be replaced by prejudice, discrimination, and social injustice? Are greed and hatred to bury the nobler attributes of human nature? Is violence to subdue peaceful coexistence, cooperation, and coordination? Is war to be the final page of history? The ultimate conclusion of entropy would suggest such outcomes, but we firmly believe that the best is not in the past. We live in an age of skepticism and disillusionment, and our own feelings of trepidation and pessimism remind us that we are tied to the world view of the present. Yet, we hold to the dream that humans can join together to achieve a society in which order and disorder are united in such a way to realize a dimension of human existence that philosophers, theologians, utopians, visionaries, and social scientists have dreamed of, but that human societies have been unable to realize.

NOTES

1. Simon Dinitz, "Nothing Fails Like a Little Success," *Criminology* 16 (August 1978), pp. 225–238.
2. Harry Elmer Barnes and Negley K. Testers, *New Horizons in Criminology,* 2d ed. (New York: Prentice-Hall, 1951), pp. 371–853; Edward Sagarin, *Odd Man In* (New York: Quadrangle, 1969).
3. See, for example, National Advisory Commission on Criminal Justice Standards and Goals, *A National Strategy to Reduce Crime,* (Washington, D. C.: U.S. Government Printing Office, 1973). This report is a summary of the findings of six task forces. See

also *Deinstitutionalization of Corrections and Its Implications for the Residual Of-fender,* Secretariat Working Paper, Sixth United Nations Congress on the Prevention of Crime and the Treatment of Offenders, A/Conf. 87/7, 9 July 1980, Caracas, Venezuela.

4. National Advisory Commission on Criminal Justice Standards and Goals, *Task Force Report on Corrections* (Washington, D.C., U.S. Government Printing Office, 1973); see also *United Nations Norms and Guidelines in Criminal Justice: From Standard Setting to Implementation,* A/Conf. 87/8, 23 June 1980.

5. Richard Quinney, *The Social Reality of Crime* (Boston: Little-Brown, 1970); An-thony Platt, *The Child Savers: The Invention of Delinquency* (Chicago: University of Chicago Press, 1969).

6. See, for example, Ernest van den Haag, *Punishing Criminals* (New York: Basic Books, 1975).

7. For an overall perspective from this position, see Marshall B. Clinard and Robert Meier, *The Sociology of Deviant Behavior,* 5th ed.; Simon Dinitz, Alfred C. Clarke, and Russell R. Dynes, eds., *Deviance: Studies in Definition, Management and Treat-ment,* 2d ed. (New York: Oxford University Press, 1975), part 1.

8. Philip Rieff, *Triumph of the Therapeutic* (New York: Harper & Row, 1966).

9. Norval Morris, *The Future of Imprisonment* (Chicago: University of Chicago Press, 1974); James Q. Wilson, *Thinking About Crime* (New York: Basic Books, 1975); Steve Van Dine, Simon Dinitz, and John P. Conrad, *Restraining the Wicked* (Lexing-ton, Mass.: Lexington Books, Heath, 1979).

10. Georg Rusche and Otto Kirchheimer, *Punishment and Social Structure* (New York: Columbia University Press, 1939).

11. Ysabel Rennie, *The Search for Criminal Man* (Lexington, Mass.: Lexington Books, Heath, 1978); Peter Conrad and Joseph W. Schneider, *Deviance and Medicalization* (St. Louis: Mosby, 1980).

12. For a review and balanced assessment of these developments, see George Vold and Thomas Bernard, *Theoretical Criminology* (New York: Oxford University Press, 1979). See also Dinitz, Clarke, and Dynes, eds., *Deviance: Studies in Definition, Management, and Treatment,* parts IV and V.

13. Rennie, *Search for Criminal Man,* chaps. 36 and 37.

14. Ibid., chap. 18; Vold and Bernard, *Theoretical Criminology,* chap. 10.

15. William Ogburn, *On Culture and Social Change: Selected Papers* (Chicago: Univer-sity of Chicago Press, 1964).

16. Clifford R. Shaw and Henry D. McKay, *Juvenile Delinquency in Urban Areas* (Chi-cago: University of Chicago Press, 1969); Edwin Sutherland and Donald R. Cressey, *Principles of Criminology,* 10th ed. (Philadelphia: Lippincott, 1979), pp. 80–82. See also Walter C. Reckless, *The Crime Problem,* 5th ed. (Pacific Palisades, Calif.: Goodyear, 1973); Daniel Glaser, ed., *Handbook of Criminology* (Chicago: Rand McNally, 1974); Glaser, "Criminality Theories and Behavioral Images," *American Journal of Sociology* 61 (March 1956), pp. 433–444.

17. Thorsten Sellin, *Culture Conflict and Crime* (New York: Social Science Research Council, 1938).

18. Hermann Mannheim, *Pioneers in Criminology* (Montclair, N.J.: Patterson Smith, 1972), contains sections on the major utilitarian writers and their social and crimino-logical thought.

19. This consensus model is described in much of the early social problems and social pathology literature. See, for example, Russell R. Dynes, Alfred Clarke, Simon Dinitz, and Iwao Ishino, *Social Problems: Dissensus and Deviation* (New York:

Oxford University Press, 1964). For a stinging review of the consensus model, see C. Wright Mills, *The Sociological Imagination* (New York: Oxford University Press, 1959).

20. See, for example, Albert Deutsch, *The Mentally Ill in America* (New York: Columbia University Press, 1949); Joseph Gusfield, *Symbolic Crusade* (Urbana, Ill.: University of Illinois Press, 1963); Alfred Lindesmith, *The Addict and the Law* (Bloomington, Ind.: Indiana University Press, 1965); Kai Erickson, *Wayward Puritans* (New York: Wiley, 1966).

21. Frederick Jackson Turner, *Frontier and Section: Selected Essays* (Englewood Cliffs, N. J.: Prentice-Hall, 1961).

22. See, for example, C. Wright Mills, *The Power Elite* (New York: Oxford University Press, 1956); August Hollingshead and F. C. Redlich, *Social Class and Mental Illness* (New York: Wiley, 1958); Floyd Hunter, *Community Power Structure* (Chapel Hill N.C.: University of North Carolina Press, 1953); W. Lloyd Warner and Paul S. Lunt, *The Social Life of a Modern Community,* Yankee City Series (New Haven: Yale University Press, 1941). An overall review of these class studies is contained in Joseph A. Kahl, *The American Class Structure* (New York: Holt, Rinehart & Winston, 1961).

23. William F. Whyte, *Street Corner Society* (Chicago: University of Chicago Press, 1955).

24. For a review of the anomie tradition literature, see Vold and Bernard, *Theoretical Criminology,* chap. 10, and Rennie, *Search for Criminal Man,* chap. 19.

25. Robert Martinson, "What Works? Questions and Answers About Prison Reform," *Public Interest* 35 (Spring 1974), pp. 22–54; C. Ray Jeffery, *Crime Prevention Through Environmental Design* (Beverly Hills, Calif.: Sage, 1971), pp. 28–29; Wilson, *Thinking About Crime,* van den Haag, *Punishing Criminals.*

26. Oswald Spengler, *The Decline of the West* (New York: Knopf, 1934).

27. For a review of the problem of terrorism in Europe within a broader crime context, see Hans Joachim Schneider, "Crime and Criminal Police in Some Western European and North American Countries," *International Review of Criminal Policy* (New York: United Nations, 1980), pp. 55–65.

28. Jorge A. Montero Castro, "Crime Trends and Crime Prevention Strategies in Latin American Countries," *International Review of Criminal Policy,* 35 (New York: United Nations, 1980, pp. 38–43.

29. *Crime in the United States, 1979 (Uniform Crime Reports),* (Washington, D. C.: U.S. Department of Justice, 1980).

30. *Jerusalem Post,* 13–19 July 1980, p. 3.

31. Van Dine, Conrad, and Dinitz, *Restraining the Wicked,* pp. 35 ff.

32. Despite verbal assurances and speeches to the contrary—e.g., at the Sixth UN Congress on Crime Prevention and the Treatment of Offenders, in Caracas on August 25–September 5, 1980—there are enough data to justify this assertion. See, for example, Walter Connor, *Deviance in Soviet Society* (New York: Columbia University Press, 1972).

33. Data presented at the Sixth UN Congress on Crime Prevention and the Treatment of Offenders, Caracas, August 25–September 5, 1980.

34. See David Biles, "Australian Working Paper on Crime Prevention and the Treatment of Offenders," 1980.

35. Ezra Vogel, *Japan as Number One* (Cambridge, Mass.: Harvard University Press, 1979); see also "Japan Working Paper," UN Social Defense Research Institute (New York: United Nations, 1977).

36. See Conrad and Schneider, *Deviance and Medicalization,* chapts. 9 and 10.

37. Jeffery, *Crime Prevention,* chap. 11; Center for Residential Security Design, *A Design Guide for Improving Residential Security* (Washington, D. C.: U. S. Government Printing Office, 1975).

38. National Advisory Commission, *A National Strategy to Reduce Crime.*

39. See, for example, William Fairley and Michael Liechenstein, *Improving Public Safety in Apartment Dwellings* (New York: New York City Rand Institute, 1971).

40. John Decker, "Curbside Deterrence," *Criminology* (August 1972), pp. 227–242.

41. National Advisory Commission, *A National Strategy to Reduce Crime,* p. 88.

42. Jane Jacobs, *The Life and Death of Great American Cities* (New York: Random House, 1961).

43. Oscar Newman, *Defensible Space* (New York: Macmillan, 1972).

44. William Yancey, "Architecture, Integration and Social Control," in *Environment and Social Services,* ed. Wohhill and Carson, American Psychological Association, 1972. See also Newman, *Defensible Space,* chap. 11.

45. Newman, *Defensible Space.*

46. Robert Sommer, *Tight Spaces* (Englewood Cliffs, N. J.: Prentice-Hall, 1974); Jeffery, *Crime Prevention,* chap. 11.

47. For a review of the crime displacement literature, see Thomas Gabor, "Crime Displacement: The Literature and Strategies for Its Investigation," *Crime and/or Justice* 6 (1978), pp. 100–107; Thomas Gabor, "The Crime Displacement Hypotheses: An Empirical Examination" (Student First Prize Award Paper, American Society of Criminology Annual Meeting, San Francisco, 8 November 1980).

48. Unpublished manuscripts of the Rural Crime Center, The Ohio State University, Columbus.

49. For a general review of this complex field, see Harold Goldman, "The Limits of Clockwork: The Neurobiology of Violent Behavior" in *In Fear of Each Other,* ed. John P. Conrad and Simon Dinitz (Lexington, Mass.: Lexington Books, Heath, 1977), chap. 4; Saleem Shah and Loren Roth, "Biological and Psychophysical Factors in Criminality," in *Handbook of Criminology,* ed. Daniel Glaser (Chicago: Rand McNally, 1974); Vernon H. Mark, William H. Sweet, and Frank R. Ervin, "Role of Brain Disease in Riots," *Journal of the American Medical Association* 201 (1967), p. 895; Vernon H. Mark and Frank R. Ervin, *Violence and the Brain* (New York: Harper, 1970); Kenneth E. Moyer, *The Control of Aggression and Violence,* (ed. J. L. Singer (New York: Harper, 1969); Conrad and Schneider, *Deviance and Medicalization;* Dinitz, Clarke, and Dynes, *Deviance,* part V; Simon Dinitz, "The Anti-Social Personality," in *Modern Legal Medicine, Psychiatry and Forensic Science,* ed. William Curry, Charles Petty, and Louis McGarry (Baltimore: Davis, 1980), chap. 33; C. Ray Jeffery, ed., *Biology and Crime* (Beverly Hills, Calif.: Sage, 1980), especially Article 6.

50. Vold and Bernard, *Theoretical Criminology.*

51. Harold Goldman, *op. cit.,* p. 64.

52. See Edward O. Wilson, *Sociobiology* (Cambridge, Mass.: Belknap Press, Harvard University Press, 1975).

53. For general coverage of these areas in historical perspective, see Rennie, *Search for Criminal Man.*

54. Nicholas Kittrie, "Will the XYY Syndrome Abolish Guilt?" *Federal Probation* 35 (1971), pp. 26–31.

55. Benjamin Pasamanick and Hilda Knobloch, "Retrospective Studies on the Epidimi-

ology of Reproductive Causality," *Merrill-Palmer Quarterly of Behavioral Development* 12 (1966), pp. 7–26.

56. Linda Sleffel, *The Law and the Dangerous Criminal* (Lexington, Mass.: Lexington Books, Heath, 1977).
57. Ibid., pp. 1–20.
58. Ibid., pp. 41–100.
59. Goldman, p. 60.
60. Rennie, *Search for Criminal Man,* pp. 87 ff.
61. See Georg K. Sturup, "Treatment of Sexual Offenders in Herstedvester Denmark: The Rapists" (Third Isaac Ray Lecture, Munksgaard, Copenhagen, 1968).
62. For experience in Switzerland, Holland, and Denmark up to 1968, see Sturup, "Treatment of Sexual Offenders," pp. 11–13.
63. For a concise analysis of recent developments and of the general issues involved in psychosurgery, see Rennie, *Search for Criminal Man,* chap. 32.
64. Goldman, "Limits of Clockwork," pp. 57–58.
65. Dr. Moniz and his colleage Dr. Lima actually elaborated the prefrontal lobotomy in the 1930s. The Nobel Prize compensated in part, I suppose, for the tragedy which had befallen him: a lobotomized patient shot him in the spine and left him a hemiplegic for life. See Elliott S. Valenstein, *Brain Control: A Critical Examination of Brain Stimulation and Psychosurgery* (New York: Wiley, 1973), p. 55; E. Moniz, "How I Succeeded in Performing the Prefrontal Leukotomy," in *The Great Psychodynamic Therapies in Psychiatry,* ed. A., M., and R. Sackler and F. Marti-Ibanez (New York: Harper & Row, 1956), p. 131.
66. B. J. Culliton, "Psychosurgery: National Commission Issues Surprisingly Favorable Report," *Science* 194 (1976), p. 299; Rennie, *Search for Criminal Man,* p. 234.
67. H. Narabayshi, "Stereotaxic Amygdalectomy," in *The Neurobiology of the Amygdala,* ed. B. E. Eleftherion (New York: Plenum, 1972), p. 459 ff.
68. M. Goldstein, "Brain Research and Violent Behavior," *Archives of Neurology* 30 (1974), p. 1.
69. Goldman, "Limits of Clockwork," pp. 58–59.
70. M. H. Brown, "Further Experience with Multiple Limbic Lesions for Schizophrenia and Sociopathic Aggression" (Paper presented at the Third World Congress of Psychosurgery, Cambridge, England, 14–19 August 1972).
71. Moyer, *Control of Aggression and Violence,* p. 61.
72. Mark and Ervin, *Violence and The Brain,* Mark, Sweet, and Ervin, "Brain Disease," p. 895.
73. Mark and Ervin, *Violence and The Brain,* p. 70.
74. Rennie, *Search for Criminal Man,* p. 233.
75. Murray Glusman, "The Hypothalamic 'Savage' Syndrome," in *Aggression,* ed. S. H. Frazier), *Research Publications of the Association for Nervous and Mental Diseases,* 52, (1974), p. 52 ff.; Samuel Yochelson and Stanton Samenow, *The Criminal Personality* (New York: Aronson, 1977).
76. Jose M. R. Delgado, *op. cit.*
77. Ibid., p. 259.
78. Ibid., p. 262.
79. Goldman, "Limits of Clockwork," pp. 49–51.
80. O. Resnick, "Use of Psychotropic Drugs with Criminals," *Psychopharmacology Bulletin* 5 (1969), p. 17.
81. Nathan S. Kline, "Drugs Are the Greatest Practical Advance in the History of Psychiatry," *New Media Materia for Diagnosis, Prevention, Treatment* 4 (1962), p. 48.

82. J. Swazey, *Chlorpromazine: The History of a Psychiatric Discovery* (Cambridge, Mass.: MIT Press, 1974).

83. Jonathan O. Cole, "Psychoactive Drugs" in *Modern Legal Medicine,* ed. Curran, McGarry, and Petty, chap. 40.

84. O. Resnick, "The Psychoactive Properties of Diphenylhydenation," *Intervention Journal of Neuropsychology* 3 (1967), Supplement 2, S20.

85. S. Dinitz, Harold Goldman, Lewis Lindner, Harry Allen, and Thomas Foster, "Drug Treatment of the Sociopathic Offender: The 'Juice Model' Approach," 3:20–28, 1972.

86. S. D. Morrison, C. W. Ervin, D. T. Gianturco, and C. J. Gerber. "Effect of Lithium on Combative Behavior in Humans," *Diseases of the Nervous System* 34 (1973), p. 186.

87. See Saleem A. Shah and Loren H. Roth, "Biological and Psychophysiological Factors in Criminality," in *Handbook of Criminology,* ed. Glaser, pp. 151–152.

88. H. Hoffet, "On the Application of the Testosterone Blocker Cyprotone Acetate (SH 714) in Sex Deviants and Psychiatric Patients in Institutions," *Praxis* 7 (1968) p. 221; U. Laschet, "Antiandrogens in the Treatment of Sex Offenders: Mode of Action and Therapeutic Outcome," in *Contemporary Sexual Behavior: Critical Issues in the 1970s,* ed. J. Zubin and J. Money (Baltimore, Md.: Johns Hopkins University Press, 1973).

89. For a comprehensive review of the effectiveness of cyproterone acetate and other antiandrogens, see Franco Ferracuti and R. Bartilotti, "Technical and Legal Aspects in the Pharmacologic Treatment of Sex Offenders," in *Sexual Behavior: Pharmacology and Biochemistry,* ed. M. Sandler and G. L. Gessa (New York: Raven Press, 1975), p. 205.

90. See *The Diversion and Use of Methadone Used to Treat Drug Addicts,* Report of Committee of the Judiciary of the U. S. (Washington, D.C.: U.S. Government Printing Office, 1973); National Advisory Commission, *A National Strategy To Reduce Crime,* p. 59.

91. Richard Rawson, Michael Glazer, Edward Callahan, and Robert P. Liberman, "Naltrexone and Behavior Therapy for Heroin Addiction," in *Behavioral Analysis and Treatment of Substance Abuse,* ed. Norman A. Krasnegor, NIDA Research Monograph 25 (June 1979), chap. 3.

92. Simon Dinitz, "Home Care Treatment as a Substitute for Hospitalization," *New Directions for Mental Health Services* 1 (1979), p. 13. The pioneering study in the field was Benjamin Pasamanick, Frank Scarpitti, and Simon Dinitz, *Schizophrenics in the Community: An Experimental Study in the Prevention of Hospitalization* (New York: Appleton-Century-Crofts, 1967). See also Ann E. Davis, Simon Dinitz, and Benjamin Pasamanick, *Schizophrenics in the New Custodial Community* (Columbus, Ohio: Ohio State University Press, 1974).

93. Harry E. Allen, Simon Dinitz, Thomas Foster, Harold Goldman, and Lewis Lindner, "Sociopathy: An Experiment in Internal Environmental Control," *American Behavioral Scientist* 20 (1976), pp. 215–226. For the theory underlying this program, see Harold Goldman, "Sociopathy and Diseases of Arousal," *Quaderni di Criminologia Clinica* (1979).

94. For a technical discussion and appropriate scientific references, see Jean L. Marx, "Learning and Behavior (1): Effects of Pituitary Hormones," *Science* 190, 24 October 1975, pp. 367–370, and Marx, "Learning and Behavior (2): The Hypothalamic Peptides," *Science* 190, 7 November 1975, pp. 544–545. A less technical article, written by a journalist specializing in science, presents the history of the origin and development of the polypeptide revolution for the informed reader: Joan Arehart

Treichel, "Using the Brain's Chemicals to Improve the Mind," *Washington Post*, 20 March 1977, p. C-3.

95. Ibid.
96. For a brief history of the origins and use of behavior modification, see Rennie, *Search for Criminal Man*, pp. 196–201.
97. The two critical decisions are: *Kaimowitz* v. *Michigan Department of Health* (1973) 42 U. S. L. W. 2063 (Mich. Cir. Ct.), and *Mackey* v. *Procunier* (1973) 477 F. 2d (9th Cir.).
98. The most detailed description of these and other such procedures and programs can be found in Ralph K. Schwitzgebel, *Development of Legal Regulation of Coercive Behavior Modification Techniques with Offenders,* Department of Health, Education and Welfare Publication No. (HSM) 73-9015 (Washington, D.C.: U.S. Government Printing Office, 1971).
99. Rennie, *Search for Criminal Man,* p. 199; Schwitzgebel, *op. cit.,* p. 5–12.
100. Schwitzgebel, *op. cit.,* p. 5–12.
101. John Conrad has outlined the correctional dilemmas posed by the bio-medical revolution in a short article. See John P. Conrad, "Right, Wrong and Sheer Indifference," in *In Fear of Each Other* (edited by John P. Conrad and Simon Dinitz), *op. cit.,* pp. 133–141.
102. Schwitzgebel, *Legal Regulation,* pp. 5–12.
103. See, again, the *Kaimowitz* decision in Michigan.
104. Rennie, *Search for Criminal Man,* pp. 196–201.
105. For a review of the general problem of pharmacology as a means of social control see, above all, Nicholas Kittrie, *The Right to Be Different* (Baltimore: Johns Hopkins University Press, 1971). Professor Kittrie has devised a therapeutic bill of rights that should be standard reading for all who are concerned with the ethical problems inherent in the biomedical revolution. The Hastings Institute and especially Dr. Willard Gaylin also have been much concerned and have produced monographic materials on the issues involved. Two psychiatrists, in particular, while divergent in their views to some degree, nonetheless are perturbed by the medicalization of deviance for the purpose of social control: see the work of Thomas Szasz and of Seymour Halleck in this respect.

Glossary

Accreditation process   Standards established to upgrade the police and corrections programs of nearly every state.

Actus reus   Thoughts do not constitute a crime; a crime has not been committed as long as the thoughts about it do not result in action.

Administrative regulations   Laws and rulings made by federal, state, and local agencies to deal with such contemporary problems as wage and hour disputes, pollution, automobile traffic, industrial safety, and the purity of food and drugs.

Aggravated assault   Unlawful attack by one person upon another for the purpose of inflicting severe or aggravated bodily harm; a weapon is usually used in this attempt to inflict great harm or to produce death.

Allocution   The convicted offender's address to the court at the sentence hearing.

Areal decentralization   Crime prevention facilitated through the process of neighborhood groups or block organizations working directly with the police.

Arraignment hearing   The step following a criminal charge in which the defendant or accused is read the charges and advised of his or her rights. The accused may plead guilty, not guilty, no contest, or not guilty for reason of insanity at this step.

Arson   Any willful or malicious burning or attempt to burn, with or without intent to defraud, a dwelling house, public building, motor vehicle or aircraft, or personal property of another.

Assigned counsel defense system   A system whereby an indigent defendant is provided counsel, selected by a judge, at the public's expense.

Autocratic warden   Warden who takes total responsibility over prison life; he is suspicious of the intentions of inmates and uses whatever measures necessary to control their behavior.

Bail hearing   A hearing in which the defendant is assessed a monetary amount to insure his or her return to court.

Behavior modification   A technique in which rewards or punishment are used to alter or change one's behavior.

Bench or unsupervised probation   A type of probation in which probationers are not subject to supervision.

Beyond a reasonable doubt   The standard required to prove guilt and convict a defendant of a crime.

Bill of Rights   No person shall be deprived of life, liberty, or property without due process of law. The intent of the Bill of Rights is to protect the individual against coercive government action, unless it is exercised in conformity with a previously stated legal grant of power.

Biological positivism   The belief that criminals are driven into crime because of biological or constitutional limitations.

Blackstone's Commentaries   Legal commentaries that influenced the criminal procedures adopted in the American colonies.

Born criminals   Cesare Lombroso argued that certain individuals who represented an earlier stage of evolutionary development were more likely to become involved in crime.

Bureaucracy   A system with a clearly outlined organizational hierarchy.

Burglary   The breaking and entering into a structure, usually for the purpose of committing a theft or an assault.

California Community Treatment Project   Under this project, wards in Youth Authority institutions were randomly divided into control and experimental groups; those in the experimental group were immediately released to community supervision, while the controls were released after serving normal sentences.

Capacity limitations   Refers to the limited ability of the justice system to provide adequate protection for society.

Carroll Doctrine   Allows a vehicle search when there is probable cause to believe that contraband is being transported.

Case law   Law based on previous judicial decisions.

Case overload   An excessive number of cases that must be handled by public defenders or others in the system.

Certiorari   This writ needs a vote of four U.S. Supreme Court justices to order a lower court to send up the records of a case.

Challenge for cause   A request by either the prosecution or defense to remove a juror from serving because of a concern about that person's ability to be fair and impartial.

Charging decision   The determination of the police officer, prosecutor, and judge as to the crime for which the person arrested will be formally charged.

Chief of police   The top administrator of a law enforcement agency.

Citation   A written notice ordering a suspect to appear in court of law to answer for a certain offense.

Civilianization   The increased use of civilians to carry out certain police tasks.

Civil law   Law governing the relationships among persons or groups.

Classical school   Proposed that human beings are rational persons who, being free to choose their actions, can be held responsible for their behavior.

Clearance rate   Represents the number of crimes solved expressed as a percentage of the total number of crimes reported to the police.

Closing argument   After the evidence for both the prosecution and the defense has been presented, each side has an opportunity to make one final plea to the jury.

Common law   The basis for common law was custom and tradition; common law was judge-made law, in that the laws were molded, refined, examined, and changed as decision making took place from one period to the next.

Computer theft   The most common technique of this white-collar crime involves the unauthorized modification, replacement, insertion, or deletion of data before or during their input to a computer system.

Concurrent sentence   Prison terms served simultaneously for two or more crimes.

Conflict perspective   The organizing principles of this perspective are these: (1) at every point society is subject to change; (2) society displays at every point dissension and conflict; (3) every element contributes to change; and (4) society is based on the coercion of some of its members by others.

Conjugal visitation   Prisoners can enjoy private visitation with their families.

Consensus perspective   The organizing principles or assumptions of this model are these: (1) society is a relatively persistent and stable structure; (2) society is well integrated; and (3) a functioning social structure is based on agreed-upon values.

Consent   In terms of search and seizure, a person voluntarily allows the police to conduct a search.

Constitutional order   The order codified or laid down in criminal law.

Containment theory   A control theory that addresses the variety of internal and external forces restraining individuals from crime.

Continuance   An order from the court continuing a case, usually for the purpose of gathering more information.

Contract defense system   A system providing counsel to indigent defendants, using an attorney appointed under contract with the court or government jurisdiction.

Control theory   Contends that human beings must be held in check, or somehow controlled, if criminal tendencies are to be repressed.

Corporate crime   Organizational crime occurring in the context of the complex relationships among boards of directors, executives, and managers, on the one hand, and among parent corporations, corporate divisions, and subsidiaries, on the other hand.

Counterfeiting   A crime related to forgery in that it represents an alternative method of producing illegal tender.

County sheriff   An elected official of a county who usually provides criminal law enforcement and essential public services to the county.

Courtroom team   The group consisting of the prosecutor, the defense attorney, and the judge, which has developed a legal culture, or informal rules, to guide decision making.

Courts of general jurisdiction   Trial courts that hear more important matters, such as felony trials, than the courts of limited jurisdiction.

Courts of limited jurisdiction   The jurisdiction of the lower courts usually encompasses petty offenses, serious misdemeanors, lesser felonies, and, in a few jurisdictions, felonies punishable by five years imprisonment or more.

Crime   Derived from the Latin *crimen,* meaning judgment, accusation, and offense. Crime is an intentional act in violation of criminal law (statutory and case law), committed without defense or justification, and sanctioned by the state as a felony or misdemeanor.

Crime control model   Law enforcement is the key element in this model. The police apprehend factually or probably guilty suspects, and the other actors in the system—prosecutors, defense attorneys, judges—play their specialized roles in converting factual or probable guilt into legal guilt according to the rules and constraints of the adversarial format.

Criminal law   The idea behind the criminal law is that a criminal violation against any member of a society represents a criminal violation against the entire society. When such a violation takes place, society has not only the right but also the obligation to take corrective and retaliatory action.

Criminology   The scientific study of crime. The objective of criminology is the development of a body of general and verified principles regarding the process of law, crime, and treatment.

Crisis in confidence   Term currently used as descriptive of the present attitudes toward political and legal institutions of American society.

Cultural conflict   Thorsten Sellin contends that individuals are members of many groups (family, work, political, religious, play), and each group has specific conduct norms.

Cultural deviance theory   That the lower class has its own culture and the motivation to become involved in criminal activities.

Cytogenetic studies (XYY studies)   Research related to the contention that those males with an extra Y chromosome are more likely to become involved in crime.

Deferred sentence   Delays conviction on a guilty plea until the sentenced offender has successfully served his or her probation term.

Demodernization   A gradual erosion of humanitarian values taking place in Western societies.

Determinate sentencing   Its main forms are flat-time sentences, mandatory sentences, and presumptive sentences. In flat-time sentencing, the judge may choose between probation and imprisonment but has limited discretion in setting the length of any sentence to prison. The presumptive sentence is based upon the concept of "just deserts," which has been proposed by David Fogel, by Andrew von Hirsh, and by the Twentieth Century Fund in *Fair and Certain Punishment.* Mandatory sentencing sets a required number of years of incarceration for specific crimes.

Deterrence   A crime control strategy used to prevent crime and protect the social order.

Differential association   According to Edwin H. Sutherland, criminals learn crime from others because crime is a product of social interaction. Sutherland adds that criminal behavior is to be expected of those who have internalized a preponderance of definitions favorable to law violations.

Direct evidence   Evidence that was observed firsthand.

Direct verdict   A judge's ruling during a trial that the prosecution has failed to establish a case of guilt beyond reasonable doubt against the defendant; charges are dismissed.

Discretion   The exercise of judgment in making a decision from various choices or options; in police work, an officer may decide after investigating a crime or observing a crime being committed whether to arrest or release.

Disorder   A threatening lack of predictability in the behavior of others; disorganization, cultural conflict, normlessness or anomie, norm erosion, disconsensus, and entropy.

Double jeopardy   The Fifth Amendment states that a citizen cannot be punished more than once for the same offense.

Drift theory   The process of becoming a delinquent, according to David Matza, begins when a juvenile neutralizes himself or herself from the moral bounds of the law and drifts into delinquency.

Due process rights   Guarantees citizens fair and proper treatment by government officials.

Duress (defense against responsibility)   Is involved when the accused was forced or coerced by another into doing the illegal act.

Durham Rule   Based on the supposition that insanity is a product of many personality factors and is more complex than the ability to know right from wrong.

Eighth Amendment   Prohibits excessive bail and fines and the infliction of cruel and unusual punishment.

Elements of a crime   The act, the surrounding circumstances, and the state of mind of the accused.

Excessive use of force   Use of more force than was necessary either to control a situation or to make an arrest.

Exclusionary rule   Excludes any illegally seized evidence from use in a criminal trial.

Federal police   Agencies established for the purpose of investigating and enforcing the federal laws.

Feudalism A system whereby almost all of the rural land is divided into large estates, owned by absentee lords or nobles, managed by landlords, and farmed by peasants.

Field training A rookie police officer is assigned to a field training officer and receives on-the-job training.

Fifth Amendment Protects against self-incrimination and against double jeopardy.

Fiscal constraints Restriction of revenues.

Forcible rape Legally, the sexual penetration of a women's body without her consent and with either the use or the threat of force.

Formal system The rules, regulations, policies, and procedures of the criminal justice system.

Fourth Amendment Prohibits "unreasonable" searches.

Fragmentation The lack of interdependence and cooperation of the components of the criminal justice system.

Fraternal twins Develop from two eggs that were separately fertilized during the act of conception, hence sharing about half their genes.

Gambling Usually includes the exchange of money in order to make more money.

Good faith exception Determines whether the police acted within the scope of the Constitution or in good faith.

Grand jury A body of persons selected to hear evidence against a person or persons and to determine if sufficient evidence has been presented to bring them to trial.

Hands-off doctrine phase A period during which the U.S. Supreme Court refused to become involved in corrections because of the belief that the prisoner had no rights when sentenced to prison.

Harmless error rule A U.S. Supreme Court ruling that a denial of a constitutional right at times may be of insufficient magnitude to require that the conviction be overturned.

Hearsay evidence Information heard or obtained secondhand.

House of refuge Juvenile institutions in the nineteenth century based upon the belief that they provided a means of control that would provide an orderly, disciplined environment similar to that of the "ideal" Puritan family.

Identical twins Develop from a single fertilized egg that divided into two embryos, hence sharing all their genes.

Immaturity (defense against responsibility) Can be used as a defense for children under the age of seven on the grounds that children under this age are immature and are not responsible for their actions.

Incapacitation Isolating offenders to protect society.

Incident to arrest Police are permitted to search a person or the surrounding area at the time of or immediately after an arrest.

Indeterminate sentencing Permits early release of a prisoner from a correctional institution after the individual has served a portion of his or her sentence.

Industrialization Process during which the worker becomes part of a larger economic organization, and his or her task is only part of a broad operation requiring the combined efforts of other parts; this process pulled a mass of rural workers together into cities.

Inevitable discovery exception Evidence is admissible because it would have inevitably been found.

Informal codes The values of the police or corrections culture, which vary among departments; these unwritten procedures are not covered in the formal system.

Informal probation Supervising an offender without placing him or her under the jurisdiction of the formal justice system.

Initial hearing   A hearing shortly after arrest in which the defendant is informed by a judge or magistrate of the crime he or she has been charged with by the police and is then informed of such constitutional rights as the right to remain silent and to have an attorney appointed.

Intensive supervision   Supervision based on the belief that increased contact and referral result in more positive adjustments to society, such as a higher employment rate and a lower rate of involvement in crime.

Irresistible impulse rule   Excuses the defendant from responsibility of a crime when a mental disease controls his behavior.

Jury instructions   The judge tells the jury the elements of the offense charged or those of any lesser offenses charged; the type of evidence needed to prove each element of the offense or lesser offense; and the evidence needed to prove guilt beyond a reasonable doubt.

Just deserts   The criminal is punished proportionately to the damage inflicted on society.

Knapp Commission   The most famous of the commissions formed to investigate police corruption in the city of New York; it found that more than half of the city's police department had been involved in some form of corruption.

Labeling perspective   That society creates the deviant by labeling those who are apprehended as different from others. The labeling perspective, sometimes called the "interactional theory of deviance" or the "social reaction" perspective, emphasizes the causal power of response, both verbal and nonverbal, to classes of people and classes of acts.

Larceny   Unlawful taking, carrying, or leading away of property that belongs to another, without the use of force or fear.

Law Enforcement Assistance Administration (LEAA)   Created to distribute funds to local governments for improved crime control.

Leviathan   Thomas Hobbes believed that without the lawlike restraints of the sovereign state, social life would collapse into an ongoing war of individuals with conflicting interests.

Local ordinances   Cover such matters as traffic regulations, health regulations, and liquor controls.

Lower courts   Their jurisdiction usually encompasses petty offenses, serious misdemeanors, lesser felonies, and, in some jurisdictions, felonies punishable by five years imprisonment or more.

Management culture   Those persons, usually progressive thinkers, who make up the upper management of the police agency and demand higher levels of professionalism from street officers.

Management style   The style used by managers to make decisions and handle subordinates in an organization.

Mandatory sentence   A required number of years of incarceration for specific crimes.

Marxist perspective   Views the state and the law as tools of the ownership class, reflecting the economic interests of that class.

Medicalization of deviance   The process by which certain categories of deviant or criminal behavior became defined as medical rather than moral problems and how medicine, rather than the family, church, or state, became the primary agent of social control for those so identified.

Medical model (rehabilitation)   Regards the criminal as sick with the disease of criminality.

Mens rea   A guilty mind is present; a person has not committed a crime unless he or she has this state of mind. To show *mens rea,* it must be proven that an individual intentionally and purposefully, knowingly, or negligently behaved in a certain manner or caused a given result.

Metropolitan Police Act   An English act set up to establish regulations for the hiring, training, and supervision of police officers.

Minnesota Community Corrections Act (CCA)   The CCA had four major purposes: (1) reduction of commitments to state prisons; (2) encouragement of local units of government to maintain responsibility for offenders whose crimes are not serious (those who would receive a sentence of less than five years in a state facility); (3) promotion of community corrections planning at the local level; and (4) improved coordination among local components of the criminal justice system.

Minority hiring   Hiring of women and minorities.

MINS   Minors in need of supervision.

M'Naughten Rule   A person cannot be found guilty if at the time of committing the wrongful act he or she was suffering from a disease of the mind so as to not know the nature and quality of his or her act.

Motor vehicle theft   The theft or attempted theft of a motor vehicle.

Murder   The unlawful killing of a human being.

Nationalization   The growth of the state.

Necessity (defense against responsibility)   May be claimed as a defense when the accused has been faced with a choice of evils.

Occasional offenders   Do not normally perceive of themselves as criminals and are likely to become involved in crime only when opportunity or situational inducements exist.

Opening statement   The prosecutor generally outlines the case and states that the government will prove beyond a reasonable doubt that the defendant did the crime with which he or she is charged.

Order   A condition in which every part or unit is in its right place or in a normal or efficient state; the condition brought about by good and firm government and obedience to the laws.

Organized crime   The two basic approaches to dealing with organized crime are the structural view and the process view. The structural approach usually argues that the criminal syndicate is a highly structured network of sustained relationships. The process view argues that group relation networks labeled "mafia" are best understood as an extension of the interaction and exchange processes inherent in social life.

Parens patriae **philosophy**   The belief that the state was established as a surrogate parent whose actions were to rehabilitate the child.

Parole guidelines   A three-step process is typically involved: First, upon reviewing a prisoner's case, the examiner panel gives the case a salient factor score, ranging from zero to 11. Second, the case is then given an offense severity rating on a scale of 1 to 8. Finally, equipped with the salient factor score and the offense severity rating, the examiners refer to another chart, which reveals the amount of time a prisoner should serve, assuming good prison performance.

Participatory management   Based on developing a team approach and on sharing the decision-making responsibilities throughout the organization.

Penitentiary   Also known as prison or reformatory, used to house persons found guilty of a felony.

Pennsylvania penitentiary   A product of the idealism of the Jacksonian period, which saw the young American nation believing it had an unlimited capacity to solve its social problems. Its purpose was to make up for a bad environment by providing offenders with a properly structured, or ordered, environment, which would enable offenders to repent of their wrongdoings and become useful citizens upon their return to the community.

Perks   Offers (coffee, cigarettes, drinks, etc.) from others used to persuade a police officer to accept wrongdoing.

Pickpocketing   The robbery of money from a person without his or her cooperation or knowledge.

Plain view search   An officer can conduct a search of objects that are in plain view.

Plea bargaining   A process that presumes the assumption of guilt, rather than the innocence mandated by the Constitution and the Bill of Rights.

Pluralist perspective   Recognizes the existence of a multiplicity of social groups with different and competing interests and values.

Police academy   Training institution for police recruits.

Police brutality   Unreasonable force used by the police in order to control a situation or to make an arrest.

Police-community reciprocity   Implies that police serve, learn from, and are accountable to the community.

Police culture   The officers' value systems and informal code of conduct.

Police stress   Comes from a number of areas: department pressures for allegiance to the formal rules and regulations, boredom from doing the same unexciting activity, isolation, problems in marital and family relationships.

Politicization of crime   Politicians blamed crime for the social disorder perceived to be apparent in the larger society.

Popular justice   The means by which the politically powerful impose their notions of what constitutes a good community and often take the lead in vigilante movements.

Positivism   The belief that human behavior is caused by specific factors and that it is possible to know what these factors are.

Preemptory challenge   An objection by either prosecution or defense to a prospective juror; no cause need be given.

Preliminary hearing   Usually occurs within seven to ten days after arrest. The charges are read to the accused at the initial appearance, and he or she is reminded of the right to remain silent and to have an attorney appointed by the court if he or she cannot afford to retain one.

Presentence investigation (PSI)   The primary purpose of the PSI is to help the court decide whether or not to grant probation, to determine the condition of probation, to determine the length of the sentence, and to decide upon community-based or institutional placement for the defendant.

Pretrial detention   The detention or holding of a defendant prior to the time of trial.

Pretrial release   Permits a person to be released from jail or pretrial detention centers pending adjudication of the case.

Preventive detention   Statutes passed in many states for stricter bail practices to help decrease crime and prevent pretrial flight of defendants.

Prison abolition   The strategy of doing away with detention or confinement for convicted criminals.

Prison democracy   The principle of equality of rights for convicted criminals.

Private police   People hired by the private sector to maintain policing functions (except for making arrests).

Proactive policing   Being aware of emerging trends a community or nation demonstrates; being flexible and able to change and adapt quickly.

Probation   Permits the convicted offender to remain in the community, under the supervision of a probation officer and certain conditions set by the court.

Procedural criminal law   Accused persons must be given certain rights and assurances that they will be tried according to legally established procedures.

Professionalism   Establishes standards of behavior based on education, a code of ethics, pride, and dignity.

Progressive Era   A period in American history, from the late 1800s to the early 1900s, characterized by ideas of reform.

Prostitution   The provision of sexual stimulation and/or gratification for profit.

Psychological positivism   Focuses on the differences between the personality traits of criminals and of noncriminals.

Psychopathy   The psychopath or sociopath generally is not delusional or irrational and does not exhibit nervousness or psychoneurotic manifestations; he or she is unreliable, lacking in either shame or remorse, willing to commit all kinds of misdeeds for astonishingly small stakes, and characterized by poor judgment.

Psychotherapy   The treatment of a mental disorder which involves communication between a patient and a trained professional.

Public defender defense system   Usually involves a full-time staff of lawyers hired by public funds to provide legal services to indigent defendants.

Public order crimes   Laws against prostitution, gambling, substance abuse, public drunkenness, pornography, and homosexuality are examples of society's attempts to control the willing exchange of socially disapproved of but widely demanded goods or services.

Public safety exception   The U.S. Supreme Court held that the "overwhelming" need for the safety of the public in some situations justifies not giving Miranda warnings.

Quantitative genetics   Patterns of correlations among blood relatives and among people who share common environments even though they may not be blood relatives.

Real evidence   Refers to concrete objects introduced during a trial.

Reality theory   The theory that an individual's mental activity can be adjusted to meet the demands of his environment.

Rebuttal   The prosecution may present additional witnesses to refute evidence presented by the defense.

Reformatory model   Confinement of youthful offenders based on indeterminate sentencing and parole, classification of prisoners, educational and vocational training, and privileges for positive behavior.

Rehabilitation   To change an offender's character, attitudes, or behavior patterns so as to diminish his or her criminal propensities.

Reintegrative philosophy   That offenders' problems must be solved in the community where they began; society has a responsibility for dealing with its own problems, and it can partly fulfill this responsibility by helping law violators reintegrate themselves into community living.

Release on Recognizance (ROR)   The release without bail of those defendants who appear to have stable ties in the community and are a good risk to appear for trial.

Reliability   Related to the consistency found in answers given on a questionnaire or in an interview. The crucial issue of reliability is whether repeated administration of a questionnaire will elicit the same answers from the same individuals when they are questioned more than once.

Reparation   Requires the offender to make amends for a wrong or an injury; the defendant must pay compensation to the victim or society for the harm resulting from the criminal offense.

Residential programs   Probation centers, work-release centers, restitution centers, prerelease centers, and halfway houses are the main residential programs for adult offenders.

Retribution   The retributive philosophy wants to punish an individual for what he or she has done in the past.

Revocation of probation   A judicial procedure that takes place when a probation officer recommends to the court that probation should be revoked because a probationer has committed a new crime or violated the conditions of probation.

Right to jury trial   If it appears the suspect will be sentenced to jail for more than a short period (six months), the possibility of a jury trial must be offered.

Robbery   The taking of property or something of value from a person through force or the fear of force. The use of a deadly weapon (armed robbery) makes the offense more serious.

Search warrant   A document issued by a judicial officer that gives police officers the legal means to conduct a search.

Selective incapacitation   Researchers have discovered that individual offending rates are highly skewed, with a small number of offenders responsible for a large portion of crimes or arrests. Therefore, the potential exists to achieve major crime reduction benefits from incarceration by selective imprisonment of high-rate offenders.

Self-defense (defense against responsibility)   Has to do with the legal right to ward off an attack from another, if a person thinks that he or she is in immediate danger of being harmed.

Self-growth program   Programs developed to promote personal gain and improvement.

Self-report studies   Studies that ask juveniles or adults to tell about the crimes they have committed at an earlier period of time.

Sentencing hearing   For those defendants who have either pleaded guilty or been found guilty during a trial, the judge must decide upon the appropriate sentence during a sentencing hearing.

Serial killers   Murderers of more than one person who kill their victims on different occasions.

Shock probation   The offender, his or her attorney, or the sentencing judge can submit a motion to suspend the remainder of the sentence after a felon has served a period of time in prison.

Simultaneous killers   Mass murderers who kill their victims at the same time or in one episode.

Sixth Amendment   Provides the right to counsel, to a speedy, and public trial, and to an impartial jury.

Social construction of the law   Crime is ultimately defined in terms of the range of behavior socially accepted in a given community at a given time.

Social contract   Cesare Beccaria and Jeremy Bentham viewed humans as rational creatures who are willing to surrender enough liberty to the state so that society can establish rules and sanctions for the preservation of the social order.

Social control theory   Theory that criminal behavior is controlled by the social bond or processes of socialization. Travis Hirschi states that "delinquent acts result when an individual's bond to society is weak or broken."

Social disorganization   Emphasizes the importance of social rules in maintaining social organization; when such means of social change as immigration, rural-urban migration, and high mobility accompany the development of an urbanized and industrial society, social conditions begin to be characterized by anonymity, impersonality, and different laws and traditions.

Social injustice   The thrust of the perspective is that the criminal justice system is biased to weed out the middle and ruling classes so that the vast majority of those found in the system come from the lower classes.

Sociobiology   The study of the relationship between biological and environmental factors.

Sociological positivism   The theory that explains how interactions between individuals and their environments influence them to become involved in criminal behavior.

Somatotyping   Body build correlates with behavioral tendencies, temperament, susceptibility to disease, and life expectancy. A person's "somatotype" is a characterization of his or her physique in terms of three components, endomorphy (roundness), mesomorphy (heavy bone and muscular), and ectomorphy (linearity).

State appellate courts   The main task of these approximately 207 state-administered courts is to hear appeals from lower state courts.

State police   Agencies in each state for the purpose of patrol and investigation for that state.

Station house citation   Allows for release after a suspect has been arrested and brought to the police station.

Statutory law   Laws passed by state legislators.

Stop and frisk   A "pat down" check of the body for weapon detection.

Strain theory   Contends that status frustration takes place when an individual cannot obtain the cultural goals or the means of achieving these goals.

Street officer culture   Learned by a police officer from the informal code that fills the void the formal system does not cover.

Subculture of violence   Contends there is a subculture of violence among young males in the lower classes that legitimizes the use of violence in various social situations.

Substantive capacity test   A test for insanity which does not require that a defendant be totally unable to distinguish right from wrong.

Substantive criminal law   That no one can be punished for an offense unless that offense is prohibited by the law.

Symbolic interactionism   Individuals are constantly being changed as they take on the expectations and points of view of the people with whom they interact in small groups.

Systems approach   Focuses on the interrelationships among components of the criminal justice system.

Terrorism   Involves the intentional use of violence or threat of violence by the precipitator(s) against an instrumental target in order to communicate to a primary target a threat of future violence if demands are not answered.

Testimonial evidence   Testimony of witness under oath to the facts in the case.

Third industrial revolution   This revolution is built on brain power rather than tools and hard human labor; achievement is the basic work ethic of the new industrial revolution.

Transactional analysis (TA)   A form of psychotherapy that attempts to bring into balance the three states of the ego—parent, adult, child.

Uniform Crime Reports   Annual reports of the FBI covering arrests and crimes in the United States. The FBI gathers data from over 15,000 law enforcement agencies throughout the nation, covering about 98 percent of the population.

Urbanization   Migration to the cities, especially by young adults, for the purpose of employment.

U.S. Courts of Appeals   The 11 federal courts of appeals hear all appeals from federal district courts and the decisions of specified administrative and regulatory agencies.

U.S. District Courts   Criminal matters involving the violation of a federal law are brought to these courts.

U.S. Supreme Court   The final court of appeals is the U.S. Supreme Court. Cases reach this final court of appeals from a variety of routes: from federal courts of appeals, from the special three-judge federal courts, from petition from paupers (generally state and federal prisoners), and from a small number of cases involving disputes between states.

Utilitarian philosophy   Looks to the future rather than the past; when applied to crime, this position attempts to accomplish some socially desirable outcome in the future from criminal sanctions, such as protection of society or criminal rehabilitation.

Validity   In statistics, concerned with the question, How can researchers be certain that juveniles or adults are telling the truth when they fill out questionnaires?

Victimization surveys   National surveys that ask people to tell about the crimes committed against them.

Vigilante justice   Americans will take justice in their own hands when their dissatisfaction with the institutions of public order reaches a certain level.

Voir dire   The process of placing those selected for jury panel under oath and examining their fitness and qualifications to serve.

War on crime   The political strategy in the 1970s and 1980s of taking a hard-line approach to control crime.

White-collar crime   Crime committed by a person of respectability and high social status in the course of his or her occupation.

Wisconsin system (NIC Model Probation Client Classification and Case Management System)   Under the Wisconsin system, a risk/needs assessment instrument is completed on each probationer at regular intervals. The scores derived from the assessment are used to classify probationers by required level of supervision—intensive, medium, or minimum.

Working personality   Certain behaviors and attitudes of the police; key elements are danger, authority, and efficiency.

Name Index

Abadinsky, Howard, 312, 316n, 511n
Abbott, Jack Henry, 198, 220n
Abraham, Henry J., 444n
Abrahams, Alan, 280n, 316n
Acton, Lord, 113
Adams, William P., 510n
Adler, Freda, 72, 212, 314n
Adler, Patricia A., 312, 345, 346n
Afanasyer, V., 248
Ageton, Suzanne S., 210, 222n, 252n
Agnew, Spiro, 16, 246, 421
Aichhorn, August, 155n
Akers, Ronald, 199, 220n
Albanese, Jay S., 312, 315n
Albini, J., 315n
Alex, Nicholas, 401, 402, 408n
Alexander, Yonah, 282n
Alinsky, Saul, 166, 190n
Allen, Francis A., 10, 27n, 444n
Allen, Harry E., 510n, 512n, 544n
Alpert, Geoffrey P., 474, 474n
Amir, Menachem, 260, 279n
Anderson, Andy B., 120n
Arehart, Joan, 544n
Aristotle, 247
Aron, Nan, 477n
Augustus, John, 356
Austin, James, 234, 248, 250n, 251n,
    445n, 512n

Bachman, Jerald, 221n
Bailey, William, 117, 123n
Balkan, S., 233, 250n
Ball, Richard Allen, 201, 220n, 492,
    509, 511n
Banfield, Edward C., 8, 26n, 101,
    102, 104, 105, 119, 121n, 122n
Barlow, Hugh D., 346n
Barnard, Thomas, 191n
Barnes, Harry Elmer, 539n

Bartilotti, R., 544n
Bartollas, Clemens L., 122n, 475n,
    513n
Bartollas, Linda Dippold, 330
Bayley, David H., 387, 389, 390, 404,
    406, 407n, 409n
Bazelon, David, 140
Beach, F. A., 347n
Beccaria, Cesare, 9, 10, 26n, 30, 31,
    37, 54n, 55n, 95, 96–98, 100, 120n,
    121n
Beck, Richard, 390
Becker, Craig, 376n
Becker, Howard S., 208, 209, 219,
    222n, 346n
Bedau, Hugo Adam, 345, 345n
Beers, Clifford, 520
Beirne, Piers, 248
Bendix, R., 249n
Bennett, Lawrence A., 501, 511n,
    512n
Bentham, Jeremy, 9, 30, 37, 54n,
    98–100, 116, 121n, 340, 347n
Bequai, August, 294, 314n
Berger, R. J., 250n
Berk, Richard A., 120n, 192n, 251n,
    389, 406, 407n
Bernard, Thomas J., 25n, 189n,
    190n, 192n, 248, 250n, 540n–542n
Besharov, Douglas J., 265, 280n
Bias, Len, 318
Biles, David, 541n
Bittner, Egon, 407n
Black, Algernon, 387, 407n
Black, Donald, 52, 56n
Blackman, John, 409n
Blackmun, Harry, 423
Blau, J. R., 234, 251n
Blau, P. M., 234, 251n
Block, Marilyn R., 269, 281n

Blumberg, Abraham S., 43, 55n, 406,
    407n, 443, 444n–446n
Blumstein, Alfred, 187, 192n
Bohlander, Edward, Jr., 510n
Bonanno, Joseph, 284–285, 308, 312,
    316n
Boneseana, Cesare, 95
Bonger, William, 226, 249n
Bonn, Robert L., 314n
Boorkman, David, 510n
Bowker, Lee, 473, 474n, 476n
Box, Steven, 220n
Boyer, Andrew, 153n
Bradley, F. H., 109, 122n
Braithwaite, John, 184, 189, 192n,
    234, 250n
Brenner, Harvey M., 234, 250n
Brockway, Zebulon, 356
Brown, Frank, 88n
Brown, Lee, 384
Brown, M. H., 543n
Brown, Michael K., 406, 407n,
    409n
Brown, Richard Maxwell, 65, 90n,
    376n
Browning, Frank, 278, 315n
Bundy, Ted, 259
Burdman, Milton, 481
Burger, Warren E., 392, 423, 472
Burgess, Earnest W., 162, 163, 164,
    189n, 190n, 519
Burgess, Robert L., 199, 219, 220n
Burt, Cyril, 526
Burton, Sir Thomas, 99

Cadoret, R. J., 154n
Cain, C. A., 154n
Callahan, Edward, 544n
Calvin, A. D., 234, 250n
Calvin, John, 6, 7, 26n

Cameron, Mary Owens, 290, 312, 313*n*
Camp, Camille Graham, 473, 476*n*
Camp, George M., 473, 476*n*
Canter, Rachelle J., 222*n*, 252*n*
Capone, Al, 58, 62
Carlson, K., 476*n*
Carroll, George, 395
Carroll, Leo, 234, 250*n*, 251*n*, 473, 474*n*
Carter, Jimmy, 16
Carter, Robert M., 509, 510*n*, 512*n*
Carter, Timothy, 184, 192*n*
Castellano, Thomas C., 183, 192*n*
Casper, Jonathan D., 33, 44, 54*n*, 55*n*, 444*n*
Castro, Jorge A. Montero, 541*n*
Cavender, Gray, 312
Cernkovich, Steven, 212, 213
Chafetz, Henry, 347*n*
Chaiken, Jan, 107, 117, 123*n*, 316*n*
Chaiken, Marcia, 107, 117, 123*n*, 316*n*
Chambliss, William J., 45, 47, 49, 55*n*, 56*n*, 219*n*, 227, 240, 251*n*, 313*n*
Chandler, Paul M., 510*n*
Chapman, J., 235, 251*n*
Chesney-Lind, Media, 213, 251*n*
Chimel, Ted Steven, 395
Chiricos, Theodore, 117, 123*n*
Christiansen, Karl, 132, 153*n*, 154*n*, 526
Clark, Malcolm, 54*n*
Clark, Ramsey, 375*n*
Clark, Richard, 272
Clarke, Alfred C., 540*n*, 542*n*
Clear, Todd R., 372, 377*n*, 509, 511*n*
Cleckley, Hervey, 142, 143, 156*n*
Clelland, Donald, 184, 192*n*
Clemmer, Donald, 467, 474, 475*n*, 477*n*
Clinard, Marshall B., 21, 27*n*, 179, 191*n*, 192*n*, 299, 300, 303, 311, 312, 315*n*, 316*n*, 540*n*
Cloninger, C. R., 154*n*
Cloward, Richard A., 168, 170, 172, 175, 176, 178, 189, 190*n*, 191*n*, 212, 475*n*, 522
Coates, Robert M., 513*n*
Cohen, Albert K., 168, 170, 172–176, 189, 191*n*, 219, 220*n*
Cohen, B., 280*n*
Cohen, Jacqueline, 120*n*, 187, 191*n*, 192*n*, 220*n*, 522
Cole, George F., 372, 377*n*
Cole, Jonathan O., 544*n*
Colvin, Mark, 222*n*, 236, 237, 248, 250*n*, 251*n*, 252*n*, 476*n*
Conger, J. J., 139, 156*n*

Conklin, John E., 261–262, 279*n*, 280*n*
Conley, John A., 375, 376*n*
Connor, Walter, 541*n*
Conrad, John P., 474*n*–478*n*, 481, 509, 510*n*, 511*n*, 540*n*, 542*n*, 545*n*
Conrad, Peter, 148, 149, 153*n*, 157*n*, 280*n*, 341, 345, 348*n*, 459, 540*n*–542*n*
Cook, Philip J., 114, 122*n*
Cooley, Charles H., 220*n*
Cortes, Juan B., 153*n*
Coser, Lewis A., 225, 248, 249*n*
Course, Keith, 25*n*
Cramer, James A., 429, 445*n*
Crepin, Ann E., 462, 476*n*
Cressey, Donald, 44, 55*n*, 145, 157*n*, 296, 314*n*, 376*n*, 430, 444*n*, 445*n*, 456, 475*n*, 540*n*
Crites, Laura, 72, 73
Cromwell, Paul F., Jr., 376*n*
Cronin, Tania Z., 443*n*
Cronin, Thomas E., 443*n*
Crouch, Ben M., 462, 474*n*, 476*n*
Cullen, B., 212
Cullen, Francis T., 114, 123*n*, 212, 302, 312, 314*n*, 375*n*, 446*n*, 509
Currie, Elliott, 6, 25*n*, 26*n*, 115, 123*n*, 184, 187, 189, 192*n*, 235, 241, 250*n*, 251*n*, 278, 278*n*, 282*n*
Curry, William, 542*n*
Curtis, Tom, 408*n*
Czajkoski, Eugene H., 511*n*

Dahrendorf, Ralf, 225, 226, 228, 248, 249*n*
Daley, Richard Major, 233
Datesman, Susan, 212
Davis, Ann E., 544*n*
Davis, K., 407*n*
Davis, William S., 25*n*
De Brenes, E. Acosta, 221*n*
Decker, John, 542*n*
DeFleur, Melvin, 199, 220*n*
Deleuze, Gilles, 246
Dershowitz, Alan M., 413
Deutsch, Morton, 190*n*, 520, 541*n*
De Wied, David, 534
Dietz, Mary Lorenz, 256, 278, 279*n*
Dightman, Cameron R., 512*n*
Dill, Forest, 509*n*
Dinitz, Simon, 145, 157*n*, 203, 204, 210, 221*n*, 222*n*, 280*n*, 474*n*, 475*n*, 477*n*, 478*n*, 539*n*, 540*n*–542*n*, 544*n*, 545*n*
Dix, Dorothea, 520
Doerner, William G., 155*n*
Durkheim, Emile, 5, 25*n*, 26*n*, 170, 190*n*, 204, 517, 519
Dynes, Russell R., 540*n*, 542*n*

Eastland, Terry, 423
Edelhertz, Herbert, 293, 294, 312, 314*n*
Egger, Steven A., 279*n*
Ehrlichman, John, 11
Einstadter, Werner J., 357, 375, 509, 510*n*, 511*n*, 512*n*, 513*n*
Eisenstein, James, 443, 444*n*, 446*n*
Eitzen, D. Stanley, 250*n*, 251*n*, 313*n*
Eleftherion, B. E., 543*n*
Elliott, Delbert S., 178, 183, 192*n*, 207, 210, 222*n*, 252*n*
Empey, Lamar T., 251*n*
Engels, Friedrich, 225, 248, 249*n*
Epps, P., 13
Erasmus, 523
Ericson, Richard V., 380, 406, 406*n*, 409*n*
Erikson, Kai T., 6, 26*n*, 153*n*, 541*n*
Erlander, Howard, 190*n*
Ermann, M. David, 315*n*
Ervin, C. W., 544*n*
Ervin, Frank R., 530, 542*n*, 543*n*
Erwin, Billie S., 509, 510*n*, 511*n*
Estrich, Mark H., 443
Eysenck, Hans, 137, 153*n*, 155

Faine, John R., 510*n*
Fairley, William, 542*n*
Farberow, Norman L., 347*n*
Farrington, D. P., 135, 155*n*, 192*n*, 270, 281*n*, 476*n*
Faupel, Charles, 279*n*
Faust, Cleon, 478*n*
Feeley, Malcolm M., 417, 430, 438, 443, 443*n*, 444*n*, 446*n*
Ferracuti, Franco, 160, 168–170, 204, 189, 190*n*, 221*n*, 522, 544*n*
Ferri, Enrico, 23
Figlio, Robert M., 281*n*
Finestone, Harold, 190*n*, 220*n*, 222*n*
Finger, Seymour Maxwell, 282*n*
Finkelhor, David, 280*n*
Finsterbush, Kurt, 282*n*
Flanagan, Timothy J., 510*n*
Fleming, John, 180
Fogel, David, 109–112, 119, 122*n*, 373, 375*n*–377*n*, 435, 446*n*, 477*n*, 478*n*, 489, 510*n*, 513*n*
Fogelson, Robert M., 282*n*, 354, 376*n*
Ford, C. S., 347*n*
Ford, Daniel, 511*n*, 512*n*
Ford, Gerald, 86, 254
Forer, Lois G., 37, 55*n*
Forster, Brenda, 192*n*
Forte, David, 423
Fortune, E. P., 263, 280*n*
Foster, Jack, 210, 222*n*
Foster, Jodi, 139
Foster, Thomas, 544*n*

Foucault, Michel, 357, 375
Fowler, Floyd J., Jr., 347*n*
Fox, James Alan, 82, 278, 279*n*, 467
Frankel, Marvin E., 495, 512*n*
Frankfurter, Felix, 412
Franklin, Alice, 297, 314*n*
Franklin, Benjamin, 352
Freed, Daniel, 445*n*
Freud, Sigmund, 10, 26*n*, 138, 153*n*,
   155*n*, 205, 517
Friedenburg, Edgar Z., 157*n*
Friedlander, Kate, 139, 155*n*
Friedman, Lawrence M., 375
Friedrichs, David O., 25*n*, 249*n*, 276,
   278, 278*n*, 282*n*
Funke, Gail S., 478*n*
Fyfe, James J., 399, 406, 408*n*

Gabor, Thomas, 526, 542*n*
Gacy, John Wayne, 259
Gallagher, Kenneth W., 511*n*
Garland, Bonnie, 150
Garofalo, Raffaele, 23
Gatti, Florence M., 153*n*
Gatz, N., 435, 446*n*
Gayland, William, 150, 157*n*
Gaylin, Willard, 545*n*
Geis, Gilbert, 303, 315*n*
Gelles, Richard J., 268, 280*n*, 281*n*
George, Henry, 8
Gerassi, John, 88*n*, 278, 315*n*
Gerber, C. J., 544*n*
Gessa, G. L., 544*n*
Gettinger, Stephen, 476*n*, 509, 510*n*,
   511*n*
Gianturco, D. T., 544*n*
Gibbons, Donald C., 153*n*, 313*n*,
   347*n*, 348*n*
Gibbs, Jack, 211, 222*n*
Gilbert, James N., 259, 279*n*
Gilbert, Karen E., 375*n*, 446*n*
Gillespie, Robert, 184, 192*n*
Gilmore, Gary, 87
Giordano, Jeffrey A., 281*n*
Giordano, Nan Hervig, 281*n*
Giordano, Peggy, 212, 213
Glaser, Daniel, 199, 219, 220*n*, 509,
   510*n*, 512*n*, 520, 540*n*, 542*n*,
   544*n*
Gleick, James, 4, 25*n*
Glueck, Eleanor, 131, 139,
   153*n*–155*n*
Glueck, S., 139, 153*n*–155*n*
Glusman, Murray, 543*n*
Goddard, H. H., 134, 155*n*
Godwin, John, 259, 279*n*
Godwin, William, 99, 100
Goetz, Bernhard, 65, 66, 102
Golden, K. M., 212
Goldman, Harold, 150, 157*n*, 531,
   542–544*n*

Goldstein, Herman, 381, 397, 406,
   407*n*, 408*n*, 543*n*
Goldwater, Barry, 17, 86, 525
Gompers, Samuel, 520
Goodstein, Lynne, 451, 458, 475*n*
Gordon, C. Wayne, 337, 347*n*
Gordon, Robert, 135, 155*n*
Goring, Charles, 128, 129, 154*n*
Gottfredson, Don M., 446*n*
Gottfredson, Michael, 192*n*, 252*n*
Grant, Douglass, 481
Greeley, Horace, 12
Greenberg, David F., 175, 191*n*, 234,
   235, 241, 250*n*, 251*n*, 376*n*, 384
Greenwood, Peter, 107, 263, 280*n*,
   316*n*
Griffin, Brenda S., 199, 220*n*
Griffin, Charles T., 199, 220*n*
Griffiths, Keith, 512*n*
Grosser, George H., 475*n*
Groth, A. Nicholas, 260, 279*n*
Grupp, Stanley, 109, 122*n*
Guattari, Felix, 246
Gunn, John, 476*n*
Gurr, Ted Robert, 3, 13, 15, 16, 25*n*
Gusfield, Joseph, 46, 55*n*, 541*n*

Haas, Kenneth C., 474, 474*n*
Hageman, Mary Jeanette C., 386,
   407*n*
Hagan, John, 170, 190*n*–192*n*, 294,
   314*n*
Haldeman, H. R., 115
Hall, Jerome, 38, 45, 54*n*, 55*n*, 296,
   314*n*, 443*n*
Halleck, Seymour, 545*n*
Haller, Mark, 347*n*
Hammond, W., 270, 281*n*
Hamparian, Donna Martin, 271, 281*n*
Handy W. J., 264, 280*n*
Hannel, Lawrence, 527
Hans, Valerie P., 157*n*
Harding, Richard, 276, 282*n*
Hare, R. D., 281*n*
Harlow, Nora, 509, 510*n*
Hart, H. L. A., 340, 345, 347*n*
Hassler, Alfred, 448, 474*n*
Hathaway, Starke, 141, 142, 156*n*
Hawkins, Gordon, 59, 89*n*, 315*n*,
   323, 329, 345, 346*n*–348*n*, 466,
   469, 474, 477*n*, 503, 513*n*
Healy, William, 139, 155*n*
Hearst, Patricia, 273
Hegel, Georg F., 225
Henry, Jack, 220*n*
Hepburn, John R., 250*n*, 310, 315*n*,
   316*n*, 451, 462, 475*n*, 476*n*
Heraclitus of Ephesus, 247
Herodotus, 247
Herrin, Richard, 150
Herrnstein, Richard, 94, 113, 120*n*,

   136, 143, 146–148, 153*n*, 154*n*,
   157*n*, 526
Hess, H., 315*n*
Heumann, Milton, 445*n*
Hickley, J., 156*n*
Hinckley, John, Jr., 139, 150
Hindelang, Michael, 136, 153*n*, 155*n*,
   192*n*, 207, 222*n*
Hippchen, Leonard, 153*n*
Hirschi, Travis, 136, 153*n*, 155*n*, 175,
   183, 191*n*, 192*n*, 201, 202,
   204–206, 212, 219, 221*n*, 252*n*,
   509, 511*n*
Hitler, Adolf, 526
Hobbes, Thomas, 7, 8, 25*n*, 26*n*, 112,
   122*n*, 205
Hobson, Barbara Meil, 345, 346*n*
Hochstedler, Ellen, 400, 408*n*
Hoffet, H., 544*n*
Hollingshead, August, 521, 541*n*
Holmes, Oliver Wendell, 528
Honderich, Ted, 282*n*
Honig, Paul, 316*n*
Hooker, Evelyn, 331, 347*n*
Hooton, E. A., 128, 130, 154*n*
Horne, Peter, 408*n*
Horowitz, Irving Louis, 248*n*
Howard, John, 99
Hubay, Charles, 316*n*
Huberty, James Oliver, 258
Hudson, Joe, 375*n*, 377*n*, 478*n*
Huff, C. L. Ronald, 73, 90*n*, 248,
   249*n*
Hugon, Daniel, 527
Huizinga, David, 183, 192*n*
Humphries, D., 376*n*
Hunt, Jennifer, 408*n*
Hunt, Morton, 331
Hunter, Floyd, 521, 541*n*
Hutchins, Robert M., 244, 251*n*

Iadicola, Peter, 513*n*
Ianni, Francis A. J., 304, 312, 315*n*
Ignatieff, Michael, 474, 477*n*
Inciardi, James A., 248, 249*n*, 279*n*,
   292, 313*n*, 314*n*
Irwin, John, 426, 445*n*, 454, 456, 474,
   475*n*, 502
Ishino, Iwao, 540*n*

Jackson, Bruce, 222*n*
Jackson, Pamela I., 234, 251*n*
Jacob, Herbert, 443, 444*n*, 446*n*
Jacobs, James B., 250*n*, 449, 451,
   458, 461–463, 467, 474, 474*n*–478*n*
Jacobs, Jane, 542*n*
Jacobs, P. A., 133, 134
Jacoby, Joan E., 116, 123*n*
James, J., 280*n*
James, William, 144
Jankovic, I., 234, 250*n*

Jeffrey, C. Ray, 132, 153*n*, 220*n*, 525, 541*n*, 542*n*
Jenkins, Brian M., 273, 278, 282*n*
Jenkins, Philip, 120*n*, 153*n*
Jenkins, Richard, 157*n*
Jennifer, James, 155*n*
Jensen, Gary F., 203, 210, 221*n*, 526
Johnson, Kenneth A., 318, 345, 346*n*
Johnson, Lyndon B., 481, 525
Johnson, Richard E., 207, 219, 222*n*, 252*n*
Julian, Joseph, 346*n*
Jurik, N., 251*n*
Justice, Blair, 278, 280*n*
Justice, Rita, 278, 280*n*

Kahl, Joseph A., 541*n*
Kalinich, David B., 458, 474, 474*n*, 475*n*
Kant, Immanuel, 109, 122*n*
Kanter, Rosabeth Moss, 222*n*
Kaplan, H. B., 204, 221*n*, 446*n*
Karacki, Larry, 291, 313*n*
Karpman, Benjamin, 143, 144, 156*n*
Kauffman, K., 156*n*
Kaufman, Gerald, 477*n*
Kaufman, Irving R., 343
Kaysman, Benjamin, 376*n*
Kelling, George L., 337, 339, 347*n*, 409*n*
Kennedy, Anthony, 423
Kennedy, John F., 254
Kennedy, Robert, 254
Kesner, Idalene F., 315*n*
Kidder, Robert L., 156*n*
Killinger, George C., 376*n*
King, Harry, 219*n*, 284, 313*n*
King, L. J., 156*n*
King, Martin Luther, Jr., 254
Kirchheimer, Otto, 467, 474, 477*n*, 540*n*
Kittrie, Nicholas N., 156*n*, 157*n*, 445*n*, 542*n*, 545*n*
Kleck, Gary, 446*n*
Kline, Nathan S., 543*n*
Kloss, Robert Marsh, 249*n*
Kobrin, Solomon, 190*n*
Kohlberg, Lawrence, 144, 145, 156*n*
Kornhauser, Ruth R., 178, 189, 191*n*
Kosberg, Jordan, 281*n*
Knobloch, Hilda, 542*n*
Krajick, Kevin, 512*n*, 513*n*
Krasnegor, Norman A., 544*n*
Kretscher, Ernst, 130
Krisberg, Barry, 227, 234, 248, 250*n*, 251*n*, 445*n*
Krohn, Marvin D., 206, 221*n*
Ku, Richard, 512*n*

Lalli, Sergio, 316*n*
Lamont, Bruce Y., 315*n*

Lane, R., 375
Lange, Johannes, 132, 526
Lardner, George, Jr., 408*n*
Laschet, U., 544*n*
Latessa, Edward J., 510*n*
Lau, Elizabeth, 281*n*
Laub, John H., 189, 189*n*, 190*n*
Lavin, Marvin, 280*n*
Lee, Robert W., 444*n*
Leinen, Stephen, 402, 406, 408*n*
Lemert, Edwin M., 208, 209, 219, 222*n*, 509*n*
Lenihan, K., 251*n*
Lentini, Joseph B., 331, 333, 345, 347*n*
Levin, Jack, 82, 278, 279*n*, 446*n*
Levin, Martin A., 443
Lewis, Dorothy O., 265, 266, 280*n*, 520
Liberman, Robert P., 544*n*
Liebow, Elliot, 522
Liechenstein, Michael, 542*n*
Lilly, J. Robert, 492, 509, 511*n*
Lincoln, Abraham, 61, 352
Lindensmith, Alfred, 219, 220*n*, 541*n*
Lindner, Lewis, 544*n*
Lipset, S. M., 249*n*
Lipton, Douglas, 512*n*
Littrell, W. Boyd, 424, 443, 445*n*
Lively, E. D., 204, 221*n*
Lombardo, L., 476*n*
Lombroso, Cesare, 10, 23, 26*n*, 128, 131, 154*n*
Lorenz, Konrad, 526
Lucas, Henry Lee, 259
Luckenbill, David F., 279*n*
Lundman, Richard J., 315*n*
Lunt, Paul S., 541*n*
Lupsha, Peter, A., 304, 312, 315*n*

Maakestad, William J., 312
Mabbott, J. D., 109, 122*n*
MacKintosh, Sir James, 99
MacNamara, Donal E. J., 10, 27*n*
Madison, James, 40
Maguire, Mike, 288, 313*n*
Mangione, Thomas W., 347*n*
Mannheim, Hermann, 540*n*
Marin, Peter, 339
Mark, Vernon H., 530, 542*n*, 543*n*
Marmor, Judd, 347*n*
Marquart, James W., 449, 474
Marti-Ibanez, F., 543*n*
Martin, Susan E., 389, 400, 406, 407*n*, 408*n*
Martinson, Robert, 358, 376*n*, 512*n*, 541*n*
Marx, Jean L., 544*n*
Marx, Karl, 225, 239, 241, 248, 249*n*–251*n*, 534

Massey, James L., 206, 221*n*
Mather, Lynn, 431, 446*n*
Matlin, Matthew, 476*n*
Matza, David, 153*n*, 154*n*, 175, 191*n*, 200, 201, 215, 219, 220*n*–222*n*
McAnany, P., 489, 510*n*
McCaghy, Charles, 297, 314*n*
McCahill, Thomas W., 279*n*
McCleery, Richard, 475*n*, 500, 512*n*
McDonald, William F., 445*n*
McGarrell, Edmund F., 510*n*
McGarry, Louis, 542*n*, 544*n*
McGee, Richard, 481
McGillis, Daniel, 443
McKay, Henry D., 160–166, 189, 189*n*, 190*n*, 208, 212, 247, 507, 540*n*
McKenna, George, 282*n*
McKenzie, Roderick D., 190*n*
McKinely, J. C., 156*n*
McNall, Scott G., 246, 248, 252*n*
Mead, George, 220*n*, 246
Mednick, Sarnoff A., 132, 133, 135, 153–155*n*, 526
Megargee, E. I., 156*n*
Meier, Robert E., 116, 123*n*, 251*n*, 540*n*
Meiselman, K. C., 280*n*
Mendelsohn, G. A., 156*n*
Merry, Sally Engle, 114, 123*n*
Merton, Robert K., 170–173, 175, 176, 189, 190*n*, 191*n*, 208
Messinger, Sheldon L., 475*n*
Meyerding, J., 280*n*
Michalowski, Raymond J., 46, 54*n*, 56*n*, 227, 231, 248, 248*n*, 250*n*, 477*n*
Mieczkowski, Tom, 307, 315*n*
Mielke, Kurt L., 281*n*, 282*n*
Milakovich, Michael E., 443*n*
Mill, John Stuart, 340, 345, 347*n*
Miller, Eleanor M., 327, 345, 346*n*
Miller, J. L., 120*n*
Miller, Stuart J., 222*n*, 280*n*
Miller, Walter B., 160, 166–168, 189, 190*n*, 272, 281*n*, 522
Miller, W. C., 139, 156*n*
Mills, C. Wright, 517, 521, 541*n*
Mitchell, John, 115, 520
M'Naughten, Daniel, 140
Moitra, Soumyo, 192*n*
Monachesis, Elio, 97, 121*n*, 141, 142
Money, J., 544*n*
Moniz, E., 528, 543*n*
Moore, Mark H., 89*n*, 278, 278*n*, 282*n*, 443, 446*n*
Moore, Richard, 512*n*
Morris, Desmond, 526
Morris, Norval, 59, 89*n*, 281*n*, 323, 329, 345, 346*n*–348*n*, 373, 376*n*, 377*n*, 407*n*, 477*n*, 540*n*

Morrison, S. D., 544n
Moyer, Kenneth E., 542n, 543n
Mullen, Joan, 376n
Murchison, Carl, 134, 135, 155n
Murphy, G., 156n
Murphy, Patrick V., 408n
Myers, Barbara A., 267

Nader, Ralph, 294
Nagin, Daniel, 117, 120n, 123n
Narabayshi, H., 543n
Nardulli, Peter, 54n
Neithercutt, M. G., 510n
Nelson, E. K., 509, 510n
Ness, Eliot, 62
Nettler, Gwynn, 170, 178,
  190n–192n, 220n–222n, 296, 314n
Neubauer, David W., 424, 443,
  443n–445n
Newman, David, 445n
Newman, Graeme, 109, 122n
Newman, Oscar, 525, 542n
Newton, Phyllis J., 390, 407n
Niederhoffer, Arthur, 386, 387, 406,
  407n
Niederhoffer, Elaine, 406, 407n
Nixon, Richard M., 86, 114, 115, 412,
  423

O'Connor, Sandra Day, 423
Ogburn, William, 519, 540n
Ohlin, Lloyd E., 168, 170, 172, 175,
  176, 178, 190n, 191n, 212, 475n,
  522
Ohmart, Howard, 509, 510n
O'Leary, Vincent, 509
Orne, M. T., 156n

Packer, Herbert, 41, 43, 54n, 55n,
  329, 345, 347n
Palmer, John W., 476n
Park, Robert E., 162, 189n, 519
Parker, Patricia, 294, 314n
Parker, William H., 383
Parnell, W. R., 131
Parrillo, Vincent N., 346n
Pasamanick, Benjamin, 542n, 544n
Paulus, Paul B., 476n, 477n
Pauly, John, 222n, 236, 237, 248,
  251n, 252n
Paust, Jordan J., 272
Pearson, Frank S., 511n
Pedrick-Cornell, Claire, 281n
Peel, Robert, 140
Penn, William, 99
Pepinsky, Harold, 227, 248n, 249n
Petersilia, Joan, 263, 280n, 316n,
  377n, 407n, 425, 443, 446n, 474,
  475n–477n, 490, 502, 509,
  510n–512n
Peterson, Joyce, 316n

Petty, Charles, 544n
Pfau-Vicent, Bettye A., 204, 221n
Pfohl, Stephen J., 219, 220n
Piaget, Jean, 144, 153n, 156n
Pittman, David, 264, 280n, 337, 347n
Platt, Anthony M., 227, 231, 248,
  250n, 540n
Pogrebin, Mark, 297, 314n
Pokorny, A. D., 204, 221n
Polybius, 247
Poole, Eric, 201, 220n, 297, 314n,
  408n
Pound, Roscoe, 47, 56n
Powell, Jody, 16, 27n
Powell, Lewis, 423
Pratter, Fredrick E., 347n
Priestino, Ramon R., 512n
Prisi, Nicolette, 510n
Prus, Robert C., 500, 512n

Quarles, Benjamin, 393
Quay, H. C., 156n
Quinney, Richard, 5, 26n, 49, 56n,
  199, 220n, 226, 227, 233, 235, 248,
  249n–251n, 316n, 346n, 540n

Rafter, Nicole Hahn, 356, 375,
  376n
Ragen, Joe, 454
Rankin, Ann, 445n
Rathus, S., 346n, 347n
Rawls, John, 242, 251n
Rawson, Richard, 544n
Reagan, Nancy, 319
Reagan, Ronald, 8, 26n, 36, 66, 86,
  87, 139, 151, 254, 272, 343
Reasons, Charles, 477n
Reckless, Walter C., 202–204, 210,
  220, 221n, 222n, 540n
Redlich, F. C., 541n
Regoli, Robert, 201, 220n, 297, 314n,
  408n
Rehnquist, William, 423
Reid, Sue Titus, 346n
Reiman, Jeffrey H., 61, 89n, 238,
  251n, 376n
Reiss, Albert J., 199, 220n
Rennie, Ysabel, 30, 44, 54n, 55n, 61,
  64, 89n, 519, 540n, 541n, 543n,
  545n
Resnick, O., 543n, 544n
Reussi-Ianni, Elizabeth, 406, 407n
Reuter, Peter, 345, 347n
Rhodes, A. Lewis, 199, 220n
Rieff, Philip, 149, 157n
Richards, Pamela, 192n
Richardson, James F., 375, 376n
Ricoeur, Paul, 246
Rieff, Philip, 540n
Rivera, Ramon, 191n
Roberts, Ron E., 206, 249n

Robertson, John A., 443n
Robin, Gerald D., 290, 313n, 377n
Robins, L. N., 139, 156n, 270, 281n
Robinson, James, 512n
Roebuck, Julian B., 449, 474
Rogers, Don, 318
Romilly, Sir Samuel, 99
Rosenberg, Bernard, 248, 249n
Rosett, Arthur, 44, 54n, 55n, 430,
  444n, 445n
Ross, H. L., 117, 123n
Ross, Irwin, 303, 313, 315n
Rossi, P., 251n
Rossman, Henry H., 445n
Rossum, Ralph A., 375, 377n
Roth, Loren H., 155n, 542n, 544n
Rothman, David J., 60, 89n, 354,
  356, 375, 376n, 466, 474, 477n
Rothman, Mitchell Lewis, 314n
Rowe, Alan, 117, 120n, 123n
Rowe, David C., 133, 154n
Rubenstein, Jonathan, 406
Rubin, Lillian B., 89n
Ruhl, J., 251n
Rumbart, Ruben G., 407n
Ruppert, James, 257
Rusche, Georg, 467, 474, 477n, 540n
Rush, Benjamin, 352
Ryan, John Paul, 417, 443, 444n

Sackler, R., 543n
Sade, Marquis de, 99, 100
Sagarin, Edward, 539n
Salem, Richard, 221n, 222n
Samenow, Stanton, 543n
Sampson, Robert J., 183, 192n
Sandberg, Carl, 526
Sandler, M., 544n
Scarpitti, Frank, 544n
Schafer, Stephen, 342
Schaling, D., 281n
Scharf, Peter, 156n
Schauss, Alexander, 153n
Scheingold, Stuart A., 33, 34, 54n,
  89n, 418, 446n
Schelling, Thomas C., 324
Schessler, K. F., 145
Schmidt, Annesley K., 511n, 512n
Schmidt, J., 250n, 251n
Schneider, Hans Joachim, 541n, 542n
Schneider, Joseph W., 148, 149, 153n,
  157n, 341, 345, 347n, 540n
Schoen, Kenneth, 504
Schubert, Glendon, 422, 444n
Schuessler, Karl F., 153n, 157n, 219,
  220n
Schur, Edwin M., 222n, 345, 345n,
  347n
Schwartz, M., 204, 221n
Schwendinger, Herman, 227, 233,
  235, 250n, 251n, 279n

Schwendinger, Julie R., 227, 233, 235, 250n, 251n, 279n
Schwitzgebel, Ralph K., 545n
Scott, J. E., 509, 511n
Scott, Joseph H., 512n
Scull, Andrew T., 505, 513n
Seidman, R., 47, 56n, 240, 251n
Sellin, Thorsten, 66, 90n, 229, 248, 249n, 520, 540n
Senna, Joseph J., 155n
Sergio, Lalli, 312
Serrill, M. S., 446n
Shah, Saleem A., 153n, 154n, 155n, 542n, 544n
Shapiro, Susan, 315n
Shaw, Clifford R., 160–166, 189, 189n, 190n, 208, 212, 247, 507, 520
Sheldon, William H., 130, 131, 153n, 154n
Sherman, Lawrence W., 120n, 389, 397, 406, 407n, 408n
Sherman, Michael, 466, 469, 474, 477n, 503, 513n
Sherrill, Patrick Henry, 258
Shichor, David, 249n, 358, 359
Shockley, William, 526
Shoemaker, Donald J., 219, 222n
Short, James F., Jr., 175, 190n, 191n, 250n, 252n
Short, James S., Jr., 198, 220n
Shover, Neal, 357, 375, 509, 510n, 511n, 512n, 513n
Siegel, Larry J., 155n, 156n, 347n
Sigvardsson, S., 154n
Silberman, Charles E., 89n, 279n, 280n, 282n, 375, 418, 435, 440, 443, 446n
Silverman, Ira J., 189n, 192n, 263, 313n, 315n, 346n
Simmel, George, 225, 229, 249n
Simon, James, 444n
Simon, Rita J., 72, 314n
Singer, J. L., 542n
Singer, Richard, 446n
Sinnott, Jan D., 269, 281n
Skogan, Wesley G., 89n
Skolnick, Jerome H., 380, 386, 387, 389, 390, 404, 406, 406n, 407n, 409n, 424, 445n
Sleffel, Linda, 543n
Smith, B., 476n
Smith, Douglas A., 192n, 315n
Snodgrass, Jon, 24, 28n, 166, 190n
Sommer, Robert, 525, 542n
Sorensen, Lis K., 135, 155n
Speck, Richard F., 257, 527
Spelman, William, 443
Spencer, Herbert, 519
Spengler, Oswald, 541n
Spitzer, Stephen, 227, 249n

Stahura, John M., 73, 90n
Stanley, Amy Dreu, 376n
Stanley, David T., 510n
Stastny, Charles, 474, 476n, 477n
Steer, D., 270, 281n
Steffensmeier, Darrell J., 72, 73, 287, 313
Steinmetz, Suzanne, 268, 280n, 281n
Stephens, Sir James Fitzjames, 37, 55n
Sterling, James W., 385, 407n
Stewart, James K., 446n
Stimson, Ardyth, 346n
Stimson, John, 346n
St. James, Margo, 327
Stratton, John R., 500, 512n
Straus, Murray, 268, 280n
Strodtbeck, Fred L., 175, 191n
Studt, Elliot, 510n, 512n
Sturup, Georg K., 528, 543n
Sudnow, David, 445n
Sullivian, Dennis, 249n
Sumner, William G., 517
Sutherland, Edwin H., 23, 27n, 45, 55n, 135, 176, 195–197, 199, 208, 212, 213, 219, 220n, 248n, 293, 300, 313, 314n, 315n, 376n, 520, 540n
Swazey, J., 544n
Sweet, Ellen, 279n
Sweet, William H., 542n
Sykes, Gresham M., 201, 219, 221n, 456, 474, 475n
Szasz, Thomas, 545n

Takagi, Paul, 227
Tangri, S. S., 204, 221n
Tannenbaum, Frank, 208
Tappan, Paul W., 38, 55n
Tarde, Gabriel, 195, 219n, 519
Taylor, Ian, 201, 221n, 248, 249n
Tennenbaum, D. J., 145, 157n
Tennyson, Ray, 191n
Terry, W. Clinton, III, 409n
Testers, Negley K., 539n
Thomas, Charles W., 315n, 456, 475n
Thomas, R. L., 489
Thompson, D., 489, 510n
Thompson, E. P., 231, 232, 245, 248, 250n, 251n
Thornberry, Terrence P., 251n
Thornton, William, Jr., 155n
Tifft, Larry, 248n, 249n
Tiger, Lionel, 526
Timmer, Doug A., 250n, 251n, 313n
Titchener, Edward, 144
Tittle, Charles, 117, 123n, 183, 192n
Tonry, M., 281n
Torny, Michael, 407n
Tracy, Paul E., 281n
Travis, Lawrence F., 509

Turk, Austin T., 228, 249n
Turner, Frederick Jackson, 521, 541n
Turner, Jonathan H., 249n
Tyce, Francis A., 504
Tyler, Gus, 344, 348n
Tyrnauer, Gabrielle, 474, 476n, 477n

Useem, Bert, 474n, 476

Valachi, Joseph, 308
Valenstein, Elliott S., 543n
Van den Haag, Ernest, 101, 102, 105, 108, 118, 119, 122n, 123n, 375n, 376n, 540n, 541n
Vanderwood, Paul J., 2, 25n, 63
Van Dine, Steve, 540n, 541n
Van Maanen, John, 386, 406, 407n
Vaughan, Diane, 303, 313, 315n
Vega, M., 263, 280n
Velde, Richard W., 426
Vetri, Dominick, 445n
Vetter, Harold J., 189n, 192n, 313n, 315n, 346n
Victor, Bart, 315n
Vigil, James Diego, 281n
Villemez, Wayne J., 192n
Vito, F. G., 435, 446n, 510n
Vogel, Ezra, 541n
Vold, George B., 189n–192n, 229, 248, 250n, 540n–542n
Vollmer, August, 383
Von Hentig, Hans, 342, 348n
Von Hirsch, Andrew, 111, 122n, 446n, 512n
Voss, Harwin L., 178

Waid, W. M., 156n
Wald, Patricia, 445n
Waldo, Gordon, 120n, 145, 157n, 312, 315n
Waldron, Ronald J., 377n
Walker, N., 270, 281n
Walker, Samuel, 84, 89n, 91n, 282n, 375, 375n, 376n, 407n
Wallerstein, J. S., 80, 90n
Walton, Paul, 221n, 248, 249n
Warner W. Lloyd, 521, 541n
Warnock, Mary, 347n
Warren, Earl, 102
Warren, Marguerite, 481
Wasby, Stephen L., 444n
Weber, Max, 227, 228, 249n, 519
Webster, D. Robert, 478n
Weiner, Neil Alan, 278, 280n, 281n
Weinstein, M. A., 282n
Weis, Joseph, 192n
West, D. J., 135
Wheeler, Stanton, 294, 314n, 475n

Whitehead, John T., 511*n*
Whyte, William I., 521, 541*n*
Wiatrowski, 206
Wicks, R. J., 476*n*
Wilkins, Leslie T., 446*n*, 509, 510*n*, 512*n*
William, Gayland, 156*n*
Wilson, Edward O., 519, 526, 542*n*
Wilson, James Q., 6, 8, 25*n*, 26*n*, 89*n*, 94, 101, 102, 104–106, 108, 113, 118, 119, 120*n*, 122*n*, 123*n*, 136, 143, 146–148, 153*n*, 154*n*, 156*n*, 157*n*, 375*n*, 376*n*, 540*n*, 541*n*
Wilson, O. W., 383

Wilson, Rob, 510*n*
Wineman, David, 156*n*
Wirth, Louis, 519
Witte, Ann, 117, 123*n*
Witkin, H. A., 155*n*
Wohhill, 542*n*
Wolfgang, Marvin E., 160, 168–170, 189, 190*n*, 270, 278, 279*n*, 280*n*, 281*n*, 522
Wolkes, Judith, 512*n*
Wolpin, Kenneth I., 117, 123*n*
Wonziak, John F., 509
Woodruff, R. A., Jr., 156*n*
Wright, Erik Olin, 474*n*
Wundt, Wilhelm, 144
Wylie, C. J., 80, 90*n*

Yablonsky, Lewis, 156*n*
Yancey, William, 542*n*
Yeager, M. G., 234, 250*n*
Yeager, Peter C., 179, 192*n*, 299, 300, 303, 311, 312, 315*n*, 316*n*
Yochelson, Samuel, 543*n*
Young, Jack, 221*n*, 248, 249*n*

Zahn, Margaret, 259, 279*n*
Zangwill, Israel, 519
Zenoff, Elyce H., 445*n*
Zimbardo, Philip, 103
Zimmer, L., 476*n*
Zimring, Franklin E., 120*n*, 270, 281*n*, 495, 511*n*
Zubin, J., 544*n*

Subject Index

Abuse
 of the elderly, 268, 269
 and neglect, 265, 266, 284, 532
Academy of Management Journal, 301
Actus reus, 38, 39
Adoptions, 132, 133
AIDS (acquired immune deficiency syndrome), 318, 325, 331, 340, 341, 452
Alabama, 465
Alaska, 321
Alcohol abuse, 14, 139, 149, 217, 217, 284, 532, 535
Alcoholics Anonymous, 217, 218
Allocution, 436
American Correctional Association, 373, 517
American Revolution, 32
American Sociological Association, 293
Appellate review, 369
Argersinger v. *Hamlin,* 416
Arizona, 272
Arkansas, 459, 465, 536
Arraignment, 369
Arrest, 70, 117, 492
Attica, 5, 460, 467
Attorney General's Task Force on Violent Crime, 270
Auburn System, 355
Autonomous morality, 144

Bail, 354, 368
Bartley-Fox Gun Law, 435
Baumes Law, 527
Bearden v. *Georgia,* 493, 494
Bexter v. *Palmigiano,* 465
Beyond a reasonable doubt, 434
Bill of Rights, 32, 40, 42, 50, 51, 53

Biological determinism, 30
Biological positivism, 127, 128, 131, 148, 151
Biomedical intervention, 526–536, 538
Black Act, 231, 233
Born criminals, 10
Brewer v. *Williams,* 392, 394
Briggs Act, 527
Brown v. *Board of Education,* 517
Bruno v. *Maguire,* 268
Buck v. *Bell,* 528
Bureau of Justice Statistics (BJS), 77, 288, 297, 458, 470
Burger Court, 402

California, 80, 103, 117, 165, 205, 234, 244, 257, 259, 263, 266, 272, 273, 321, 338, 339, 390, 400, 459, 481, 490, 502, 503
Call Off Your Old Tired Ethics (COYOTE), 327
Capitalism, 3, 226
Capital punishment, 16, 17, 97, 107, 108, 113, 437, 439, 440
Career Criminal Prosecution (CCP) programs, 425
Carroll v. *U.S.,* 394, 395
Census Bureau, 76
Center for Rape Concern, 260
Centers for Disease Control, 169, 319
Chaos theory, 4
Chicago Area Projects, 161, 165, 507
Child abuse and neglect, 265, 266
Child sexual abuse treatment program, 266
Chronic offenders, 210
CIA (Central Intelligence Agency), 244, 245, 331
Civil Rights Act, 400, 423, 465
Civil suits, 399, 417

Civil War, 61, 353
Class action suit, 268
Classical school of criminology, 94
Code of Hammurabi, 32
Cognitive psychologists, 144
Cohort studies, 169, 270
Coleman v. *Peyton,* 463
Collective jeopardy, 243
Colonies, 351, 402
Colorado, 297, 321, 334, 452, 470, 471
Commentaries (Blackstone), 32
Committee on Gambling Law Enforcement, 336
Common law, 32
Communal societies, 3
Communication systems, 525
Community-based corrections, 360, 374, 380, 483
Community Resource Management Team (CRMT), 489
Community restitution programs, 485
Conflict perspectives, 230
Conflict theory, 224, 225, 226, 228, 239, 240, 242, 246
Congress, 360, 362, 423
Connecticut, 265, 417, 455
Constitution, 50, 51, 392, 402, 423, 430
Constitutionally guaranteed rights, 392, 402
Containment theory, 202, 204, 217
Control theory, 202
Conviction, 21
Corrections, 366, 369, 372
 administrators, 460
 agencies, 364, 458
 task force, 481, 482
Countries
 Australia, 276, 523, 527
 Canada, 18

Denmark, 528
England, 18, 45, 99, 234, 288, 351,
   353, 523
Germany, 231
Holland, 523
Israel, 523
Japan, 18–20, 22, 23, 254, 523
Mexico, 185, 187, 323
New Zealand, 276
Scandinavia, 18, 523
Scotland, 234
Soviet Union, 523
Switzerland, 18, 21, 22, 23, 523
Third World, 18
County attorney. *See* Prosecutor
Courts, 350, 354, 363, 365, 392, 393,
   395, 396, 413, 463
Crime. *See also* Federal crimes
   arson, 285, 293, 460
   assault, 17, 62, 254, 264
   bank robbery, 238
   bookmaking, 334, 335
   bribery, 16
   "bugging," 16
   burglary, 16, 70, 180, 285–288, 395
   child abuse, 17
   child molestation, 62
   computer, 297–299
   conspiracy, 37
   corporate, 63, 64, 113, 114, 119,
      284, 299–303
   destruction of criminal evidence, 16
   disorderly conduct, 17
   embezzlement, 238, 296, 297
   extortion, 16
   forgery and counterfeiting, 295, 296
   fraud, 16
   homicide, 21, 77, 168
   juvenile, 173
   kidnapping, 523
   larceny, 261, 285, 288–289
   loitering, 14
   manslaughter, 254, 255
   misuse of public funds, 16
   money laundering, 344
   murder, 62, 70, 198, 254–259, 392,
      523
   obstruction of justice, 16
   organized, 114, 119, 304–309, 336,
      341, 343, 344
   perjury, 115
   pickpocketing, 288–289
   political, 114
   prostitution, 14, 213, 267, 318,
      325–331, 356
   rape, 62, 233, 254, 259–261, 392,
      536
   robbery, 21, 62, 70, 254, 261–263
   sexual assault, 17, 535
   shoplifting, 289–290
   spousal assault, 389–391

tax evasion, 16
terrorism, 272–275
theft, 14, 180, 285, 288–289
vagrancy, 14, 45, 336
vandalism, 460
white-collar, 37, 114, 118, 119, 235,
   293–295
wife battering, 233
withholding information, 115
Crime control model, 43, 44
Crime-control strategies, 5
Crime Index, 288
Crime rates, 117
Criminal courts, 413–415
   case type, 414
   general jurisdiction, 417–418
   lower courts, 416–417
   state appellate courts, 418
   structure, 413–415
   trial courts, 419
Criminal justice data, 19
Criminal justice system, 16, 20, 21,
   33, 37, 49, 104, 110, 114, 116,
   118, 357, 361–366, 368, 371–373,
   413
Criminal law, 31, 38, 51, 59
Criminal subculture, 176, 178
Criminal trial, 431–434
Criminal victimization, 83
Criminologists, 2, 112, 116, 135, 137,
   138, 276, 301, 336, 340
Criminology, 23, 24, 30, 99, 100, 161
Cruel and unusual punishment, 464,
   465
Cultural conflict theory, 188, 229
Cultural deviance theories, 160, 165,
   166, 180
Cytogenetic studies, 133, 134

Darwinism, 518, 521
Death penalty. *See* Capital
   punishment
Declaration of Independence, 32
Decriminalized marijuana, 321
Decriminalized prostitution, 330
Defendants, 44, 51, 102
Defense counsel, 44, 418, 429
Delinquency. *See* Juvenile,
   delinquency
Delinquency prevention programs,
   178
Delinquency rates, 2
Determinate sentencing, 187, 451,
   505, 506
Deterrence, 116
Differential association theory, 195,
   196, 197, 198, 199, 200, 217, 218
Discrimination, 243
District attorney, 268. *See also*
   Prosecutor
District of Columbia, 140

Diversion, 428–429
Domestic violence, 264
Double jeopardy, 40
Draconian Code, 32
Drift theory, 200, 201, 217
Drug Enforcement Administration,
   319
Drugs, 177, 213, 217, 218, 233, 284,
   328, 458, 462
   addict, 324, 342, 533
   dealing, 272
   subculture, 22
   treatment, 531
Due process, 40, 41, 51, 437
Due process rights, 110, 460
Durham Rule, 140
Durham v. *United States,* 140

Eastern Penitentiary, 354
Economic inequality, 184
Electric shock, 536
Elmira Reformatory, 356, 357
Emotionally disturbed, 151, 181
Employment Opportunity
   Commission (EEOC), 400
English Common Law, 32
Enlightenment, 100
Enomoto v. *Clutchette,* 465
Europe, 8, 12, 467, 523
Exclusionary rule, 392, 402

Family violence, 218, 268
Federal Bureau of Investigation
   (FBI), 66, 67, 70, 244, 255, 261,
   287, 331, 384
Federal Bureau of Narcotics, 520
Federal Bureau of Prisons, 360
Federal Child Abuse Prevention and
   Treatment Act, 265
Federal Courts, 297, 420, 422, 484.
   See also Criminal courts
   chief justice, 422
   per curiam decision, 422
   U.S. Court of Appeals, 421
   U.S. District Courts, 263, 420–
      421
   U.S. Supreme Court, 421–423
   writ of certiorari, 422
Federal crimes, 41
Federal penitentiary, 134
Federal probation system, 498
Federal Tort Claim Act, 465
Federal Trade Commission Act, 301
Felicific calculus, 98, 99
Felony, 368, 502
Female offender, 212, 213
Feudalism, 3, 8, 30
Firearms, 261, 264, 524
Flat-time sentencing, 435
Florida, 259, 263, 333, 459, 465
Ford Motor Company, 302

Gagnon v. *Scarpelli,* 493, 494
Gamblers Anonymous, 217
Gambling, 14, 217, 318, 333, 462
Gangs, 165, 166, 168, 170, 173, 175,
    176, 178, 233, 272
Gay-rights ordinance, 333
Georgia, 491
Gestalt psychology, 144
"Get-tough" policy, 6, 14, 17, 18, 61,
    88, 108, 109, 112, 118, 119, 505
Global disorder, 276
Grand jury, 368
Great Depression, 14

Halfway houses, 504
Hard-core offenders, 151, 188
Harrison Act, 527
Harris v. *U.S.,* 395
Hawaii, 203
Heteronomous morality, 144
High-risk offenders, 502
Home furlough programs, 502
Homeless, 338
Homosexuality, 318, 331, 535
House of refuge, 355
Husband abuse, 268
Hyperkinetic children, 149, 531, 532

Idaho, 488
Illegal markets, 334
Illinois, 41, 45, 82, 212, 233, 257,
    259, 272, 290, 306, 339, 424
Immigration, 11, 85, 162, 521
Incapacitation, 107
Incest, 266
Indeterminate sentence, 106, 111
Indiana, 488
Industrialization, 11–13, 17, 18, 352
Infant mortality, 181
Injunction, 31
Insanity defense, 150
Intelligence, 134–136
International Association of Chiefs of
    Police, 66
Iowa, 366, 452, 483, 488
Irresistible impulse rule, 140

Jackson v. *Bishop,* 464
Jails, 44, 107, 117, 238, 351, 352, 364,
    374, 426, 459
Johnson v. *Avery,* 463
Judges, 32, 368, 417, 418, 426, 433,
    435, 436, 438, 463
Jury, 51, 417, 434, 436
"Just deserts," 16, 37, 101, 109–112,
    119, 435
Justice model, 489
Juvenile
    court, 231, 358
    delinquency, 2, 14, 22, 79, 131,
        135, 137, 139, 141, 160, 161,

163–166, 176, 178, 179, 180, 184,
    188, 189, 199, 200, 203, 205–207,
    212, 213, 236, 266, 270, 365
    institution, 265
Juvenile Justice and Delinquency
    Prevention Act, 270
Juvenile justice system, 328

Kansas, 268, 366, 483, 490, 508
Kent State, 5
Kentucky, 488
Knapp Commission, 397, 398
Korean War, 86
Ku Klux Klan, 65, 353

Labeling theory, 208–211, 216, 217
Latin America, 523
Law enforcement, 361, 365, 373, 524.
    See also Police
Law Enforcement Assistance
    Administration (LEAA), 384,
    426, 525, 527
Law of the twelve tables, 32
Legalized prostitution policy, 332
Legislating morality, 318
Legislature, 353
Louisiana, 304, 459, 465, 470
Lower-class, 164, 166, 188, 202, 231,
    233, 238, 242, 247, 260, 320
    boys, 175
    culture, 167, 170
    minorities, 350
    persons, 171, 181, 183
    subcultures, 179
    values, 168
    youth, 176, 180, 184
Lower courts, 418

McKay Commission, 460
McNabb v. *U.S.,* 397
Maine, 321
Mandatory sentences, 106, 187, 435,
    470
Mapp v. *Ohio,* 392, 393
Marxist, 3, 228, 235, 236, 238, 244,
    276, 519
Marxist criminology, 224, 226, 230,
    233, 234, 239, 240–246, 247, 276
Marxist theorists, 224, 230, 231, 233,
    247
Maryland, 322, 366, 527
Massachusetts, 108, 165, 234, 262,
    353, 356, 527
Massachusetts v. *Sheppard,* 393
Mass production, 12
Meachum v. *Fano,* 465
Meachum v. *Haymes,* 465
Medicaid, 303
Medicalization of deviance, 148, 149,
    152
Medical model, 358

Mempa v. *Rhay,* 493
Mens rea, 38, 39
Mental disorder, 143, 522
Mental retardation, 141
Michigan, 80, 117, 256, 272, 458, 459,
    470
Middle-class
    delinquency, 179, 180
    persons, 181
    values, 173, 174, 175, 176
    youth, 180
Minnesota, 117, 141, 366, 442, 483,
    504, 505, 508
Minnesota Multiphasic Personality
    Inventory, 141, 142
Minority women, 260
Miranda v. *Arizona,* 393, 396, 402
Misdemeanor, 368
Mississippi, 465
Missouri, 139, 452
M'Naughten Rule, 140
Modernization, 12, 13
Morrisey v. *Brewer,* 500

Narcotics, 435, 520
National Advisory Commission on
    Criminal Justice Standards and
    Goals, 482, 508
National Association of
    Manufacturers, 311
National Council on Alcoholism, 320
National Crime Survey, 259, 261, 264,
    267
National Guard, 430
National Institute of Drug Abuse, 321
National Traffic Highway Safety
    Administration, 302
Nebraska, 218
Neglect, 181, 265
Neuroscientists, 151
Neutralization theory, 201
Nevada, 330, 452, 459, 465
New England, 6, 306
New Hampshire, 140, 465
New Jersey, 51, 169, 260, 272, 290,
    353, 455, 491, 507
New Mexico, 459, 460
Newsweek, 275
New York, 61, 66, 80, 165, 178, 198,
    207, 234, 268, 284, 304, 305, 308,
    323, 334, 337, 353, 355, 397, 399,
    401, 402, 459, 491, 527
New York v. *Quarles,* 393
North Carolina, 117
North Dakota, 490
Nuclear arms race, 276

Ohio, 6, 201, 203, 204, 257, 271, 321,
    353, 417, 451, 455, 465, 470–472,
    488, 523, 537
Oklahoma, 258, 459

Opportunity theory, 176, 178
Oregon, 321, 330, 366, 470, 471, 483, 508
Organized Crime Commission, 343

Parens patriae, 106, 358
Parole, 356, 364, 370, 495–500. *See also* Community-based corrections
   adults, 496–497
   board, 111, 506
   discretion, 495
   guidelines, 498–499
   officers, 366
   supervision, 499–501
Pedophiles, 535
Peer groups, 167, 207, 211, 213, 236, 237
Pennsylvania, 61, 351, 352, 354, 355, 455, 490
Personality disorders, 203
Philosophical rationalism, 30
Physical abuse, 181, 213, 214, 265
Physiognomy, 127
Plain view doctrine, 394
Plea bargaining, 21, 51, 354, 369, 429–431, 437, 441
Police, 20, 260, 293, 296, 354
   administrators, 383
   brutality, 398–400
   civilianization, 404
   community-oriented policing, 389
   corruption, 397–398
   culture, 385–387, 404
   deadly force, 399
   department, 268, 360
   discretion, 391–392
   informal code, 388–389
   interrogation, 396–397
   management, 404
   minority officers, 400–401
   officers, 8, 264, 337, 400, 524
   professionalism, 382–384, 399
   search and seizure, 393–396
   stress, 405
   training, 400
Pornography, 318
PORT Corrections Center, 504, 505
Poverty, 59, 61, 118, 233, 522
Preliminary hearing, 368
Presentence investigation (PSI), 436, 493–494
President's Commission on Law Enforcement and Administration of Justice, 384, 428, 481
President's Commission on the Causes and Prevention of Violence, 170
President's Crime Commission, 343, 366, 482, 508

Pretrial programs
   diversion, 428
   percentage bail program, 427
   release on recognizance (ROR), 427
   supervised release, 368, 424–428
Prison, 111, 117, 143, 169, 186, 187, 198, 234, 238, 263, 374, 429
   abolitionists, 466
   administration, 449–451
   big house, 454
   contemporary, 457–458
   contraband market, 458
   correctional institution, 455
   deprivation model, 456
   gangs, 461–462
   guards, 462
   humane, 470
   importation model, 456
   inmate code, 454–455
   management information systems (MIS), 451
   maximum-security, 449, 468, 470, 473
   overcrowding, 458–460, 469–471, 484
   prisoners, 291, 320, 354, 357
   prisoners' rights, 463–465
   programs, 452–454
   services, 452–454
   "snitch system," 449
   social control, 450
   staff, 462
   violence, 460–462
   women, 455, 459
Probation, 111, 238, 356, 366, 485–492
   adults, 486–487
   departments, 364
   officers, 268, 293, 321, 358, 369, 492–494
   shock, 488
Procunier v. *Martinez,* 463
Professional criminal, 214, 292
Prohibition, 35, 527
Prompt arraignment rule, 397
Property crimes, 14, 44, 45, 67, 184, 186, 213, 215, 235, 254, 284–293, 309, 312, 374. *See also* Crime
Prosecutor, 365, 418, 431, 435
Protestant Reformation, 7
Psychiatric characteristics, 142–143
Psychiatrists, 358
Psychoanalysis, 138, 151
Psychological positivism, 138, 139, 145, 146, 148, 151
Psychopathology, 138, 142–144, 187, 256
Psychosurgery, 528–531
Psychotropic drugs, 531–536
Public defenders, 429
Puerto Rico, 204, 274, 507

Punishment, 5, 9, 10, 15, 21, 33, 39, 40, 45, 52, 96, 99, 101, 103, 104, 105, 108, 109, 111, 112, 116–119, 139, 169, 238, 473
Punishment model, 359

Quakers, 352

Racial unrest, 455
Racism, 239
Rand Survey, 263
Recidivism, 88, 103, 187, 263, 290, 291, 441
Rehabilitation, 10, 11, 15, 16, 100, 103, 104, 111, 119, 186, 358, 359, 517
Reinforcement theory, 146
Reintegration model, 483, 488
Repeat offender project (ROP), 389
Residential facilities, 484, 502
Retribution, 37
Revolutionary War, 12
Rhode Island, 465
Riots, 22, 359
Risk assessment, 490, 491, 500, 501
Rockefeller Drug Law, 435
Ruffin v. *The Commonwealth of Virginia,* 463

Schizophrenia, 141, 142, 246, 533
School, 178, 206, 207, 211, 217, 218, 235, 266
Scientific determinism, 10
Select Committee on Aging, 269
Self-concept, 203, 204
Self-report studies, 80, 81, 205, 206
Senate Committee on Organized Crime, 334
Sentencing, 369, 434–437, 441
Sex discrimination, 342
Sex offenders, 150, 527, 537
Sexual abuse, 213, 265, 267
Sexual psychopath laws, 45
Shaker Communities, 216
Sheriff, 351
Social bond theory, 205
Social control theory, 5, 13, 204, 206, 207, 212, 217, 247
Social disorganization theory, 161, 164, 166, 185, 208, 520
Social disruption, 6, 9, 10
Social pathology, 521
Social process theory, 194, 214, 218
Social reaction theory of deviance, 209. *See also* Labeling theory
Social scientists, 4
Social stratification theory, 227
Social structural theories, 160, 182, 188, 189
Sociobiology, 131, 132, 135, 137, 150, 151

Sociopaths, 138, 141, 187
Sociopsychological theories, 194
South Carolina, 470, 471
Southeast Asia, 323
Spouse abuse, 181, 267
State Attorney. *See* Prosecutor
Stateville Penitentiary, 449, 451, 458, 462, 463, 467
Stop-and-frisk, 394, 402
Strain theory, 170, 180
Street crime, 64, 88, 102, 114, 238, 277, 538. *See also* Crime
Subculture of violence, 168, 170, 179
Substance abuse, 318, 319–323
   alcohol, 320
   cocaine, 321
   marijuana, 321
   Mothers Against Drunk Drivers (MADD), 320
   opiates, 322–323
   Remove Intoxicated Drivers (RID), 320
   Students Against Drunk Drivers (SADD), 320
Substantial capacity test, 140
Suicide, 21, 22, 170
Suspended sentences, 21
Symbionese Liberation Army, 273
Symbolic interactionism, 195, 196

Talley v. *Stephens,* 464
Target hardening, 524–526
Tennessee, 470, 471, 488, 501
Terry v. *Ohio,* 394, 395
Texas, 80, 117, 257, 459, 465, 488, 491
Theory of anomie, 170, 171, 172

Theory of delinquent subculture, 173, 174, 175
Therapeutic communities, 217, 218
Transvestites, 536
Treatment Alternatives to Street Crime, 428
Trial, 351, 369, 416, 424, 431, 437
Twin studies, 132, 133, 526
Typology of syndicate model, 307

Unemployment, 218, 233, 234
Uniform Crime Reports (UCR), 66, 70, 72–74, 77, 117, 255, 259, 261, 285, 286, 291–293, 295, 296, 319, 325, 333, 336, 384
United Nations, 518
U.S. Attorney General, 66
U.S. Board of Parole, 498
U.S. Chamber of Commerce, 311
U.S. Constitution, 33, 34, 40
U.S. Department of Justice, 66, 235
U.S. Government Report on Alcohol and Health, 320
U.S. Supreme Court, 384, 392, 393, 394, 395, 397, 416, 423, 429, 463, 465, 493, 517, 528
U.S. v. *Leon,* 393
Upper-class persons, 181
Utilitarian, 37

Victim, 200, 201, 213, 233, 235, 256, 341–342
Victimization/deterrence model, 507
Victimization surveys, 77, 79, 183
Victimless crime, 14, 15
Vietnam War, 5, 86, 338, 380, 482

Vigilante, 65, 278, 352
Violent crimes, 17, 44, 62, 184, 215, 233, 235, 255, 259, 275–277, 278, 311
Violent subculture, 169, 275
Virginia, 85, 351
Volstead Act, 46, 527

War on crime, 372
War on drugs, 323
War on poverty, 178
Warren Court, 402, 422, 423
Washington, 258, 259, 456, 491
Watergate affair, 16, 115, 244, 246, 421
Weight Watchers, 217
Welfare, 105, 519, 522
West Virginia, 455
Wickersham Commission, 384
Williams v. *New York State,* 494
Wing span search, 396
Wisconsin, 490
Wolff v. *McDonnell,* 464
Wood theft law, 231
Work-release programs, 503
World War I, 12, 527
World War II, 70, 86, 361, 384, 418, 448, 450, 455, 521
Writ of certiorari, 422
Wyoming, 465

XYY chromosomal abnormality, 526–527

Youth crime, 22, 270–272
Youth service bureau, 328